Death of the Covenant Code

Supplements to the Journal for the Study of Judaism

VOLUME 211

The titles published in this series are listed at *brill.com/jsjs*

Death of the Covenant Code

Capital Punishment in Old Greek Exodus in Light of Greco-Egyptian Law

By

Joel Korytko

BRILL

LEIDEN | BOSTON

The Library of Congress Cataloging-in-Publication Data is available online at https://catalog.loc.gov
LC record available at https://lccn.loc.gov/2023028479

Typeface for the Latin, Greek, and Cyrillic scripts: "Brill". See and download: brill.com/brill-typeface.

ISSN 1384-2161
ISBN 978-90-04-68203-0 (hardback)
ISBN 978-90-04-68204-7 (e-book)

This book is printed on acid-free paper and produced in a sustainable manner.

Contents

Acknowledgments

The ideas represented in this monograph are the culmination of nearly half a decade of work, beginning with the final project of a master's degree. So many have been a support to me during what seems like a lifetime. Above all, I could not have made it far past the starting line if it were not for my family. My wife, April, has been my greatest advocate and the one to keep me grounded when the vicissitudes of life tried to deter me. My children continually brought a smile to my face amidst the challenges of moving across the sea to a new culture and country. Birthing and raising a newborn only one month into our new living arrangements is also a feat of which my wife deserves untold credit. For the days spent with our children in that small, "insane-asylum white" apartment while I was away putting this research together, I will always be grateful. For bearing with me in an intense season of chronic pain during my studies, and ultimately helping me to finally overcome it, what could I say?

Without the academic mentoring and partnership of Larry Perkins it is very possible that this project's hypothesis would have remained hidden for some time. My thanks belong to him for guiding me in the earlier stages of our work together. Likewise, I am astonished at the dedication of Dr Alison Salvesen who took me on in doctoral supervision while at the same time dealing with so many other unexpected and pressing matters. Never once did I feel neglected, and the final year and edition of my project was successful thanks to her. Appreciation must also be expressed for scholars who have come alongside me over the years. Here the advice, opportunities, and friendship from Robert Hiebert and more recently Benjamin Wright stand out. To them can be added others who showed me both personal and professional concern while living in Oxford. For this I owe thanks to John Screnock, Jean Maurais, Hindy Najman, and the late James Aitken. Part of this research's success is owed to the editorial support provided by Steel Lane and Jacob Cerone. Thank you both for your assistance.

This project could not have been completed without the doctoral fellowship provided to me by The Social Sciences and Humanities Research Council of Canada. I am grateful for their support in my doctoral studies. Similarly, thank you, dad (and Susan), for helping me get off on the right foot in my first year. Thank you, mom, for assisting with our housing as we lived in Oxford. Both of your support means the world to me. Thank you, Chandehl and David, for your early financial support.

Learning to succeed in a project like this under the circumstances I faced is the result of a family taking me in as a young man. Thank you, Bentley, for helping me discover the wisdom to get here. The endless days and nights you and Stella gave to me taught me how to walk in the world.

Finally, my thanks go out to Northwest Seminary & College (particularly to Howard Andersen and Jonathan Numada) for believing in my scholarship, encouraging me to publish this monograph, and providing me with the means and time to write.

ἐξ αὐτοῦ καὶ δι᾽ αὐτοῦ καὶ εἰς αὐτὸν τὰ πάντα· αὐτῷ ἡ δόξα εἰς τοὺς αἰῶνας

Tables

Abbreviations

Sigla and abbreviations generally follow *The SBL Handbook of Style*, 2nd ed. (Atlanta, SBL Press, 2014). Sigla for the texts of papyri and inscriptions follow the edition cited. Documentary sources are abbreviated according to John F. Oates, William H. Willis, et al., *Checklist of Editions of Greek, Latin, Demotic and Coptic Papyri, Ostraca and Tablets*, https://papyri.info/docs/checklist.

In addition to abbreviations found in *The Handbook of Style*, the following are used:

Gen	translation of Greek Genesis
Ex	translation of Greek Exodus
Lev	translation of Greek Leviticus
Num	translation of Greek Numbers
Dt	translation of Greek Deuteronomy
OG	Old Greek version of LXX text
SSF	superficial semantic fidelity
GCC	The Greek Covenant Code
LXX.D	Martin Karrer and Wolfgang Kraus, eds., *Septuaginta Deutsch: Das Griechische Alte Testament in Deutscher Übersetzung: Text* (Stuttgart: Deutsche Bibelgesellschaft, 2009)
CGL	Diggle, James, ed., *The Cambridge Greek Lexicon* (Cambridge: Cambridge University Press, 2022)

Dates of papyri or inscriptions are given in the main body of work and when relevant in the footnotes. Insignificant chronological ranges are cited according to the earliest possible date, and larger ranges are noted.

CHAPTER 1

Approaching Greek Exodus and Greco-Egyptian Law

1.1 A New Hypothesis

Multistable perception is the phenomenon that occurs when an image is identified as depicting one thing or another depending on how the image is viewed. Such images often appear in pop psychological discourse and media. Multistable perception can also be guided into a preconditioned response. A subject may be told that a picture is of a rabbit, and the viewer then sees only a rabbit. However, from a different vantage point the picture might be better characterized as a duck. The onlooker has been inured to see one image and not the other. It is the claim of the present work that, in a similar way, it is not only in pop psychology where pre-guided illusions occur—they are also found in the world of texts. In the field of Septuagint Studies, it is incumbent upon the scholar to look at both the Hebrew parent text and its rendering in the Greek target text in order to assess the character and nature of the translation. In this process it is easy to default to the assumption that the Greek text by and large represents the Hebrew text's meaning, despite other smaller aspects of potential interference resulting from the linguistic transfer that comes with translating from one language to another, or perhaps rhetorical embellishments or the like. In the case of the laws involving the death penalty within the portion of Exodus often labelled "The Covenant Code," this default has historically prevailed. The insistence of the present volume is that previous scholarship has been unduly swayed by the Hebrew text to see these laws as "a rabbit" when in fact the picture more appropriately represents "a duck." When the translation of these regulations is viewed in light of the Greek language as represented in the literary and documentary sources from the time period around that of the translation, there are strong reasons to suggest that previous readings of the text have been misguided.

In this monograph, therefore, I (1) attempt to provide a comparative analysis of these sources to establish a more accurate reading of the Greek text, and in tandem with this linguistic analysis, (2) look to the world of Classical and Greco-Egyptian law and their language to see if further light can be shed upon the translation transformations under discussion.[1] Here I will propose that the

1 "Greco-Egyptian law" is defined in a general sense referring to Greek law as it came to be in the Ptolemaic Egyptian setting. It does not refer to native Egyptian law as it is found in the

 DOI:10.1163/9789004682047_002

translator may have drawn upon various aspects of Greco-Egyptian legal practice, language, and formulations when rendering the Hebrew text. The resulting conclusion from these two investigative strata, should they prove true, would be that the translator rendered these laws involving the death penalty in such a way so as to intentionally conform to Greco-Egyptian law.

1.2 Superficial Semantic Fidelity

The translator uses various maneuvers in order to achieve this outcome, all while staying relatively close to the source text. Here we find some commonly maintained isomorphic categories such as quantitative and serial fidelity.[2] Added to these would be what could be called "superficial semantic fidelity." This category is coined for the purpose of this study, and it seems to have been the driving force behind why previous scholarship did not pick up on the translational differences that will be argued to be present in the text. By "superficial semantic fidelity" (henceforth SSF) I refer to the translational practice of rendering the Hebrew text with a Greek term that shares some sort of baseline commonality of concept with the Hebrew yet means something quite distinct in the Greek language. The varied ways in which the translator goes about using this technique will be discussed as the present work unfolds. An illustration of SSF in the Greek Covenant Code has, in reality, been the subject of discussion for two millennia. In Exod 22:27 (22:28 LXX) the translator rendered θεοὺς οὐ κακολογήσεις, "you shall not revile gods."[3] The underlying Hebrew for θεούς is אלהים ("God"). While there is discussion as to the original intent of אלהים, it is very unlikely that the Hebrew text referred to deities other than the God of Israel. The Greek meaning is therefore quite distinct from the Hebrew parent text, but a surface representation of אלהים is maintained with a Greek term

Ptolemaic period. See *1.5.3* for a discussion of Ptolemaic legal practice and its background. Often "Greco-Egyptian law," "Greek law," and "Ptolemaic law" will be used interchangeably throughout this work.

2 That a general idea of isomorphism defines the translation of Exodus see Larry J. Perkins, "Exodus: To the Reader," in *A New English Translation of the Septuagint and the Other Greek Translations Traditionally Included under That Title*, ed. Albert Pietersma and Benjamin G. Wright (Oxford: Oxford University Press, 2007), 43.

3 See, e.g., Pieter Willem van der Horst, "'Thou Shalt Not Revile the Gods': The LXX Translation of Ex. 22:28(27), Its Background and Influence," in *The Studia Philonica Annual: Studies in Hellenistic Judaism*, vol. 5 of *The Studia Philonica Annual: Studies in Hellenistic Judaism*, ed. David T. Runia, Alan Mendelson, and David Winston (Atlanta: Scholars Press, 1993), 3–8, and Robert Goldenberg, "The Septuagint Ban on Cursing the Gods," *JSJ* 28, no. 4 (1997): 381–89, who both outline some of this verse's interpretive history.

that also refers to divinity. There is a superficial semantic correspondence in concept—both אלהים and θεός refer to spiritual entities, often god/God—but using the plural Greek noun θεούς to refer to foreign deities besides Israel's God is out of step with the Hebrew text. The translator seems to have exploited the stereotypical plural ending on אלהים, resulting in a superficial representation of the Hebrew.

Now I do not presently intend to discuss Exod 22:27 (22:28 LXX) at length. Rather, this text is used to highlight a famous example of interpretive transformation via SSF in the Greek Covenant Code recognized among Septuagintalists and biblical scholars alike. Whether the rendering of אלהים here originated with the translator or a previous interpretive tradition, it should not be immediately controversial that a similar pattern of SSF could be present throughout other laws. This is not the only technique employed by the translator, but it is a significant and consistent one. As this study progresses, examples of SSF will multiply and it will become more apparent how the translator treats the Hebrew text.

Perhaps the most convincing example that could serve as an introduction is the rendering of מות יומת ("he shall surely die") with θανάτῳ θανατούσθω (lit. "by death let him be put to death"; Exod 21:12, 15) as compared to θανάτῳ τελευτάτω (lit. "by death let him come to an end"; 21:16–17). I attempt to demonstrate that these two collocations are not synonymous phrases in sections 2.2–2.5 through an analysis of the terminology used for the death penalty in Classical and Ptolemaic Greek law. Note that both renderings involve Greek terms often used to refer to "death" (i.e., θανατόω as in "to put to death" and τελευτάω as in "to come to an end," i.e., "to die"). A shared superficial semantic concept regarding "death" connects both terms to מות יומת. Whereas θανάτῳ θανατούσθω will be seen to refer to capital punishment, θανάτῳ τελευτάτω will instead refer to an imprecation with no here-and-now consequences. This change in meaning is achieved despite the use of a verb that commonly indicates "death" (τελευτάω). Documenting this and other superficial semantic correspondences to the Hebrew text will occupy a large portion of the present volume. The rationale for the translator's employment of this kind of translation technique will be the other focal point. I hypothesize that Greek law as represented in its late Classical and early Ptolemaic varieties offer a probable framework that might stand behind the changes found in Greek Exodus. For example, the interchange between θανάτῳ θανατούσθω/θανάτῳ τελευτάτω in Exod 21:15, 17 (21:16 LXX) can be explained based on how Greek law treated abuse towards parents. In the one instance, striking of parents could warrant death, and so the translator rendered with θανάτῳ θανατούσθω. In the other, abusive speech did not warrant death and so the translator instead inserted the imprecation θανάτῳ τελευτάτω. In this way the translator has maintained a superficial representation of the Hebrew text while also conforming the translation to Greek legal expectations. While in-depth analyses are only undertaken for laws involving the death penalty here, other examples have been noted for the future.[4]

1.3 The Scope of the Inquiry

The present volume is primarily concerned with the laws containing the death penalty within what is often labelled "The Covenant Code," the section of legal materials from approximately Exod 20:22 until 23:33.[5] The exact limits of the Covenant Code are not important for the present study since I only analyze laws involving the death penalty. How the translator divided up the text is also a question worth considering, but it is on the periphery of the investigation at hand.[6] Which laws get categorized as involving the death penalty is also debatable. For instance, there is the repeated use of מות in penal apodoses, often with an accompanying infinitive absolute, which is quite universally accepted as referring to capital punishment.[7] In addition to laws with מות as the penal

4 Laws not involving the death penalty will be the focus of future publications. Preliminary analyses have been completed for the whole Covenant Code. Some of the ideas expressed in the present volume represent refined arguments that stem from my master's thesis (Joel F. Korytko, "The 'Law of the Land' in the Land of the Lagids: A Comparative Analysis of Exodus 21.1–32," [M.A. Thesis, Trinity Western University, 2018]). This monograph is also a revised version of my doctoral dissertation at Oxford (Joel F. Korytko, "Death of the Covenant Code: Evaluating the Translation of Laws with Capital Punishment in Old Greek Exodus 21:1–23:19 in Light of Graeco-Egyptian Law" [DPhil Diss., The University of Oxford, 2022]), which partially relied on ideas from that earlier work as well.

5 There is debate on the date of this section of Exodus. See, e.g., Bernard M. Levinson, "Is the Covenant Code an Exilic Composition? A Response to John Van Seters: Proceedings of the Oxford Old Testament Seminar," in *In Search of Pre-Exilic Israel: Proceedings of the Oxford Old Testament Seminar*, ed. John Day (London: T&T Clark, 2004), 272–325. For the label "Covenant Code" see Raymond Westbrook, "What Is the Covenant Code?" in *Law from the Tigris to the Tiber: The Writings of Raymond Westbrook: The Shared Tradition*, vol. 1 of *Law from the Tigris to the Tiber: The Writings of Raymond Westbrook*, ed. Bruce Wells and Rachel Magdalene (Winona Lake: Eisenbrauns, 2009), 97–118.

6 Some implications of section 2.7 may speak to this matter.

7 21:12, 14–17, 29; 22:18 (22:19 LXX). Virtually all modern commentaries agree that מות יומת refers to the same reality of the death penalty in these verses (e.g., Cornelius Houtman, *Exodus*, vol. 1 of *Exodus*, HCOT 2 [Leuven: Peeters, 2000], 38–39; William Henry Covici Propp, *Exodus 19–40: A New Translation with Introduction and Commentary* [New York: Doubleday, 2006], 5–7, 204–205). "Capital punishment," "the death penalty," "the death sentence," "capital crimes," and other similar phrases will all refer to this same reality henceforth.

verb, this work also focuses on Exod 21:20–21; 22:2 (22:3 LXX),[8] 17 (22:18 LXX), and 22:19 (22:20 LXX). Each of these laws also arguably refer to the death penalty in the Hebrew text (except 22:2 [22:3 LXX]).[9] This project does not extend beyond Exodus, though some of its conclusions may point towards implications for other Greek translations, particularly the Pentateuchal materials.[10] This is not to say that I do not use data from other LXX translations, but rather that the focal point is on the text of Exodus as presented and not in other translations. There are a few special instances where it is warranted to mention how the data apply to other books, since the identical techniques seem to be employed in parallel contexts. Most implications from the data will, however, be focused upon Exodus. This is partially on account of spatial constraints, but also because Exodus, for reasons yet unclear, seems to render laws with parallel content in the Pentateuch in significantly different ways.[11]

Working together with the data from sections 2.2–2.5 that describe formulae for the death penalty, in 2.7 I will propose that the translator also employs a translation tactic taken from Ptolemaic legal syntax. This legal formulary is signalled through the employment of the third person imperative as the penal command verb of a given law in contrast to the future tense used for the penal command verb. It has the effect of downgrading the punishment from an absolute command to a possible outcome, depending on other legal considerations. This syntactic trait is found with laws involving the death penalty as well as a few others. It has the effect, similar to SSF, of maintaining a semblance of the source text while introducing a new element that transforms the law. Here the influence of Ptolemaic law comes in part from Greco-Egyptian legal scribal practice.

Both of these examples from Chapter 2 serve as foundations for the examination of particular laws found in Greek Exodus in Chapter 3. This chapter stands together with Chapter 2 whereas Chapter 4 only partially draws from the conclusions of Chapter 2. This is due to the nature of the translational transformations found in Exod 22, which require different approaches. These laws, too, will be shown to depart from the Hebrew source text in significant ways that could comport with Greco-Egyptian law.

8 The death penalty is present here in the Greek text in contrast to any known Hebrew text.

9 The present volume does not cover Exod 21:23 in detail. It is uncertain whether this law is meant to establish the death penalty or a more generic principle of equity (cf. Propp, *Exodus*, 228–229).

10 Connections are noted throughout this work as relevant.

11 See section 5.1.2 for some potential reasons as to why this may be the case.

1.4 Septuagint Studies and Exodus

The present volume stands upon the shoulders of giants within the field of Septuagint Studies. Its work could not have begun without a critical edition of the Greek text as provided by Wevers.[12] His commentaries for both text-critical and exegetical matters are also invaluable.[13] Added to his materials are a disparate set of commentaries often distinct in foci, length, and age.[14] The somewhat annotated translations of Perkins, Sandevoir and LeBoullec, and Schaper together provide any scholar working in Greek Exodus with a sturdy frame from which a foundation for interpretation can begin to be built. It is not necessary to provide a complete bibliography of work done on Greek Exodus here as the foreword to the commentary in LXX.D contains a relatively comprehensive list up until the time of its publication.[15] Articles have, of course, sprung up and will continue to do so.[16] Probably the closest work to the pres-

12 John William Wevers, *Exodus*, vol. 2 of *Vetus Testamentum Graecum, Auctoritate Academiae Scientiarum Gottingensis editum* (Göttingen: Vandenhoeck & Ruprecht, 1991).

13 John William Wevers, *Notes on the Greek Text of Exodus* (Atlanta: Scholars Press, 1990); idem, *Text History of the Greek Exodus* (Göttingen: Vandenhoek & Ruprecht, 1992).

14 Alain Le Boulluec and Pierre Sandevoir, *L'Exode*, vol. 2 of *La Bible D'Alexandrie* (Paris: Cerf, 1989); Zacharias Frankel, *Ueber den Einfluss der palästinischen Exegese auf die alexandrinische Hermeneutik* (Leipzig: J. A. Barth, 1851); idem, *Vorstudien zu der Septuaginta* (Leipzig: F. C. W. Vogel, 1841); Daniel Gurtner, *Exodus: Commentary on the Greek Text of Codex Vaticanus*, SCS (Leiden: Brill, 2013); Perkins, "Exodus: To the Reader"; Joachim Schaper, "Exodos: Das zweite Buch Mose," in *Septuaginta Deutsch. Erläuterungen und Kommentare zum griechischen Alten Testament. Band I: Genesis bis Makkabäer*, vol. 1 of *Septuaginta Deutsch. Erläuterungen und Kommentare zum griechischen Alten Testament*, ed. Martin Karrer and Wolfgang Kraus (Stuttgart: Deutsche Bibelgesellschaft, 2011), 258–324; John Screnock, *Traductor Scriptor: The Old Greek Translation of Exodus 1–14 As Scribal Activity*, VTSupp 174 (Leiden: Brill, 2017); Martha Lynn Wade, *Consistency of Translation Techniques in the Tabernacle Accounts of Exodus in the Old Greek*, SCS 49 (Atlanta: Society of Biblical Literature, 2003); Wevers, *Notes*; idem., *Text History*.

15 See Schaper, *Erläuterungen*, 273–277.

16 E.g., Eberhard Bons, "The Lord is the One who Crushes Wars: A Fresh Look at the Septuagint Translation of Exodus 15:3," in *Die Septuaginta—Geschichte, Wirkung, Relevanz*, ed. Martin Meiser et al., WUNT 405 (Tübignen: Mohr Siebeck, 2018), 158–167; Christopher Fresch, "The Peculiar Occurrences of οὖν in the Septuagint of Genesis and Exodus," in *XV Congress of the International Organization for Septuagint and Cognate Studies: Munich, 2013*, ed. Wolfgang Kraus, Michaël N. Van Der Meer, and Martin Meiser, SCS 64 (Atlanta: Society of Biblical Literature, 2016), 455–472; Christian Lustig, "Moses eigenes Zelt. Zur Unterscheidung zweier Zelkonzeptionen im griechischen Exodusbuch," in *Die Septuaginta—Geschichte, Wirkung, Relevanz*, ed. Martin Meiser et al., WUNT 405 (Tübignen: Mohr Siebeck, 2018), 168–180; Larry Perkins, "'Glory' in Greek Exodus: Lexical Choice in Translation and its Reflection in Secondary Translations," in *Translation is Required: The Septuagint in Retrospect and Prospect*, ed. Robert J. V. Hiebert, SCS 56

ent study would be that of my colleague at Oxford, Jelle Verburg. He, too, has looked to the documentary legal sources as well as to Ptolemaic legal practice in order to shed light on the Old Greek Covenant Code.[17] His research does not intersect with the contents of this work, although it does support my broader hypothesis. For the future, *The Society of Biblical Literature Commentary on the Septuagint* (SBLCS) and its volume for Exodus seems to be the next comprehensive volume on Greek Exodus to arise.[18]

More broadly, the relationship of biblical texts to the documentary sources of Ptolemaic Egypt has not been without discussion.[19] Here we have Deissmann, Moulton and Milligan, Horsley and Llewelyn, Spicq, and Lee.[20] The lexicons of Lust and Muraoka cannot go without mention, along with the latter's recent

(Leiden: Brill, 2011), 87–106; idem, "Israel's Military Characterization in Greek Exodus," in *Die Septuaginta—Orte und Intentionen* (ed. Sigfried Kreuzer, Martin Meiser, and Marcus Sigismund, WUNT 361 (Tübingen: Mohr Siebeck, 2016), 550–563; idem, "The Greek Translator of Exodus—Interpres (translator) and Expositor (interpreter)—His Treatment of Theophanies," *JSJ* 43/3 (2012): 1–41; idem, "The Translation of אהל מועד/משכן and שכן in Greek Exodus," *JSCS* 48 (2015): 8–26.

17 Most notably, Jelle Verburg, "The LXX of the Law of Deposit in Exodus 22:6–14," *JSCS* 51 (2018): 66–83.

18 I am working with Larry Perkins on this volume and it does not yet have a definite publication date.

19 "Biblical texts" here and throughout this work refer to the traditional corpus of sacred texts under that label. It is recognized that sacred texts were not categorized so neatly in ancient Judaism.

20 Respectively, Adolf Deissmann, *Licht vom Osten. Das Neue Testament und die neuentdeckten Texteder hellenistisch-römischen Welt*, 4th ed. (Tübingen: Mohr Siebeck, 1923); James H. Moulton and George Milligan, *The Vocabulary of the Greek Testament Illustrated from the Papyri and Other Non-literary Sources* (London: Hodder and Stoughton, 1930); Greg H. R. Horsley and Stephen R. Llewelyn, eds., *New Documents Illustrating Early Christianity*, 10 vols. (Sydney: Macquarie University, 1976–2008); Ceslas Spicq, *Theological Lexicon of the New Testament*, trans. and ed. James D. Ernest, 3 vols. (Peabody: Hendrickson, 1994); John A. L. Lee, *A Lexical Study of the Septuagint Version of the Pentateuch* (Chico: Scholars Press, 1983); idem, *The Greek of the Pentateuch: Grinfield Lectures on the Septuagint 2011–2012* (Oxford: Oxford University Press, 2018); idem, "The Vocabulary of the Septuagint and Documentary Evidence," in *Die Sprache der Septuaginta*, vol. 3 of *Handbuch zur Septuaginta*, ed. Eberhard Bons and Jan Joosten (Gütersloh: Gütersloher Verlagshaus, 2016), 98–108. Michaël N. van der Meer, "Papyrological Perspectives on the Septuagint of Isaiah," in *The Old Greek of Isaiah: Issues and Perspectives*, ed. Arie van der Kooij and Michaël N. van der Meer, CBET 55 (Leuven: Peeters, 2010), 110 and fn. 22–24 provide a list of Italian papyrological scholarship which also relate to LXX lexicography; see also Franz Winter, "Die dokumentarischen Papyri Ägyptens und die Septuaginta: Studien zu Köln," *Tyche* 17 (2002): 197, fn. 27, for a listing of Anna Passoni dell'Acqusa's works in LXX and documentary texts.

grammar.[21] Similarly, Trevor Evans has provided exceptional syntactic and lexicographic commentary.[22] Others have honed in on the legal sphere of Ptolemaic Egypt with undertakings ranging from lexicographic investigations to cultural analyses regarding the place of the LXX and Jewish legal practice in Ptolemaic Egypt.[23] To the present author's knowledge, these enquiries into law and the LXX have not touched upon the subject matter in the present work.

21 Johan Lust, Erik Eynikel, and Katrin Hauspie, A *Greek-English Lexicon of the Septuagint*, rev. ed., (Stuttgart: Deutsche Bibelgesellschaft, 2003); Takamitsu Muraoka, *A Greek-English Lexicon of the Septuagint* (Louvain: Peeters, 2009); idem, *A Syntax of Septuagint Greek* (Leuven: Peeters, 2016).

22 E.g., *Verbal Syntax in the Greek Pentateuch: Natural Greek Usage and Hebrew Interference* (Oxford: Oxford University Press, 2001); idem, "The Nature of Septuagint Greek: Language and Lexicography," in *The Oxford Handbook of the Septuagint*, ed. Alison G. Salvesen and Timothy Michael Law (Oxford: Oxford University Press, 2021), 91–104.

23 E.g., Sheldon H. Blank, "The LXX Renderings of Old Testament Terms for Law," *Hebrew Union College Annual* 7 (1930): 259–283; Hélène Cadell, "Vocabulaire de la législation ptolémaïque: problème du sens de dikaioma dans le Pentateuque," in *Kata tous O' "Selon les Septante": Trente études sur la Bible grecque des Septante*, ed. Gilles Dorival and Olivier Munnich (Paris: Cerf, 1995), 207–221; Cécile Dogniez, "Le vocabulaire de la loi dans la Septante," in *Die Sprache der Septuaginta*, vol. 3 of *Handbuch zur Septuaginta*, ed. Eberhard Bons and Jan Joosten (Gütersloh: Gütersloher Verlagshaus, 2016), 350–354; Robert A. Kugler, *Resolving Disputes in Second Century BCE Herakleopolis: A Study in Jewish Legal Reasoning in Hellenistic Egypt* (Leiden: Brill, 2022); particularly idem, "Uncovering a New Dimension of Early Judean Interpretation of the Greek Torah: Ptolemaic Law Interpreted by Its Own Rhetoric," in *Changes in Scripture: Rewriting and Interpreting Authoritative Traditions in the Second Temple Period*, ed. Hanne von Weissenberg, Juha Pakkala, and Marko Marttila (Berlin: de Gruyter, 2011), 165–175; idem, "Dispelling an Illusion of Otherness? Juridical Practice in the Herakleopolis Papyri," in *The "Other" in Second Temple Judaism: Essays in Honor of John J. Collins*, ed. Daniel C. Harlow et al. (Grand Rapids: Eerdmans, 2011), 457–470; idem, "Uncovering Echoes of LXX Legal Norms in Hellenistic Egyptian Documentary Papyri: The Case of the Second-Century Herakleopolite Nome," in *XIV Congress of the International Organization for Septuagint and Cognate Studies, Helsinki 2010*, ed. Melvin K. H. Peters (Atlanta: Society of Biblical Literature, 2013), 142–153; John A. Lee "A Lexical Study Thirty Years on, with Observations on 'Order' Words in the LXX Pentateuch," in *Emanuel. Studies in Hebrew Bible, Septuagint and Dead Sea Scrolls in Honor of Emanuel Tov*, ed. Shalom M. Paul et al. (Leiden: Brill, 2003), 513–524; Joseph Mélèze-Modrzejewski, "La Septante comme nomos. Comment la Torah est devenue une loi civique pour les Juifs d'Égypte," *Annali di scienze religiose* 2 (1997): 143–158; Laurent Monsengwo Pasinya, *La notion de NOMOS dans le Pentateuque grec* (Rome: Biblical Institute Press, 1973); Anna Passoni Dell'Acqua, "Il Pentateuco Dei LXX Testimone Di Istituzioni Di Età Tolemaica," *Annali Di Scienze Religiose* 4 (1999): 171–200; idem, "La terminologia dei reati nei προστάγματα dei Tolemei e nella versione dei LXX," in *Proceedings of the XVIIIth International Congress of Papyrology*, vol. 2 of *Proceedings of the XVIIIth International Congress of Papyrology*, ed. Vasileios G. Mandēlaras (Athens: Greek Papyrological Society, 1988), 335–350; idem, "Ricerche Sulla Versione Dei LXX e i Papiri II. Nomós," *Aegyptus* 62, no. 1/2 (1982): 173–94.

This is no doubt due in part to the fact that Greek Exodus makes use of translation strategies that are somewhere in between the Greek legal formulae of the day and the translator's own invention (due to the aforementioned SSF) in these cases involving the death penalty. These kinds of translations would not show up in typical lexical searches of legal terms.

The following investigation into LXX Exodus hopes to contribute to the conversation begun by these forebears and colleagues working in the field. Some of their research will find greater resonance with its findings due to shared presuppositions when it comes to interpreting the text.

1.5 Methodological Considerations

1.5.1 *Hebrew and Greek Texts*

As basic texts for reference, *BHS* and the Göttingen edition of the Septuagint corpus will be used. Rahlfs's edition supplements any texts not yet complete in the Göttingen series.[24] I do not assume that MT stands behind the Greek text as its *Vorlage*. At the same time, it is not controversial to claim that there is a great deal of congruity between what we now know as MT and the *Vorlage* of Greek Exodus.[25] Cases where this assumption needs to be questioned will be dealt with on a case-by-case basis. It is also not appropriate to claim that the eclectic text produced by Wevers completely represents the oldest iteration of the translation. Even still, this study will presuppose its accuracy and tentatively label it the Old Greek (OG). This decision is in part influenced by the desire not to be biased towards other readings that could support my foundational claims. This rule is only broken in one case where there are significant factors lending support against Wevers's text (see section 4.4.2.8).

Greek literary texts are consulted from both TLG as well as from the translations and editions provided online by the Loeb Classical Library.[26] Documentary sources are in large part accessed through papyri.info or trismegistos.org for papyrological texts and inscriptions.packhum.org or https://scholarlyeditions.brill.com/sego/ for inscriptional materials. These websites are supplemented with hard-copy resources when texts are not available online and they are documented as used. Translations of documentary sources are either cited from a secondary source or are my own.

24 As found in Alfred Rahlfs, *Septuaginta: With Morphology* (Stuttgart: Deutsche Bibelgesellschaft, 1979), electronic edition.

25 Perkins, "To the Reader," 43.

26 Found at https://www.loebclassics.com.

1.5.2 *Interpreting the Septuagint*

Alive and vigorous is the discussion on how to interpret the Septuagint.[27] The present work situates its analysis within a few confines that are relatively well established in the field. One such limitation will be the assumption that the Greek translation of Exodus belongs to the third century BCE and was made in Egypt.[28] Another would be that LXX Exodus can and will be approached from the perspective of the text-as-produced rather than the text-as-received.[29] That is, no attention is given to how Greek Exodus was interpreted by later communities after its initial production.[30] Rather, I attempt first to understand the translator's choices based on the assumption that the translation is "an entity dependent on its source text in distinction from the translated text."[31] The brass tacks of this approach are that the Hebrew parent text must act as the point of origin from which all interpretive enterprises take motion. This method entails that priority is given to explanations of the Greek text that emerge from a judicious examination of the Hebrew source text. It asks what types of potential linguistic interference could emerge when moving from the Hebrew language to the Greek language. While such comparisons and evaluations sound easy in theory, working from the angle of text-as-produced brings along with it a world of questions that play no small part in the interpretive

27 A wonderful synopsis of the current points of consideration, methodologies, and schools of thought can be found in Jean Maurais, *Characterizing Old Greek Deuteronomy as an Ancient Translation*, JSJS 203 (Leiden: Brill, 2022), 49–97, particularly 49–92. See also Martin Rösel, "From the Torah to Nomos: Perspectives of Research on the Greek Pentateuch," in *Introduction to the LXX*, ed. Siegfried Kreuzer (Waco: Baylor University Press, 2019), 65–73.

28 See, e.g., James K. Aitken, *The T&T Clark Companion to the Septuagint* (London: Bloomsbury, 2015), 3; Jennifer M. Dines and Michael A. Knibb, *The Septuagint* (London: T&T Clark, 2005), 41–44; Natalio Fernández-Marcos, *The Septuagint in Context: Introduction to the Greek Versions of the Bible* (Boston: Brill Academic, 2001), 40; Henry Barclay Swete, Henry J. Thackeray, and Richard Rusden Ottley, *An Introduction to the Old Testament in Greek* (Cambridge: Cambridge University Press, 1914), 9–28.

29 Albert Pietersma, "The Society of Biblical Literature Commentary on the Septuagint: Basic Principles," in *The SBL Commentary on the Septuagint: An Introduction*, ed. Dirk Büchner (Atlanta: SBL Press, 2017), 2–8. An example at work would be Albert Pietersma, "A Commentary on Psalm 15 in Greek: Text-Production and Text Reception," in *Die Septuaginta—Texte Theologien, Einflüsse*, ed. Wolfgang Kraus and Martin Karrer with Martin Meiser (Tübingen: Mohr Siebeck, 2010), 523–542.

30 This is not to say that the translator did not translate in ways that diverge from the Hebrew source text based on extenuating factors such as the original expected audience(s) of the translation. Only later reception of Greek Exodus is precluded here. For a helpful overview of the distinction between interpretation based in text-as-produced as opposed to text-as-received see Maurais, *Characterizing Old Greek*, 49–58.

31 Pietersma, "The Society," 2.

process: How do we quantify what constitutes linguistic interference or adaptation? Should a translation be considered literal or free, and are these kinds of divisions even appropriate?[32] Is it possible to lay claim to the 'norms' of a translation? How might we quantify or categorize them? If a translator does maintain a typical translation equivalent, does that particularly stereotypical translation choice represent merely a 'symbol' or 'stand-in' that points back to its Hebrew referent? All these questions are current points of contention and concern in Septuagint scholarship. Maurais gives a helpful summary of the avenues that can be explored when beginning to answer such questions:

> Factors explaining particular renderings may include the linguistic background of the translator (including his familiarity with other languages such as Aramaic), his reading tradition of a given book, interference from the source text, linguistic challenges in the target language, theological/ideological tendencies, and many others. These all come into scope as one examines the strategies employed. Nevertheless, apparent departures from the source text need to be understood in the broader context of the verbal make-up of the translation and the overall norms governing it, insofar as they can be inferred … The outcome of this analysis is the ability to further refine our understanding of how the translator worked by examining the many strategies that he adopts in specific contexts and taking steps towards identifying his overall norms and preference values. In this way, departures from the source text are interpreted in an appropriate context, that of the constitutive character of the text.[33]

Strategies such as these undergird the inquiries into the translation of the death penalty laws found in the present work. In addition, along with the assumption of the importance of the source text in determining the rationale behind a translation choice, I leave room to compare the Greek text with contemporary Greek literary and documentary sources in order to gain insights into the translation. This process is part of discerning the give-and-take between the mediating influence of the source text and the target text. Pietersma notes this interpretive back-and-forth: "Crucial for determining the linguistic make-up of

32 James Barr, *The Typology of Literalism in Ancient Biblical Translations* (Göttingen: Vandenhoeck & Ruprecht, 1979), famously breaks down the literal-free divide. See also, e.g., Cameron Boyd-Taylor, "The Classification of Literalism in Ancient Hebrew-Greek Translation," in *Die Sprache der Septuaginta*, vol. 3 of *Handbuch zur Septuaginta*, ed. Eberhard Bons and Jan Joosten (Gütersloh: Gütersloher Verlagshaus, 2016), 121–142.

33 Jean Maurais, "Translated Torah: Characterizing Old Greek Deuteronomy as an Ancient Translation" (PhD diss., McGill University, 2020), 84–85.

the text-as-produced, or rather its constitutive character, is, on the one hand, to map the translated text onto its source text, in order to establish what sort of translation one is dealing with, and, on the other, to consult Greek composition literature of the period in order to determine what sort of Greek document it is."[34] One must, in a sense, be cross-eyed when attempting to discern the steps taken by the translator. It is here where the greatest certainty can begin to emerge as to the process and intent of the translator in his renderings. To this end, Maurais gives a helpful table describing the relationship between the Hebrew parent text with its expression in the Greek target text:[35]

TABLE 1.1 Aspects and levels of analysis

Adequacy	Level of analysis	Acceptability
Tension with literary conventions and ideological values	Literary and cultural	Features of the source text brought in compliance with literary and ideological norms
Disruptions to the coherence and cohesion of the target text	Textual-Linguistic	Features of discourse and style introduced by the translator
Interference at the level of grammar, syntax, and the lexicon	Linguistic	Conventional grammatical and lexical uses

Here he draws on the language of adequacy and acceptability as means of describing the character of the resulting text.[36] The former can be defined as "the analytical category that is concerned with the description of translational strategies and their regulative norms."[37] Adequacy analyzes the connection between the translation and its source text. Acceptability, on the other hand, "seeks to describe the translation in relation to the textual and linguistic conventions of the target culture, i.e., those attested in monolingual productions."[38] These categories "are meant to be non-prescriptive descriptors of the translation's relationship to both its source text and target conventions"

34 Pietersma, "The Society," 7.
35 Maurais, *Characterizing Old Greek*, 79.
36 For further discussion on these categories see Maurais, *Characterizing Old Greek*, 76–81.
37 Maurais, *Characterizing Old Greek*, 77.
38 Maurais, *Characterizing Old Greek*, 77.

whose relationship to each other should be perceived more as on a continuum than as rigid divides.[39] I investigate each of these respective levels of analysis as potential explanations for a given rendering. Any facet of the translation will be weighed against both the source text and the target text in light of the translation's adequacy or acceptability, with explanations of a given rendering necessarily ascending each level of analysis.[40] This kind of approach is necessary as it places the burden of proof on the interpreter, who must show how a particular rendering demonstrates adequacy or acceptability, should either one of them be claimed.

When it comes to the use of documentary sources, appeals to legal terminology or the legal genre will be supported with appropriate evidence. However, not many claims about a specific word or phrase being exclusive to a specific legal genre will be made. Rather, the documentary sources are mostly drawn upon when making broader claims about the Greek language in general as it was operative at the time of the translation.[41] In this way, the data presented here are not much different from the material presented by those who in the past have drawn upon the documentary sources for LXX research. My work differs primarily with respect to which items are investigated.

A helpful limitation of the present research is that I do not intend to provide a full portrait of the Old Greek translation of Exodus. Instead, I ask very focused questions relating to a set of laws involving a single topic, namely, the death penalty. That the project focuses on this sphere of law also allows for the data to be analyzed within a more controlled setting than a study looking to a plethora of legal categories might. A large portion of the data relates only to a single Hebrew term (מות) and its translation in a string of casuistic penal clauses in the Covenant Code. Chapter 4 does diverge into alternative cases, and here greater pains are undertaken to solidify the relationship between the Hebrew and Greek texts. What emerge from an examination of these laws are strong indications that in multiple places not enough scholarly concern has been placed on the meaning of the Greek text in relation to what can be seen in the contemporary sources. This is to say that the Greek text does not seem to reflect the meaning of the Hebrew text in contexts where there is arguably no viable reason for some sort of interference from that source text. These arguments should stand on their own as the first and most important facet of this study. They are the point of departure from which I present a new hypothesis.

39 Maurais, *Characterizing Old Greek*, 77.

40 That is, beginning from linguistic up to literary.

41 In some cases there is a mix of common terms within genre-specific analyses, such as with πᾶν as it is used in documentary legal sources (section 4.4.2).

The undoubtedly more controversial element of this research is the postulation that these text-linguistic transformations find parallels with Greco-Egyptian law as it is known at the time of the translation. I admit from the outset that these translation choices cannot be unambiguously proven to be influenced by Greco-Egyptian law. It is not possible to have certainty regarding the mind of the translator in extra-textual factors like these. The comparison should be seen then within the realm of heuristic devices that could lead to fruitful discussions and potentially further insights into the translation and its environs. This is not to say that this hypothesis does not have teeth. Something must explain the transformations, and this perspective has much to merit its consideration. It should be emphasized that other studies in the Greek Pentateuch have uncovered significant cultural adaptations made in the translations which correspond to the Greco-Egyptian context.[42] That the translator might adapt the text is not overly controversial, even though this has not been discussed much with regard to the Ptolemaic legal context. Even still, the merits of the present hypothesis are not immediately obvious to those who do not know the cultural and legal situation in which Greek Exodus was translated. The interdisciplinary nature of this approach requires some prolegomena before more formal assessments can take place.

1.5.3 *The Ptolemaic Legal System and Greco-Egyptian Legal Practice*

Scholarly deliberations concerning a wealth of legal practices during the Ptolemaic era have been ongoing for more than a century.[43] Some matters are still unresolved or disputed, and those that intersect with the subject matter of the present study will be mentioned when required. Fortunately, the broader contours of the system introduced by the Ptolemies are relatively

42 E.g., Martin Rösel, "The Septuagint: Translating and Adapting the Torah to the 3rd Century BCE," in *Times of Transition: Judea in the Early Hellenistic Period*, ed. Sylvie Honigman, Christophe Nihan, and Oded Lipschits (Grand Rapids: Eisenbrauns, 2021), 253–262, particularly 253–257, gives a recent and succinct list of adaptations away from the Hebrew text of the Pentateuch towards both the cultural environment of Ptolemaic Egypt as well as to developing Jewish thought. Cf., e.g., Gilles Dorival, "The Septuagint Between Judaism and Hellenism," in *Die Septuaginta—Text, Wirkung, Rezeption*, ed. Wolfgang Kraus et al., WUNT 325 (Tübingen: Mohr Siebeck, 2014), 29–31.

43 See, e.g., many entries in *JJP*. Classic synopses for Ptolemaic Egypt are Erwin Seidl, *Ptolemäische Rechtsgeschichte* (Glückstadt: Augustin, 1962), and Raphael Taubenschlag, *The Law of Greco-Roman Egypt in the Light of the Papyri 332 BC–640 AD*, rev. ed. (Warsaw: Panstwowe Wydawnictwo Naukowe, 1955). More recent is the capstone work of Joseph Mélèze-Modrzejewski, *Loi et coutume dans l'Egypte grecque et romaine* (Varsovie: Faculty of Law and Administration of the University of Warsaw, 2014).

agreed upon.[44] In order to speak to the potential influence of legal norms on the translation, it is essential to understand both this system as well as the legal influences and kinds of Greek law found in Ptolemaic Egypt.

Ptolemaic Egypt was a diverse and multicultural environment that did not feature cultural or ethnic unity outside of, perhaps, some syncretistic religious initiatives.[45] Such ethnic freedom is echoed in Ptolemaic Egypt's legal practices as well. Instead of creating a monolithic set of regulations by which all residents of Egypt must abide, the Ptolemies designed a system that allowed for judicial diversity as based on a few contributing factors.[46] Mélèze-Modrzejewski gives a helpful summary:

> Ptolemaic Egypt offers the legal historian a particularly interesting example of legal pluralism … Egyptian local law, which the Greeks called *nomoi tes choras* (νόμοι τῆς χώρας), the 'law of the land', was still in force for the indigenous population. The immigrants had imported their own legal traditions: the Greek *nomoi*. In the cities—Alexandria, Naucratis, Ptolemais—these took the traditional form of written legislation, often influenced by the reigning monarch. In the *chora*, they spread as a substantially homogeneous customary law, the 'common law' of the Greeks. Over and against the Greek and Egyptian *nomoi*, the will of the Ptolemaic sovereign was expressed in royal regulations, *diagrammata* (διαγράμματα), and orders, *prostagmata* (προστάγματα). Faced with the problems created by the existence of legal rules of unequal weight and of various provenance, the Ptolemies did not strive to unify the content of these various legal sources. Another solution was found: the kingdom was blanketed by a double network of jurisdictions, each one authorized to deal with the cases falling within its specific nationally-determined competence: the dicasteries in the cities and in the *chora* for the Greek-speaking

---

44 See previous footnote. For a recent and more minimalistic approach see Uri Yiftach, "Law in Ptolemaic and Roman Egypt," in *The Oxford Handbook of Ancient Greek Law*, ed. Edward M. Harris and Mirko Canevaro (Oxford: Oxford University Press, 2020), 1–54.

45 Mélèze-Modrzejewski, *Loi et Coutume*, 185–188. Naphtali Lewis, *Greeks in Ptolemaic Egypt: Case Studies in the Social History of the Hellenistic World* (Oxford: Clarendon Press, 1986), 4, 154; See section 4.5.4 for religious syncretism. Joseph Manning, "Hellenistic Egypt," in *The Cambridge Economic History of the Greco-Roman World*, ed. Walter Scheidel, Ian Morris, and Richard P. Saller (Cambridge: Cambridge University Press, 2007), 435, points out that there was more cohesion in economics.

46 See Mélèze-Modrzejewski, *Loi et Coutume*, 142–150, particularly 147 and Chapter 3, for an in-depth discussion on the diversity in this legal system. For another summary see Gerhard (Graz) Thür, "Legal pluralism," BNP: http://dx.doi.org/10.1163/1574-9347_bnp_e1019600.

> immigrants, and the courts of *laocritae* ('people's judges'), staffed by Egyptian priests, for cases involving the indigenous population; the king reserved the right of intervention in any and all litigation, either directly or indirectly, through the *chrematistae*, royal judges.[47]

This ingenious approach circumvented the difficult task of creating a unifying law code. It also avoided the problems that would arise from imposing such a constraint on a variegated set of subjects each accustomed to their own differing legal heritages and moral norms. For instance, Egyptians were traditionally inclined to follow customs rather than a set legal manual or code (though such codes are attested in part), and the Ptolemies permitted this to continue under their supervision.[48] Indeed, custom and tradition seems to have played a considerable legal role at the outset of the era for many groups, especially in the *chora* outside of the three main cities.[49] Here would be found a mix of Greek and Egyptian legal traditions, of which the Greek aspect "peuvent bien remonter, quant au fond, à l'activité législative des cités grecques anciennes" since this is where many would have immigrated from.[50] Added to the vocabulary introduced by Mélèze-Modrzejewski is the phrase πολιτικοὶ νόμοι. This collocation has in more recent times been understood, generally, to refer to some sort of judicial means for persons of various nationalities and legal heritages to bring their own traditions to court to act in a given legal process.[51]

47 Joseph Mélèze-Modrzejewski, "Jewish Law and Hellenistic Legal Practice in the Light of Greek Papyri from Egypt," in *An Introduction to the History and Sources of Jewish Law*, ed. Neil S. Hecht et al. (Oxford: Oxford University Press, 1996), 82.

48 Mélèze-Modrzejewski, *Loi et Coutume*, 86–87 (cf. 102). It is not known if Egyptian courts were able to carry through with penalties themselves (Andréas Helmis, "Crime et châtiment dans l'Égypte ptolémaïque. Recherches sur l'autonomie d'un modèle penal" [DPhil diss., Université de Paris x – Nanterre, 1986], 143), but some inferences can be made for small crime (cf. ibid., 152 and P.Enteux. 50 and 83). Sandra Lippert, "Law Courts," UEE: 8, https://escholarship.org/uc/item/4136j3s7, suggests that the *laocritae* were "limited to civil cases and minor criminal ones." This is based in part on the crimes attested from their court documents. A list can be found in Ursula Kaplony-Heckel, *Die Demotischen Tempeleide: Teil 1: Text*, vol. 1 of *Die Demotischen Tempeleide* (Wiesbaden: Harrassowitz, 1963), 27, where she directs towards more comments on these texts throughout her work.

49 Helmis, "Crime et châtiment," 140; Mélèze-Modrzejewski, *Loi et Coutume*, 109.

50 Mélèze-Modrzejewski, *Loi et Coutume*, 109. Cf. James G. Keenan et al., "The Judicial System in Theory and Practice," in *Law and Legal Practice in Egypt from Alexander to the Arab Conquest: A Selection of Papyrological Sources in Translation, with Introductions and Commentary*, ed. James G. Keenan, Joseph G. Manning, and Uri Yiftach-Firanko (Cambridge: Cambridge University Press, 2014), 472; Helmis, "Crime et châtiment," 143.

51 See Mélèze-Modrzejewski, *Loi et Coutume*, 151–169 for the various meanings ascribed to this collocation. Of note, Hans J. Wolff, "Plurality of Laws in Ptolemaic Egypt," *RIDA* 7 (1960): 219, thought the phrase refers to actual physical foreign laws brought to court (cf.

In other words, in Ptolemaic Egypt one could bring their own legal tradition to a judge who could then decide whether to arbitrate based on that custom. Of course, cases in which persons of different nationalities or legal traditions were opposed to each other would create tension, but this is a friction that the Ptolemies seemed to readily accept.[52]

Into this world we can insert the legal traditions of the Jews, the Torah. It seems more than likely that most Jewish residents of Ptolemaic Egypt could draw on their legal heritage as πολιτικοὶ νόμοι[53]—whether or not they would actually be acted upon by a judge/official is another matter and these laws would be subject to any other Ptolemaic diktats that could override their authority.[54] This data point should serve as a potential first stop in delimiting the rationale for the changes found in Ex, should they be derived from this Ptolemaic legal milieu. Torah was respected in Ptolemaic Egypt in that it could be at least brought to court.[55] No one was telling Jews to 'throw out their scrolls' before arriving. This acceptability of Jewish law could stand behind

Mélèze-Modrzejewski, *Loi et Coutume*, 158 for the impracticality of this view). Another option suggested is that they are the city laws of Alexandria (James L. O'Neil, "Royal Authority and City Law under Alexander and His Hellenistic Successors," *CLQ* 50, no. 2 [2000]: 427). Helmis comments specifically on the *punishments* of these possible legal heritages being applied ("Crime et châtiment," 152).

52 Cf. Michael Rostovtzeff, "Chapter IV: Ptolemaic Egypt," in CAH: *The Hellenistic World*, vol. 7, pt. 1 of CAH, ed. John B. Bury et al. (Cambridge: Cambridge University Press, 1923), 123, stating that laws "undoubtably often contradicted each other."

53 Joseph Mélèze-Modrzejewski, "The Septuagint as Nomos: How the Torah Became a 'Civic Law' for the Jews of Egypt," in *Critical Studies in Ancient Law, Comparative Law and Legal History: Studies in Honour of Alan Watson*, ed. John W. Cairns and Olivia F. Robinson (London: Hart Publishing, 2001), 183–200; Keenan et al., "The Judicial," 472; Seth Schwartz, "Law in Jewish Society in the Second Temple Period," in *The Cambridge Companion to Judaism and Law*, ed. Christine Hayes (Cambridge: Cambridge University Press, 2017), 59–64, particularly 59–61.

54 Joseph Mélèze-Modrzejewski, "La sanction de l'homicide en droit grec et hellénistique," in *Mélanges Pierre Lévêque. Tome 7: Anthropologie et société*, vol. 7 of *Mélanges Pierre Lévêque*, ed. Marie-Madeleine Mactoux and Évelyne Geny (Paris: les Belles lettres, 1993), 255; Leiv Amundsen, "The Classical Greek background of Ptolemaic law and Administration of Justice," in *Acta Congressus Madvigiani* (*Proceedings of the Second International Congress of Classical Studies*) 1, ed. Carsten Hoeg, Per Krarup, and P. J. Riis (Copenhagen: Ejnar Munksgaard, 1958), 257–258. Despite such overruling, even at the start of the era Alexander began exemplifying respect and sensibility for the civic codes that existed (O'Neil, "Royal Authority," 425). Schwartz, "Law in Jewish Society," 59, suggests that the scope of any enduring πολιτικοὶ νόμοι was relegated to "the realm of religion and limited areas of private law."

55 For evidence of this practice and Jewish law vis-à-vis Ptolemaic legal practice, see section 1.6 below.

the translation. However, there is an alternative paradigm that should also be considered.

It is widely acknowledged that the three *poleis* of Ptolemaic Egypt, Alexandria, Naucratis, and Ptolemais, held some degree of autonomy in political and legal matters.[56] These cities had their own set of codified laws[57] which were likely quite similar to one another.[58] P.Hal. represents part of this civic code for Alexandria.[59] Yet outside of this document and a few other more minor items, "The civic laws and institutions of Alexandria and the other Greek cities of Egypt … are poorly known."[60] Likewise, the details of these cities are scarcely discernable.[61] Even still, if it is true that there were civic codes in these *poleis*, then it is harder to imagine that Jewish Torah could have been brought as a counterclaim to such laws in a given legal dispute. Jews could do this in the *chora* but maybe not in the major cities, lest we might conceive of a gap in these civic laws where nothing was written on a subject. Most of the laws discussed in the present work would be matters falling under typical Greek legislative aims, so this would not likely be the case. So, from the perspective of law as practiced in the cities, it might be the case that the translator worked in such a way as to conform to these civic legal standards. From this angle the translation choices could be situated as emerging from necessity, since there would be the legal pressures of the city that stood opposed to some of the prescriptions found in the Hebrew laws.[62] There is one piece of evidence that might suggest that the translation was intended to be read within the confines of these cities. Previous commentators point out that in rendering τὰ ἰατρεῖα ("the medical fees") as paid for by the assailant in Exod 21:19, the law now conforms to the practice of Ptolemaic Egypt, and that specifically of a Greek city and

56 Sandra Coussement, *Because I Am Greek: Polyonymy as an Expression of Ethnicity in Ptolemaic Egypt* (Leuven: Peeters, 2016), 129; Taubenschlag, *The Law of Greco-Roman*, 572–573.

57 Thür, "Legal pluralism;" Taubenschlag, *The Law of Greco-Roman*, 576.

58 Amundsen, "The Classical Greek," 258.

59 Peter Marshall Fraser, *Ptolemaic Alexandria: Text*, vol. 1 of *Ptolemaic Alexandria* (Oxford: Clarendon Press, 2001), 109; Joseph Mélèze-Modrzejewski, "La règle de droit dans l'Egypte ptolemaique: état des questions et perspectives de recherches," in *Essays in Honor of C. Bradford Wells*, ed. Alan C. Samuel (New Haven: The American Society of Papyrologists, 1966), 131.

60 Roger S. Bagnall and Peter Derow, *The Hellenistic Period: Historical Sources in Translation* (New York: John Wiley & Sons, 2008), 206.

61 "The most serious absence of evidence is our restricted knowledge of the Greek urban centers (Alexandria, Naucratis, Ptolemais)" (Manning, "Hellenistic Egypt," 434).

62 Why the translator would feel the need to conform the text to these laws is another question altogether and will be considered in 5.1.2.

not an Egyptian city.[63] Predominantly Egyptian cities like those in the *chora* received free medical care. There may be other indicators of the Greek city present in Ex, but as of yet they are not obvious.

It is not my present intention to take a stance on either of these potential legal frameworks that may be active in the translation's backdrop. Rather, my purpose is broader in that it is only the similarities with Greek law that are being presented. So, what place did the subject matter of the laws covered in the present volume have in Ptolemaic Egypt?

When it comes to the cases covered in this study, that is, matters of (mostly) private law that led to the death penalty, it might come as a surprise that the Lagids rarely dictated royal decrees concerning private law.[64] Rather, private law including matters of assault, murder, and theft "restant ainsi régis par des règles d'essence coutumière."[65] Or, more broadly, they were based on "la pratique contractuelle, aux statuts des associations, aux lois poliades d'Alexandrie."[66] This is not to say that capital jurisdiction was given to any case asking for it, but rather that it was particularly the inherited legal traditions of Greeks and Egyptians that would have defined the heinousness and culpability of offenders in these areas.[67] The actual sanctioning of a death in these

63 Le Boulluec and Sandevoir, *L'Exode*, 219, and Schaper, *Erläuterungen*, 302. For the distinction between Greek and Egyptian cities see Fraser, *Ptolemaic*, 373–374; Willy Clarysse and Dorothy J. Thompson, *Counting the People in Hellenistic Egypt. Volume 2: Historical Studies*, vol. 2 of *Counting the People in Hellenistic Egypt* (Cambridge: Cambridge University Press, 2006), 162, with the caveat that "evidence is conflicting" concerning public funds that may been allocated to the Greek community as well (fn. 204). Darrel W. Amundsen and Gary B. Ferngren, "The Forensic Role of Physicians in Ptolemaic and Roman Egypt," *Bulletin of the History of Medicine* 52, no. 3 (Fall, 1978): 339, claim that it is unclear whether everyone received free healthcare or only specific classes of people.

64 Hans Julius Wolff, "Law in Ptolemaic Egypt," in *Essays in Honor of C. Bradford Wells*, ed. Alan C. Samuel (New Haven: The American Society of Papyrologists, 1966), 71. Matters like homicide seem to have been on the border of the private and public legal spheres (Helmis, "Crime et châtiment," 151). The Ptolemies still seemed to leave such cases to the normal judicial measures and did not interfere with trials (ibid.). Frédéric Bluche, "La peine de mort dans l'Égypte ptolémaïque," *RIDA*, 3ᵉ série, 22 (1975): 145, believes that cases such as murder would become public. In Athens cases involving the death penalty were public (see section 3.3.2). Even still, as will be discussed, the Ptolemies were relatively removed from personal injuries and their legal compensation.

65 Helmis, "Crime et châtiment," 146 (cf. 140–143, 146–148). Helmis quite boldly states that the Ptolemies bowed to legal customs in the third century despite being in the height of their power (154). If they interfered, it would be discreetly (ibid.).

66 Méleze-Modrzejewski, "La sanction," 256, here referring to homicide specifically.

67 Helmis, "Crime et châtiment," 148, notes that the only governmental aspect of private legal cases like these would be the court, but the sentence would be according to the respective legal traditions presented. Cases involving death may have been more complex

cases would more than likely belong to high Ptolemaic authorities, as was in line with Pharaonic tradition.[68] Greek officials took over the role of the great courts from Egypt, which previously judged cases of capital punishment.[69] Private or borderline private legal cases like these would need to be brought by the offended party to the local officials.[70] So then, if one were to look for Greco-Egyptian legal expectations concerning private laws like those covered in the Covenant Code, it is the Greek (and to a degree Egyptian) legal traditions brought into and inherent within Ptolemaic Egypt that must be consulted. The question is, of course, what legal customs and norms were found in Egypt, and what evidence do we have for them? These questions will continually be asked as each respective subject matter is addressed. For now, the nature and sources of Greek law imported to Egypt need to be established, since it is Greek influence that is posited for the changes found in Ex. This is not to say that traditional/inherited Greek legal norms are the only thing that might influence the translation. The translational changes seem to reflect a consciousness towards both traditional Greek law and royal/Ptolemaic legal concerns, depending on the issue at hand. It is the whole force of Greek legal expectations (both royal and civic) that I postulate drive the changes. It must also be emphasized that, as much as can be demonstrated, I will give prominence to the evidence measurable from Ptolemaic Egypt and then use Classical law as a means of responsibly filling in lacunae. This, of course, prompts the question: Does Classical Greek law even fit into Ptolemaic Egypt?

It would be remiss to claim that the Mediterranean world broadly, along with Pharaonic Egypt and the Persian incursion, did not influence the legal

(see section 1.8). Greek and Egyptian private law never merged (Herwig Maehler, "Greek, Egyptian and Roman Law," *JJP* 35 [2005]: 134–135), so one imagines capital crimes for each respective tradition remained.

68 See section 1.8. Individual crimes and the death penalty are discussed in their respective section related to the biblical laws. It appears legal matters began with the *strategos* in the third century (Taubenschlag, *The Law of Greco-Roman*, 480, 485–486 [cf. 544]; Rostovtzeff, "Ptolemaic Egypt," 122, 125). He would examine a case and direct it towards the relevant official (Victor Tcherikover et al., eds., *Corpus Papyrorum Judaicarum*, 4 vols. [Cambridge: Harvard University Press, 1957], 1:182; Lippert, "Law Courts," 9).

69 Lippert, "Law Courts," 1.

70 Erich Berneker, *Zur Geschichte der Prozesseinleitung im ptolemäischen Recht* (Ansbach: C. Brügel & Sohn, 1930), 107. The Demotic private legal documents also show this trait (Erwin Seidl, "La preuve d'après les documents demotiques," *RecSocJB* 16 [1964–1965]: 54–55). To highlight this feature of Ptolemaic legal practice, P.Hal. 124–165, 166–185 show that a magistrate who was struck in Alexandria had to bring a private suit himself, whereas previously in Athens the culprit immediately lost civic rights (Amundsen, "The Classical Greek," 261).

world of Ptolemaic Egypt.[71] The Ptolemies took on a system that was already in motion and that did not need a complete overhaul. Even still, Amundsen remarks about "how strongly the royal Ptolemaic legislation was permeated with Greek thought and spirit."[72] Some of this influence is found simply in terminological borrowing where Greek legal terms are adopted but take on new definitions suited to Egypt.[73] Similarly, institutions are carried over.[74] When it comes to the specific Greek legal influences found in Ptolemaic Egypt—as expected based on their aforementioned *modus operandi* concerning πολιτικοὶ νόμοι—there are numerous *poleis* and geographical regions represented.[75] While this fact eliminates the possibility of Athenian law being transplanted into Egypt, it remains the case that Athenian law was more than likely the pervading legal tradition brought to Egypt. Méléze-Modrzejewski states, "Nous sommes en presence d'influences diverses, parmi lesquelles le rôle d'exemples athéniens a pu être dominant, mais non pas d'une réception pure et simple du droit athénien par Alexandrie."[76] To this could be added Amundsen's comment that there are "numerous differences existing between Athenian law and the Greek law in Egypt, *in spite of their comprehensive agreement*" due to the "the dominating influence radiating from Athens."[77] Alexandria itself seems to have founded its laws on an Athenian basis[78] and our surviving civic laws from that city show in their style an "unmistakable" correspondence to the Athenian

71 Amundsen, "The Classical Greek," 256.

72 Amundsen, "The Classical Greek," 256–257, noting also the opinion of Rostovtzeff, as found in Michael Ivanovitch Rostovtzeff, *The Social & Economic History of the Hellenistic World*, 3 vols. (Oxford: Clarendon Press, 1998), 1:273. For more on Classical Greek law in general see e.g., Mark Sundahl, David C. Mirhady, and Ilias Arnaoutoglou, *A New Working Bibliography of Ancient Greek Law, 7th–4th centuries BC* (Athens: Academy of Athens, 2011), and David D. Phillips, *The Law of Ancient Athens. Law and Society in the Ancient World* (Ann Arbor: University of Michigan Press, 2013).

73 Amundsen, "The Classical Greek," 257.

74 Claire Préaux, "Les continuités dans l'Egypte gréco-romaine," in *Conclusions du xe Congrès de Papyrologues, Actes du xe Congrès International de Papyrologues, Varsovie-Cracovie, 3–9 septembre 1961*, ed. Jozef Wolski (Wrocław: Zakład Narodowy im. Ossolińskich, 1964), 234.

75 Raphael Taubenschlag, "The Ancient Greek City Laws in Ptolemaic Egypt," in *Actes du ve Congrès international de Papyrologie, Oxford, 30 août-3 septembre 1937* (Bruxelles: Fondation égyptologique reine Élisabeth, 1938), 471–489, is the classic study.

76 Méléze-Modrzejewski, *Loi et Coutume*, 124. See also Fraser, *Ptolemaic*, 110–112; Taubenschlag, *The Law of Greco-Roman*, 8–9.

77 Amundsen, "The Classical Greek," 262, 265, emphasis added.

78 Amundsen, "The Classical Greek," 254 and Michael Ivanovitch Rostovtzeff, *The Social & Economic History of the Hellenistic World*, 3 vols. (Oxford: Clarendon Press, 1998), 2:1067; Julie Vélissaropoulos, *Ἀλεξανδρινοί νόμοι. Πολιτική αυτονομία καί νομική αυτοτέλεια της πτολεμαϊκής Ἀλεξάνδρειας* (Αθήνα: Σάκκουλας, 1981), 85–89; Lippert, "Law Courts," 8.

model.[79] Even in private law, Athens is the "notable" influence in Egypt.[80] There is therefore warrant for turning to Athenian law when looking to the expectations of Greeks in Ptolemaic Egypt. Athens was also the epicenter of what is called the "legal koine" that had begun to form among Greek cities in the fourth century of which "the different civil codes of the Greek world … resembled one another increasingly from the fourth century onwards."[81] The tectonic plates of various *poleis*' legal practices had begun to shift under each other before the third century, and this fact should in turn provide at least a measure more of connectivity between Athens and average Greek legal expectations in Egypt.

It is due in part to the influence of Athenian law on the Greek laws of Ptolemaic Egypt that I will predominantly use Athenian examples in this study as points of comparison as to what Greeks 'on the ground' in Ptolemaic Egypt would have expected in legal cases. This would especially be the case in Alexandria, the favored locale for the Greek Pentateuch's translation among Septuagint scholars. Such an expectation would be all the more true of recent immigrants, since Athenians memorized and studied their laws as part of their education.[82] Greek immigrants from Athens and her subject cities would no doubt know something of the legal koine and legal traditions of Athens, and this knowledge would come unadulterated to Egypt. Moreover, the Greeks in Egypt were driven to maintain their distinctness from the Egyptians, which would safeguard against these traditions being contaminated by or assimilated

79 Amundsen, "The Classical Greek," 255. Cf. Marja Vierros, *Bilingual Notaries in Hellenistic Egypt. A Study of Greek as a Second Language* (Brussels: Koninklijke Vlaamse Academie van België, 2012), 31, fn. 21, who also connects the administrative language of Ptolemaic Egypt to that of educated Athenians.

80 "On pourrait multiplier les exemples à propos desquels il serait possible de constater une ligne d'évolution continue depuis les sources concernant le droit privé des poleis avant Alexandre, notamment Athènes, jusqu'aux documents grecs d'Égypte" (Mélèze-Modrzejewski, *Loi et Coutume*, 131). Cf. Raphael Taubenschlag, "Die Geschichte der Rezeption des griechischen Privatrechts in Ägypten," in *Atti del IV Congresso Internationale di Papirologia* (Milano: Società editrice "Vita e Pensiero," 1936), 259–281.

81 Fraser, *Ptolemaic*, 112; Mélèze-Modrzejewski, *Loi et Coutume*, 148, warns of connecting this legal koine to private law early on in this process. Given the public status of capital punishment cases in late fourth century Greek practice, laws involving such would likely be part of this unification.

82 Yun Lee Too, "Legal Instructions in Classical Athens," in *Education in Greek and Roman Antiquity*, ed. Yun Lee Too (Leiden: Brill, 2001), 111–132, particularly 123–130; Ronald F. Willetts, *The Law Code of Gortyn* (Berlin: Walter de Gruyter, 1967), 8 and fn. 3 for list of source material references.

to broader (non-Greek) cultural values.[83] Athenian law is also used as the primary source of Classical Greek law because it is this tradition more than any other that has survived in our source materials.[84] Greek law exhibited idiosyncrasies across the *poleis*,[85] despite some degree of growing uniformity in the fourth century. Giving Athens a priority is a bias in this study.[86] At the same time, there is indication from Antiphon (*De caede Her.* 47) and the inscriptions that many cases that involved capital punishment and that stemmed from Athens' subject cities were directed to Athens. Antiphon states: "An allied state is denied the right of inflicting the death-penalty in such fashion without the consent of the Athenian people."[87] This could serve as an indicator that what constituted capital crimes in Greek thought was at least somewhat more unified than other more minor matters of illegal activity. This would be true at least among the cities subject to Athens. Moreover, in Classical Greek law cases involving the death penalty belonged to public suits, a category which would be within the broader unified legal koine developing at the time.[88] This further affirms that these kinds of crimes and their punishments would have been well known in the legal koine of Ptolemaic Egypt.

For these reasons the following investigation will supplement Ptolemaic data with Classical legal data, mostly from Athens. The pervasiveness of Athenian law in Alexandria and the Athenian influence among her *poleis* whose residents streamed into Egypt allow for these kinds of comparisons. Information will be drawn from any applicable source of the Ptolemaic documentation that refers to legal practice, which can include anything from petitions to

83 Préaux, "Les continuités," 243; Lewis, *Greeks in Ptolemaic*, 4–5. Mélèze-Modrzejewski, *Loi et Coutume*, 192, points out that the division between Greek and Egyptian law seems sharpest in the third century.

84 Cf. Ilias Arnaoutoglou, *Ancient Greek Laws: A Sourcebook* (London: Routledge, 2010), xvi; Catherine Darbo-Peschanski, "La prononcé de la peine de mort en Grèce ancienne," in *La peine de mort: droit, histoire, anthropologie, philosophie*, ed. Ioannis S. Papadopoulos and Jacques-Henri Robert (Paris: Université Panthéon-Assas, 2000), 130.

85 Arnaoutoglou, *Ancient Greek*, xv–xvi.

86 It should also be cautioned that "Lawcourt speeches ... preserve to a large extent the ideology, interests, values, and ambitions of these [elite of the *polis*]" (Arnaoutoglou, *Ancient Greek*, xiv).

87 See Kenneth J. Maidment, trans., *Antiphon, Andocides, Minor Attic Orators, Volume I: Antiphon*, LCL (Cambridge: Harvard University Press, 1941), 193, fn. b, for a discussion on the inscriptions supporting Antiphon's statement, of which he notes the Erythraean Decree, the Chalcidian Decree, and the Milesian Decree. Each has differing stipulations, and all involve capital punishment being directed towards Athens.

88 Gustav Gilbert, *The Constitutional Antiquities of Sparta and Athens*, trans. E. J. Brooks and T. Nicklin (New York: Macmillan, 1895), 414. This is to be contrasted with private law that was not brought into the legal koine immediately.

royal decrees. In addition to these legal data, this research will often include accompanying relevant cultural data that supports a given legal analysis. This information will also aid in filling in some of the gaps left where there are no surviving legal texts.

1.5.4 *Egyptian Law as a Source of Data*

While this study is positing a Greek influence on the translation of the Covenant Code, it will, at times, refer to Egyptian legal or cultural standards that either align or contrast with the Greek view. The reasoning for including this material is sometimes to provide a counterpoint that further demonstrates that it is specifically a *Greek*-legal paradigm that might influence the translation. In some cases, the other (and numerically more dominant) force of the Egyptians held a different standard on a particular issue. In contrast, when Egyptian and Greek standards align with the translation choice, it cannot be said that this information proves Greek influence, but it does point to the overall cultural legal milieu and what would have likely been practiced by natives and non-natives alike. This information does serve a purpose: to whatever degree regional judges sometimes based their decisions on a more subjective perception of equity and moral intuition when there was a deficiency in other sources of law, as can be at least assumed based on this practice documented in the phrase γνώμηι τῆι δικαιοτάτη[ι], "by the most just opinion" (P.Gurob 2.45, 226 BCE), then Egyptian standards would sometimes come into play.[89] Egyptian law and custom could at least in theory inform a judge as how they ought to proceed to maintain order, especially in moral rural and tight-knit communities. A place where the Egyptian legal background and a judge's decision on a lacuna in the law might come into play is Exod 22:18 (22:19 LXX) where bestiality would not be considered under either Greek or Egyptian law, and hence a judge's decision would likely be the final say on the matter.[90] Despite the helpfulness of the Egyptian legal data in some cases, Egyptian law codes are next to

89 For this translation and practice see Mélèze-Modrzejewski, *Loi et Coutume*, 213–215. This kind of judgement would be subsidiary to royal decree or civic law. Whether the formal Athenian Greek category of ἐπιείκεια is being drawn on (Amundsen, "The Classical Greek," 258) is debatable (Mélèze-Modrzejewski, *Loi et Coutume*, 214, disagrees and places ἐπιείκεια within broader Greek practice and values). For more examples of "the most just opinion" as a concept for filling in gaps or uncertainties in law see the Hellenistic world, see Julie Vélissaropoulos-Karakostas, *Droit grec d'Alexandre à Auguste (323 av. J.-C.–14 ap. J.-C.): personnes, biens, justice* (Athens: Centre de Recherches de l'Antiquité grecque et romaine, 2011), 78–82. Inasmuch as the legal subject matter veers into criminal law, it should be stated that the relationship between Egyptian and Greek criminal law is "somewhat patchy and has not been properly explored" (Maehler, "Greek, Egyptian," 123).

90 See section 4.4.

non-existent, and "our understanding of Egyptian law and order is taken from more indirect evidence: a random mixture of court documents, civil contracts, private writings, observed behavior and fictional tales, plus a series of royal decrees that detail particular crimes and their specified punishments."[91] The insufficiency of documentary sources here is lamentable and serves to sideline these data as they relate to the present discussion.

1.6 Jewish Law and Legal Practice in Ptolemaic Egypt

A further measure of confidence can be placed in the hypothesis that there could be Greco-Egyptian legal interference in the Septuagint when one considers what is known about Torah and its legal observance in early Ptolemaic Egypt. We are in fact able to ask, so far as evidence exists, what kind of involvement the Torah played in the legal lives of Jewish residents in Ptolemaic Egypt, and to what degree we can see external influences upon their legal activities in the third century BCE?[92]

When it comes to the first question, the degree to which even the most privileged Jews had legal freedom to practice Torah norms is debated.[93] Given the

91 Joyce A. Tyldesley, *Judgement of the Pharaoh: Crime and Punishment in Ancient Egypt* (London: Weidenfeld & Nicolson, 2000), 9. There exists a law code from the temple archives of Hermopolis West from the third century BCE, but the contents of this code do not cover the same materials as those discussed here.

92 Definitive data on legal practice and institutions in Ptolemaic Judea have been called a "black hole," and the lack of materials there do not aid in providing insight into the question for Ptolemaic Egypt (Michael LeFebvre, *Collections, Codes, and Torah: The Re-Characterization of Israel's Written Law*, LHB/OTS 451 [New York: T&T Clark, 2006], 173).

93 E.g., Aryeh Kasher, *The Jews in Hellenistic and Roman Egypt: The Struggle for Equal Rights* (Tübingen: Mohr Siebeck, 1985), 32, suggested the spheres of "religion, matrimony, and national customs." He is here commenting on the rights of a possible Jewish *politeuma*. These kinds of rights may not have existed in the third century since *politeumata* are not evidenced then (see Sylvie Honigman, *The Septuagint and Homeric Scholarship in Alexandria A Study in the Narrative of the Letter of Aristeas* [London: Routledge, 2012], 99; Mélèze-Modrzejewski, "Jewish Law," 77). Schwartz, "Law in Jewish Society," 59, comments to a similar end, including also some small matters of private law (cf. fn. 81 above). For recent discussions on the legal practices of Ptolemaic Jews which revolve around the second century BCE see James M. S. Cowey, "Das ägyptische Judentum in hellenistischer Zeit—Neue Erkentnisse aus jüngst veröfftenlichten Papyri," in *Im Brennpunkt: Die Septuaginta. Studien zur Entstehung und Bedeutung der griechischen Bible*, vol. 2 of *Im Brennpunkt: Die Septuaginta*, ed. Siegfried Kreuzer and Jürgen P. Lesch, BWANT 8 (Stuttgart: Kohlhammer, 2004), 24–43; Sylvie Honigman, "Jewish Communities in Hellenistic Egypt: Different Responses to Different Environments," in *Jewish Identities in Antiquity: Studies in Memory of Menachem Stern*, ed. Lee I. Levine and Daniel R. Schwartz (Tübingen:

apparent function of the πολιτικοὶ νόμοι mentioned above, it can be claimed that the Torah did not govern the Jewish residents as a constituent body across Egypt, but residents might have availed themselves of that tradition in individual legal cases.[94] They would have brought such cases to the appropriate court.[95] Still, if the Egyptian Jews did in fact use the Torah in their legal dealings, the papyri are "rather disappointing" in demonstrating this.[96] Instead, they "contain rich evidence of Jews using freely the common Hellenistic law."[97] Jewish legal documents included a prescript with the title of deified Ptolemaic kings.[98] Jews had Ptolemaic notary offices draw up forms.[99] The court to which Jews most often brought legal disputes was Greek.[100] Tcherikover sums up the situation: "If the contract, the office, the court, were Greek, so were the laws and regulations, and thus we are faced with the likelihood that Egyptian Jews lived not according to the precepts of the Bible but according to the principles of Hellenistic common law."[101] The papyri even provide evidence that some Jews lent at an interest rate of 24% when Exod 22:24 (22:25 LXX)/Deut 23:20 prohibit the charging of interest to fellow Israelites.[102] It must be concluded that

---

Mohr Siebeck, 2009), 117–135; idem, "*Politeumata* and Ethnicity in Ptolemaic Egypt," *Ancient Society* 33 (2003): 61–102; idem, "The Jewish *Politeuma* at Heracloepolis (review of J. M. S. Cowey and K. Maresch, *Urkunden des Politeuma der Juden von Herakleopolis* [*144/3–133/2 v. Chr.*] [*P.Polit.Iud.*])," SCI 21 (2002): 251–266. For more views with a particular focus on Pentateuchal integration into the legal culture see Keenan et al., "The Judicial System," 472, arguing especially for family law being practiced; Kugler, *Resolving Disputes*, along with his collection of articles (see bibliography at ibid., 2, fn. 3).

94 Mélèze-Modrzejewski, *Loi et Coutume*, 155.

95 See Mélèze-Modrzejewski, *Loi et Coutume*, 201–212, for the various courts for immigrants. Jews who had privileges could also find themselves in Greek courts like the δικαστήριον.

96 Tcherikover et al., *Corpus Papyrorum*, 33.

97 Tcherikover et al., *Corpus Papyrorum*, 33.

98 P.Hib. 96; P.Tebt. 820; P.Tebt. 817; P.Tebt. 818.

99 P.Tebt. 817; P.Freib. 12b.

100 Tcherikover, et al., *Corpus Papyrorum*, 33; Notably, P.Petr. 3 21g (226 BCE) documents a Jew bringing a πρόσταγμα (royal decree) to the Greek court for the ruling (line 8). It is possible that Jews as immigrants were considered Hellenes and only went to Greek courts (so Elias Bickerman, "Two Legal Interpretations of the Septuagint," in *Studies in Jewish and Christian History*, 56 vols., ed. Amram Tropper [Leiden: Brill, 1976], 1:207–208). While there were previously Jewish courts in Elephantine, their jurisdiction and continued practice is unknown (Kasher, *The Jews*, 39; Rostovtzeff, "Ptolemaic Egypt," 120).

101 Tcherikover et al., *Corpus Papyrorum*, 34; cf. Martin Hengel, *Jews, Greeks, and Barbarians: Aspects of the Hellenization of Judaism in the Pre-Christian Period* (Philadelphia: Fortress Press, 1980), 90; Mélèze-Modrzejewski, "The Jewish Law," 79.

102 P.Tebt. 815, fr. 2, r, 2.17–22 (228 BCE); P. Tebt. 818 (174 BCE); cf. Joseph Mélèze-Modrzejewski and Robert Cornman, *The Jews of Egypt: From Rameses II to Emperor Hadrian* (Princeton: Princeton University Press, 1997), 114–119.

"leur 'hellénisation juridique' est indéniable."[103] Added to this Hellenization is the fact that, even if the Jews could abide by Mosaic law in some elements of life, Taubenschlag states that "in criminal cases ... where members of various nationalities were involved, it was the Greek law that exclusively applied."[104] Civil cases between non-Greek residents in foreigners' courts did not even have the right of *res iudicata* in and of themselves, which highlights that legal decisions like these would make their way to the higher up Greek officials.[105] Indeed, "papyrological documents show the Jews in Egypt bringing their claims and business affairs before the regular instances of State justice."[106] If these legal traditions contradicted Ptolemaic concerns, they would likely be dismissed.[107] And so, despite the possibility of Jews using the Torah in legal proceedings, the degree of legal Hellenization of the Jewish residents of Ptolemaic Egypt cannot go unnoticed. A distinctive integration of Greek practice is documented and this should increase the probability of my hypothesis concerning Greco-Egyptian legal influences on Greek Exodus.[108] The reason for Jewish adherence to Hellenistic law in Egypt at the time was probably due to the strong influence of Hellenistic culture in general, to weak social structures within the Jews communities,[109] and due to the fact that certain laws were absolutely binding on the entire population (e.g., those concerning slaves). Not to mention, Jews were categorized as Hellenes at this time.[110] This was not so much an ethnic but a cultural marker that pressed towards assimilation into Greek ideals and customs.[111] Such coalescence of ethnic boundaries is indeed also attested in the material evidence of Ptolemaic

103 Helmis, "Crime et châtiment," 75.

104 Taubenschlag, *The Law of Greco-Roman*, 20; Kasher, *The Jews*, 146. For what seems to be a Jew, one Mousaios, being sentenced to hard labor by Greek royal judges, see P.Eleph.Wagner 1, col. 1 (third century BCE; cf. Keenan et al., "The Judicial," 473).

105 Taubenschlag, *The Law of Greco-Roman*, 26–27; Méléze-Modrzejewski, *Loi et Coutume*, 202–203, 206.

106 Méléze-Modrzejewski, "The Jewish Law," 82.

107 Méléze-Modrzejewski, "La sanction," 255.

108 Though note something like CPR XVIII 9 (232 BCE) where the 50% additional fee from a returned dowry is in line with Jewish practice and not Greek (cf. Méléze-Modrzejewski, "The Jewish Law," 87, fn. 70). Given the fluidity of acceptable legal practice in Ptolemaic Egypt, blanket claims should not be made.

109 Tcherikover et al., *Corpus Papyrorum*, 9.

110 Nathalie LaCoste, *Waters of the Exodus: Jewish Experiences with Water in Ptolemaic and Roman Egypt* (Leiden: Brill, 2019), 3. With the caveat: "provided they spoke Greek and served the royal dynasty" (Méléze-Modrzejewski, "The Jewish Law," 76).

111 LaCoste, *Waters of the Exodus*, 3, fn. 6; cf. Dorothy Thompson, "Hellenistic Hellenes: The Case of Ptolemaic Egypt," in *Ancient Perceptions of Greek Ethnicity*, ed. Irad Malkin (Cambridge: Harvard University Press, 2001), 301–322.

Egypt.[112] In these ways, the documentary evidence makes clear that Jews in early Ptolemaic Egypt practiced Greek law as Hellenes, which colors in the background of the LXX translation. Yet this is not to say that there is no evidence for the Torah being integrated into legal practice.

The only early[113] reference to Jewish law is probably P.Enteux. 23.2–3 (218 BCE), which mentions "[τὸν νόμον π]ο̣λ̣ιτικὸν τῶν ['Ιου]δαίων" ("the civic law of the Jews").[114] Any reference to specific legal matters that this phrase may have referred to has been lost because of the fragmentary state of this papyrus. If this reconstruction is correct, it does lend credence towards the hypothesis that Jews could present their own legal traditions in Greek court settings and that they did so on occasion. The second century BCE attests to Jews drawing on their legal heritages in instances that exhibit some extraordinary interpretive maneuvers that meld together both Torah and Greek practice. These have recently been discussed at length by Kugler.[115] He and others comment on P.Polit.Iud. (144–132 BCE), a collection of 20 papyri from a Jewish *politeuma* which contain references to a Jewish "ancestral oath" and "ancestral law" (P.Polit.Iud. 9.7–8, 28–29; 132 BCE).[116] One example (P.Polit.Iud. 8.15–16) has a Jewish man charging 24% interest according to Greek law and contra Torah (Exod 22:24; Lev 25:35–38; Deut 23:20–21). At the same time, he seems to try to honor Torah, however superficially, by writing a loan in his (presumably non-Jewish) wife's name, Philista.[117] Honigman explains this by referring to a Demotic manual of law,[118] which also has a Greek translation and which contains many outdated/unused laws alongside current/used laws.[119] The point Honigman makes is that it was commonplace for a law code to contain prescripts

112 LaCoste, *Waters of the Exodus*, 7.

113 This is the only reference in the third century. P.Pol.Iud. contains references from the second century (see Kugler, "Uncovering Echoes," and Sylvie Honigman, *The Septuagint and Homeric*, 109–111). P.Pol.Iud. 4.22–24 is arguably the only clear reference to the Septuagint being appealed to as a legal authority (see Stewart Alden Moore, *Jewish Ethnic Identity and Relations in Hellenistic Egypt: With Walls of Iron?* [Leiden: Brill, 2015], 83–86, particularly 85–86).

114 For the persisting debate on this phrase see Honigman, *The Septuagint and Homeric*, 111; Tcherikover et al., *Corpus Papyrorum*, 36. For the alternative reading "[πρὸς τὸ ἀρχεῖον π]ο̣λ̣ιτικὸν" see Kasher, *The Jews*, 150 and the comments in Tcherikover et al., *Corpus Papyrorum*, 36.

115 Kugler, *Resolving Disputes*.

116 For the role of this *politeuma*, a Jewish military settlement with some judicial autonomy, see ibid., 18–26.

117 See Kugler, "Uncovering Echoes," 148; idem., *Resolving Disputes*, 179–204.

118 For the text see Koenraad Donker van Heel, *The Legal Manual of Hermopolis (P. Mattha). Text and Translation* (Leiden: Brill, 1990).

119 Honigman, *The Septuagint and Homeric*, 109–111.

that could be disregarded while maintaining others right beside them. This might be how some Jews viewed the Mosaic law in light of Greek legal practice: one law was superseded by the more relevant/current law, or if one aspect was missing from one law, the other could fill in the 'gap.' Mélèze-Modrzejewski likewise sees Jewish law here being overtaken by Greek influence by means of exploiting particular technicalities.[120] Kugler's approach to these papyri contrasts to those like Mélèze-Modrzejewski who claim a more thoroughgoing Hellenistic bent in their Jewish legal practice.[121] What is seen in P.Polit.Iud. has instead led Kugler to conclude that "the Jews of the Herakleopolite demonstrably knew and used legal principles derived from familiarity with Torah, while also relying on Greek (and even in limited cases Egyptian) legal norms; they were legal pluralists firmly rooted in their own legal traditions."[122] His conclusion must be taken as a caution against presupposing an overwhelming Greek influence in these papyri. Even still, outside of P.Polit.Iud. there are papyri like P.Petr. 3 21 from the third century (225 BCE). This is a text where a Jewish woman draws on Greek law instead of Jewish practice, and it might be explained in similar ways to what was seen above in P.Polit.Iud. 8.15–16: she does not lay claim to the battery laws in Exodus (21:18–19) because the assailant did not show up in court, a situation that then evoked the Greek law with respect to that kind of occasion.[123] Examples like these could illustrate how Greek and Jewish legal practice functioned side-by-side.[124]

Mélèze-Modrzejewski effectively sums up the predominant view concerning Jewish Hellenization towards Greek law in Ptolemaic Egypt:

> Fidelity to Jewish law is demonstrable in family life. Occasionally, we can observe a kind of convergence between Jewish tradition and Hellenistic custom. Sometimes, an apparent deviation was in fact a manifestation of the pluralistic character of Jewish law itself during the Second Temple period. The hypothesis of a *halakhah* proper to the Jewish diaspora in Egypt could also be envisaged ... In the majority of cases, however, the choice of language and of formulae appears decisive. Language is the vehicle of law. Jews who drew up Greek contracts followed Greek law. From Alexander the Great to the revolt of 115–117 C.E., the Jews in Egypt

120 "The Jewish Law," 89–90.
121 See his rebuttal to the prevailing view in *Resolving Disputes*, 26–30.
122 *Resolving Disputes*, 2.
123 Mélèze-Modrzejewski and Cornman, *The Jews of Egypt*, 111.
124 For other examples, though not expressly stated to be within this same framework, see Mélèze-Modrzejewski and Cornman, *The Jews of Egypt*, 114–119; see also Bickerman, "Two Legal," 208; Kugler, *Resolving Disputes*.

> applied, by anticipation and in a manner that modern orthodox Judaism might deem excessively liberal, the well-known principle which the Babylonian Amora Mar Samuel was to enunciate in the third century C.E.: *dina demalkhuta dina* … 'the law of the governing State is law.'[125]

Whether we adopt a more moderate Hellenizing perspective like Kugler or accept a more pervasive Greek influence like Mélèze-Modrzejewski, the legal Hellenization of Jews is still not disputed and it could serve as evidence as to why the translator of Exodus adapted certain aspects of the Covenant Code towards Greek legal practice. If Hellenization was occurring at some and at any rate, why not include this practice within the translation itself so as to reflect what was already becoming a reality? Perhaps the changes made by the translator could be seen in the same stream of practice concerning things like lending with interest as found above: Torah and Greek law were being mixed and various justifications for such confluences were at hand. The bottom line is that Jews were significantly influenced by Greek legal norms at the time and to some degree followed them. Should it be surprising that these Greek standards might have influenced the translation of their laws—laws that, on the face of it, were already beginning to be tinged with pigments of Hellenism according to the documentary sources? And it is not as though the Pentateuchal legal corpus is alone here. There is substantial evidence regarding other translational projects at the time that may provide additional supporting information for this notion.

1.7 Parallel Activity of Translation

In recent times, particularly during the Grinfield Lectures of 2021, the late James Aitken brought to the fore the importance of comparing the Septuagint translation-technical data with the parallel translational techniques found in the documentary evidence.[126] He quite convincingly illuminated the similarities between translations of Demotic materials into Greek and the kinds

125 Mélèze-Modrzejewski, "The Jewish Law," 90.

126 James Aitken, "The Septuagint—A Translation Among Translations," "The Septuagint, Editing, and Textual Production in Ancient Judaism," and "The Septuagint and Scribal Creativity in Egypt" (papers presented at The Grinfield Lectures, Oxford, Feb. 15–16, 24, 2021). See also idem, "The Septuagint and Egyptian Translation Methods," in *XV Congress of the International Organization for Septuagint and Cognate Studies: Munich, 2013*, ed. Wolfgang Kraus, Michaël N. Van Der Meer, and Martin Meiser, SCS 64 (Atlanta: Society of Biblical Literature, 2016), 269–293.

of translation choices found in the LXX corpus. It seems as though a similar translational methodology was appropriated. As a heuristic for internal translation-technical information, this approach is undoubtedly productive. Common scribal practice and expectations in translation seem to have been at work.[127] No doubt there were variations of expectations based on the occasion. We see, for example, that Ptolemaic decrees written in Demotic and in Greek contain the same information, whereas other bilingual documents can use supplemental language to facilitate comprehension and not just convey identical information.[128] Brock notes a particular literalism for legal texts among translations.[129] Within this legal world of translation others have also compared the Septuagint to the known translation of an Egyptian manual for case law that was rendered from Demotic to Greek in the third century BCE.[130] The translation is similar to the Greek Pentateuch (and Covenant Code for that matter) in that it follows the source text quite closely.[131] However, it does not often maintain Demotic idiom or phraseology that would compromise the meaning of the Greek.[132] The text needs to be comprehensible Greek for Greek legal scribes.

That these Greek translations were written in idiomatic Greek is understandable, since, more than such translations simply being an interest of the royal authorities, it seems that "Greek versions facilitated the enforcement of legal prescriptions not originally formulated in Greek."[133] Due to the position of one's national legal practices within the Ptolemaic legal system, it could be hypothesized that the LXX legal corpus was desired in Greek, since, "for its effective application, the royal judges and officials needed a Greek translation" in a similar way that they needed Egyptian legal texts.[134] Moreover, it

127 For an overview of translators in Hellenistic Egypt see Rachel Mairs, "Hermēneis in the Documentary Record from Hellenistic and Roman Egypt: Interpreters, Translators and Mediators in a Bilingual Society," *Journal of Ancient History* 8 (2020): 1–53.

128 Sandra Lippert, "What's New in Demotic Studies? An Overview of the Publications 2010–2013," *JJP* 43 (2013): 39.

129 Sebastian P. Brock, "The Phenomenon of the Septuagint," *OtSt* 17 (1972): 17, 19.

130 See Mélèze-Modrzejewski, "The Jewish Law," 81 and P.Oxy.XLVI 3285, which is based on a later version of the Demotic text from the temple archives of Hermopolis.

131 Pieter W. Pestman, "Le manuel de droit égyptien de Hermoupolis," in *Textes et études de papyrologie grecque, démotique et copte*, ed. Pieter W. Pestman (Leiden: Brill, 1985), 115–144: "La traduction en grec suit assez fidelement le texte demotique" (118).

132 See the various assessments from Pestman, "Le manuel," throughout the work.

133 Keenan et al., "The Judicial System," 472.

134 Mélèze-Modrzejewski, "The Jewish Law," 80. Wolfgang Orth, "Ptolemaios II. und die Septuaginta-Übersetzung," in *Im Brennpunkt: Die Septuaginta. Studien zur Enstehung und Bedeutung der Griechischen Bibel*, vol. 1 of *Im Brennpunkt: Die Septuaginta*, ed. Heinz-Josef Fabry and Ulrich Offerhaus (Stuttgart: Kohlhammer, 2001), 107, 111, also

seems that in legal appeals to the king it was only petitionary documentation written in Greek that was permitted.[135] Legal concerns of various ethnicities were then, in one way or another, funnelled through the Greek language. This channelling also meant the adoption, to one degree or another, of Greek legal terminology as opposed to the terminology of a source text or foreigner's language.[136] Such rendering was no doubt difficult for scribes not natively Greek. Thompson points out some mistakes by Egyptian scribes in Greek syntax and vocabulary in particular contracts.[137] Likewise, Aitken documents abnormal uses of case endings in other types of translated materials.[138] Surely a degree of error or at the least unwieldiness was expected. Even still, translations of legal texts into Greek would be plugged into the Greek system and be read in light of the Greek legal categories and terminology employed. Texts translated for officials needed to be comprehensible to them as Greek documents and not simply as a reference material for the source text.

If the Covenant Code (and other Pentateuchal law) were to be perceived as participating in this system, then this could provide a further rationale for why the translator was so inclined to make the changes that will be discussed: the translator may have anticipated that this legal corpus was going to make its way into that Greek legal system. Whether or not the translator actually intended for the laws of the Covenant Code to be a part of that system, one can imagine that the translator might have known that it would inevitably become part of it as the translation was read abroad. Added to this pressure is the fact that, "unlike many Near Eastern law codes [e.g., The Hebrew Covenant Code], Greek legislation was meant to be used in actual litigation."[139] Greeks perceived legal texts as functional. Whether or not the Hebrew Bible was viewed this way

observes the potential connection between other legal translations at the time and the Greek Pentateuch's production.

135 Demotic is arguably not attested for petitions (Gert Baetens, "Demotic Petitioning," *JJP* 44 [2014]: 43–47, 60–61, 63).

136 Roger S. Bagnall and Uri Yiftach-Firanko, "Law in Graeco-Roman Egypt: Hellenization, Fusion, Romanization," in *The Oxford Handbook of Papyrology*, ed. Roger S. Bagnall (Oxford: Oxford University Press, 2011), 541–542, comment on the separate formulae and traditions of language from Egyptian and Greek legal texts. Demotic legal documents did not use Greek formulae or wording (Lippert, "What's New," 39–40).

137 Dorothy J. Thompson, "Literacy and Power in Ptolemaic Egypt," in *Literacy and Power in the Ancient Near East*, ed. Alan K. Bowman and Greg Woolf (Cambridge: Cambridge University Press, 1994), 74–75. This is not to say that these are translations but rather that Greek and especially its legal jargon could be difficult to apprehend for a non-native.

138 "The Septuagint and Egyptian," 19–22.

139 Michael Gagarin, "Early Greek Law," in *The Cambridge Companion to Ancient Greek Law*, ed. Michael Gagarin and David Cohen (Cambridge: Cambridge University Press, 2005), 92.

at this juncture in the Second Temple Period is not presently important.[140] When the Covenant Code was translated into Greek, it was to some degree bound to be perceived within the confines of Greek legal terminology and practice, as was the case with other contemporary legal translations. These laws would be seen in the Greek system as functional legislation for litigation or other legal purposes. Perhaps part of the pressure as to why the translator would make adaptations such as I propose is then due to his expectation that the translated Code would be read by Greek officials as was customary for translated legal texts.

It is here that we must begin to look more closely at the specific legal subject matter pertaining to the present study in order to attempt to discern why such a potential admixture of Torah and Greek law may present itself in the death penalty materials found in the Greek Covenant Code.

1.8 The Death Penalty in Classical Greek, Egyptian, and Greco-Egyptian Law

1.8.1 *Introduction*

In the same way that the Ptolemaic legal system is indebted to a variety of legal traditions, the Ptolemaic stance on capital punishment must be viewed considering these forebears. These legal traditions help to define and set expectations for the Greco-Egyptian context and potentially to fill in a few lacunae.[141] Before specific cases can be discussed, the historical framework within which these crimes are to be viewed is a necessary component of understanding the death penalty in Ptolemaic Egypt. In-depth discussions concerning explicit crimes and their punishment with death are to be found in the sections dealing

140 See section 5.1.3.

141 Many studies have been done on the death penalty in Greek legal practice. For Greco and Greco-Egyptian capital punishment, see, e.g., Bluche, "La peine de mort"; Eva Cantarella, *Les peines de mort en Grèce et à Rome: Origines et fonctions des supplices capitaux dans l'Antiquité classique* (Paris: Albin Michel, 2000); Darbo-Peschanski, "Le prononcé de la peine"; J. J. Farsedakis, "θανάτῳ ζημιοῦν: Contribution à l'étude du droit criminel athénien à l'époque classique" (DPhil diss., Strasbourg, 1978); Jan Kucharski, "Capital Punishment in Classical Athens," *Scripta Classica* 12 (2015): 13–28; Essam Safty, "Les principales catégories de crimes passibles de la peine capitale dans le droit attique aux temps des orateurs," *Cahiers des études anciennes* 33 (1997): 161–172; Stephen C. Todd, "How to Execute People in Fourth-Century Athens," in *Law and Social Status in Classical Athens*, ed. Virginia Hunter and Jonathan Edmondson (Oxford: Oxford University Press, 2000), 31–51; Julie Velissaropoulou "He poine tou thanatou," *Archaiologia* 11 (1984): 36–44.

with the law of Exodus to which they correlate. This discussion focuses on all the other matters that help to inform the explanation of those cases.

1.8.2 *Athenian Capital Punishment*

The use of capital punishment in the Ancient Near East has a long history and is well documented from the third millennium onward.[142] Its practice was within the expectations and purview of the peoples living there over a broad period of time. To this day, the word "Draconian" continues in the Western legal consciousness due to the notorious (and hyperbolized) early history of Greek law concerning the death penalty. Irving comments concerning early Athenian history:

> A careful perusal of the sources leads to the conclusion that human life was little valued by the Athenians when balanced against the letter of the law. Capital punishment was resorted to very frequently. The code of Draco prescribed the death penalty for offenses generally, small or great. A man who stole vegetables was punished with the same severity as a perpetrator of sacrilege or homicide, according to Plutarch's account … Solon's revision of the laws brought sanity into the penal system and a mitigation of the penalties in many cases. A distinction was drawn between various crimes, and the penalties were made more or less proportionate to the gravity of the offenses.[143]

This increasingly proportional prescription of the death penalty applied later to "high-treason, temple-robbery, kakourgemata … illegal practices in connection with the grain supply"[144] as well as premeditated murder and other crimes of a religious nature.[145] These violations would normally be assessable cases fixed in codified law, whereas non-assessable cases could be decided through the deliberation of the *dicasts*/judges.[146] In the Classical Greek and Athenian setting as far back as the fifth century, Athenian law required that the court

---

142 See Hans Neumann, "Death Penalty I: Ancient Orient," BNP, 20 vols., ed. Christine F. Salazar (Leiden: Brill, 2004), 4: 136–137.

143 Irving Barkan, *Capital Punishment in Ancient Athens* (Chicago: University of Chicago, 1936), 1.

144 Barkan, *Capital Punishment*, 1.

145 Gottfried Schiemann, "Death Penalty II: Graeco-Roman," BNP, 20 vols., ed. Christine F. Salazar (Leiden: Brill, 2004), 4:137.

146 Barkan, *Capital Punishment*, 1–2; Darbo-Peschanski, "Le prononcé de la peine," 131.

(δικαστήριον) approve of a death under the death penalty.[147] This policy was heightened after 350 BCE.[148] Even still, certain crimes such as grievous assault, violent burglary, and seduction/adultery could permit an on-the-spot slaying of the offender without any consequence on the part of the slayer.[149] Should one be freed from formal capital punishment, the offender "might be required to pay a fine so heavy … that either his family and friends would be ruined in paying it or he would be indefinitely excluded, as a debtor to the state, from exercise of his civic rights."[150] Cases regarding the death penalty would also belong to public suits which could involve the community.[151]

The Classical Greek practice of the death penalty is, then, an orderly judicial sentence that was prescribed through various fixed or discretionary legal recourses. Capital punishment was a civic affair decided upon through the democratic court system. Greeks prior to the Hellenistic period would expect death to be the outcome of various criminal trials as this was well-situated in their legal history. In contrast to the purposes and functions of capital punishment in ancient Greek history is the somewhat less documented ancient Egyptian practice of capital punishment.

1.8.3 *Egyptian Capital Punishment*

In Pharaonic Egypt it was the prerogative of the Pharaoh and not the democratic court to officially sanction death. Part of his duty was in "rubber-stamping the death penalties imposed by his courts."[152] Likewise, he held the right to put to death his own people.[153] The use of the death penalty in Ancient Egypt contrasts starkly with Classical Greek practice in that its use, as far as is documented, was reserved almost exclusively for rebellion against the king.[154]

147 Mogens Herman Hansen, *Eisangelia: The Sovereingty of the People's Court in Athens in the Fourth Century B.C. and the Impeachment of Generals and Politicians* (Odense: Odense University Press, 1975), 20.

148 Hansen, *Eisangelia*, 15.

149 Darbo-Peschanski, "Le prononcé," 132.

150 Kenneth James Dover, *Greek Popular Morality in the Time of Plato and Aristotle* (Indianapolis: Hackett, 2008), 290.

151 Gilbert, *The Constitutional Antiquities*, 414.

152 Tyldesley, *Judgement of the Pharaoh*, 31; cf. Kerry Muhlestein, *Violence in the Service of Order: The Religious Framework for Sanctioned Killing in Ancient Egypt* (Oxford: Archaeopress, 2011), xxii.

153 Tyldesley, *Judgement of the Pharaoh*, 24.

154 Muhlestein summarizes: "Rebellion was not the only reason for sanctioned killing. Concurrently, rebellion was the overwhelming reason for the act" (322, emphasis his; cf. xxii). See also Tyldesley, *Judgement of the Pharaoh*, 71; David Lorton, "The Treatment of Criminals in Ancient Egypt Through the New Kingdom," *JESHO* 20, no. 1 (1977): 14; Renate Müller-Wollermann, "Todesstrafe und Folter im pharaonischen Ägypten," in *Strafe und*

Cases of capital punishment are far-and-away connected to treasonous acts in the surviving sources. Muhlestein lists a few other crimes punished with death: "Murder, adultery, theft of royal property, being false in office, tomb desecration or interference with funerary or temple cult."[155] It is likely that interpersonal crimes like adultery would be capitally punished only with the permission of the king.[156]

We can also look to Diodorus, who lauds the ancient Egyptian laws that he (and others) claim affected even Classical Athens after Lycurgus's and Solon's visits to Egypt (*Bib. hist.* 1.68, 96, 98).[157] He recounts ancient Egyptian laws that afford the death penalty for perjury, not aiding a person suffering violence or injury, false accusation concerning the death penalty, falsely recording one's livelihood, and murder (1.77). The historicity of these laws is questionable. Diodorus's recollection would portray ancient Egypt as more prone to capital punishment for variegated crimes than the other documentary sources seem to indicate. We can surmise from the historical data that Ancient Egypt was different from Ancient Greece in that the Pharaoh held power over capital punishment and that such authority was exercised mostly in the realm of rebellion against his charges and whims. There is a distinct focus on Pharaoh's concerns and prerogatives when it comes to sanctioning death.

When the Ptolemaic context is investigated in light of the Classical Greek and Egyptian perspectives on the death penalty, it can be seen that elements

---

Strafrecht in den antiken Welten: unter Berücksichtigung von Todesstrafe, Hinrichtung und peinlicher Befragung, ed. Robert Rollinger, Martin Lang, and Heinz Barta (Wiesbaden: Harrassowitz Verlag, 2012), 148.

155 Muhlestein, *Violence in the Service*, 322; For a corroborating reiteration of this data see Tyldesley, *Judgement of the Pharaoh*, 65–72. See also Russ VerSteeg, *Law in Ancient Egypt* (Durham: Carolina Academic Press, 2002), 154, who relays "murder, conspiracy to assassinate the king (treason), robbery of royal tombs, perjury, and judicial bribery" as crimes warranting the death penalty in the New Kingdom, and Ellen Dailey Bedell, "Criminal Law in the Egyptian Ramesside Period" (PhD diss., Brandeis University, 1973), 146–153, who documents the following as meriting capital punishment during the Ramesside Period: crimes against the state, attempt on the pharaoh's life, theft of sacred materials, tomb robbery, theft of important local items (149, 151 questions if the theft here is of sacred items), misuse or mishandling of sacred animals, corrupt officials, and high treason. However, Müller-Wollermann, "Todesstrafe und Folter," 148, believes that only high treason and grave robbery can be objectively classified as crimes that did have people put to death.

156 Müller-Wollermann, "Todesstrafe und Folter," 156; though see Tyldesley, *Judgement of the Pharaoh*, 157–158, who suggests that the seducer could be killed on the spot much like in the Greek traditions. Whether adultery was a crime definitively deserving death is debated (Muhlestein, *Violence in the Service*, 156–157).

157 See also Herodotus, *Hist.* 2.177. Whether these recollections coincide with historical fact is uncertain.

of both systems and practices show themselves in unique ways, while other novelties appear in light of the new Greco-Egyptian milieu.

1.8.4 *Ptolemaic Capital Punishment*

That the Greek and Egyptian traditions on the death penalty converge in Ptolemaic Egypt is widely accepted. Bluche makes this connection:

> Successeur des Pharaons, le roi est juge suprême en Égypte … Le roi est souverain juge en pays égyptien. La tradition pharaonique subsiste en son entier au profit du Lagide, rejoignant sur ce point le courant monarchique de la pensée politique grecque qui se concrétise dans la royauté hellénistique. Le roi a droit de vie et de mort sur ses sujets dans le cadre des lois. Mais le monarque ne se déplaçait pas en personne pour juger chaque procès capital. Il a délégué ses pouvoirs.[158]

It is not particularly clear who received such delegated power in the early Ptolemaic period. Suggestions have been made for the *diocete* (second in command to the king),[159] or the *chrematists* (itinerant royal judges).[160] Whether the three Greek cities of Ptolemaic Egypt (Alexandria, Naucratis, Ptolemeis) had judicial autonomy in capital cases is debated.[161] Alexandria held this authority

158 Bluche, "La peine de mort," 152–154. Cf. Préaux, "Les continuités," 231, for the continuation of the Pharaonic kingship. Préaux, "Les continuités," 236, also notes that the Egyptians addressed the Ptolemaic king with religious titles like that of Pharaoh, whereas the Greeks maintained the simple reference of "king" (cf. Peter M. Fraser, "Inscriptions from Ptolemaic Egypt," *Berytus* 7 [1960]: no. 1, 123–161 and no. 2, 133–134 for the inscriptional evidence). For the same practice among the Seleucids see Elias Bickerman, *Institutions des Séleucides* (Paris: Geuthner, 1938), 13–14. Préaux states: Nous croyons pouvoir montrer qu'en réalité l'Égypte a deux royautés juxtaposées et non point une royauté gréco-égyptienne ("Les continuités," 236).

159 This is the prevailing opinion according to Bluche, "La peine de mort," 154.

160 See Bluche, "La peine de mort," 154, and fn. 48–49, 50. For the *chrematists* judging a case of capital punishment see P.Berl.13.771 (unpublished) in Diedrich Schäfer, "Zwei Spätptolemäische Ladungsprogrammata," *Aegyptus* 13, no. 3/4 (1933): 617, fn. 1. A date for the text is not given. SEG 9 1, 8.48–50 show Ptolemy Soter investing this authority to the *Gerousia*, a group given significant authority above that of the *strategos* in Ptolemaic Egypt (cf. Théodore Reinach, "La charte ptolémaïque de Cyrène," *Revue Archéologique* 26 [1927]: 7). That the earlier Egyptian "great courts" acceded power over death to the Ptolemaic officials see Lippert, "Law Courts," *i*. It would not be the case that the *strategos* held capital competency at this time. These were an authority with respect to the death penalty in the first century (BGU 8 1816), but their limited role as delegators in the third century make such a claim doubtful for that time.

161 See Bluche, "La peine de mort," 154, fn. 51, noting Jean Colin, *Les villes libres de l'Orient gréco-romain et l'envoi au supplice par acclamations populaires* (Bruxelles: Latomus,

later on around the first century, but even in this time when the death penalty's pronouncement was somewhat more liberal, Alexandria was still "très limitée par la 'suprématie judiciaire' du roi."[162] Cases involving death might have been prosecuted *ex officio*,[163] with the proper Ptolemaic authority exercising this prerogative as a consequence of Pharaonic authority. There is a contrast here between the Greek city-states, which internally condemned criminals to death in each of their respective locales, and the Egyptian pharaoh from whom the authority to kill emanated. If the suggestion were made that someone must die for a particular crime, such a request would need to make its way up the ranks until it was received by the appropriate authority delegated by the kingship.[164] This peculiarity of the Greco-Egyptian position on capital punishment should not be overlooked as it may provide insight into the interpretation of the legal materials involving the death penalty in the Septuagint Pentateuch.

Another point, which leads to the most controversial aspect of this subject for my present purposes, is to look at the Ptolemaic application of the death penalty in the early Hellenistic period. Here a problem emerges for which solutions can only be suggested. Based on the surviving documentation, Helmis points out the problem:

> En effet, toutes les ordonnances du IIIe et du IIe siecle qui prévoient la peine de mort ne répriment que des comportements des fonctionnaires. Les objets sur lesquels elles portent sont assez variés, mais se réfèrent tous au fonctionnement régulier de l'économie royale … Dans tous ces cas, les personnes exposées à la peine capitale sont des agents de l'administration, comme si le roi ne se permettait d'ôter la vie qu'à ses propres serviteurs.[165]

While it is true that the early documentation only explicitly refers to capital punishment against Ptolemaic officials, it is not clear whether this means that the Ptolemies would not permit the death of laypersons convicted of various

1965), 176, who uses the information from SEG 9 1 to inform his decision in favor of the autonomy of the cities. On SEG 9 1 see below. Perhaps as a contrast, Bluche points out the limitations for these cities to enact the death penalty later in the Ptolemaic period when capital matters were less tightly regulated. This could press against Colin's hypothesis.

162 Bluche, "La peine de mort," 154, fn. 51.

163 Bluche, "La peine de mort," 154.

164 Even if the Greek cities held autonomy in this regard, a request like this would still need to ascend to the necessary higher authority. Claims for capital punishment also traditionally ascended a hierarchy in Egypt (Lippert, "Law Courts," 4–5).

165 Helmis, "Crime et châtiment," 197.

crimes. Helmis thinks that the death penalty was a sort of "scarecrow" for those outside of the royal administration.[166] Later on the death penalty would come into play for regular persons in specific situations, but not early on.[167] On the other hand, Bluche agrees that the Ptolemies mainly prescribed death in places where the economy was at risk on account of their servants' disobedience, but he does not limit capital punishment to this more internal sphere.[168] Others have suggested that the Ptolemies would not provide violent reparations for non-economic concerns at all but would instead offer monetary compensation.[169] Part of the problem here lies with the nature of the surviving documentation. A fair share of Ptolemaic royal decrees survive, but it seems to be the case that the Ptolemies did not write their own laws concerning matters that were outside of economic and fiscal concerns.[170] Their hierarchy of 'royal decree—civic/native law—judicial decision' allowed for the traditions and laws of the peoples governed to arbitrate these concerns. These civic laws in the Ptolemaic period, unfortunately, are almost completely unattested in our documentation. None survive that concern the death penalty.

Lending potential support to the idea that civic laws could govern what would be capitally punishable is SEG 9 1 (321 BCE). This is the earliest διάγραμμα from the then satrap Ptolemy Soter. It concerns not Egypt but the neighboring Cyrene. A section is devoted to applying the death penalty (lines 34–43). Here we find that Ptolemy allows for either his court or the Cyrenian laws to govern capital cases (lines 39–40). After a period of three years, the Cyrenian laws are to be the sole source of recourse (line 42). Vélissaropoulos-Karakostas points out an important caveat in this text: "Une condemnation à la peine capitale ne peut résulter que de l'application des lois de la cité ou d'une disposition de Ptolémée. La coutume, pourtant présente dans la charte de Cyrène, ne peut conduire à la condamnation d'une personne à la peine de mort."[171] There needed to be definitive legal precedent and not just unwritten customs that governed capital cases. If allowed to act as corroborating evidence, this could suggest that in Ptolemaic Egypt it would likewise be necessary to draw on established laws (like those from Greek *poleis* or perhaps Egypt prior) when

166 Helmis, "Crime et châtiment," 198.

167 Helmis, "Crime et châtiment," 198. See also Bernard Legras, *Hommes Et Femmes D'Égypte: IVe S. Av. N. è.–IVe S. De N. è: Droit, Histoire Et Anthropologie* (Paris: A. Colin, 2010), 244–248.

168 Bluche, "La peine de mort," 171–172.

169 See section 3.3.2.2. Bluche, "La peine de mort," 167–169, notes the absence of typical interpersonal crimes in the sources but does not conclude that this means they were not outside of the Ptolemies' application of justice.

170 See section 1.5.3.

171 *Droit Grec*, 93.

addressing the death penalty. Perhaps, in this view, the three Greek cities with their more formal legislation would be the milieu for trial and adjudication. Whatever the case, SEG 9 1 provides a point of comparison as to the force of civic laws in capital crimes, and this could have been what was similarly prescribed for Egypt.[172] Likewise, we find in that document the pronouncement that anyone contravening *any* order from Ptolemy will be put to death (lines 51–52). This, too, points to at least the potential of death for any person, not just officials. Such a command should also serve to indicate that there was likely no formal and unchanging list of crimes that merited death in the Ptolemaic period.[173] Despite Ptolemy's warning, the death penalty was not something randomly pronounced, and it would need to be based on an obvious act of disobedience.[174] With respect to the crimes that are documented in Ptolemaic Egypt as meriting death, these were "grec par ses techniques et égyptien par les objectifs visés."[175] Even still, Greek and Egyptian concerns could and would often overlap.[176] However, economic and fiscal concerns were primarily guided by the Egyptian milieu.

So, what can be concluded about capital punishment in Ptolemaic Egypt? There are certainly blurry lines as to how traditional Egyptian and Greek laws were used in cases involving death. It has been suggested that native legal traditions held a greater legal authority in the early third century, while continuing to be a basis of legal practice throughout the Ptolemaic period.[177] It is likely that traditions expressed in civic Greek/native Egyptian law were the legal sphere in which crimes penalized with death were dealt with.[178] This is the policy found in the earliest known διάγραμμα for the neighboring Cyrenians

172 Bluche, "La peine de mort," 162, allows for this text to speak broadly of the era. Cf. Colin, *Les villes libres*, 176.

173 So Bluche, "La peine de mort," 162 and fn. 98. For an example of a case-specific application of the death penalty see Rostovtzeff, *The Social & Economic*, 2:909.

174 "elle ne pouvait être prononcée au hazard" (Bluche, "La peine de mort," 151–152; cf. 173–174).

175 Bluche, "La peine de mort," 175; see 173–174, fn. 154, and the caveat in fn. 153 that "Le fond du droit n'est pas entièrement égyptien, ni les techniques exclusivement grecques. Cette problématique vaut pour une vision globale: elle ne saurait s'appliquer à tous les cas particuliers." An example of discontinuity would be the secularization of capital punishment, which was a religio-sacrificial matter in Ancient Egypt (Bluche, "La peine de mort," 156, fn. 61; 158, fn. 77; 161, fn. 90).

176 Cf. Bluche, "La peine de mort," 163.

177 Section 1.5.3.

178 Mélèze-Modrzejewski, "La sanction," 257, seems to imply this, though it comes across as unclear as to whether he takes on the monetary compensation model alone (see 258 and fn. 56). While the continuity of Egyptian customary law is certain, exactly which aspects of their law continued is debated (see Mélèze-Modrzejewski, *Loi et Coutume*, 115–120).

(SEG 9 1). Of course, Greek and Egyptian traditions cannot be excised from the earlier periods and placed in the third century. There were certainly changes introduced in the transition as well as sources from various locations.[179] Rather, these traditions provide a framework that can help at least point to the norms and expectations of the residents of Ptolemaic Egypt. Knowing whether Greeks or Egyptians traditionally expected capital punishment for specific crimes could be a helpful way of filling in some of the gaps regarding Greco-Egyptian civic and native laws. Even if it cannot be proven that a particular crime was punished with death in Ptolemaic Egypt, it is possible to point to the legal heritages of Greeks and (to a lesser extent) Egyptians so as to suggest what was likely legislated at the civic/customary level of law.[180] At the very least, it is possible to see what punishments were expected, even if they could not be actualized due to the prerogative of the Pharaoh-King who had the right over death and whether other penalties would be prescribed besides execution.

1.8.5 *Application of Data Concerning the Death Penalty*

There are three main contributions this elaboration on the death penalty offers to this study:

(1) The first is to consider the nature of the influence from Greek law. If it is true that the civic/native laws of the Greeks and Egyptians did govern actual cases where the death penalty would actually be applied, then the translational changes would be born out of a desire to match the biblical text with the on-the-ground realities of the day. If, on the other hand, the death penalty was reserved mainly for Ptolemaic officials, then these changes could be based on a desire to present the biblical laws as comporting with earlier *ideals or expectations* of Greek justice, not necessarily what was able to be practiced at the time.[181] The difference between these two translational aims would then be that one is based in an *actualized* legal practice whereas the other in *idealized*

179 Méléze-Modrzejewski, *Loi et Coutume*, 120–142, discusses the continuities of classical Greek law into Ptolemaic Egypt. He states, "Il n'est pas possible de considerer que les règles juridiques importées de Grèce dans le royaume des Lagides reposent sur une réception pure et simple de codes ou de lois de telle ou telle cite grecque ancienne" (ibid., 122). For example, the law of ὕβρις in Athens was a public γραφή, but a private δίκη in Alexandria (cf. P.Hal. 1. 115–123; Amundsen, "The Classical," 260–261). ὕβρις could be punished with death in Athens, given their corporate civic loyalty. The privatization of this crime in Alexandria may suggest a moving away from such a Greek value and consequence. See also Taubenschlag, "The Ancient Greek."

180 For the Ptolemies taking Egyptian customary law into consideration see Mélèze-Modrzejewski, *Loi et Coutume*, 89.

181 That immigrant Greeks desired legal continuity with their homeland see ibid., 104.

legal practice. To what degree a particular translational change comports with one or the other (or both) will be discussed in each individual case. Here it is only important to stress that, due to insufficient data, the changes found in the laws under discussion could reflect the influence of either actualized or idealized legal practice. In some cases it seems plausible that both actualized and idealized legal practice are being combined. This may be the case with the laws on homicide where the translator maintains the expected death penalty (θανάτῳ θανατούσθω) yet couches the apodosis in the imperative.[182] The link between the imperative and the death penalty in the Greek Pentateuch is also consistent and requires an explanation. The relationship may be that the imperative, itself being what seems to be legal shorthand that limits the authority and practicability of the penalty, is used so as not to encroach on Pharaonic authority in declaring the death sentence. This is discussed further in section 2.7.

(2) That the death penalty may have been relegated to the realm of civic/native law in interpersonal affairs also acts as a further justification in the presentation of earlier legal traditions for the upcoming case laws. It becomes more plausible that these legal traditions influenced the decisions on the ground in Ptolemaic Egypt since at this early time these legal heritages would be what came with Greek immigrants to Egypt.[183] If the translation is being written in the latter half of the third century BCE, then there have only been a few generations of Greeks who came as a result of their foreign conquests. It is doubtful that this amount of time would be enough to lead to a dissolution of their legal-moral framework from the homeland, especially since Greeks prided themselves on their cultural separation from others in Ptolemaic Egypt.[184] Likewise, Egyptians would have their legal customs ingrained from earlier times as well. The influence of these sources on the legal decisions in the early third century should not therefore be overlooked and can provide insight into what might have been practiced or expected at that early time.

(3) There is no indication from the documentary evidence or in the general framework concerning the death penalty in either the Greek or Egyptian iterations that Jews in Ptolemaic Egypt would have authority to try capital cases in their own community. It is plausible that they could bring their own laws to a judge to be considered in litigation, but they would not have autonomy to practice capital punishment. They would need to go through the official channels and processes like everyone else. Perhaps this reality, too, stands in part behind

182 See section 2.7 with 3.3.

183 Even if only in memory (see fn. 82 above).

184 Coussement, *Because I am Greek*, 12–15.

the delimitation found in the LXX text through the imperative command verb in legal pronouncements (see section 2.7).

1.9 Conclusion: The Validity of Inferences from Greco-Egyptian Law

To situate the text-linguistic changes found in the laws involving the death penalty in Exodus as emanating from Greco-Egyptian legal expectations is inferential. However, if my text-linguistic analyses hold true, then an explanation of these translational changes is warranted. The various macro-influences from the Ptolemaic legal milieu that have been outlined provide both a basis for the more specific legal texts furnished in upcoming chapters as well as a hypothetical historical framework as to why the translator might have been inclined to translate in the ways outlined. The welcoming of ethnic texts and legal practice into the Ptolemaic system, the pervasive practice of translation into Greek for institutional and not just religious use, and the adoption of Hellenised legal practice by the Jewish population provide a strong impetus to view the translator as concerned with rendering in light of this legal situation. That Athenian law permeated the early Ptolemaic context, especially with respect to capital crimes, also provides warrant for comparisons with those legal materials. These factors substantiate why the translator of Exodus could have translated in light of Greco-Egyptian law. Moreover, these historical and legal cues are parallel in time and location to Ex, whereas other possible recourses for sourcing the interpretive changes would need to be inferred from more remote contexts. Even still, this framework is not the only plausible explanation of the text-linguistic changes.

1.10 Other Possible Sources of Influences on the LXX Legal Corpus

There are many developments and evolutions in the understanding of biblical law that occur not only within the corpus known as the Hebrew Bible itself but also in the Second Temple period. These oft-labelled *halakhot* continue to take on lives of their own across the Mediterranean and cross the chronological border into the Common Era.[185] Such legal debates are famously present in

185 For an overview see Neil. S. Hecht et al., eds., *An Introduction to the History and Sources of Jewish Law* (Oxford: Oxford University Press, 1996), and within this work particularly, Daniela Piattelli and Bernard S. Jackson, "Jewish Law during the Second Temple Period," 19–51. Alex P. Jassen, *Scripture and Law in the Dead Sea Scrolls* (Cambridge: Cambridge

the New Testament and Dead Sea Scrolls, and they continue into the Tannaitic Period and beyond. Each has been drawn upon for materials that could be retroverted back onto the Septuagint as possible parallel interpretive traditions.[186] It is necessary for these interpretive mores to be scavenged for data that might combat, correct, or supplement the findings presented here. Added to these would be the fragmentary legal practices attested in the Aramaic papyri of pre-Ptolemaic Egypt.[187] While each of these sources are invaluable, they are not drawn upon in any substantial way in this work.[188] The present author welcomes any contribution that could illuminate this apparent lacuna in the future. Such work will indeed be a personal focus in the future. It might be that a synthetic approach is in order where the translator is seen as working both with a more formally internal Jewish dialogue and within the influence

University Press, 2014), 18–40, gives a wonderful but less textually quantitative overview with a greater focus on hermeneutics.

186 This has been especially the case for Rabbinic materials: see, e.g.: Dirk L. Büchner, "On the Relationship Between *Mekilta De Rabbi Ishmael* and Septuagint Exodus 12–23," in *IX Congress of the International Organization for Septuagint and Cognate Studies, Cambridge 1995*, ed. Bernard A. Taylor, SCS 45 (Atlanta: Scholars Press, 1997), 403–420; Johann Cook, "Hellenistic and/or (Pre-)Rabbinic Traditions in the Septuagint," in *Florilegium Lovaniense: Studies in Septuagint and Textual Criticism in Honour of Florentino García Martínez*, ed. Hans Ausloos, Bénédicte Lemmelijn and Marc Vervenne, BETL 224 (Leuven: Peeters, 2008), 119–132; Frankel, *Ueber den Einfluss*; Timothy Law and Alison Salvesen, eds., *Greek Scripture and the Rabbis* (Leuven: Peeters, 2012); Martin Vahrenhorst, "Zwischen Alexandria und Tiberias—Berührungen zwischen dem Text der LXX und rabbinischen Traditionen," in *Die Septuaginta—Text, Wirkung, Rezeption*, ed. Wolfgang Kraus et al., WUNT 325 (Tübingen: Mohr Siebeck, 2014), 483–500. Likewise, the case is made for the Dead Sea Scrolls (e.g., Lawrence H. Schiffman, "The Septuagint and the Temple Scroll: Shared 'Halakhic' Variants," in *The Courtyards of the House of the Lord: Studies on the Temple Scroll*, ed. F. García Martínez [Leiden: Brill, 2008], 85–98).

187 See e.g., Alejandro F. Botta, *The Aramaic and Egyptian Legal Traditions at Elephantine: An Egyptological Approach* (New York: T&T Clark, 2009).

188 Some comments on their approaches to the death penalty will be included in the conclusion. This delimitation is in part due to spatial constraints. It is also the case that, when researching for this topic, very few explicit parallels could be found in these sources. Consultation with experts at Oxford during the course of this research led to no salient comparisons being uncovered. This is not to say that the hermeneutical and interpretive underpinnings allegedly appropriated by the translator cannot be found in other places, but rather that the specific laws that are changed do not seem to find comparative materials elsewhere. The translator's view of the text and interpretive method are discussed in section 5.1. Here there is room to discuss how the text was perceived as well as the traditions of updating or revising previous law in the ancient Near East and within Jewish practice.

of Greco-Egyptian legal practice. There is precedent to view these together. Such *halakhic* conversation does say as much later on: דינא דמלכותא דינא ("the law of the state is the law").[189]

189 b. Giṭ. 10*b*; b. Ned. 28*a*; b. B. Qam. 113*a* and *b*.

CHAPTER 2

Greek-Legal Paradigms and Techniques

2.1 Potential Objections

A few preliminary matters need to be considered before a formal analysis can get underway. First, the underlying assumption that the translator of Exodus is aware of Greek legal practice and terminology is not controversial. Kugler comments on Septuagint lexicographic scholarship as a whole: "That the Greek of the Septuagint version of the Pentateuch depended heavily on the koine Greek of the Egyptian documentary papyri of the third century BCE particularly for its legal and administrative terminology has long been recognized."[1] This is not to say that the translator wholesale adopts the verbiage and patterns of Ptolemaic legal documentation. The translator is keen to stay close to the source text so as to represent it in certain qualitative ways. Some examples would be a general imitation of word order and quantitative fidelity. It is also my claim that the translator is determined to often maintain translation equivalents that share similar conceptual domains between the Hebrew and Greek texts (SSF). Understanding the translator's choices requires, then, intense scrutiny of the translation and the language chosen.

I document the terminology for the death penalty in Greek law in sections 2.2–2.5 and conclude that the translations θανάτῳ τελευτάτω (lit. "by death let him come to an end") and θανάτῳ θανατούσθω (lit. "by death let him be put to death") for מות יומת ("he shall be put to death") are not synonymous phrases.[2] This is despite the fact that both phrases use Greek verbs that are often used to refer to death. In this way the translator superficially represents the Hebrew while at the same time accomplishes different things by each respective expression. This translation technique is what I outlined and labelled superficial semantic fidelity (SSF) in the previous chapter. I will argue that θανάτῳ τελευτάτω would be understood to refer to an imprecation and not the death penalty. It will be seen that the translator, due to this desire to represent the Hebrew superficially, utilizes a Greek legal category of apodotic punishment, namely, imprecation, but he does not draw on the typical legal vocabulary. This kind of translation strategy, then, prevents a consistently straightforward

1 Kugler, "Uncovering a New Dimension," 165.

2 θανάτῳ ἀποκτενειτε in 22:18 (22:19 LXX) is likewise not exactly synonymous with these other two syntagms. See section 4.4.2.6.

 | DOI:10.1163/9789004682047_003

adoption of Greek legal terminology. The translator seems instead to work on a case-by-case basis, utilizing legal terms when they fit the particular context and source text lexeme. This strategy should serve as a deterrent against the arguments of those who might retort that presupposing a Greco-Egyptian legal framework on the Greek Covenant Code is unwarranted due to the absence of a wealth of legal vocabulary or formalities.

Another potential objection—here thinking particularly of the posited difference between θανάτῳ τελευτάτω and θανάτῳ θανατούσθω—would be to insist that the translator is merely using stylistic flourish and rhetorical embellishment in his translation, such as synonymous phrases woven together to create a more embellished and readable text. Synonymy and rhetorical ornamentation has been the explanation of previous scholars for the difference between θανάτῳ τελευτάτω and θανάτῳ θανατούσθω.[3] There are two issues with this assumption. The first is that the translator of Exodus is prone both to flatten his terms in the Covenant Code lexically and to maintain the same translation equivalents elsewhere. The other would be that two different phrases in the penal apodosis would not be considered insignificant in Greek law. Precise wording was part and parcel of their legal practice. These considerations will be taken in order.

2.1.1 *Lexical Fidelity and Flattening in Exodus 21:1–23:19*

Part of the problem in tracing the strategy of Exodus's translator is that the materials he is translating in the Covenant Code are often wildly disparate in their contents. This range of Hebrew vocabulary and context, in general, makes it difficult to discern if synonymous renderings are a trait of the translator here.[4] When certain Hebrew terms do crop up, however, the translator does not seem to render with synonyms. The following serve as examples of

3 Evans, *Verbal Syntax*, 192, fn. 92; Frankel, *Ueber den Einfluss*, 93–94; Gurtner, *Exodus*, 99, 389; Le Boulluec and Sandevoir, *L'Exode*, 217 (implied); John A. L. Lee, "Translations of the Old Testament," in *Handbook of Classical Rhetoric in the Hellenistic Period 330* B.C.–A.D. *400*, ed. Stanley E. Porter (Leiden: Brill, 1997), 777; Wevers, *Notes*, 328, 330.

4 Whether the translation renders with synonyms purely for stylistic reasons is worth exploring. The present volume is focused on the legal, case-law genre and the renderings therein. Should someone present a study for the whole of Greek Exodus on this topic, it would be worth considering in comparison to the present research. As it stands, such work remains a desideratum. Perkins, "To the Reader," 43–44, suggests this is a general trait of the translation but does not provide broad-scale data. Rösel, "From the Torah," 67, and fn. 1, points out previous work done to establish that laws are translated with a greater strictness than narrative in the Pentateuchal materials (cf. Brock, "The Phenomenon," 20).

lexical fidelity in 21:1–23:19, of which alternative renderings are discussed in the references:[5]

שׁלם = ἀποτίνω (14× in 21:34, 36–37; 22:2 [3 LXX]–6 [7 LXX], 8 [9 LXX], 10 [11 LXX]–14 [15 LXX])[6]
נתן = δίδωμι (11× in 21:4, 22–23, 30, 32; 22:6 [7 LXX], 9 [10 LXX], 16 [17 LXX], 28 [29 LXX])[7]
יצא = ἀπέρχομαι/ἐξέρχομαι (8× in 21:2–7, 11)[8]
נכה = πατάσσω (6× in 21:12, 15, 18, 20, 26; 22:1 [2 LXX])[9]
מצא = εὑρίσκω (6× in 21:16; 22:1 [2 LXX], 3 [4 LXX], 5 [6 LXX]–7 [8 LXX])[10]
מכר = ἀποδίδωμι (4× in 21:7, 17 [16 LXX], 35, 37)[11]
גנב = κλέπτω (4× in 21:16 [21:17 LXX], 37; 22:6 [7 LXX], 11 [12 LXX])
נגח = κερατίζω (3× in 21:28, 31–32)[12]
שׁית = ἐπιβάλλω (3× in 21:22, 30 [2×])[13]

---

5 How the context is or is not influential is of course a decision of the present interpreter. A more detailed analysis is desirable but is not within the focus of this work.

6 Infinitive absolutes are not counted with their cognate verb. 22:2 [22:3 LXX] with ἀνταποθανεῖται is a major point of this monograph and is discussed in section 4.2.2.

7 21:19 renders with ἀποτείσει due to the need to specify that the idle time and medical costs are being compensated for and not in some way performed by the culprit. 22:29 (22:30 LXX) probably renders ἀποδώσεις due to the context focusing on the time the animal is with the mother and then subsequently "returned" to the owner, God.

8 The change in prefix is reflective of formal legal terminology for manumission. ἀπέρχομαι and its present/imperfect form ἀποτρέχω are terms for manumission (see Lee, *A Lexical Study*, 125–127) and in the contexts specifically focusing on this, Ex exhibits these terms. 21:11 does not render with either of these lexemes because the focus is not on manumission but on possessions the slave will leave with (i.e., ἄνευ ἀργυρίου). For the phrase ἐὰν δὲ γυνὴ συνεισέλθῃ μετ' αὐτοῦ (21:3) see Korytko, "The 'Law of the Land,'" 39–41.

9 τύπτω (21:15) and πλήσσω (22:1 [22:2 LXX]) represent different forms relating to πατάσσω with respect to different tense/grammatical operations and should still be considered to represent lexical fidelity (see LSJ for each term respectively). The use of the present tense in 21:15 is probably significant and is discussed in section 3.2.2.

10 22:3 [22:4 LXX] and the rendering of the infinitive absolute phrase with καταλημφθῇ, καὶ εὑρεθῇ is a departure from the source text. καταλημφθῇ likely helps to return the reader back to the initial capture of the thief and to an alternative scenario than death or debt-slavery, since the previous verse had elaborated on these punishments later on in the judicial process. See the interpretation of 22:2 (22:3 LXX) in section 4.2.

11 מכר is translated πωλέω (21:8) and πιπράσκω (22:2 [22:3 LXX]). πωλέω appears here as a contrast to ἀποδίδωμι, since the former is used as a contrast to the latter in order to indicate a potential sale (compare LSJ, ἀποδίδωμι, III., notably Xenophon, *Mem.* 2.5.5, with LSJ, πωλέω, I.). πιπράσκω is discussed in 4.2.4.5.

12 κυρρίσω would be the other common term to refer to the same thing (at least in the literary sources).

13 23:1 renders an idiom and the change from תשׁת ידך ("set/join/lift your hand") to συγκαταθήσῃ ("deposit with") may reflect the on the ground reality of witness documents

These examples only serve to point to a tendency and not to an absolute rule.[14] Even still, these represent some of the most repeated terms, often in very close proximity, and do present a case against stylistic synonymy being a concern of the translator in this legal section. In addition, the translator lexically flattens multiple Hebrew terms into one Greek term. He seems to prefer redundant repetition of a given Greek lexeme over against representation of each distinct Hebrew lexeme in these laws. Ostensibly, this is to create a clearer text. The following examples of lexical flattening in 21:1–23:19 are not necessarily exhaustive but do highlight this discernable trait of the translation's style in these laws:

אדן + בעל = κύριος (בעל in 21:28, 29 [2×], 34 [2×], 36 [implied from plus]; 22:7 [8 LXX], 10 [11 LXX], 11 [12 LXX], 13 [14 LXX], 14 [15 LXX]; אדן in 21:4 [2×], 5, 6 [2×], 8, 32)[15]
פדיון + כפר = λύτρα (21:28)
נגף = κερατίζω (21:35; elsewhere נגח for goring laws in 21:28, 31–32)[16]
שור + בקר = μόσχος (21:37 [22:1 LXX])
צאן + שה = πρόβατον (21:37 [22:1 LXX])
בעיר = κτῆνος (22:4 [5 LXX]; elsewhere בהמה = κτῆνος in 22:9 [10 LXX], 18 [19 LXX])
שקל = ἀποτίνω (22:16 [17 LXX]; elsewhere שלם = ἀποτίνω in 21:34, 36–37, 22:2 [3 LXX]–6 [7 LXX], 8 [9 LXX], 10 [11 LXX]–14 [15 LXX])
ענה + ינה = κακόω (22:20 [21 LXX]–22 [23 LXX])
חמס + רשע = ἄδικος (23:1)
אביון + דל = πένης (23:3, 6)[17]

---

submitted at the local legal office which were part and parcel of the Greek legal system at the time (e.g., P.Hal. 1.10.224–225 [259 BCE]).

14 For example, ὑποζύγιον (20:10, 17; 22:8–9 [9–10 LXX]; 22:29 [30 LXX]; 23:4–5, 12) and ὄνος (21:33; 22:3 [4 LXX]) might be synonymous translations of חמור. Even here one wonders if ὑποζύγιον is used in contexts where animals who work the field are in view. This is speculative, but it may be supported by the rest of the Pentateuchal data. Further research is required.

15 Excluding 21:3, 22 due to the problems created in rendering κύριος in these laws due to this term referring to the legal guardian of a woman in Greco-Egyptian law (see Korytko, "The 'Law of the Land,'" 39–41).

16 Eveline Staalduine-Sulman argues that נגף is a term that specifies an unintended strike ("Between Legislative and Linguistic Parallels: Exodus 21:22–25 in Its Context," in *The Interpretation of Exodus: Studies in Honour of Cornelis Houtman*, ed. Riemer Roukema [Leuven: Peters, 2006], 217) and this nuance may be lost in the translation due to lexical flattening. This interpretation of נגף is not agreed upon by all (cf. e.g., Calum Morgan Carmichael, *The Origins of Biblical Law: The Decalogues and the Book of the Covenant* [Ithaca: Cornell University Press, 1992], 121–122).

17 אביון seems to be rendered with πτωχός in 23:11 in order to indicate that it is the beggars of the land in view, not just poor day-workers.

שנא + איב = ἐχθρός (23:4–5)
שקר = ἄδικος (23:7; see רשע + חמס)

These data again suggest that the translator preferred to have a succinct and simple text over against a text with variegated terminology. It appears that terms that occur only once are the most likely to be flattened with other similar lexemes. This trait of lexical flattening might deter one from thinking the translator would introduce synonymous phrases as in the case of θανάτῳ τελευτάτω and θανάτῳ θανατούσθω when elsewhere they opt for one term instead of two for a given concept.[18]

Both the translator's consistency in rendering the same Hebrew terms successively as well as the merging of various Hebrew terms into one Greek term suggest that he was seeking first to render in a simple and unambiguous way in this legal section. The introduction of synonymous phrases would be counterproductive to that goal. At the same time, when approaching the Greek Covenant Code from the perspective of formulaic Greek legal language, it becomes even clearer that these alternative apodoses would not go unnoticed.

18 Perhaps Exod 22:9 (10 LXX)/13 (14 LXX) and 21:28/35 could be used as counter evidence. In both cases the translator renders almost identical phrases and contexts of מות with τελευτάω and ἀποθνήσκω. However, 22:9 (10 LXX) makes clear that *it is not known what happened to the animal* whereas in 22:13 (14 LXX) it is implied that *the cause of death is known*. In this former instance τελευτάω might have been more appropriate in that it could express the idea of the animal meeting its end in an unspecific manner and without a specific agent. A case could be made that τελευτάω is marked for non-agency. This seems to fit with how τελευτάω is used elsewhere in Exodus, if it is conceded that the plague activities were considered a sort of secondary causation. In the same way, 21:35 may use τελευτάω because deaths within the animal realm may have been considered agentless in a manner somewhat akin to the plagues. Likewise, this fits the uses of τελευτάω elsewhere in the Pentateuch. Elsewhere in Exodus ἀποθνήσκω is used when there is an immediate agent present in the context who might do the action of killing. This verb seems to be able to indicate either agency or non-agency, in contrast to τελευτάω. A formal linguistic analysis needs to be undertaken to further substantiate these observations. Note as well that Ex does not switch between τελευτάω and ἀποθνήσκω in contexts with repeated מות (7:18, 21; 9:4, 6[2x]–7, 19; barring translations of the substantive participle המת in 21:34 [τὸ τετελευτηκός] and 21:36 [ὁ τετελευτηκώς] compared to 21:35 [τὸν τεθνηκότα] where the only difference is that 21:35 is an attributive participle and not a substantival participle like 21:34/36). That τελευτάω would be used to refer to an unknown less exact cause of death does comport with its use in the Ptolemaic papyri (see section 2.4). It would be also interesting to research whether τελευτάω is used in Greek thought to refer to those presumed dead and not those who are known to be dead. Despite all this, even if τελευτάω and ἀποθνήσκω represent synonymous variation, it does not negate the conclusion of section 2.2–2.5. τελευτάω and ἀποθνήσκω might be used synonymously in places that are not the command verb in legal penal clauses, but 2.2–2.5 provide strong evidence that these terms should be distinguished in this specific context.

2.1.2 *Formulaic Language in Greek Law*[19]

Formulaic language is "a sequence, continuous or discontinuous, of words or other elements, which is, or appears to be, prefabricated: that is, stored and retrieved whole from memory at the time of use, rather than being subject to generation or analysis by the language grammar."[20] These kinds of rote and stock formulae are well-appreciated within the ancient Greek legal traditions. Vera Stolk comments on formulaic language in relation to Greek law:

> Legal language is highly specialized with its own conceptions of meaning based on a prior written discourse. This does not only apply to customized technical vocabulary, but also to the complete phrases that are employed in legal formulas … legal phrases are expected to be written in (conservative) standard language, especially as they are likely to be modelled on existing legal formulas rather than being *ad hoc* formulations which may be subject to on-going changes in the grammar of the language of the writer.[21]

These kinds of formulations can be seen in the Classical poets and orators, who use the correct legal terminology when a respective context required it.[22] Mélèze-Modrzejewski comically accentuates the importance of using precise terminology in one's legal dispute in a brief excursus:

> « Tuer » ou « être meurtrier » est-ce bien la même chose? La question peut paraître ridicule, mais si l'on ne respecte pas la loi à la lettre, on perdra le procès à cause d'un mot, comme perdait à Rome à la même

19 Sections 2.1.2–2.6 largely depends on and in many places represents the exact wording of my article, "The Death Penalty in OG Exodus in Light of Graeco-Egyptian Legal Formulations," *JSCS* 54 (2021): 77–94. This article is relied upon here with permission from Peeters Publishers.

20 Alison Wray, *Formulaic Language and the Lexicon* (Cambridge: Cambridge University Press, 2002), 9.

21 Joanne Vera Stolk, "Scribal and Phraseological Variation in Legal Formulas: ὑπάρχω + Dative or Genitive Pronoun," *JJP* 45 (2015): 258–259. See also the comments of Bagnall and Yiftach-Firanko, "Law in Graeco-Roman Egypt," 546: "If the document was introduced in court, the judge had to be familiar with these clauses in order to consider and interpret them properly. Accordingly, one of the most important measures in the formation of the court system in early Ptolemaic Egypt was to direct disputes among Greeks, with their Greek documents, to the Greek court of the *dikastêrion* and those among Egyptians to the Egyptian board of the *laokritai* (Wolff, 1970, 37–53). The existence of an interpretative tradition in the courts also required the maintenance of some uniformity by the scribes; for the expedient administration of justice with regard to leases, for example, the judge had to find a similar scheme and content in every lease contract."

22 Edward M. Harris, "Did Solon Abolish Debt-bondage?" *ClQ* 52, no. 2 (2002): 429, fn. 43, where he lists even Greek poets using legal language appropriately.

> époque le sien un plaideur qui, à propos d'une coupe de vignes, parlait de « vignes », comme le lui dictait le bon sens, au lieu de s'en tenir aux « arbres », comme l'exigeait le régime des actions de la loi.[23]

The specific words chosen in law and its discourse are of significant import when working within a Greek legal framework.

This quality of exactness also extends to all geographic locales in the Hellenistic and Classical Greek-speaking worlds and not just in Athens. We can clearly see this when looking at the genre of the royal decree, concerning which Amundsen comments, "The wording of the decree formulae, so conservatively fixed in Greek communities, is in early Ptolemaic time identical to such a degree that it has sometimes been difficult to decide the origin of an inscription, whether it really belongs to Alexandria or Ptolemais or has been imported from overseas."[24] When Greeks wrote law, they wrote it with formulaic legal language as is starkly portrayed in the decrees. It is for this reason that it can be said that "la précision du langage des bureaux ptolémaïques était remarquable."[25] Greeks expected their laws to conform somewhat rigidly to formulae, and hence if alternative terminology were employed at key junctures such as a punishment clause, it would not be considered without purpose. This is not to say that all laws were written with equal elegance, as this is not the case. One need only compare the embellished laws of Dracon to the drabber Gortyn Code.[26] The Gortyn Code does not abandon legal formulae, of course. Such formulae are only draped with less elegant robing. There was certainly a spectrum for style. While acknowledging this stylistic give-and-take, the importance of formulae and clarity in Greek legal language is essential to understand when approaching the Greek translation of the Covenant Code from a Greco-Egyptian legal perspective. The changing of terminology as represented in the different terms used in rendering the death penalty clauses would not go unappreciated.[27] This is especially the case when it comes to the death penalty, as Greeks had devised formulae to indicate this practice. It is to these syntagms that we now turn in order to shed light upon the translation choices in Ex.

23 Joseph Mélèze-Modrzejewski, "« Paroles néfastes » et « vers obscènes ». À propos de l'injure verbale en droit grec et hellénistique : Anthropologies juridiques," *Dike* 1 (1998): 161.

24 Amundsen, "The Classical Greek," 264.

25 Élias Bikerman, "Διάγραμμα," *RPh* 12, (1938b): 307.

26 See the comments concerning their stylistic difference in Michael Gagarin, *Drakon and Early Athenian Homicide Law* (New Haven: Yale University Press, 1981), 159, 161.

27 Perhaps this aspect of Greek law also explains the rationale for the lexical fidelity and flattening previously described.

2.2 Terminology for the Death Penalty in Classical Greek Law

2.2.1 *Varied Contexts for Terminology*

Table 2.1 indicates that a necessary distinction must be made between legal discourse and formal legal commands within a law code when approaching a study of the terminological boundaries involved in the thought-world of Greek law. When, for example, a fourth-century orator is involved in a lengthy *exposition* on a law and legal topic, the language will be tempered by the appropriate terminology. There is, however, also a great deal of freedom permitted in expressing their ideas. Compare this to the marked difference in freedom expressed when stating a *legal command* such as from a law code or decree, which, from the examples we have in both the Classical and Ptolemaic contexts, are to the point and are not characterized by terminological embellishment.[28] One should expect the most formulaic language to be found in the written legal code, since this is the basis on which the legal orations are built.[29] For this reason, I will distinguish between terminology for the death penalty found *within formal legal documents*[30] and terminology for the death penalty used *when speaking about the practice*. It will be seen that there are quite a few more expressions in the latter category.

The main body of source material on the death penalty for the century before the Ptolemaic era "come[s] from the law-court speeches of the Attic orators and here the terminology is surprisingly unimaginative: there is no slang and rarely unnecessary detail."[31] A few examples in the following delineation express the death penalty in epigraphic documentary sources. The ensuing chart (Table 2.1) documents references to the death penalty from the fourth and fifth centuries BCE, mostly from the orators. There are, of course, nearly innumerable references to death and to people being killed in these texts. Some will have been killed unlawfully and on the spot. This examination will only focus on places the orators speak about the formal, legal death penalty being enacted by an authoritative rulership.[32] I am indebted to the

28 I am unaware of any comparisons between formal law codes and orations with respect to the fixity or fluidity of stock legal language. The relevant sections on style in Sundahl, Mirhady, and Arnaoutoglou, *A New Working Bibliography*, neither provide any relevant studies.

29 The orators are constantly citing law codes as the authorial foundation of their argument: see, e.g., Andocides, *Myst.* 85.5–7; 87.1–5, 8–10; 96.3–13; Aeschines, *Timarch.* 12.1–12; 16.1–9; 21.1–9; 35.1–13; Demosthenes, *Mid.* 47.1–12; 94.3–5; 113.4–7, etc.

30 This category is intentionally broad and ambiguous, as there are many kinds of formal legal documents which stick to strict language such as νομοί, ἐντολαί, ψηφίσματα or προστάγματα/διαγράμματα (in the Ptolemaic era). The common trait among these items is that they stick closer to formal language and are in some way binding on a constituency.

31 Todd, "How to Execute," 36.

32 Whether these deaths were morally accepted does not affect the data.

article by Safty, who has collected and elaborated upon all the crimes punishable by death during this period.[33] Table 2.1 uses Safty's article as a point of departure, since there are no studies solely on the terminology used for the death penalty in Classical Greek law. The reason may be rather plain: as Todd stated above, "the terminology is surprisingly unimaginative."[34] Todd does not give a comprehensive list of phrases for the death penalty but his list does match the predominant phrases found in Table 2.1 below.[35] This should serve as corroborating evidence that Table 2.1, though not exhaustive, does present the most common formulations.

The following chart contains all the citations from Safty's article that speak about the death penalty. Safty's data have been the springboard from which all terminological searches have been done. The corroborating data with Todd's article and the extreme funneling of terms into only a few categories gives a sufficient picture of what type of language was used. Direct citations of legal documents are separated from general speech. Places where an indication of the death penalty is not precisely clear are not included.[36] The terms ἀποκτείνω, ἀποθνήσκω, θνάσκω, and ἀπόλλυμι do not have references cited in the "Speech Outside of Legal Documents" section due to their numerous uses in various contexts. They are not solely legal terms and this section is the least important for the present study. Inscriptions that have replicates are only cited once. Finally, Plato's *Laws* is treated as a formal legal document (law code), since he presents his laws in the syntactical form that Greek city laws did.[37] Even if the morality he promotes did not reflect real practice, his language still represents the formal legal genre. Likewise, it is understood that some law codes found in the orators are later scribal additions.[38] These insertions do not affect my argument, since these scribes still use the appropriate verbiage. Citations of law codes and formal legal documents come from direct quotes in the orators and the documentary evidence.

---

33 Safty, "Les principales catégories."

34 Todd, "How to Execute," 36.

35 See Todd, "How to Execute," 36, fn. 22, for his brief listing.

36 E.g., Aeschines, *Timarch.* 14, 72; Demosthenes, *C. Phorm.* 37; Lysias, *Epicr.* 8, etc.

37 The conditional sentence frame for a law goes back to some of the earliest Greek legal cases (Michael Gagarin, *Early Greek Law* [Berkeley: University of California Press, 1986], 36, fn. 51). Greek law is normally written with the third person singular conditional sentence and in prose (Gagarin, *Early Greek Law*, 54) with the apodosis being an infinitive or third person imperative (most frequently the present tense; cf. Gagarin, *Early Greek Law*, 85, fn. 13). All the laws cited by the orators contain either an infinitive or third person imperative in the apodosis or as the command verb. The documentary evidence likewise exhibits this same trait.

38 Cf. Mirko Canevaro, "Thieves, Parent Abusers, Draft Dodgers ... and Homicides? The Authenticity of Dem. 24.105," *Historia* 62/1 (2013): 27–28 and the bibliographic information there.

TABLE 2.1 Terminology for the death penalty in the fifth and fourth centuries BCE

Death penalty terminology	Safty: citation from legal documents	Safty: speech outside of legal documents	Citation of legal documents	Speech outside of legal documents
θάνατος + ζήμια (predicative relationship)	(2×) Plato, *Leg.*, 869c; Demosthenes, *Timocr.* 212[a]	(11×) Aeschines, *Timarch.* 87; *Ctesiph.* 250; Demosthenes, *Aristog.* 24; *Fals. leg.* 126, 131; *Lept.* 167; [2] *Steph.* 80; *Timocr.* 113; Isocrates, *De pace*, 50; Lysias, *Agor.* 68	(2×) IG I^3 70.8; SEG 50:1304.12	(49×)[b] All occurrences are within the formal legal context outlined above.
θανάτῳ + ζημιόω	(4×) Plato, *Leg.*, 871d; 942a; Demosthenes, *Lept.* 135;[c] Aeschines, *Timarch.* 21	(16×) Aristotle, *Ath. pol.* 52.1; Aeschines, *Timarch.* 91, 113, 184; *Ctesiph.* 224, 252; Demosthenes *Mid.* 49, 182; *Aristocr.* 31, 80; Dinarchus, *Phil.* 20; Lysias, *Agor.* 91; *And.* 15; Lycurgus, *Leocr.* 117; Xenophon, *Hell.* 1.7.10; 1.7.33	(5×) Aeschines, *Timarch.* 12; Plato, *Leg.* 866c; IG I^3 1453,C.21; IG II^2 43, face A front.I. 59–60; SEG 34:849.14	(49×) 47×;[d] Mylasa 112.9; TM 65795, col. 3.8 All occurrences are within the formal legal context outlined above.
θάνατος + καταγινώσκω	(0)	(5×) Andocides, *Myst.* 13; Isocrates, *Paneg.* 157; *Loch.* 6 Lycurgus, *Leocr.* 93; Plutarch, *Alc.* 22.2	(1×) IG II^2 125.12–13	(41×) 39×;[e] IG II^2 111.30, 35, 38; IG XII,6 1:42, frag. ab.I.14 All occurrences are within a formal legal context.

a It is debatable whether Demosthenes is citing a law directly here.
b According to TLG. Citations have been left out to keep the chart from becoming unwieldly.
c It is debatable whether Demosthenes is citing a law directly here.
d According to TLG.
e According to TLG.

TABLE 2.1 Terminology for the death penalty in the fifth and fourth centuries BCE (*cont.*)

Death penalty terminology	Safty: citation from legal documents	Safty: speech outside of legal documents	Citation of legal documents	Speech outside of legal documents
θάνατος + τιμάω	(0)	(1×) Lysias, *Epicr.* 7	(1×) IG II² 43, Face A, Front 1.61	(19×) Plato, *Gorg.* 486b; 516a; Plato, *Leg.* 946e; Lysias, *Fr.* Or. 22, frag. 52c; Demosthenes, *Aristocr.* 167; *Timocr.* 103; 1 *Aristog.* 74, 80, 83, 92, 94; *Zenoth.* 15; *Nicostr.* 18, 26; Aeschines, *Fals. leg.* 5, 59, 159; Dinarchus. *Dem.* 1; *Phil.* 2 All occurrences are within a formal legal context.
θνάσκω	(3×) Andocides, *Myst.* 95,[f] 96,[g] 110[h]	(3×) Demosthenes, *Mid.* 182; *Pant.* 51; Herodotus, *Hist.* 4.165.3	(13×) Plato, *Leg.* 874c(2×);[i] 933e; 938c; 946e; 952d; 955d; Aeschines, *Timarch.* 16; Demosthenes, *3 Philip.* 44;[j] *Aristocr.* 60; SEG 31:67.19; SEG 57:1409,A.7; Hatzopoulos, Mac. Inst. II 40.10; IG I³ 104.38	N/A

f νηποινί indicates on-the-spot slaying.
g νηποινί indicates on-the-spot slaying.
h It is debatable whether Andocides is directly citing a law here.
i These refer to on-the-spot slayings, as indicated by the additional νηποινί and indication of agency via ὑπό.
j This refers to an on-the-spot slaying, as is made clear from the immediate context. The next line is "This simply means that anyone slaying a member of Arthmius's family would be free from blood-guilt" (James H. Vince, trans., *Demosthenes with an English Translation* [London: Harvard University Press, 1930], 249). The whole law must have made this clear.

TABLE 2.1 Terminology for the death penalty in the fifth and fourth centuries BCE (*cont.*)

Death penalty terminology	Safty: citation from legal documents	Safty: speech outside of legal documents	Citation of legal documents	Speech outside of legal documents
ἀποκτείνω[k]	(0)[l]	(10×) Aeschines, *Ctesiph.* 224; Lycurgus, *Leocrit.* 65, 115; Lysias, *Nicom.* 25; Demosthenes, *Timocr.* 138; [*Tim.*] 10; Isocrates, *Big.* 8; Dinarchus, *Aristog.* 2; Xenophon, *Hell.* 1.7.26–27(2×)	(0)	N/A
ἀποθνήσκω	(2×) Plato, *Leg.*, 874b; Xenophon, *Hell.* 1.7.20[m]	(8×) Demosthenes, *1 Philip.* 47; Antiphon, *1 Tetr.* 2.9; Andocides, *Myst.* 51, 94; Hypereides, *Demosth.* 6; Lysias, *Nichom.* 15; Xenophon, *Hell.* 1.7.34–35(2×)	(1×) IPArk 17, B.112–113	N/A

k Instances where the text clearly refer to the on-the-spot slaying of a criminal are not included here. These references are cases where the court/ruling body put people to death through the established formal means.

l Demosthenes, *Aristocr.* 28 is a cited by Safty and is a case of on-the-spot slaying and not the formal death sentence. See the notes below on ἀποκτείνω.

m It is debatable whether Xenophon is directly citing a law here.

TABLE 2.1 Terminology for the death penalty in the fifth and fourth centuries BCE (*cont.*)

Death penalty terminology	Safty: citation from legal documents	Safty: speech outside of legal documents	Citation of legal documents	Speech outside of legal documents
θανατόω	(0)	(1×) Aristotle, *Ath. pol.* 52.1	(1×) Xenophon, *Ec.* 14.5[n]	(19×)[o] Xenophon, *Hell.* 2.3.15; 2.3.51; *Anab.* 2.6.4; *Cyr.* 7.5.31; Plato, *Leg.* 868c; 872c; Aristotle, *Ath. pol.* 37.1; 52.1; [*Mir. ausc.*] 836a; [*Oec.*] 2.1347b.34; *Rhet.* 1397b;[p] *Fr.*, 8,44,429.8–10; Alcidamas, *Fr.*, frag. 2.73; Philochorus, *Fr.*, Volume-Jacoby#-F 3b,328,F, frag. 66.12–13; Hecataeus, *Fr.*, Volume-Jacoby#-F 3a,264,F, frag. 25.743; frag. 25.1201–1202; frag. 25.1216; Megasthenes, *Fr.*, frag. 27.44–45; Priene 50, B.11.28.50
ἐπὶ θανάτῳ + εἰσάγω	(0)	(1×) Demosthenes [*Lacr.*] 47	(0)	(0)
θάνατος + τάσσω	(0)	(1×) Lycurgus, *Leocrit.* 65	(0)	(0)[q]
τῷ δημοκοίνῳ + παραδίδωμι	(0)	(1×) Antiphon, *Noverc.* 20	(0)	(0)

n Carleton L. Brownson, trans., *Xenophon in Seven Volumes* (Cambridge, MA: Harvard University Press, 1979), 507, states that this Solon law citation is an imprecise recall of this law and may be textually corrupt.

o The following examples from before the Septuagint Pentateuch (fifth century and prior) also use θανατόω but do not refer to the death penalty: Aesoph, *Fab.* 51 version 3, delta.5; 81.7, 11, 13; 192.6; Aeschines, *Fr.* Tetralogy 44, play A, frag. 597e.3; Aeschylus, *Prom.* 1054; Herodotus, *Hist.* 1.113.1; Antiphon, 2 *Tetra.* 3.11; Empedocles, *Test.* frag. 15.3; Stesimbrotus, *Fr.* frag. 2.5; Plato, *Leg.* 865d; Hippocrates, *Fract.* 26.30; *Liq.* 2.10; *Mul.* 1.4.47; Straton, *Fr.* frag. 124.11(2×). The following are uncertain if the death penalty is in mind: Plato, *Phaed.* 64b(2×); Plato, *Leg.* 862c; Socrates, *Epistles*, 14.6.7–12. It is worth commenting that after the fifth century there are no uses of θανατόω until the first century BCE that do not refer to the death penalty (when referring to humans).

p The text is uncertain here.

q There are a few examples with 'θάνατος + τάσσω + another item.'

TABLE 2.1 Terminology for the death penalty in the fifth and fourth centuries BCE (*cont.*)

Death penalty terminology	Safty: citation from legal documents	Safty: speech outside of legal documents	Citation of legal documents	Speech outside of legal documents
θάνατος + κολάζω	(0)	(1×) Lysias, *Erg*. 3	(0)	(4×) Euripides, *Hel.* 1173; Andocides, *Alcib.* 4; Plato, *Resp.* 492d; Demosthenes, *Mid.* 176
θάνατος + καταχειροτονέω	(0)	(1×) Demosthenes, *Fals. leg.* 31	(0)	(2×) Plato, *Spuria*, 368e; Lysias, *Philocr.* 2
ἔσχατος + πάσχω	(0)	(0) Demosthenes, *Lept.* 100[r]	(0)	(9×) Xenophon, *Hell.* 2.3.49; 6.4.5; *Anab.* 2.5.24; *Cyr.* 3.1.9, 3.1.22; Lysias, *And.* 13; *Agor.* 60; Aeneas, *Pol.* 10.23; Posidippus, *Epig.* Epigram 57
θάνατος + ἐπιτίμιον	(0)	(1×) Demosthenes, *Lept.* 156	(0)	(2×) Aristotle, [*Oec.*] 2.1349b; 1350a
ἀπόλλυμι	(0)	(3×) Demosthenes, *1 Boeot.* 33; Xenophon, *Hell.* 1.7.24; 1.7.25	(0)[s]	N/A
μέγιστος + τίμημα	(0)	(1×) Lycurgus, *Leocrit.* 8	(0)	N/A
ἔσχατος + τίμημα	(0)	(1×) Lycurgus, *Leocrit.* 8	(0)	(0)

r It is uncertain if Demosthenes is citing a law here, but since the phraseology used is not found in any other formal legal material, it will be considered a rhetorical flourish by Demosthenes.

s This term is used in imprecatory cursing, not in establishing a formal death penalty. See, e.g., Nomima I, 105, A.2–10 (470 BCE); Nomima I, 104 (*c.*475 BCE); for a curse in the same context as the formal death penalty see IK Kibyra 2 (167 BCE); for judicial cursing see, e.g., Aeschines, *Fals. leg.* 87; Andocides, *Myster.* 98; Demosthenes, *Fals. leg.* 71, 172; *Con.* 41; Dinarchus, *Aristog.* 16; Plutarch, *Sol.* 24. For studies see: Angelos Chaniotis et al., "SEG 60–2024. Religion. Magic: Witchcraft and Divine Vengeance in Cases of (Untimely) Death," *SEG* (2010), http://dx.doi.org/10.1163/1874-6772_seg_a60_2024, who are argue that curses like these were used when legal recourse could not be availed; John G. Gager, *Curse Tablets and Binding Spells from the Ancient World* (New York: Oxford University Press, 1992), 116–150 and 175–199; Henk S. Versnel "Les imprecations et le droit," *RHD* 65 (1987): 5–22.

The data presented in Table 2.1 are quite conclusive. The phraseology used when encoding or speaking of the death penalty demonstrates both a terminological framework from which the orators were heavily drawing, as well as other more creative ways of speaking about this practice. Notice that there are few creative measures taken in formal law codes/legal documents. Only a few lexemes are used to designate the death penalty in codified law, and certain terms are never used.[39] A few brief comments on the main syntagms will elucidate these data.

A mass of terminological appropriation comes from 'θάνατος + ζήμια/ζημιόω' (e.g., Aeschines, *Timarch.* 12: ἐὰν δέ τις παρὰ ταῦτ' εἰσίῃ, θανάτῳ ζημιούσθω, "if anyone might enter in violation to these [prescripts], he will be punished with death"). In *every single* context using these terms, a formal court or authoritative body is viewed as committing the deed. Thus, such phraseology is reserved most exclusively for the officially sanctioned death penalty. In formal law, these terms are only numerically superseded by θνήσκω when used to refer to capital punishment (e.g., Aeschines, *Timarch.* 16: οὗ δ' ἂν τὸ δικαστήριον καταψηφίσηται … τεθνάτω, "Whoever the court condemns … put to death"). This is only by a small margin, and the data are skewed of course by the fact that they are based on extant documentation. What can be deduced is that both 'θάνατος + ζήμια/ζημιόω' and θνήσκω were used very frequently in law to indicate the formal death penalty. The latter term can also refer to an immediate and informal slaying if further indicators are present (cf. Plato, *Leg.* 874c[2×]; Demosthenes, *3 Philip.* 44), whereas the former seems to be reserved only for an officially performed death by execution. Moreover, θνήσκω is used outside of legal contexts, whereas 'θάνατος + ζήμια/ζημιόω' never is.[40] ἀποθνήσκω ("to die") is not frequently found to refer to the death penalty in codified law. This is probably because the perfect tense is employed stereotypically when θνήσκω refers to the death penalty and "the simple Verb [θνήσκω] is regularly used in early Prose in pf. and plpf.; for pres., fut., and aor. the compd. ἀποθνῄσκω is substituted."[41] Because the perfect tense is idiomatically used, ἀποθνήσκω rightly does not present itself often in the documentation.[42]

39 At least in the existing evidence.

40 Crates, *Fr.* Play Eif, frag. 1.2 uses 'θάνατος + ζήμια' outside of a formal legal context, but the author seems to be referring to a legal practice (the reproach of youth is not a capital crime in his culture).

41 LSJ, θνῄσκω, I.1.

42 In the case of Ex, since the translator was bound to use the future tense, ἀποθνήσκω had to be utilized in 21:29 and 22:3.

Two phrases are used to refer to sentencing to death: 'θάνατος + καταγινώσκω' (e.g., "θάνατον κατέγνωτε" [Andocides, *Myst.* 13]) and 'θάνατος + τιμάω' (e.g., "θανάτου τιμήσητε" [Lysias, *Epicr.* 7]). Both designations are only used in formal legal contexts in the extant literature. They do not seem to appear with any frequency in encoded law to refer to being punished with death by the ruling body.

ἀποκτείνω/κτείνω ("to kill") occur frequently in Classical Greek legal documents, *but not as the formal death penalty*. These terms are never used for capital punishment in formal legal documentation but instead are used for cases of homicide (i.e., the murderer is said to have ἀποκτείνω-ed the victim)[43] or on-the-spot slayings instead of a formally appointed death (i.e., if one encounters a criminal and they resist arrest).[44] Harris speaks towards the set definition of this term in the Classical Period: "poets and prose authors [do not] use the term ἀποκτείνειν, found in homicide statutes, in different ways."[45] It is used in many contexts and can refer to both immediate and non-immediate causality with respect to the death.[46] Outside of formal law documents, it most definitely can refer to the formal death penalty enacted by officials.[47] Plato's *Laws* provides a lengthy excursus on homicide (9.864e–874) and speaks ubiquitously of crimes involving killing with κτείνω and αποκτείνω, yet capital punishment is not spoken of with that verb. In fact, nowhere in the massive *Laws* is κτείνω/αποκτείνω used for the verb indicating the death penalty, despite the numerous locutions employed for capital punishment.[48] Instead, when not

43 κτείνω/ἀποκτείνω are the normative terms for homicide in Classical Greek law (cf. Edward M. Harris, "How to Kill in Attic Greek. The Semantics of the Verb [ἀπο]κτείνειν and their Implications for Athenian Homicide Law," in *Symposion 1997, Vorträge zur griechischen und hellenistischen rechtsgeschichte* [*Altafiumara, 8–14 September 1997*], ed. E. Cantarella and G. Thür [Cologne/Vienna: Böhlau, 2001], 75–87; idem, "Did Solon Abolish," 429, fn. 43]. See, e.g., the famed laws of Drakon in *IG* I³ 104.11, 16–17, 18, 20–21(2×), 27, 28–29, 38, which utilize no synonyms.

44 See, e.g., the law cited in Demosthenes, *Aristocr.* 28 (τοὺς δ' ἀνδροφόνους ἐξεῖναι ἀποκτείνειν ἐν τῇ ἡμεδαπῇ [cf. 31, 41]), IG I² 115.30 (409 BCE), and this use in Lycurgus, *Leocrit.* 121, 125–127; Lysias, *And.* 54.

45 Harris, "Did Solon Abolish," 429, fn. 43.

46 Harris, "How to Kill," 75–88.

47 E.g., Aristotle, *Fr.* 8.44.429.10; Demosthenes, *Aristocr.* 217.

48 A case could be presented for 873b: ἐὰν δέ τις ὄφλῃ φόνου τοιούτου, τούτων κτείνας τινά, οἱ μὲν τῶν δικαστῶν ὑπηρέται καὶ ἄρχοντες ἀποκτείναντες. Bury translates this as "and if any man be convicted of such a murder, and of having slain any of the persons named, the officers of the judges and magistrates shall kill him" (Robert G. Bury, *Plato in Twelve Volumes*, vols. 10–11 of *Plato in Twelve Volumes*, LCL [London: Harvard University Press, 1967–1968], 265). However, the aorist participle ἀποκτείναντες is more likely referring to a

referring to homicide, *Laws* likewise uses ἀποκτείνω in the previously mentioned way, in relation to an informal on-the-spot slaying (cf. 871d–e). The only exception found in the present study's research is SEG 57:1409, A. 5–9.12–13 (333-200 BCE), where the formal death penalty is announced (τεθνάτωσαν, "they [the criminals] shall be put to death"), and is then followed by instructions for the officials who are to kill the transgressors ([ἀ]ποκτεινάτωσαν δ' αὐτούς, "and they [the officials] shall kill them"). Given that the normal means of indicating the death penalty is used here, this example should probably not be considered an exception to the rule.

θανατόω ("to put to death") is an interesting case. It is used before the fourth century to refer to deaths of various sorts, though always with a focus on agency, as in, there is no case where the active agent of the verb θανατόω has done the act of killing incidentally or accidentally. The verb ἀποκτείνω can be used in this way, but not θανατόω. This makes sense, given the factitive omicron ending of the verbal form. Even more fascinating is that after the fifth century and all the way until the first century BCE, θανατόω is only found in the literary sources referring to the formal death penalty when it is used of humans.[49] Did it become colloquially reserved for this act, but only outside of law? Is this mere coincidence? If not, maybe its sole use in referring to the formal death

past action, that is, "after the judges and magistrates have killed him." This is clear from the context. The previous line states: "The warnings of exclusion from customary places, and the sureties, are the same as those prescribed for former cases" (Bury). These former prescriptions involve the death penalty for the murderer spoken of in this law. In this way, ἀποκτείναντες is looking back to that mandate and assuming it for the present discussion. In other words, this is not a case prescribing the death penalty but looking back on a former prescription.

49 33 total occurrences with the following texts (not included in enumeration) being uncertain: Aristotle, *Rhet.* 1397b; Socrates, *Epistles* 14.6.7–12; Philodemas, Περὶ εὐσεβείας (pars i), frag. 53.1520. Texts with dates ranging into the Common Era are also not included. The next table (2.2) will provide the rest of the references not found in Table 2.1. While the Septuagint texts have not been included in these charts, it is worth mentioning that Gen only uses θανατόω once (38:10) when the evil of the person described is a transgression of Mosaic law (Deut 25:5–10). This might indicate that the translator was envisaging this death within a legal framework. Likewise, Deut 17:7 only uses the verb once in a court setting (compare to 13:10 where ἀποκτείνω is used likely for an on-the-spot slaying). Leviticus and Numbers both maintain the formal legal sense with Num 21:6 being a possible exception, though here the deity/authoritative ruler is the one issuing the killing order and it may be presented as a capital punishment from God for their disobedience to the covenant. The later LXX texts are worth investigating in the future but have not been included here due to their uncertain dating and potential influence from the Greek Pentateuch.

penalty (when referring to humans) provides another rationale for the translator's choice of this verb. This will be discussed more in the conclusion below. In any case, this verb is used commonly in the vernacular to refer to the death penalty, but it does not appear in actual laws (besides, perhaps, Solon's law cited in Xenophon, *Oec.* 14.5).

Table 2.1 also demonstrates that outside of formal law, there was a degree of freedom allowed in expressing this severe penalty. Many syntagms appear only once, with a few others sharing select mentions (e.g., 'θάνατος + κολάζω' or 'ἔσχατος + πάσχω').

It is interesting that when a writer wants to employ rhetorical synonymy when citing the formal death penalty, the combinations of 'θάνατος + ζήμια/ζημιόω,' θνῄσκω, ἀποθνήσκω, ἀποκτείνω, θανατόω are drawn upon, just as Table 2.1 would indicate:

> τὸ δ᾽ ἄν τις τῶν θηρίων τούτων ἀποκτείνῃ, ἢν μὲνἑκών, **θάνατος ἡ ζημίη**, ἢν δὲ ἀέκων, ἀποτίνει ζημίην τὴν ἂν οἱ ἱρέες τάξωνται. ὃς δ᾽ ἂν ἶβιν ἢ ἴρηκα ἀποκτείνῃ, ἤν τε ἑκὼν ἤν τε ἀέκων, **τεθνάναι** ἀνάγκη.
>
> Whoever kills one of these creatures intentionally is punished with death; if he kills accidentally, he pays whatever penalty the priests appoint. Whoever kills an ibis or a hawk, intentionally or not, must die for it.[50]
>
> HERODOTUS, *Hist.* 2.65.5

> ἡ δὲ βουλὴ πρότερον μὲν ἦν κυρία καὶ χρήμασιν ζημιῶσαι καὶ δῆσαι καὶ **ἀποκτεῖναι**. καὶ Λυσίμαχον αὐτῆς ἀγαγούσης ὡς τὸν δήμιον, καθήμενον ἤδη μέλλοντα **ἀποθνῄσκειν**, Εὐμηλίδης ὁ Ἀλωπεκῆθεν ἀφείλετο, οὐ φάσκων δεῖν ἄνευ δικαστηρίου γνώσεως οὐδένα τῶν πολιτῶν **ἀποθνῄσκειν**: καὶ κρίσεως ἐν δικαστηρίῳ γενομένης, ὁ μὲν Λυσίμαχος ἀπέφυγεν, καὶ ἐπωνυμίαν ἔσχεν ὁ ἀπὸ τοῦ τυπάνου, ὁ δὲ δῆμος ἀφείλετο τῆς βουλῆς τὸ **θανατοῦν** καὶ δεῖν καὶ χρήμασι ζημιοῦν
>
> The Council formerly had sovereign power to pass sentences of fine, imprisonment and death. But once it had brought Lysimachus to the public executioner, when, as he already sat awaiting death, Eumelides of the deme Alopece rescued him, saying that no citizen ought to die without sentence by a jury; and when a trial was held in a jury-court Lysimachus

50 Godley, LCL.

> got off, and he got the nickname of "the man from the drum-stick" and the People deprived the Council of the power to sentence to death and imprisonment and to impose fines[51]
>
> ARISTOTLE, *Ath. pol.* 45.1

> ἂν μὲν ὁμολογῶσι, **θανάτῳ ζημιώσοντας**, ἂν δ᾽ ἀμφισβητῶσιν, εἰσάξοντας εἰς τὸ δικαστήριον, κἂν μὲν ἀποφύγωσιν, ἀφήσοντας, εἰ δὲ μή, τότε **θανατώσοντας**
>
> to punish with death [if they] confess their guilt, but if they deny the charge to bring them before the Jury-court, and if they are acquitted discharge them, but if not then to execute them[52]
>
> ARISTOTLE, *Ath. pol.* 52.1

> ἄλλο τι οὖν ἢ ἀξιοῖς **ἀποθανεῖν**, εἴ τι πεποίηκας παρὰ τοὺς νόμους, ἐφ᾽ οἷς **θάνατος ἡ ζημία**
>
> Must you not, then, expect to be put to death, if you have committed a breach of the laws for which death is the penalty?[53]
>
> LYSIAS, Κατὰ τῶν σιτοπωλῶν, 5

> **θανάτῳ ζημιῶσαί** τινες ὑμῶς ᾤοντο χρῆναι, καὶ **τέθνηκεν** ἁλοὺς παρ᾽ ὑμῖν … οἱ μὲν **τεθνᾶσιν**
>
> [He] was thought by some of you to deserve capital punishment, and he was convicted in your court and put to death … who were put to death.[54]
>
> DEMOSTHENES, *Mid.* 182

These examples further suggest that these expressions were the most common for the death penalty. Unfortunately, there are few instances of back-to-back mentions of capital punishment, so a study in synonymy is not fully possible.[55]

---

51 Rackham, LCL.

52 Rackham, LCL.

53 Lamb, LCL.

54 Murray, LCL.

55 If one looks to imprecatory apodoses, however, we can see in the civic oaths of Nomima I, 104 (ca. 475 BCE) and Nomima I, 105 (470 BCE) that ἀπόλλυσθαι ("perish") is used five and four times in a row, respectively (cf. also IG XI,4 1296 [third century BCE]). Similarly, if another stock legal lexeme is chosen, we find back-to-back uses of something like ἀποτίνω ("to pay") in, e.g., P.Hal. 1.190, 195, 198; P.Hib. 2 197, frag. 6.49, 52; frag. 7.58, or SB 8

It is important again to point out that τελευτάω ("to come to an end"/"to die") is not attested as a synonym to refer to the act of killing via the death penalty in any of the literary texts. Instead, when τελευτάω is paired with the contents of Table 2.1—which almost never occurs—it refers to the person killed in an act of murder,[56] to a death that could have occurred in a multitude of ways,[57] to a natural death,[58] as a synonym in contexts referring to generic death,[59] or to a death that was not caused by a doctor as compared to an unintentional but culpable death via a non-doctor (Plato, *Leg.* 865b). This is not to say that τελευτάω cannot refer to a dead person who has already been put to death by means of capital punishment (e.g., Aeschines, *Ctesiph.* 235; Lycurgus, *Leocr.* 122), but the verb is never used to refer to the act of killing itself. As such, τελευτάω is never—and this seems to be an absolute rule—used to refer to the act of killing or sentencing to death when an author speaks of capital punishment.

2.2.2 *Conclusions on Terminology for the Death Penalty in the Fifth–Fourth Centuries*

Table 2.1 does not represent a complete picture of every reference to the death sentence in the fifth–fourth centuries BCE. The purpose of the chart is to illustrate the most common syntagms, to establish the difference between actual legal documents and general speech about legal matters, and above all to document that τελευτάω is not a term used in relation to the death penalty in the time preceding the translation of Septuagint Exodus. It remains to be seen if it is a term used for the death penalty in the Ptolemaic period, and what its use is in legal documentation. This will be explored below after a look into the phraseology found for the death penalty in the Ptolemaic period.

2.3 Terminology for the Death Penalty in Greco-Egyptian Law

Whereas in the previous chart it was necessary to expand upon the data presented in Safty's article, it is fortunate that Bluche has written an article on

9841.7, 9, 12. Another example, though not the penalty verb, would be *IG* i[3] 104.11, 16–17, 18, 20–21(2×), 27, 28–29, 38, which utilize no synonyms for ἀποκτείνω.

56 Plato, *Leg.* 866b, 868b, 869a; Demosthenes, *Pant.* 59; Dinarchus, *Dem.* 6; Lycurgus, *Leocr.* 45.

57 Demosthenes, *Aristocr.* 47; Xenophon, *Apol.* 26; Plato, *Leg.* 831a.

58 Herodotus, *Hist.* 6.136.3; Xenophon, *Hell.* 3.5.25 (note that τελευτάω is almost used as an opposite to the death penalty here); Plato, *Symp.* 179e; Demosthenes, *Mid.* 179.

59 Lysias, *De caede Erat.* 7; Plato, *Leg.* 766c, 924e.

the death penalty in Ptolemaic Egypt that is essentially exhaustive.[60] For this reason the following chart (Table 2.2) will only have two categories: "Speech Outside of Legal Documents" and "Citation of Legal Documents." There are a few references to the death penalty in formal legal documents that Bluche does not include, which have been added to the data. Some of these are found outside of Egypt for the Ptolemaic era, and all the additions are inscriptions. Additionally, some cases of 'θανάτῳ + ζημιόω' and θανατόω have been added to "Speech Outside of Legal Documents" because Bluche limited his work to Egypt and to actual cases where the death penalty was practiced, but there are mentions in literary texts for these expressions both outside of Egypt and just at the close of the Ptolemaic period. This table does not include references to the Septuagint as it is seeking to establish norms outside of those traditions.

Table 2.2 might be clearer than Table 2.1. There are few formal ways to indicate the death penalty in known Ptolemaic legal codification, and, like the Classical period, many more ways to express it outside of formal law.[61] The most popular formulation, 'θανάτῳ + ζημιόω,' can be seen to have come from the Classical era. 'θανάτῳ + ἔνοχος + εἰμί' is not attested as a formulation for the death penalty before the Ptolemaic period according to TLG. The only third century reference to this formula is found in Gen 26:11 (translating מות יומת, "he shall be put to death"), showing that this legal phrase was used at this time, though the documentary evidence could lead one to think otherwise. θανατόω is found exclusively referring to the formal death penalty (when referring to humans) from the fourth century onward until Philo.[62] That θανατόω is only used this way helps to explain the translator of Exodus's choice to utilize this verb, but more must be said. In any case, both main phrases in the Ptolemaic period contain the dative θανάτῳ, which further solidifies that θανάτῳ in Exodus would likely be associated with the legal jargon concerning capital punishment. In fact, in all the formal legal terminology from the Classical to the Ptolemaic periods, a form of θάνατος is included in the syntagm.[63] In none of these formulations is τελευτάω paired with θάνατος.

60 Bluche, "La peine de mort."

61 The formal ways of indicating the death penalty charted here are corroborated by Helmis, "Crime et châtiment," 197.

62 Excluding LXX texts, which generally fit the framework of an authoritative ruler or their emissaries killing people(s). It is debatable if all fit this category and the later translations are less fixed in their dating.

63 Or there is the shared root as in θνήσκω and ἀποθνήσκω.

TABLE 2.2 Terminology for the death penalty in the Ptolemaic period

Death penalty terminology from Bluche	Speech outside of legal documents	Citation of legal documents
θανάτῳ + ζημιόω	(11×) Heraclides, *Descr. Graec.* frag. 1.16.6; Dionysius Halicarnassensis, *Ant. Rom.* 2.25.6.6; 5.8.3.7; 5.9.3.3; 7.17.5.6; 7.25.3.6; 7.30.3.6; 10.31.6.6; Nicolaus, *Fr.* frag. 114.10, 128.3, 143.9;	(7×) P.Hib. 2 198 v,7.159; SEG 37:1372.14; P.Tebt. 3 1 699, frag. 2.21;[a] PSI 14.1401.8;[b] P.Tebt. 1.5, 4.94–95; BGU 6 1250.14; P.Gen. 3 136 R, FrA,v,i.7; SEG 16 784.17
θανάτῳ + ἔνοχος + εἰμί	(0)	(7×) Aphrodisias 179.18; Rizakis, Achaïe III 5.20; P.Tebt. 3 1 700, 2.49; P.Yale 1 56.13–14; C.Ord.Ptol. 73.8; Fayoum 2:116.30
θανατόω	(22×)[c] Diogenes, *Test. fr.* frag. 110.2; Posidonius, *Fr.* frag. 22.38; Diodorus Siculus, *Bib. hist.* 1.60.4; 1.70.9; 1.78.2; 3.39.6; 11.23.3; 13.1.93; 16.45.9; 16.56.5; 16.73.2; 16.82.3; 16.82.4; 17.80.2; 17.80.3; 18.40.4; 18.48.4; 18.66.4; 18.69.3; 20.71.5; Dionysius Halicarnassensis, *Din.* 3.41; Nicolaus, *Fr.* frag. 130.4	(0)
θανάτῳ + περιπίπτω	(4×) Diodorus Siculus, *Bib. hist.* 1.77.3, 5; 1.83.6(2×)	(0)

a The original editors have presupposed an error on the part of the scribe here and corrected accordingly. See Arthur S. Hunt and Josiah Gilbart Smyly, eds., *The Tebtunis Papyri*, vol. 3, pt. 1 of *The Tebtunis Papyri* (London: Milford, 1933), 39.

b Cf. Bluche, "La peine de mort," 164, for the reconstructed death penalty here.

c References of uncertain date (e.g., Testament of the 12 Patriarchs) are not included here. Philodemus, Περὶ εὐσεβείας (pars i), frag. 53.1520 is unclear as to whether it refers to the formal death penalty.

TABLE 2.2 Terminology for the death penalty in the Ptolemaic period (*cont.*)

Death penalty terminology from Bluche	Speech outside of legal documents	Citation of legal documents
θάνατος + πρόστιμον (predicative relationship)	(2×) Diodorus Siculus, *Bib. hist.* 1.77.2; 1.78.2	(0)
ἀποθνήσκω	(1×) Diodorus Siculus, *Bib. hist.* 1.77.6	(0)
πίπτω + ὑπὸ πικροτέραν διάληψιν[d]	(1×) SB 3 6152–6153.25–26	(1×) BGU 8 1812.6–7
θανάτῳ + καταδικάζω	(1×) Diodorus Siculus, *Bib. hist.* 1.77.9	(0)
θάνατος + ὁρίζω	(1×) Diodorus Siculus, *Bib. hist.* 1.77.7	(0)
ἀποκτείνω	Plutarch, *Ag. Cleom.* 38.823; Polybius, *Hist.* 22.17	(0)
ἀποτυπανίζω	(1×) UPZ I. 119, V.37	(0)
ἐμπαίζω + τραχήλωι	(1×) P.Tebt. 3 1 758.1–4	(0)
θάνατος + ?	(1×) BGU 8 1816, r.24[e]	(0)
κρεμάννυμι[f]	(0)	(0)

d This refers to the death penalty according to Bluche, "La peine de mort," 164, who notes its correspondence to Greek traditional language.

e The papyrus is fragmentary here. The phrase could not be one of the more prevalent choices since θάνατος is nominative, whereas it is more popularly in the dative.

f P.Cair.Zen. 59202 may at first glance seem to be referring to the death penalty but Bluche, "La peine de mort," 158, fn. 75, argues for this to refer to bodily punishment.

2.4 τελευτάω as a Legal Term in Classical and Ptolemaic Contexts

A brief examination will further demonstrate that τελευτάω is not used for the death penalty in Greek legal parlance. First of all, when Todd gives a small and inexhaustive list of terms and phrases used for the death penalty in the fourth century, he does not mention the verb τελευτάω in his data.[64] Second, though τελευτάω does not appear in the laws cited by the orators, it does occur in Plato's *Laws* (766d–e) as a synonym with ἀποθνήσκω to refer to simple death, and again later in inheritance passages to refer generically to the end of life (922–923). It can even be used in the context of the death penalty:

> 'λύουσι γάρ,' ἔφη, 'οἱ ἕνδεκα Σωκράτη καὶ παραγγέλλουσιν ὅπως ἂν τῇδε τῇ ἡμέρᾳ τελευτᾷ'
>
> "For," he said, "the eleven are releasing Socrates from his fetters and giving directions how he is to die today."[65]
>
> PLATO, *Phaed.* 59e.6–7

Yet even here, note that the verb is employed due to the unspecified method or agent by which Socrates was to die, not to refer directly to the formal death penalty.[66] But there is more to gain from looking at the Ptolemaic context.

τελευτάω does occur frequently both in the Ptolemaic papyri of the third century and in the inscriptional evidence. In the inscriptions it is frequently found referring to the end of a person's life (however or whenever that might come about).[67] The death referred to is often in reference to an ensuing will or testament. There are no instances of the verb as the penalty in the apodosis of a legal, casuistic inscription. In the papyri of the third century BCE, τελευτάω refers to the death of individuals or animals, without itself detailing with or indicating how or why they died; it is a simple way of referring to death.[68] Like the inscriptions, the verb is used frequently in the context of

64 Todd, "How to Execute," 36 and fn. 22.

65 Fowler, LCL.

66 It is possible that τελευτάω is marked for non-agency (see fn. 18 above).

67 E.g., SGDI II 1719.14; 1752.8; 1755.14; 1757.13–14; 1767.22; 1775.24; 1776.34; 1784.17; 1796.6; 1826.7; 1829.10; 1830.18; 1846.10; 1858.9; 1874.22; 1882.28; 1890.23; 1924.16; 2006.10; 2014.11; 2036.14; 2049.12; 2065.12; 2072.11; 2227.21; 2246.8.

68 Some of the texts with this verb are fragmentary, but for clear contexts see, e.g., CPR 18 21.8; P.Cair.Zen. 3 59341 c, v.5; P.Col. 3 9, r.5; P.Count 23, col. 8.97; P.Enteux. 13, r.6; P.Enteux. 20, r.4; P.Hib. 1 120, FrC.31–32; P.Lond. 7 2000, 2.15–16; P.Mich. 1 67, r.25–26; P.Tebt. 3 1 701, 4.145;

wills or inheritance to refer to the end of the testator or fortune-holder's life.[69] The third century documentary evidence is split nearly in half between the verb describing generic death and the verb describing death in the context of a will or possessions. Given that many of these attestations come from the petitionary papyri, which are full of stock sayings and terminology, along with the consistent usage in the inscriptions, it is safe to assume that τελευτάω was the stock verb used for wills and inheritances when referring to the death of the testator. This makes sense as it is used to indicate an undefined point and cause of death when looking to the future.[70]

All these factors suggest that τελευτάω would not be understood as referring to the death penalty when viewed from both the legal and the colloquial perspectives. There is another aspect of this discussion that might further substantiate that this is the correct assumption.

2.5 'θανάτῳ + (Verb of Death)' as a Means of Expressing "Untimely Death"

As early as Homer and well into the Hellenistic era there are similar cases to Ex where θανάτῳ modifies a verb that relates to death (i.e., θανάτῳ τελευτάτω).[71]

P.Zen.Pestm 44, r.3; SB 20 14577 DAHT 8066 (15×); SB 20 14578, v.19. P.Köln 6 272 DAHT 3202.11, refers to someone who died via murder, though more descriptors make this clear.

69 Formal will: P.Eleph. 2, r.15. For the same context of a death relating to possessions and inheritance see P.Enteux. 8, r.4, 9; P.Enteux. 9, r. 4; P.Enteux. 10, r.3; P.Enteux. 17, r.2; P.Enteux. 18, r.3; P.Enteux. 22, r.1, 3; P.Enteux. 32, r.2–3; P.Enteux. 51, r.4; P.Enteux. 52, r.4; P.Enteux. 95, r.6; P.Hib. 1 81.5, 12; P.Lille 1 4, 2,ctr.27; P.Sorb. 3 89, r.2; P.Sorb. 3 110, r.4; P.Yale 1 46, 1.8; SB 1 4303.2.

70 The translator of Genesis renders מות with this verb to indicate this same undefined death in the future (25:32).

71 Homer, *Il.* 21.281 & *Od.* 5.312, με λευγαλέῳ θανάτῳ εἵμαρτο ἁλῶναι ("by a miserable death was it fated for me to be cut off"); 11.412, θάνον οἰκτίστῳ θανάτῳ ("I died by a most pitiful death"; cf. 24.34); 15.359, ἀπέφθιτο … λευγαλέῳ θανάτῳ ("she perished … by a miserable death"); 22.462, καθαρῷ θανάτῳ … ἑλοίμην (I take [the lives] by a clean death [i.e., an honorable death]); Pindar, *Pyth.* Ode 3.41–42, ὀλέσσαι οἰκτροτάτῳ θανάτῳ ("to destroy by a most pitiful death"); Xenophon, *Hell.* 6.2.36, αὐθαιρέτῳ θανάτῳ ἀποθνῄσκει ("he died a self-inflicted death"); Hippocrates, *Artic.* 64.4–5, ἀποθανεῖται … τοιούτῳ θανάτῳ ("he will die … by this kind of [early] death"); Theano, *Fr.* pg. 198, l. 21, αὐτόχειρι θανάτῳ μεταστᾶσαι ("to be removed by a self-inflicted death"); Lysias, *And.* 1, θανάτῳ τῷ ἀλγίστῳ ἀπώλετο ("in the most painful death he perished"); Heraclides, *Fr.* frag. 50.7, παρανομωτάτῳ θανάτῳ διέφθειραν ("they perished in a most lawless death"); Crantor, *Fr.* 10.23, κεῖται μοιριδίῳ θανάτῳ ("he lies by means of a doomed death"); SEG 38:440.4–5, θάν' … ἀδίκωι θανάτωι ("he died by an unrighteous death"; fourth century BCE); IG IX,2 638.3, ὤλεο δὴ στυγερῶι θανάτωι ("you perished by a terrible death [dying in childbirth]"; third century BCE);

Using the dative case, these texts describe the manner by which someone dies. Examples crop up particularly in the the fifth century with the phrase βιαίῳ θανάτῳ ("in a violent death"), where this collocation modifies various verbs used to indicate death such as ἀποθνήσκω,[72] ἀποκτείνω,[73] τελευτάω,[74] διαφθείρω,[75] or ἀπόλλυμι.[76] On all occasions where θανάτῳ modifies a verb that relates to death, the death described is unnatural and undesired. A good example is from Dinarchus where 'βιαίῳ θανάτῳ + τελευτάτω' is used in the same context as the death penalty:

> καὶ τοῖς μὲν βιαίῳ θανάτῳ τετελευτηκόσι βοηθῆσαι, τοὺς δὲ παράνομόν τι τῶν ἐν τῇ πόλει διαπεπραγμένους ἐκβαλεῖν ἢ θανάτῳ ζημιῶσαι
>
> to take up the cause of those who have met a violent end and banish or execute any in the city who have broken the law.[77]
>
> DINARCHUS, *Dem.* 6

Here βιαίῳ θανάτῳ τετελευτηκόσι refers to meeting a violent end and θανάτῳ ζημιῶσαι refers to capital punishment. The pairing of 'θανάτῳ + τελευτάτω' does not refer to the death penalty. Another example where 'θανάτῳ + verb of death' is used in contrast to capital punishment is in Demades:

Diodorus Siculus, *Bib. hist.* 2.57.5, μεταλλάττειν ἐξηλλαγμένῳ θανάτῳ ("to make away with themselves by a strange manner of death [suicide]"); Philo, *Names*, 62, καθαρῷ θανάτῳ τελευτήσῃ ("he might die a clean death"); cf. Jer 14:15; 16:4; 21:6. Diodorus Siculus, *Bib. Hist.* 38/39.15.1, ἰδίῳ ἀπεβίω θανάτῳ ("he ceased to live by his own death"), might refer to a natural death (so Diodorus Siculus, *Library of History, Volume XII: Fragments of Books 33–40*, trans. Francis R. Walton, LCL [Cambridge: Harvard University Press, 1967], 261). However, see the comments of Plutarch, *Sull.* 36 and other ancient authors (see Pliny the Elder, *Natural History*, trans. John Bostock and Henry T. Riley [London: Henry G. Bohn, 1855], 191 and fn. 84) who point out that the death of Sylla described in Diodorus Siculus was from some sort of terrible, flesh-consuming disease. This does seem to fit the category of an untimely/early demise.

72 Xenophon, *Hier.* 4.4.1; Herodotus, *Hist.* 7.170.3; Demosthenes, *Aristocr.* 82; Aristotle, *Fr.* 8.44.515.4; Philochorus, *Fr.* Volume-Jacoby#-F 3b,328,F, frag. 137.2; IG I[3] 57.9–10; IG I[3] 227.22–23; IG II[2] 37.11–12; IG II[2] 38.5–6.

73 Plato, *Resp.* 566b; IG I[3] 161.5–6; IG I[3] 179.6–7; IG I[3] 228, fr. b.11–12; IG II[2] 73.6–7; IG II[2] 226.35–36.

74 Aeschines, *Timarch.* 172; Demosthenes, [*Theocr.*] 28; Dinarchus, *Dem.* 6.

75 Demosthenes, *Mid.* 107; Theopompus, *Fr.* Volume-Jacoby#-F 2b,115,F frag 114.22.

76 Lysias, *And.* 1.

77 Translation from Burtt, LCL.

μετὰ τὴν Θηβαίων κατασκαφὴν ἐξήτησεν Ἀλέξανδρος τοὺς ῥήτορας· ὁ δὲ δῆμος ἔπεμψε Δημάδην παραιτησόμενον αὐτούς. ὁ δὲ τοῦτο εἰπὼν ἔπεισεν ὅτι 'ἔασον αὐτοὺς Ἀθήνησι ῥητορικῷ θανάτῳ ἀποθανεῖν.'[78]

After the Thebian destruction Alexander demanded the orators. But the *demos* sent Demades to beg for them. This [Demades] persuaded [Alexander] saying, "Permit them to die a rhetorical death at Athens."

DEMADES, *Fr.*, frag. 52.1–4

Murphey summarizes the historical situation behind this quote:

> In 336 Greece was stunned by the news that Philip had been assassinated. When his son Alexander succeeded him, many Greeks believed that freedom was about to be restored. But within a year Alexander proved that he was an even more implacable foe than his father—for, when the city of Thebes rebelled against him in 335, he destroyed it. A string of victories emboldened Alexander to demand that Athens surrender Demosthenes and seven other orators who had opposed his father and himself; only a special embassy to Alexander succeeded in having that order rescinded. Shortly thereafter, Alexander began his invasion of Asia that took him as far as India and left Athens free of direct military threat from him.[79]

While Demades is a fragmentary text, he clearly refers to this event, given the reference to Thebes and to the demand for the orators' lives. If this assumption is correct, then fragment 52 provides an example where 'ῥητορικῷ θανάτῳ + ἀποθνήσκω' is used in contrast to the immediate death penalty. In context, Alexander is seeking formally to put to death the eight orators. Demades is sent to pacify Alexander and asks that instead of the death penalty, Alexander would allow the orators "ῥητορικῷ θανάτῳ ἀποθανεῖν." This means that whatever the phrase ῥητορικῷ θανάτῳ ἀποθανεῖν referred to, it was not the immediate death penalty. Otherwise, Demades's comment would be incomprehensible. He would be saying, "Instead of putting them to death, put them to death."

78 Ferdinand Schultz, *Aeschinis Orationes* (Leipzig: Teubner, 1865), 253–355, has a slightly different text but it does not affect the argument here.

79 James J. Murphy, "Demosthenes," *Encyclopaedia Britannica*, https://www.britannica.com/biography/Demosthenes-Greek-statesman-and-orator.

This is an obvious tautology. The force of ῥητορικῷ θανάτῳ ἀποθανεῖν must be a contrasting reality to capital punishment in this context.

Now it could be insisted that 'θανάτῳ + τελευτάω' (as found in Ex) is not precisely equivalent to 'βιαίῳ θανάτῳ + τελευτάω' or 'ῥητορικῷ θανάτῳ + ἀποθνήσκω.' This is a fair critique. It is important to point out that when θανάτῳ is paired with a verb relating to death, there is another descriptor modifying θανάτῳ (e.g., βιαίῳ, ῥητορικῷ, etc.). The surviving literary evidence does not suggest that θανάτῳ as an instrumental dative is colloquially paired with a verb describing death without such a modifier. This linguistic situation could be somewhat akin to how one can say "he died by a painful death" but not "he died by a death" in English. Perhaps this might lead one to conclude that the Greek Pentateuch is not using colloquial Greek when θανάτῳ is paired with verbs describing death (e.g., 'θανάτῳ + τελευτάω' or 'θανάτῳ + ἀποθνήσκω'). These phrases might also be described as redundant: "he died by death" gains no semantic content from the addition of "by death." While it is possibly the case that this phenomenon of 'θανάτῳ + verb of death' in the Greek Pentateuch does represent something atypical to Greek parlance, it may not be the case that these turns of phrase are redundant. When one surveys the rest of the uses of θανάτῳ (with no additional descriptor) as an instrumental dative in the literary sources, it appears that θανάτῳ refers to an untimely manner of death.[80] That is to say, the death described is unnatural and undesired in the same way that is seen in cases involving 'θανάτῳ + verb of death.' The most prominent and exceedingly numerous example of θανάτῳ in this function has already been documented above: the death penalty. 'θανάτῳ + ζημιόω' is used to refer to "punishing by means of (an early) death." It might be the case that

80 Cypria, *Fr.* 1.6, κενώσειεν θανάτωι βάρος ("to empty the weight [of overpopulation] by death [in the Trojan War]"); Herodotus, *Hist.* 2.177.8, ἰθύνεσθαι θανάτῳ ("to be guided by death [i.e., put to death]"); 3.127.18, καταλαμπτέος ἐστὶ ἡμῖν θανάτῳ ("he [the king] is stayed by death [=murders]"); 7.83.6, θανάτῳ βιηθεὶς ("being forced by death [in war]); Euripides, *Fr.* frag. 11.2, ἀρετὰν ἀποδείξασθαι θανάτῳ ("to exhibit virtue by death"); Demades, *On the Twelve Years* 4, κτήσασθαι … ἰδίῳ θανάτῳ ("to win [public favor] by his own death [i.e., giving up his life]"); Theocritus, *Id.* 24.59, θανάτῳ κεκαρωμένα ("being lulled to sleep by death [= murder]"); Aelian, *NA* 4.7, τὸ ἀσέβημα διελύσαντο θανάτῳ, πηδήσαντα κατὰ κρημνοῦ ("they atoned for their impious deed by death, throwing themselves over a precipice"); IG II^2 6146.9–10, λυσαμένη θανάτωι ("freed by death [at an early age]"; first century BCE) There are, of course, cases where θανάτῳ is not instrumental and instead the dative case might be a part of the semantics of the accompanying verb or where θανάτῳ is simply the indirect object of the verb. These cases are not included here. Plato, [*Epin.*] 922b, θανάτῳ … τὴν αὑτοῦ μοῖραν ἀναπλήσει ("someone might complete his fate by death"), could be read with instrumental θανάτῳ referring to someone's natural death. Whether this text refers to an early death in context is not clear.

when an action occurs θανάτῳ ("by death") in Greek, that "death" is early and untimely. Perhaps, then, what we see in the Pentateuch and in Ex is in fact a sort of middle of the line translation. A bare θανάτῳ paired with a verb relating to death is not typical Greek, but θανάτῳ modifying a verb to indicate that the action was completed by means of an untimely demise is typical. By rendering with 'θανάτῳ + verb of death' the translators are indicating that the death in view was untimely (signalled by instrumental θανάτῳ), even though this use of θανάτῳ without a modifier was normally reserved for verbs that did not refer to dying. This understanding of instrumental θανάτῳ is further supported by the Septuagintal data and helps to explain a unique translational phenomenon.

One can find θανάτῳ instrumentally modifying verbs in the LXX in the same way that can be seen in the literary sources. In Exod 9:15, θανάτῳ is a translation of בדבר ("by the plague"): אך אותך ואת עמך בדבר ("I could have struck you and your people by the plague") = πατάξω σε καὶ τὸν λαόν σου θανάτῳ ("I will strike you and your people by death"). That the translator of Exodus considered θανάτῳ to be a fitting translation of בדבר in this context suggests that θανάτῳ refers to an early demise—as would occur through a plague—and not just death more generically. This use of instrumental θανάτῳ (without a modifier) paired with a verb that does not refer to death (πατάσσω) is the same pattern found in the literary texts. The same translational strategy is found elsewhere in the Pentateuch in Numbers 14:12 (בדבר אכנו = πατάξω αὐτοὺς θανάτῳ). Later translations also exhibit the same practice with some frequency.[81] Of particular note in these later translations are two occurrences of 'θανάτῳ + τελευτάω,' which connect to this same translational strategy:

> οἱ δὲ περιόντες αὐτοῦ ἐν θανάτῳ τελευτήσουσιν = שרידו במות יקברו
>
> And those of his who survive will end in death[82] = Those who survive them the pestilence buries[83]
>
> Job 27:15

81 Ezek 5:12 (בדבר ימותו = ἐν θανάτῳ ἀναλωθήσεται); 6:11 (בדבר יפל = ἐν θανάτῳ … πεσοῦνται); 28:8 (מתה ממותי חלל = ἀποθανῇ θανάτῳ τραυματιῶν); 33:27 (בדבר ימותו = θανάτῳ ἀποκτενῶ); 38:22 (נשפטתי אתו בדבר = κρινῶ αὐτὸν θανάτῳ); Jer 14:12 (בדבר אנכי מכלה אותם = ἐν θανάτῳ ἐγὼ συντελέσω αὐτούς); 18:21 (יהיו הרגי מות = γενέσθωσαν ἀνῃρμένοι θανάτῳ).

82 Cox, NETS.

83 NRSV.

ὁ δὲ μακρὰν ἐν θανάτῳ τελευτήσει = הרחוק בדבר ימות

the one who is far away shall come to an end by death[84] = Those far off shall die of pestilence[85]

Ezekiel 6:12

While these books are largely regarded to be later translations than the LXX Pentateuch and could therefore be influenced by this earlier work, it is still valuable to mention them, because the translators have both chosen to use 'θανάτῳ + τελευτάω' as a translation of Hebrew texts that do not isomorphically conform to such a rendering. In fact, they seem to translate with ἐν θανάτῳ τελευτήσει based on the same principle and understanding as seen above with בדבר. As for the Joban translator, one would expect a translation like "with death they will be buried," but, as HALOT indicates, Job 27:15 may be an idiom: "c. בַּמָּוֶת יִקָּבֵרוּ they are buried by death ... meaning either they are killed through a plague ... or they are not actually buried at all."[86] Assuming these two possible intentions of the Hebrew, the translator might be rendering based on sense. In context, and as NETS renders, this phrase refers to an imprecation on the wicked:[87] "And those of his who survive [their youth] will end in death, and no one will pity their widows." The idea being conveyed seems to be that of an untimely death before these new adults grow to old age. The Joban translator seems to use θανάτῳ here in the same way as seen above with בדבר and as can be seen in Ezekiel.

The immediately preceding context in the passage from Ezekiel says ἐν ῥομφαίᾳ καὶ ἐν θανάτῳ καὶ ἐν λιμῷ πεσοῦνται ("they will fall by sword and by death and by famine"; v. 11). This context is also about certain persons meeting an early death via various undesirable means. Note the use of 'ἐν θανάτῳ + πεσοῦνται' that corresponds to the sense described above. The following ἐν θανάτῳ τελευτήσει seems to refer to "the one who is far away" meeting an unspecified early demise. Perkins has argued that Ezekiel might be influenced by the translator of Exodus in the use of θάνατος (v. 11) to refer to a "plague," and one could then infer that the whole phrase (θανάτῳ τελευτήσει) has been lifted from Exodus.[88] This is possible. One might also consider that the translator of

84 Hubler, NETS.

85 NRSV.

86 Ludwig Koehler et al., *The Hebrew and Aramaic Lexicon of the Old Testament* (Leiden: Brill, 1994–2000), 1065.

87 Cf. v. 13.

88 Larry Perkins, "Observations on the Plague Narrative in Greek Exodus: Strategies Used by the Translator to Shape the Narrative," *JSCS* 52 (2019): 73–90. Cf. MGS, claiming that the

Job could be influenced by Greek Exodus, whether directly or intermediately through texts like Ezekiel. Even still, the context in which the Ezekiel translator employed θανάτῳ τελευτήσει suggests that it is suited to imprecation and early death, in line with what is seen elsewhere with instrumental θανάτῳ in the LXX and literary sources, rather than the formal death penalty. In fact, the translator of Ezekiel uses 'θανάτῳ + θανατόω' in contexts referring to the legal death penalty for transgression of laws (Ezek 3:18; 18:13; 33:8, 14). This also suggests that this translator did not view θανάτῳ τελευτήσει as the formal death penalty.

It is no great leap, then, to posit that 'θανάτῳ + τελευτάω' means an "meet an early death" in Ex. Surely the translator could have translated with something other than 'θανάτῳ + τελευτάω' if this phrase were not comprehensible Greek.[89] The translator of Exodus has no problem not translating the infinitive absolute in places where (it seems) there was no suitable translation equivalent. The use of 'θανάτῳ + τελευτάω' elsewhere in the LXX likewise suggest the suitability of this translation. Other cases of 'θανάτῳ + (verb of death)' in the Greek Pentateuch can also now be explained.

Exodus 19:12 translates כל־הנגע בהר מות יומת ("anyone touching the mountain shall be put to death") with πᾶς ὁ ἁψάμενος τοῦ ὄρους θανάτῳ τελευτήσει ("anyone touching the mountain shall meet an untimely end"). The warning here relates to human or beast who would ascend mount Sinai before horn is blown. The next verse makes the consequence apparent, namely, death by stones or an arrow (ἐν γὰρ λίθοις λιθοβοληθήσεται ἢ βολίδι κατατοξευθήσεται, "for he shall be stoned with stones or with an arrow he shall be struck down"). θανάτῳ τελευτήσει describes the death that will occur, namely, an untimely one. The kind of untimely demise that will occur is then expounded upon. It is unclear if God was expected to enact one of these punishments or if Israel was supposed to. Arrows are not a means used for the death penalty in the Hebrew Bible but are a typical weapon associated with Israel's deity.[90] Perhaps

definition of "pestilence" for θάνατος is not found outside of the LXX. However, if the present argument is correct, θανάτῳ should probably not be glossed as "pestilence" but rather more broadly as "early demise."

89 Chris Wonjae, "'For in the Day that You Eat of it, You Shall Surely Die': The Early Reception History of the Death Warning in Genesis 2:17," PhD diss., The University of Edinburgh, 2019, 110, claims that the rendering of the Hebrew infinitive absolute מות with θανάτῳ was prompted by the literalism of the translator(s): "the cognate dative θανατω ('death') does not read smoothly with the intransitive verb ἀποθανεῖσθε ('to die') in normal Greek". It is uncertain if "not reading smoothly" is a claim that the phrase is redundant. This study would suggest the pairing does not express redundancy, though it might not be a typical turn of phrase.

90 Num 24:8; Deut 32:23, 42; Job 6:4; Pss 7:12–13; 18:14; 21:12; 38:2; 58:7; 64:7; 77:17; 144:6; Lam 3:12–13; Ezek 5:16; Hab 3:9, 11; Zech 9:13–14.

the translator presumed this would be a divine arrow. The death narrated is also not part of a formal legal procedure, which might be why θανατόω was not selected at this juncture.

In Num 26:65 the translator renders כי־אמר יהוה להם מות ימתו במדבר ולא־נותר מהם איש ("because the LORD said to them, 'they will certainly die in the wilderness.' And not a man was left over from them") with ὅτι εἶπεν κύριος αὐτοῖς Θανάτῳ ἀποθανοῦνται ἐν τῇ ἐρήμῳ· καὶ οὐ κατελείφθη ἐξ αὐτῶν οὐδὲ εἷς ("because the Lord said to them, 'They will meet an untimely demise in the wilderness.' And there was not left even one of them"). Here the Israelite deity's words are remembered. All the unfaithful Israelites were appointed to die in the wilderness over a broad period of time, and this is in fact what happened and is being recounted. Each of them "met an untimely demise" in the wilderness. They were not put to death in any formal or immediate way. This same notion could fit what is found in Gen 2:17 and 3:4. We find 'θανάτῳ + (verb of death)' used with reference to eating from the tree of the knowledge of good and evil: ᾗ δ' ἂν ἡμέρᾳ φάγητε ἀπ' αὐτοῦ, θανάτῳ ἀποθανεῖσθε, "and in whichever day you might eat of it, you will meet an untimely demise" (2:17; cf. 3:4). There has always been debate regarding what the nature of the death warned against here would be, and it is not important to establish this here. Rather, had 'θανάτῳ + θανατόω' been used, a formal death penalty would have been envisaged, which, ostensibly, would mean the primeval couple would need to be killed forthwith. We know the text does not include such a killing, and so it is fitting that the translator can leave open the timing and nature of this 'death.'

There are a fair few other uses of 'θανάτῳ + (verb of death)' in the later LXX translations which can likewise be rendered along the lines of "meet an untimely demise" or "die an early death."[91] Whether or not these later texts borrow from the Pentateuch, they at least suggest the comprehensibility and suitability of the syntagm. Admittedly, it is still possible that instances of 'θανάτῳ + (verb of death)' were not colloquial and represent a redundant phrase in which θανάτῳ conveys no further meaning.[92] However, I have provided a plau-

91 Jer 26:8 (33:8 LXX); Judg 13:22; 21:5; 1 Kgdms 14:39, 44; 20:14; 2 Kgdms 12:14; 14:14; 3 Kgdms 2:37, 42; 4 Kgdms 1:4, 6, 16; 8:10. 1 Kgdms 22:16 is a good example that shows that while 'θανάτῳ + (verb of death)' generically refers to dying an early death, that death could in fact end up being the death penalty, since the king puts someone to death afterwards in this context (cf. Judg 13:22). Other contexts see 'θανάτῳ + θανατόω' used when a ruler utilizes their powers to exert the death penalty (Jer 38:15 [45:15 LXX]; Judg 15:13; 3 Kgdms 3:26, 27; 4 Kgdms 11:15) or in reference to the death penalty prescribed in law codes (Ezek 3:18; 18:13; 33:8, 14).

92 It is possible that instrumental θανάτῳ could refer to death in an undefined sense without the narrower meaning of "untimely death." This concession does not affect the argument concerning τελευτάω that I outlined—it does not refer to the death penalty—nor does my

sible basis for translating these passages in Septuagint Exodus as, "Whoever does ___, let him meet an untimely demise." This translation is particularly supported by the fact that τελευτάω is not a term used for the death penalty in Greek law, and it is also suggested by what I highlighted concerning the collocation of 'θανάτῳ + (verb of death).' In this understanding, the apodosis in laws with 'θανάτῳ + τελευτάω' have become an imprecation, with no concrete or defined here-and-now punishment. This is, in fact, a trait of contemporary Greek law.

Arnautoglu notes a kind of Greek law whereby "no penalty is provided either for the offenders or officials; only curses are pronounced."[93] He cites SEG 33.679.20–24 (third–second century BCE): εἴ τις εἰς τὸν λοιπὸν χρόνον ἀδικήσειέ τι ἢ ἐ[ξ]αλείψειεν ἢ ἐνγράψειεν τῶν μνημονικῶν [γρ]αμμάτων τῶν ἀναφερομένων … ἐξώ[λ]η εἶναι αὐτὸν ("If anyone has abused or erased or tampered with any of the entries in the existing archive … let him perish").[94] There are many instances, of which the following are examples:[95]

> εἰ δέ τις … ποίη … κάταρος ἔστω
>
> If someone … might do (this) … let him be accursed
>
> IPArk 24.14 (273 BCE)[96]
>
> 'ἥτις δ' ἂν μὴ παρῇ πόλις … ἔσται καὶ τῇ ἀρᾷ ἔνοχος
>
> Whichever city might not come out … will be guilty with respect to the curse
>
> AESCHINES, *Ctesiph.* 122

While the phrase 'θανάτῳ + τελευτάω' is not used in the surviving texts as the imprecation, the same idea can easily be conveyed in light of defining 'θανάτῳ + τελευτάω' as "meeting an early demise." All that this comparison needs to

suggested translation of 'θανάτῳ + τελευτάω' in Ex change. If θανάτῳ refers to death more generically, the imprecatory element still remains by virtue of the use of τελευτάω.

93 Arnaoutoglou, *Ancient Greek Laws*, 115 (cf. 63, "sometimes imprecations may have been considered as an exclusive strategy").

94 *Ancient Greek Laws*, 115.

95 For more examples and literature on this trait see Table 2.1, fn. s above.

96 Taken from Gerhard Thür and Hans Taeuber, "Rechtshilfevertrag zwischen Stymphalos und Demetrias (273 BCE)," in *Prozessrechtliche Inschriften der griechischen Poleis: Arkadien* (*IPArk*) (Vienna: Verlag der Österreichischen Akademie der Wissenschaften, 1994), 163.

establish is that a law with an imprecation as the punishment is not foreign to the Greek legal traditions. This trait of Greek law acts as corroborating evidence that the translator of Exodus meant for θανάτῳ τελευτάτω to be read not as the death penalty but rather as an imprecation.

2.6 Conclusion of Terminological Analyses: Motivations for the Translator's Choices

While it is not possible to know the mind of the translator with certainty, this analysis provides indicators as to his motivations when choosing between 'θανάτῳ + τελευτάω' and 'θανάτῳ + θανατόω' in rendering the death penalty מות יומת. First, the translator's desire to represent the Hebrew text must be acknowledged. If all he wanted to do was indicate that the perpetrator is not to be killed, there were obviously much clearer ways to do this. He could have just written μὴ θανάτῳ θανατοῦσθω. One could speculate as to why the translator did not feel comfortable adding a negation, but perhaps the most basic answer would be that he desired to represent the Hebrew source text, even if somewhat superficially (SSF). Both θανάτῳ τελευτάτω and θανάτῳ θανατούσθω represent מות יומת on a surface level in that they both use verbs broadly associated with death. A measure of fidelity to the Hebrew is therefore achieved. Yet the translator not only removes the death penalty, but also adds that the criminal should meet an untimely or unnatural demise (θανάτῳ τελευτάτω). While an imprecation is not a tangible punishment, per se, it is nonetheless a greater penalty than simply saying the guilty person should not be put to death. This aggrievement maintains a degree of justice that μὴ θανάτῳ θανατοῦσθω would not. Perhaps this is another reason he translated as he did. Yet more can be said about the translator's rationale.

The translation choice of θανατόω makes sense now. θανατόω seems to be reserved for the formal death penalty in the common vernacular (not codified law), as it is only found used this way in the extant non-biblical literary and documentary evidence from the fourth to the first centuries BCE. The translator's choice to include the fronted θανατῳ is not only keeping in step with typical formulaic language for the death penalty within the Greek tradition, seeing as there almost always is a form of θάνατος in each syntagm (see Tables 2.1 and 2.2), but also in the Ptolemaic period θανάτῳ is nearly always included in these formulations when it comes to legislation. The translator has mimicked this trait by using θανάτῳ. With θανατόω already likely being a term used for capital punishment and θανάτῳ being part of the formulary, the translator has created a pairing that is as close as one could get to 'θανάτῳ + ζημιόω' or 'θανάτῳ + ἔνοχος + εἰμί.'[97] Additionally, the Classical data also suggest that θανάτῳ τελευτάτω would not be perceived as a synonymous rendering for the death penalty since τελευτάω is not used when authors utilize synonyms for capital punishment. It should be emphasized again that even if the argument for 'θανάτῳ + (verb of death)' is not accepted, the non-use of τελευτάω for the death penalty in Greek law still remains a significant reason to not read penal clauses with this verb as the death penalty. This understanding of τελευτάω might also indicate that Exod 35:2 and Lev 24:16 (both penal clauses with τελευτάτω) should be considered imprecatory.[98]

So, can we take a step further and derive any greater conclusions about the translation and the translator's aims from these data? Did the translator maintain a semblance of the Hebrew parent text purely for aesthetic reasons? Maybe. One cannot help but wonder if the translator anticipated that certain groups reading this translation would not pick up on the changed meaning here. Those untrained in Greek law might not know that θανάτῳ τελευτάτω did not mean the same thing as θανάτῳ θανατούσθω, especially if they were more accustomed to reading the Hebrew scriptures in either Aramaic or Hebrew. The parent text's meaning might have been assumed. Alternatively, someone thoroughly educated in Greek law and language would know θανάτῳ τελευτάτω did not refer to the death penalty and would need to know the *Vorlage* and its language in order to discern that the source text had a different meaning. Was the translator intending for this ambiguity? What end would this achieve? These questions will be resumed in the conclusion of the present volume. We must look first to a more pressing matter.

There remains now a burning question if the conclusion that θανάτῳ θανατοῦσθω does refer to the death penalty but θανάτῳ τελευτάτω only refers to an imprecation and does not indicate an immediate punishment: Why did the Exodus translator change the meaning of the Hebrew text in these places? Was this a conscious process? What could account for these adjustments? I maintain that a tentative answer can be found in the moral and legal milieu of the translation, namely that of Greco-Egyptian law. For an immediate comparison

97 That 'θανάτῳ + θανατόω' might have been somewhat of a redundant phrase, note Hauspie's comment that "the dative expresses exactly the same as the verb (there is no question of instrumentality)" (Katrin Hauspie, "Ἐν with Dative Indicating Instrument in the Septuagint of Ezekiel," in *XII Congress of the International Organization for Septuagint and Cognate Studies Leiden*, ed. Melvin K. H. Peters (Leiden: Brill, 2006), 205. The translator of Exodus might have suffered such redundancy to match the legal formulary typical with θανάτῳ.

98 35:2 is discussed briefly in fn. 200 below. Lev 24:16 will be the focus of later research.

of laws in Ex in light of the data on terminology for the death penalty, Chapter Three begins the comparisons with Greco-Egyptian law. For the moment, one other aspect of the Greco-Egyptian legal world should be discussed, as it also affects the interpretation of all the laws that pertain to the death penalty in Ex.

There is a peculiar legal scribal trait that Ex–Num seem to utilize when rendering laws with a command to capitally punish. This is the employment of a command verb in the imperative rather than the typical future tense in their law codes. While a subtle and unassuming change in translational practice, the switch from the future tense to a sudden imperative in a command verb was meaningful within the Greek legal system at the time. It is another indication of the potential influence of Greek law on these translations and is a key exegetical factor moving forward.

2.7 Ptolemaic Legal Syntax: Imperative vs. Future Tense in the Command Verbs of Laws

2.7.1 *Introduction*

In Greek Exod 21:1–23:19 there are 133 occurrences of the future tense verb formation. The Hebrew imperfect or prefixed conjugation is the typical form being translated in these cases, and there is a degree of analogy between the two that makes this a fitting pairing. Concomitantly, the use of the future in legal materials in the Ptolemaic era has been noted as a rationale for the translator to follow suit.[99] In light of this use of the future tense, a comparison can also be made to the legal genre of royal decree. The προστάγματα and διαγράμματα, two forms of such decrees, are also prone to utilize the future tense when making commands (see below).[100] We find the translator rendering מצות ("commands") as τὰ προστάγματα instead of the expected ἐντολαί ("commands") at the outset of the legal materials in question (20:6).[101] Exodus 18:16 also renders את חקי האלהים ואת־תורתיו ("the statutes of God and his instructions") as

99 See, e.g., Anwar Tjen, *On Conditionals in the Greek Pentateuch: A Study of Translation Syntax* (London: T&T Clark, 2010), 193.

100 These terms can both be generally translated as "decrees." Their different uses in Ptolemaic law are discussed below.

101 These terms were still in fact closely related at the time. See Friedrich Bechtel et al., *Dikaiomata. Auszüge aus alexandrinischen Gesetzen und Verordnungen in einem Papyrus des philologischen Seminars der Universität Halle* (*Pap. Hall., 1*) (Berlin: Weidmann, 1913), 43–44; P.Tebt. 6.10.

τὰ προστάγματα τοῦ θεοῦ καὶ τὸν νόμον αὐτοῦ ("the decrees of God and his law").[102] In the past, the translation choice in 20:6 has been pointed out to be worthy of further exploration and explanation.[103] That the translator of Exodus framed these laws as προστάγματα could be significant as it could point to the form of law to which the Septuagint Covenant Code could most resemble in the Greco-Egyptian legal context. These προστάγματα were part of a genre of royal decree and law introduced in the third century by the Ptolemies.[104] The focal point of this chapter is, then, to compare the patterns and types of command verbs found in Greek law with an eye towards the genres of legal texts found in the Ptolemaic setting. From this comparison a line can be drawn to the LXX text. There are a few occasions in Exodus where the translator suddenly renders not with a future tense command verb but rather an imperative. These imperatives appear a scant few times in the legal materials of the translations[105] and only on ten occasions in Exod 21:1–23:19, six of which are in laws involving the death penalty. This switch from future tense commands to imperative commands is also a trait found in the royal decrees and, as I will argue, seem to express a specific function and meaning in Ptolemaic legal and scribal practice.

Wevers suggests that these imperatives result from the Hebrew cognate free infinitive.[106] If no infinitive absolute pairs with a verb in the Hebrew, a Greek future tense is used for the translation.[107] This is an understandable theory from

102 The second noun is singular in the Greek and could imply that τὰ προστάγματα comprise the totality of τὸν νόμον (cf. 18:20; 20:6). SamP reads the singular התורה in v. 20, from which it might be inferred that the translator of Exodus had a *Vorlage* with the singular reading here. Additionally, τὰ προστάγματα τοῦ θεοῦ is found in v. 20, which reflects a harmonization with v. 16. Whether this harmonization is an introduction by the translator or based in the *Vorlage* is uncertain.

103 Blank, "The LXX Renderings," 262. Noted in Leonard J. Greenspoon, "Textual and Translation Issues in Greek Exodus," in *The Book of Exodus*, ed. Thomas B. Dozeman, Craig A. Evans, and Joel N. Lohr (Leiden: Brill, 2014), 328. In commenting that πρόσταγμα is a more specific legal term than νόμος, Le Boulluec and Sandevoir, *L'Exode*, 42, also invite such a discussion.

104 See section 2.7.3 for a discussion on Ptolemaic decrees. Outside of the legal genre πρόσταγμα can refer more broadly to a generic command of a God (cf. IG XI,4 1299.2 [end of third century BCE] with πρόσταγμα τοῦ θεοῦ).

105 Exod 21:12, 15–17, 20; 22:2 (22:3 LXX), 30 (31 LXX); 23:13–15 (and to a degree 35:2, which is difficult to explain); it is possible that this trait explains Lev 13:45; 18:24; 19:3, 26; 20:2, 9–13, 15–16, 27; 23:4; 24:16–18, 21; 25:14, 17, 31, 45; Num 1:51, 53; 2:2; 15:35; 18:9; 35:16–18, 21, 28. There is a great deal of work that needs to be done on delimiting the genre of the texts in Lev–Num. Research as to how the imperative is employed in their texts exhibiting directives elsewhere (which is very infrequent) is also to be desired.

106 Wevers, *Text History*, 229.

107 He cites v. 21 as an example. Note that he does state that verbs without the infinitive are "usually in the future" (Wevers, *Text History*, 229). He gives no further explanation why these other cases are not.

a translational point of view, but it does not give any explanation as to why an imperative would be better suited than a future for these command verbs. Moreover, he does not provide an explanation why cases like 21:22 include the Hebrew free infinitive and no imperative verb (see also 21:28, 22:15 [22:16 LXX], 22 [23 LXX], 23:4).[108] On this same topic Tjen comments, "This interesting situation [of the use of the imperative] deserves a detailed study on its own, *to examine usage in different genres*."[109] The ensuing analysis aims to undertake the study Tjen desired. It should be emphasized that the following argumentation is based within the Greek legal genre. In normal Greek parlance one could use either an imperative or future tense verb to issue a command without any semantic difference. In order to demonstrate the significance of this changed command verb in the legal genre, it is essential to grasp certain aspects of the syntax of Greek law from Greek history and in the Ptolemaic context.

2.7.2 *Overview of Command Verbs in Classical Greek Law*

Here we are looking at a small cross-section of Classical Greek law. I only focus on the νόμοι ("laws") that governed the whole populace/*polis* in Classical Greece for their syntactic norms. The rationale for this approach will become apparent. However, to be clear, there were distinct categories of law, namely, νόμιμα ("norms"), νόμοι ("laws"), and ψηφίσματα ("decrees"), that guided the Athenians during the fifth and fourth centuries.[110] For example, ψηφίσματα were used for a specific temporal situation and a subsection of the city's populace.[111] Likewise, contracts and obligations between individuals do not seem to be subject to the same syntactic formulae as the laws governing the whole populace. These legal genres are not included in these data, but I will mention their syntactical traits briefly.

It takes little time searching the available sources to come to see that Greek civic laws were formulaically written with their command verbs in the third person imperative and infinitive.[112] Even still, a brief demonstration is helpful. Unlike the papyri of Ptolemaic Egypt, there are not many papyrological items from the Classical period that provide documentary data. This is mostly due to the inability for such materials to survive in less arid places than Egypt. It is also because Greeks inscribed most of their legal materials; they did not often

108 Or 21:36, 22:5 (22:6 LXX), and 22:13 (22:14 LXX), which do not render the infinitive absolute at all.

109 Tjen, *On Conditionals*, 193, emphasis added.

110 Gagarin, *Early Greek Law*, 55, and fn. 13.

111 Gagarin, *Early Greek Law*, 55.

112 For instance, one would only need to look up the texts cited in something like Arnaoutoglou, *Ancient Greek Laws*, ch. 1–3, to see this.

write them on impermanent surfaces. The Classical orators regularly cite such law codes and specify that they are doing so. Whether they are citing from inscriptions or otherwise is not obvious. Whatever the case, they provide a reading of a law code as preserved from our literary sources and not from the inscriptions. Table 2.3 illustrates the command verb utilized in the citations of their law codes. Here "command verb" refers to the verb that issues a prescription that is to be followed, such as χρῆσθαι in the law "ἀγράφῳ δὲ νόμῳ τὰς ἀρχὰς μὴ χρῆσθαι μηδὲ περὶ ἑνός" ("In no circumstances shall magistrates enforce a law which has not been inscribed").[113]

The data are clear. There are arguably no examples of a command verb in the future tense, whereas the imperative and infinitive are found throughout. One could add the entirety of Plato's *Laws* to this table as well. Plato mimics Greek legal formulations, and as such it could be included as literary evidence. That the orators cite laws using these formulae is in no way surprising to anyone who has even begun to wade through the documentary inscriptions, which are our primary source of Greek law.

Greeks were accustomed to writing laws on semi-permanent surfaces of which numerous examples persist. Gagarin comments: "The sheer quantity of inscribed legislation in Greece is striking. The inscriptions discovered to date probably constitute only a small fraction of all archaic legislation."[114] Such an extensive data set allows for syntactical norms within laws to become apparent. In this vein Jacobsthal confirms that "die überwiegende syntaktische Form der Hauptsätze in den Inschr. ist die imperativische und die infinitivische."[115] It is essential to grasp that this is the rule in Greek city law.

There is, though, an illuminating text that breaks this rule. Agora inv. no. I 7557 (374 BCE) contains a string of future tense verbs. Stroud has commented on this strange text and discusses the peculiar and rare switch from an imperative to future command verb.[116] This shift occurs consecutively in lines 9–36

113 Andocides, *Myst.* 85 (Maidment, LCL).

114 Gagarin, "Early Greek Law," 93.

115 Hans Jacobsthal, *Der Gebrauch der Tempora und Modi in den kretischen Dialektinschriften* (Strassburg: Trübner, 1907), §34; cf. §75: "die Imperative … sie (und die imperativen Infinitive) die fast ausschließliche Form der Hauptsätze bilden." Jacobsthal is commenting on Cretan legal inscriptions but makes known elsewhere that the lack of a future tense in the apodosis is common among the other dialects (§73). He notes the exception of payment verbs, which will be seen to be the only real exception that is found among the multiple dialects.

116 Ronald S. Stroud, *The Athenian Grain-Tax Law of 374/3 B.C.* (Princeton: American School of Classical Studies at Athens, 1998).

TABLE 2.3 Command verbs in the orators' citations of law codes

Command verb[a]	**Reference**
Infinitive	Andocides, *Myst.* 85, 87; Demosthenes, *Cor.* 120; *Lept.* 27; *Aristocr.* 22, 28, 37, 44, 51, 53, 60, 62, 82, 86, 87; *Timocr.* 33, 39–40, 45, 54, 56, 59, 71; [*Macart.*] 62; 2 [*Steph.*] 14, 18, 20, 24, 26; Isaeus, *Hagn.* 11; Lysias, 1 *Theomn.* 8
Third person imperative	Aeschines, *Timarch.* 12, 16, 21, 35; Andocides, *Myst.* 96; Demosthenes, *Mid.* 47, 94, 113; [*Macart.*] 75; [*Neaer.*] 16, 52, 87
Combination of infinitive & third person imperative	Demosthenes, *Mid.* 8, 10; *Aristocr.* 42; *Timocr.* 50, 63 (repeated in 64), 105; [*Lacr.*] 51; [*Macart.*] 51, 54, 57–58, 71
Future tense	(0×)[b]

a It would almost be fitting to label this category "apodotic command verb" since "apodotic" describes the second part of a conditional sentence, and many Greek laws are written in conditional sentences. But this is not always true. For the infinitive used as a command without being in a conditional sentence, see Demosthenes, 2 [*Steph.*] 8, 10, 22. For the third person imperative used as a command without being in a conditional sentence, see e.g., Demosthenes, 2 [*Steph.*] 10.

b There is one future tense found in Demosthenes, [*Macart.*] 16, but here it seems as though the future is not prescribing anything but rather states that a particular outcome was no longer an option since the legal claim was already settled. The text reads ἐὰν δὲ μὴ προσκαλεσάμενος ἐπιδικάσηται, ἀτελὴς ἔσται ἡ ἐπιδικασία τοῦ κλήρου ("And if he wins an adjudication without citation, the adjudication of the estate shall be of no effect" [Murray, LCL]). Similar functions of the future will be seen in the exceptions to the rule as discussed below. Tjen, *On Conditionals*, 190, also quotes Plato, *Leg.* 921a: "If any craftsman fail to execute his work within the time named, owing to baseness—he not revering the god who gives him his livelihood, but deeming him (in his blindness of mind) to be merciful because of his kinship,—he shall, in the first place, pay a penalty to the god, and, secondly, there shall be a law enacted to suit his case" (ἂν δή τις δημιουργῶν εἰς χρόνον εἰρημένον ἔργον μὴ ἀποτελέσῃ διὰ κάκην, μηδὲν τὸν βιοδότην θεὸν ἐπαιδεσθείς, ἡγούμενος ὡς οἰκεῖον συγγνώμονα εἶναι θεόν, οὐδὲν τῷ νῷ βλέπων, πρῶτον μὲν δίκην τῷ θεῷ ὑφέξει, δεύτερον δὲ ἑπόμενος αὐτῷ νόμος κείσθω). If everywhere else in the hundreds of laws Plato writes the command with an imperative/infinitive in line with typical Greek law, this future should be considered either an error, or perhaps, due to the nature of the case, Plato is giving a command that is not considered to be an actual law. Note the very next line says "secondly, there shall be a law enacted to suit his case"—indicating that a law needs to be formulated on this matter. This suggests that the previous item, "he shall, in the first place, pay a penalty to the god," was not being presented as an actual law. It is more a matter of Plato stating something that should happen but is not legislation—legislation needs to be made or appealed to on the matter. Finally, this is a future tense found with a payment verb, and, as will been seen, future verbs of payment are sometimes an exception in Greek law for use of the future.

(of 61 total lines) and such a change, he claims, is not "a slip or an isolated stylistic quirk."[117] Stroud's commentary is informative here:

> Such variety of construction is very unusual in Attic public inscriptions and, to my knowledge, a consecutive string of thirteen finite verbs in the future indicative is completely without a parallel in the main body of an Athenian law ... All other surviving Athenian laws on stone couch their instructions in either imperatives or infinitives, or a combination of both ... Nor have I found valid parallels for this concentration of future indicatives in the main text of decrees from Attica.[118]

Stroud notices that the focus of the law changes in this section with future tense verbs, and when the imperative is resumed, the main thrust shifts once again.[119] The future-laden section involves those to whom land is being farmed out, namely, the πόλις ("the city") and ὁ πριάμενος ("the buyer"). Stroud compares this section to *IG* II^2 244 (337 BCE), which, in an appended section (lines 47–113) of συγγραφαί ("contracts" or "leases"), adds future tense commands to a law composed only with the regular infinitive.[120] Other Athenian συγγραφαί also show a preponderance of future tense commands.[121] From this information Stroud concludes:

> Clearly, then, in this syntactic environment of contracts and leasing documents in 4th century BC. Athens, obligations to the πόλις undertaken by ὁ μισθωσάμενος, ὁ πριάμενος, *vel sim.* were often spelled out in the future indicative ... Perhaps [the inscriber's] own previous experience as

117 Stroud, *The Athenian*, 44.

118 Stroud, *The Athenian*, 44–45. He notes the only exception from *IG* II^2 140.25, 27 (353 BCE), which he does not comment further on. It is difficult to explain this inscription. In the place where the future occurs Alessandrì comments that "E' questa la sezione più controversa di tutta l'epigrafe: le lacune sono abbastanza ampie e mancano utili riscontri in altri documenti" ("This is the most controversial section of the whole inscription: the gaps are quite large and there is no useful evidence in other documents") (Salvatore Alessandrì "IG II 2, 140 [Una Proposta Di Lettura]," *Annali Della Scuola Normale Superiore Di Pisa. Classe Di Lettere E Filosofia*, Serie III, 10, no. 4 [1980]: 1147). It may be that the future does not represent a command but a summary (Alessandrì gives this as the view of other editors [1148]). The lacunae make it exceptionally difficult to determine and for this reason this example is not discussed further. Another example with indecipherable lacunae is IG V,1 1498.2 (second century BCE).

119 Stroud, *The Athenian*, 45.

120 Stroud, *The Athenian*, 45.

121 E.g., *IG* II^2 1668; 1670–1671; 1675; 1678; 1685; Demosthenes, [*Lacr.*] 10–13; see Stroud, *The Athenian*, 46.

> a tax-farmer, his familiarity with contracts, finance, and banking, and his involvement at least one prolific importer of grain to the Peiraieus led him to depart from the customary imperatives and infinitives employed by contemporary lawgivers in favor of a more vivid, perhaps even more technical, style. As a result, I suggest that his text of lines 9–36 closely resembles in many respects the form of a contract ... lines 9–36 of our inscription are themselves, in a sense, a written contract, publicly displayed.[122]

It is quite astonishing that by simply changing the form of the command verb a Greek writer can signal the switch of genre from city law to contract. This is how fixed the imperative and infinitive were within that system. Likewise, that a change in genre would likely be perceived by this kind of syntactic maneuver bodes well for what is to be seen in the Ptolemaic documentation, where switching the command verb within a decree, in a similar way, signals to the reader/legal interpreter that something is afoot. What is seen here in Agora inv. no. I 7557 at least gives Classical precedent for such an interpretation. A change from the norm in the command verb is significant.

Despite this regularity of imperative/infinitive in the pre-Ptolemaic era, the future tense is rarely found as a volitive/command verb within city law when the verb is a payment verb. This is true in the Cretan texts and the same trait will be seen in the Ptolemaic texts.[123] It is the only exception to the rule for volitional/command verbs being written with the future tense. Admittedly, I am unsure where this trait's origins lie. Its genesis does not, however, affect the ensuing argument. Apparently using the future for a payment verb was a longstanding trait of Greek law that came into Greco-Egyptian legal syntax.

2.7.3 *Command Verbs in Greco-Egyptian Law*

Since it is true that the earlier Greeks wrote their laws with an imperative or infinitive command verb, one should expect that, upon the Ptolemies entry and exertion of dominance in Egypt at the end of the fourth century, the same kind of syntax would be introduced in any laws they write or import into that context. Such is the case. Throughout the bevy of legal prescriptions found in the papyri and the inscriptions, the imperative and infinitive are likewise

---

122 Stroud, *The Athenian*, 46–47. Others have also commented that contracts demonstrate a consistent use of the future tense: e.g., Jacobsthal, *Der Gebrauch*, §73; Konrad Meisterhans and Eduard Schwyzer, *Grammatik Der Attischen Inschriften* (Berlin: Weidmann, 1900) §88.5.

123 Jacobsthal, *Der Gebrauch*, §73.

pervasive.[124] However, there is one significant difference that becomes apparent when browsing these sources: the future tense is also used for legal commands governing the populace, a distinction from the Classical sources. The type of legal document that future commands appear in is even more interesting,[125] which are almost exclusively in a new type of judicial authority and document, namely, the Ptolemaic decrees as expressed in the διαγράμματα and προστάγματα.[126] Whereas in the *poleis* it was city law alone that acted to broadly govern the people, in Ptolemaic Egypt there were a hierarchy of legal authorities.

In section 1.5.3, I explained that there were essentially three sources of influence and hierarchy when it came to Ptolemaic law. In ascending order, these were (1) judicial discretion, (2) civic/national laws, and (3) the royal decrees embodied in the διαγράμματα and προστάγματα that the king issued. These decrees overrode the other two types of authority[127] and could speak to issues from most areas of law, such as slavery or the process and rules associated with execution of penalties.[128] This hierarchy comes to exist due to monarchal authority; the word of the king is now final.[129]

The διαγράμματα were probably published yearly and consisted of two sorts: "Those dealing with the courts, especially those defining the methods of execution upon property; and those of an economic character, dealing with the relations between officials and subjects."[130] Tcherikover describes a διάγραμμα as "a proclamation of the king regulating some juridicial or administrative

124 Similarly, the change from the imperative to the infinitive in a given document is considered "a frequent occurrence in the style of laws and decrees" (William Linn Westermann, *Upon Slavery in Ptolemaic Egypt* [New York: Columbia University Press, 1929], 34, fn. 91).

125 Once again, this study distinguishes between laws that govern a populace and contracts or leases or the like. For example, contracts do exhibit the future tense.

126 Mostly documented in Appendix 1.1, Table A1.1.

127 Fraser, *Ptolemaic*, 107; Mélèze-Modrzejewski, *Loi et Coutume*, 213, 215–220; O'Neil, "Royal Authority," 427; see, e.g., P.Lille 29, 1.10ff. (257 BCE) and P.Gurob 2.42 (226 BCE) for documentation of this kind of correction through hierarchy.

128 Taubenschlag, *Law of Greco-Roman*, 14; Rostovtzeff, "Ptolemaic Egypt," 119.

129 Tcherikover et al., *Corpus Papyrorum*, 5–6. That this kind of authority was already beginning to form in Greek thought before the Ptolemaic era, see Claude Mossé, *La fin de la démocratie athénienne. Aspects sociaux et politiques du déclin de la Cité grecque au IV siècle avant J.-C* (Paris: Presses Universitaires de France, 1962), 375–397. For Alexander's practice of it see O'Neil "Royal Authority," 425.

130 Westermann, *Upon Slavery*, 31–32. Westermann suggests the annual dissemination of this kind of decree. Cf. Bechtel et al., *Dikaiomata*, 42, for more on the function of the διάγραμμα.

question on a grand scale."[131] Westermann lists some of the known διαγράμματα, and it is evident that they cover issues that have very little to do with the more personal and inter-relational matters found in Ex.[132] This is not to say they do not cover measures involved in private law, but rather that if they do cover such matters, it is usually in relation to some economic or fiscal concern directly related to the Ptolemies.[133]

πρόσταγμα is a specific legal term that likely came to be used in the Ptolemaic legal sense around 286 BCE during the reign of Philadelphus.[134] It continued to be employed in this specific royal sense into the Roman era.[135] In contrast to the διάγραμμα, the πρόσταγμα could refer to individual matters as well as to general issues.[136] The πρόσταγμα could be written in an epistolary or non-epistolary form.[137] This kind of decree, too, is not particularly focused on private law but rather on the concerns of the Ptolemies. Perhaps it is the more personal nature of this type of decree that could have led the translator to render with this term instead of διαγράμματα.[138]

Within this authoritative structure and with the royal decrees at the top of the hierarchy, the use of the future for the command verb *within decrees* takes on a new light.[139] The future is now used within a genre distinct from

131 Tcherikover et al., *Corpus Papyrorum*, 164, emphasis added. Joseph Mélèze-Modrzejewski, "Note sur la législation royale des Lagides," in *Mélanges d'histoire ancienne offerts à William Seston*, ed. Pierre Courcelle (Paris: de Boccard, 1974), 370–372, points out that the διαγράμματα may have been more influential and prominent than the προστάγματα in the third century.

132 Westermann, *Upon Slavery*, 30–33, notes examples about court proceedings, broad economic structures, land execution, and rules for officials.

133 Mélèze-Modrzejewski, "Note sur la législation," 373, 376–377.

134 Wolff, "Law in Ptolemaic," 69; See Rostovtzeff, "Ptolemaic Egypt," 127, who dates the related διάγραμμα to the very end of the fourth century under Soter. Le Boulluec and Sandevoir, *L'Exode*, 43, also comment that this term is specific with respect to Ptolemaic governance. Note that πρόσταγμα is also found outside of the legal sphere in reference to divine commands in dreams (Honigman, *The Septuagint and Homeric*, 109).

135 Joseph Mélèze-Modrzejewski, "The πρόσταγμα in the Papyri," *JJP* 5 (1951): 201.

136 Cf. Mélèze-Modrzejewski, "The πρόσταγμα in the Papyri," 196–197.

137 Mélèze-Modrzejewski, "The πρόσταγμα in the Papyri," 187.

138 Alternatively, maybe this term was perceived to be a measure less formal and authoritative than the διάγραμμα and the translator avoids διάγραμμα in order to keep away from unwanted offense to the royals (cf. fn. 131 above). Likewise, the broader scope of what is covered by a διάγραμμα may have directed away from using this term, especially if there were separate fiscal and legislative διαγράμματα (cf. Joseph Mélèze-Modrzejewski, "Papyrologie et histoire des droits de l'antiquité," in *École pratique des hautes études. 4e section, Sciences historiques et philologiques. Annuaire 1973–1974* [Paris, 1974], 238).

139 Admittedly, it is uncertain if some other genres of documents governing the populace were written with the future tense. For example, a διόρθωμα ("correction") from P.Rev. is

the traditional imperative/infinitive found in Classical city law. Now, when it comes to city law in Ptolemaic Egypt, it must be acknowledged that "the civic laws and institutions of Alexandria and the other Greek cities of Egypt ... are poorly known."[140] Few city laws have survived. Even still, when what has survived is viewed along with the knowledge that Classical city law is written with the imperative/infinitive, it can be claimed or strongly inferred that city law in Ptolemaic Egypt was written just like city law in the Classical *poleis*, that is, with the imperative/infinitive. The surviving city laws from Ptolemaic Egypt do show this. To assume this to be the case makes sense, since the category of 'civic law' continued into Ptolemaic Egypt within their legal hierarchy.

A few delimitations are in order before the data can be properly framed. First, decrees can use either the future tense or the imperative for their command verb. However, *a decree does not switch between the two*. The Ptolemies seem to have created a fixed form and rule where a law must be written with the same command verb throughout—either the future or the imperative. Exceptions to the rule are significant. The infinitive can be found mixed in with either future tense or imperative and does not seem to be part of the rule. Second, while there exists a unified set of προστάγματα in the literature,[141] the διαγράμματα have (to the present author's knowledge) never been formally collected together.[142] I do not claim to have assembled every διάγραμμα, though I have made an earnest effort. Part of the problem lies in the fact that scholars debate which fragmentary texts are διαγράμματα since they do not have a preamble to identify them like a πρόσταγμα often does.[143] This is also true, to a degree, for city laws. Despite this, a good assortment of both is clear and tabulated in Appendix 1.1.[144] It must also be acknowledged that other genres of legal texts existed that cannot be categorized so easily, such as the διόρθωμα

written with the future tense. What survives of the evidence shows that this was a particular trait for the decrees. Even if this delineation were to be challenged, the argument that a change in command verb signalled something to the reader would still be applicable.

140 Bagnall and Derow, *The Hellenistic Period*, 206.

141 Marie-Thérèse Lenger, *Corpus des ordonnances des Ptolémées* (*C. Ord. Ptol*) (Bruxelles: Palais des Académies, 1980). For the sake of simplicity there has been no distinction made in this study between a πρόσταγμα in epistolary form or otherwise. The rules stated seem to remain the same.

142 This study relies on various secondary sources noted in Appendix 1.1.

143 These texts are still included in Appendix 1.1, Table A1.1. Even if they were not included, the argument herein would remain valid. Cf. Bikerman, "Διάγραμμα," 303.

144 Some texts quoted do not belong to Egypt. The διαγράμματα functioned differently in different regions (Bikerman, "Διάγραμμα," 309). That their content and function differed does not mean that the style and syntax did not follow the same rules, as seems to be the case.

of the oil laws in P.Rev. where the future is employed.[145] Similarly, some προστάγματα are a mere line or single verb in length. They can also represent a command to put another decree into effect. Perhaps these examples should not be considered equivalent to more formal legislation. I am not attempting to allocate airtight categories for the legal genres of Ptolemaic Egypt. This is probably impossible given the surviving documentation and is also not necessary. Rather, I attempt to note the broader categories of law that are substantially attested and then demonstrate that fixed syntactic patterns existed for Ptolemaic law in general. Even if some of the texts are obscure in their genre or precise classification, the argumentation still holds together. Its surety is dependent on the fixity of the syntactic rules, not the proper taxonomy of every text. All texts and their classifications can be viewed in Appendix 1.1.

2.7.3.1 Discussion of Common Syntax

Much remains to be desired for the quantity and quality of the documentary resources pertaining to Greco-Egyptian/Hellenistic law. Despite the dearth of texts, it is still possible to fill in some of the gaps and to come to some conclusions. The data collected for this study are not confined to Ptolemaic Egypt, but this should not be considered suspect. The legal syntax used in the Hellenistic world was quite stock. Amundsen's assessment bears repeating here:

> The wording of the decree formulae, so conservatively fixed in Greek communities, is in early Ptolemaic time identical to such a degree that it has sometimes been difficult to decide the origin of an inscription, whether it really belongs to Alexandria or Ptolemais or has been imported from overseas.[146]

We see this consistency in the collected findings. Far and away the most prominent feature in the royal decrees in relation to their command verbs is the consistent tense formation chosen. If a document is written with the future tense, it keeps the future tense. Likewise for the imperative and the infinitive. The infinitive can be found in some cases with the imperative and future, but the future and the imperative do not regularly mix.[147] When they do, it is in specific circumstances. This consistency is in line with earlier Greek law where

145 Cf. Col. 57–60.17. It is possible that the first-person voice exhibited here from the king is the reason for the future and that the future in combination with the first person expressed the tone and tenor of a royal decree. See the discussion in Appendix 1.1.

146 Amundsen, "The Classical Greek," 264.

147 Texts with only infinitives do not seem to use imperatives sporadically, though perhaps if more documentation survived we would see this.

the imperative and infinitive are maintained. It is unclear why some decrees are written with the future and others with the imperative or infinitive.[148] Did the future tense have a novel and regal air about it? Was it used in specific legal contexts or perhaps to instill a certain solemnity? Was it used to highlight the royal voice and concerns? There may be some legitimacy to these suggestions.[149]

The most prominent aspect of this data set is that there are fixed rules when it comes to the syntax of Ptolemaic decrees/law, just as in previous Greek law. If these rules and their exceptions seem obtuse, cumbersome, or pedantic to us, it can be assured that this was likely always the case. Thompson comments on how the Ptolemaic administration had a language of its own:

> The language of surviving Ptolemaic documents, of decrees and depositions, of applications and appeals, lends support to the argument of Wilcken for further technical training for would-be scribes and bureaucrats. This is a subject on which there is more work to be done, but the complex vocabulary and syntax of both official communications and legal writings suggest the development of both a legal and a bureaucratic jargon. Existing Greek vocabulary was extended in meaning ... and the use of unusual vocabulary, of abstract nouns for instance ... or colourful and unusual verbs ... in legal and in bureaucratic writing suggests a professional system in which training and practice served to complicate and even to mystify. If some of the bureaucratic words and phrases are found also in contemporary literary usage, in the Septuagint or in Polybius, suggesting their adoption into the language of the time, the *koine* of the Hellenistic world, the same fortunately cannot be said of the complicated sentence structure which combines with linguistic usage to typify the documents of the Ptolemaic administration ... Those who dealt in these writings learnt the jargon with the job and made it difficult

148 Commenting on the Ptolemaic data in tandem with the LXX, Tjen states that the use of the future in conditional clauses signifies, "'minatory and monitory' force, expressing either covert threat, warning, or indignant rejection" (*On Conditionals*, 123 [cf. 183–184, 189]; see also Antonius Jannaris, *An Historical Greek Grammar: Chiefly of the Attic Dialect* [London: Macmillan, 1897], §1890; Edwin Mayser, *Grammatik der griechischen Papyri aus der Ptolemäerzeit. Band II 1: Satzlehre, Analytischer Teil, Erste Hälfte*, vol. 2, part 1 of *Grammatik der griechischen Papyri aus der Ptolemäerzeit* [Berlin & Leipzig: De Gruyter, 1926], 283; Herbert Weir Smyth and Gordon M. Messing, *Greek Grammar*, rev. ed. [Cambridge: Harvard University Press, 1956] §2328).

149 See "Imperative Dominant with Added Future (Not Payment Verb)", Table A1.1.

> for any outsider to gain access to the system and the information they controlled.[150]

The most common forms of communication concerning commands in Ptolemaic decrees were, it seems, when a document used primarily the imperative, primarily the future tense, or only the infinitive.[151] The abnormal cases, however, are perhaps part of this "jargon" that was more in the wheelhouse of legal scribes.

2.7.3.2 Discussion of Abnormal Syntax

As far as I am aware, previous scholarship has noted that commands change from imperative to future or the like, but no one has sought to explain each aberration. In earlier works such as Bikerman's, the command verb was noted and in part explained geographically:

> Comme une loi, le diagramme devient ici insaisissable. Comme une loi, le diagramma de cette espèce est rédigé à l'impératif: les textes de Cyrène, d'Andania, de Chalcis, d'Amphipolis et de Thessalonique prennent cette forme. Les diagrammata ptolémaïques sont conçus plutôt au futur. Cette difference est conforme à celle entre le diagramma qui sert de directive économique et le diagramma législatif.[152]

That διαγράμματα only use the future tense in Ptolemaic Egypt is contested by the data in this study, provided the labels of other scholars for at least some of the texts are correct. Westermann observes the use of the imperative from a διάγραμμα in P.Rev. col. 75–78 as compared to the future in col. 73–74.[153] He states that "hard and fast rules cannot as yet be made regarding the forms of speech employed in *diagrammata* and laws."[154] It seems that Westermann had considered these changing forms but did not attempt to reconcile them, was unable to find a solution, or did not think it possible at the time. More

---

150 Thompson, "Literacy and Power," 76–77. In a similar vein is Bikerman ("En effet, la précision du langage des bureaux ptolémaïques était remarquable; "Διάγραμμα," 307) and Vierros ("A legal and bureaucratic jargon developed, which strengthened the position of the scribes, since only they could correctly use and understand it … the [mostly Egyptian] scribal class was upholding a strict administrative language form," *Bilingual Notaries*, 33–34). Vierros, *Bilingual Notaries*, 38, comments that the scribal class seems to have intentionally maintained an elitist distance from the masses in this regard.

151 These are the first three lefthand columns in Table A1.1 from Appendix 1.

152 Bikerman, "Διάγραμμα," 310.

153 Westermann, *Upon Slavery*, 30.

154 Westermann, *Upon Slavery*, 30. He echoes the opinion of Ulrich Wilcken.

recently, Mandēlaras has mentioned the relationship between the imperative and future in commands, but he only gives one citation from before the Common Era (P.Rev. 54.15–19).[155] He claims that "the relationship between these two modes of expression is well illustrated in passages where both occur together."[156] This comment is difficult to understand and does little but affirm that this phenomenon exists. Similarly, Tjen notes the future and imperative in this same text but does not explain it.[157] He also remarks that: "This [use of the imperative] may have a significant implication for the interpretation of the Pentateuch in the light of its historical circumstances."[158] This "significant implication" might in fact be what I am describing in this chapter. If it is true that a fixed form of command verb is the norm, then a change from that norm is not random but calculated. This seems to be the case. What remains to be seen are the contexts and applications of these deviations from the normal legal syntactic patterns.

2.7.3.3 Future Tense in Relative Clauses of Imperative-Based Texts

The most straightforward category of future tense verbs appearing in imperative-dominant Greek laws is when they are found in a relative clause.[159] These instances do not need much of an explanation. The future in a relative clause is not a command but is used to describe an anticipated event related to the legal materials at hand. It is used as a descriptor and is not itself a command. One example suffices to demonstrate this function:

> ἐὰν δέ τι βασιλικὸν κώλυμα γένηται, παρ'] ὃ οὐ δυνήσεται βεβαιοῦν Πτολέμαρχος τὴν [μίσθωσιν, ἀποδότω Πτο[λέμαρχος
>
> But if there may be some royal hinderance, on account of which Ptolemarchos will not be able to confirm the rent, Ptolemarchos shall give
>
> P.Freib. 3 34, Fr2.29–30[160]

155 Vasileios G. Mandēlaras, *The Verb in the Greek Non-Literary Papyri* (Athens: Hellenic Ministry of Culture and Sciences, 1973), §719, p. 303.

156 Mandēlaras, *The Verb in the Greek*, 303.

157 Tjen, *On Conditionals*, 192, fn. 23.

158 Tjen, *On Conditionals*, 193, fn. 24.

159 See also Jacobsthal, *Der Gebrauch*, §74, p. 80; Meisterhans and Schwyzer, *Grammatik*, §88, no. 6.

160 This example is from a contract but it demonstrates the point none the less. Likewise, it might suggest that some of these rules crossed the boundaries of genre, as is the case with the future tense used for payment stipulations.

The rest of the examples collected align with the usage seen here. The future can be used in relative clauses as a descriptor that is not a command.

2.7.3.4 Future Tense Payment Verb Exception

I have already shown that the volitional future tense for payment verbs is found in early Cretan texts.[161] This same phenomenon occurs in the Ptolemaic period. Only two verbs are used in this way in the Ptolemaic data: (1) a form of πράσσω and (2) ἀποτίνω. Outside of Egypt, only one text breaks this pattern, SEG 49:722: δοθήσεται τοῦ πραχθέντος with πράσσω as a modifying genitive participle. Of the irregularities regarding the same command verb type established in Appendix 1.1, this well-defined trait accounts for almost half. Of course, considering that πράσσω and ἀποτίνω are found innumerable times elsewhere in the documentary legal sources with the imperative, one cannot help but wonder why a scribe would feel compelled to make this change on certain occasions. While this conclusion must remain tentative, a pattern can be discerned when this trait is found: the future tense of either a form of πράσσω or ἀποτίνω is invoked when referring to monies owed to the royals and their treasury (τό βασιλικόν).[162] All non-fragmentary texts with these payment verbs demonstrate a connection to the royal treasury.[163] For this reason, it seems expedient to surmise that the future tense was used, on occasion, to

161 See fn. 115 above.

162 C.Ord.Ptol. 8.6 (276 BCE), εἰσ̣πραχθήσονται τρίπλουν with the next line (7) reading οἱ γὰρ σ̣[ταθ]μοί ε̣[ἰσι] β̣α̣σ̣ι̣λικοί; C.Ord.Ptol. 7.5–6 (276 BCE), ε[ἰσπ]ρ̣[α]χ[θ]ή̣σεται ἐπίτιμο̣ν εἰς τὸ βασιλικ[ὸ]ν τὸ βασιλικὸν; P.Hib. 1 29, FrA,1.23 (265 BCE), ἀπο]τείσει is contextually linked to royals (line 25); P.Rev. 13.12 (259 BCE), ἀποτεί]σ̣ει [εἰς τὸ] βα[σι]λικὸν; P.Rev. 14.13, [πραχθήσε]ται μ̣[νᾶ]ς τριάκ[οντ]α is the same context and law as 15.1 that mentions τὸ βασιλικὸν; P.Rev. 15.1, ἀποτεί[σ]ει εἰς τὸ βασιλικὸν; P. Rev. 15.9, ἀπο]τίσει δ̣ρ̣[αχμὰς is from the same context as the previous law but is exceedingly fragmentary; P.Hib. 2 198, r,2.17 (242 BCE), εἰσπραχθ]ήσεται τὴν τι[μὴν, while fragmented, is followed by ο]ἱ γὰρ σταθ̣μοὶ βασιλ[ικοί εἰσι; IG VII 3172, face B 1.28 (222–200 BCE), πραχθήσονται, is followed by κατὰ τὸν νόμον (this ψήφισμα, which affects a smaller body of people than the city, points towards more broad regulations and uses the future here only. Perhaps this a nod to royal authority and debt?); Hatzopoulos, Mac. Inst. II 13.45 (221–197 BCE), πραχθήσεται is preceded by (εάν) ὁ βασιλεὺς παρ᾽ ἑτέρου πύθηται; SEG 49:722.4 (late third to second century BCE), δοθήσεται τοῦ πραχθέντος is preceded by lines 2–3 that are reconstructed as ἀποτινέτωσαν εἰς μὲν τὸ βασι]λικὸν while later the typical payment verbs are not in the future tense (ἀποτινέτω [line 6]; πρασσέσθω [line 9]); P.Bingen 45.9 (royal act of 33 BCE), πραχθήσεται is within a royal statement that the benefactor will not need to pay taxes to the royal treasury or to the rulers' own private account (οὐδὲν οὔτε εἰς τὴν διοίκησιν οὔτε εἰς τὸν ἴδιον ἡμῶν κα[ὶ τέκν]ων λόγον καθ᾽ ὀντινοῦν τρόπον πραχθήσεται; see Bagnall and Derow, *The Hellenistic Period*, 110, for this reading).

163 The following are too fragmentary to discern a connection: P.Hib. 2 198, r,2.36, πράξετα[ι; P.Hib. 2 198 v,Fr4.2, εἰσπ]ραχθή[σεται.

refer to payments owed to the royals. Did this future tense amidst imperatives connote something beyond the obvious deontic force of a legal admonition? If the future did have a stronger force than the imperative, as Tjen claims, then perhaps when it came to royal goods and monies owed to them, the future represented a more forceful royal tenor.[164] On the other hand, perhaps this was simply a context in which it was customary for a scribe to write the future and no further deontic thrust would be perceived. Further investigation into this matter might be fruitful. In any case, the use of πράσσω and ἀποτινω in the future tense when referring to payments is a consistent pattern, particularly when referring to the royal treasury. So far this pattern corroborates the claim that a switch in command verb is not haphazard. It is also not random when the future tense is found without these payment verbs.

2.7.3.5 Imperative-Dominant Examples with Added Future (Not Payment Verb)

As a reminder, Ptolemaic decrees maintain the same type of penal verb throughout a given document. If penal commands are in the imperatival mood, then all commands are in the imperative (infinitives can also be included). The same pattern holds true with the future tense. It is, therefore, strange to find cases where sporadic future tenses appear in imperative-laden contexts. The examples in this category are not always easy to interpret. It does not help that most cases come from the notoriously complex Papyrus Revenue Laws.[165] Even so, there do seem to be consistent traits that can help to synthesize the data.

The easiest examples come from Rev. 49.21, 93.6; 97.2; C.Ord.Ptol. 19.2–3, 18–19, all of which use the phrase ὁ βασιλεὺς διαγνώσεται ("the king will make it known")—διαγνώσεται being a future tense amidst imperatives in each respective context. The future tense here is obvious in its intention: "The king will make it known" is a way of deferring the consequence of a particular crime until the king makes a formal decision on the matter later. There is no here-and-now sentence/consequence because such a sentence will be taken up later. The future, then, indicates a matter that is not part of the commands being set up at the present time and instead points to the future action of the king. This phrase ὁ βασιλεὺς διαγνώσεται is actually a stock phrase in the papyri.[166] Because it is an unmalleable phrase of sorts, it is not clear that it

164 Tjen, *On Conditionals*, 189.

165 Citations of P.Rev. will be according to the first edition in order to align with the translation of Bernard P. Grenfell, and John P. Mahaffy, *Revenue Laws of Ptolemy Philadelphus* (Oxford: Clarendon Press, 1896).

166 P. Petr. 3 42, F fr. C, 15 (250 BCE); P. Petr. 3 43, fr. 2, r 1.27; r 3.7; v 3.14 (246 BCE); C.Ord.Ptol. 21.14; 22.10–11; Tjen, *On Conditionals*, 192–193, refers to P.Rev. 49.21 and the future tense as noteworthy but does not recognize that the future here is a stock phrase.

should be included among the next examples. What can be verified is that the future tense is used to refer to the action of the royals and assumes the king will in fact undertake this action at a later date. The action/decision is outside of the authority and specifics of the legislation at hand. Such traits will find commonalities among the ensuing examples when using the future tense.

> παρα[κ]αταστήσουσι δὲ οἱ πριάμενοι τὴ̣ν [ὠ]νὴν καὶ ἀν[τιγ]ραφεῖς
>
> The contractors shall also appoint clerks[167]
>
> P.Rev. 54.15–16

Those unacquainted with P.Rev. should understand that it is a massive set of legal materials that contains many scribal hands. The laws therein are often inserted in patchwork manner. So, while the scribes attempt some divisions and organizational tools, it cannot be assumed that the text is a cohesive whole. For this reason, segmenting the text and paying attention to how previous editors have divided the legal materials is important. For the future tense of 54.15–16, the content before 54.2 should probably be disconnected from what follows because 53.27–54.2 may have originally formed a separate section.[168] From 54.7 onward we find only imperatives in this large section except for παρα[κ]αταστήσουσι ("they shall appoint") in 54.15. Immediately discernable in this example is that, (1) this is the first directive in the section (segmented with a line by the scribe),[169] and (2) the scribe is referring to a one-time event in which the contractors are to set up individuals in the role of clerk. There is no behavior being moderated, but rather this instruction acts as a prerequisite to the upcoming directives (in the imperative) for these clerks. The future is used for the appointment of the clerks to a role of authority. This directive forms a necessary and obvious prerequisite for what is about to be stipulated. This same context describes some of the other uses of the future in P.Rev. as well.[170] These uses represent a structuring of the economic system through

167 Translation from Grenfell and Mahaffy, *Revenue Laws*, 156.

168 Grenfell and Mahaffy, *Revenue Laws*, 155.

169 The scribal division line is called a "division-mark" in Grenfell and Mahaffy, *Revenue Laws*, (vi) and indicates a new section. How that section relates to its broader context, and if the new section could be an excerpt from another law, is not mentioned.

170 P.Rev. 46.8–10: οἱ δὲ τὴν ὠνὴν ἔχοντες καὶ ὁ ἀντιγραφεὺς ὁ κατάστα[θε]ὶς ὑπὸ τοῦ οἰκονόμου καὶ τοῦ ἀντιγραφέ[ω]ς κυρι[εύσου]σιν τῶν ⟦γεωργῶν⟧ \ἐλαιουργῶν/ πάντων τῶν ἐν τ[ῶι τ]όπωι ("The contractors and the clerk appointed by the oeconomus and antigrapheus shall have joint authority over all the workmen in the nome" [translation from Grenfell and Mahaffy, *Revenue Laws*, 140]); P.Rev. 3.2–3: [κ]υριεύσ[ο]υσιν οἱ [ἀντιγ]ραφεῖς οἱ κατασταθέντ[ε]ς ὑπ[ὸ τοῦ οἰκον]όμου ("The clerks appointed by the oeconomus shall have authority").

the appointment of certain groups to roles of authority. The Ptolemies are setting up the prerequisite positions in order for these groups to be told what to do—prescripts that are then formed with the imperative. Each of these future tense verbs from P.Rev. represents a single action that is prerequisite and is not part of the formal directives to be consistently performed. In some cases, there is no actual action performed. For example, when the Ptolemies simply appoint someone to authority (e.g., 3.2–3), this is no more than a statement establishing jurisdiction. It is a statement of structure, a structure that needs to be put in place before anyone can be instructed. Perhaps the royal voice is also to be heard in the future tense since it is the royal authority that is setting up each of these lesser authorities. Indeed, it is both the royal voice and the prerequisite actions that also seem to unite the use of the future in the rest of the sections involving the future tense amidst imperatives in P.Rev. These remaining sections also share unifying themes and topics.

A particular group of texts all have one trait in common: each relates to the setting of fixed prices for goods (P.Rev. 34.1–8; P.Rev. 40.9–20; P.Rev. 53.4, 18–19, 23; P.Rev. 56.14–18).[171] This commonality should immediately suggest that the appearance of the future tense is not random. A particularly clear example of sudden future tense verbs comes in 40.9–20:

> πωλήσουσι δὲ τὸ ἔλαι[ο]ν ἐν τῆι χώραι ⟦τοῦ μ̣ὲν⟧
> \τό τε/ σησάμινον καὶ τὸ κν[ή]κινον \καὶ τοῦ κίκιος καὶ τοῦ κολυκυντίνου καὶ ἐπελλυχνίου/ πρὸς χαλκὸν
> τὸμ μετρητὴν τὸν [δωδε]κάχουν (δραχμῶν) μη,
> ⟦τοῦ δὲ κίκιος καὶ κολοκ[υνθίνο]υ καὶ \ἐ/πελλυχνίου⟧
> ⟦τὸμ μετρητὴν (δραχμῶν) λ⟧ τὴν δὲ κοτύλην (διωβόλου),
> ——
> ἐ[ν Ἀ]λεξανδρείαι δὲ κ[αὶ] τῆι Λιβύηι πάσηι
> τοῦ σησ[α]μίν[ου] \καὶ τοῦ κίκι[ος]/ τὸμ με[τρη]τὴν (δραχμῶν) μη, \τὴν δὲ κοτύλην
> (διωβόλου)/, ⟦καὶ τοῦ⟧
> ⟦κ[ί]κιος τὸμ μ[ετ]ρητὴν [(δραχμῶν)] μη⟧ \{τὴν}/ καὶ πα[ρέ]ξουσιν

171 It is possible that P.Rev. col. 73–74 should be lumped in with these texts and their use of the future. See the discussion in Appendix 1.1, fn. b. Grenfell and Mahaffy, *Revenue Laws*, 174, connects this fragmented section to the others that refer to set prices and states that a section "fixing the rate of interest" may have been lost here. If this is the case, the future tenses are again located in a place referring to the Ptolemies' setting up of a specific price. Col. 74.1 seems to refer to similar instructions to the fragmented 52.4 and 53.4, which both appear to be preliminary actions setting up the laws to come. Admittedly, this is all uncertain.

ἱ[κανὸ]ν τοῖς [βου]λομένοις ὠνεῖσθαι π[ω]λο[ῦ]ντες
δ[ιὰ χώ]ρας ἐν [π]άσαις ταῖς πόλεσιν [καὶ κώ]μαις
... μ]έτ[ρ]οις τοῖς ἐξετα[σθεῖσιν] ὑπὸ[τοῦ οἰκονόμου καὶ τοῦ ἀν]τιγραφέω[ς].

The contractors shall sell the oil in the country at the rate of 48 dr. for a metretes of sesame oil containing 12 choes and for a metretes of cnecus-oil, accepting payment in copper, and at the rate of 30 dr. for a metretes of cici, colocynth oil, and lamp oil [altered to 'the contractors shall sell the oil in the country, both sesame oil, cnecus oil, cici, colocynth oil, and lamp oil at the rate of 48 dr. for a metretes of 12 choes, accepting payment in copper, and 2 obols for a cotyle']. In Alexandria and the whole of Libya they shall sell it at the rate of 48 dr. for a metretes of sesame oil, and 48 dr. for a metretes of cici [altered to '... 48 dr. for a metretes of sesame oil and cici, and 2 obols for a cotyle'], and they shall provide an amount sufficient to meet the demands of buyers, selling it throughout the country in all the towns and villages, (measuring it) by measures which have been tested by the oeconomus and antigrapheus.[172]

P.Rev. 40.9–20

This example is prominent because the preceding context is not fragmentary. Lines 9–20 do seem to be a part of the broader law, though line 9 does come after a scribal division marker. Five lines fill lacunae after line 20, and then imperatives pick up again. It is apparent in lines 9–20 that the section concerns fixed prices for oils being set *by the Ptolemies*. No one is being commanded, per se, but the Ptolemies are establishing the rates their servants will charge. When it comes to the exaction of payments by their servants, we do find the imperative (e.g., 39.13–18). It seems that once again the future tense is used for prerequisite matters. No action is being prescribed, but rather a rate is being set. Additionally, Grenfell comments on the exorbitant increase in price here for the lesser quality oils.[173] Perhaps, given the tenor of such a command for an outrageous price, the future tense would be perceived not only as prerequisite data but also with an air of royal authority? Similar patterns can also be discerned in the other texts relating to the topic of fixed prices.[174]

Despite the difficulty in interpreting these often cryptic and fragmentary laws, there are at least designs that connect each of these texts that suggest reasons for the use of the future tense amidst imperatives. It is possible that

172 Translation from Grenfell and Mahaffy, *Revenue Laws*, 129.

173 Grenfell and Mahaffy, *Revenue Laws*, 129.

174 See Appendix 1.2 for P.Rev. 34.1–8; P.Rev. 53.4, 18–19, 23; P.Rev. 56.14–18.

I have not discerned these purposes exactly. Still, the connections made suffice to point out that the future tense is not employed randomly. This conclusion allows us to move to the final example in this category, namely, SEG 9 1 (321 BCE):

> Ὃς ἂν τὰς Πτολεμ̣αί̣ου γ̣ν̣ώ̣μ̣α̣ς̣ [λύσηι ἅς ἐς Κυρην]αίους Πτολεμαῖος κα[θεῖ]σε, θανάσιμος ἔσται
>
> Whoever [will undermine] the decisions imposed by Ptolemy [on the Cyre]naeans should be liable to death penalty.[175]
>
> ὃς δ' ἂν φρουρῶ[ν] α̣ὐ̣τ̣ο̣μ̣ο̣λ̣ή̣σ̣η̣ι̣, [ἡ δίκη] θάνατος ἔσται
>
> Whoever will desert his post of guard, to him the penalty should be death.[176]
>
> SEG 9 1.52–53, 71–72

These excerpts come from a massive διαγράμμα of the first Ptolemy (Soter) that is too large to cite in full. The two citations above are not part of prolegomena or background matters, so that use of the future should be dismissed. These lines are equal parts vexing and illuminating.[177] Two of the other future tenses (lines 2, 56) are easily explained, and the rest of the text is laden with imperatives (lines 5–70).[178]

---

175 Translation from Catherine Dobias-Lalou et al., "Diagramma of Ptolemy I," IGCyr (2022), http://doi.org/10.6092/UNIBO/IGCYRGVCYR, file name: IGCyr010800.

176 Translation from Catherine Dobias-Lalou et al., "Diagramma of Ptolemy I."

177 These futures have not been discussed beyond a superficial documentation that they exist, as far as the present author is aware. André Laronde, *Cyrène et la Libye hellénistique. Libykai historiai de l'époque républicaine au principat d'Auguste* (Paris: Centre National de la Recherche Scientifique, 1987), 90, calls the use of the imperative throughout a "leitmotiv;" G. Oliverio, "Iscrizioni di Cirene," *RFIC* 56 (1928): 196–197, comments that the verbal forms are "le stesse adoperate nelle cancellerie di molti Stati" and then documents 4 futures, 29 imperatives, and one infinitive (ibid.). He makes no comment on the unequal distribution of verb forms or why they occur. His comparison to OGIS 229 B is likewise unhelpful because it is a document of a different genre than a Ptolemaic royal decree (cf. 197). Most do not comment on the tense change: e.g., M. Cary, "A Constitutional Inscription from Cyrene," *JHS* 48, pt. 2 (1928): 233–235; Silvio Ferri, "Note d'epigrafia cirenaica," *Historia* 3 (1929): 381–400; Peter M. Fraser, "Inscriptions from Cyrene," *Berytus* 12 (1958): 120–127.

178 Whether this text is written by the Ptolemies or by the Cyrenians under the influence of the Ptolemies is uncertain (Mélèze-Modrzejewski, "Note sur la législation," 370).

Line 2 states that "they will be citizens" (Πολ]ῖται ἔσονται) with the future tense. It goes on to label which groups are considered citizens who will be under the auspices of the upcoming regulations.[179] This is not a law but rather prolegomenon to the upcoming set of laws beginning in line 6. It is part of the introduction. Likewise, in a similar fashion to what was seen previously, line 56 refers to future laws that will be put in place and not to a current item being commanded.[180] Both of these futures are also at the outset of a section.

In contrast to these, we find lines 52 and 72. Out of all the future tenses examined here, these two are the most difficult to comprehend. What is doubly unexpected is that both futures refer to the death penalty. Lines 52 and 72 are embedded in the διάγραμμα and do not, as far as I can apprehend, represent anything other than the command to put to death particular individuals. A more nuanced reading of these laws is not possible either. Fraser remarks that "any attempt to recover more than the most general sense must be abandoned" due to the fragmentary nature of the text.[181] It is possible that the future tense in these two death penalty commands somehow represents a later action or consequence that is outside of the current prescriptions in the same way that ὁ βασιλεὺς διαγνώσεται does in P.Rev. In those cases, the future action is indefinite as to its time of completion, and the responsibility for their completion lies with the king. Are we to suppose this kind of use here? Could the death penalty be pushed into the indefinite future? One could make the argument that SEG 9 1 sets the death penalty in the indeterminate future since it includes a section on the death penalty (lines 36–43) where it specifies that those under capital punishment could choose to be judged by the local laws or the court of Ptolemy (lines 39–41). How and when the death penalty might come into play would depend on the authority chosen and the verdict given. However, this tolerance for local laws is explicitly not applicable if the current διάγραμμα made a statement on the death penalty otherwise (lines 35, 37–8).[182] In other words, someone under capital punishment for the matters in lines 52 and 72 would have no choice in the matter since Ptolemy had already decided that

179 See the English translation from Dobias-Lalou et al., "Diagramma of Ptolemy I." For a similar phrase and function of the future to describe who are citizens and then the law binding on them, see Smyrna 14.39 (245 BCE).

180 Laronde, *Cyrène*, 90, has already made this claim.

181 Fraser, "Inscriptions from Cyrene," 125. The commentary from Dobias-Lalou et al., "Diagramma of Ptolemy I," likewise agree with Fraser's sentiment.

182 Ll. 35, 37–38: Πάσας τὰς θανάτου δίκας … χρέσθωσαν δὲ τοῖς νόμοις τοῖς προ[τέ]ροις ὅσοι μὴ ὑπεναντίοι τῶιδε τῶι διαγράμματι, "All cases with a risk of death penalty … should use the former laws, provided that they do not infringe the present *diagramma*" (translation from Dobias-Lalou et al., "Diagramma of Ptolemy I").

these cases were worthy of death and this decision could not be deauthorized. Unless we presuppose that those liable to death were held in waiting until a later time when the king would (again) authorize their deaths, the future tenses in these laws do not seem to correspond to what is found elsewhere in the documentary papyri.

What then could the function of the future tense verbs in lines 52 and 72 be? Perhaps the usage indicates—and this is very much a speculation—something of a solemn royal voice akin to what may be seen with the future used for payments to the royal treasury (and possibly for setting prices) as described above. If it is true that the Ptolemies intended to use the future tense in their decrees and that such a use was novel when it came to corporate Greek law, then perhaps the future tense here represents this tenor. Tjen comments that the "imperatival future seems to have a stronger force than the imperative."[183] If this intuition is correct, then perhaps SEG 9 1 represents the first documentation of this "stronger force" in a legal command of the Ptolemies. Ptolemy already indicated earlier in the inscription that some matters concerning the death penalty were to come, so the future tense in lines 52 and 72 would likely not be misunderstood as anything other than a direct command for capital punishment. It may be that these future tenses came across as stark and solemn royal directives, befitting the severe measure that they describe. If these futures represent a solemn royal directive, then it is not insignificant that they occur in a context referring to the death penalty. In the LXX Pentateuch we find, quite remarkably, that laws with the death penalty are those that almost exclusively receive the changed command verb. In those instances, we find the opposite phenomenon, namely, the future tense command verb is switched to the imperative. The change from future to imperative is a trait to be discussed momentarily, but it is striking that the first Ptolemy seems to have considered the death penalty a matter worthy of this kind of change of legal syntax.

2.7.3.6 Conclusion on Future Tense in Imperative-Dominant Examples

So then, whatever the function of the future tense in SEG 9 1.52, 72, all other attestations in the relevant legal materials demonstrate patterns of use. Future tenses do not appear arbitrarily in imperative or infinitive-dominant documents. When they appear, they describe matters outside of the present recourses being set up. These matters may be prolegomena, as in the appointment of persons to authority or in prices being established, or they may be future actions of the king in the indefinite future. The use of the future tense for payments to the royal treasury could suggest that the future tense was used

183 Tjen, *On Conditionals*, 189.

to indicate a more solemn admonition or a certain royal backing and concern. Perhaps this tone should be read into all the laws with the future tense (outside of those in relative clauses). These futures also seem to be contained either in their own section (as divided by the scribe) or at the beginning of a section when setting up preliminary matters.

This project does not aim for a perfect explanation of the phenomenon at hand. Rather, it seeks to demonstrate at least a plausible explanatory framework for these examples. If this plausibility is granted, then the final category of syntactic abnormality to be discussed should likewise be considered something intentional rather than random. A function should be prescribed, and indeed one does come to light when examining documents that switch from a future-dominant command verb to the imperative.

2.7.3.7 Future-Dominant Examples with Added Imperative (Equivalent to Greek Exodus)

To put the following argument succinctly: in Ptolemaic legal syntax the function of switching from a future tense command verb to an imperative indicated that the command in the imperative was not the final say on a matter, but its performance or non-performance was a choice, as constrained by other related regulations. While only three texts with this syntactic trait survive, they all represent this function. The first example is helpfully from a relatively complete text.

> τῶν δὲ καταβολῶν σύμβολα λαμβανέτωσαν παρὰ τοῦ τραπεζίτου ὑπογραφὰς ἔχοντα παρὰ τῶν ἐπακολουθούντων. ἐὰν δ' ἄ[λλ]ως οἰκονομῶσιν, ἄκυροι αὐτοῖς ἔσονται αἱ δόσεις.
>
> For the payments (the collectors) should receive receipts from the bank manager, which bear the signatures of the witnesses. If they act differently, the payments should be invalid.[184]
>
> P.Paris 62, r,5.12–15 (204 BCE)

Lines 12–15 are a contained section and are set apart by the scribe. In P.Rev. the future tense was usually found within its own segmented section, but here in P.Paris the imperative and future tense are found *in the same segmented section*. It cannot then be argued that the tense change is based on scribal

184 Based on translation from Ulrich Wilcken, *Urkunden der Ptolemäerzeit. Erster Band: Papyri aus Unterägypten*, vol. 1 of *Urkunden der Ptolemäerzeit* (Berlin & Leipzig: de Gruyter, 1927), 509, and Lewis, *Greeks in Ptolemaic*, 18–19.

segmentation and a different section. P.Paris is a large document, and it must be stressed that there are some 150 lines of text that only exhibit the future tense command. Only in r,5 line 12 is the imperative used. That by itself should make the reader stop and consider that, excluding scribal error, there must be some significance to this change.[185] What is particularly helpful with this example in comparison to the other two is that the law and section in view is small and uncomplex.

This terseness is helpful in commenting on the imperative. Here the law refers to those who bring collected tax monies to the royal bank and who need to receive a receipt from said bank that includes witnesses' signatures.[186] If this specific receipt and signatures are not sought out, the payments are null as far as it concerns the Ptolemies and their legal agreement with the tax-farm leasers.[187] It is important to point out that the law acknowledges that the person bringing the collected monies to the bank may act in a different way. The law admits as much with the phrase ἐὰν δ' ἄ[λλ]ως οἰκονομῶσιν, "but if he might manage differently." If the depositor does not follow this protocol, then the payments will not be recognized by the royals and their benefits/acknowledgement of payments received will be withheld. *There is no punishment for the depositor not completing the collection of such a receipt.* This lacking consequence contrasts with an earlier fragmented section where a punishment for "managing differently" is stated in r,2.17–18 to r,3. 1–2: [ὃ]ς δ' ἂν ἄλλως [οἰκ]ον[ομῆι …] περὶ ταῦτα κα̣ [… ἀποτείσει] εἰς τὸ βασιλικὸν καθ' ἕκαστον ἀδίκημα (τάλαντα) ε καὶ πρὸς τὸν διοικητὴν καταποσταλήσεται μετὰ φυλακῆς ("But whoever might manage differently … concerning these things … he will pay five talents to the royal treasury for each injustice and he will be sent down to the *dioketes* with a guard"). Here such mismanagement is called ἀδίκημα and is penalized with a hefty sum along with an escort from a guard. In contrast, r,5.12–15 assumes the leaser is free to withhold from the royal records the payments he has collected from the populace, but such an act will prevent the royals acknowledging their payment, and hence they will still owe the royals in the future. The subject matter right before lines 12–15 is in fact the loss of contracts to these leasers should they not act in accordance with the monarch's desires. The reason λαμβανέτωσαν is in the imperative, then, is because it is permissible not to undertake this action, though this is not without some consequence as is spelled out in the next sentence, i.e., the payments not being validated. This

185 Oddly, Wilcken, *UPZ*, 516 does not make any note of this change in verb tense.

186 See Grenfell and Mahaffy, *Revenue Laws*, 129, for receipts and their importance.

187 For tax-farming in Ptolemaic Egypt and a full translation of this text, see Lewis, *Greeks in Ptolemaic*, 18–19.

means amounts are still owed to the royals. The imperative λαμβανέτωσαν functions as a shorthand way of acknowledging that this command may or may not be followed. Such a choice, however, is subject to the legal consequences spelled out in the immediate context.

Another richly preserved text provides the next example:

> αἴ κα ἐπὶ βωμῶι θύσηι ἱαρῆιον, ὅ τι μὴ νόμος θύεν, τ[ὸ] ποτιπίαμμα ἀφελὲν ἀπὸ τῶ βωμῶ καὶ ἀποπλῦναι καὶ τὸ ἄλλο λῦμα ἀνελὲν ἐκ τῶ ἱαρῶ, καὶ τὰν ἴκνυν ἀπὸ τῶ βωμῶ καὶ τὸ πῦρ ἀφελὲν ἐς καθαρόν· καὶ τόκα δὴ ἀπονιψάμενος, καθάρας τὸ ἱαρὸν καὶ ζαμίαν θύσας βοτὸν τέλευν, τόκα δὴ θυέτω ὡς νομ[...]οκώχιμος μέστα ἐς ἀδελφεῶν τέκνα.
>
> If one sacrifices on the altar a sacrificial animal which it is not customary to sacrifice, he is to remove the residue of grease from the altar and wash it off and remove the remaining refuse from the sanctuary and remove the ash from the altar, and the fire to a pure (place). And only then after having washed himself off, having purified the sanctuary and sacrificed as a penalty an adult animal, precisely then let him sacrifice as one liable to the law up to the children of brothers.[188]
>
> SEG 9 72.26–32 (325–300 BCE)

There is little known about which populace this set of laws governed, and much discussion exists on this and other aspects of the decree.[189] Even if the genre and exact audience of this law is uncertain, the syntactic anomaly in question does clearly appear here. Across this massive inscription future tense verbs dominate, including θύω in lines 11, 37, 46, 57, 61, 67, 74, 87, 96 (ἐπιθύω), 130. Only here we find the imperative θυέτω among future tense (and infinitive) command verbs.

The thrust of the law is that the person who has sacrificed wrongly is commanded to ameliorate the situation, and then once such cleansing has occurred, may offer rightly. Depending on how the text is reconstructed, either the sacrificer will offer according to the law (ὡς νόμος) or as one liable to the law (νομοκώχιμος).[190] Two things are apparent here. (1) θυέτω refers to an offering

---

188 Translation from Dobias-Lalou et al., "Sacred Laws," IGCyr (2022), http://doi.org/10.6092/UNIBO/IGCYRGVCYR, filename: IGCyr016700.

189 See Jan-Mathieu Carbon, Saskia Peels, and Vinciane Pirenne-Delforge, "CGRN 99: Dossier of Purity Regulations at Cyrene," *CGRN* (2022), http://cgrn.ulg.ac.be, filename: CGRN 99, introduction commentary.

190 There is also the option to create a new paragraph after νόμος which then removes -κώχιμος μέστα ἐς ἀδελφεῶν τέκνα from defining the law further. This does not affect the discussion

the sacrificer is not mandated to make. We know this because the previous clause says they must make amends for the improper sacrifice through another sacrifice (ζαμίαν θύσας βοτὸν τέλευν, "having sacrificed as a penalty an adult animal"). It is only after this that they can offer proper sacrifices once again. The law would be tautological if it said that they must make amends through a sacrifice as a penalty and then give another sacrifice. That second sacrifice, if it were required, would then be another penal sacrifice. It makes much more sense to read that θυέτω is only speaking towards their newfound ability to do so if they chose to. (2) The sacrifice, should they choose to make it, must be in accordance with some sort of law, the contents of which are not specified here. Depending on how one segments the text, it could be that the law is one "up to the children of brothers" (μέστα ἐς ἀδελφεῶν τέκνα)—whatever that might mean[191]—or the law is undefined (ὡς νόμος).[192] Whatever the case, the relevant legal data are elsewhere and must be taken into account when it comes to making this next sacrifice. We see, then, that the imperative is found in a similar context to P.Paris 62. Both texts use the imperative in a situation where the specific action in the imperative might not be followed while the performance or non-performance of that action is subject to effects from other legislation. SEG 9 72 only refers to such legislation (via ὡς νόμος/νομοκώχιμος), whereas in P.Paris 62 it is described in the immediate context. In the final text under examination, the same function of the imperative is also found.

> τῶν δὲ στρατευομένων καὶ τῶν ἄλλων τῶν κατοικούντων ἐν Συρίαι καὶ Φοινίκηι, ὅσοι συνοικοῦσιν γυναιξὶ λαικαῖς, [ἃς] ἀνειλήφασιν, μὴ ἀπογραφέσθωσαν.
>
> καὶ εἰς [τὸ] λοιπ[ὸν] δὲ μηδενὶ ἐξέστω ἀγοράζε[ιν] μηδὲ [ὑ]ποτί[θε]σθαι σώματα λαικὰ ἐλεύθερα παρευρέσει μηδ[ε]μιᾶι, πλὴν τῶν ὑπὸ τοῦ διοικοῦντος τὰς κατὰ Συρίαν καὶ Φοινίκην προσόδους ἐν προσβολῆι διδ[ο]μένων, ὧν ἡ πρᾶξις καθήκει, καὶ ἐκ τοῦ σώματος γίνεσθαι, καθότι ἐν τῶι νόμωι τῶι ἐπὶ τῆς μισθώσεως γέγραπται.
>
> Whoever of the soldiers on active duty and the other military settlers in Syria and Phoenicia are living with native wives whom they have captured need not declare them.

at hand. For the various reconstructions offered see Dobias-Lalou et al., "Sacred Laws," and the textual notes on lines 31–32.

191 There is no certainty regarding this phrase's meaning. See also previous footnote.

192 Perhaps ὡς νόμος would be a shorthand way of referring to all pertinent laws on the matter.

> And for the future no one shall be allowed to buy or accept as security native free persons on any pretext, except for those handed over by the superintendent of the revenues in Syria and Phoenicia for execution, for whom the execution is properly on the person, as it is written in the law governing farming contracts.[193]
>
> SB 5 8008 (2).49–59 (= C.Ord.Ptol. 22; 260 BCE)

If the laws in Exod 21–23 were intended to be viewed under the heading and genre of προστάγματα, then this text offers the closest analogy of a syntactic parallel within that genre. Moreover, the dating of this text to the middle of the third century likely aligns closely with the translation project itself. It is again fortunate that the surviving text in the document is so large. There are some 63 lines of text and only in lines 52–53 do we find the imperative instead of the future tense (i.e., μὴ ἀπογραφέσθωσαν ... μηδενὶ ἐξέστω). The two consecutive imperatives come from separate injunctions within the same general legal topic.

Lines 49–52 command soldiers who have taken wives from the native or lower-class population (τῶν δὲ στρατευομένων καὶ τῶν ἄλλων τῶν κατοικούντων ἐν Συρίαι καὶ Φοινίκηι, ὅσοι συνοικοῦσιν γυναιξὶ λαικαῖς, [ἃς] ἀνειλήφασιν, μὴ ἀπογραφέσθωσαν).[194] Bagnall and Derow translate ἀνειλήφασιν as "captured" which gives the impression that a certain kind of acquisition is in mind. The terminology for captured or seized free folk is found earlier in the text: εἴ τινες τῶν κατὰ Συρίαν καὶ Φοι[νίκην] ἀγοράκασιν σῶμα λαικ[ὸ]ν ἐλεύθερον ἢ ἐξε-νέν[κασιν] [κ]αὶ κατεσχ[ή]κασιν ἢ κατ' ἄλλον τρόπον κέκ[τηνται] (lines 33–36). There is nothing specific about the term ἀναλαμβάνω that would indicate only capture.[195] It might be that the free folks acquired by these soldiers could have been attained through any means, whether that be sale, capture, or the like. However, Westerman understands ἀνειλήφασιν in a more neutral sense as "taken up with," referring to cohabitation.[196] In any case, the soldiers who have these wives are not required to register them. This command is expressed in the imperative (μὴ ἀπογραφέσθωσαν). Registration of acquired natives has been

193 Translation from Bagnall and Derow, *The Hellenistic Period*, §64, p. 112.

194 William Linn Westermann, "Enslaved Persons Who Are Free," *AJP* 59, no. 1 (1938): 3–4, argues that λαικά refers not to natives but to those of a lower farming class.

195 The verb is used twice before in this document to refer to items confiscated by the royals (lines 15, 31), and as such the meaning, inasmuch as it might be used in the same way regarding persons, could refer to taking something/someone by force. Such an act could be done through purchase, capture, or the like. LSJ or DGE likewise have no specific category for ἀναλαμβάνω referring to capture alone for this kind of context.

196 Westermann, "Enslaved Persons," 8.

the topic of this legislation up until this point (lines 33–49). The extreme repercussions of not registering were the loss of the slave, 6,000 drachmas per head, and a further decision by the king (lines 39–43) provided one did not register within twenty days of the posting of the decree (lines 37–39). μὴ ἀπογραφέσθωσαν represents the soldiers' exemption from these matters. So why then does the imperative appear here?

The simplest explanation would be that the imperative is used because the soldiers could register these wives if they wanted to. It appears non-registration was a privilege and benefit granted by the royals, not necessarily what the Ptolemies might have preferred.[197] So, if soldiers were to register their native wives, all the better. Moreover, the exorbitant fines and penalties associated with not registering could themselves press a keen soldier to want to make sure everything was above board and documented. If we are to understand ἀνειλήφασιν as a negative term for forceful acquisition, one can imagine a host of situations where, after the twenty days had passed, an unhappy native wife of a soldier could go to the authorities and claim that she was acquired illegally. Registration by the soldier, though not mandatory, could then have been prudent for some soldiers. This is because their exemption only included these kinds of wives purchased or captured up until the end of twenty days. After that, soldiers could not purchase or capture them of their own accord. Sales had to be mediated through the governing bodies at that point. In this reading, μὴ ἀπογραφέσθωσαν and the choice to or to not register a wife applies in a limited way for the next twenty days, since in the future these purchased wives will only be mediated through registered sales according to what "is written in the law governing farming contracts" (ἐν τῶι νόμωι τῶι ἐπὶ τῆς μισθώσεως γέγραπται). On the other hand, if ἀνειλήφασιν is a neutral term referring to peaceful cohabitation, then this kind of rationale does not fit as well. In this reading, soldiers are simply given the choice whether they want to register these relationships and this segment of the decree does not seem to directly connect to the following command.

The conditions surrounding the next imperative in the document (ἐξέστω) are easier to discern than μὴ ἀπογραφέσθωσαν. In the future, assumedly after the twenty days, it would be illegal to purchase or accept as security those labelled σώματα λαικὰ ἐλεύθερα (either native or lower-class free persons). The limitation on the prohibition is evident given that one could theoretically purchase

197 Note the commentary of Reinhold Scholl, *Corpus der ptolemäischen Sklaventexte. Teil 1: Text Nr. 1–114*, vol. 1 of *Corpus der ptolemäischen Sklaventexte* (Stuttgart: Steiner, 1990), 22: "Diese Regelung bevorzugt eindeutig das Militär, zumal kein schriftlicher Ehevertrag vorliegen muß."

a slave or take them as security and then go register them before the deadline was up. This is a caveat that must be considered and seems to be embedded in the syntax by using the imperative. Additionally, note that the text goes on to create another caveat in that this universal prescription did not apply to one group, namely, "those handed over by the superintendent of the revenues in Syria and Phoenicia for execution" (πλὴν τῶν ὑπὸ τοῦ διοικοῦντος τὰς κατὰ Συρίαν καὶ Φοινίκην προσόδους ἐν προσβολῆι διδ[ο]μένων). Such an exception is apparently laid out in another legal document since the scribe claims that this is "as it is written in the law governing farming contracts" (καθότι ἐν τῶι νόμωι τῶι ἐπὶ τῆς μισθώσεως γέγραπται). This other law was meant to inform exactly in which cases it would still be legal to sell or accept as security such subjugated persons.[198] In this way, it was not *always* illegal (μηδενὶ ἐξέστω) to purchase these persons. Under certain circumstances one might make the choice to make a purchase through governmentally sanctioned sales. All in all, SB 8008 provides us with two exceptions to the command issued with ἐξέστω: one is immediate within the twenty days; and another is based on other legal materials that must be consulted for such a sale to be permitted. Just as with μὴ ἀπογραφέσθωσαν, the action commanded with the imperative is understood to be one that may or may not be followed, depending on other legal materials and considerations. This is the same usage we have seen in the other documentary evidence where an imperative is used in a future tense-dominant document.

2.7.3.8 Conclusion on Future-Dominant with Added Imperative Examples and Its Implications for Septuagint Law

Just as I established patterns of use for the sporadic future tense used in imperative-dominant decrees and city law, so also is a pattern evident in future tense-dominant documents with the infrequent imperative. The imperative is used to indicate that the command in question may or may not be followed, with this choice being dependent on additional exceptions that delimit one's performance of it. The imperative functions not as an outright command but as a command with an asterisk, so to speak. This "asterisk" directs the reader to other laws or prescriptions that affect the performance of the imperative verb. In the cases above, this other legal material was either in the immediate context or the scribe directed the reader towards it by mentioning other legal sources. This "asterisk" also indicates that the command may or may not be followed. It seems that this kind of imperative verb was a form of legal shorthand and was part of the Ptolemaic legal syntax. Perhaps the reason the imperative found this use was due to its connection to Greek city law and the hierarchies

198 See Westerman, "Enslaved Persons," 9.

within Ptolemaic law. City law was less authoritative than decree, and city laws were not written with the future tense. When an imperative appeared in a future tense document, it represented this lower authority through the analogous syntax of civic law. Whether this is the genesis of this phenomenon is speculative. In any case, the function of this kind of imperative is significant for the legal sections of the Greek Pentateuch.

The LXX versions of Exodus, Leviticus, and Numbers almost always utilize the imperative when rendering the death sentence.[199] Only three examples do not, namely, Exod 31:14–15, Lev 27:29, and Num 35:31.[200] If the hypothesis

199 A distinction can be made between the formal pronouncement of the death penalty and the subsequent procedure. For example, Lev 20:2 sentences to death one who gives seed to a ruler with the imperatival phrase θανάτῳ θανατούσθω (ὃς ἂν δῷ τοῦ σπέρματος αὐτοῦ ἄρχοντι, θανάτῳ θανατούσθω) and then proceeds to describe the procedural action with the future tense (λιθοβολήσουσιν). 20:15–16 is a similar situation that uses the future tense of ἀποκτείνω between two pronouncements (θανάτῳ θανατούσθω and θανάτῳ θανατούσθωσαν). These texts comport with the documentary evidence that ἀποκτείνω can be used to describe the death after the pronouncement has been made (an example seems to be SEG 57:1409 [333–200 BCE] with τεθνάτωσαν in line 7 compared to [ἀ]ποκτεινάτωσαν in line 8 [cf. line 13]). ἀποκτείνω describes the procedure after the death sentence is ratified, rather than the pronouncement. Alternatively, we see in Lev 24:16 that the verb for stoning is in the imperative: θανάτῳ θανατούσθω· λίθοις λιθοβολείτω αὐτὸν πᾶσα συναγωγὴ Ἰσραήλ. Here, in contrast to 20:2, it specifies that Israel is to do the killing. This would likely not be permitted in the Ptolemaic context and hence the imperative continues. In 20:2 it only states that τὸ ἔθνος τὸ ἐπὶ τῆς γῆς λιθοβολήσουσιν, which leaves ambiguous the identity of the people group doing the killing.

200 Lev 27:29 is discussed briefly in section 4.4.2.1, p. 190. Num 35:31 is discussed below. Exod 31:14–15 is admittedly difficult to ascertain exactly why the translator renders the first iteration of the Sabbath law without the imperative (θανάτῳ θανατωθήσεται/θανατωθήσεται) and later on with τελευτάτω in the imperative (35:2). Some options present themselves: (1) the translator was not translating as though within a formal legal genre in these texts; (2) 35:2 represents the second and updated version of the law (which is now a deregulated imprecatory punishment), since at this junction in the narrative the laws of 31:14–15 were smashed along with the tablet; (3) 31:14–15 represent internal religious conflict and the translator did not care, for whatever reason, about changing every law that did not have implications for those outside of the Jewish community; (4) GCC was expected to circulate by itself and these other Sabbath laws would not be included; (5) 35:2 does not include an infinitive absolute in its formulation for the death penalty and it is possible that this indicates (for narratival reasons?) a less certain outcome for the perpetrator (cf. 21:29 and the option for ransom). Any combination of these views could offer reasons for this difference. Perhaps a case could be made that Exod 21:23 with δώσει ψυχὴν ἀντὶ ψυχῆς should be considered another example of the death penalty without the imperative mood. This law is notoriously debated and it might refer to a more general principle of equity rather than a literal call for exact, talionic retribution. Even if it does refer to the death penalty, the immediately preceding clause indicates that the compensation for the plaintiff is to be adjudicated through official channels (δώσει μετὰ ἀξιώματος,

presented here is accurate, then these translators have used this shorthand form of legal syntax to indicate that a law may or may not be practiced based on other legal considerations. What those other considerations are remains relatively elusive. One option for capital cases that Num 35:31 seems to support is that the imperative is used deferentially, that is, in order not to presume upon a *de jure* right to capital sentencing. It is interesting that while Num always uses the imperative with the collocation 'θανάτῳ + θανατόω,' in 35:31 the future tense is used when the text states that the killer has *already* been condemned to death: καὶ οὐ λήμψεσθε λύτρα περὶ ψυχῆς παρὰ τοῦ φονεύσαντος **τοῦ ἐνόχου ὄντος ἀναιρεθῆναι**· θανάτῳ γὰρ θανατωθήσεται ("and you will not receive a ransom concerning a life from the murderer *who is sentenced to be killed*; for by death he shall be put to death"). This law, unlike all the others with the death sentence, indicates that the culprit has already been labelled guilty of death (τοῦ ἐνόχου ὄντος ἀναιρεθῆναι).[201] In a similar way, Exod 21:29 does not use the imperative for the death penalty in a context where an alternative is presented. Here, the death sentence is not assumed, but rather an (unstated) agent can decide between financial compensation or death.[202] A similar pattern is seen in Exod 22:2 (22:3 LXX).[203] Elsewhere, the future tense remains in contexts where the death penalty is negated, seemingly because there is no claim being laid on this repercussion.[204] All these contexts avoid outright declaring the death penalty. There are a few other laws in the Covenant Code that likewise suddenly switch to the imperative without any warrant from the Hebrew source text or any noticeable linguistic constraint forcing such a decision.[205]

If my conclusions withstand scrutiny, then a potential rationale for the change in command verb in all these laws could be suggested: *The translators used the imperative as a legal shorthand in order to mitigate the binding nature of the translated command.* Why this trait of legal syntax is applied almost exclusively to the death penalty is not entirely clear, though some suggestions

---

"he [the defendant] will give [compensation to the plaintiff] with an [approved] claim"). This means that the penalty would need to be condoned by the authorities. If approval of the death penalty by the government is the reason for the imperative in laws with the death penalty, then the translation may already conform to this standard without the imperative.

201 For the use of ἔνοχος as a legal term for declaration of guilt see, e.g., P. Koeln. 6 272.16–17, ἔνοχος γένηται περὶ τοῦ φόν[ο]υ (250–201 BCE); SB 8008, 1.4–6, 26–27, ἐὰν [δ]έ τινε[ς μή ποιῶ]σιν ... στε[ρηθήσονται καὶ ἔνοχοι] ἔσονται (260 BCE).

202 See section 3.6.

203 See section 4.2.1–4.2.3.

204 οὐκ ἐκδικηθήσεται (Exod 21:21; see 3.5); οὐκ ἀποθανοῦνται (Lev 19:20).

205 Exod 22:2 (22:3 LXX), 30 (31 LXX); 23:13–15; it is possible that this legal syntax could also explain a number of other texts (see fn. 105).

could be made. A reason could presumably be found in the historical context concerning capital punishment in Egypt: it is the Pharaoh who holds the keys to life and death. The royal authorities must be the ones to give approval to exercise capital punishment. To write a law indicating otherwise would be to step outside of a subjugated people group's rightful place. This rationale for the imperative in these texts must remain speculative with other options being possible, but it is nevertheless plausible. Another explanation could be that capital punishment was either not permitted or frowned upon by the Ptolemies as a means of recourse for interpersonal injustices; monetary compensation might have been preferred.[206] Finally, if city laws or Greek/Egyptian custom were the legal recourse for matters concerning the death penalty, then the actual performance of capital punishment was often not the resulting consequence of someone sentenced to death. In the Greek tradition it was also possible that one condemned to death might face exile or monetary compensation. The imperative may be a nod to these other legal recourses.

It is also worth considering that Jews likely did not have the authority to execute by themselves at this time. If they brought someone for execution, it seems as though the crime would need to be investigated by the government and then a suit would ensue (likely) within the civic legal sphere. The imperative could also be a shorthand way of pointing to these kinds of broader legal hedges without adding anything to the text.

When we look at the other laws in OG Exodus with the imperative and compare them to what we know about Ptolemaic legal practice, the hypothesis herein seems to be further substantiated. This study is limited to laws involving the death penalty and does not exhaustively cover the content of some of the other laws with the imperative. Exodus 22:2 (22:3 LXX) and πραθήτω are discussed in section 4.2 and its imperative also coincides with what we know about Ptolemaic legal practice.[207] Likewise, a case could be made for 22:30 (22:31 LXX) and 23:13–15. These laws involve matters that concern the broader economy and property of the Ptolemies. In other words, they are economic concerns to which the Ptolemies paid special attention.[208]

It is worth asking whether a normal citizen of Ptolemaic Egypt, here thinking of a Jewish resident, would pick up on the function of the imperative in these translated laws. It is hard to know. Greek citizens memorized laws as part of their upbringing and perhaps some Jews with a Greek education would also do so. It is possible that this trait of legal syntax was known to those who had

206 See section 3.3.2.2, particularly fn. 74.

207 See section 4.2.2.

208 Exod 22:30 (22:31 LXX) and 23:13–15 will be the topic of future research.

this kind of education. At the same time, Carbon, Peels, and Pirenne-Delforge comment on SEG 9 72, stating, "The rules were presumably displayed prominently, for the use and consultation of sacred officials (these are seldom mentioned, however; cf. line 98), but also, quite clearly, for both men and women worshippers."[209] If regular worshippers were reading this text that includes the imperative among future tense verbs, it seems reasonable to think that they understood what the change in syntax indicated.[210] Greek speaking Jews in Ptolemaic Egypt would likely be exposed to similar laws and would, presumably, understand this syntactic trait. While distanced from the translation, Josephus evidences a parallel phenomenon when he wrote biblical law. Consider the following from Altshuler:

> The general structure of the Josephus-tradition on biblical law is intended to impose not only sequence but also emphases on certain types of laws. Josephus carefully separates the laws of Exodus 25–40, Leviticus and Numbers (AJ 3:102–286; cf. 4:67–75) from those of Exodus 20–28 and Deuteronomy (AJ 4:199–301). The former collection includes mostly cultic and particularistic regulations, while the latter is more civil-secular in nature and contains many universalistic ethical precepts … *Without exception, Josephus narrates the laws of Exodus 25–40, Leviticus and Numbers in indicative verbs, but he phrases the laws of Exodus 20–23 and Deuteronomy in imperatives.*[211]

In other words, based on content, Josephus changed the command verb in the biblical laws. He did this based on what he viewed as universal law as opposed to cultic or particularistic law. One should not presuppose the categories

209 Carbon, Peels, and Pirenne-Delforge, "CGRN 99."

210 Contrast the comment of Carbon, Peels, and Pirenne-Delforge with Fraser's claim that it seems as though προστάγματα were not often posted publicly but rather stored in archives ("A Prostagma of Ptolemy," 179–180). However, Bikerman, "Διάγραμμα," 300–301, claims that διαγράμματα were publicly posted and were expected to be copied for litigation. There is evidence that διαγράμματα were placed out in the public, even by farmers: see P.Hib. 29 r, fr.A.8–9 (265 BCE), reconstructed as τὸ [διά]γραμμα τ[όδε] by Adolf Wilhelm, *Beiträge zur griechichen Inschriftenkunde* (Vienna: A. Hölder, 1909), 247; Charles B. Welles, "New Texts from the Chancery of Philip v of Macedonia and the Problem of the <<Diagramma>>," *AJA* 42 (1938): 255, fn. 6, agrees with this restoration and suggests that the farmer, perhaps along with the royal official, would be the one displaying the decree. This reconstruction is doubted by Westermann, *Upon Slavery*, 39, fn. 113. See also P.Rev. col. 53.10–11 for the public display of the document. That Greeks often posted laws for those passing by to read see Vélissaropoulos-Karakostas, *Droit grec*, 82.

211 David Altshuler, "On the Classification of Judaic Laws in the Antiquities of Josephus and the Temple Scroll of Qumran," *AJS Review* 7 (1982): 4, emphasis added.

presented in this chapter to be operative at the time he wrote, however, he witnesses to the normalcy and comprehensibility of this kind of change as a Jew in the Greco-Roman world.

Broader Jewish aptitude towards Greco-Egyptian law notwithstanding, the use of this kind of imperative leads one to suppose that the translator of Exodus, and perhaps also those of Leviticus and Numbers, were particularly adept in Ptolemaic law and Greek law more broadly. These translators' use of known legal terminology already suggested this, and that they draw on this specific trait of legal syntax points all the more in that direction. By using the imperative, the translators were also able to maintain an element of isomorphism in their translation practice while also indicating that a given legal command may or may not be practiced, in line with other legal considerations. They have added meaning and depth to the laws without sacrificing a superficial representation of the Hebrew through the exploitation of the Greek legal genre and Greek morpho-syntax.

CHAPTER 3

Exodus 21 and Laws Involving the Death Penalty

3.1 Prolegomena

This chapter is in large part based on the data presented in Chapter Two. Given now what is known about the terminology for the death penalty in Greek law, and particularly how that informs the laws in Exod 21, it is appropriate to look at the Greek legal background that could explain the translation choices found in Exodus, and to make more specific comments on the biblical text itself.

Instead of proceeding sequentially, this chapter begins with Exod 21:15, 17 (21:16 LXX) due to the similarity in subject matter in these two verses that allows for a close comparison. Both laws deal with disrespectful conduct against parents. However, the translator renders with apodoses of different meaning (θανάτῳ θανατοῦσθω vs. θανάτῳ τελευτάτω; see sections 2.2–2.5). The content of each of these verses will be analysed from the perspective of Greek law as demonstrable first from the Classical and then from Ptolemaic sources (see section 1.5.3). From here the rest of the chapter continues, beginning from Exod 21:12 and moving sequentially to the end of Exod 21 and its materials on the death penalty. The same examination of the Classical and Ptolemaic legal spheres will accompany each respective biblical law.

3.2 Exodus 21:15, 17 (21:16 LXX): On Abuse towards Parents

ומכה אביו ואמו מות יומת

Whoever strikes his father or his mother shall surely be put to death.

Ὃς τύπτει πατέρα αὐτοῦ ἢ μητέρα αὐτοῦ, θανάτῳ θανατούσθω.

Whoever is striking his father or his mother, by death let him be put to death.

Exodus 21:15

ומקלל אביו ואמו מות יומת

Whoever curses his father or his mother shall surely be put to death.

ὁ κακολογῶν πατέρα αὐτοῦ ἢ μητέρα αὐτοῦ θανάτῳ τελευτάτω.

Let the one speaking ill of his father or his mother meet an untimely end.
Exodus 21:17 (21:16 LXX)

3.2.1 *Introduction*

The primary difference in the translation is between θανάτῳ θανατοῦσθω vs. θανάτῳ τελευτάτω and how that reflects the broader concerns about parental mistreatment in Greek law. In turn, these data will help at least to shed some light on why the translator might have introduced the marked present tense τύπτει whereas all other laws involving striking are aorist (21:12, 18, 20, 26; 22:1 [22:2 LXX]), and to provide a possible reason for rendering ומקלל with ὁ κακολογῶν. The distinct renderings of θανάτῳ θανατοῦσθω vs. θανάτῳ τελευτάτω coincide with Greek legal expectations when it came to punishing wayward children. Striking a parent could be punished with death, whereas ill-speech towards them would likely not be. The two renderings thus correspond to these values. We begin with the Classical data.

3.2.2 *Classical Greek Law on Abuse towards Parents*

There was a class of prosecutable offenses in Athens called κάκωσις γονέων[1] ("mistreatment of parents") which was, quite distinctly, available to the public to bring to court.[2] Normally private offenses would be dealt with by kin, but "the patriarchal traditions of the Greeks, like those of the Jews, paid a high regard to the dignity and authority of a parent. The duty of reverence for parents is described as the 'third commandment' in Aesch[ines]."[3] Parents were due "honours on par with the gods" (Aeschines, *Timarch.* 28), and reverence for parents was one of the highest moral obligations.[4] This criminal category (κάκωσις γονέων) "was provided against those who struck or reviled or simply disobeyed their parents, or who refused them the means of support while they

1 See the notes from Demosthenes, *1 Boeot.* 33 (Murray).
2 Gagarin, *Early Greek Law*, 69.
3 Notes on Demosthenes, *1 Boeot.* 33 (Murray).
4 Dover, *Greek Popular Morality*, 273.

lived, or due honours after their death."[5] The antiquity of this kind of legislation can be seen in Diogenes Laertius, *Lives* 1.2 Solon (55), who allegedly cites a Solonian law (from 594 BCE): ἐάν τις μὴ τρέφῃ τοὺς γονέας, ἄτιμος ἔστω ("If anyone should not support his parents, he shall be deprived of rights").[6] The idea of providing material support for one's parents is the common theme in the discourse of the fifth to fourth centuries, and there were probably only a few exceptions to this requirement.[7] With respect to punishments for this crime, only a few texts suggest the death penalty (cited below), whereas the rest prescribe ἀτιμία ("loss of rights").[8] Phillips provides a comprehensive list of literary references to the crime of κάκωσις γονέων, only one of which mentions striking parents (Lysias, *Agor.* 91).[9] This study would add to Phillips's list Plato, *Leg.* 877b and Aeschines, *Timarch.* 28. These three texts are as follows:

> ὅστις οὖν τόν τε γόνῳ πατέρα τὸν αὑτοῦ ἔτυπτε καὶ οὐδὲν παρεῖχε τῶν ἐπιτηδείων, τόν τε ποιητὸν πατέρα ἀφείλετο ἃ ἦν ὑπάρχοντα ἐκείνῳ ἀγαθά, πῶς οὐ καὶ διὰ τοῦτο κατὰ τὸν τῆς κακώσεως νόμον ἄξιός ἐστι θανάτῳ ζημιωθῆναι
>
> Therefore, just as much as the man who struck his own natural father and denied him all necessaries of life, he who robbed his adoptive father of the means that he possessed is certainly, on this one score, as provided by the law of such maltreatment, deserving of the penalty of death.[10]
>
> LYSIAS, *Agor.* 91[11]

5 Notes on Demosthenes, *1 Boeot.* 33 (Murray).

6 Cf. Phillips, *The Law of Ancient Athens*, 207.

7 See Phillips, *The Law of Ancient Athens*, 207–210 and Plutarch, *Sol.* 22.1.

8 Aeschines, *Timarch.* 28–30, 32; Diogenes Laertius, *Lives* 1.2 Solon (55); Xenophon, *Mem.* 2.2.13; Demosthenes, *Timocr.* 103, 107; Andocides, *Myst.* 73–79. Cf. Phillips, *The Law of Ancient Athens*, 208. Plato, *Leg.* 932a–d suggests corporal punishment as a possibility and is not mentioned in Phillips.

9 See Phillips, *The Law of Ancient Athens*, 207–210. Cf. Lysias, *1 Theomn.* 8.

10 Lysias, *Agor.* 91 (Lamb).

11 The translator's (Lamb) notes on this text claims that this is a rhetorical expansion by a later hand. It does not matter if this is the case or not for the present study. This work is attempting to show only that such a law and punishment were within the moral and legal paradigms of Greek thought. Phillips, *The Law of Ancient Athens*, 208–209, does not mention this extra hand, and Farsedakis, "θανάτῳ ζημιοῦν," 85, seems to consider this text to be spurious in origin.

> γονέας δ' ἂν παῖς ἢ δοῦλος δεσπότην ὡσαύτως ἐκ προνοίας τρώσῃ, θάνατον εἶναι τὴν ζημίαν
>
> If in like manner, deliberately, a son should wound his parents or a slave his master, death shall be the penalty.[12]
>
> PLATO, *Leg.* 877b
>
> ἐάν τις λέγῃ ἐν τῷ δήμῳ τὸν πατέρα τύπτων ἢ τὴν μητέρα, ἢ μὴ τρέφων, ἢ μὴ παρέχων οἴκησιν:' τοῦτον οὐκ ἐᾷ λέγειν
>
> If anyone attempts to speak before the people who beats his father or mother, or fails to support them or to provide a home for them. Such a man, then, he forbids to speak.[13]
>
> AESCHINES, *Timarch.* 28

It is interesting that the striking in Lysias and Aeschines is presented in the present and imperfect tenses (ἔτυπτε/τύπτων), potentially pointing to a repeated occurrence rather than a singular infraction being criminal in Greek thought. The present tense is also found in Exod 21:15 (τύπτει), which unexpectedly breaks the translator's unmarked use of an aorist in the protases of the laws, most notably in laws also describing striking. Whether a singular infraction or multiple strikes warranted criminal proceedings in Greek law is unknown. The prescription in Plato only speaks generally about wounding (τρώσῃ) a parent. Lysias and Plato suggest the death penalty for such crimes, with the addition of deprived material goods also included in Lysias. Aeschines is only focused on the loss of public rights and so only that facet of a punishment is mentioned. Demosthenes, *1 Boeotus* 33 also generally suggests that disobedient children ought to die, and Plato, *Leg.* 932a–d suggests pecuniary *and corporal* punishments for depriving parents of their necessities. Taken together and across approximately a century, these texts suggest that the death penalty was within the moral and legal framework of Greeks when it came to the harm of parents, which is usually depicted as depriving parents of material necessities but also includes striking parents. This outlook is found in the century prior to the Septuagint translation and should be considered a possible legal framework that was brought to Egypt in the wake of Hellenization. This outlook is even more possible as Greek laws were known to remain unchanged

12 Plato, *Leg.* 877b (Bury).
13 Aeschines, *Timarch.* 28 (Adams).

for lengthy periods.[14] It is unfortunate that more detail as to the exact crimes that were brought to court are not found.

What can be said about disrespectful speech against parents? Nothing in these references to parental abuse make mention of it. Dover has created a list of references describing parental respect in the Classical Greek world and nothing within his enumeration connects ill speech towards parents as being worthy of serious punishment.[15] This is probably because "Greek society did not carry such respect to the point of serious irrationality."[16] Taking family to court was considered utterly shameful,[17] which might be why disrespectful speech was not worth bringing to court or mentioning in the literature.

3.2.3 *Greco-Egyptian Law on Abuse towards Parents*

Most of the evidence regarding legal treatment of parents in Ptolemaic Egypt is documentary. A recent publication by Velissaropoulos-Karakostas has fortunately gathered the relevant data,[18] though she does fail to mention P.Eleph. 2, plate 7 (284 BCE).

I acknowledge that no texts speak directly about children striking parents in the Ptolemaic documentation. There are, still, five sources regarding parental maltreatment in general. All five deal mainly with the lack of provisions given to parents. Velissaropoulos-Karakostas and Taubenschlag both agree that there was probably no specific law requiring that children provide materially for their parents in Ptolemaic Egypt.[19] Rather, individual contracts probably mediated these issues.[20] Even so, "l'indifférence à l'égard des parents n'est pas dépourvue de conséquences" and P.Enteux. 22 (see below) shows "à l'entourage social le comportement cruel d'un fils envers un père vieux, pauvre et malade,"[21] which indicates a social stigma for this crime. A child could thus face at least social ostracization, and at the most a push from the Ptolemaic officials to make a deal with their parents.

The first text from Velissaropoulos-Karakostas is not Egyptian but Delphian. She cites a text which is still within the Hellenistic empire and that dates from after Alexander during a period where his influence was still being felt

14 Méléze-Modrzejewski, "La sanction," 247.
15 Dover, *Greek Popular Morality*, 275.
16 Dover, *Greek Popular Morality*, 275. Dover's comment is a bit of an overstatement and is ethically situated within his own views of what is rational or ethically justifiable. His point seems to be that not every infraction against parental honor would be acted upon.
17 Dover, *Greek Popular Morality*, 275.
18 Vélissaropoulos-Karakostas, *Droit grec*, 330–334.
19 Vélissaropoulos-Karakostas, *Droit grec*, 334; Raphael Taubenschlag, "Γηροκομία," *RIDA* 3 (1956): 173–179.
20 Velissaropoulos-Karakostas, *Droit grec*, 332.
21 Vélissaropoulos-Karakostas, *Droit grec*, 334.

(315–300 BCE).[22] This official document seeks to enshrine a law against those who "do not provide the material necessities" (τὸν μὴ τρέφοντα; line 10) for their parents.[23] The inscription cuts off just after mentioning that those guilty of this crime should be imprisoned (lines 10–11), and thus if further punishments were employed, they are lost in lacunae. If we proceed chronologically, the next example is from P.Eleph. 2, plate 7.11–13 (284 BCE), which is a will/contract not included in Velissaropoulos-Karakostas. The contract says, "If any one of [the sons] should not be willing to support them (τράφειν = τρέφειν) or join in repaying their debts or should not join in burying them, let him repay one thousand drachmas of silver, and let there be requisition from the one who is insubordinate and does not act in accordance with what is written."[24] Once again the focus here is on material support for one's parents with the consequence being pecuniary with the potential for further penalties. P.Enteux. 25 (222 BCE) follows this as a petition to the king from a father concerning his ungrateful children. Here the focus is again on material provisions (τρέ̣ψαι in line 3 and lines 3–6 generally), though the father is also angry about disrespectful intrusions into his house and hurtful speech (lines 6–9). If it is true that no contract existed between this father and his son, this document shows that the government would still get involved in matters of parents and children without any binding regulation. This at least highlights the broader morality of Ptolemaic Egypt concerning parents; leaving them desolate was unconscionable. It does not seem a far stretch to assume that a parent being physically beaten would also have the government to call upon to rectify the situation.

P.Enteux. 26 (221 BCE) indicates that a father had grown old and his daughter had promised to care for him financially in a written oath (lines 2–8). She shirks this duty on account of the influence of a certain Dionysius (lines 8–10). The father asks the *strategos* to compel (ἐπαναγκάσαι; line 14) his daughter to act upon her commitment and for Dionysius to be treated as the *strategos* sees fit (line 13). A similar account has a father asking for help to get back his daughter so that he can be provided for in his old age (P.Lond. 7 1976 [253 BCE]). A formal officer is not appealed to but rather Zenon (of the Zenon papyri). It is likely, however, that Zenon would have taken measures to involve the law.

22 The text is from "J. Bousquet, "Inscriptions de Delphes II," *BCH* 54/55 (1940/1941): 90 (lines 1–7)," as found in Velissaropoulos-Karakostas, *Droit grec*, 330.

23 The verb used here (τρέφω) is the typical verb used in the Classical literature for this crime. Note, too, that Delphi is different from Ptolemaic Egypt in that they were seeking formal legislation on this matter.

24 Translation from Bezalel Porten and Jay Joel Farber, *The Elephantine Papyri in English: Three Millennia of Cross-Cultural Continuity and Change* (Atlanta: Society of Biblical Literature, 2011), 413.

It can be concluded from these documents that the Ptolemaic (and more generally Hellenistic) government(s) did intrude in matters involving the physical protection of parents. Would such physical protection extend to parents being habitually struck by their child? One must imagine so. Indeed, if the Attic attitude was in any way imbibed in Ptolemaic Egypt, then one might associate not providing for one's parents with striking them as Lysias does. Both acts put the parent's life in immediate danger. That both imprisonment and major fines are connected with parental deprivation point to the serious treatment that harming a parent brought. Would the Ptolemies put to death a person for habitually striking a parent? There is no direct evidence, so any claim would be inferentially based on an assumed Greek legal heritage. While this is not an outlandish proposition, it is probably best to leave this as an open case with presently inconclusive data.

A standout feature of these documentary texts is the lack of a mention of verbal abuse against parents. The legal inscription at Delphi focuses on material provisions, as does P.Eleph. 2, plate 7. The latter, being a contract with the provisions desired from a parent included, does not mention being disrespected verbally. P.Enteux. 25 does mention a son mocking a father (line 7: λοιδορεῖ με τὰ αἴσχιστα ["he reviles me most shamefully"]; lines 8–9: καταφρονῶν μου ὅτι πρεσβύτερός εἰμι καὶ ἀσθενῶ τοῖς ὀφθαλμοῖς ["looking down on me because I am old and I see poorly"]), concerning which the father requests that the official put such insult to an end (line 12). However, when it comes to the evaluation of the case by the *strategos*, it is *only* the monetary and provisional aspect of the case that is rectified or even mentioned (verso, lines 1–3). The verbal abuse is left out. P.Enteux. 26 does not include λοιδορέω ("to verbally abuse") but does indicate that the daughter is "despising [the father] through (his) old age and no inheritance belonging [to him]" (καταφρονοῦ[σά μου διὰ τοῦ γ]ήρως κ[αὶ τ]ῆς ὑπαρχούσης μ̣οι ἀκληρίας, lines 9–10). Whether this includes verbal assault is not clear, but one could imagine that a daughter persuaded against family by another man would not have kind words to say about their parental figure. Once again, the focus of the text is on material provision with no concern for verbal abuse.

Méléze-Modrzejewski has written on verbal assault against *royalty* in the Ptolemaic context.[25] Here there is found an association with the death penalty, as opposed to the context of fourth century Athens where degrading speech against the rulers was punished with fines.[26] This discrepancy leads Méléze-Modrzejewski to conclude that the Attic legal sources would not be

25 Méléze-Modrzejewski, "Paroles Néfastes."
26 Méléze-Modrzejewski, "Paroles Néfastes," 162.

the only influencing factor in Ptolemaic Egypt[27] and that royal insult was differentiated from the crime of λοιδορ- and its cognates.[28] These latter crimes would fit under the category of ὕβρις ("serious offense") and were met with a pecuniary fine and thus not the death penalty.[29] Presumably, insulting a parent would fit in this category.

3.2.4 *Ancient Egyptian Law on Abuse towards Parents*

It is lamentable that "we have no extant ancient Egyptian texts dealing with a physical attack upon a person, although it is probable that corporal punishment was the result of this type of complaint."[30] One would need to make inferences about parental treatment in these matters. There are still numerous crimes that are documented as meriting death in Ancient Egypt, but these almost exclusively involve crimes against the state.[31] It is not well-known which crimes in the private sphere would merit capital punishment. Muhlestein only documents adultery and murder.[32] One could imagine that, just like the *familial* division and damage that adultery causes, extreme parental maltreatment would have likewise been a familial crime ending in death. It is known that "Children were supposed to look after their sick or aged parents, see to their burial and perform the cult of the dead. If they were not prepared to do so, they could lose their inheritance or part of their inheritance."[33] Bontty lists a few examples of sons taking on the responsibility of caring for their fathers and highlights that ancient Egyptians held this task in high esteem.[34] In this way the same concerns can be seen here as with the Greek contexts. The punishments for neglect in this matter are not known, though Bontty suggests that banishment may have been the sentence for children who did not abide by their parents' requests.[35] Whether violence against parents was seen differently is difficult to know, but an analogy—albeit a speculative one—could be drawn from the prescriptions against adultery to the familial situation.

Whether to include Diodorus Siculus, *Bib. hist.* 1.77.8–9 as evidence for this study is hard to decide. Diodorus writes about ancient Egyptian law (cf. 77.1),

27 Mélèze-Modrzejewski, "Paroles Néfastes," 162.
28 Mélèze-Modrzejewski, "Paroles Néfastes," 166–167. Cf. Exod 21:18.
29 Mélèze-Modrzejewski, "Paroles Néfastes," 166–167.
30 Bedell, "Criminal," 179.
31 See chapter 1, fn. 154–156.
32 Muhlestein, *Violence in the Service*, 332.
33 Erika Feucht, "Family: II., Egypt," *BNP*, 20 vols., ed. Christine F. Salazar (Leiden: Brill, 2004), 5:333.
34 Mónica Marie Bontty, "Conflict Management in Ancient Egypt: Law as a Social Phenomenon" (PhD diss., University of California, 1997), 98–100.
35 Bontty, "Conflict Management in Ancient Egypt," 107–109.

which might refer to a time before the Ptolemaic era, refer to a time in the Ptolemaic era, or his data could be in error. If he does relay accurate information, it is helpful whichever era it comes from. He says,

> But for children who had killed their parents they reserved an extraordinary punishment; for it was required that those found guilty of this crime should have pieces of flesh about the size of a finger cut out of their bodies with sharp reeds and then be put on a bed of thorns and burned alive; for they held that to take by violence the life of those who had given them life was the greatest crime possible to man.[36]

Diodorus probably speaks in hyperbole calling patricide "the greatest crime possible to man."[37] This claim reinforces that Egyptians held parental respect in high regard. That a torturous death was given to such criminals beyond the death penalty also illumines this same attitude. Whether Egyptians would put to death those beating parents is not clear from this text. Perhaps it could be broadly inferred.

A lack of sources also plagues any investigation into the verbal abuse of parents, because "Egyptian law had a cause of action for some form of defamation, but we know very little regarding the particulars."[38] VerSteeg mentions that insulting the pharaoh was worthy of 100 blows (cf. Ostracon Cairo 25556). In another case where a person or item was cursed, the punishment was likewise 100 blows (Papyrus Deir el-Medina 26 A).[39] It is interesting that even insulting the pharaoh was not worthy of death, which perhaps reveals that Egyptians did not view verbal insult as deserving the death penalty, no matter the person insulted. Ancient Egyptian offenses against honor, like verbal abuse, would have been a private matter and would likely have faced pecuniary penalties as did other offenses against honour.[40] If this legal framework carried on into the early Ptolemaic period, one would expect the insulting of parents not to qualify for serious punishment.[41] The Ptolemaic sources seem to bear this out.

36 Diodorus Siculus, *Bib. hist.* 1.77.8–9 (Oldfather).

37 Note the next section where the phrase "the greatest of evils" is used to refer to dishonor (78.2).

38 VerSteeg, *Law in Ancient Egypt*, 179.

39 VerSteeg, *Law in Ancient Egypt*, 179.

40 Wolfgang Boochs, *Strafrechtliche Aspekte im altägyptischen Recht* (Sankt Augustin: Academia Verlag, 1993), 121.

41 For the drastically static nature of the Egyptian culture see Tyldesley, *Judgement of the Pharaoh*, 15; for similar heavy reliance on legal precedent, see ibid., 140.

3.2.5 *Conclusion*

Outside of the Attic sources, the death penalty as a punishment for striking parents is not documented. There are strong indications from the Ptolemaic sources that legal recourse for physically harming a parent existed and was practiced. Whether capital punishment came into play is not known, but imprisonment and heavy fines are indicated. Ancient Egyptian law permitted capital punishment for familial matters like adultery, but a lack of documentation prevents knowledge regarding parental abuse. It is at least conceivable that the solemnity with which Attic Greeks treated parental abuse would be found in Greeks or educated Greek-speakers in Egypt. Even on the more extreme end of punitive measures, the death penalty as a punishment for parental physical abuse as found in the Classical sources does not seem to be outside of the moral and legal *Zeitgeist* of Ptolemaic Egypt.

Verbal abuse is not mentioned in the Classical resources, and it is only a passing matter in what we have from the Ptolemaic period. It is reasonable from this evidence to assume verbal abuse towards a parent was not considered a matter worthy of death or even serious punishment in these contexts. Given the same verbiage used between Classical and Ptolemaic law (τρέφω) and the same focus across these centuries, there is a case to be made that the general concerns of Attic law are found in Ptolemaic Egypt. Ancient Egyptians, likewise, did not associate verbal abuse with the death penalty. Greeks and Egyptians cared primarily about physical and material protection of parents. Extreme cases of habitual, physical abuse ostensibly could warrant the death sentence, but verbal abuse would not. This conclusion corresponds to the changes made in Ex.

Therefore, it is plausible that the translator of Exodus has removed the death penalty in the law involving parental verbal abuse (21:17 [21:16 LXX]) by translating with θανάτῳ τελευτάτω so that the translation would be more in line with the legal standards of third-century Ptolemaic Egypt. Likewise, the translator has maintained the death penalty in 21:15 with the rendering θανάτῳ θανατούσθω because recurring physical violence against a parent may have been punished with death according to the legal traditions at the time.[42] It is

42 Note that Lev 20:9 maintains the death penalty for disrespectful speech in the Greek version yet still couches it with the deferential imperative. Perhaps this points to a different expected audience for each text, or that the imperative was enough to indicate that the consequence still may not be practiced. In this way Leviticus is less concerned with being in line with Greco-Egyptian norms. More is said concerning the translator's audience in section 5.1.2. The conclusion concerning the removal of the death penalty in Exod 21:17 (21:16 LXX) contrasts with 11QT[a] LXIV, 2–6 which still maintains the death penalty for disrespectful children (though referring to Deuteronomy in the scroll). Likewise, compare b. Sanh. 84b:1 which lists crimes punishable by death and includes striking parents,

admitted that classical standards must here support the inconclusive evidence from Ptolemaic Egypt to make this claim. These contrasting apodoses between 21:15 and 21:17 (21:16 LXX) could also be the reason that the Greek version of the text presents a differing order of laws from MT. The translator might have placed these laws covering the same topic side-by-side in order to emphasize the contrast in treatment.

The Greek legal framework that stipulates multiple or habitual striking of a parent (noted with the present tense) as culpable of the death penalty could also form the backdrop to the unexpected translation of ὅς τύπτει.[43] It could also be hypothesized that the translator rendered מקלל with ὁ κακολογῶν because Greek law does not speak to nor specifically care about cursing a parent. A more generalized rendering like "ill-speaking" would then cover both cursing and other disrespectful comments. However, given that "ill-speaking" is a rendering of קלל (Piel) elsewhere in the Greek Pentateuch's legal materials (Lev 19:14, 20:9 = 'κακῶς + λέγω'; cf. Exod 22:27 [22:28 LXX]), the specific Greek-legal aspect regarding parental mistreatment should not be stressed. It seems like "ill-speaking" was seen as an appropriate rendering for the translators when קלל (Piel) referred to activity between humans.[44]

---

to b. Sanh. 85b:3–18 which also lists cursing parents as warranting death. The rabbinic witness seems to regard dishonoring parents as worthy of death, regardless of whether they could put that in effect (see David de Sola Pool, *Capital Punishment Among the Jews* [New York: Bloch, 1916], 18). Lastly, Josephus, *A.J.* 13.10.6 recalls that the Pharisees did not consider reproaches to be a matter deserving the death penalty and that they were in general less obliged to carry out severe sentencing. In this context Josephus mentions the extra-biblical traditions of the forefathers, which could suggest that the removal of capital punishment for reproach might be a tradition of theirs. If so, it could correspond to the change in 21:17 (21:16 LXX; and perhaps Lev 24:16), which may have been an influence on their tradition. Perhaps new light could also be shed on Mark 7:10 and Matt 15:4 and their citation of Exod 21:17 (21:16 LXX). If the Pharisees used it to corroborate their tradition not to penalize with death those who reproached, maybe Jesus cited it back to them in an ironic manner, since they would be rejecting the tradition within their Scriptures that was itself already departing from the Hebrew source text. Despite this musing, it seems more likely that the text in the Gospels is simply a reproduction of the LXX without any of these finer details.

43 Parallel laws on striking in P.Hal. 1.196, 203, 205, 207 (259 BCE) use the aorist in their protases and when multiple strikes are in view the legislation includes additional comments to make that known (line 205: ἐὰν δὲ πλείονας πληγῆς μιᾶ[ς] πατάξηι; cf. lines 200–201). Multiple strikes were liable to greater punishments. It is difficult to discern if any weight should be placed upon the choice not to render Exod 21:15 as a typical conditional clause. Perhaps the indicative mood was more apt in emphasizing the habitual or reoccurring nature of the striking indicated by τύπτει.

44 It is possible that the "cursing" envisioned in the Hebrew version of this law might be translated as "treating lightly" in the sense of not providing provisions for one's parents. This does not seem to be how the translator understood קלל.

A word can also be said about the imperatival mood in these verses. θανάτῳ θανατοῦσθω does represent the death penalty, and I have suggested reasons why penalties with capital punishment were couched with the imperative. Why θανάτῳ τελευτάτω included the imperative is not so clear. If it is true that the imperative is a Greek legal-syntactic cue that indicates a consequence may or may not be practiced as based on other legal concerns (see section 2.7), then why did the translator feel the need to use this cue when the punishment stated is only an imprecation? It is unclear. Perhaps the translator is leaving open the possibility that other, less dire, consequences could be an option in cases of children disrespectfully speaking against their parents. It is not as though Greeks did not care about parental disrespect but rather that speech was not a focal point warranting solemn discourse concerning litigation. It is plausible that in the Greek system some egregious cases of disrespectful speech could have some sort of action taken up. For example, Taubenschlag notes the category of crime labelled δίκη κακηγορίας ("suit of defamation") in Attic law which refers to disrespectful speech in general.[45] He documents analogous cases that appear in the Ptolemaic papyri for Alexandria and the *chora*.[46] Perhaps the translator leaves open punishment fitting within this realm of minor crime.[47] It is worth bearing in mind that the translator seems to have had competing values, one of which was superficially representing the source text (SSF). Only so much could be done. Another option could be that the translator wanted to avoid any chance that the death penalty would be read here, and then included the imperative as a caution.

From the comparison of laws involving mistreating parents, we now return to the first instance of the death penalty in GCC and proceed sequentially.

3.3 Exodus 21:12–14: On Homicide and Homicide with Refuge

3.3.1 *Introduction*

There are many aspects of the text-linguistic make-up of Exod 21:12–14 that merit discussion, but the focus of the present study is to come to terms with the translator's choice of θανάτῳ θανατούσθω/θανατῶσαι as the respective penal clauses of vv. 12, 14. If the findings of sections 2.2–2.5 are applied to these apodotic punishments, then a few matters become apparent. These require more commentary.

45 See Raphael Taubenschlag, *The Law of Greco-Roman Egypt in Light of the Papyri 332 B.C.–640 A.D.* (New York: Harold Square Press, 1944), 331 and fn. 41 for references.

46 Taubenschlag, *The Law of Greco-Roman*, 331.

47 The category of ὕβρις is also an option, as previously mentioned.

Concerning 21:15 and 21:17 (21:16 LXX) I hypothesized that the former maintained the death penalty in line with Greco-Egyptian standards while the latter removed the death penalty and replaced it with an imprecation. If it is true that 21:15 and 21:17 (21:16 LXX) correspond to Greek legal expectation in this way, then one must expect that the other laws in Exodus with θανατόω are of a character that would be compatible with Greco-Egyptian expectations. This means that one should expect to find that homicide was expected to be punished with death, since it is the topic of 21:12, which uses θανατόω. Likewise, the following verses (13–14) continue to speak about homicide with the added stipulations of the killing either being unintentional (οὐχ ἑκών; v. 13) or anticipated (ἀποκτεῖναι ... δόλῳ; v. 14). In the first instance, refuge is permitted (δώσω σοι τόπον, οὗ φεύξεται ἐκεῖ ὁ φονεύσας). Where this refuge is supposed to be located is not indicated explicitly in this verse (it is labelled τόπον). The second instance does not permit refuge, and here details that one who has fled for refuge (καταφύγῃ) is to be taken from the altar (ostensibly the place of refuge) and put to death (ἀπὸ τοῦ θυσιαστηρίου μου λήμψῃ αὐτὸν θανατῶσαι). The three topics intertwining in these verses are then homicide, its intentionality, and subsequent refuge. Of these only homicide and intentional homicide with (refused) refuge prescribe death. One should expect, if Greco-Egyptian norms were in the mind of the translator, that capital punishment would be expected or appreciated in cases involving these subjects at the time of the translation. This is in fact the case. Beginning with homicide and then moving to refuge and intentionality, the Classical and Ptolemaic data will be discussed.

3.3.2 *Exodus 21:12: Homicide and the Death Penalty*

מכה איש ומת מות יומת

Whoever strikes someone and he dies shall surely be put to death.

Ἐὰν δὲ πατάξῃ τίς τινα, καὶ ἀποθάνῃ, θανάτῳ θανατούσθω.

And if someone strikes someone and he dies, by death let him be put to death.

Exodus 21:12

3.3.2.1 Classical Greek Law and Homicide

In the Ancient Near East there is no question that the death penalty was often prescribed for homicide.[48] As with the other case studies, the Classical

48 Neumann, "Death Penalty," 4:136–137.

Greek context also provides ample evidence for the practice in question. The Greek perspective on homicide is stable from the time of Dracon until the Ptolemies.[49] Solon did not edit Dracon's homicide statutes and "homicide laws were the least subject to change" for Greeks.[50] The fourth century attests to this continuing legal lineage as well.[51] Ancient tradition held homicide to be more of a matter of private justice, but in the Classical period the governing bodies became involved.[52] In a survey of all classical Greek literature, Safty finds four categories of crime punishable by death: homicide, indecent assault, crimes against the State, and impiety.[53] There was an alternative to capital punishment for intentional homicide, which was permanent exile.[54] How it was decided whether a person was to be capitally punished or permanently exiled for intentional homicide is not altogether clear, and there is no evidence this was based on the severity of the homicide.[55] It may have been a choice of the killer, though before the verdict was given.[56] This kind of redress, according to Polydeukes, *Onomastikon* 8.117, was not available to those who killed their parents. In addition to exile, intentional homicide garnered the confiscation and sale of one's property.[57] It should be clarified that while citizens, metics, and slaves were all considered to be humans under Greek law when they were murdered, the punishment meted out for each was based on "considérations d'un autre ordre."[58] As such, the punishment for killing a slave, stranger, or metic was exile.[59]

---

49 Méléze-Modrzejewski "La sanction," 246. For the most archaic Greek laws on homicide see Gagarin, *Early Greek Law*, 90, fn. 23.

50 Barkan, *Capital Punishment*, 51; Mélèze-Modrzejewski, "La sanction," 247. For the insistence on maintaining laws rather than changing them, see Mirko Canevaro, "Making and Changing Laws in Ancient Athens," in *The Oxford Handbook of Ancient Greek Law*, ed. Edward M. Harris and Mirko Canevaro (Oxford: Oxford University Press, 2015), 1–43.

51 See IG I^2 115.4–5, 83; Demosthenes, *Lept.* 158; *Aristocr.* 51; [*Euerg.*] 71; cf. Douglas M. MacDowell, *Athenian Homicide Law in the Age of the Orators* (Manchester: University Press, 1963), 118.

52 Farsedakis, "θανάτῳ ζημιοῦν," 43–44.

53 Safty, "Les principales," 163–172.

54 Safty, "Les principales," 164; cf. Mélèze-Modrzejewski, "La sanction," 253.

55 MacDowell, *Athenian Homicide Law*, 113.

56 MacDowell, *Athenian Homicide Law*, 114–115; cf. Safty, "Les principales," 165; Mélèze-Modrzejewski, "La sanction," 252. On p. 254, Mélèze-Modrzejewski claims that later classical law may have removed the ability for the murderer to choose to flee to exile, instead offering the victim's family the choice.

57 Lysias, *De caede Erat.* 50; Aristotle, *Ath. pol.* 47.2; Polydeukes, *Onom.* 8.99; Demosthenes, *Aristocr.* 45; MacDowell, *Athenian Homicide Law*, 115–116.

58 Farsedakis, "θανάτῳ ζημιοῦν," 43, and fn. 110.

59 Safty, "Les principales," 164, who comments that the length of exile is unknown.

Greeks also distinguished between intentional and unintentional killings.[60] When it came to accidental manslaughter, late fifth century-law in Athens stated that it was punished with exile unless the entire family forgave the killer.[61] Demosthenes, *Aristocr.* 53 likewise attests the same punishment of exile for the fourth century.

It is uncontroversial to conclude that Classical Greek law punished homicide with death. This did not always occur, but it was certainly one of what seems to be two usual options. The Greek perspective on homicide was also one of the most longstanding and unchanging legal traditions. There can be little doubt this tradition was brought to Ptolemaic Egypt. Whether this tradition was put into practice is to be discussed.

3.3.2.2 Greco-Egyptian Law on Homicide Meriting Capital Punishment

Greeks of the *poleis* would find themselves at home with Egyptians in that they agreed upon a compensatory life or severe costs for homicide.[62] Despite this congruity, it is unfortunate that "the [Ptolemaic] papyri do not give positive information about the kind of punishment meted out in homicide cases."[63] This is due in part to the fact that our documentary sources deal mostly with local disputes, whereas cases of homicide were likely brought to higher tribunals of which we have scant evidence.[64] For certain there was a "public penalty" in the case of premeditated murder which was applied as a principal or additional penalty.[65] P.Tebt. 14 (114 BCE), by indicating an inventory of the murderer's goods, likely suggests the Attic law of confiscation was still in effect.[66] BGU 8 1816 (60 BCE) does have a victim ask that certain assailants be put to death, but this text is late and may reflect a more liberal stance on the death penalty than earlier times.[67] Likewise, P.Köln VI 272 (third century BCE) only speaks of the murderer being brought to justice "so that he might be guilty concerning the murder" (ὅπως ἔνοχος γένηται περὶ τοῦ φόν[ο]υ; lines 15–17). The punishment is probably not stated because the Ptolemies would only feel

60 Plato, *Leg.* 871a; Demosthenes, *Aristocr.* 50.

61 Arnaoutoglou, *Ancient Greek Laws*, 54. For a list of items considered under the rubric of "unintentional" see MacDowell, *Athenian Homicide Law*, 75–80 and Safty, "Les principales," 165–166.

62 Tyldesley, *Judgement of the Pharaoh*, 10–11, assumes this with the noted contrast that Egyptians mostly seemed to have dealt with these matters outside of a court setting. Diodorus Siculus, *Bib. hist.* 1.78 is the only talionic Egyptian legal text we have.

63 Taubenschlag, *The Law of Greco-Roman* (1955), 432.

64 Helmis, "Crime et châtiment," 18.

65 Taubenschlag, *The Law of Greco-Roman* (1955), 432.

66 Taubenschlag, *The Law of Greco-Roman* (1955), 432. Cf. Kugler, *Resolving Disputes*, 104.

67 Bluche, "La peine," 170.

comfortable establishing guilt rather than penalty, the latter of which was reserved for civic/traditional laws. There is, therefore, little data to work from. Regardless, some Ptolemaic legal experts have pointed out that this does not mean that capital punishment for homicide was not the case in Greco-Egyptian Egypt. Bluche's comments are helpful:

> A partir de ce faisceau d'indices, la conclusion s'impose: puisque la confiscation dans la conception grecque accompagne la peine de mort, que l'ancien droit égyptien punissait déjà de mort l'homicide volontaire, qu'il s'agit enfin du crime par excellence dans l'Antiquité, il était certainement puni de mort sous les Lagides, le criminel pouvant peut-être s'exiler comme à Athènes pour échapper au supplice ... De toute façon la rareté des sources peut avoir une explication naturelle : les législateurs de l'Antiquité omettent souvent les dispositions qui vont de soi. En ce cas précis, c'est la mort.[68]

He connects the Greek practice of confiscated property with the established Egyptian tradition for capitally punishing homicide.[69] Added to this is the previously described Athenian heritage.[70] The absence of a text with this specific punishment is in this view due to the presumption of all parties and peoples that homicide could warrant death. Such an assumed lacuna may have been part and parcel of ancient legislation according to Bluche.[71]

Mélèze-Modrzejewski offers another reason as to why capital punishment for homicide is hardly mentioned:[72]

---

68 Bluche, "La peine," 170.

69 For the Greek practice of confiscated property see also Taubenschlag, *The Law of Greco-Roman* (1955), 431–432. Though note that Egyptians also often confiscated the goods (and persons!) of those under the sentence of death (Müller-Wollermann, "Todesstrafe und Folter," 151). For Egyptian capital punishment for homicide see Diodorus Siculus, *Bib. hist.* 1.77 and 1.91; this penalty for homicide is only attested after the New Kingdom (Muhlestein, *Violence in the Service*, xxii, 240–241) and seems to have continued into the fourth century BCE (ibid., 255–256).

70 For more comparisons between Athens and Hellenistic Egypt with respect to homicide, see Helmis, "Crime et châtiment," 135.

71 Bluche, "La peine," 170, fn. 151: "Le Code de Hammurapi, qui distribue la peine capitale dans des cas particuliers d'homicide (116, 153, 210, 229, 230), ne sanctionne pas l'homicide volontaire en général. Il s'agit d'un recueil d'une précision telle que la conclusion s'impose—dans un autre domaine, la loi successorale athénienne omet de mentionner le fils du de cujus, dont la vocation successorale est évidente."

72 Mélèze-Modrzejewski, "La sanction," 256, fn. 47 considers Bluche's claim about the unspoken nature of this punishment to be unfounded.

> Le roi ne s'intéresse pas à la vie privée des habitants du royaume … l'État lagide abandonne la sanction de ces comportements délictuels à la pratique contractuelle, aux statuts des associations, aux lois poliades d'Alexandrie. Selon toute vraisemblance, l'homicide fait partie de cet ensemble de relations individuelles et familiales qui sont laissées à l'initiative des particuliers et des familles sans qu'une sanction étatique préétablie indique d'avance les conséquences légales … L'État lagide, on l'a dit, se limite à protéger les intérêts du roi et le bon fonctionnement de l'économie royale. Pour peu que soient remplis les devoirs fiscaux qu'il impose aux habitants du royaume, ceux-ci sont sûrs de pouvoir vivre sous le régime de leurs coutumes nationales que le roi place sous la protection des organes de la justice et de l'administration.[73]

This explanation attributes the lack of royal mention of capital punishment for homicide to a governmental disinterest in personal matters. There is no effect on the economy, so the royals do not legislate on the matter themselves. Mélèze-Modrzejewski goes on to presuppose from here that an act of counter-violence such as the death penalty for a personal matter like homicide may have been excluded by the Ptolemaic government, which would only offer compensation as a means of reparation.[74] This outcome is not clear, and it might still be that civic laws could punish homicide with death, whereas the Ptolemies have simply left no mention of this in their royal decrees.[75] Whatever the case, in this view the death penalty for homicide was intentionally outside of Ptolemaic jurisdiction—their concern was the economy.

It is difficult to decide which conclusion is more probable. It cannot be concluded that Greeks and Egyptians did not have inherited traditions that expected the death penalty for homicide.[76] This is certain. Whether these heritages could be brought to bear in the Ptolemaic reality is another, less clear story. National customs probably did play a more prominent role in legal decisions in the less organized first decades of the third century BCE.[77] Of such

---

73 Mélèze-Modrzejewski, "La sanction," 256–257.

74 Helmis, "Crime et châtiment," 165–166 (also referenced by Mélèze-Modrzejewski, "La sanction," 258, fn. 56), agrees likewise.

75 Mélèze-Modrzejewski, "La sanction," 256, seems to admit as much: "l'État lagide abandonne la sanction de ces comportements délictuels à la pratique contractuelle, aux statuts des associations, aux lois poliades d'Alexandrie."

76 Though see Mélèze-Modrzejewski, "La sanction," 258, fn. 58, who notes that it is possible that capital punishment for homicide was an Athenian particularity in the Greek world. We do not have significant data on this punishment elsewhere.

77 Helmis, "Crime et châtiment," 140.

customs Helmis states, "Vol, coups et blessures, meurtre, sont ainsi considérés comme l'apanage de règles ancestrales qui survivent en tant que coutumes à côté de la législation transcendante du souverain."[78] All of this suggests that at some level homicide would have been dealt with according to Greek and Egyptian traditional law and norms at the time of the translation. Each of these would affirm capital punishment for homicide.

3.3.2.3 Implications for Exodus 21:12

If it is true that the death penalty for homicide was within the expectations of both Greeks and Egyptians (and the broader ANE/Hebrew *Vorlage*), then the translator has translated with θανάτῳ θανατούσθω in line with such expectations. Death is prescribed for homicide. However, this penalty is couched in the imperative, which is a means of diminishing the absolute nature of a command. For this reason, it is unnecessary to reach a conclusion as to whether the death penalty was actually practiced for homicide in third-century Ptolemaic Egypt. The translator has deferred such a punishment to other authorities/laws, admitting, in a sense, that it might not be feasible based on other considerations, which might be things such as exile or compensation instead of death. If death were not actualized in the Ptolemaic context, the translator could be, in effect, nodding to the Greek heritage with the use of θανατόω (indicating the death penalty), while at the same time acknowledging with the imperative the Ptolemaic authorities' potential overruling of such a decision with the imperative.

3.3.3 *Exodus 21:13–14: On Homicide, Intentionality and Refuge*

These considerations apply to Exod 21:13–14 since both these verses deal with homicide. Classical Greeks arbitrated between intentional and unintentional homicide and Greek and Egyptian law both distinguished between premeditated and unpremeditated murder.[79] There is not enough data to indicate the measures taken in cases of unintentional manslaughter. The Classical perspective would be exile or forgiveness from the victim's family.

---

78 Helmis, "Crime et châtiment," 147.

79 For Classical Greek homicide see, e.g., Demosthenes, *Aristocr.* 48: ἐάν τις ἀποκτείνῃ, ἄκων ἢ ἑκών; (if any man, might kill, with or without intention). For premeditation in murder see Taubenschlag, *The Law of Greco-Roman* (1955), 431; for Egyptian law see, e.g., Diodorus Siculus, *Bib. hist.* 1.77.6: εἰ δέ τις ἑκουσίως ἀποκτείνει ("if someone murders intentionally"); for Greek papyri, e.g., C.Ord.Ptol. 53.6: φόν]⟨οι⟩ς ἑκουσίοις. Cf. Helmis, "Crime et châtiment," 87–89.

ואשר לא צדה והאלהים אנה לידו ושמתי לך מקום אשר ינוס שמה

If he did not lie in wait, but God let him fall into his hand, then I will appoint a place for you to which he shall flee.

ὁ δὲ οὐχ ἑκών, ἀλλὰ ὁ θεὸς παρέδωκεν εἰς τὰς χεῖρας αὐτοῦ, δώσω σοι τόπον, οὗ φεύξεται ἐκεῖ ὁ φονεύσας.

The one not acting willfully, but God delivered him into his hands—I will give you a place, there where the killer shall flee.

Exodus 21:13

Exodus 21:13 renders in the language of Greek law with ὁ δὲ οὐχ **ἑκών** ("the one not *acting willfully*")[80] rather than in metaphoric conformity to the Hebrew parent text (ואשר לא צדה, "if he did not lie in wait"). Outside of this rendering, the translation continues in a relatively straightforward representation of the Hebrew (ושמתי לך מקום אשר ינוס שמה = δώσω σοι τόπον, οὗ φεύξεται ἐκεῖ ὁ φονεύσας). The only major change is the addition of ὁ φονεύσας ("the killer") which clarifies the already implied subject.[81] While there is the obvious Classical background of exile that could be read into the "place where the manslaughterer shall flee," the fact that departing from the Hebrew text in any substantial way prevents discerning any such intention. τόπος is the main translation equivalent for מקום (both "place"), which leaves next to no room to consider the translator's intent outside of a stereotypical rendering.[82] Greek readers who did not know about the cities of refuge, which this text was likely originally speaking about, may have read their own traditions into the text. However, there is no way to know if the translator was considering this. Exodus 21:13 fortuitously coincides with the Greek practice of exile for unintentional homicide. What then can be said about intentional homicide and Exod 21:14?

---

80 See previous two footnotes; for the same form see, e.g., P.Enteux. 81, r.12 (220 BCE) with ἑκών.

81 Emmanuel Tov, "Textual Harmonization in Exodus 1–24," *JBTC* 22 (2017): 11, claims that ὁ φονεύσας is not a plus here but a translation of הרצח which was harmonized from Num 35:6 in the translator's *Vorlage*. The translator frequently adds the subject to clauses in which the subject is implied and obscure. This is seen nearby in 21:19 with ὁ ἄνθρωπος (which Tov does not comment on). Tov's assumption is therefore possible but not necessary.

82 The only exception is 23:20. See next section for more on τόπος and places of refuge.

וכי־יזד איש על־רעהו להרגו בערמה מעם מזבחי תקחנו למות

If someone acts presumptuously against his neighbour to kill him by treachery, you shall take him from my altar to die.

Ἐὰν δέ τις ἐπιθῆται τῷ πλησίον ἀποκτεῖναι αὐτὸν δόλῳ, καὶ καταφύγῃ, ἀπὸ τοῦ θυσιαστηρίου μου λήμψῃ αὐτὸν θανατῶσαι.

If someone makes an attempt on his neighbour to kill him by treachery, and he flees, you shall take him from my altar to put him to death.

Exodus 21:14

Similar to the rendering of צדה in 21:13, Ex departs from the Hebrew semantics of זיד, "to be presumptuous" or "to be arrogant,"[83] with the contextual rendering of ἐπιθῆται, which is used in the papyri to refer to a premeditated attack, as in, "to make an attempt upon."[84] Here again we seem to see the translator making use of the common legal phrases with respect to a crime's premeditation and intentionality.[85] The Greek text contains the addition of καὶ καταφύγῃ ("and he flees"), which is not paralleled in any known Hebrew text of Exodus.[86] The translator seems unconcerned when adding helping phrases like this if necessary (see, e.g., μὴ βούληται in 22:16 [22:17 LXX]). Whether or not this is a true plus, the verb is significant. The root καταφυγ- is used frequently in petitions to royal authorities, whether metaphorically or literally, to indicate one's

---

83 David J. A. Clines, "זיד," *DCH* 6:101; זיד could also be a synonym to צדה (Propp, *Exodus*, 206). In this way it could be closer to ἐπιτίθημι in meaning.

84 BGU 6 1215 (third century BCE) [τοὺ]ς φύλα[κ]ας ἐπιθεμένων τῶν Αἰγυ[π]τίων καὶ ἐνεδρ[ε]υσάντων ἐπὶ τὸ φρουρίον ("The Egyptians made an attempt on the guards and set an ambush at the garrison"); P.Petr. 3 28 R (e), v a.1 (224–218 BCE), Βερενίκη ἐπ[ιθέσ]εως λῃστῶν ("Berenice, concerning an attempt of robbers"). Note that the stock phrase introducing the petitioned item is ἐπιθέσεως, which suggests this is a categorical term for this kind of attack; SB 8 9792.7–9 (162 BCE) λῃστηρίου ἡμῖν ἐπιθεμένου κάθοδον ὤϊχεσθαι ("A band of robbers made an attempt upon us as we descended"); P.Heid. 9 428.7–8 (158 BCE) ἐπιθεμένους τινὰ[ς ... ἐπὶ τὸ προωνομ]ασμένον πλ[οῖον ("Certain individuals made an attempt upon the aforementioned ship"). If בערמה indicated premeditation (Propp, *Exodus*, 208), then this could have been a guiding factor in the choice of ἐπιτίθημι.

85 See Jelle Verburg, "The Septuagint and Legal Traditions" (DPhil diss., The University of Oxford, 2021), 159–162 who also argues that the LXX here presents the death penalty even for attempted—and unsuccessful—murder based on his understanding of ἐπιτίθημι ("to attempt [and fail]") and its use in Classical Greek law. This example from his work could provide another example of the law conforming to Greek legal norms.

86 Tov, "Textual Harmonization," 11, claims that the LXX text is based on a harmonization with ונס from Num 35:25.

"fleeing for refuge" or "fleeing for mercy" in light of a legal problem.[87] It is a technical term that spans centuries, usually with a preceding 'ἐπι + second person personal pronoun' to indicate who is being asked to supply refuge.[88] If the translator did not have a *Vorlage* that prompted καὶ καταφύγῃ, his desire to clarify the text and situate it within the legal category of refuge is noteworthy, even more so when one considers that 21:14, at face value, refuses legal refuge for a murderer. This seems to contradict Ptolemaic legal practice.

Legal refuge was both pervasive and abused in Ptolemaic Egypt.[89] It was so important to that culture that the death penalty was applied to those who violated the rights of the refugee, though the evidence for this practice comes from later in the Ptolemaic era.[90] Legal refuge was a sacrosanct situation, from which "the offender could not forcibly be removed; the State had, therefore, to wait until he had left the asylum."[91] Exodus 21:14, in contrast, mandates that one can be forcibly removed from refuge when guilty of intentional homicide.[92] The translator represents his *Vorlage* when rendering the places of refuge mentioned in his text (i.e., τόπος from 21:13 and ἀπὸ τοῦ θυσιαστηρίου μου in 21:14). It is helpful to ask what locales were permitted to be places of refuge and to make a comparison.

Rostovtzeff comments that "under the early Ptolemies a few sanctuaries of high reputation possessed the right of *asylia* … but this right of *asylia*, though recognized by the government, was gradually restricted by several royal edicts."[93] He only documents such restriction after the third century. In the third century it may be possible that some synagogues held this status, though only one inscription survives to document it, and that with an

---

87 P.Enteux. 2.11 (218 BCE); P.Enteux. 12.7 (244 BCE); P.Enteux. 13.8 (222 BCE); P.Enteux. 14.10 (222 BCE); P.Enteux. 15.10 (218 BCE); P.Enteux. 24.6 (221 BCE); P.Enteux. 26.15 (221 BCE); P.Heid. 6.376.17 (220 BCE); P.Hib. 2.238.10 (246–221 BCE), etc.

88 The place of refuge (signaled with ἐπι) is likely not paired with καταφύγῃ here because this is not a formal petition and due to a desire to keep additions to a minimum. The cognate noun καταφυγή is used in 17:15.

89 See P.Fuad Univ. 3–4 (246–222 BCE) in Bagnall and Derow, *The Hellenistic Period*, 145–146, for the pervasiveness of asylum. Its abuse is recounted in Francoise Dunand, "Droit d'asile et refuge dans les temples en Égypte lagide," in *Hommages à la Mémoire de Serge Sauneron. Tome II: Egypte post-pharaonique*, vol. 2 of *Hommages à la Mémoire de Serge Sauneron*, ed. Jean Vercoutter (Paris: Institut Français D'archéologie Orientale du Caire, 1979), 77–97.

90 Taubenschlag, *The Law of Greco-Roman* (1955), 477, citing W.Chr. 70.17–19 (57 BCE).

91 Taubenschlag, *The Law of Greco-Roman* (1955), 552. On p. 84, Taubenschlag states that slaves were always not safe if they ran away from their masters to a sanctuary, so there seem to be limits on one's immunity.

92 Or attempted homicide. See fn. 85 above.

93 Rostovtzeff, *Social and Economic*, vol. 2, 899.

uncertain date.[94] In the first century BCE such a practice seems more common. OGIS 129 (42–30 BCE) documents that later Ptolemaic kings "granted to some synagogues the same right of asylum as was commonly granted to Egyptian temples."[95] Rajak also points to a few times in the Augustan era where a Roman decree might use τόπος to refer to a synagogue.[96] That this would be inferred in the third century from τόπος in 21:13 cannot be determined. Of more importance is to ask where the altar of Israel's deity (θυσιαστηρίου μου) was considered to reside at that time, since 21:14 is the law that presses up against Ptolemaic practices of refuge. Was this altar in Jerusalem? We know of an earlier temple that had been destroyed and then abandoned in the fourth century BCE at Elephantine and of the later second century BCE temple at Leontopolis. Was there a temple in Egypt at the time of the translation? Were synagogues a *de facto* replacement at the time?[97] Did any of these places hold the status of legal refuge? There is not enough data to make claims about a distinctly Jewish place of legal refuge in this period. If it is true that the early Ptolemies only gave this right to "sanctuaries of high reputation" early on, one might expect that Jewish places of worship were not granted this right. If so, then there would be no tension with Ptolemaic practice from the law of 21:14. The death penalty could be maintained, along with the refusal of refuge to a place which was already not granted such a right. While no definitive answers can be given concerning refuge, there is another matter in 21:14 that is also problematic for the hypothesis of the present work.

In section 2.7, I argued that the imperative command verb amidst future command verbs is a form of Ptolemaic legal syntax that indicates the deregulation of the command to a status where it may or may not be practiced, as regulated by other legal concerns. This deregulation occurs frequently with the death penalty within the Greek Covenant Code. In Exod 21:14, however, there is no imperative. The text reads λήμψῃ αὐτὸν θανατῶσαι (probably "you will take him to die"). There are a few ways to solve this dilemma. First and foremost, it must be acknowledged that in the LXX materials the infinitive seems to be

94 CIJ II no. 1449, IV.3 in Margaret H. Williams, *The Jews Among the Greeks and Romans: A Diasporan Sourcebook* (London: Duckworth, 2001), 87. It is uncertain if this dedication dates to Ptolemy III Euergetes I (246–222 BCE) or Ptolemy VIII Euergetes II Physkon (145–116 BCE).

95 Tcherikover et al., *Corpus Papyrorum*, 8, 125. Cf. Kasher, *The Jews*, 110.

96 Tessa Rajak, "Synagogue and Community in the Graeco-Roman Diaspora," in *Jews in the Hellenistic and Roman Cities*, ed. John R. Bartlett (London: Routledge, 2002), 29. Cf. Josephus, *A.J.* 14.235, 260.

97 For various views on the function of the *proseuchai*/synagogue in Hellenized Egypt, see LaCoste, *Waters of the Exodus*, 62, fn. 176.

colloquially paired with the aorist for the verb θανατόω (28× of 30).[98] These examples are all arguably in contexts where the infinitive is dependent, which could point towards the aorist infinitive being the default when in this kind of construction.[99] Even if the aorist is simply the default, there are a few other considerations that can be made.

Significantly, the infinitive can function by itself as a command verb in Greek law.[100] From a non-translational perspective, it is possible to read two directives here instead of one, namely: "you shall take him (from the altar), (then) you shall put him to death." This would mean not taking θανατῶσαι as a complementary infinitive to λήμψῃ. This is acceptable Greek.[101] The other laws with θανατούσθω are asyndetic before this command verb and a parallel could be drawn, although in their cases they are the only apodotic verb. Additionally, because the infinitive is considered a 'floating form' in legal documents, it would then be understood in relation to the command verbs surrounding it. In this reading the translator could have expected θανατῶσαι to be perceived as a proxy for θανατούσθω.

But taking θανατῶσαι as a stand-alone command does not explain why θανατῶσαι is in the aorist instead of the present tense like the rest of the commands with θανατούσθω. Why not simply translate as θανατοῦν? This would sustain continuity. In the Ptolemaic legal documentary texts the present tense is solely used when formulating the death penalty:[102] Ptolemaic legal syntax, including

98 The present appears in an ingressive context in 1 Macc 5:2 (ἤρξαντο τοῦ θανατοῦν), and the future infinitive appears in 1 Kgdms 30:15.

99 The literary texts do not have enough examples to bring any clear indications. It could be that θανατόω defaults to aorist when strictly a dependent infinitive, but this would not include when it relates to a copula or when nominalized. After looking at all the examples, one would need to conceive of Diodorus Siculus, *Bib. hist.* 18.66.3 as using βούλεται as more of a copula, as in "They decide/are going to put to death") for this distinction to hold (διδοὺς τὴν ἐξουσίαν τῷ δήμῳ εἴτε βούλεται θανατοῦν εἴτ᾽ ἀπολῦσαι τῶν ἐγκλημάτων; lines 3–4).

100 Smyth and Messing, *Greek Grammar*, 448; Mayser, *Grammatik*, 2:1:150–151.

101 While it is difficult to find a direct parallel to Ex here, the literary texts show that an infinitive following λαμβάνω does not need to be taken as complementary: Aesop, *Fab.* 46.5, ὁ πίθηξ καὶ τοῦ δικτύου **λαβόμενος ἀγρεῦσαι** δῆθεν δι᾽ αὐτοῦ ἐπεχείρει; Aeschylus, *Pers.* 365–366, εὖτ᾽ ἂν φλέγων ἀκτῖσιν ἥλιος χθόνα λήξῃ, κνέφας δὲ τέμενος αἰθέρος **λάβῃ, τάξαι** νεῶν στῖφος μὲν ἐν στοίχοις τρισὶν ἔκπλους φυλάσσειν καὶ πόρους ἁλιρρόθους; Thucydides, *P. W.* 2.5.4, ἐβούλοντο γὰρ σφίσιν, εἴ τινα **λάβοιεν, ὑπάρχειν** ἀντὶ τῶν ἔνδον; Herodotus, *Hist.* 3.29.2, ταῦτα εἴπας ἐνετείλατο τοῖσι ταῦτα πρήσσουσι τοὺς μὲν ἱρέας ἀπομαστιγῶσαι, Αἰγυπτίων δὲ τῶν ἄλλων τὸν ἂν **λάβωσι** ὁρτάζοντα **κτείνειν**; Isoc. *Euth.*7 ὅτε καὶ οἱ μετὰ μαρτύρων δανεισάμενοι ἐξηρνοῦντο, τότε ἃ μόνος παρὰ μόνου **ἔλαβεν ἀποστερῆσαι**. Certainly, the grammatical complexity of these texts could be used as a counterargument to claim dissimilarity to Ex.

102 Barring when the future tense is appropriated. The aorist appears in literary texts but not in formal law code (Aristotle, *Ath. pol.* 29.5.1; Dinarchus, *Dem.* 6). For the infinitive always

tense in some cases, is rigid and formulary. The aorist might then be unidiomatic and marked in Ex.[103] One then wonders if the aorist was chosen because the translator expected θανατῶσαι to be read as the complementary infinitive to λήμψῃ. Had the translator rendered λήμψῃ αὐτὸν θανατοῦν, this law could have been perceived as prescribing the death penalty without any reference to the mitigation conveyed through the imperative command verb elsewhere. However, one attuned to legal syntax might raise an eyebrow to the aorist here. Perhaps the aorist would indicate an undefined action in that the only thing being stated is that the action is to occur and be completed.[104] In this way, the context of θανατούσθω and its limited application indicated by the imperative could be read into θανατῶσαι. The dependent aorist infinitive does seem to be consistently differentiated from the present tense infinitive in the papyri, so the tense formation here would likely distinguish the action from the present tense represented by θανατούσθω.[105] At the very least the aorist would not be immediately perceived as the same type of action as the present tense θανατούσθω.

It is also possible to read θανατῶσαι as an aorist imperative (2p.sg.) in the middle voice. This interpretation would maintain the imperative consistency with θανατούσθω and also accommodate the sudden second person, singular voice from λήμψῃ. The use of the aorist instead of the present tense like

being in the present tense see SEG 37:1372.14 (145 BCE); P.Tebt. 3 1 699, fr.2.21 (135 BCE); P.Tebt. 1 5, 4.94–95 (118 BCE); BGU 6 1250.14 (second century BCE); SEG 16 784.17 (145 BCE); potentially also CPR 28 14, fr. 4,5,6,12 (second or first century BCE). Cases involving the copula and a present infinitive are not cited here.

103 ζημιόω is used in that formula, which could affect the tense used. The present θανατούσθω seems to prevent this conclusion.

104 Mayser, *Grammatik*, 2:1:150–168 provides a host of ways in which the aorist and present tense compare and contrast in the papyri. It is uncertain which category 'λήμψῃ + θανατῶσαι' is most comparable to, and precise aspectual allocations concerning the aorist and present infinitive should be approached "ohne Zwang und Pedanterie" despite the generally consistent usages (159).

105 "Bei einzelnen Verben läßt sich entsprechend ihrer Bedeutung eine Tendenz für einen der beiden Infinitive konstatieren, auch hier in der Regel mit fühlbarer Unterscheidung der Aktionsart, doch ohne Zwang und Pedanterie: der Aorist herrscht vor, wo ein Willdensakt oder Entschluß, eine Bitte oder Aufforderung, eine Möglichkeit oder Notwendigkeit eine einmalige und damit abgeschlossene Erscheinung oder Handlung zum Ziele hat; wo dagegen eine durativ-lineare oder wiederholte Tätigkeit gewollt, befohlen, versucht, ein dauernder Zustand als möglich oder notwendig bezeichnet wird, steht der Infini. des Präsens" (Mayser, *Grammatik*, 2:1:159). For the use of the aorist tense in law, see fn. 147 below. It is hard to determine whether a dependent infinitive would fit the category presented there.

θανατούσθω could be explained as a consequence of the present tense imperative (2p.sg.) not being attested with θανατόω.

Whatever explanation is correct for θανατῶσαι, it is possible that the translator knew that θανατῶσαι could be perceived in multiple ways. My findings seem to exhibit reactionary and exploitative changes rather than systematic and wholesale changes to the text. The aorist θανατῶσαι might reflect such tendencies. If the translator wanted to avoid or ambiguate certain readings of the text while maintaining a superficial representation of the Hebrew text, this example could be representative of one of the more obscure cases.

3.4 Exodus 21:16 (21:17 LXX): On Abducting an Israelite

וגנב איש ומכרו ונמצא בידו מות יומת

> Whoever steals a person and sells him or he is found in his hand, he shall surely be put to death.

> Ὃς ἂν κλέψῃ τίς τινα τῶν υἱῶν Ἰσραὴλ, καὶ καταδυναστεύσας αὐτὸν ἀποδῶται, καὶ εὑρεθῇ ἐν αὐτῷ, θανάτῳ τελευτάτω.

> Whoever steals someone of the sons of Israel and, having subdued him, sells him, and he is found with him, let him meet an untimely end.
> Exodus 21:16 (21:17 LXX)

3.4.1 *Translation-Technical Comments*

The syntagm ὅς ἄν occurs six other times in Ex, each with a different underlying Hebrew text.[106] It represents a break from the rhythmic and stock phraseology in the majority of the laws in GCC which utilize 'ἐάν δέ τις + subjunctive verb.' In 21:16 (21:17 LXX) the ו is not represented, and 21:37 (22:1 LXX) translates similar Hebrew phraseology and content with the typical ἐὰν δέ τις. The choice of ὅς ἄν seems intentional as compared to ἐάν δέ τις. ὅς ἄν creates a future more vivid construction when combined with a subjunctive verb in the protasis and a corresponding verb that looks to the future in the apodosis.[107]

106 Exod 12:15, 19; 21:17 (21:16 LXX); 30:33(2x), 38.

107 Smyth and Messing, *Grammar*, §2560–2561, p. 576. For this construction in the legal papyri see e.g., P.Hib. 2, 1.9 (298–269 BCE) or for legal literary sources see, e.g., Demosthenes, *Aristocr.* 62.

It is equivalent to ἐάν τις.[108] Perhaps, since the function is the same, the translator is contrasting ὃς ἂν κλέψῃ here with ὃς τύπτει in 21:15 in order to contrast the aspectual nuance intended in 21:15. That law seems to represent either an iterative striking, whereas here the abduction is pictured as a singular infraction. The translator might be relying on the assumption of strictness in legal syntax to accomplish this contrast. The translator may also be seeking to imitate the Hebrew participial phrase by including ὃς. Otherwise, the rendering could be chalked up to stylistic variation since the phrase is essentially equivalent to ἐάν δέ τις.

The phrase καὶ εὑρεθῇ ἐν αὐτῷ (possibly "and he is found with him") and its counterpart ונמצא בידו (possibly "and he is found in his hand") are vexingly ambiguous.[109] One expects the translator to translate ἐν τῇ χειρὶ αὐτοῦ here, as he renders a similar phrase in v. 13 (cf. v. 20) with εἰς τὰς χεῖρας αὐτοῦ.[110] This is the only place where ἐν αὐτῷ is found translating a phrase with יד. The subject of εὑρεθῇ could be the captor, the captee, the theft itself, or its monetary proceeds, and likewise with the referent of αὐτῷ. Such an unclear rendering is surprising for the translator, though he may be nodding to the already ambiguous Hebrew with this translation. It is also possible that, due to the imprecatory penalty, the translator was not concerned with an exact reading since there would be no here-and-now penalty issued.

Lastly, in comparison to MT, the sequence τῶν υἱῶν Ἰσραήλ, καὶ καταδυναστεύσας αὐτόν ("of the sons of Israel and, having subdued him") is a plus. One option is to conclude that the translator renders from a *Vorlage* that contained something like מבני ישראל והתעמר בו ("from the sons of Israel and he treats him brutally"), which is paralleled in the similar law from Deut 24:7.[111] This explanation entails that the translator had a pre-harmonized Hebrew text. Another option is that either the translator of Exodus or the translator of Deuteronomy has harmonized their Greek text according to the other. This would explain the same translation of the two. Aejmelaeus suggests that the translator of Deuteronomy was influenced by the translator of Exodus here.[112] This is based

108 Smyth and Messing, *Grammar*, §2560, p. 576.

109 See Propp, *Exodus*, 212–213, for options on the Hebrew. For an ancient reading see Samuel Iwry, "הנמצא—a Striking Variant Reading in 1QIsa," *Textus* 5 (1966): 37.

110 Though phrases with יד can be rendered without a form of χείρ (e.g., 2:5, 19; 9:35; 10:25; 16:3).

111 Deuteronomy reads כי־ימצא איש גנב נפש מאחיו מבני ישראל והתעמר־בו ומכרו ומת הגנב ההוא.

112 Anneli Aejemeleaus, "What Can We Know About the Hebrew *Vorlage* of the Septuagint," in *On the Trail of the Septuagint Translators: Collected Essays* (Leuven: Peeters, 2007), 108–110.

on the translator of Deuteronomy's rendering of two lexemes in parallel laws, ἀθετέω ("to deal faithlessly"; see Exod 21:8 and Deut 21:14) and καταδυναστεύω ("to subdue"; see Exod 21:16 [21:17 LXX] and Deut 24:7). In both laws the Hebrew text of Deuteronomy contains the rare word התעמר ("to treat brutally"). Exodus has different Hebrew terms in these parallel laws (בגד = ἀθετέω in 21:8 and [possibly] והתעמר = καὶ καταδυναστεύσας in 21:16 [21:17 LXX]). Despite the different Hebrew text of Exodus, the translator of Deuteronomy renders *with the same terminology of Greek Exodus* in these parallel laws. Aejmelaeus concludes that the translator sought help with התעמר in his Hebrew text and looked to *the Greek text* of Exodus in these parallel laws.[113] The translator of Deuteronomy does not seem to perceive that the Hebrew text underlying Exodus is different, though this is debatable. If these considerations are correct, then it seems likely that the translator of Exodus translates from a Hebrew *Vorlage* that includes מבני ישראל והתעמר־בו.

Why is it important that the translator had a Hebrew text with this phrase? It is possible that, if the translator has an eye towards the Ptolemaic legal milieu, a Hebrew *Vorlage* without מבני ישראל would not have been problematic and in need of the change from (the expected) θανάτῳ θανατούσθω to θανάτῳ τελευτάτω. The singling out of Israelites may very well have been the problem. If we consider the historical situation involving Jewish captives at and around the time of the translation, a potential rationale for the translator's choice of θανάτῳ τελευτάτω might become apparent.[114] In short, through the rendering θανάτῳ τελευτάτω, the translation might avoid contravening the actions and authority of the Ptolemaic government that would have ordered the enslavement of Jewish captives in war, while at the same time nullifying any notion of concrete retribution that an enslaved Jew might find justification for in Exod 21:16 (21:17 LXX).

113 Le Boulluec and Sandevoir, *L'Exode*, 218, agree with Aejmelaeus' assessment.

114 Perhaps the use of καταδυναστεύω could act as evidence against this interpretation, since the only other occurrence of the verb in Exodus is when it is used of the Egyptian subjugation of ancient Israel (1:13 translating עבד). There is a potential element of intertextuality with 21:14. If the translator wanted to mitigate the way the law would be perceived, perhaps he would not want to draw a connection between the ancient despots and anyone who acts similarly in his day and age (i.e., the Ptolemies). At the same time, καταδυναστεύω is a common term for unwilling detainment in the papyri, so the translator may have just been using proper legal terminology and a direct connection is unwarranted (see P.Lond. 7 2039.11 [275–226 BCE]; P.Koeln.13.516.3 [225–176 BCE]; P.Tarich. 1.10, 26 [188 BCE]; P.Tebt.3.2 953.7 [181 BCE]).

3.4.2 *Abduction and Israelite Captivity in Ptolemaic Egypt*

Theoretically, had the translator translated a Hebrew text like MT without the specification concerning Israelites, the law would have been a basic condemnation concerning abduction. In the ancient Greek context, abduction of a free person was punishable by death.[115] This is the prevalent standard found in the Ancient Near East.[116] It is possible it also existed in Pharaonic Egypt.[117] Interestingly, it does not seem that abduction was punished with death in Ptolemaic Egypt.[118] This does not mean that the legal traditions of the Greeks were not known or sought out, only that for this particular crime other major penalties are attested. Imprecation, however, would not be a suitable punishment. So then, why does θανάτῳ τελευτάτω appear in this law? What could have pressed upon the translator? It is difficult to determine, though a case can be made from our knowledge of the early Ptolemaic period.

It is generally accepted that in the third century[119] Ptolemaic Egypt gained a population of captured Syrian/Palestinian peoples.[120] Westermann gives four categories for how people became slaves in Ptolemaic Egypt, the first two

115 Aristotle, *Ath. pol.* 52.11: κλέπτας καὶ τοὺς ἀνδραποδιστὰς ... ἂν μὲν ὁμολογῶσι, θανάτῳ ζημιώσοντας, εἰ δὲ μή, τότε θανατώσοντας, "thieves and kidnappers ... if they might confess [to kidnapping], in death they will be punished and if [they are] not [acquitted in trial], then they will be executed." Cf. Aeschines, *Timarch.* 91 and Arnaoutoglou, *Ancient Greek Laws*, 113. Farsedakis, "θανάτῳ ζημιοῦν," 78, maintains that other aggravating factors would need to be included for abduction (categorized within the class labelled κακοῦργοι) to be punished with death.

116 See Bluche, "La peine," 169, and fn. 143; Neumann, "Death Penalty," 136–137.

117 Bluche, "La peine," 169; Jean-Joseph Thonissen, *Études sur l'histoire du droit criminel des peuples anciens. (Inde brahmanique, Égypte, Judée)*, vol. 1 of *Études sur l'histoire du droit criminel des peuples anciens* (Bruxelles, 1869), 153; See also Herodotus, *Hist.* 2.115 and Diodorus Siculus, *Bib. hist.* 1.78.1.

118 Bluche, "La peine," 170.

119 In reality from 320 BCE onward.

120 Clarysse and Thompson, *Counting the People*, 263; Fraser, *Ptolemaic*, 57, 74; Tcherikover et al., *Corpus Papyorum*, 2, 4; Westermann, *Upon Slavery*, 57; Let. Aris. 12–14. Mélèze-Modrzejewski, "Jewish Law," 76, draws attention to the tradition of Hecataeus of Abdera and further knowledge of Jewish settlements as counter evidence to the claims about mass deportation. He still acknowledges the presence of Jewish slaves at the time (ibid.; cf. Scholl, *Corpus der ptolemäischen*, 27, who also limits the amount of captured Jewish people, but nevertheless acknowledges their existence). Note as well that "Syrian" was a moniker for Jewish peoples at the time in Egypt. Distinctions between Jews and Syrians were not often made (Victor Tcherikover, *The Jews in Egypt in the Hellenistic-Roman Age in the Light of the Papyri* [Jerusalem: Hebrew University Press Association, 1945], 4–5.). Outside of this mass enslavement event, "There is no other information on Jewish slaves in Egypt in the Ptolemaic period" (Tcherikover, *Hellenistic Civilization*, 342). For the practice of taking captives in war in Ptolemaic Egypt in general see Peter J. van Minnen, "Prisoners of War and Hostages in Graeco-Roman Egypt," *JJP* (2000): 155–157.

being by (1) becoming prisoners of war and (2) by being purchased. He claims that "The Zenon papyri indicate that Palestine and lower Syria were the chief sources of purchased slaves in the third century B.C."[121] Jews were a significant portion in both of these instances. As prisoners of war their sale would have been by direct order of the king himself.[122] These captees would either be the king's slaves, privately auctioned, or given to soldiers as booty.[123] Jews would have, therefore, been distributed throughout Ptolemaic Egypt as those taken from their homeland and given to slavery. This all would have been commanded by the king.

One could imagine how a law seeking the death penalty for those who are involved in capturing Israelites for slavery might be perceived in this context. Such a law might be considered rebellious against the government's actions and prerogatives. In a sense, it could be tantamount to suggesting the death of the king, who had issued commands in direct opposition to the content of the law of 21:16 (21:17 LXX). The Egyptian pharaonic tradition would hold a law with such an implication as treasonous and itself worthy of death.[124] This law could also suggest that those who owned Israelite slaves ought to die as well. Given the presence of peoples who owned Jewish slaves, this would be undoubtably problematic should such a law be circulating in Ptolemaic Egypt, regardless of whether it had the power to be practiced.[125] Exodus 21:16 (21:17 LXX) with θανάτῳ θανατούσθω would be both deeply offensive to the population and to the king—not to mention utterly impossible to practice legally. In these ways 21:16 (21:17 LXX) would be problematic in two different sectors of Ptolemaic law: the king's decree and the practice of slavery. It is interesting that slavery was, unlike some of the other interpersonal matters in Ex's laws, a direct concern of the Ptolemies. Slavery was highly regulated and a matter of economic importance. Other laws involving slavery in Ex seem to have been changed based on Ptolemaic legal concerns, so the law here in 21:16 (21:17 LXX) is not

121 Westermann, *Upon Slavery*, 60.

122 Taubenschlag, *The Law of Greco-Roman* (1955), 71; cf. Scholl, *Corpus der ptolemäischen*, 21–22, for commentary on SB 5 8008 (260 BCE) where it may refer to the royal auctioning of prisoners of war.

123 Taubenschlag, *The Law of Greco-Roman* (1944), 53.

124 To plan to kill the king was "the unforgivable heresy and ultimate rebellion combined" given the semi-divine status the king held (Tyldesley, *Judgement of the Pharaoh*, 89; see the whole chapter [6] on regicide in Egypt). Rebellion against the king of this sort is itself consistently punished with capital punishment (Muhlestein, *Violence in the Service*, 312–319; cf. Tyldesley, *Judgement of the Pharaoh*, 71, 100).

125 See fn. 120 above for the presence of Jewish slaves in Ptolemaic Egypt.

anomalous in this regard.[126] For the Jewish law to take such a strong stance (i.e., the death penalty) against slave practices in 21:16 (21:17 LXX) would, then, be doubly problematic. The king and his economy would be threatened. As such, this background could make sense of why the translator rendered with the imprecation θανάτῳ τελευτάτω in 21:16 (21:17 LXX).[127]

It could be argued that θανάτῳ τελευτάτω still entails a measure of ill will towards those capturing Israelites and would be problematic all the same. This is unlikely. There is a stark contrast between a law actually calling for an action to kill and a law calling for no action at all. It is hard to imagine that abductors would have expected their captees to look on them with smiling faces. That these victims would have a negative disposition towards their captors yet take no action would be par for the course. One envisions that a law confirming the non-retaliation of Israelites in this situation would actually be looked upon favourably by the State. Added to this is the fact that θανάτῳ τελευτάτω is presented with the imperative. Based on the findings of section 2.7, this suggests that the 'punishment' here is not being presented as the final say on the matter. This recourse of curse may or may not be practiced, based on other legal considerations constraining its practice. In a way, this lessens the force of the curse all the more. Perhaps also the imperative leaves open the possibility for alternative consequences for cases of Israelite abduction that are not within the confines of war or the expansion of Ptolemaic dominance.

While it is possible to look to the Greek and then Ptolemaic legal stance on abduction for background to the translator's choice, the specificity regarding Jewish captivity is difficult to ignore given their plight in the third century.[128] Their transfer to Egypt as slaves was a royal mandate, and disobedience or contrary opinions to such decrees were often met with the utmost severity.[129] Such a law also threatened the Ptolemies' realm of legal concern, namely, the economy. In this perspective, the translation choice of θανάτῳ τελευτάτω would be

126 See Joel Korytko, "Slaves to the Septuagint: Applying Greek Legal Terminology for Slaves to Ex. 21.7," in *Themes and Texts, Exodus and Beyond* (Bloomsbury, T&T Clark, forthcoming), which replaces the comments from Korytko, "The 'Law of the Land,'" 27–31, and the commentary on 21:7 and 26–27. The commentary on 21:6, 10 remains valid.

127 It is also possible that somehow the law could have been offensive to Greek legal beliefs because of its sole protection of *Israelite* captees and (perhaps tacitly) not other people groups.

128 It is probably true that captives of war and abduction of free persons should be categorized separately, but the underlying act remains similar in that a person is unwilfully taken (stolen) and sold into slavery.

129 See, e.g., SEG 9 1, an early Cyrenian and Ptolemaic text (discussed in section 2.7.3.5, pp. 100–102) where any disobedience to a direct command of Ptolemy is met with capital punishment.

a clever means of ameliorating some of that potential animosity while also superficially representing the Hebrew *Vorlage*.

3.5 Exodus 21:20–21: On a Master Killing a Slave

וכי־יכה איש את־עבדו או את־אמתו בשבט ומת תחת ידו נקם ינקם: אך אם־יום או יומים יעמד לא יקם כי כספו הוא

If someone strikes his male slave or his female slave with a staff and he dies under his hand, he shall surely suffer vengeance. But if he stands a day or two, he shall not suffer vengeance; for he is his money.

Ἐὰν δέ τις πατάξῃ τὸν παῖδα αὐτοῦ ἢ τὴν παιδίσκην αὐτοῦ ἐν ῥάβδῳ, καὶ ἀποθάνῃ ὑπὸ τὰς χεῖρας αὐτοῦ, δίκῃ ἐκδικηθήτω. ἐὰν δὲ διαβιώσῃ ἡμέραν μίαν ἢ δύο, οὐκ ἐκδικηθήσεται· τὸ γὰρ ἀργύριον αὐτοῦ ἐστιν.

If someone strikes his male slave or his female slave with a staff, and he dies by his hands, in a trial let him suffer vengeance. But if he survives a day or two, he shall not suffer vengeance; for he is his money.
Exodus 21:20–21

3.5.1 *Translation-Technical Comments*

This law concerns any variety of blows against a slave. The translator of Exodus, in contrast to the Hebrew, seems to translate with different terms for slaves depending on the content of a given law.[130] παῖς/παιδίσκη ("male slave"/"female slave") found here in 21:20 are generic terms for slaves in Ptolemaic Egypt within which various categories were subsumed. Within the categories of παῖς/παιδίσκη, the punitive measures (δίκῃ ἐκδικηθήτω/οὐκ ἐκδικηθήσεται, "in a trial let him suffer vengeance/he shall not suffer vengeance") are given for abuse of any slave of any type or class. It is the meaning of these judicial sentences, namely, δίκῃ ἐκδικηθήτω/οὐκ ἐκδικηθήσεται, that occupies the following discussion. I will argue that, while it is uncertain whether ἐκδικέω ("to avenge") was understood to refer to the death penalty, the preceding δίκῃ ("in a suit") is a means of redirecting whatever possible consequence might fall upon the master to the courts in a private suit. This redirection finds resonances with the Greek legal traditions on injuries to slaves caused by masters and might represent a more realistic rendering of a law that could hardly be put to practice

130 See Korytko, "Slaves to the Septuagint."

in Ptolemaic Egypt. The imperative will likewise point to the impracticality of the consequence described by ἐκδικηθήτω. It is to this punishment that we first turn.

There is some debate concerning what the verb נקם ("to avenge") originally meant in the Hebrew legal context. This collocation of נקם ינקם ("he shall surely suffer vengeance") only occurs here in the biblical legal corpus. Many interpreters view נקם ינקם as essentially equivalent to מות יומת ("he shall surely be put to death").[131] This would entail that נקם ינקם sentences the slave-killer to death. The reason that מות is not utilized in 21:20–21 could be explained by virtue of the slave having no blood redeemer and hence the need to be avenged by either the community or God.[132] Alternatively, נקם ינקם could more vaguely refer to criminal prosecution of which the punishment would be adjudicated by the appropriate legal body.[133] The rendering that the translator gives seems to provide an interpretation that lands somewhere in the middle of these options and constitutes a creative translation of the Hebrew infinitive absolute construction.[134]

Two terms form the translation: δίκη and ἐκδικέω. The first item finds a significant place in Greek legal discourse. From early times in the Classical period δίκη meant a "private suit" or sometimes more broadly a "legal process" or "law."[135] The reason for these varied definitions is due to the fact that "the early Greeks probably did not distinguish sharply between a just procedure and a just final settlement. The word *dikē* can designate either the procedure, or the settlement, or both. In the system for settling disputes that prevailed in early Greece, in which disputes were voluntarily submitted for settlement, a just settlement (that is, a settlement acceptable to both sides) would be the normal result of a just procedure."[136] A δίκη stood in contrast to a γραφή, a "public suit." It was only possible for the former to be brought forward "by the victim or his relatives" while the latter "by anyone who wished."[137] In cases of homicide this distinction might not have been such a hard and fast rule.[138]

---

131 See Propp, *Exodus*, 219. SP reads מות יומת.

132 Propp, *Exodus*, 219; Shalom M. Paul, *Studies in the Book of the Covenant in the Light of Cuneiform and Biblical Law* (Eugene, OR: Wipf & Stock, 2006), 70.

133 Houtman, *Exodus*, 157–159.

134 For translations of this construction in the Pentateuch see Raija Sollamo, "The LXX Renderings of the Infinitive Absolute Used with a Paronymous Finite Verb in the Pentateuch," in *La Septuaginta en la investigacion contemporanea* (*V Congreso de la IOSCS*), ed. Natalio Fernández Marcos (Madrid: Instituto Arias Montano CSIC, 1985), 101–113.

135 Gagarin, *Early Greek Law*, 47, 69; Phillips, *The Law of Ancient Athens*, 29.

136 Gagarin, *Early Greek Law*, 100.

137 Gagarin, *Early Greek Law*, 69; cf. Phillips, *The Law of Ancient Athens*, 30.

138 MacDowell, *Athenian Homicide Law*, 17–18.

In the Ptolemaic context, Bluche goes so far as to claim that the greatest continuity between Greek law and the law of Ptolemaic Egypt was the continuance of the δίκη and γραφή.[139] The term δίκη appears frequently in the Ptolemaic papyri and is understood to refer to something like a "suit" or "case,"[140] which accords with the Classical usage. Wolff defines it as a "claim to proceed against a person or to seize a thing, [that] might arise out of a situation."[141] The dative form that is equivalent to Exodus is found a few times in the relevant papyri. The first is P.Rev. 33.15–16 (259 BCE; also reconstructed in 84.8 and 97.4). This text reads [ἐ]ὰν δὲ μὴ ἀπογράψωσιν ἢ μὴ δικαίως φα[ί]νω[ν]τα[ι ἀπογ]εγραφηκότες, δίκηι νικηθέντες ("If they fail to make out the list, or it is discovered to be incorrect, they shall be condemned in a court of law").[142] Grenfell and Mahaffy translate δίκηι here as "in a court of law" whereas others like Bagnall and Derow render the same text and term with "in a suit."[143] Whether one translates with "in a court of law" or "in a suit" or "in a case," the same idea is conveyed. δίκῃ refers to an action occurring within a formal legal process. P.Hal. 1 (259 BCE) also uses δίκηι on six occasions (lines 111, 113, 188, 191, 205, 208) and all in the same sense of "in a suit" or the like.[144] If this sense could be applied to Ex, then the Greek-legal semantics of δίκῃ would be to limit through what means and where the apodotic verb's action (ἐκδικηθήτω) takes place. The slave should receive said justice in a private formal case via the Ptolemaic court system.

The question then arises as to what kind of justice ἐκδικηθήτω anticipates. ἐκδικέω consistently renders verbal נקם in the Greek Pentateuch. In the papyri it is found once in P.Tor. Choach. 12 6.8 (117 BCE): ἐ[[κ]]δικήσαντες (τὴν κρίσιν), translated as "defend (the case)" by Bagnall and Derow.[145] LSJ provides the definition of "decide (a case)" when the object of the verb is something like δίκην.[146] κρίσιν from P.Tor. Choach fits this criterion as well. It is possible then to read δίκῃ ἐκδικηθήτω as "in a legal suit (the case) shall be decided," but implying a subject of the verb that is essentially the same as the dative object seems cumbersome and unwarranted. The grammatical subject of ἐκδικηθήτω is more likely either the slave or the homicidal master. ἐκδικέω could be

139 Bluche, "la peine," 174, fn. 157. Cf. Mélèze-Modrzejewski, "La sanction," 256.
140 See, e.g., Bagnall and Derow, *The Hellenistic Period*, 187, 236, etc.; Tcherikover et al., *Corpus Papyorum*, 155.
141 Wolff, "Law in Ptolemaic," 73.
142 Translation from Grenfell and Mahaffy, *Revenue Laws*, 109.
143 Bagnall and Derow, *The Hellenistic Period*, 187.
144 Bagnall and Derow, *The Hellenistic Period*, 208–210.
145 Bagnall and Derow, *The Hellenistic Period*, 222.
146 LSJ, ἐκδικέω, I.2.

translated in the passive as either "be avenged" (assuming the slave as subject) or "suffer vengeance" (assuming the master as subject), and it is plausible for either to be the case. Even so, in the parallel homicide and death penalty laws before this (vv. 12–17), the perpetrator has been the grammatical subject of the apodotic verb, and so that can probably be assumed here. The text would then read "the master shall suffer vengeance in a suit."

What kind of vengeance would this entail? There is nothing concrete established by the verb alone, while δίκῃ delimits whatever punishment might be envisioned through a necessary court procedure where judicial authorities would have their say. It is probably fair to suggest that Exod 21:12 provides a background to 21:20 in that the death sentence is assumed for any willful and unprovoked act of homicide. This is an easy inference from 21:12. Such an assumption would also make sense of the use of the imperative instead of the future tense for the verb in the apodosis (ἐκδικηθήτω). It has already been proposed that Ex couches laws with the death penalty in the imperative as a legal shorthand that indicates the possibility that this punitive measure may not be practiced based on other legal considerations. That the translator uses the imperative here might then point to the fact that he believed ἐκδικηθήτω would be perceived as a call for the death penalty. It is also possible that the imperative appears for other reasons (e.g., like πραθήτω [22:2 (22:3 LXX)]). That the next verse does not render with the imperative but rather the indicative (οὐκ ἐκδικηθήσεται) also supports the imperative hypothesis. οὐκ ἐκδικηθήσεται either expresses that no penalty should be suffered or that the death penalty is no longer applicable to the master. In either case, no capital measures are being prescribed, and hence the translator does not need to use the imperative to defer the possibility of the consequence.

A further line of inquiry can be made of the translator's choice of the aorist tense with ἐκδικηθήτω. While verbal aspect and tense are relatively variable and interchangeable in many aspects of Greek speech, in law these tenses have more particular functions when making commands. The aorist tense is used frequently in Greek law to make a command of which the action is understood to be immediately performable and completable, whereas the present tense often functions to indicate that an action's completion may take more time.[147] That the death penalty is encoded in formal law in the present tense (as also in Exod 21:12, 15) makes sense within this framework. A trial, judicial

147 Mayser, *Grammatik*, 2:1:§36a, p. 145 (cf. §36, no. 3, p. 149); Meisterhans and Schwyzer, *Grammatik*, 243, no. 12; cf. 243–244. Though see Jacobsthal, *Der Gebrauch*, §62, p. 66–67, who warns against overstating confidence in the function of the tenses in the legal language of the Greeks.

decision, confiscation of goods, payment of potential fines, etc., are all possible actions preceding the actual execution. That ἐκδικηθήτω is aorist may be an attempt to distance the reader from assuming the death penalty in 21:20. In the legal sense, the "avenging" seems to be conceived of as easily and immediately completable (aorist). It could be that δίκῃ provides the conceptual end of the "avenging" in that the law only looks as far as the legal suit for its resolution. Whether that suit would lead to death is then a more distant possibility outside of the purview of the solution provided. By rendering with the aorist tense, the translator might also avoid the assumption that ἐκδικηθήτω is simply a proxy for θανατούσθω. If not, perhaps it was only δίκῃ that motivated the choice of the aorist tense—if δίκῃ provides the means of vengeance anticipated (i.e., "by means of a trial he shall suffer vengeance"). The trial is the end point and is the quickly performable action envisioned.

While the translator does maintain his typical technique in rendering the 'Hebrew infinitive absolute + cognate verb' with Greek terms of a shared root or concept (here δικ-), it is worth considering why he did not render with ἐκδίκησις, the direct cognate of ἐκδικέω. Exodus 7:4 and 12:12 use ἐκδίκησις in reference to God's judgment on Egypt.[148] An appropriate rendering for these contexts would be "vengeance."[149] Had he translated ἐκδικήσει ἐκδικηθήτω, the text would mean something like "in (an act) of vengeance he shall be inflicted with vengeance." Other texts pair these terms together (e.g., Num 31:2: נקם נקמת = ἐκδίκει τὴν ἐκδίκησιν), so the combination should not necessarily be considered unconventional.[150] The pairing of 'ἐκδίκησις + ἐκδικέω' would probably express that the slave's life would be avenged more generically, whereas δίκῃ ἐκδικηθήτω more specifically points to the need for legal recourse to be initiated via formal means. The other cognate related to the δικ- word group that could have been drawn on is καταδίκη. In some of the contemporary documentary sources this term refers to a "fine."[151] Presumably, καταδίκῃ ἐκδικηθήτω would be understood as "he shall suffer vengeance with a fine." I suggested that the

148 בשפטים גדלים = σὺν ἐκδικήσει μεγάλῃ (7:4); שפטים = τὴν ἐκδίκησιν (12:12). For extrabiblical use see Aesop, *Fab.* 3.2.20 and 246.11 (both in the dative); Quintus Fabius Pictor, *Fr.* 18.35 (third century BCE); Polybius, *Hist.* 3.8.10.6. In the papyri: P. Strasb. 1 79.7 (16 BCE).

149 So NETS, 55, 59. LSJ defines the term with respect to "avenging."

150 See also Judg 16:28; Jer 51:36 (28:36 LXX); Ezek 24:8; 25:12; 1 Macc 2:67; 9:42; Sir 28:1. Lev 26:25 and Deut 32:43 choose 'δίκη + ἐκδικέω' when rendering phrases with two forms of נקם. The former verse is in reference to a covenant, and one wonders if perhaps a legal register is to be considered. In this way ἐκδικοῦσαν δίκην διαθήκης, "(a sword) deciding a case of the covenant," could be an apt translation (see LSJ, ἐκδικέω, I.2). The poetic context of Deuteronomy seems less amenable to such a reading.

151 P.Hal. 1.52 (third century BCE); P.Hib. 1 32.7–8 (245 BCE); IG XII,8 267.16 (third century BCE). LSJ also gives the gloss of "judgement given against" or "sentence" (LSJ, καταδίκη, I.1.).

Ptolemies preferred monetary compensation in lieu of violence, so this may have been a fitting contextual translation. Helmis defines καταδίκη as the term for "la condamnation du défendeur dans la procédure accusatoire."[152] In this reading καταδίκη in 21:20 would only serve to proclaim that the slave-striker is guilty. However these might be understood, the data from the Classical and Ptolemaic legal contexts point to variegated matters that would leave both renderings (καταδίκη or ἐκδικήσει) inadequate.

3.5.2 *Classical Greek Law on a Master Killing a Slave*

In early Greek legal thought we find Plato advocating that a master who kills his slave ought to be put to death.[153] Later fourth-century Athenian law does not seem to allocate penalties for a master killing a slave, though legally-sanctioned killings should have been performed by the authorities, and a master himself killing a slave would be seen as problematic.[154] Wiedemann states that, "The existence of religious sanctions or even legal pronouncements against killing one's own slave does not imply mechanisms for making the owner answerable before a court of law."[155] A law cited in Demosthenes does seem to act to restrain abuse if an Athenian should make known a case of an abused slave.[156] In these cases slaves might have had a γραφή or a δίκη issued when they were struck.[157] There may then have been some recourse should the slave find advocates in the broader society, but this was not guaranteed by law, because slaves "had barely any legal protection."[158] Not only did the slave lack legal recourse but they were doubly troubled due to social taboos. Fischer comments that

152 Helmis, "Crime et châtiment," 150.

153 Plato, *Leg.* 872c.

154 Thomas Wiedemann, *Greek and Roman Slavery* (London: Croom Helm, 1983), 171–172; Gilbert, *The Constitutional Antiquities*, 172, states that, "the slave's life could not be forfeited except by judicial sentence." Likewise, the death penalty could neither be enacted upon a slave without a tribunal (ibid., 172, fn. 1). See also Antiphon, *De caede Her.* 47–48 and the comments of the translator in Antiphon, *De caede Her.* 47–48 (Maidment), 195, fn. a, where he notes that Antiphon distorts the facts of the case at hand since the slave murdered was the property of the murderers, whereas Antiphon applies legal logic as though the slave belonged to another.

155 Wiedemann, *Greek and Roman*, 172.

156 Demosthenes, *Mid.* 47; Ibid., 172.

157 Ilias Arnaoutoglou, "The Fear of Slaves in Ancient Greek Legal Traditions," in *Fear of Slaves—Fear of Enslavement in the Ancient Mediterranean* (*Actes du XXIXe colloque du GIREA—Rethymnon 4–7 novembre 2004*), ed. Anastasia Serghidou (Besançon: Presses universitaires de Franche-Comté, 2007), 134. Arnaoutoglou mentions only the master bringing these cases forth, whereas Wiedemann, *Greek and Roman*, 172, seems to think it could be any Athenian.

158 Arnaoutoglou, "The Fear of Slaves," 134.

"Homicide by a slave owner might in theory be prosecuted by another citizen, but it is not easy to imagine this happening in view of the general solidarity among slave owners."[159] Further, in court slaves were often beaten, flogged, or tortured depending on the reason for their presence.[160] Outside of court, likewise, "In everyday life it seems that a master could vilify, strike, or beat his slave with impunity."[161] In cases of severe abuse, slaves may have been able seek refuge in a temple and pursue their sale to someone else.[162]

While there are no specific laws available concerning a master killing a slave, it could be inferred that in the fourth century there would be at most a fine for such an act, if it were ever prosecuted, because killing *another* person's slave seems to have been punished with either a fine[163] or (temporary?) banishment[164] under prosecution for either homicide or damages.[165] Even still, there does not seem to be a strong reason to suggest that slaves would have justice served on their behalf should their master murder them. The master was the slave's legal representative in cases of their death,[166] and the slave was an object, mere property almost solely at their disposal. Such an attitude towards slaves is quite close to the content of Exod 21:20–21. In this text, slaves are only avenged should they die immediately and in a manner where direct causation between the master's attack and the death can be determined.[167] Otherwise, the slave is a possession in much the same way with the Greeks. If justice were sought for the murder of a Greek slave in similar cases, it was likely due to the altruism of a member of society getting involved rather than any set procedure.

---

159 Nick Fisher, "Citizens, Foreigners and Slaves in Greek Society," in *A Companion to the Classical Greek World*, ed. Konrad Kinzl (Oxford: Blackwell, 2006), 336.

160 Farsedakis, "θανάτῳ ζημιοῦν," 59–63; cf. Arnaoutoglou, "The Fear of Slaves," 134, and 138–140 for the reasons slaves were physically punished. For a particular brutality against slaves on display see Plato, *Leg*. 872b–c.

161 Dover, *Greek Popular Morality*, 284.

162 Gilbert, *The Constitutional Antiquities*, 172.

163 Safty, "Les principales," 165, and MacDowell, *Athenian Homicide Law*, 127, pointing out Lycurgus, *Leocr*. 65. The death penalty may have been practiced earlier on for killing another's slave (Safety, "Les principales," 165).

164 Demosthenes, [*Neaer.*] 10; Safty, "Les principales," 164, notes that the length of exile is unknown.

165 Fisher, "Citizens, Foreigners and Slaves," 336.

166 Gilbert, *The Constitutional Antiquities*, 384. A slave was not allowed to have their family legally act for them.

167 Of course, in the Hebrew text a struck slave who is maimed can receive emancipation. It is worth noting that Ex uses different terms for slaves in those laws (21:26–27). This phenomenon will be explored in the upcoming *SBLCS* volume on Exodus. That 21:20–21 concerns only whether the death penalty is applied is found also in Mek. 21.20.1.

3.5.3 *Greco-Egyptian Law on a Master Killing a Slave*

The Ptolemaic data are quite scarce on these legal matters.[168] Like the Greeks of prior times, slaves could be corporeally punished within the household.[169] Likewise, the courts conferred the same rights.[170] There is uncertainty as to whether corporal punishment of slaves within a household was mitigated by law.[171] The one text that might support it (P. Lille. 1.29.13–16 [third century BCE]) likely refers to punishment in a legal suit, not in the home.[172] Murdering another person's slave was a legal matter to be investigated, as seen in BGU 6 1244 (225 BCE). The accusers in this text seem to assume compensation of goods as a penalty, though their claims and actions are dubious. They might be lying about who or what killed the slave. Like the Classical Greek setting, it is difficult to establish how a murdered slave would have any judicial vengeance enacted on their behalf.[173] This is because: "in personal relations to their masters slaves are considered as objects" in a similar way as the Classical period.[174] If slaves died by their master's hand, who would advocate for the dead slave? Added to this, in the Ptolemaic context there was no automatic action taken by the Ptolemies in cases of personal injustice. To the contrary, plaintiffs were responsible for bringing their cases to the local authorities.[175] Besides, when a plaintiff did not come to court, a δίκη ἐρῆμος ("vacant trial") was declared and the case thrown out.[176] The problem for legal action with respect to the content of 21:20–21 is apparent. Moreover, if δίκη is taken in the

168 Note P.Polit.Iud. 6 which refers to issues adjacent to the content of Exod 21:20–21. A slave dies under the employ of another and Exod 21:20–21 may be drawn upon as a legal recourse in this situation involving Jewish participants. For this argument see Kugler, *Resolving Disputes*, 96–110.

169 Taubenschlag, *The Law of Greco-Roman* (1944), 58.

170 See P. Lille. 1.29 and Rotman, Scholl, and Straus, "Slavery in Greco-Roman Egypt," 447–449.

171 Compare interpretations of P. Lille 1.29.13–16 (third century BCE) in e.g., Taubenschlag, *The Law of Greco-Roman* (1944), 58 to Rotman, Scholl, and Straus, "Slavery in Greco-Roman," 447.

172 See previous footnote. The present author views the latter argument as compelling.

173 There may have been less recourse: "As compared with earlier Attic law, a decline in the legal protection afforded slaves is to be noted in Ptolemaic Egyptian law in the failure of the *politikoi nomoi* of Alexandria, the city-state laws, to provide protection for slaves against acts of hybris perpetrated upon them by free persons" (William Linn Westermann, *The Slave Systems of Greek and Roman Antiquity*, MAPS 40 [Philadelphia: American Philosophical Society, 1955], 38).

174 Taubenschlag, *The Law of Greco-Roman* (1944), 69 (cf. 57). If a slave commits a crime by themselves, they could be held accountable without reference to their master (Helmis, "Crime et châtiment," 101, and P. Hal. 1.190–191, 197–199, where the master could intervene with compensation if he desired).

175 Berneker, *Zur Geschichte der Prozesseinleitung*, 107.

176 Berneker, *Zur Geschichte der Prozesseinleitung*, 107.

sense of "*private* suit," then there might be some issues regarding who would stand as plaintiff in place of the dead slave, since a private suit needed to be brought by the injured party or their representative.[177] Slaves' legal advocate was their master and, in Classical law at least, they could not be defended by their relatives.[178] In the case of Exod 21:20–21, the master is in fact the offender. Who then would bring the dead slave's case to the authorities? Since the slave was the property of the master, no one could lay claim to compensation for their death. At most, someone who knew the slave could suggest injustice to the Ptolemies, and here we would have to presume that δίκῃ is to be understood more generally as a legal process of any kind so as to be open to the public. Even still, given that it is only the master who has lost property in this case, one can imagine that the Ptolemies might dismiss cases like these as irrelevant to their concerns. This would be particularly the case if, as Kugler claims, there was a "reluctance in Ptolemaic practice to hold slaveholders and employers of debt servants to account for injury or death of a worker in their employ."[179] At the same time, it has been noted that "the Ptolemaic kings also intervened in the relationships between slave owners and slaves, notably within the sphere of criminal law."[180] It is, therefore, possible that they could have intervened in a case like this. Intervention might have come due to the loss of tax revenue from the slave or out of a desire to maintain order or the like. In this perspective, it is possible that the trial (δίκῃ) would be instigated by the government themselves.

3.5.4 *Conclusion*

Considering this legal milieu, a few comments can be made concerning the choice to translate with δίκῃ ἐκδικηθήτω. Perhaps the translator was aware that the law of 21:20–21 would meet a dead end in that (1) there was likely no one who would or could represent the dead slave as a legal advocate in a private suit, and (2) the Ptolemies might not have shown interest in a case like this. If δίκῃ is to be understood more broadly to refer to a court case in which

177 Gilbert, *The Constitutional Antiquities*, 404.

178 Adolf Philippi, *Der Areopag und die Epheten: Eine Untersuchung zur athenischen Verfassungsgeschichte* (Berlin: Weidmann, 1874), 98. That a master was liable for a slave's actions in some respects in the Ptolemaic period does seem to indicate similar practice in Ptolemaic Egypt (see Taubenschlag, *The Law of Greco-Roman* [1944], 69–70, 72).

179 Kugler, *Resolving Disputes*, 253. It should be highlighted that Kugler's claim here is speculative. There is no explicit data on the subject (as he admits [ibid., 103]), so his claim here should not be taken for granted.

180 Rotman, Scholl, and Straus, "Slavery in Greco-Roman," 446. See also Stephen R. Llewelyn, "'Slaves, Obey your Masters': The Legal Liability of Slaves," in *NewDocs*, 7:169, fn. 22, for some of the protections afforded to slaves by the government.

anyone could bring a charge against the abusive master, it is still possible that (2) would be the result. One also wonders if it could be said that the translator is adding an additional deterrent to justice for the slave, if δίκη refers to a private suit. This term seems to bar any hope of a public legal recourse, and, since the slave likely had no private legal advocate, what avenues would be left to pursue justice? These issues could also explain the deregulating imperative verb: a case such as this would not often (or ever?) be pursuable in the Ptolemaic legal milieu. On the other hand, perhaps the translator knew there were no specific penalties for cases such as this and rendered only so as to defer the consequences to the decision of a court, if such a hearing should ever take place. Perhaps the hearing would be something instigated by the government. Given the tight grip the Ptolemies had on slave registration and documentation, it is certain that their legal offices would be interested in the death of the slave. The question is whether they would pursue consequences for the master. That the translator defers to the court rather than prescribing a more definitive penalty like the translations ἐκδικήσει ἐκδικηθήτω/καταδίκη ἐκδικηθήτω might suggest is more comprehensible in view of the legal difficulties a case like this entails. Perhaps these problems, as well as the possible association of ἐκδικηθήτω with the death penalty in GCC, also led to the rendering with the imperative. It is difficult to know.

What is relatively clear, however, is that another law with connections to the death penalty has been rendered with the deregulating imperative command verb. The appellation of δίκη seems to further distance the law from sanctioning the death penalty.[181] If ἐκδικηθήτω is understood as a proxy for "he shall be put to death," then the law envisions a formal trial accompanying this possible outcome. Alternatively, it is possible that δίκη defines the means by which "he shall suffer vengeance." This would lead to a translation such as "he shall suffer vengeance by means of a trial." In this interpretation the death penalty falls outside of the purview of the consequences.

181 For a similar distancing consider the comment from Joshua Ezra Burns, "Practical Wisdom in 4QInstruction," *DSD* 11, no. 1 (2004): 27: "the rabbinic discussion of this law … limits its applicability to a case where the slave's ownership is completely in the hand of a single master; any status less than full ownership would warrant the release of the slave (Bava Kamma 90a:12; Mekhilta d'Rabbi Yishmael 21:20:4). The Rabbis bowed to the prescription of the verse, but clearly had an uneasy opinion over the idea of uninhibited violence against slaves."

3.6 Exodus 21:29–30, 32: On Goring

ואם שור נגח הוא מתמל שלשם והועד בבעליו ולא ישמרנו והמית איש או אשה השור יסקל וגם־בעליו יומת: אם־כפר יושת עליו ונתן פדין נפשו ככל אשר־יושת עליו ... אם־עבד יגח השור או אמה כסף שלשים שקלים יתן לאדניו והשור יסקל

If the ox has been prone to goring previously and it has been borne witness to its owner but he has not restrained it, and it kills a man or a woman, the ox shall be stoned, and its owner also shall be put to death. If a ransom is imposed upon him, he will give the redemption price of his life according to whatever is imposed upon him ... If the ox gores a male slave or a female slave, he will give thirty shekels to his owner and the ox shall be stoned.

ἐὰν δὲ ὁ ταῦρος κερατιστὴς ᾖ πρὸ τῆς ἐχθὲς καὶ πρὸ τῆς τρίτης, καὶ διαμαρτύρωνται τῷ κυρίῳ αὐτοῦ, καὶ μὴ ἀφανίσῃ αὐτόν, ἀνέλῃ δὲ ἄνδρα ἢ γυναῖκα, ὁ ταῦρος λιθοβοληθήσεται, καὶ ὁ κύριος αὐτοῦ προσαποθανεῖται. ἐὰν δὲ λύτρα ἐπιβληθῇ αὐτῷ, δώσει λύτρα τῆς ψυχῆς αὐτοῦ ὅσα ἂν ἐπιβάλωσιν αὐτῷ ... ἐὰν δὲ παῖδα κερατίσῃ ὁ ταῦρος ἢ παιδίσκην, ἀργυρίου τριάκοντα δίδραχμα δώσει τῷ κυρίῳ αὐτῶν, καὶ ὁ ταῦρος λιθοβοληθήσεται.

If the ox is prone to goring before yesterday and the day before, and they are bearing witness to its owner, and he does not conceal it, but it kills a man or a woman, the ox shall be stoned, and its owner shall be put to death with it. But if a ransom price is imposed on him, he will give as the ransom price of his life as much as they might impose upon him ... If the ox gores a male slave or a female slave, he will give thirty didrachmas to their owner and the ox shall be stoned.

Exodus 21:29–30, 32

3.6.1 *Translation-Technical Commentary*

Capital punishment presents itself again in the laws concerning gored persons (vv. 28–32). A repeat offending animal is to be stoned "and also his owner shall be put to death" (וגם־בעליו יומת). The translator renders the death penalty with προσαποθανεῖται ("he shall be put to death with"). Tov believes this verb to be a neologism.[182] The translator seems to have assimilated גם ("also") into the

182 Emmanuel Tov, "Compound Words in the Septuagint Representing Two or More Hebrew Words," in *The Greek and Hebrew Bible: Collected Essays on the Septuagint* (Leiden: Brill, 1999), 151.

verb representing the death penalty (ἀποθανεῖται). גם has then become the prefix προσ-. A translational decision like this is not unprecedented in Ex.[183] The animal's owner is prescribed death along with the ox in both the Hebrew and Greek texts. What is unique about this case as compared to what has been seen up until this point is that the translator does not render the death penalty with an imperatival form, and he selects a new lexeme (ἀποθνῄσκω). This seems to be an intentional departure from the previous renderings of θανατόω/τελευτάω. The new term is used in a new context where there is an alternative to the death penalty present within the text (i.e., the possibility of a ransom payment) that was not present in any previous law. This alternative also stands behind the choice not to render the penal verb with the deregulating imperative, since no unmitigated call for capital punishment is present.

ἀποθνῄσκω, as sections 2.2–2.3 outlines, is typical in Greek legal formulations for the death penalty. It should be understood as such.[184] This verb also occurs in 22:2 (22:3 LXX) with a different prefix (ἀντι-). That prefix also seems to be drawn from the Hebrew text, though in a different way from גם here.[185] There is also a unique similarity between 21:29 and 22:2 (22:3 LXX). Both laws present explicit alternatives to capital punishment within the text.[186] The verse after 21:29 offers the possibility of monetary compensation with ἐὰν δὲ λύτρα ἐπιβληθῇ αὐτῷ ("if a ransom is imposed on him"). λύτρον is a colloquially plural noun when referring to ransom money.[187] It appears in the papyri in the same way.[188] This stereotypical usage explains the plural noun despite the singular Hebrew nouns (כפר and פדיון, both basically "ransom"). Moreover, the translator semantically levels כפר and פדיון when rendering both with λύτρα. Perhaps two terms here would have made it unclear that the ransom imposed (λύτρα ἐπιβληθῇ)[189] was the same as that which the owner must pay (δώσει λύτρα τῆς ψυχῆς αὐτοῦ). If so, then the translator has shown a greater desire for clarity than isomorphic representation of the Hebrew.[190] This clarity ensures that the reader understands that capital punishment can be averted through λύτρα.

183 This kind of assimilation may also occur at 7:11 with συνεκάλεσαν (for ויקרא גם); 12:38 is also a possible example (συνανέβη for עלה + גם).

184 This would run contrary to Frankel, *Ueber den Einfluss*, 93–94, who offers this to be a case (parallel to the rabbis) where God is left to judge the crime and the death penalty is not enacted (so also 22:2 [22:3 LXX]).

185 See section 4.2.2.3, p. 171.

186 See section 4.2.2 for this reading of 22:2 (22:3 LXX).

187 See LSJ, λύτρον, I.1.

188 SB 28 16855.16, 21 (167 BCE); P.Koeln 13 524.5 (second century BCE); P.Lugd. Bat. 19 7 B. 4. (109 BCE); BGU 6 1260.12 (101 BCE).

189 LSJ, ἐπιβάλλω, I.2.; CGL, 3, for this verb indicating a fine.

190 See section 2.1.1 for lexical flattening in GCC.

While the translator habitually makes explicit the unstated agent in passive verbs,[191] that the singular passive יושת ("it is imposed") is translated both as singular (ἐπιβληθῇ, "it is imposed") and then plural (ἐπιβάλωσιν, "they impose") could point to an external group of governmental adjudicators in addition to the offended party.[192] Compensation would in fact often be through these official channels.[193]

It does not seem to be a coincidence that both laws offering alternatives to the death penalty display a different lexeme from what has been established (θανατόω thus far in the legal materials). The translator could have simply added prefixes to θανατόω.[194] Perhaps the change in lexeme is a means of indicating the difference between these laws and the others, since they alone explicitly present alternatives to the death penalty.

3.6.2 *Cultural and Legal Analysis*

Exodus 21:30 presents monetary compensation as a possible substitute for the death penalty, which might have been the preferred penal measure of the Ptolemies.[195] Because an alternative is presented, the future tense seems to be permissible for προσαποθανεῖται. The ransom option of 21:30 would present a happy alternative in the eyes of the governing authorities.

Unfortunately, no evidence for animals killing humans can be found in the Ptolemaic documentary sources,[196] although a few texts on animal damages

191 10:24, 26; 20:26; 21:29, 30, 31; 22:5 (22:6 LXX), 18 (19 LXX); 25:29 (28 LXX), 31; 31:15; 35:2.

192 See a close parallel in 21:22 with καθότι ἂν ἐπιβάλῃ ὁ ἀνὴρ τῆς γυναικός, δώσει μετὰ ἀξιώματος. Here the compensation is channeled through governmental means as indicated by μετὰ ἀξιώματος. Shemesh claims that ἀξιώμα "means that the court will evaluate the damages and exact compensation from the assailant accordingly" (Aharon Shemesh, "4Q251: Midrash Mishpatim," *DSD* 12, no. 3 [2005]: 284); Deissmann defines the term as a "request preferred before a higher tribunal" (Adolf Deissmann, *Bible Studies: Contributions, Chiefly from Papyri and Inscriptions, to the History of the Language, the Literature, and the Religion of Hellenistic Judaism and Primitive Christianity* [Edinburgh: T&T Clark, 1901], 93); Le Boulleuc and Sandevoir translate accordingly with "avec le concours d'un dignitaire" ("with the support of a dignitary/official"; *L'Exode*, 220); Kugler defines ἀξιώμα as "that which is thought fit" (*Resolving Disputes*, 46). The term also appears in the rote phraseology typical of the end of petitions which further solidifies its stock association with appeals to the king/government (P.Enteux. 17.9–10 [218 BCE]; P.Sorb. 3 128.15 [219 BCE]). Research I am currently working on indicates that ἀξιώμα should be precisely translated as "a claim," a definition which differs from these other translations. This "claim" would go through the Ptolemaic courts and is an indication of compensation mediated through the Ptolemaic government within the translation.

193 Taubenschlag, *The Law of Greco-Roman* (1955), 438.

194 Cf. Aesop, *Fab.* 69, v.2.9 with προθανατούμενόν.

195 See section 3.3.2.2, p. 131.

196 Cf. Helmis, "Crime et châtiment," 99.

survive.[197] In the Classical Greek world the Prytaneion (in Athens) was the court for homicides involving animals or inanimate objects.[198] Objects involved in the crime were thrown outside the borders of Attica.[199] Animals convicted of killing someone would themselves be killed.[200] Laws holding animals accountable for their actions were otherwise uncommon.[201] This accountability for animals creates an interesting link between these Hebrew laws and Classical Greek tradition. In Ptolemaic Egypt crimes involving animal damages needed to be formally reported, and the animal could not be killed by the victim.[202] The court fixed the price for compensation in these matters.[203] It is uncertain if the animal was considered formally guilty as in the Classical setting. The guilt of the owner is still emphasized.[204] Additional fines could also accompany cases of particular negligence with respect to the animal's owner.[205] In this respect the liability of the owner is more prominent in Ptolemaic Egypt than in Athens. That the owner was more culpable in Ptolemaic Egypt points in a direction where victims might desire that the owner be held to account with physical punishment. In any case, the provision of an alternative ransom seems to be in line with the Ptolemaic preference for compensation and it creates a law that does not claim an outright prerogative to the death penalty. For these reasons there is no need to use the imperative to defer the punitive measure provided. Whether or not Greeks expected the animal's master to face death or physical punishment is difficult to discern, but not outside of what is intimated. Even if physical punishment were outside of Greek legal expectations, the renumeration aspect of the text would fit their ideals.

---

197 See Mélèze-Modrzejewski, "Papyrologie et histoire," 231–232 for a listing of the Ptolemaic documentary texts and a list of the Classical literary references to such laws.

198 Demosthenes, *Aristocr.* 76; Polydeukes, *Onom.* 8.120; Arist. *Ath.Pol.* 57.4.

199 Aeschines, *Ctesiph.* 244; Pausanias, *Descr.* 6.11.6; Polydeukes, *Onom.* 8.120.

200 Safty, "Les principales," 163; Brian Calvert, "The Death Penalty in Plato's Laws," in *Justice v. Law in Greek Thought*, ed. Leslie G. Rubin (Lanham, MD: Rowman & Littlefield Publishers, 1997), 244. MacDowell, *Athenian Homicide Law*, 88, notes that it is uncertain whether execution occurred in Athens.

201 Mélèze-Modrzejewski, "Papyrologie et histoire," 233.

202 Cf. Helmis, "Crime et châtiment," 100, referring to P.Petr. 3 26 (240 BCE); also P.Hal. 1.80–102 (259 BCE).

203 Raphael Taubenschlag, "Die action de pastu, de pauperie und de arborius casesis im Rechte der Papyri," *JJP* 7–8 (1953–1954): 388.

204 Helmis, "Crime et châtiment," 56, 100–101.

205 Taubenschlag, *The Law of Greco-Roman* (1955), 460; he cites the late P.Ryl. 69 (34 BCE).

3.6.3 *Comments on the Goring of a Slave (Exodus 21:32)*

Verse 32 in the Hebrew text likely refers to a slave who dies when gored. This can be strongly inferred from the price named (thirty שקלים), which was the average price of a slave in earlier Near Eastern texts.[206] In third-century Ptolemaic Egypt the price of a slave was approximately two hundred to one thousand drachmas.[207] The translator renders כסף שלשים שקלים ("thirty shekels of silver") with ἀργυρίου τριάκοντα δίδραχμα ("thirty didrachmas of silver"), that is, sixty drachmas.[208] This price is remarkably lower than the cost of a slave at that time. We seem to see the translator of Genesis changing the prices of slaves in order to update the translation to a more suitable price.[209] These factors lead to the consideration that the law presented in Ex might be recognized as the price given for a maimed or injured slave and not for a dead slave. The helping

---

206 Propp, *Exodus*, 236, gives ancient Near Eastern parallels that would need to be slightly adjusted (upwardly) according to inflation: Eshnunna 55 ("If it gores a slave and thus causes his death, he shall weigh and deliver 15 shekels of silver") and Hammurapi 252 ("If it is a man's slave [who is fatally gored], he shall give 20 shekels of silver"). These translations are from Martha Tobi Roth, Harry A. Hoffner, and Piotr Michalowski, *Law Collections from Mesopotamia and Asia Minor* (Atlanta: Scholars Press, 1997), 67 and 128 respectively. Cf. Paul, *Studies in the Book*, 83, who cites a text from Nuzi also pricing the slave at thirty שקלים.

207 Westermann, "Enslaved Persons," 4, prices them at three hundred drachmas, though he may be averaging costs between Palestinian and Egyptian prices; Tcherikover prices a full-grown slave in Egypt at upwards of one thousand drachmas (Victor Tcherikover, "Palestine Under the Ptolemies: A Contribution to the Zenon Papyri," *Mizraim* 4–5 [1937]: 17), though possibly less in the early third century (ibid.); Lee, *A Lexical Study*, 64, gives the range of one hundred to three hundred drachmas, and Scholl, *Corpus der ptolemäischen*, 22, at approximately three hundred drachmas. From the papyri, see e.g., P.Cair.Zen. 3 59355 (257 BCE), which prices two female slaves at two hundred drachmas each and P.Cair.Zen. 4 59606 (256–239 BCE) at three hundred drachmas. Prices would vary depending on the abilities and traits of the slave.

208 Note the curious translation practice of transliterating שקל with σίκλος in Ex. This seems to occur when the focus of a text is not on a monetary price but on the weight of an item, with each context also being a past-historical description of a particular event (30:23–24; 38:24 [39:1 LXX], 38:25–26 [39:2 LXX], 38:26 [39:3 LXX], 38:28 [39:6 LXX]). This use of σίκλος could also have an archaizing effect, perhaps to indicate a different weight of the שקל according to a more ancient time. Regardless, שקל seems to be translated with δίδραχμα in contexts where monies and not weights are referred to (21:32; 30:13[4x], 15). This pattern might hold for Lev as well.

209 Gen 37:28 renders כסף with χρυσοῦς as a way (it seems) to increase the price paid for Joseph. This is in line with the use of χρυσοῦς as a monetary unit and shows the translator's awareness that the price of a slave was much higher at the time (see Lee, *A Lexical Study*, 64). The translator of Exodus could have used this term here, but seeing as χρυσοῦς is worth twenty drachmas (ibid., 63), five hundred drachmas for a slave may have been too high here.

verbs elsewhere added to the translation could suggest that the translator would have added καὶ ἀποθάνῃ ("and he dies") if the death of the slave were in mind (e.g., καὶ καταφύγῃ in 21:14; μὴ βούληται in 22:16 [22:17 LXX]; καὶ ὀμεῖται in 22:7 [22:8 LXX]). At the same time, the deictic article on ὁ ταῦρος connects the law back to vv. 28–31. Considering the rest of this legal context is about this ox that gores someone to death, fatality should probably be implied here. That the owner of the ox would lose the ox and its meat would have been a substantial monetary loss and could help to fill in the gap between the cost of a slave and what is penalized here.[210] However, such a loss for the ox's owner does not help the owner of the slave. It is possible that other penalties for negligence existed at the time that would have provided more compensation to the master of the slave.[211] These are simply not spelled out here. These considerations could help to situate the low cost of the slave within the Ptolemaic context. Admittedly, they are not completely compelling. The fidelity to the Hebrew text is close enough to leave this kind of reasoning as speculative.

---

210 The only text giving a direct price for a ταῦρος is P.Petr. 3 31, pricing it around 60 drachmas (183–173 BCE) or 130 drachmas (210–183 BCE) depending on the date of the papyrus (see Willy Clarysse and Eddy Lanciers, "Currency and the Dating of Ptolemaic Papyri," *Ancient Society* 20 [1989]: 126–127).

211 Taubenschlag, *The Law of Greco-Roman* (1955), 460; idem., "Die action de pastu," 65–67.

CHAPTER 4

Exodus 22 and Laws Involving the Death Penalty

4.1 Introduction

The basis for much of the discussion in Chapter 3 was the data presented in Chapter 2. Here in Chapter 4, the information from Chapter 2 will come to bear on the conclusions to a lesser degree. New analyses are presented here as each case requires it. The outcome will be to present each respective law in a new light. Exodus 22:2 (22:3 LXX) in the Greek version gains new consequences for nocturnal theft, as well as a novel reference to the death penalty that happens to be in line with Greek legal standards. In contrast, I will raise questions whether 22:17 (22:18 LXX) indicates the death penalty in its Greek version. Much labor is invested into 22:18 (22:19 LXX) where I posit that the OG does not refer to a prohibition against bestiality but rather speaks towards proper animal husbandry. The death penalty in this law is probably then directed towards wild animals and not humans. That Greeks (and Egyptians) did not legislate against most private sexual matters will be presented as a possible framework for the translational change. Finally, I will examine 22:19 (22:20 LXX) and the translation of θυσιάζω for זבח ("to sacrifice") based on a re-evaluation of the literary and documentary texts and their use of θυσιάζω, which refers not simply to being a participant in a sacrifice but rather to the one performing a θυσία ritual. This definition leads to the conclusion that 22:19 (22:20 LXX) in the Greek version permits participation in sacrifices to other gods but not the conducting of such ceremonies. A few aspects of Ptolemaic legal practice are then drawn on as possible backgrounds to such a change.

4.2 Exodus 22:2 (22:3 LXX): On Nocturnal Theft

אם־זרחה השמש עליו דמים לו שלם ישלם אם־אין לו ונמכר בגנבתו

> If the sun rises on him, there is bloodguilt for him. He shall surely make restitution. If there is nothing to him, he shall be sold for his theft.

ἐὰν δὲ ἀνατείλῃ ὁ ἥλιος ἐπ᾽ αὐτῷ, ἔνοχός ἐστιν, ἀνταποθανεῖται. ἐὰν δὲ μὴ ὑπάρχῃ αὐτῷ, πραθήτω ἀντὶ τοῦ κλέμματος.

 | DOI:10.1163/9789004682047_005

> If the sun rises on him, he is guilty. He shall die in exchange. If it (the death penalty) is not applied to him, let him be sold in place of the theft.
>
> Exodus 22:2 (22:3 LXX)

4.2.1 *Introduction*

As with other laws involving the death penalty in chapters 21–22 of Greek Exodus, here in 22:2 (22:3 LXX) some changes from the Hebrew text seem to have been either overlooked or misunderstood in previous scholarship. The misunderstanding stems again from assuming that the Greek text represents the Hebrew text in meaning (often on account of SSF).[1] A novel aspect of 22:2 (22:3 LXX) is the addition of the death penalty (ἀνταποθανεῖται ["he shall die in exchange"] translates שלם ישלם ["he shall surely make restitution"]) instead of its subtraction (as discussed in laws with θανατῷ τελευτάτω). This added corporal punishment refers to what happens to the night burglar and not the victim of the theft who acts in retaliation on the following day. This conclusion is based on an assessment of the phrase ἐὰν δὲ μὴ ὑπάρχῃ αὐτῷ, which should be translated as "if (the previous punishment [i.e., the death penalty]) is not applied to him." The addition in the law of capital punishment for the thief might have its roots in Greco-Egyptian legal traditions. Its inclusion here would be appreciated specifically by Greeks and potentially by the Ptolemaic authorities. Coming to this understanding of 22:2 (22:3 LXX) necessarily begins with a discussion on ἐὰν δὲ μὴ ὑπάρχῃ αὐτῷ.

4.2.2 *Translation-Technical Analysis*

The crux of the interpretation of 22:2 (22:3 LXX) is how to understand ἐὰν δὲ μὴ ὑπάρχῃ αὐτῷ (אם־אין לו). There are a few layers to the problem. The first is to ask what the Hebrew phrase means. Commentators indicate that אם־אין לו translates to something like "if he has no possessions."[2] The referent here is the thief, who is going to be sold into slavery if they have no goods that can replace the stolen item(s). Septuagint scholarship and translators have likewise understood ἐὰν δὲ μὴ ὑπάρχῃ αὐτῷ as essentially a Greek representation of the same idea.[3] In other words, it is assumed that this phrase conveys what the Hebrew text conveys. This is problematic since there is little reason to assert

1 See, e.g., Frankel, *Ueber den Einfluss*, 81, pointing to the difficulty in finding the grammatical subjects in 22:2 (22:3 LXX).

2 Thomas B. Dozeman, *Eerdmans Critical Commentary: Exodus* (Grand Rapids: Eerdmans, 2009), 517, 539; Houtman, *Exodus*, 185; Propp, *Exodus*, 105. 2Q3 4, 5 has אין לו לש[לם, which, if the correct emendation, might remove some of the ambiguity of MT.

3 E.g., NETS; Le Boulluec and Sandevoir, *L'Exode*, 224; LXX.D; Wevers, *Notes*, 342.

that ἐὰν μὴ ὑπάρχῃ αὐτῷ communicates this meaning in the Greek language as far as the literary or documentary texts inform. There are four contributing elements that indicate the problem: (1) ὑπάρχω does not function as an impersonal verb, which means that, (2) when paired with a dative pronoun to indicate possession it should be understood in its consistent usage where its grammatical subject is found within the immediate context (in 22:2 [22:3 LXX] it is the death penalty). This is corroborated by the fact that (3) there is stock language that the translator could have drawn upon and used here to indicate the idea of "there are no possessions belonging to the thief"—language that other Pentateuchal translators are well aware of and in fact render from similar Hebrew phraseology.[4] Finally, (4) 'ὑπάρχω + dative pronoun' is a common expression in Greek legal terminology to indicate a punishment being applied to a criminal. These aspects involving ὑπάρχω will be discussed in turn.

4.2.2.1 ὑπάρχω is Not an Impersonal Verb

For modern commentators to be correct in their reading of 22:2 (22:3 LXX), it must be assumed that ὑπάρχω ("to exist"), when found without an explicit subject, can function as an impersonal verb.[5] In 22:2 (22:3 LXX) this would mean that ἐὰν δὲ μὴ ὑπάρχῃ αὐτῷ, literally translated "and if (it) is not to him," would be a case where the reader readily supplied a subject, namely, "possessions." Such would be an example of an impersonal verb or impersonal construction where "a third person singular or plural finite verb is often found with nothing in the context that can be identified as its grammatical subject."[6] However, the Classical grammars do not mention ὑπάρχω among the verbs that are used this way.[7] Similarly, works covering Greek grammar at the time of the translation do not include any reference to ὑπάρχω functioning impersonally.[8]

---

4 E.g., בכל־אשר יש־לו = ἐν πᾶσιν τοῖς ὑπάρχουσιν αὐτῷ (Gen 39:5). The participial form of ὑπάρχω is the main colloquial expression for possessions in the documentary sources.

5 Impersonality is defined as when the subject of a verb is implied, despite that subject not being within the immediate context.

6 Muraoka, *Syntax*, 749. Muraoka does not comment on 22:2 (22:3 LXX). Ostensibly, he reads along with all other modern commentators. In that case, one assumes he would posit this is an instance where in "some cases a vague subject can be deduced from the immediate context" (§87d, p. 755). Smyth and Messing call these verbs "quasi-impersonal" (*Greek Grammar*, §933, p. 260). See Emde Boas et al., *Cambridge Grammar of Classical Greek* (Cambridge: Cambridge University Press, 2019), §36.3–36.10, and Meisterhans and Schwyzer, *Grammatik*, §79, p. 195, for more on impersonal verbs.

7 See previous footnote.

8 Mandēlaras, *The Verb in the Greek*, §890, p. 363, concerning εἰμί, γίνομαι, ὑπάρχω, and προϋπάρχω, writes "Εἰμί and γίνομαι ... occasionally possess a sense of impersonality" but does not

When consulting the TLG database, I could not likewise find any examples of conditional clauses similar to 'ἐὰν ... ὑπάρχῃ' where ὑπάρχω is without a subject that is not immediately supplied from what comes before.[9] Beyond this basic claim about ὑπάρχω not being an impersonal verb, it is possible to consult the documentary texts to look at parallel examples of the exact combination of 'ὑπάρχω + dative pronoun'—itself a distinct and studied syntagm—to determine how ἐὰν δὲ μὴ ὑπάρχῃ αὐτῷ would be understood.

4.2.2.2 'ὑπάρχω + Dative Pronoun' in the Documentary Sources

In her recent article from the *Journal of Juristic Papyrology*, Vera Stolk has written extensively on 'ὑπάρχω + dative' in the documentary papyri.[10] This is a stock phrase of which she states, "The possessive meaning is the one that occurs most often in the papyri."[11] Her article only covers this possessive meaning. Stolk provides no examples of possessive 'ὑπάρχω + dative' analogous to 22:2 (22:3 LXX) where a subject must be supplied outside of the immediate context. It might be suggested that this is an oversight on her part. However, the following table delineates occasions of 'ὑπάρχω + dative pronoun' in the papyrological sources from before the Common Era and confirms that 'ὑπάρχω (third person) + dative pronoun'[12] never functions impersonally. Each citation will include a reference to the subject.

include ὑπάρχω in this category. Mayser, *Grammatik*, 2:2:269–270, covers ὑπάρχω and does not include impersonal examples. He does mention that the immediately preceding context can supply the subject matter (he notes P.Cair.Zen. 59235.7). Mayser also covers ὑπάρχω at 2:2:§66.4, p. 68, and in 2:1:§41.1, p. 223, but does not expand any further.

9 TLG seems to show that ὑπάρχω in analogous conditional clauses means something like "if there is a chance (the previous thought) might happen." Examples without a dative pronoun are, e.g., Anaximenes, *Ars rhet.* 32.5; 35.16; Thucydides, *P. W.* 6.6.3. This same use is found in the papyri: PSI 6 581, r.2–5 (245 BCE; subject follows). Examples with the dative pronoun: Antiphon, *De caede Her.* 14; Isocrates, *Plat.* 17; Aeneus Tacticus, *praef.* 37.2.1; Aristotle, *An. pr.* 43a.4. Of course, there are other permutations that could be considered. These are examples similar to 22:2 (22:3 LXX).

10 Vera Stolk, "Scribal and Phraseological."

11 Vera Stolk, "Scribal and Phraseological," 261.

12 The table is limited to the third person since that is a requirement when using a verb impersonally. Of course, nouns in the dative case that are not pronouns could fit within the confines of this grammatical structure under investigation. Given the constraints of the present argument, only pronouns have been included in this data. Nouns with the dative do seem to follow the same patterns as pronouns.

TABLE 4.1 'ὑπάρχω (third person) + Dative Pronoun' in the Documentary Papyri

Pronoun	Source with subject from immediate context
μοί	P.Mich. 1 28, r. I.22 (256 BCE) = drachmas
	P. Cair.Zen. 2 59225, r.7–8 (253 BCE) = horse
	P.Cair.Zen. 2 59271, r.6–7 (251 BCE) = workers[a]
	P.Cair.Zen. 3 59357, r.17 (244 BCE) = written statement
	P. Hib. 1 33.6, 14 (245 BCE) = sheep
	P.Cair.Zen. 3 59509.2 (275–226 BCE) = artebas
	PSI 6 584, r.10 (275–226 BCE) = artebas
	SB 12 10859.8 (220 BCE) = contracts
	P.Enteux. 51, r.1 (222 BCE) = written statement
	P.Enteux. 22, r.8–9 (218 BCE) = written statement
	P. Enteux 6, r.2 (222 BCE) = temple
	P.Lille 1 9.12, 21 (third century BCE) = sesame
	SB 22 15213 fr.B.20 (203–178 BCE) = written statement
	P. Tebt. 1.44 and 49 (119 BCE) = written statement
	SB 14 11269.4 (first century BCE to first century CE) = house
ἡμῖν	P.Cair.Zen. 2 59170, r.6 (255 BCE) = wine
	P. Tebt. 3 1 796.18 (185 BCE) = written statement
	P.Tebt. 4 1097 (125–101 BCE) = written statement
σοί	P.Mich. 1 41, r.9 (253 BCE) = stone
	P.Cair.Zen. 3 59525, r.2 (252 BCE) = pigs
	P.Lond. 7 1993.12 (251 BCE) = remaining seeds
	P.Cair.Zen. 3 59509, r.6 (275–226 BCE) = account
	SB 3 7267, r.9 (184 BCE) = firm letters
αὐτῷ	P.Lille 1 4, 2,ctr.32 (217 BCE) = sons
	P.Mich. 18 780 a, r.14 (205 BCE) = house and plot of land
αὐτοῖς	P.Tebt. 3 1 703, r.32–33 (210 BCE) = space[b]
	P.Tebt. 1 88, 2.37 (115 BCE) = arouras
ᾧ	P.Lille 1 4, 2,ctr.26–27 (217 BCE) = land
	P.Tarich. 6 a.11 (186 BCE; cf. P.Tarich. 6 b) = kin
ὅσοις	PSI 6 554, 3.22–23 (258 BCE) = vineyards
ἡμετέροις	P.Monts. Roca 4 66.19 (second century BCE) = other people

a This may not indicate possession but loyalty (cf. LSJ, ὑπάρχω, III. 2).
b With preposition (ἐν αὐτοῖς).

In these examples ὑπάρχω always refers to a subject clearly stated within the text and never acts impersonally, as the grammars already indicate. ὑπάρχω requires a stated subject, which can be found in the immediate context.[13] In contrast, *we do have texts* showing how "if there are no possessions belonging to him" would be phrased if it were following the outline of Ex's' ἐὰν δὲ μὴ ὑπάρχῃ αὐτῷ. The following examples proceed chronologically:

ὧι μηθὲν ὑπάρχει
P.Hib. 1 113, 1.16 (260 BCE)

ἐμοὶ δὲ ὑπάρχει οὐθὲν
P.Cair.Zen. 3 59492, r.8 (275–226 BCE)

οἷς οὐθὲν ὑπ̣ά̣ρ̣χει
P.Köln 10 411, Fr3, 3.3 (178 BCE)

ὧι οὐ⟦χ⟧θεὶς ὑπάρχει
P.Tarich. 11. 14–15 (184 BCE)

οὐδὲν αὐτοῖς ὑπάρχει
P.Tebt. 3 1 742, 2.27 (157 BCE)

οὐθὲν ὑπάρχει περ⟨ὶ⟩ τὴν κώμην Ἀμινίᾳ
P.Tebt. 1 76, 2.2 (112 BCE; cf. line 11)

[οὐ]δὲν ὑμ⟨ῖν⟩ ὧδε ὑ̣πάρχ⟨ε⟩ι
SB 6 9017, Nr18.10 (CE)

These examples show that in order to state that someone does not have possessions while using 'ὑπάρχω + dative,' a numeral adjective such as οὐδέν or μηδέν must be supplied. All the translator needed to do in 22:2 (22:3 LXX) in order to indicate a lack of possessions would be to translate ἐὰν δὲ μὴ ὑπάρχῃ **οὐδὲν** αὐτῷ. Even further, there are other colloquial ways the translator could have said "if there are no possessions belonging to him" that would have sufficed here. One thinks of ἐὰν δὲ μὴ υπάρχοντα ᾖ αὐτῷ, since the participial form of ὑπάρχω is so utterly predominant in the papyri.[14] The translator of Genesis renders in this

13 E.g., P.Cair.Zen. 3 59349, r.4–7 (245 BCE) where κεράμια is assumed from the previous line.
14 Indeed, the legal title for complaints concerning goods is περὶ ὑπαρχόντων (cf. e.g., P.Enteux. 95, v.4 [222 BCE]).

way when translating a similar phrase to Exod 22:2 (22:3 LXX) where בכל־אשר יש־לו = ἐν πᾶσιν τοῖς ὑπάρχουσιν αὐτῷ (39:5). Regardless, since ὑπάρχῃ does not have οὐδὲν supplied and since it does not function impersonally, the grammatical subject of ὑπάρχω should be dictated by the previous context. In Exod 22:2 (22:3 LXX), the previous context would be the previous apodosis and punishment clause (i.e., ἀνταποθανεῖται). This would not be considered improper Greek.[15] For example, a third century inscription uses ἐὰν δὲ μὴ ὑπάρχῃ to refer to the previous apodosis of its decree (Miletos 41, A.53 [205 BCE]).[16]

4.2.2.3 'ὑπάρχω + dative' as a Legal Formula in the Literary Texts

In approaching this new reading of ἐὰν δὲ μὴ ὑπάρχῃ, the literary texts are even more arresting. It is apparent that 'ὑπάρχω + dative' is a common legal formulation to indicate a punishment being applied to someone. A fitting example is found in Demosthenes where the law mentioned is a near carbon-copy of the contents of Exod 22:2 (22:3 LXX):

> εἰ δέ τις ἰδίαν δίκην κλοπῆς ἁλοίη, ὑπάρχειν μὲν αὐτῷ διπλάσιον ἀποτεῖσαι τὸ τιμηθέν, προστιμῆσαι δ' ἐξεῖναι τῷ δικαστηρίῳ πρὸς τῷ ἀργυρίῳ δεσμὸν τῷ κλέπτῃ, πένθ' ἡμέρας καὶ νύκτας ἴσας
>
> If a man was found guilty on a private prosecution for theft, while the normal penalty was double reparation, the court was empowered to add to the fine the extra penalty of imprisonment for five days and as many nights[17]
>
> DEMOSTHENES, *Timocr.* 114

Here ὑπάρχειν αὐτῷ indicates the punishment befalling the thief (διπλάσιον ἀποτεῖσαι τὸ τιμηθέν). This same use of 'ὑπάρχω + dative' can be seen in:

---

15 It is always possible that the translator was incompetent in his translation here. Given his consistent demonstration of Greek fluency elsewhere, incompetency should be considered only when the Greek is unintelligible or truly ineloquent. Here it is perfectly ornate and common.

16 Ll. 48–53: ἐὰν δέ τινες τῶν δόντων τῆι πόλει τὸ ἐκκείμενον πλῆθος ἐγλ[ί]πωσι τὸμ βίον, τοῦ μὲν δοθέντος καὶ τοῦ ἐξαιρουμένου σιτηρεσίου ἀπολελύσθαι τὸν δῆμον, δίδοσθαι δὲ εἰς ταφὴν τοῖς προσήκουσιν ὑπὲρ ἑκάστου δραχμὰς ἑκατὸν πεντήκοντα, ὑπηρετεῖσθαι δὲ τοῦτο ὑπὸ τῶν ταμιῶν, ἐφ' ὧν ἂν ἕκαστοι τελευτήσωσιν ἀπὸ τῶν εἰς τὰ κατὰ ψηφίσματα ἐξειρημένων. ἐὰν δὲ μὴ ὑπάρχῃ....

17 Demosthenes, *Timocr.* 114 (Vince, LCL).

ἐὰν δέ τις ὄφλῃ, ὑπάρχειν μὲν αὐτῷ μήποτε τῆς ὅλης ἀριστείας ἀγωνιστῇ γενέσθαι

Any man that is convicted shall be debarred from ever competing for any distinction[18]

PLATO, *Leg.* 943b

Likewise, Aeschines uses the phrase *to refer to the death penalty being applied to someone*:[19]

ὅστις ἂν ἐθελήσειε σαφῶς τοιαύτην μαρτυρίαν μαρτυρῆσαι, ἐξ ἧς ὑπάρχει αὐτῷ, ἐὰν τἀληθῆ μαρτυρήσῃ, ἐπιδεικνύναι ἔνοχον ὄντα ἑαυτὸν τοῖς ἐσχάτοις ἐπιτιμίοις;

Now what man is so reckless that he would be willing to give in plain words testimony which, if the testimony be true, would inevitably amount to information against himself as liable to extreme punishment [i.e., death]?[20]

AESCHINES, *Timarch.* 72

εἰ μνησθεὶς τῶν προτέρων ἀδικημάτων ὁ δῆμος μὴ προσδέξαιτο τὴν συμμαχίαν, ἀλλ' ὑπῆρχεν αὐτῷ ἢ φεύγειν ἐκ Χαλκίδος, ἢ τεθνάναι ἐγκαταληφθέντι

if the people, remembering his past crimes, should refuse the alliance, since one of two things was sure, that he would be banished from Chalcis, or be caught and put to death[21]

AESCHINES, *Ctesiph.* 91

It is clear from these texts that 'ὑπάρχω + dative' was a way to indicate that a formal legal penalty is being prescribed.[22] For this reason, along with the fact that ὑπάρχω is not found impersonally in the relevant sources, ἐὰν δὲ μὴ ὑπάρχῃ αὐτῷ in 22:2 (22:3 LXX) should be understood as referring to the previously

18 Plato, *Leg.* 943b (Bury, LCL).

19 Cf. Dionysius Halicarnassus, *Ant. Rom.* 5.29.1.8–10: οὐκ ἀγνοῶν μέν, ὅτι καὶ κατορθώσαντι καὶ διαμαρτόντι τῆς ἐλπίδος **ἀποθανεῖν ὑπάρχει** μοι.

20 Aeschines, *Timarch.* 72 (Adams, LCL). The language of τοῖς ἐσχάτοις ἐπιτιμίοις reflects informal verbiage for the death penalty.

21 Adams, LCL, 381.

22 See also Aeschines, *Timarch.* 72.

mentioned punishment, namely, ἀνταποθανεῖται.[23] From a Greek legal perspective this is certainly how ἐὰν δὲ μὴ ὑπάρχῃ αὐτῷ would be understood and the ramifications of this conclusion are significant. The first such consequence is that new light is shed on the grammatical subject of ἀνταποθανεῖται.

It is odd that the translator renders שלם ישלם as ἀνταποθανεῖται since every other occurrence of the verb שלם (only found in chapters 21–22) is translated with ἀποτίνω (13×).[24] ἀποτίνω is a "forensic term which means to pay a penalty"[25] and is one of the most common verbs indicating restitution in the penalty clauses of legal documentary texts. It is not a verb used to describe the death penalty in Greek law. If one were basing an understanding of שלם on the laws in chapters 21–22, a similar meaning would be deduced, since the Hebrew verb deals with contexts involving the restitution of goods or monies. Translating שלם as to "restore" or "make compensation" is fitting.[26] The question at hand is to ask what led the translator to translate שלם ישלם as the death penalty (ἀνταποθανεῖται). Previous translations are somewhat ambiguous as to who the subject of ἀνταποθανεῖται is, whether it be the thief or the retaliating victim.[27] Wevers explains that ἀνταποθανεῖται represents the talionic principle of 21:12 in that killing someone deserves death in requital because the time had passed where the thief could be killed (i.e., during the break-in).[28] Thus the victim of the theft is the subject of ἀνταποθανεῖται and the recipient of the death penalty. It is an assumption on the part of Wevers that the subject of ἀνταποθανεῖται is the theft's victim, though it is grammatically and exegetically possible that the

23 This is also likely why the translator chose ὑπάρχω here instead of εἰμί to represent the copula.

24 21:34, 36, 37 (22:1 LXX); 22:3 (22:4 LXX), 4 (5 LXX), 5 (6 LXX), 6 (7 LXX), 8 (9 LXX), 10 (11 LXX), 11 (12 LXX), 12 (13 LXX), 13 (14 LXX), 14 (15 LXX). The translator also lexically flattens נתן (21:19) and שקל (22:16 [22:17 LXX]) into ἀποτίνω.

25 Bickerman, "Two Legal Interpretations," 212.

26 See, e.g., Francis Brown, Samuel Rolles Driver, and Charles Augustus Briggs, "שלם," *BDB*, 1022.

27 So Lancelot Charles Lee Brenton, *The Septuagint Version of the Old Testament: English Translation* (London: Samuel Bagster and Sons, 1870); NETS leaves the subject of ἀνταποθανεῖται unclear. LXX.D, given the clarification of the subject in the previous clause ("der, der ihn fing"), seems to indicate that the subject is the victim of the theft. It is unclear, however, what punishment the translation exactly indicates with "Er soll Ersatz für den Todesfall leisten." Private communications with a scholar working in German theological translation, Jacob Cerone, verified that the phrasing of LXX.D. is particularly ambiguous. Le Boulluec and Sandevoir, *L'Exode*, 223–224, state the subject of the verb to be the victim of the theft. Frankel, *Ueber den Einfluss*, 94, does not speak about this verse.

28 Wevers, *Notes*, 341–342.

translator thought the theft's victim was the subject of שלם ישלם.[29] The meaning of the Hebrew is not particularly clear. שלם ישלם could also refer to the thief needing to make restitution after having survived the night.[30] Yet, since it has been demonstrated that ἐὰν δὲ μὴ ὑπάρχῃ αὐτῷ should be understood as referring to the previous apodosis (ἀνταποθανεῖται), and since it is justifiable to read שלם ישלם with the thief as its subject, Wevers' interpretation should probably be dismissed. In the Greek text of 22:2 (22:3 LXX) the death penalty is instead being directed at the burglar.

Another indication that the translator intended ἀνταποθνήσκω to refer to the thief is found in his translation of לו דמים ("bloodguilt for him"). In Exod 22:1 (22:2 LXX) והכה ומת אין **לו דמים** is rendered as πληγεὶς ἀποθάνῃ, οὐκ ἔστιν **αὐτῷ φόνος**. The hypothetical situation is that the thief is killed in the act of night burglary. Here the translator renders לו דמים as αὐτῷ φόνος, "murder to him." It is uncertain whether αὐτῷ refers to the thief, i.e., there is no "murder with respect to the thief," or the victim, i.e., there is no "(charge of) murder for the victim." The next verse, however, translates אם־זרחה השמש עליו **דמים לו** as ἐὰν δὲ ἀνατείλῃ ὁ ἥλιος ἐπ' αὐτῷ, **ἔνοχός ἐστιν**. One would expect the translator to render דמים לו again as φόνος αὐτῷ if he wanted to make clear that it is the victim of the theft who is to die. This does not happen. Instead, ἔνοχός ἐστιν, a typical phrase from the papyri regarding legal liability, is used.[31] If φόνος αὐτῷ were rendered in 22:2 (22:3 LXX), it would clearly indicate that ἀνταποθανεῖται refers to the victim of the theft being killed. This is because φόνος αὐτῷ would highlight that a murder occurred, and hence a punishment was needed. ἔνοχός ἐστιν does not convey this. ἔνοχός ἐστιν could refer to either the thief or the victim. Given the other findings in this section, perhaps the change in translation of דמים לו should act as another clue as to the translator's intent here. ἔνοχός ἐστιν refers to the thief still being guilty after escaping the prior evening.

---

29 There is only one reference to ἀνταποθνήσκω in the literary texts in Antiphon, *De caede Her.* 8. While it is true that this reference concerns one being killed in requital for having murdered someone else—a use that supports Wevers' reading—concluding that this verb is *always* used this way would be too rash a decision. The prefix ἀντι- simply communicates that the verbal idea it is attached to will be done in return for another action. The other action could be anything, though in the case of Antiphon it was murder. Philo, *Alleg. Interp.* 3.32–35, also discusses this law. His interpretation is difficult to follow, but he seems to indicate that the whole passage is to be understood (allegorically) as referring to the thief, and as such, ἀνταποθανεῖται refers to the thief (see section 33 particularly). Still, his interpretation should probably not inform a correct reading of the original intent of 22:2 (22:3 LXX).

30 See e.g., LEB, NIV, NJB.

31 For a discussion on the phrase, see Roger S. Bagnall, "Some Notes on P. Hib. 198," *BASP* 6, no. 3/4 (1969): 91–92.

One might also ask why the translator decided to use the lexeme ἀνταποθνήσκω here. It has already been noted that a form of ἀποθνήσκω is employed in 21:29 with προσαποθανεῖται. There, it seems as though the prefix προσ- is derived from גם in the phrase וגם־בעליו יומת (= καὶ ὁ κύριος αὐτοῦ προσαποθανεῖται). Perhaps here in 22:2 (22:3 LXX) the translator wanted to represent the idea of "compensation" from the root שלם and thus added the prefix ἀντι. This would add an element of reciprocity when prefixed to the verb. We have already seen how the translator is keen to stay superficially close to the source text (SSF), and this would be another way to do so.[32] Moreover, note that the next line includes πραθήτω ἀντὶ τοῦ κλέμματος, "let him be sold in place of the theft."[33] It makes great sense for the translator to attach ἀντι- to ἀποθνήσκω in order to unite both the themes and alternative consequences to the theft.[34] Additionally 22:2 (22:3 LXX), like 21:29, is different from other laws with the death penalty in that it offers an alternative punishment, that is, the thief being sold into slavery.

With respect to this punishment of sale into slavery (expressed with πραθήτω ["let him be sold"] in 22:2 [22:3 LXX]), Ptolemaic legal syntax using the imperative in contrast to the future tense as a command verb in law indicates that a punishment may or may not be applied, provided it is in line with other legal considerations. Why the translator would include this imperative here with πραθήτω is discussed below in the legal and cultural analysis.

4.2.3 *Conclusion of Translation-Technical Analysis*

In the case of 22:2 (22:3 LXX), apart from the added death penalty, it is not always possible to know if the translation has intentionally diverged from the source text or if the translator was simply translating what the text was assumed to say.[35] The Hebrew text here is terse and at times cryptic. Despite this, having suggested that ἐὰν δὲ μὴ ὑπάρχῃ αὐτῷ in 22:2 (22:3 LXX) refers to the previous apodosis and punishment being applied to the thief, the obvious and most

32 22:4 (22:5 LXX), 13 (14 LXX) do not render the infinitive absolute of שלם so it is unlikely that the translator particularly cared that שלם were to be isomorphically represented here with ἀντι.

33 This phrase could theoretically be translated ἀντιπραθήτω and still retain the same meaning had the translator not wanted to stay close to the source text.

34 21:37 (22:1 LXX) also uses ἀντί twice, potentially setting up the connection to ἀνταποθανεῖται.

35 For example, in 22:2 (22:3 LXX) one wonders if the translator understood אין לו as referring back to שלם ישלם since there was no stated subject in the clause. There is almost always a subject included when 'אין + ל' is found in the Pentateuch (Gen 2:5; 11:30; Exod 22:1 [22:2 LXX]; Lev 11:10, 12; 22:13; 25:31; Num 5:8; 27:4, 8–10, 17; 35:27; Deut 12:12; 14:10, 27, 29; 22:26; 25:5; 28:31). The only contrary example seems to be Deut 28:32 with ואין לאל ידך (lit. "there is not to the strength of your hand [anything]").

pressing question arising from these conclusions is why the translator added the death penalty to this text when translating שלם ישלם. If it is not founded in talionic principles like Wevers claims, then what is the source of inspiration? While it is certainly possible that an ancient and unknown tradition in the Second Temple Period stands behind interpreting שלם ישלם as the death penalty, there is still, once again, ample reason to suggest Greco-Egyptian law as the impetus for the translation. This case is rather unique, since the translator is actually adding in the death penalty rather than removing it (as has otherwise been the case up until this point). The legal milieu might also help explain why ἀποτίνω was not used in this verse—mere payment might have been considered too light of a sentence. What, then, did the Greco-Egyptian context sustain regarding theft and more particularly nocturnal burglary?

4.2.4 *Legal and Cultural Analysis*

As is common, there is less information from the Ptolemaic period than from the Classical sources. Despite this deficit, the strong stance found towards nocturnal burglary in the Classical texts, as well as the seriousness with which theft was dealt with in the papyri, present a milieu where it can at least be said that it was acceptable and even normal for Greeks to consider the death penalty for burglary at night. Whether it was put into practice in Ptolemaic Egypt is not as clear as in the Classical sources. Egyptian law coincides with Classical practice in that physical punishments are documented. Confiscation of goods and enslavement likewise were potential outcomes of this crime.

4.2.4.1 Theft and Nocturnal Burglary in Classical Greek Law

There can be little doubt that Classical Greek law permitted capital punishment for nocturnal theft.[36] For example, Demosthenes recounts,

> If he stole anything, however small, by night, the person aggrieved might lawfully pursue and kill or wound him, or else put him into the hands of the Eleven, at his own option. A man found guilty of an offence for which arrest is lawful was not allowed to put in bail and refund the stolen money; no, the penalty was death.[37]

---

36 Cf., e.g., Farsedakis, "θανάτῳ ζημιοῦν," 79, fn. 232; Katelijn Vandorpe and Marc Waelkens, "Protecting Sagalassos' Fortress of the Akra: Two Large Fragments of an Early Hellenistic Inscription," *Ancient Society* 37 (2007): 32, fn. 21.

37 Demosthenes, *Timocr.* 113 (Murray, LCL). The lines before this speak of a lesser penalty for theft by day (cf. 114). See also Demosthenes, [*Lacr.*] 47 as another example of capital punishment for theft.

Such a punishment is attested frequently.[38] The heinousness of this crime seems to stem from the fact that both adultery and nocturnal theft were considered crimes against a household. They were viewed as "a dangerous violation of public order,"[39] which makes sense, since the house was an inviolable sanctuary.[40] Victims of this crime could ask for monetary compensation instead of the thief's death.[41] If thieves were brought to the court, upon confession, they would be executed immediately.[42] If the victim was to kill the thief, it is emphasized that it should be done so quickly.[43] Under certain conditions (such as at night, or accompanying other actions, etc.), those labelled κλέπτης or τοιχωρύχος were considered κακοῦργοι and punished with death.[44] Note that both terms are, in essence, used by Ex: the thief is the κλέπτης and the same image and shared root of "wall-digger" (τοιχωρύχος) is conveyed by διορύγματι.[45]

Since there is such a strong and consistent promulgation of capital punishment for night theft in Classical law, it is very difficult to imagine that this stance and norm was not at least known in Ptolemaic Egypt. Such a standard would be commonplace for Greeks, and this heritage would come with them from the *poleis*, even if the actual on-the-ground practice might not have been so strongly pursued. On the other hand, ancient Egyptian tradition does not attest the same penalties.

---

38 See, e.g., Aeschines, *Timarch.* 91; Lysias, *De caede Erat.* 36, in an address against a man breaking into a home for adultery, implies that burglary was also punishable by death (cf. 30–33). Plato, *Leg.* 874c states that a homeowner can lawfully kill a burglar entering his house but does not make clear whether the criminal should die outside of the actual act of robbery.

39 Robert W. Wallace, "On not Legislating Sexual Conduct in Fourth-Century Athens," in *Symposion 1995: Vorträge zur grieschischen und hellenistischen Rechsgeschichte*, ed. Gerhard Thür and Julie Vélissaropoulous-Karakostas (Cologne and Vienna: Böhlau, 1997), 152, fn. 3; cf. Eva Cantarella, *I Supplizi Capitali in Grecia E a Roma* (Milano: Rizzoli, 1991), 334.

40 Farsedakis, "θανάτῳ ζημιοῦν," 79, fn. 231.

41 Cantarella, *I Supplizi*, 336.

42 Arnaoutoglou, *Ancient Greek Laws*, 113.

43 Demosthenes, *Aristocr.* 60 cites a law about a thief being allowed to be killed immediately if he is in the process of stealing and using force. Lines 60–61 stresses the immediacy necessary in this killing (cf. MacDowell, *Athenian Homicide Law*, 76). Demosthenes, *Timocr.* 113 deals with night theft and the permissible killing therein—even without the thief's use of force (cf. Isocrates, *Loch.* 6; Lycurgus, *Leocr.* 65).

44 Farsedakis, "θανάτῳ ζημιοῦν," 78.

45 Both relate to ὀρύσσω and cognates.

4.2.4.2 Theft and Nocturnal Burglary in Ancient Egyptian Law

The Egyptians did not punish nocturnal theft with death, inasmuch as the fragments of sources we have attest. Tyldesley summarizes the punishment for theft, stating that the government

> depriv[ed] convicts and their families of office, property and freedom. In his Nauri decree, Seti I, for example, specifies 'beating with 100 blows plus extracting the property belonging to the House as stolen property at a rate of a hundred to one' as the appropriate, exorbitant rate of interest for theft. As here, financial penalties were more often than not combined with corporal punishments, which became more specific as the dynastic age progressed. By the New Kingdom we find many impoverished prisoners departing to work in the labour-gangs with ears and noses missing.[46]

On the other hand, theft with relation to the king or his items was in fact a capital crime.[47] If it is true that the death penalty only occurred in this setting for Egyptians, its appearance in Ex could, in theory, be posited as a purely Greek influence. Ptolemaic evidence continues to buttress this supposition.

4.2.4.3 Theft and Nocturnal Burglary in Greco-Egyptian Law

The most incontrovertible formal legal text describing capital punishment for nocturnal burglary during the early Ptolemaic era is, regrettably, not from Ptolemaic Egypt. To the north in Arkadia, IPArk 17, B.112–113 (303–300 BCE) sentences night thieves to death. One should not presuppose that such a policy was present in Ptolemaic Egypt, but it at least demonstrates that the practice was continued into the third century by Greeks nearby. Otherwise, Bluche believes that crimes against property do not have sufficient evidence to claim that capital punishment was ever applied to them.[48] Theft was met with a required restitution (often double) along with other potential penalties including the loss of one's κλῆρος ("land allotment") or additional fines.[49] Ultimately, Bluche claims that "L'application généralisée de la peine capitale au brigandage est possible, mais elle n'est pas démontrable."[50] It is noteworthy that theft

46 Tyldesley, *Judgement of the Pharaoh*, 64; cf. 64 and 75 for more examples.

47 Muhlestein, *Violence in the Service*, 320; cf. Tyldesley, *Judgement of the Pharaoh*, 28–29.

48 Bluche, "La peine de mort," 168.

49 Bluche, "La peine de mort," 144, fn. 5, 168; Taubenschlag, *The Law of Greco-Roman* (1944), 343–346. For the confiscation of property see, e.g., P Tebt. 53.23–25; P.Tebt. 5.6–9. That confiscation of property was directly linked to the death penalty, see Helmis, "Crime et châtiment," 204.

50 "La peine de mort," 168. Note that Bluche is only commenting on one form of theft.

at night is highlighted in some papyri.[51] P.Dion. 10.4 (109 BCE) mentions a night theft. In this case the perpetrators are to be hunted down to return the item. It is said in addition to the return of goods that τύχωσι τῶν ἐξακολουθούντων ("they might receive consequences"; lines 13–16). Whether this hints at something more than a pecuniary penalty is unclear. It is the case, though, that aggravating circumstances in theft were important in the Ptolemaic legal system.[52]

As in the case with the Classical sources, breaking into someone's home was particularly offensive in Ptolemaic Egypt. Taubenschlag lays out the evidence that only in very specific circumstances were uninvited individuals allowed to enter into a person's home.[53] Those who trespass were liable to charges of ὕβρις ("serious offence") and ἄδικος ἀγωγή ("unlawful entry"; e.g., P.Fay 12.31 [103 BCE]), but the exact recompense is not found in the papyri.[54] In this way a thief was doubly guilty in Ptolemaic Egypt when breaking into a home. Helmis goes as far as to surmise that theft was, in some ways, seen as more severe than murder by the government.[55] This is due to the risk of lower taxation for the victim, as well as non-taxable goods being accrued to the thief. That Exod 22:2 (22:3 LXX) adds the death penalty, in this light, would be a favorable addition for the Ptolemaic bureaucracy—even if, perhaps, the Ptolemies were influenced by the Egyptian traditions of not putting thieves to death. In the end, whether they did or did not enact capital punishment for nocturnal theft like the Classical Greeks is not clear. Perhaps, if the translation came in the middle of the third century where legal traditions and customs might have held more sway, the Classical stance involving capital punishment would have been permissible at the time.[56] It surely would have been known.

4.2.4.4 Conclusion on Theft and Nocturnal Burglary

Outside of IPArk 17, B.112–113, there is no law speaking about a sentence of death for night burglars around the time of the translation. The Classical sources strongly favor capital punishment for this crime, while the Ptolemaic data leave it uncertain if it was ever considered or put into place. If the translator of Exodus were aiming to appease Greeks who knew their patriarchal traditions

51 E.g., P.Petr. 3 34 (a).3 (210–183 BCE). For other crimes being specified at night see Helmis, "Crime et châtiment," 73.

52 Bluche, "La peine de mort," 147.

53 Raphael Taubenschlag, "The Inviolability of Domicile in Greco-Roman Egypt," *Archív Orientální* 18(4) (1950): 293–297.

54 Cf. Taubenschlag, "The Inviolability of Domicile in Greco-Roman Egypt," 293, fn. 6.

55 Helmis, "Crime et châtiment," 169.

56 Cf. Helmis, "Crime et châtiment," 147, who mentions theft as a likely category of crime within these traditions.

and laws, they almost certainly would associate the death penalty with nocturnal theft (unlike the Egyptians). It is not known whether the Ptolemies had certain pressures keeping them from imposing the death penalty where they might have liked to. It is at least highly plausible, given this context, that the death penalty added to 22:2 (22:3 LXX) was in line with broader Greek expectations, and possibly Ptolemaic practice.

4.2.4.5 πραθήτω and Exceptions to Enslavement

I have already argued in section 2.7 that the imperative used as the command verb of a law otherwise surrounded by future tenses is a form of Ptolemaic legal syntax that indicates that the command verb may or may not be practiced, while being bound to any other legal constraints relating to the topic at hand. Assuming that framework here, it must be asked why πραθήτω ("let him be sold") follows this legal syntactic pattern. Exodus 22:2 (22:3 LXX) is speaking about a consequence for the thief in the place of the death penalty (ἐὰν δὲ μὴ ὑπάρχῃ αὐτῷ, "But if [the death penalty] might not be [assigned] to him"). In the death penalty's place, it is stated πραθήτω ἀντὶ τοῦ κλέμματος, "he should be sold in place of the theft."[57] The main concern, then, is whether there were factors within the Greco-Egyptian legal context that prohibited or mitigated the sale of persons into slavery for theft. This can be demonstrated.

A distinction must be made between people *selling themselves* into slavery for debt and between those who *were sold* for debts and crimes. The former practice has too little evidence from the earlier Egyptian context to make a claim for that time period.[58] In the Ptolemaic framework self-debt slavery "was almost certainly illegal."[59] In contrast, the Ptolemies could decree that

---

57 For the use of πιπράσκω for sale into bondage, see, e.g., the law in Demosthenes, [*Neaer.*] 16 (πεπράσθω, line 11). See also πιπράσκω, I.1, LSJ; CGL, 1126.

58 "The overall evidence of the existence of slavery for debt in ancient Egypt is unfortunately very meagre" (Tomasz Markiewicz, "Security for Debt in the Demotic Papyri," *JJP* 35 [2005]: 142). The account of Diodorus Siculus which suggests that debt-slavery was eventually forbidden (*Bib. hist.* 1.79.3) is likely unreliable as it contains historical inaccuracies and a particular idealizing *tendenz* (Markiewicz, "Security for Debt," 142–143). It is uncertain whether it was the Ptolemies who introduced debt-slavery to Egypt (and that from Greece) or if it existed prior (ibid., 144). See also Richard H. Pierce, *Three Demotic Papyri in the Brooklyn Museum: A Contribution to the Study of Contracts and Their Instruments in Ptolemaic Egypt* (Oslo: Universitetsforlaget, 1972), 128–130.

59 Maehler, "Greek, Egyptian," 124. He cites PSI 5.549 (42 BCE) as evidence. Westermann, *Upon Slavery*, 51–52, argues that the specifics of which situations or who were permitted to initiative debt-slavery are not known. It seems there would have been some instigation on the part of the debtor (ibid., 53).

someone be sold into slavery "for debts to the Crown or to private persons."[60] It seems as though this would be a governmental prerogative that could not be privately executed.[61] Likewise, thieves were liable to paying double, fines, and potential loss of their κλῆρος.[62] An example is P.Tebt. 1 5 (118 BCE) which notes that thieves would have their property sold. From this practice, Taubenschlag suggests that those who faced execution/seizure of their goods would also likely be enslaved.[63]

Based on just these factors, then, there would be little reason for deregulating the law with the imperative πραθήτω, since selling a thief into slavery would be permissible. It could be that the imperative is again deferential, if the authority to do this act lay with the Ptolemies, as it seems to have. However, we also have documentation that specific groups of peoples could not be enslaved under any circumstance. For example, the law code preserved in P.Hal. 1. 219–221 (259 BCE) regulates that Alexandrian citizens could not be sold into slavery, though non-citizens could be.[64] Taubenschlag adds the βασιλικοὶ γεωργοί and the ὑποτελεῖς to those who were exempt.[65] This evidence is about as definitive as we could hope for in determining that no law would permit indiscriminately selling any persons into slavery in the Ptolemaic context. As such, it would make sense for the translator to use the imperative in order not to compose a law that directly contradicted Ptolemaic legal expectations, assuming legislation like this existed before the time of the translation.[66] Another option for the imperative is that the thief had the means to pay back what was owed and would not need to be sold to pay his penalties.

So, whether as a means of deference, an indication of the thief's ability to compensate, or in order to comply with current legislation concerning who could or could not be enslaved, πραθήτω in the imperative mood ensured that the law was not read as the final say on the matter.

60 Markiewicz, "Security for Debt," 144; Westermann, *Upon Slavery*, 50; see P.Col.Inv. 480 (198 BCE).

61 C.Ord.Ptol. 22 (262 BCE) indicates that personal execution against debtors was not permitted (at least in Syria and Phoenicia; Markiewicz, "Security for Debt," 144).

62 See fn. 49 above.

63 Taubenschlag, *The Law of Greco-Roman* (1955), 527–528.

64 Cf. Taubenschlag, *Law of Greco-Roman* (1955), 598; Westermann, *Upon Slavery*, 50, believes that this rule only applied within Alexandria. Even if true, the argument made in this section remains valid.

65 Taubenschlag, *The Law of Greco-Roman* (1955), 599. Note that b. Qidd. 22b:4 refers to a rabbinic interpretation where slaves could not be slaves of slaves, and as such acts as a parallel reading where certain groups could not be sold into slavery.

66 P.Hal. 1 is dated to approximately 259 BCE, which suggests that legislation did exist at the time of translation.

4.2.5 *Conclusion to Legal and Cultural Analysis*

It is the case that there are more definitive Ptolemaic data concerning exemptions to slavery than positive evidence that the death penalty was prescribed for nocturnal burglary. These exemptions are likely to be the rationale behind the Ptolemaic legal syntax employed with πραθήτω. The Classical position that night burglars were to be put to death could serve as an ideal from which the translator drew, or it may have been a practice in Ptolemaic Egypt if IPArk 17 is permitted to serve as evidence for parallel Greek practice at the time. Even if the Ptolemies did not prescribe death in this instance, it is almost certain that the Greek populace would be aware that their traditions did, and as such, its inclusion in 22:2 (22:3 LXX) would be in line with that heritage. It is interesting that the death penalty for this crime is a distinctly Greek notion in comparison with the Hebrew Bible and known Egyptian practice.

4.2.6 *Conclusion on Exodus 22:2 (22:3 LXX)*

Unlike other laws discussed in this study, Exod 22:2 (22:3 LXX) is unique in that the death penalty is added. If Greeks were expected to read this translation, the addition would be in line with their legal heritage from Athens and abroad. Perhaps it also coincides with actual practice at the time. Through a nuanced and legally-attuned reading of ἐὰν δὲ μὴ ὑπάρχῃ αὐτῷ it is possible to see that this phrase refers back to the death penalty (ἀνταποθανεῖται) and its application to the thief. This reading entails that the phrase does not mean "if there are no possessions belonging to (the thief)." If it is true that Greco-Egyptian law never permitted the death sentence for nocturnal burglars, then ἀνταποθανεῖται may have been included in the translation to assuage a Greek readership and not to match actual legal practice. It could also be speculated that the Ptolemies desired the death penalty for this crime but did not enact it for some unknown reason.

ἀνταποθανεῖται is an interesting case among those in this study. Other renderings of the death penalty seem to be preventative in their translational approach in that the translator removes or deregulates the call for capital punishment. The Ptolemaic data seem to suggest that pecuniary fines were normal for theft, including night theft, and so translating with ἀποτίνω as expected probably would not have raised many eyebrows. That the translator felt compelled to add ἀνταποθανεῖται might point to a desire beyond just mitigating any clashes with Ptolemaic legislation and towards the intent to bring this law into line with Greek perceptions simply for the sake of appealing to that demographic. At the same time, rendering with ἀποτίνω in 22:2 (22:3 LXX) without any further information would probably direct the reader back to the stated payment required in 21:37 [22:1 LXX]. Having the same punishment for a regular theft as compared to a nocturnal home burglary—a much more severe crime in the Greek tradition—could also have led the translator to 'up the ante,' so to speak, and include the harsher punishment that would be more appropriate within the Greek legal framework.

4.3 Exodus 22:17 (22:18 LXX): On Sorcery/Poisoning

מכשפה לא תחיה

You shall not let a sorceress live.

Φαρμάκους οὐ περιποιήσετε.

You shall not protect poisoners (from death).
Exodus 22:17 (22:18 LXX)

It is uncertain whether OG Exod 22:17 (22:18 LXX) does in fact refer to the death penalty. For this reason, the most relevant factor in this verse is how to understand περιποιήσετε. A case will be made that it is possible to read this verb as a prohibition against protecting φαρμάκους, rather than an active call to put them to death. I will also suggest that the group labelled φαρμάκους could be situated within the Greek-legal framework of those guilty of poisoning.

It is unclear as to whether περιποιήσετε should be understood similarly to תחיה. The latter is a Piel form of חיה that is regularly understood in this passage to refer to not "letting [the מכשפה] live."[67] The question is whether περιποιέω conveys the same thing in Greek. In the Greek Pentateuch περιποιέω is found in contexts contrasting someone being killed with someone being preserved

67 Brown, Driver, and Briggs, "חיה," *BDB*, 311; Koehler, Baumgartner, and Stamm, "חיה," *HALOT*, 309. Brevard S. Childs, *The Book of Exodus: A Critical Theological Commentary* (Philadelphia: Westminster Press, 1974), 478, considers that this term could be equivalent to "the ban" (Num 3:15; Deut 20:16; 1 Sam 27:9–11). It is also possible that לא תחיה, seeing as it does not use the typical terminology for the death penalty, referred to some other kind of depravation from protection, food, society, or the like (cf. Houtman, *Exodus*, 212). Propp, *Exodus*, 256, suggests that the phrase could refer to sparing a sorcerer from the death penalty once already tried and guilty. This could be in line with what is found concerning περιποιέω and the death penalty (see fn. 74 below). The translation of מכשפה with φαρμάκους is discussed below.

from death, i.e., "letting live" (Gen 12:12 = יחיו; Exod 1:16 = חיה;[68] Num 22:33 = החייתי).[69] All of these occasions, in contrast to Exod 22:17 (22:18 LXX), use the middle voice of περιποιέω. The active voice is only found in Exod 22:17 (22:18). At first glance this is curious. LSJ comments that in the LXX the middle voice of περιποιέω is used in the sense of their first definition, namely, to "cause to remain over and above, keep safe, preserve."[70] This is the usage we find in these passages contrasting killing and keeping alive. There are also more uses of περιποιέω in the active voice that distinguish it from the middle. One such use is "to procure" or "to secure."[71] The only active use in the relevant papyri attests to this use along with the other later Septuagintal texts.[72] In this vein, 22:17 (22:18 LXX) could be read, "You shall not procure φαρμάκους." This would be a prohibition against the acquisition or use of these types of peoples.

Problematic to this line of interpretation are the literary texts. It seems that the active form of περιποιέω, when speaking about humans, most frequently (perhaps always) refers to the preservation of their lives from death.[73] This consistent use of the active voice rules out the middle form found in the other LXX texts as indicating anything semantically substantial. What is more, the legal orators use the active voice of περιποιέω to refer to the act of preserving someone from the formal death penalty.[74] These are instances where people(s)/fate are blocking the death of a person through various modalities, whether that be court processes, fleeing for exile, or the like. If οὐ περιποιήσετε in 22:17 (22:18 LXX) were read in a similar way to these contexts, it would be a prohibition from stopping the death penalty and not a way of formally

68 Given the parallel consonantal representation between Qal and Piel for this form, it is possible the translator read the consonantal text as Piel. SamP also reads וחיתה which could account for the second person voice in Ex.

69 Cf. Ezek 13:19 = ולחיות; Ps 78:11 = הותר.

70 LSJ, περιποιέω, II. 2.

71 LSJ, περιποιέω, I. 4.

72 UPZ 1 14 r,2. 12 (157 BCE): περιποιῆσαι … ἀδελφῶι στρατείαν ("to procure military service for my brother"). It is active a few times in later books with the sense of "to secure": 1 Macc 6:44; Sir 19:18. 2 Macc 3:35 uses the active in a situation involving the preservation of life in the face of death. Whether this text should be translated "to the one preserving my life" or "to the one securing (my right) to live" is debatable. That God only preserved the man's life for his own purposes suggests that it was this act of divine purpose that gave him a right to live, and thus "secured" this.

73 Herodotus, *Hist.* 1.110.3; 3.36.6; 7.52.1; 7.181.1; 8.76.1; Isocrates, *Arch.* 91; Isocrates, *Phil.* (Ep 2), 7; Lysias, *And.* 47; Aristotle, [*Rhet. Alex.*] 1423a.9. Literary texts were only examined up until the beginning of the first century BCE for this data point.

74 Lysias, *Agor.* 63 (θάνατος αὐτῶν κατεγνώσθη, ἡ δὲ τύχη καὶ ὁ δαίμων περιεποίησε); Demosthenes, *2 Aristog.* 19, in light of 14; Dinarchus, *Dem.* 98 in light of 104.

declaring the death penalty. It would not speak to the act of condemning to death, only to (somehow) inhibiting its actuality.

Elsewhere the translator of Exodus renders the same Piel Hebrew verb with ζῳογονέω, a term that distinctly focuses on the production or preservation of life (1:17–18, 22).[75] In chapter 1 each use of ζῳογονέω comes successively after the translator renders וחיה with περιποιεῖσθε in 1:16. Perhaps the change of verb to something more reflective of midwifery and birthing explains the change to the more explicit ζῳογονέω. We also see ζωγρέω, a term primarily used to indicate sparing someone from death, render Piel חיה in the other Pentateuchal translators (Num 31:15; Deut 20:16).[76] It is difficult to know whether ζῳογονέω or ζωγρέω, should they have been chosen in 22:17 (22:18 LXX), would say anything more than περιποιέω. Perhaps they would not be as open to variant interpretations. If they conveyed the idea "to *cause* to live," then their negation would be equal to "do not keep alive" and hence would be tantamount to a call for capital punishment. This would distinguish their meaning from περιποιέω, which could speak only to protecting a life, not necessarily going out of one's way to end it.

The choice of περιποιέω in 22:17 (22:18 LXX) is, then, difficult to interpret. If the few literary texts could function as a guide—particularly the legal orators and their contrast to the death penalty—then οὐ περιποιήσετε would present a prohibition from saving φαρμάκους from death. It might not be a means of outright saying that these people ought to be capitally punished. It could instead be a prohibition against intervening when φάρμακοι are condemned to die. περιποιέω in the literary texts does not mean to take a life but rather to preserve it. To remove that protection is not the same thing as saying, "kill the φαρμάκους." Given the importance of wording in Greek law, such a distinction probably would not go unnoticed by a legal scribe. Likewise, another Greek-legal facet dissuades from reading περιποιήσετε as equal to condemning someone to death. If it is true that the translator of Exodus couches laws with the death penalty through the deregulating imperative, it is expected that an imperative would also be found in 22:17 (22:18 LXX).[77] That the imperative is

75 According to LSJ all its uses have to do with the propagation/preservation of life. Note that the editors believe that the LXX uses ζῳογονέω in the sense of ζωγρέω (II. 3). See also 1 Kgdms 2:6; 4 Kgdms 7:4. Perhaps the translator chooses ζῳογονέω in this context due to its use related to birthing.

76 Deut 32:39 pairs ἐγὼ ἀποκτενῶ with ζῆν ποιήσω (ואחיה), which perhaps is a more all-encompassing statement than ζωογονήσω or περιποιήσομαι, which would both only indicate the preservation of life, not the creation of it.

77 This is, of course, assuming the validity of section 2.7 and its bearing on Ex.

not present might suggest that he did not expect this περιποιήσετε to be understood as another way of calling for capital punishment.[78]

What φάρμακος might have meant should at last be briefly discussed. In Greek Exodus the term is found twice referring to a group in Pharaoh's court who encountered Moses and Aaron (7:11; 9:11). Their acumen in performing the miraculous lends towards the term being understood as "magician" or "sorcerer" in that context.[79] Here in the legal materials it is possible that the same could be said, though there are a few other definitions that should not be ignored. φάρμακος can refer to a "poisoner" as well as a "sorcerer."[80] In the Classical legal world the legal category for poisoning was φαρμάκεια.[81] The shared root with φάρμακος could direct the reader of 22:17 (22:18 LXX) towards this legal milieu. Poisoning was considered to be a form of intentional homicide.[82] Plato's *Laws* prescribes death for poisoners.[83] The act of poisoning was also taken quite seriously in the Ptolemaic legal context.[84] Bluche considers that it might have been punished by death.[85] These factors could lend credence to φάρμακος being read specifically in reference to poisoning in the Ptolemaic legal world. At the same time, another definition for φάρμακος also exists. If the accent is changed from φάρμακος to φαρμακός, then the latter category refers to a criminal who is to be executed as a scapegoat.[86] This term does not appear in the Ptolemaic papyri and does not relate to a formal legal category like φαρμάκεια, so it seems less plausible that it would be perceived in 22:17 (22:18 LXX).

While it could be argued that a reader of Greek Exodus would infer the meaning of φάρμακος as "sorcerer" from the earlier narrative sections, it is also

78 Maybe the change from the singular to the plural can be explained within this framework as well. The plural is somewhat more generic in that it does not focus on a specific case (as, e.g., ἐὰν δέ τις φάρμακος ᾖ ostensibly would) but instead looks to multiple occasions of poisoning. The various ways protection might be afforded to a φάρμακος are then highlighted. If this were a law equivalent to prescribing death, then the plural may not have been as suitable. At the same time, the plural may have been a way of avoiding the fact that the law seems only speak against female sorcerers (מכשפה is feminine singular; cf. Dozeman, *Exodus*, 542–543). See also Deut 18:10–11.

79 See LSJ.

80 See LSJ.

81 Cf. Farsedakis, "θανάτῳ ζημιοῦν," 51–52.

82 Safty, "Les principales," 164.

83 Plato, *Leg.* 933d–e.

84 Helmis, "Crime et châtiment," 20, notes that while the documentary evidence does not often speak of poisoning, the literary texts and the astrologues mention it enough to suggest it was a common crime at the time. Cf. P.Tebt. 1 43 (117 BCE).

85 Bluche, "La peine de mort," 170. Cf. Franz Cumont, *L'Égypte des astrologues* (Bruxelles: Fondation égyptologique reine Élisabeth, 1937), 174, 199.

86 See LSJ, φαρμακός.

possible that φάρμακος would be understood to refer to poisoning, since this category of crime was more within the legal concerns of Ptolemaic law. If the laws of the Covenant Code in their Greek rendition were to be circulated apart from the narrative, then these categories would have likely been presumed before "sorcerer." What φαρμάκους refers to is not particularly important for the present argument, since it is the function and use of περιποιήσετε that drives whether the law refers to the death penalty. Whether it meant a "sorcerer," "poisoner," or "scapegoat," 22:17 (22:18 LXX) may only prohibit intervention in their deaths.[87] A possible translation could then be, "You shall not protect poisoners (from death)."

4.4 Exodus 22:18 (22:19 LXX): On Bestiality/Animal Husbandry

כל־שכב עם־בהמה מות יומת

Anyone lying with an animal shall surely be put to death.

Πᾶν κοιμώμενον μετὰ κτήνους, θανάτῳ ἀποκτενεῖτε [αὐτούς].

Any animal lying with a domestic animal, you shall kill with (an act of early) death.

Exodus 22:18 (22:19 LXX)

4.4.1 *Introduction*

A close examination of the OG rendering of Exodus 22:18 (22:19 LXX)—a seemingly straightforward law in the Hebrew text—reveals some fascinating translation choices that seem to indicate that the translator has intentionally created a new law that does not coincide with the parent text's intent. In the Hebrew text, Exodus 22:18 (22:19 LXX) refers to a prescription against bestiality, namely, "Anyone lying with an animal shall surely be put to death." The consequence of breaking this command is the death penalty (מות יומת). In the OG version, I will argue, the translator seems to have transformed the Hebrew into a law about husbandry. A basic translation of the Greek in this perspective would be: "Any animal lying with a domestic animal, you shall kill with (an act of early/untimely) death." The "any animal" here could be conceived of as

87 Note that one could not harm or ransom someone accused of homicide when on trial in the Greek context at penalty of death (Safty, Les Principales, 165; Demosthenes, *Aristocr.* 28). "Preserving" the criminal was a part of their law.

a wild animal. Of course, this reading requires ample justification since it has not been suggested by previous modern translations.[88] If it is accurate, there are resounding ramifications for the translation, translation technique, and for Second Temple exegesis. That the translator so drastically changed the subject matter of the Hebrew law is perhaps an anomalous example from the Second Temple period. What, then, are the justifications for this reading?

There are three translation-technical components that lead to the conclusion that the Greek rendering of Exod 22:18 (22:19 LXX) is a law about husbandry. They are the following:

(1) the use of neuter πᾶν ("any") instead of the expected masculine πᾶς ("any").

(2) the sudden translation choice of ἀποκτείνω ("to kill") as the penal verb rather than θανατόω, τελευτάω, or ἀποθνήσκω like previous laws.

(3) the non-inclusion of the third person imperative when rendering the death penalty.

Together these items permit a discussion as to whether αὐτούς (Göttingen edition) should be considered OG.

These components also complement each other in demonstrating the intent of the translator. Each factor will be argued in full, but their basic effect is as follows:

(1) πᾶν as an anarthrous neuter, when the gender of this adjective is not bound to another word or colloquialism, refers to things, animals, or abstract concepts rather than to persons in the LXX, papyri, and inscriptions. This is especially so in formal or semi-formal legal or economic documentary texts. When πᾶν is paired with an anarthrous participle, it likewise refers to things, animals, or abstract concepts and not to persons in the LXX, documentary, and literary sources. As such, there is no strong evidence for Exod 22:18 (22:19 LXX) to suggest πᾶν would be read as referring to anything other than "any animal" (πᾶν) that can "lie with (κοιμώμενον) a domesticated animal (μετὰ κτήνους)." The animal that would be inferred from "any animal" would probably be a wild animal, in contrast to a domestic beast. Coinciding with this point is:

(2) The translation choice of ἀποκτείνω for יומת. ἀποκτείνω always refers to homicide or an on-the-spot slaying in formal Greek legal diction. It seems likely that the translator was aware that ἀποκτείνω would not be read as the formal

88 E.g., Brenton, *The Septuagint*; Le Boulluec and Sandevoir, *L'Exode*, 229; Perkins, NETS, 67, translates with "Everything lying with an animal." Private correspondence with the author confirms that he was not certain of the function of πᾶν here but translated based on the typical Classical use of πᾶν; LXX.D translates "Jeden, der mit einem Tier schläft."

death penalty like the laws with θανατόω or ἀποθνήσκω. Legally-attuned readers would then be guided in their interpretation, and ἀποκτείνω would confirm that πᾶν did not refer to humans.

(3) All other laws with the death penalty in the LXX Covenant Code—provided there is no exception clause (as in Exod 21:29–30 and 22:2 [22:3 LXX])—are written with the penal verb in the apodosis as the third person imperative. This is in keeping with the specific form of Ptolemaic legal syntax outlined in section 2.7. The use of the future tense, ἀποκτενεῖτε, does not follow this pattern and could indicate that the death penalty is not in view.

These three translation choices stand in contrast to what could be straightforward renderings of this verse, such as πᾶς κοιμώμενος μετὰ κτήνους θανάτῳ θανατούσθω or πᾶς ὁ κοιμώμενος μετὰ κτήνους θανάτῳ θανατούσθω (both "anyone lying with a domestic animal should be put to death"). These translations would keep in line with previous renderings from chapter 21. Similarly, πάντα τὸν κοιμώμενον μετὰ κτήνους θανάτῳ θανατοῦτε would be an equally eloquent rendering without any of the problems that the three translation-technical components raise. Had the translator wanted to state that any person who lies with a domestic beast should be killed, he could have made this unambiguously clear with any of these simple translations. Instead, πᾶν in Exod 22:18 (22:19 LXX) is most likely representative of a basic neuter and the phrase πᾶν κοιμώμενον should be understood as "any*thing* that lies with." This would exclude any reference to humans and is also the most natural reading, excluding other grammatical or semantic categories that are not in line with the text-linguistic makeup, genre, or linguistic register of 22:18 (22:19 LXX). Exactly which "thing" is referred to in "any*thing* that lies with" might be a wild animal. The Greco-Egyptian legal and economic data support the new reading established from the translation research. Most private sexual acts would not be legislated against in both the Greek and Egyptian worlds, and likewise the documented animal husbandry practices of Ptolemaic Egypt line up with what is presented in my proposed reading of OG 22:18 (22:19 LXX). Overall, the translation might be seen as reactionary. The translator may not have wanted to include a law on bestiality on account of his legal milieu that did not prosecute such an act. Certain elements of the Hebrew text were then exploited in translation and the translator creatively changed the subject matter to animal husbandry.

4.4.2 *Translation-Technical Analysis*

4.4.2.1 The Translator's Choice of πᾶν Instead of πᾶς

It is uncontroversial that in Classical Greek the masculine and feminine πᾶς/πάσα, are generally used to indicate "persons," whereas the neuter πᾶν is used to designate "things."[89] Animals are included within this category of "things." When both persons and things are being spoken about, the default is to resort to the masculine/feminine.[90] These rules have exceptions and the neuter case can be utilized in more unique ways, which will be discussed further. Likewise, in the inscriptions and the papyri of the Ptolemaic period, πᾶς/πᾶσα and πᾶν are used to represent these basic categories of "persons" and "things" respectively.[91] Of course, these specifications are only considered when πᾶς/πᾶσα and πᾶν are not grammatically bound to another item of a specific gender (e.g., πᾶν τὸ ἀργύριον). When governed by a gendered term, the lemma πᾶς takes on the gender of that item and the specification of "persons" or "things" is not present (e.g., πᾶν τὸ ἄρσην often refers to a male human, yet is neuter in grammatical gender). For this reason, I will only evaluate cases of πᾶς/πᾶσα/πᾶν where the gender of these adjectives is the choice of the respective author and not determined by the gender of a governing lexeme. Likewise, the phrase τὸ πᾶν ("everything," "the whole") is not included in the present evaluation, since it is often used idiomatically and is not always affected by the gender that it describes.

The following chart (4.2) supplies all cases of πᾶν that are not grammatically bound to another unalterably neuter term in the LXX. For the purposes of the present argument, cases where πᾶν is used to refer to animals or specific inanimate objects will be separated from cases where it is used more generically or abstractly. Likewise, colloquially neuter terms will be separately displayed. There are a few cases of incongruity between the gender of πᾶν and its associated lexeme. This phenomenon will be discussed below. Finally, disputable cases where πᾶν could arguably refer to humans will be noted and further discussed.[92] Where full citations are useful, examples will be from the Pentateuch.

89 LSJ, πᾶς, A III.2, does not use the neuter in their examples of πᾶς meaning "anyone." In D III.2, the neuter is specified to mean "anything" and not "anyone." LSJ does not further specify as to whether "anything" would include an amalgam of human *and* other groups. Jannaris, *An Historical Greek Grammar*, §1177^{b}, p. 315, also notes the use of this neuter adjective to denote "things," while Smyth and Messing concur that masculine and feminine substantives are used for persons and neuter for things in general (*Greek Grammar*, §1023, p. 273). Cf. Boas et al., *Cambridge Grammar*, §26.21, 26.23, pp. 318–319, who do not have a section on this function of πᾶν but do note the well-known function of the neuter to indicate "objects, concepts."

90 Smyth and Messing, *Greek Grammar*, §1058, p. 277.

91 See Appendix 2.1, Table A2.1.

92 The data from Table 4.2 will be dealt with according to each category, leaving out "Gender Disagreement" for an upcoming section of its own.

TABLE 4.2 πᾶν in the LXX

	Occasion of πᾶν in LXX corpus
Refers to persons	(8×)[a] Deut 20:16 οὐ ζωγρήσετε ἀπ' αὐτῶν πᾶν ἐμπνέον
Refers to animals/ inanimate objects	(31×) *Animals:* Gen 30:32 πᾶν διάλευκον καὶ ῥαντὸν ἐν ταῖς αἰξίν Gen 30:33 πᾶν, ὃ ἐὰν μὴ ᾖ ... ἐν ταῖς αἰξὶν καὶ φαιὸν ἐν τοῖς ἀρνάσιν Gen 30:40 πᾶν ποικίλον ἐν τοῖς ἀμνοῖς Lev 11:32 πᾶν, ἐφ' ὃ ἂν ἐπιπέσῃ ἀπ' αὐτῶν τεθνηκότων αὐτῶν Lev 27:32 πᾶν, ὃ ἂν ἔλθῃ ἐν τῷ ἀριθμῷ ὑπὸ τὴν ῥάβδον Num 18:14 πᾶν ἀνατεθεματισμένον ἐν υἱοῖς Ἰσραήλ[b] Deut 12:11 πᾶν ἐκλεκτὸν τῶν δώρων[c] Judg 13:4, 14; Ezek 34:21; 47:9; 2 Esd 7:17[d] *Inanimate objects*: Gen 2:5 πᾶν χλωρόν Exod 10:5 πᾶν τὸ περισσὸν τὸ καταλειφθέν Exod 16:23 πᾶν τὸ πλεονάζον Lev 11:35 πᾶν, ὃ ἂν ἐπιπέσῃ ἀπὸ τῶν θνησιμαίων αὐτῶν ἐπ' αὐτό Lev 13:13 πᾶν λευκόν 1 Kgdms 2:14; 1 Chr 26:28; Isa 19:7(2×); 27:11; Job 40:31a; Prov 3:15; Tob 4:16; 1 Macc 10:41
Generic/ abstract use	(25×) Gen 2:19 πᾶν, ὃ ἐὰν ἐκάλεσεν αὐτὸ Ἀδάμ Judg 7:4B;[e] 1 Kgdms 9:6; 14:7; 23:20; 1 Chron 17:2; Isa 8:12; Dan 9:14; Prov 20:8; Eccl 1:9; 2:10; 8:3; 11:8; Sir 2:4; 25:11a; 42:16a; Jdt 12:14; 1 Esd 4:3; 2 Esd 7:21, 23; 9:13; 3 Macc 3:10, 29; 5:1, 27; 7:9

a This same phrase, πᾶν ἐμπνέον, is found in Josh 10:28, 30, 35, 37, 39, 40; 11:11, 14 (ἓν ἐμπνέον). It is arguable that Judg 7:4B should be included here, as Muraoka, *A Syntax*, §661 cg), does. The phrase πᾶν, ὃν ἐὰν εἴπω πρὸς σέ refers to the selection of humans in context, but it is easy to see how πᾶν entered the tradition, given the that this phrase is repeatedly found in the neuter in the corpus (see Generic/Abstract use in Table 4.2).

b Refers to both animals and objects.

c Refers to both animals and objects.

d Refers to both animals and objects.

e See fn. a above.

TABLE 4.2 πᾶν in the LXX (*cont.*)

	Occasion of πᾶν in LXX corpus
Colloquially neuter[f]	(60×) πᾶν ἀρσενικόν[g] (23×) πᾶν πρωτότοκον[h] (20×) Exod 12:20 πᾶν ζυμωτόν Exod 13:12(2×), 13, 15; 34:19; Num 18:15;[i] Ezek 20:26 πᾶν διανοῖγον μήτραν[j] Lev 18:23(2×) πᾶν τετράπουν Num 18:21; Deut 14:27 πᾶν ἐπιδέκατον Deut 14:20; Ezek 44:31 πᾶν θνησιμαῖον 1 Kgdms 4:36; 2 Kgdms 19:8; Isa 46:3[k]
Gender disagreement	(28×) Gen 1:29; Exod 12:44; 3 Kgdms 8:37; 15:22; 21:15; 4 Kgdms 15:20; 24:14; 25:9; 1 Chron 27:1; 2 Chron 6:28; 19:11(2×); 32:21; Jer 2:20; 13:11; Ezek 20:28; 28:13; 34:6; 36:10; 38:21; Dan 6:15(Θ); 11:37(Θ); Job 20:26; 40:11b; Ruth 4:7; Jdt 4:15; Pss. Sol. 3:8; 8:20
Disputable	(3×) Lev 27:29 πᾶν, ὃ ἂν ἀνατεθῇ ἀπὸ τῶν ἀνθρώπων … θανάτῳ θανατωθήσεται Isa 23:9 ἀτιμάσαι πᾶν ἔνδοξον ἐπὶ τῆς γῆς Esth C:3 πᾶν θαυμαζόμενον ἐν τῇ ὑπ' οὐρανόν

f As based on LSJ unless otherwise noted.

g This adjective is always neuter in the Göttingen LXX (55×) with the one exception of Ezek 16:17. Here it is bound to a feminine noun and does not refer to people. For ἀρσενικόν with πᾶν see Gen 17:10; 34:15, 22, 25; Exod 12:48; 23:17; 34:23; Lev 6:18; Num 1:18; 3:15, 28, 34, 39; 18:10; 26:62; 31:7, 17; Deut 16:16; 20:13; Judg 21:11; 1 Macc 5:28, 35, 51.

h If multiple firstborn are in view, the LXX always renders πρωτοτοκός as neuter. If a singular, specific firstborn is in view, the masculine can be used (cf. e.g., Gen 25:13, 25; 27:19, 32; Exod 4:22; Num 3:2; Deut 21:15, etc.). For πᾶν πρωτότοκον see Exod 11:5; 12:12; 12:29; 13:2; 13:13; 13:15(2×); 34:20; Lev 27:26; Num 3:13(3×), 40, 42; 8:17(2×); 33:4; Deut 15:19; Ps 77:51a; 104:36a.

i Refers to τὰ πρωτότοκα from 15b.

j Referring to τὰ ἀρσενικά.

k κατάλοιπος is sometimes colloquially neuter, and it is so here in Greek Isaiah; cf. 15:9; 21:17.

The data regarding πᾶν in the LXX corpus are quite clear. A phrase in Deut 20:16, which is repeated in Joshua, is the only example where πᾶν does seem to refer to humans. Yet it does so in a highly hyperbolic and expressive context that is not only derived from a Hebrew idiom, but also fits within a specific classification of πᾶν found in the Classical sources. The phrase לא תחיה כל־נשמה, "you will not keep alive anything that breathes," in context, refers to *the people groups* that Israel will "utterly destroy" (החרם תחרימם; v. 17).[93] The phrase כל־נשמה ("anything that breathes") is hyperbolic in that it semantically refers to all living creatures but pragmatically is only concerned with humans. The illocutionary force is that these condemned people groups are to be put to death. The Greek translator seems to replicate this expression and intent. πᾶν ἐμπνέον, "anything breathing," like its Hebrew counterpart refers to all lifeforms, which mirrors a Classical usage of 'πᾶν + participle' that refers to the entirety of creation or life with no eye to specific creatures or their actions. "πᾶν … τὸ ἀναπνέον" (Aristotle, *An. post.* 1.78b, 27) is a nearly parallel example, the rest of which are delineated in Appendix 2.3, Table A2.5. This specific all-encompassing use of 'πᾶν + participle' is not feasible in Exod 22:18 (22:19 LXX).

Of the sixty terms or phrases that are colloquially neuter, forty-nine of those refer to the concepts of either "firstborn" (πᾶν πρωτότοκον) or "males" (πᾶν ἀρσενικόν). The etymological history as to why these terms are perceived as neuter is not important here. The only relevant fact is that they are always neuter. For this reason they are not helpful in determining the intention of the translator in Exod 22:18 (22:19 LXX).

Likewise, the generic uses of πᾶν (25×) shed no light on Ex. These are contexts where nothing concrete is described. This category is well-attested in the Classical and documentary sources (see Appendix 2, Tables A2.3–A2.5).

When there is a concrete object referred to by πᾶν and the gender is determined by the translator, the LXX uses πᾶν to refer to either animals or inanimate objects (31×). This same property will be seen in the inscriptions and papyri. Reading πᾶν as either an animal or object would be the first and most natural reading in Exod 22:18 (22:19 LXX), since there are no colloquially neuter terms, nor specific Hebrew expressions, and the passage is written in a legal genre (law code) that is often known for its precise terminology. Finally, there are a few disputable cases of πᾶν.

---

93 It is also possible that humans and animals are in view on account of the reference to the practice of חרם, which often involved the destruction of an enemy's goods as an offering to God (cf. Josh 6:24). If so, then πᾶν ἐμπνέον neatly fits within the category of 'πᾶν + participle' that refers to all living creatures (see Appendix 2.3, Table A2.5).

Leviticus 27:29 is one such difficult case. In my view the same translational technique employed for כל in Exod 22:18 (22:19 LXX) is likely occurring here in Lev 27:29. That is, the translator is exploiting the Greek gender system in order to avoid translating an unbridled cultic law that leads to the unalterable death of a human, which would not be practicable or legally acceptable in Ptolemaic Egypt.[94] Moreover, note that *only here* in Lev is the imperative not present when rendering the death sentence (θανάτῳ θανατωθήσεται).[95] What could explain this? If the hypotheses of section 2.7 and the present discussion are correct, then the translator of Leviticus is not limiting the authority of this penal clause because he does not need to—it refers to animals.[96]

Besides Lev 27:29, Isa 23:9 and Esth C:3 are both hyperbolic and expressive like Deut 20:16. When the Isaianic translator writes ἀτιμάσαι πᾶν ἔνδοξον ἐπὶ τῆς γῆς, "to dishonour every glorified (thing) on the earth," it is uncertain whether this is meant to refer to people who are characterized by glory or to deeds/objects that are characterized by glory. It could mean both, but given that ἔνδοξοι is used in the masculine in verse 8 to refer to the traders (οἱ ἔμποροι), and is consistently plural (cf. τῶν ἐνδόξων for singular צבי), then the translation of the plural phrase כל־נכבדי־ארץ as the singular πᾶν ἔνδοξον ἐπὶ τῆς γῆς seems to indicate that the traders are not in mind. While this is not perfectly clear, it is obvious that Isa 23:9 is a hyperbolic statement and pertains to a different literary genre from Exod 22:18 (22:19 LXX). Esther C:3 states πᾶν θαυμαζόμενον ἐν τῇ ὑπ' οὐρανόν, "everything marveled at under heaven." This seems to be a case like Deut 20:16 where πᾶν refers to all life or creation indiscriminately. This is an acceptable Classical use.[97]

πᾶν has a variety of distinct functions in the LXX. It is used for animals/things, generic or abstract concepts, colloquially neuter terms, and can refer generically to all life. These categories found in the LXX are the same categories that will be seen in the documentary and literary sources.[98] There are arguably no clear cases of πᾶν referring only to humans. Given only the data in the LXX,

94 That the translator of Leviticus is keenly aware of the πᾶς/πᾶν distinction, see Lev 11:31 and v. 36b compared to v. 32–36a; 15:20 compared to vv. 21–22.

95 It is in the imperative 13× elsewhere and with the same underlying penal verb מות: 20:2, 9–13, 15–16, 27; 24:16–17, 21.

96 A more detailed study on Lev 27:29 is a desideratum and will be undertaken in the future. For the present, the data in this section will support reading πᾶν as referring to an animal in Lev 27:29.

97 See Appendix 2.3, Table A2.5.

98 Cf. Lee, *The Greek*, 248, who claims that all occasions of πᾶς in the Greek Pentateuch fit within typical Greek usage.

Exod 22:18 (22:19 LXX) with πᾶν κοιμώμενον would likely be understood as a basic neuter referring to animals.

4.4.2.2 The Neuter Gender with Human Referents

Muraoka disagrees with this conclusion for 22:18 (22:19 LXX) by noting the use of the neuter throughout the LXX in places where it is used to refer to humans.[99] However, it is not disputed that the neuter can be used of humans in a collectivizing manner, as is clear from the Classical texts.[100] The question is how this neuter function is found with the lemma πᾶς, particularly in combination with participles.[101] Muraoka claims that "in Septuagint Greek, unlike in Classical Greek, this usage [of the neuter] does not require the use of the article nor is confined to the singular."[102] Muraoka's claim that the article does not need to be present for the collective sense of the neuter is contradicted by the present data. According to Appendix 2.3, there are no examples of 'πᾶν + participle' in the collective sense without the article in any texts at least up until the first century CE (where I ended my analysis). The anarthrous examples given by Muraoka are Lev 18:6, Deut 20:16, and the law in Exodus under discussion (22:18 [22:19 LXX]).[103] Deuteronomy 20:16 was already discussed above.

The only other OG example of an anarthrous neuter referring to humans is then as a plural in Lev 18:6:[104] Ἄνθρωπος ἄνθρωπος πρὸς πάντα οἰκεῖα σαρκὸς

99 Muraoka, *A Syntax*, 102–103.

100 See Raphael Kühner, *Ausführliche Grammatik der griechischen Sprache: Satzlehre*, vol. 1, pt. 2 of *Ausführliche Grammatik der griechischen Sprache* (Hannover/Leipzig: Hahnsche Buchhandlung, 1898), 14, stating, "Das Neutrum im Singular von Adjektiven mit vorgesetztem Artikel wird oft in kollektivem Sinne gebraucht; zuweilen auch von Partizipien." This use of the neuter is also seen in later texts: see James Hope Moulton, Wilbert Francis Howard, and Nigel Turner, *A Grammar of New Testament Greek. Vol. III: Syntax*, vol. 3 of *A Grammar of New Testament Greek* (Edinburgh: T&T Clark, 1963), 21, who only gives examples with the article as well (barring Matt 12:6, 41, where μεῖζον and πλεῖον seem to be abstractions rather than parallels to the collective use of the neuter seen elsewhere. Each example also has, arguably, a neuter antecedent). Kühner points out examples of collectives, groups sharing a common trait like infantry or citizens of a particular city. If this use of the neuter were operative, it is hard to see how or why those committing bestial acts would be singled out and categorized in such a way.

101 An example of πᾶν in the collective sense noted by Kühner would be Xenophon, *Cav.* 9.3 with πᾶν τὸ ἱππικὸν ("the whole force").

102 Muraoka, *A Syntax*, 102, fn. 1.

103 Muraoka, *A Syntax*, §20 ee, pp. 102–103). He gives other examples that are plural and articular. These warrant their own discussion, but do not affect the argument at hand.

104 Judg 3:29B would be the only later tradition that uses the qualitative neuter with πᾶν. Jer 9:26SAQ (cf. 32:9BA) is another possible example, though this could be explained in another way. Both texts are discussed in Appendix 2.2.

αὐτοῦ οὐ προσελεύσεται ἀποκαλύψαι ἀσχημοσύνην ("Person by person shall not approach any of the household of his flesh to uncover shame").[105] A brief look at the use of πάντα οἰκεῖα ("any of the household") from Lev shows that it is an idiom in which gender does not play a role. Looking through the literary texts, the plural of πᾶς is found modifying οἰκεῖος in a variety of contexts. The idiom, whether in the masculine or neuter (it does not seem to matter), finds its specific referent(s) based on the surrounding context.[106] So, Lev's employment of this idiom in a non-isomorphic context with the appellation σαρκός indicates that the translator means to refer to those belonging to the kin of the legal subject. This is not equivalent to Ex, which does not employ an idiom, and a straightforward rendering of the text is in play. The neuter is idiomatic in Lev whereas it is by choice in Ex. If this is true, then Exod 22:18 (22:19 LXX) is the only place in the OG (according to the current standard texts) where a neuter form of πᾶς could refer to humans in non-hyperbolic or expansive statements like those described above with Deut 20:16. Certainly, it is the only *law* with such a possible function of πᾶν.[107]

Regarding Exod 22:18 (22:19 LXX), Muraoka states that the neuter is "used when referring to humans in a generic, gender-neutral sense, not to particular humans."[108] This is a surprising claim, since πᾶς invariably obtains this status throughout the LXX Pentateuch in cases involving this adjective.[109] πᾶς always introduces laws or prescriptions referring to humans in general.[110] The translators can even be seen to switch immediately back and forth between πᾶς when referring to humans and πᾶν when referring to animals/objects.[111] An exception could be Lev 11:42(2×), which is an anomalous case where πᾶς could refer

105 Büchner, NETS.

106 It can refer to: one's household (Herodotus, *Hist.* 3.119.2; Callisthenes, *Fr.*, 2b,124,F [neuter but refers to father and sons]); friends (Isaeus, *Pyrrh.* 27); a set of items related to each other (Plato, *Resp.* 491c; Theophrastus, *Caus. plant.* 2.4.12.6–7); one's belongings (Aristotle, *Rhet.* 1331a, 7, line 3 [cf. lines 1–2]; Polybius, *Hist.* 7.9.15).

107 Barring Lev 27:29 which is under the same suspicion as 22:18 (22:19 LXX).

108 *A Syntax*, 102. Ostensibly, Robert Hiebert, *The SBL Commentary on the Septuagint: An Introduction*, ed. Dirk Büchner (Atlanta: SBL Press, 2017), 58, fits into this category as well when he says that the "neuter adjectival form πᾶν [can be] used for a generalizing purpose." However, 22:18 (22:19 LXX) is not mentioned in texts enumerated in his commentary.

109 This is the Classical standard as well. See fn. 89 above.

110 See Exod 12:15, 19, 43; 19:12; 29:37; 30:14, 29; 31:14–15; 35:2; Lev 6:18, 27; 7:15; 11:24, 26–27, 31; 15:10, 19, 21–22, 27; 17:14; 18:29; Num 17:13; 18:11, 13; 19:13–14, 16; 31:19; 35:11, 30; Deut 18:12; 21:23; 22:5; 25:16(2x). The feminine is not used as often as the masculine or neuter to idiomatically refer to a living being: "Bei lebenden Wesen überwiegt nicht nur das Maskulinum über das Femininum, sondern auch das Neutrum über das Femininum" (Meisterhans and Schwyzer, *Grammatik*, §82 A, 1, p. 197).

111 E.g., Lev 11:31 and v. 36b compared to v. 32–36a; 15:20 compared to vv. 21–22.

to animals alone, though the animal referent is made explicit by the context. Despite this passage, that animals can be considered under πᾶς does not mean the opposite, that is, that πᾶν would be read as referring solely to persons. Again, πᾶν arguably never does this in the Septuagint nor in the documentary texts from the time before or around the translation, nor in the literary texts when modifying an anarthrous participle. Given that the masculine πᾶς is the default gender for person *and* things together, animals being subsumed under πᾶς makes sense.[112]

In fact, just before Exod 22:18 (22:19 LXX), the translator does this very thing. Exodus 19:12 includes beasts and humans (cf. v. 13, ἐάν τε κτῆνος ἐάν τε ἄνθρωπος ["whether animal or whether human"]) under the heading πᾶς: πᾶς ὁ ἁψάμενος τοῦ ὄρους θανάτῳ τελευτήσει ("anyone touching the mountain shall meet an untimely demise"). It is also helpful that 19:12 is almost the same syntax, form, and meaning as 22:18 (22:19 LXX). This comparison is strong evidence that, had the translator wanted to indicate both humans and animals in the translation, πᾶς would have sufficed. Perhaps, then, the translator would have added αὐτούς (as per the Göttingen edition) to further indicate that they would both be put to death. At the very least, the translator could have made the apodotic verb plural (e.g., θανατούσθωσαν; cf. Lev 20:16). Even in parallel contexts to this bestiality law such as Lev 20:15–16 or more particularly Deut 27:21 (Ἐπικατάρατος ὁ κοιμώμενος μετὰ παντὸς κτήνους), there are no such interpretive glosses with the neuter. One must assume this is the only case of πᾶν with this use in any of the LXX legal materials, and that without any impetus from the Hebrew text or contextual clues to make clear that this was the intent. These conclusions regarding πᾶν are even more stable when considering the use of πᾶν in the contemporaneous documentary sources.

4.4.2.3 πᾶν in the Papyri and Inscriptions

The use of πᾶν in the papyri and inscriptions proves informative as to how πᾶν would be colloquially perceived at the time of the translation. Given the large deposit of legal documentary texts, or at the very least, semi-formal business, religious, or economic dealings, we can see how πᾶν is used in these linguistically formal and semi-formal registers. The documentary sources are about as clear as one could hope.[113] This data illuminates that πᾶν is arguably not used to refer to humans in this broad expanse of texts when the gender of πᾶς is determined by the author. A close parallel to 22:18 (22:19 LXX) would be

112 Smyth and Messing, *Greek Grammar*, §1058, p. 277.

113 All uses of πᾶν when it is not modified by a gendered noun are included in Appendix 2.1, Table A2.1.

P.Hamb. 1 57.19–23 (160 BCE) with τ⟨ο⟩ θηρευθη[σό]μενον … [ἄγριον] πᾶν, where, if the conjectural text in the lacuna is disregarded, this would be a case where a wild animal is presupposed by πᾶν with a similar syntax (passive participle). If the linguistic register of many of these references is in any way akin to that of the casuistry in Exodus, then πᾶν would be perceived as referring to an animal. One does not find, at least with πᾶν, any correspondence to the articular, collective neuter from the Classical sources, which refers to humans. This is, of course, the same conclusion reached with the LXX data. However, there is an opposition that could be mounted against the reading presented for 22:18 (22:19 LXX) thus far.

4.4.2.4 πᾶν = πάντα in Exodus 22:18 (22:19 LXX)

Some commentators have opted to read πᾶν as a shortened, grammatically "accidental" variation of πάντα (ms.sg.acc. of πᾶς).[114] In other words, πᾶν would be understood to be a 'short form' of πάντα. This is probably the strongest argument against reading πᾶν as a full-fledged neuter in 22:18 (22:19 LXX). An examination of this gender discrepancy is informative. It occurs outside of the biblical corpus in Antipater, *Testimonia et fragmenta*, frag. 62.6, T. Reu. 1.10, and UPZ 1 5.11 (163 BCE). These examples suggest, as Thackeray already notes, that this is not simply a biblical phenomenon.[115] Muraoka comments on this so-called vulgarism, saying, "We note that in every case πᾶν is acc. sg. and mostly followed immediately by a substantive or adjective ending in -ον, which may have led to a confusion of m.acc. καλόν for n. acc. καλόν."[116] He indicates that this pattern is not always the case, as in πᾶν ἄνδρα from 1 Kgdms 11:8B and πᾶν ὑβριστήν from Job 40:11.[117] His explanation, then, seems to be rooted in the prevention of confusion concerning a term's gender. Thackeray likewise gives an explanation: "Assimilation of the masc. to the neuter form of the accusative is not surprising in the κοινή: the analogy of μέγαν and the preference for accusatives in ν (such as νύκταν, εὐγενῆν) might be responsible for the vulgarism."[118] He goes on to cite Gen 1:29 (πᾶν χόρτον σπόριμον σπεῖρον σπέρμα, ὅ, "any herbage, sowable, seeding seed which" [NETS]) and its use of the neuter participle and relative pronoun to indicate that "πᾶν is regarded as a true neuter."[119] What he means by "true neuter" is not particularly clear, as this seems to be a case where

114 Wevers, *Notes*, 350. For a discussion of this feature see Henry J. Thackeray, *A Grammar of the Old Testament in Greek* (Cambridge: Cambridge University Press, 1909), 174–175.

115 Cf. Thackeray, *A Grammar*, 143–174.

116 Muraoka, *A Syntax*, 661, cg.

117 Muraoka, *A Syntax*, fn. 4.

118 Thackeray, *A Grammar*, 174.

119 Thackeray, *A Grammar*, 174.

the text is grammatically neuter yet is still understood to be referring to the masculine χόρτον. There is no semantic function to the neuter. The participle and relative pronoun seem simply to be participating in the construction. Still, Thackeray proposes on the basis of Gen 1:29, that "It seems possible therefore in the remaining passages to explain πᾶν as a neuter in apposition with the masc. substantive, a sort of extension of πᾶν ἀρσενικόν ... though it is simpler on the whole to regard it in all these passages as = πάντα."[120]

While both Muraoka and Thackeray's explanations are helpful and possible, they do not help determine how to understand Exod 22:18 (22:19 LXX). Neither author provides solid criteria for *when* this kind of construction is used and if such criteria fit 22:18 (22:19 LXX). The following chart delineates all occasions of this phenomenon.

TABLE 4.3 Cases in which, according to critical editions, πᾶν occurs for πάντα[a]

Potential syntactic difficulty for πάντα	**Cases where πᾶν = πάντα**
List	Gen 1:29; Exod 12:44; 1 Kgdms 11:8B; 3 Kgdms 8:37; 21:15; 4 Kgdms 15:20; 24:14; 25:9; 1 Chron 27:1(2×); 2 Chron 6:28; 19:11(2×); Ezek 20:28; 34:6; 36:10; Dan 6:15(Θ); Antipater, *Test. fr.* frag. 62.6
Infinitive construction	Ruth 4.7; Jdt 4:15
Two proximal adjectives modifying noun	3 Kgdms 15:22; 2 Chron 32:21; Ezek 28:13;[b] Pss. Sol. 3:8[c]
Unclear	Ezek 38:21; Job 40:11b; T. Reu. 1.10; UPZ 1 5.11 (163 BCE).

a Hiebert, *The SBL Commentary*, 58, includes P.Mil. 1.2.27 and UPZ 1.99, 1,1. 22–23; 2.45 in the category of πᾶν paired with an incongruently gendered item, but these are examples of τὸ πᾶν, and, as has been stated above, should not be included in this discussion due to gender not always being at play with this phrase.
b Could also fit in "infinitive."
c This could also fit in "list."

120 Thackeray, *A Grammar*, 175.

This table only demarcates when πᾶν = πάντα in what scholars believe to be the oldest recoverable form of OG, as presented in the current critical editions. There are a few places outside of the current critical edition texts where this same phenomenon occurs, and seemingly for the same kinds of reasons listed above.[121] There seem to be, generally, three such reasons for the occurrence of this construction, all of which suggest 22:18 (22:19 LXX) is not an example where πᾶν = πάντα. These are:

(1) the pairing of πᾶν with a well-defined masculine noun. By well-defined it is meant that the reader would know that πᾶν is being matched with an incongruently gendered noun.
(2) A syntactically obtuse construction where παντα could be perceived as either ms.acc.sg. or nt.nom./acc.pl.
(3) The author did not want to include an article.

These commonalities among the texts help to explain where this construction might occur and push the discussion a bit further than previous commentators.

4.4.2.4.1 *Criterion 1*

Probably the most significant aspect of this grammatical oddity is that when πᾶν = πάντα, πᾶν always modifies a noun that is uniformly masculine and very common in the Greek language.[122] Anyone versed in Greek would know the gender of these terms. The words πᾶν modifies are as follows:

ἀνήρ = 1 Kgdms 11:8; Pss. Sol. 3:8
ἄρτος = T.Reu. 1.10
βουνός = 3 Kgdms 15:22; Ezek 34:6
λίθος = Ezek 28:13

121 Jer 2:20 (see comments on Ezek 34:6); 13:11 (οἶκος; list); Ezek 20:28 (see comments on Ezek 34:6); Dan 11:37(Θ) (θεός; string/list of ἐπί phrases); Pss. Sol. 8:20 according to Rahlfs' text has πᾶν σοφόν whereas it is πάντα σοφόν in Robert B. Wright, *Psalms of Solomon: A Critical Edition of the Greek Text* (New York: Bloomsbury Academic & Professional, 2007), 118. It is the opinion of the NETS translators that Rahlfs is to be preferred over Wright (see Kenneth Atkinson, "To the Reader of Psalms of Solomon," in *A New English Translation of the Septuagint and the Other Greek Translations Traditionally Included under That Title*, ed. Albert Pietersma and Benjamin G. Wright [Oxford: Oxford University Press, 2007], 763). In this instance, given that πᾶν = πάντα is found almost exclusively with masculine nouns that do not have a neuter counterpart (the only exception being δυνατόν; see discussion below), πᾶν σοφὸν ἐν βουλῇ should probably be understood as a true neuter phrase, as in "every wise (matter) in plan." It is not important, then, whether it is original to the translation or a matter of text-reception history. It does not fit the criteria. Even so, if this were a case of πᾶν = πάντα, then it might occur in order to aid in the stichometry of the poem.

122 The only exception to the noun rule is the adjective δυνατόν, which is discussed below. Some of these terms also gain a neuter form in the Byzantine period. Job 20:26 and πᾶν σκότος should not be included in this discussion, since σκότος is definitively neuter elsewhere in Greek Job (e.g., 15:30; 18:18; 19:8; 24:14a) and is found in the neuter frequently before and within the LXX.

λόγος = Ruth 4:7; 1 Chron 27:1(2×)
ὄγκος = Antipater, *Test. fr.* frag. 62.6
οἰκέτης = Exod 12:44
οἶκος = 4 Kgdms 25:9; Ezek 36:10; Jdt 4:15
ὁρισμός = Dan 6:15(Θ)
πολεμιστής = 2 Chron 32:21
πόνος = 3 Kgdms 8:37; 2 Chron 6:28; 2 Chron 19:11(2×)
τέκτων = 4 Kgdms 24:14
τόπος = UPZ 1 5.11 (163 BCE)
ὑβριστής = Job 40.11b
υἱός = 3 Kgdms 21:15
φόβος = Ezek 38:21
χόρτος = Gen 1:29
The only exception is, possibly, δυνατόν in 4 Kgdms 15:20:

> καὶ ἐξήνεγκεν Μαναημ τὸ ἀργύριον ἐπὶ τὸν Ισραηλ, ἐπὶ πᾶν δυνατὸν ἰσχύι, δοῦναι τῷ βασιλεῖ τῶν Ἀσσυρίων, πεντήκοντα σίκλους τῷ ἀνδρὶ τῷ ἑνί
>
> And Manaem brought out the money against Israel, against every powerful man with strength, to give to the king of the Assyrians, fifty shekels for one man.[123]

It is uncertain if this instance should be classified as a case of πᾶν = πάντα or as a true neuter functioning to qualitatively describe the men of Israel (i.e., "every powerful one"). If it is the latter, this is the only case where πᾶν is used this way in the texts of the critical editions. The Brooke-McLean edition cites BANhinv as including πᾶν with the rest of the manuscripts reading πάντα.[124] Should the consistent pattern of pairing πᾶν with a masculine noun when πᾶν = πάντα dissuade from reading πᾶν as original here? It is difficult to make a judgment call. Added to the trouble of this case is the fact that this verse falls within the sections of Kingdoms denoted "Kaige," which could further complicate its dating and translational tenor. In any case, if this is an example of πᾶν = πάντα, then the fact that ἐπὶ πᾶν δυνατὸν ἰσχύι is in apposition to ἐπὶ τὸν Ισραηλ is probably enough contextual warrant for the reader to understand that a masculine noun is being modified (through apposition), as is in line with criterion 1.[125] Note the inclusion of the article before Ισραηλ, which is not a

---

123 NETS.

124 Alan England Brooke and Norman Maclean, eds., *The Old Testament in Greek, Volume 2: The Latter Historical Books. Part Two: I–II Kings*, vol. 2, pt. 2 of *The Old Testament in Greek* (Cambridge: Cambridge University Press, 1930), 350.

125 Likewise in 2 Chron 32:21, πᾶν δυνατὸν πολεμιστήν, despite δυνατόν, would surely be understood as the construction in question due to πολεμιστήν.

common trait when translating על ישראל.[126] The translator wanted to make certain the grammatical case of Ισραηλ. This would then ensure that sg.acc. πᾶν would be read in apposition to ἐπὶ τὸν Ισραηλ rather than Ισραηλ being declined differently and potentially being understood as referring to something else. πάντα δυνατόν is found elsewhere in 1 Esd. 4:49 without the πᾶν = πάντα construction.[127] Given the approximately twenty-nine other occurrences of πᾶν = πάντα recorded, 4 Kgdms 15:20 should probably be considered within the rule that this construction operates with a masculine noun, if indeed it is a case of πᾶν = πάντα. Additionally, if criterion 2 is valid, namely, that πᾶν = πάντα is used in situations where πάντα could be perceived as neuter plural in order to remove that ambiguity, then one could ostensibly see why that would happen here. The verse could also make sense if πάντα were neuter plural: "And Manaem brought out the money against/with regards to[128] Israel, against/with regards to all things (occurring/or to be paid for), in order to give strong ability to the king of the Assyrians." In this reading δυνατὸν ἰσχύι would be the object of δοῦναι. In any case, whatever the explanation for δυνατόν in 15:20, it is the only place where a substantival adjective is found in the πᾶν = πάντα construction. The rest of the examples are always masculine nouns.

In comparison, Exod 22:18 (22:19 LXX) is a substantival participle (πᾶν κοιμώμενον), of which the gender is determined by the author, and there are no other surrounding contextual clues to lead one to conclude otherwise. There is no reference to a masculine noun that would indicate to the reader that πᾶν here is meant to represent πάντα.[129] κοιμάω in the medio-passive is likewise attested with all genders and is used to refer to animals or humans "lying."[130] One would not presuppose a masculine subject here. The only clue to the gender would be the attributive adjective πᾶν. Likewise, there are no cases of πᾶν = πάντα with a participle in the texts of the critical editions. Exodus 22:18 (22:19 LXX) does not then fit the first criterion for when πᾶν = πάντα.

---

126 Anarthrous: 3 Kgdms 1:34–35; 4:1; 6:1; 9:5; 12:20; 15:25(2×), 33; 16:8, 16(2×), 23, 29; 19:16; 20:26; 22:52; 4 Kgdms 1:18a; 3:27; 9:3 (translates אל ישראל); Articular: 3 Kgdms 2:11; 4 Kgdms 9:6. This last example (9:6) is similarly an appositional phrase like 4 Kgdms 15:20.

127 1 Kgdms 14:52, likewise, but with ἀνήρ as an additional gender clarification.

128 It is debatable whether "against" is the best translation of ἐπί with the accusative here, as per Brooke-Maclean.

129 It could be argued that αὐτούς is the masculine that signals πᾶν = πάντα. This is discussed below.

130 E.g., animal referent: Aesop, *Fab.* 130.1; 211,1 κοιμώμενον (snake); Aesop, *Fab.* 137.1(2×) κοιμώμενον (dog; cf. *Fab.* (dodecasyllabi) 185aliter); 237.1 (dragon); 254.1 (hare). Philoxenus, *Fr.* fr. 139* κοιμώμενον (lion). Human referent: Plato, *Ep.* 7.326b κοιμώμενον; Polybius, *Hist.* 6.36.4 κοιμώμενον (subject implied from previous lines).

4.4.2.4.2 *Criterion 2*

Upon evaluating the various cases of πᾶν = πάντα, one cannot help but puzzle over why the translators chose to employ this construction in one place over against another. For example, Gen 1:29 reads καὶ εἶπεν ὁ θεός Ἰδοὺ δέδωκα ὑμῖν πᾶν χόρτον σπόριμον σπεῖρον σπέρμα ("And God said, 'See I have give you any herbage, sowable, seeding seed'").[131] Here the construction occurs. Yet later in the same sentence and once again as an accusative object of the same verb (δέδωκα), Gen reads καὶ πάντα χόρτον χλωρὸν εἰς βρῶσιν ("and every green grass for food"). Why did the first instance require πᾶν but not the next? Is there a requirement, or is its use simply at the whim of the author? Could it be both? It is interesting to note that, arguably, across every example of πᾶν = πάντα, this construction occurs in places where πάντα could legitimately be read as nt.pl.acc. rather than ms.sg.acc. In Gen 1:29, had the translator written δέδωκα ὑμῖν πάντα χόρτον, the text could read "I have given to you all things, (namely), grass. …" Later in the sentence, however, the syndetic καὶ πάντα χόρτον includes καὶ before πάντα, which makes clear that πάντα is to be taken as modifying χόρτον. πάντα as nt.pl.acc. would be nonsensical here.

Table 4.3 points out some similar syntactic situations where the construction occurs. Quite often it is when πάντα is in a list of items, in which it seems that πάντα could have been perceived as a separate item in the list rather than as an adjectival modifier. Another pattern is when πᾶν is within an infinitive construction. For example, Ruth 4:7 reads:

> καὶ τοῦτο τὸ δικαίωμα ἔμπροσθεν ἐν τῷ Ἰσραὴλ ἐπὶ τὴν ἀγχιστείαν καὶ ἐπὶ τὸ ἀντάλλαγμα τοῦ στῆσαι πάν λόγον· καὶ ὑπελύετο ὁ ἀνὴρ τὸ ὑπόδημα αὐτοῦ
>
> And this was the statute in former times in Israel concerning the right of inheritance and concerning exchange:[132] to confirm every agreement, a man would take off his sandal

It is plausible that, had the translator left πάντα, a reader could understand the text as "And this was the statute … in order for everything (i.e., the pertaining matters) to be confirmed (as) an agreement." By using the shorthand πᾶν = πάντα, which ostensibly any reader at the time would know, this reading is avoided. Of course, this is speculation, but the continual ambiguity of whether πάντα is ms.sg.acc. or nt.pl.acc. is seemingly always present in these texts. Another area of interest is when two adjectives are modifying a noun, in

131 Hiebert, NETS.

132 Note the differing punctuation than the Göttingen edition.

which one imagines πάντα could also have been seen as a separate substantival adjective rather than as an attributive adjective. One example would be 3 Kgdms 15:22: καὶ ᾠκοδόμησεν ἐν αὐτοῖς ὁ βασιλεὺς Ασα πᾶν βουνὸν Βενιαμιν καὶ τὴν σκοπιάν ("and king Asa built with them all the hill of Benjamin and the look-out"). Perhaps, here too, πάντα could have been construed as neuter plural and thus obscure the meaning by creating another object of the verb, namely, "he built ... all things, the hill of Benjamin, and the lookout." There might be multiple reasons for this construction in some cases.[133] The common denominator is the syntactic ambiguity involving πάντα in each case.

While certain texts do not fit into any specific category, the same principle applies in that each text could genuinely read πάντα as nt.pl.acc. It is also important to compare πᾶν βουνὸν ὑψηλόν in Ezek 34:6 to Ezek 20:28. These two texts are closely paralleled, but 20:28 does not include the construction. So, barring some aspect of ancient Greek that would be more obvious to a native speaker, based on the comparison of Ezek 20:28 to 34:6, it would probably be best to consider the construction πᾶν = πάντα as a matter of choice, to be employed judiciously if an author saw fit, and likely if the instance matched Criteria 1–3.

With respect to syntax, then, πᾶν = πάντα seems to occur mainly in places where πᾶν provides fewer interpretive options than πάντα. Perhaps the accumulation of this construction in the Septuagint is due to the generally isomorphic serial fidelity found in the LXX, which led to more cases where πάντα was problematic. In any case, the law in Exod 22:18 (22:19 LXX) represents a simple sentence with no other interpretive options for πάντα, should that have been included.[134]

4.4.2.4.3 *Criterion 3*

All cases of πᾶν = πάντα do not include an article, except for UPZ 1 5.11. Perhaps this should be reason enough to claim that UPZ 1 5.11 is a scribal error that unintentionally mimics the construction in question. Why the article is absent in these texts is also not obvious. The article would clear up most ambiguity in each of these attestations. It is also strange that πᾶν = πάντα is not found in the mass of documentary papyri and inscriptions more than once (UPZ 1 5), and that single text itself is debatable. It is found outside the LXX corpus in T. Reu. 1.10 and Antipater, *Testimonia et fragmenta*, frag. 62.6. Perhaps it is again the translational nature of the Septuagint that informs the absence of

133 For example, 4 Kgdms 15:20 could be categorized as a list or perhaps as a place where the object of the preposition could be confused.

134 See *Interpretive Possibilities: 'πάντα/πᾶν + Participles'* below.

the article: πᾶν = πάντα provides an opportunity to stay closer to the source text by not adding the article. This is not to say that translators do not add the article frequently but rather that they have possibly exploited something from Hellenistic diction that suited their translational aims.

Should, then, the anarthrous state of πᾶν κοιμώμενον serve as evidence for πᾶν = πάντα occurring in Exod 22:18 (22:19 LXX)? Perhaps. Though, as Kühner points out, in Classical Greek the neuter article would be included with the adjective in order to signify that a collective reading is intended (e.g., πᾶν τὸ κοιμώμενον μετὰ κτήνους, "any animal-bedder").[135] By not including the article, at least by Classical standards, the translator avoids this potential misreading.[136] Additionally, the documentary example Thackeray provides has an article, so it seems as though the article is not an absolute determining factor for this construction, provided UPZ 1 5 is not simply a scribal error.[137] Likewise, syntactically similar situations to Exod 22:18 (22:19 LXX) in the LXX are both articular and anarthrous.[138]

There are a few passages where πᾶν arguably represents a true neuter as opposed to πᾶν = πάντα. These need not be discussed here.[139] It is instead helpful to ask whether there are other ways that πᾶν κοιμώμενον in 22:18 (22:19 LXX) could be read. An in-depth analysis of 'πάντα/πᾶν + medio-passive participle ending in -μενον'[140] proves that not to be the case.

4.4.2.5 Interpretive Possibilities: 'πάντα/πᾶν + Participles'

If πᾶν κοιμώμενον were a case of πᾶν = πάντα, and if this construction might be used when πάντα could be misread as nt.pl.acc., what would it be about 'πάντα + medio-passive participle ending in -μενον' that would necessitate the change from πάντα to πᾶν?

The only potential interpretive option in 22:18 (22:19 LXX) that would be excluded by this change would be reading πάντα as the neuter plural

135 Kühner, *Ausführliche Grammatik*, 14.

136 Muraoka, *Syntax*, 102, fn. 1, believes that Septuagint Greek does not follow exclusive categories as does Classical Greek in this respect. This has been contested in the present work. For the article's addition to similar syntactical situations see 33:7 and 35:24.

137 P.Paris 37.10–11 (163 BCE): ἐρευνήσαν[τ]ες οὖν πᾶν τὸν τόπον οὐθὲν εὗρον.

138 For anarthrous see Num 18:14 (πᾶν ἀνατεθεματισμένον ἐν υἱοῖς Ισραηλ σοὶ ἔσται); for articular see Isa 19:7; Eccl 11:8; 1 Macc 10:41; for definite see Gen 30:33; 1 Kgdms 9:6.

139 See Appendix 2.2: πᾶν as a True Neuter Instead of πᾶν = πάντα.

140 While this descriptor is cumbersome, it is important to maintain since participles ending in -μενον occupy a unique spot where the participle can function as both masculine and neuter accusative as well as neuter nominative. There are, then, more interpretive options and potentially confusing syntactic permutations because of this.

adverbial object of κοιμώμενον,[141] i.e., "one lying with a domesticated animal *in all ways*." However, an analysis of the primary sources confirms that 'πάντα + medio-passive participle with -μενον' would likely construe πάντα as a neuter plural only under specific circumstances. Appendix 2.3, Table A2.2 lists the cases when πάντα functions as the subject or object of the verbal action of the singular medio-passive participle ending in -μενον. While the reservoir of examples leaves something to be desired, these texts do suggest that there would be nothing syntactically unclear about the role of πάντα in 'πάντα + medio-passive participle ending in -μενον' that would lead to using πᾶν = πάντα. Had the translator wanted to make clear that πάντα is the subject of κοιμώμενον, the article simply needed to be added to make it so (i.e., πάντα τὸν κοιμώμενον). This is the way to make known that πάντα (ms.sg.acc.) is functioning as the subject of the participle. This pattern does not hold when πᾶν precedes this same form of participle.[142] The significance of this article's inclusion and placement is seen especially when comparing texts using πάντα and βουλόμαι (see Appendix 2.3, Table A2.2), where anarthrous cases assume πάντα to be the object of the participle, but in arthrous cases it functions as the subject. This is a clear-cut distinction.

Therefore, since πᾶν κοιμώμενον does not fit into the typical categories for πάντα = πᾶν, and since 'πάντα + medio-passive participle ending in -μενον' is a syntactically clear expression—especially since the simple addition of an article seems always to indicate that πάντα is the subject of the participle—πᾶν κοιμώμενον should be excluded from the grammatical "vulgarism" argument.[143] The translator of Exodus shows no hesitation in adding articles (as the very next verse does with זבח = ὁ θυσιάζων), so any claim of a desire for isomorphism should be disregarded. This conclusion can be substantiated even further when looking at genuine cases of 'πᾶν + sg. medio-passive participle ending in -μενον' in the literary and documentary sources. In these instances πᾶν *always* functions as the subject of the participle and *never* as the object or adverbial object of the participle.[144] There is, then, only one way to understand πᾶν κοιμώμενον according to Greek standards. Moreover, when extending the data to include all instances of πᾶν with a participle, πᾶν always functions as the subject of the participle.[145] This, then, seems to be an absolute rule in the Greek language

141 πάντα as pl.nom.nt. could not be the subject of the participle because their number would be incongruent—a trait not found in the literary texts.

142 See Appendix 2.3, Table A2.3.

143 As Muraoka does (*Syntax*, 102).

144 See Appendix 2.3, Table A2.3.

145 See Appendix 2.3, Tables A2.4–A2.5.

(at least up until the first century BCE).[146] Exodus 22:18 (22:19 LXX) fits into one of the analyzed categories ('πᾶν followed by anarthrous participle') and every case indicates that πᾶν is easily read as the verbal subject of the participle ending in -μενον.[147] Note as well that there are no examples of this kind of construction referring to humans, metaphorically or otherwise. A good example is Hermarchus, *Fragments*, fr. 34, line 102, with πᾶν κτεινόμενον where πᾶν is simply assumed to refer to animals, despite using a verb that is often paired with human referents.[148]

It is apparent that when using πᾶν with an anarthrous participle in the Classical and Post-classical periods, humans are never the sole referent of such a construction. In fact, of the countless examples, there are just a few (from Josephus) that use πᾶν with a participle to refer to humans—but all of these occasions are with the article.[149] The article activates the classical collectivizing usage and is not equivalent to the anarthrous case of Exod 22:18 (22:19 LXX).[150] The data surveyed in this project distinguish between the semantics of how πᾶν is colloquially paired with participles in the Greek language in the Classical period and the centuries following (up until the Common Era). There are enough examples to come to a substantial conclusion: πᾶν does not refer to humans alone when colloquially paired with an anarthrous participle. The article seems to be required for the collective sense.

It is worth mentioning that there are some cases of 'πᾶν +participle' where πᾶν refers generically to all living beings.[151] When πᾶν refers to living creatures in this construction, it is always in a generic and all-encompassing manner. It is a means of totalizing the entirety of living beings, not referring to specific subcategories and their behaviors. This use is in fact what seems to happen with πᾶν ἐμπνέον, "anything that breathes," in the previously discussed example of Deut 20:16.[152] This usage is excluded from Exod 22:18 (22:19 LXX) as it

146 The present volume does not include examples where πᾶν modifies a neuter noun with a participle. Even with a neuter noun, πᾶν seems to still always functions as the subject of the participle. This data is not included due to spatial restraints.

147 See Appendix 2.3, Table A2.3.

148 See Gillian Clark, trans., *Ancient Commentators on Aristotle* (London: Bloomsbury Academic, 2000), 35: "Ruthless killing of all harmful creatures, and protection of everything which was useful for destroying them, worked together to provide absence of fear."

149 E.g., Josephus, *J. W.* 3.463 with πᾶν τὸ νεωτερίζον. For a discussion of these texts see Appendix 2.3, Table A2.5.

150 Perhaps a case could be made that it is definiteness that activates the collective use (cf., e.g., John 6:37, 39; 17:2).

151 See Appendix 2.3, Table A2.5.

152 Note the similar phrase in Aristotle, *An. post.* 1.78b.27 with "πᾶν … τὸ ἀναπνέον." Deut 20:16 (and the phrase's repetition elsewhere) is the only instance the present author has found

would be nonsensical in that context: to put to death "every creature (human or animal) that lies with a domesticated animal" (πᾶν κοιμώμενον μετὰ κτήνους) would then be stating that normal animals in the flock that are reproducing with each other should be killed. This is hardly a tenable reading.

Therefore, having analyzed every single unequivocal attestation of 'πᾶν + sg. participle' in the relevant time period, it is clear that (1) πᾶν always functions as the subject of the participle it modifies and (2) πᾶν refers to objects/animals, generic abstractions, or to all living creatures together when paired with a participle. It does not refer solely to humans in a qualitative/collectivizing manner without the article. There are only a few such attestations with the article. It seems clear that Greeks speakers paired πᾶν with participles in these particular ways and not in others. Consequently, the most plausible conclusion is that there would be nothing strange or ambiguous about the meaning of πᾶν κοιμώμενον in Exodus, and it would be read in a straightforward manner as referring to animals. This is even clearer when it is recognized that κοιμάω is a verb regularly used of animals.[153]

4.4.2.6 Translating with ἀποκτείνω instead of θανατόω, τελευτάω, or ἀποθνήσκω

Another piece of translation-technical evidence supports the conclusion made about πᾶν. This is the choice to render מות יומת with θανάτῳ ἀποκτενεῖτε. ἀποκτείνω only translates Hiphil forms of מות elsewhere in Exodus (1:16; 4:24; 16:3; 17:3), and the Hophal יומת finds various translations in the Covenant Code that I have already discussed.[154] Considering that ἀποκτείνω generally functions

---

pragmatically referring to only humans within any Greek discourse. This is apparently not a way Greeks hyperbolically or metaphorically expressed themselves. This data presses against Muraoka's claim that this phrase is an example of the neuter referring to humans without the article (*Syntax*, §20, ee, p. 102). This text is using the phrase that refers semantically to all creatures in a pragmatic way that refers to humans. Semantically, the phrase refers to all creatures, which is a stock way Greeks used 'πᾶν + participle' in the source materials. Alternatively, if the concept of חרם described here included the slaying of animals, the phrase would fit neatly into typical Greek use of 'πᾶν + participle' as documented in this work.

153 See LSJ, κοιμάω, II.1; CGL §7. It may be that, due to the translator's attempt to represent the *Vorlage* on a superficial level (i.e., the concept of "lying down" present in the Hebrew and Greek terms), there would be better terms for animal copulation. Even so, this does not mean that the translation was not clear in its meaning.

154 Exod 21:29 might render with ἀναιρέω because ἀποκτείνω is used in Greek law for homicide that can be performed with various degrees of causality and intermediation. The verb may have been read with the ox's owner as the subject (who killed via the ox), especially because there is a sudden and unspecified switch in verbal subject here. ἀναιρέω helps to remove this ambiguity and more graphically describe the action of goring.

as the active form of ἀποθνήσκω, one might suppose all that is occurring here is that the translator has decided to render the passive מות יומת as an active phrase.[155] However, in codified Greek law ἀποθνήσκω and ἀποκτείνω are used differently and are not synonymous, as was laid out in Chapter 2 (see particularly section 2.2.1). Moreover, the translator renders מות יומת with the active θανάτῳ τελευτάτω in 21:16–17, so why not a translation like that here?

If πᾶν were understood to be in the accusative case, it would normally require a transitive verb. This would then explain the choice of ἀποκτείνω rather than ἀποθνήσκω or τελευτάω which are both intransitive verbs. But this is too quick a judgment. The translator could have simply chosen θανατόω for this purpose, which would be in keeping with previous translations in Exod 21. One might expect that the translator would have simply translated πᾶς κοιμώμενος μετὰ κτήνους θανάτῳ θανατούσθω in order to avoid any ambiguity and to keep in line with previous translations. Even πάντα τὸν κοιμώμενον μετὰ κτήνους θανάτῳ θανατοῦτε would have been perfectly clear. The translator seems to have felt the need to translate with ἀποκτείνω. This need probably explains why the translator has chosen to render the apodosis in the second person instead of the typical third person. The future passive or passive imperative are not options for the transitory verb ἀποκτείνω. From here the data presented in sections 2.2–2.5 come into play, which demonstrated that ἀποκτείνω/κτείνω occur frequently in Classical Greek legal documents, *but not as the formal death penalty*. In law codes, these terms only refer to homicide or on-the-spot slayings. If ἀποκτείνω would be understood by a Greek reader as an on-the-spot slaying and not as the formal death penalty, then this lends credence to the interpretation of πᾶν being a generic neuter indicating animals or things and not humans.

Generally speaking, there would be no issue slaying an animal without regard to the governing bodies. Those under the sentence of death, on the other hand, needed to be brought before the Ptolemaic authorities. Anyone trained in Greek and Greek law would know that ἀποκτείνω would not refer to the formal death penalty here. It is possible, of course, assuming that πᾶν somehow did refer to humans, that ἀποκτείνω would refer to killing someone engaged in bestiality immediately and without recourse to the authorities. But again, if Ptolemaic law is in the background of the translation, this would likely not be a possible outcome.[156] It is better to take πᾶν and ἀποκτείνω together as evidence for what the original translator intended, namely, to create a prescription about killing an animal. ἀποκτείνω can be used this way in Greek legal language, though finding laws about killing animals is difficult since few either

155 LSJ, ἀποκτείνω, 1.

156 See section 4.4.4.

have survived or were ever legislated. Animal death was not an overly pressing matter.[157] Herodotus, mimicking typical Greek legal syntax and terminology, does refer to an Egyptian law on this subject:

> τὸ δ᾽ ἄν τις τῶν θηρίων τούτων ἀποκτείνῃ, ἢν μὲν ἑκών, θάνατος ἡ ζημίη, ἢν δὲ ἀέκων, ἀποτίνει ζημίην τὴν ἂν οἱ ἱρέες τάξωνται. ὃς δ᾽ ἂν ἶβιν ἢ ἴρηκα ἀποκτείνῃ, ἤν τε ἑκὼν ἤν τε ἀέκων, τεθνάναι ἀνάγκη.
>
> Whoever kills one of these creatures intentionally is punished with death; if he kills accidentally, he pays whatever penalty the priests appoint. Whoever kills an ibis or a hawk, intentionally or not, must die for it.[158]
>
> HERODOTUS, *Hist.* 2.65.5

In this excerpt we can see both Herodotus's proper employment of terminology for the formal death penalty (θάνατος ἡ ζημίη and τεθνάναι) and the use of ἀποκτείνω for an on-the-spot and informal slaying of the sacred wild animals. This example is only meant to show that ἀποκτείνω can be used to refer to slaying animals within Greek legal discourse.

All these data together suggest that ἀποκτείνω would not be perceived as a formal proclamation of the death penalty from a Greek legal perspective.

4.4.2.7 The Non-use of the Third Person Imperative

In Exod 22:18 (22:19 LXX) the translator renders with the future tense ἀποκτενεῖτε whereas in other instances the imperative is used when there are no alternatives presented to the death penalty. The use of the imperative was a specific trait of Ptolemaic legal syntax.[159] Here in 22:18 (22:19 LXX), the use of the future tense suggests that the translator did not have the death penalty in mind. If the translator felt the need to couch the laws with the death penalty by means of the deregulating third person imperative everywhere else, then one would certainly expect it here. But the future tense is chosen, which suggests the translator was not worried that this law would be read as the death penalty within a Greek legal framework.

---

157 See p. 219 below.

158 Herodotus (Godley, LCL).

159 See section 2.7.

4.4.2.8 Questioning the Inclusion of αὐτούς as Representative of the OG in the Göttingen Edition

Given the preceding translation-technical analysis, it seems prudent to re-evaluate whether αὐτούς belongs to the original translation. The pronoun is problematic to the interpretation taken so far due to its masculine gender. Many witnesses do not include it.[160] The addition of a pronoun like αὐτούς is not uncharacteristic of the translator (e.g., 18:21; cf. 22:3 [22:4 LXX] for αὐτά),[161] and should not be considered outside of the translator's typical translation technique. In Wevers's *Text History*, Exod 22:18 (22:19 LXX) with αὐτούς is among the list of texts *sub obelo* that have witnesses that have removed the term in question.[162] Wevers notes that A seems to have affinities with prehexaplaric revisional activity towards MT,[163] which could include the omission of αὐτούς found in the traditions. The omission of αὐτούς finds a high degree of quantitative support among the obelized items found in Wevers' list.[164] Wevers seems to include αὐτούς in OG due to his assumption that the traditions with its omission were correcting towards MT. If the aforementioned internal translation claims are justified, however, then αὐτούς very well may be a later addition that corrects towards the meaning of MT, but not as to represent MT in a lexically quantitative manner. This would coincide with the fact that, as Wevers himself states, "The text tradition tends to expand the text as it left the hands of the translator."[165]

It should not be argued that αὐτούς was added because it is somehow more eloquent Greek, since, as Wevers claims, "In good Greek style a pronoun is better left out" when the antecedent is nearby.[166] The removal of the pronoun in other textual traditions might then fit under stylistic changes rather than changes based on recensional activity towards the Hebrew parent text. However, Wevers claims that αὐτούς is included in order to indicate that both man and beast are to be put to death, as per the parallel command in

160 A F M^{txt} *oI C''* 118′-537 106 458 30′-$85'^{txt}$-130^{txt}-343′ z 18 46 55^{c} 76′ 424 426 646 Arm, according to the Göttingen apparatus.

161 αὐτούς also functions as nothing more than a personal pronoun (Jannaris, *An Historical Greek Grammar*, 351, §1421, stating that αὐτός "serves as a mere personal pronoun" in its oblique cases).

162 Wevers, *Text History*, 37.

163 Wevers, *Text History*, 40.

164 Wevers, *Text History*, 36–39.

165 Wevers, *Text History*, 238.

166 John William Wevers, "PreOrigen Recensional Activity in the Greek Exodus," in *Studien zur Septuaginta—Robert Hanhart zu Ehren: aus Anlass seines 65. Geburtstages*, ed. Detlef Fraenkel, Udo Quast, and John W. Wevers (Göttingen: Vandenhoeck & Ruprecht, 1990), 136; cf. 137.

Leviticus.[167] The addition is thus intertextual and exegetical in his view. A close parallel text in Num 8:17 shows that neuter πᾶν can later be referred to with the masculine αὐτούς: πᾶν πρωτότοκον ἐν γῇ Αἰγύπτῳ, ἡγίασα αὐτοὺς ἐμοί (cf. 3:15). Here πᾶν πρωτότοκον is colloquially neuter (see Table 4.2). That the firstborn is grammatically neuter but conceptually masculine shows that αὐτούς can properly fit into grammatical scenarios like this. Of course, one must assume that πᾶν κοιμώμενον would fit the categories of neuter expressions at the time of the translation in order for the masculine αὐτούς to make sense.[168] I have argued that πᾶν κοιμώμενον would only be perceived as referring to animals at the time of the translation, so the masculine αὐτούς would not make much sense; there are no humans in view, and if both animals in the copulating act were being referred to, then αὐτά should be used. Likewise, it is possible that αὐτούς was added to the text in order to activate πᾶν = πάντα, since it might be the case that a masculine noun indirectly or appositionally modifying πᾶν was sufficient to indicate this construction.[169]

It is hard to make a case for αὐτούς in 22:18 (22:19 LXX) one way or the other. On the one hand, there is recensional activity attested before the third century CE, though with only five fragmentary papyri of Greek Exodus in this period.[170] None cover 22:18 (22:19 LXX) and inferences from such activity could only be made for 22:18 (22:19 LXX). This activity could explain the removal of αὐτούς in the traditions. On the other hand, given that the original text tends to expand in its reception history and that the translation-technical evidence marshalled in this study gives reason to think that the translator intended for the text to refer to animals and not humans, it makes a great deal of sense that αὐτούς would be added by a later hand in order to correct the text towards the Hebrew. This correction would then be done without changing the original wording of the text that had already been passed down. Adding αὐτούς is less invasive than changing the received text, though there are texts that do correct πᾶν back to πάντα.[171]

It is wise to ask how αὐτούς would relate to the interpretation of 22:18 (22:19 LXX) taken thus far, should it be considered part of OG. One option would be that πᾶν = πάντα through the masculine apposition of αὐτούς. This view is problematic because there is no obvious reason why the translator would need to use the construction in the first place. There is no interpretive difficulty here

167 Wevers, *Notes*, 350.

168 Note that this study has demonstrated that if both male and females were in view, the translator would still need to use πᾶς. πᾶν does not function to refer to both genders.

169 See pp. 197–198 and Appendix 2.2 of the present volume.

170 Wevers, "Pre-Origen," 122.

171 F^{b} *O*-15–707 df^{-56*} *n* $85^{\prime txt}$-130^{txt}-343–344^{txt} ty^{-392} 128′-628 426 646 Cyr *Ad* 549.

in 22:18 (22:19 LXX), and a simple translation of something like πᾶς ὁ κοιμώμενος or πάντα τὸν κοιμώμενον would also permit the inclusion of αὐτούς or the like without the added obscurity that comes with πᾶν. In this view, one would have to presuppose that the translator made the text harder to understand for no specific reason. The only other real option, then, would be to consider that πᾶν κοιμώμενον was a true neuter phrase that referred to humans, parallel to something like πᾶν πρωτότοκον ἐν γῇ Αἰγύπτῳ, ἡγίασα αὐτοὺς ἐμοί in Num 8:17. πᾶν κοιμώμενον would need to be understood as a collective or quality-focused neuter, as in something like "every animal-bedder." One would need to assume that this is colloquial Greek, and thus the translator understood that πᾶν κοιμώμενον was morphologically neuter but semantically masculine. In this way, αὐτούς would fit the original translation and might refer then to both human and beast who were to die. Even if one accepts this reading over and against my interpretation, it must be admitted that it is exceedingly odd that this meaning of 'πᾶν + (anarthrous) participle' never appears elsewhere in the LXX nor in the contemporary literary or documentary texts. As well, all other laws exhibit the typical uses of πᾶς in the LXX, with this law being the only case to the contrary.[172] If αὐτούς is then original, we must presuppose that the translator has translated in a wildly idiosyncratic manner, and then other explanations for ἀποκτενεῖτε and the future tense would need to be devised.

Perhaps a case could be made that αὐτούς and ἀποκτενεῖτε could be explained by an intertextual link with Lev 20:15–16:

> ואיש אשר יתן שכבתו בבהמה מות יומת ואת־הבהמה תהרגו: ואשה אשר תקרב אל־כל־בהמה לרבעה אתה והרגת את־האשה ואת־הבהמה מות יומתו דמיהם בם:
>
> If a man has sexual relations with an animal, he shall be put to death; and you shall kill the animal.16 If a woman approaches any animal and has sexual relations with it, you shall kill the woman and the animal; they shall be put to death, their blood is upon them.[173]
>
> καὶ ὃς ἂν δῷ κοιτασίαν αὐτοῦ ἐν τετράποδι, θανάτῳ θανατούσθω, καὶ τὸ τετράπουν ἀποκτενεῖτε. καὶ γυνή, ἥτις προσελεύσεται πρὸς πᾶν κτῆνος βιβασθῆναι αὐτὴν ὑπ' αὐτοῦ, ἀποκτενεῖτε τὴν γυναῖκα καὶ τὸ κτῆνος· θανάτῳ θανατούσθωσαν, ἔνοχοί εἰσιν.

172 Lev 27:29 seems to exploit πᾶν in the same way as Exod 22:18 (22:19 LXX) and is briefly discussed on p. 190. It will be the focus of later research.

173 NRSV.

> And he who gives his sleeping-with to a quadruped, by death let him be put to death, and you shall kill the quadruped. And a woman who shall approach any animal for her to be mounted by it—you shall kill the woman and the animal; by death they shall be put to death; they are liable.[174]
>
> Leviticus 20:15–16

Here we find the command to kill both the animal and human as well as the verb form ἀποκτενεῖτε. Ostensibly, the translator of Exodus could be representing the animal and human with αὐτούς, as Wevers claims.[175] Wevers adopts the reading of πᾶν = πάντα, which seems to give room for αὐτούς to refer to the human and animal. In the neuter reading of πᾶν κοιμώμενον, it appears harder to establish this. Either πᾶν κοιμώμενον is a genuine and comprehensible (though unattested) collectivizing neuter, or αὐτούς should be taken as a cue that πᾶν κοιμώμενον is a neuter expression which needs to be interpreted as semantically masculine, especially because there is no definite article to signal the normal classical use of the collective neuter. In order to accept the reading that animals and humans are to die, one would then need to either assume πᾶν = πάντα or, perhaps, adopt that αὐτούς plays double duty in both pointing to the masculine intention behind πᾶν κοιμώμενον as well as to the human and animal. This latter reading seems tendentious, again, because πᾶν is cumbersome and unnecessary in the first place. That Lev 20:15–16 uses ἀποκτενεῖτε is a strong point of connection with Exod 22:18 (22:19 LXX), but in Lev it is clear that the translator is simply representing the source text's lexeme הרג whereas the known Hebrew tradition for Exodus only reads מות יומת. It could be argued that the translator knew the Levitical law that used הרג and then decided to render as though translating that lexeme over against מות. Perhaps then the intention would be to use ἀποκτενεῖτε/תהרגו as a way of informing the reader that both the animal and human were in view, as in Lev. However, θανάτῳ θανατούσθωσαν also refers to killing both the animal and human in Lev, so would an intertextual echo with ἀποκτενεῖτε/תהרגו really be that noticeable? Would drawing on the lexeme alone provoke the reader enough to remember the parallel command? Even if ἀποκτενεῖτε were an allusion to Leviticus, one still needs to explain why πᾶν was chosen, since this does not seem to refer to animals and humans. As it stands, basing the translation of Exod 22:18 (22:19 LXX) solely upon intertextual grounds seems spurious.

---

174 Büchner, NETS.

175 See fn. 167 above.

4.4.3 *Conclusion of Translation-Technical Analysis*

While there are a few possible explanations for the use of πᾶν instead of πᾶς in Exod 22:18 (22:19 LXX) that have been given by previous scholars, these seem unlikely given a robust analysis of the relevant factors. πᾶν in this collocation should be understood in its frequently attested sense, whether in the documentary sources, the LXX, or the early literary texts—that is, as a basic neuter adjective describing animals/things. This claim is corroborated by the translator's choice to use ἀποκτείνω in this legal text, which, from a Greek-legal perspective, would not be read as capital punishment but as an on-the-spot slaying. Finally, the use of the future tense rather than a third person imperative in the apodosis of the law further points towards the translator viewing this law as distinct from the other laws that contain the death penalty without any other preventative factors.

The law in 22:18 (22:19 LXX) seems to no longer be about bestiality but rather about killing an animal that lies with a domestic animal (κτῆνος). The implied subject for πᾶν is likely a wild animal that is not part of the flock. Inter-special (animal) relations could also be covered under πᾶν, but given κτῆνος is one of two subcategories of animals, namely, wild and domestic, it does not seem that this is a more likely reading. The immediate contrast to κτῆνος would be apparent. πᾶν could also refer to a neighbor's animals, but the semantic and legal context of the translation might suggest otherwise. These contextual interpretations of πᾶν will be explored further. It must be emphasized that the changes to this law should probably be conceived of as reactionary. The translator's concern is not about animal husbandry, per se, but about creating a law that does not refer to bestiality. That the translator could transform the Hebrew into a Greek law about animal husbandry (through SSF) was a convenience of the interface between the Hebrew and Greek texts. כל and יומת were conveniently exploited when translated into Greek. But why did the translator not want a law on bestiality to be present in the Greek translation? For this, we must turn to the legal framework of Greeks and Egyptians when it came to sexual 'deviancy' and its criminality.[176]

4.4.4 *Legal and Cultural Analysis*

4.4.4.1 Sexual Crime in Classical Greek and Greco-Egyptian Law

The standards evidenced from the Classical, Egyptian, and Greco-Egyptian settings together point to a unified legal stance where one's private sexual

176 "Deviancy" will be used from here out assuming a sexual practice as perceived by the respective ancient culture. Sexual mores are, of course, standards set differently throughout time.

behavior, outside of a very few constraints, was not the subject of litigation or legal consequence. These contexts will be taken in order.

Very few men would have ever been prosecuted for sexual deviancy in the Athenian Greek setting.[177] Political degradation could occur for misbehavior, but likely little else.[178] Only adultery had significant consequences.[179] In fact, "before about 350 the Athenian democracy had no laws … [for] victimless sexual conduct … all such conduct went unregulated by law for those content to play no role in government."[180] When the Athenian government became more conservative in 355 BCE under new leadership, while some matters of personal life did now come under scrutiny and legislative domain, "in sexual matters they did not do so."[181] Private sexual behaviour was kept just that—private—and Athenians had significant tolerance towards even what could be considered mildly harmful.[182] When it comes to the acts that were legislated against, there were only specific situations prohibited or considered morally suspect. For homosexual activity, being the passive partner in this act would disallow a man to participate in some public political and religious offices or tasks at the risk of death, but otherwise there were no penalties for this act.[183] Similarly, male prostitution faced minor consequences.[184]

There is an ubiquitous hatred of incest in the Greek world, but "tout au plus le droit civil interdisait-il le mariage pour cause de parenté … l'inceste, dont la répression n'était pas expressément visée dans le droit criminel, tombait ainsi sous le coup d'une action pour adultère (γραφή μοιχείας) que pouvait intenter le κύριος de la femme séduite."[185] Even this deviant activity was barely touched upon in legal contexts.

177 John J. Winkler, "Laying Down the Law: The Oversight of Men's Sexual Behavior in Classical Athens," in *Before Sexuality: The Construction of Erotic Experience in the Ancient Greek World*, ed. David M. Halperin, John J. Winkler, and Froma I. Zeitlin (Princeton: Princeton University Press, 1991), 171–210, especially 195.

178 Winkler, "Laying Down the Law," 195; John G. Younger, *Sex in the Ancient World* (London: Taylor and Francis, 2009), 66.

179 Younger, *Sex in the Ancient*, 66.

180 Wallace, "On not Legislating," 151–152.

181 Wallace, "On not Legislating," 153.

182 Giulia Sissa, *Sex and Sensuality in the Ancient World* (New Haven: Yale University Press, 2008), 54.

183 MacDowell, *Athenian Homicide Law*, 134. Cf. Aeschines, *Timarch.* 19–20, 87; Demosthenes, *Andr.* 30.

184 Safty, "Les principales," 166: "l'acte même n'était visé par les lois répressives à Athènes que dans certaines conditions."

185 Safty, "Les principales," 167. Cf. Plato, *Leg.* 838a–c; Lysias, *1 Alc.* 41.

Without addressing bestiality directly, it should already be clear from Athenian practice that such activity was not and would not be legislated against. Even still, looking into Greek perceptions of this practice suggests the same. In Greek art, bestiality is seen among drunken satyrs, "amoral creatures who obey their impulses."[186] In contrast, "a youth ... penetrating an animal is a rare subject."[187] The depictions of the satyrs reflect the fringe fantasies of the Greeks, not necessarily what they actually practiced.[188] The not infrequent bestial practices of the Greek gods also suggests the topic was not overly taboo.[189] So, conjoined with the fact that sexual practices were not often the subject of legislation, "Il n' y avait aucune loi contre la bestialité, probablement parce qu'elle n'était pas pratiquée par les Grecs."[190]

It is also helpful to consider the moral and legal tendencies regarding sexual behavior of Egyptians prior to the Ptolemaic period, since their perceptions and laws could affect what was legal or on the fringes of legality in this later period.

Ancient Egyptians also seemed to relegate sexual crime to the private sector. Tyldesley states that "[a]dultery was not a crime against the state but a private matter, one that might occasionally be reported to a local magistrate or even to a local court, but that was far more likely to be dealt with by the individuals or families concerned."[191] When the offended party acted against the adulterer, it was legally justifiable to act with physical recourse.[192] Adultery in and of itself did not incur a legal penalty since it was not technically illegal and would likely only be brought to court as a last measure.[193] Diodorus Siculus, *Bibliotheca historica*, 1.78 records one thousand blows for a seducer and a lost nose for the adulterous wife; rape was penalized with castration,[194]

186 Kenneth J. Dover, *Greek Homosexuality* (Cambridge: Harvard University Press, 1989), 97; François Lissarrague, "The Sexual Life of Satyrs," in *Before Sexuality: The Construction of Erotic Experience in the Ancient Greek World*, ed. David M. Halperin, John J. Winkler, and Froma I. Zeitlin (Princeton: Princeton University Press, 1991), 61–66.

187 Dover, *Greek Homosexuality*, 97.

188 Lissarrague, "The Sexual Life," 66.

189 For a listing of their acts see Younger, *Sex in the Ancient*, 19.

190 Georges Androutsos and Aristide Diamantis, "La vie sexuelle des grecs anciens," *Andrologie* 17, no. 4 (2007): 344.

191 Tyldesley, *Judgement of the Pharaoh*, 154.

192 Tyldesley, *Judgement of the Pharaoh*, 157–158.

193 Tyldesley, *Judgement of the Pharaoh*, 159–160. Papyrus Deir el-Medina 27 shows a case where adultery occurs but the court is not invoked. Instead, the offender is confronted in their home; see ibid., 160, 162 and Jac J. Janssen, "Marriage Problems and Public Reactions," in *Pyramid Studies. Other Essays Presented to I. E. S. Edwards*, ed. John Baines et al. (London: Egypt Exploration Society, 1988), 134–137.

194 These are likely exaggerated (Tyldesley, *Judgement of the Pharaoh*, 160).

although rape was likewise generally considered a private matter.[195] Cumont points out that there might have been necrophilic practices in Egypt, such that Herodotus (*Hist.* 2.89) warns that bodies were not given to embalmers for a few days.[196] It can be inferred that "necrophilia, if not a crime, was certainly considered a moral outrage."[197] Likewise, "homosexuality was not considered to be a crime."[198] Incest and polygamy were not condemnable by law, and these were practiced almost exclusively in the royal families.[199]

Finally, a few resources depict bestial practices in Egypt, which further solidify that some sexual practices were not formally criminal. Two ancient historians mention bestiality in Egypt, the first being Herodotus:

> καλέεται δὲ ὅ τε τράγος καὶ ὁ Πὰν Αἰγυπτιστὶ Μένδης. ἐγένετο δὲ ἐν τῷ νομῷ τούτῳ ἐπ᾽ ἐμεῦ τοῦτο τὸ τέρας: γυναικὶ τράγος ἐμίσγετο ἀναφανδόν. τοῦτο ἐς ἐπίδεξιν ἀνθρώπων ἀπίκετο.
>
> In the Egyptian language Mendes is the name both for the he-goat and for Pan. In my lifetime a strange thing occurred in this district: a he-goat had intercourse openly with a woman. This came to be publicly known.[200]
>
> HERODOTUS, *Hist.* 2.46.4

The commentary by How and Wells adds that the Greeks believed the Egyptians practiced bestiality often in private, and that it was the openness of the act here that was astonishing.[201] Modern commentators on sex practices in Egypt cite Herodotus, though with a measure of skepticism towards his reliability.[202] Strabo, however, cites Pindar (*Fr.* 201 [215], fifth century BCE) to the same effect:

195 Tyldesley, *Judgement of the Pharaoh*, 161, who says it could be brought to authorities if needed.

196 Cumont, *L'Égypte des astrologues*, 183.

197 Tyldesley, *Judgement of the Pharaoh*, 116.

198 Tyldesley, *Judgement of the Pharaoh*, 163.

199 Tyldesley, *Judgement of the Pharaoh*, 155.

200 Herodotus (Godley, LCL).

201 Walter W. How and Joseph Wells, *A Commentary on Herodotus* (Oxford: Clarendon Press, 1964), 209.

202 See, e.g., Charlotte Booth, *In Bed with the Ancient Egyptians* (Chalford: Amberly Publishing, 2015), 225; Lise Manniche, *Sexual Life in Ancient Egypt* (London: Kegan Paul, 1997), 28.

> Μένδης, ὅπου τὸν Πᾶνα τιμῶσι καὶ τῶν ζῴων τράγον· ὡς δὲ Πίνδαρός φησιν, οἱ τράγοι ἐνταῦθα γυναιξὶ μίγνυνται· Μένδητα παρὰ κρημνὸν θαλάσσης, ἔσχατον Νείλου κέρας, αἰγιβάται ὅθι τράγοι γυναιξὶ μίσγονται[203]
>
> Mendes, at which place they worship Pan and, among animals, a he-goat; and, as Pindar says, the he-goats have intercourse with women there: "Mendes, along the crag of the sea, farthermost horn of the Nile, where the goat-mounting he-goats have intercourse with women.[204]
>
> STRABO, *Geogr.* 17.19:

These two sources suggest that bestiality could have been known and was perhaps infamous in Egypt, at least in some areas, before the Ptolemaic period. It should be asked, however, whether Pindar's and Herodotus's accounts are in some way dependent on each other, since they refer to the same area and practice. Despite this, the relationship between religious practice and bestiality should be noted, which might suggest the legality of the practice.[205] Whether these practices go back to the Pharaonic period is uncertain, but some do think it is likely that bestiality did take place in the Greco-Roman period.[206] Bestiality is also depicted in dream books, "which show[s] that these relationships existed in the erotic imagination of the Egyptians, if not in actual fact."[207] Tyldesley comments on this trait in these books: "The dream books include a number of erotic dreams, many of which concern bestiality, which is also

---

203 Μένδητα and μίσγονται in Pindar's citation are contested among editors, but this does not affect the argument here. See Strabo (Jones and Sterrett, LCL), vol. 1, 68, fn. 1.

204 Translation from of Strabo from Jones and Sterrett Strabo, LCL, vol. 1, 68.

205 Tyldesley, *Judgement of the Pharaoh*, 155–156, notes the connection between sex and religion in Egypt, and how they celebrated the fertile Nile and the reproductive cycles in nature.

206 Booth, *In Bed*, 225–226; Dominic Montserrat, *Sex and Society in Graeco-Roman Egypt* (London: Kegan Paul International, 1996), 83, who suggests rural Egypt as a more likely setting. Two other sources that mention bestiality in Greco-Roman Egypt are included in Cumont, *L'Égypte des astrologues*, 183, fn. 5: Wilhelm Gundel, *Hermes: Neue astrologische Texte des Hermes Trismegistos; Funde und Forschungen auf dem Gebiet der antiken Astronomie und Astrologie* (München: Verlag Der Bayerischen Akademie Der Wissenschaften, 1936), 58, with "molles, concubitores bestiarum (unknown date. early AD or BC)" and Ptolemy, *Tetrabiblos* 3.160 (second century CE), with παρανόμων καὶ θηριωδῶν μίξεων ἐπιθυμητάς, which depicts this act as a vice. These might serve as evidence for bestial practices in Egypt.

207 Manniche, *Sexual Life*, 28.

apparently not a crime although it is certainly a moral outrage … Where bestiality does get mentioned in the court it is in the form of a curse."[208]

So then, as with the Classical Greek legal system, so also with the Ancient Egyptian: bestiality is not proscribed. It might even be the case that bestiality was practiced in Egypt, whereas it would have been more of a matter of fantasy in the Greek realm. This is in large part due to both cultures' legal stance towards sexuality, namely, that it is not to be legislated against in most cases—especially when it did not involve marital bonds or gaining positions of leadership. If Ptolemaic Egypt is largely the confluence of Greek and Egyptian culture, then it should be considered fair to bring the knowledge of this legal distancing from sexual matters into the Ptolemaic period, to which we now turn.

There is an interesting silence when it comes to the Ptolemaic legal stance on sexual practices. That is, the documentary sources reveal next to nothing.[209] Neither is there a legal text involving bestiality.[210] It is possible that this is due to happenstance and that the gaps in our sources, if filled, would reveal legal dealings on sexual matters. On the other hand, this silence might speak to the inheritance previously expanded upon in this study: Greeks and Egyptians do not legislate against most private sexual practice. Helmis maintains that this legislative quality of the two cultures likely forms the backdrop for the Ptolemaic period and "en replaçant dans une perspective historique les lacunes de la documentation papyrologique, nous pouvons, peut-être, parvenir à éclaircir quelques ombres, à rendre éloquents les silences."[211] Bluche remarks, in line with Helmis, that it was not until the Roman era that pederasty, incest (including with mothers), and other sexual deviancies were more stringently restricted.[212] For the Ptolemaic period he claims, "L'adultère, l'inceste en ligne directe, le viol, la bestialité n'étaient certainement pas punis de mort," while noting that the stricter standards of ancient Egypt had been relaxed over time, a trend and policy which seems to have continued and advanced in

208 Tyldesley, *Judgement of the Pharaoh*, 163; for this dream book see Chester Beatty II (BM 10683).

209 Helmis, "Crime et châtiment," 17, states, "celle des délits sexuels … aucun texte ne fait état; nous serons ainsi amené à nous interroger sur ce silence discret de nos documents."

210 Helmis, "Crime et châtiment," 99, mentions bestiality specifically, noting only laws involving animal damages exist.

211 Helmis, "Crime et châtiment," 25.

212 Bluche, "La peine," 146, fn. 13.

the Ptolemaic era.[213] In other words, "les infractions contre les moeurs sont tolérées ou mollement poursuivies."[214]

Helmis helpfully brings to bear the Athenian evidence previously mentioned in a discussion as to why there are no documentary texts about adultery or homosexuality, as would be expected in a culture dominated by the Greeks.[215] In contrast to the family and home-oriented view of the Classical Greeks when it came to kin, he sees a new autonomy arising in which cases of adultery might have been considered a matter only pertaining to the immediately injured parties inasmuch as the violator had transgressed a marital contract.[216] In the same way, homosexual acts that were problematic in the earlier Greek milieu, due to the change in the broader culture and context, would largely no longer need to be the subject of legislation.[217] Helmis concludes that "les lacunes de nos sources se révèlent des silences culturels."[218] The Ptolemaic period can then be viewed as particularly quiet with regard to sexual mores and law. Helmis's analysis helps to confirm that the gaps in the Ptolemaic documentation do not indicate that all that is missing are some scraps of papyri which would fill in Greco-Egyptian laws on sexual practice. These laws likely did not exist.[219] This conclusion coincides with the Classical Greek and Ancient Egyptian contexts, as well as with the aforementioned leniency towards personal moral matters exhibited by the Ptolemies. It is no leap then to posit that bestiality would not only be legal in Ptolemaic Egypt, but that it would be absurd to legislate against such a practice.

4.4.4.2 Conclusion on Sexual Crimes in Ptolemaic Egypt in Relation to Exodus 22:18 (22:19 LXX)

While the Ptolemaic documentary sources do not provide positive evidence, due to the inherited cultures of both Classical Greece and Ancient Egypt, it is possible to posit that such silence is filled with the reverberations of these previous legal milieus. The consistent stance of non-interference in sexual matters in both cultures, as well as their ambivalent stances towards dialogue about

213 Bluche, "La peine," 169. Not only was incest not punishable by death, but "la 'philadelphie' est bien ancrée dans la société hellénistique" (Helmis, "Crime et châtiment," 61).

214 Bluche, "La peine," 169.

215 Helmis, "Crime et châtiment," 24–27.

216 Helmis, "Crime et châtiment," 26. Cf. 25.

217 Helmis, "Crime et châtiment," 26. He focuses on the relationship between a free person and a slave and the changes in Hellenistic slavery from earlier periods in his example.

218 Helmis, "Crime et châtiment," 27.

219 Helmis, "Crime et châtiment," 41, suggests that P.Enteux. 50 is probably related to the sex trade, but the exact context of the papyrus is not clear. This suggests that there may have been legal infractions when it came to this business.

and practice in bestiality strongly suggest that this act would not have been in any way illegal in the Ptolemaic context. Their affirmations of personal freedom would have acted to condemn such a proscription. For these reasons, it is viable to look to Greco-Egyptian law as influencing the translational changes discussed for Exod 22:18 (22:19 LXX). The law no longer refers to capital punishment for bestiality because such a crime and punishment were both alien and (potentially) antagonistic to the legal world of Ptolemaic Egypt.

4.4.4.3 Greek Law, Animal Husbandry, and Exodus 22:18 (22:19 LXX)

If, then, Exod 22:18 (22:19 LXX) could have been changed in its Greek translation so as to distance the text from a prohibition against bestiality due to that practice not being considered worthy of any serious reprimand or law, how would this new meaning correlate to the *Sitz im Leben* of Ptolemaic Egypt? If the law now says, "Any*thing* that lies with a domestic animal, you shall kill with (an act of early) death," what is the "thing" lying with the domestic animal? It seems prudent to suppose that the translator intended the law to refer to a wild animal. This makes sense from both from a semantic and cultural perspective.

On the semantic level, note the contrast of θηρίον ("wild animal") and κτῆνος ("domesticated animal") in the Greek Pentateuch in that these are the terms most often paired in contrast to each other.[220] Leviticus 26:22 states that it is the θήρια that come in and ravage the κτῆνος. Likewise, literary texts use these terms in an antonymic fashion.[221] This is no new claim, as LSJ already defines this contrast.[222] Such a direct comparison is not found in the third-century papyri since these texts are dealing with practical matters of industry and are not concerned with wild animals. Of course, κτῆνος is in fact found referring to the domestic and agricultural animals.[223] So, from a basic conceptual standpoint, that which is not a κτῆνος would be a θηρίον in the Greek mindset. Since Exod 22:18 (22:19 LXX) is prohibiting something (i.e., πᾶν) from lying with a κτῆνος, the easily supplied referent is that which falls outside of the category of κτῆνος, namely, θηρίον. It is of course possible that another domestic animal may be in view; thus "any (other domestic animal) lying with a domestic animal." Ostensibly, this would be a neighbor's animal. In the Ptolemaic context, one would not be allowed to kill another farmer's animals, so this is less

---

220 Gen 1:25; 2:20; 3:14; 6:19; 7:14, 21; 8:1, 19; 9:10; Lev 25:7; 26:22.

221 Hippocrates, *Nat. puer.* 538; Megasthenes, *Fr.* frag. 35.45. Eudoxus, *Selen. sec.* vol. 7, 185.1–2 contrast κτήνεσιν with ἀγρίοις.

222 LSJ, κτῆνος, 2, "in sg., a single beast, as an ox or sheep ... horse or mule for riding ...; *of a domestic animal, opp. θηρίον*" (emphasis added).

223 E.g., P.Tebt. 703. 66 (210 BCE). There are twenty-six uses in the third century according to Papyri.info.

likely.[224] It is also possible that a domestic animal of another species is being considered here, though one wonders what, if any, problems that would cause a farmer. The best option is a wild animal, since this animal could throw into ruin the breeding practices of a farmer, and he would be legally allowed to kill the animal. This is all the more applicable when a farmer was in the care of royal cattle, which required extra care and caution in their breeding and treatment.[225] Before we turn to these practices, a brief note on the legal provisions regarding wild animals is in order.

Wild animals are not a significant concern in ancient, codified law. Mélèze-Modrzejewski comments that across ancient legal systems laws focus on domestic and not wild animals, since damages caused by wild animals are not the responsibility of any person.[226] As such, it is admitted that there is no law in any of the Greek sources (to my knowledge) saying that a wild animal copulating with a domestic animal must be killed in any of the ancient Greek sources. This is not a very significant absence as things that were common sense were often not included in codified law. If a wild animal was causing trouble, it is common sense to put a stop to it. This is all the more the case when the breeding habits of the ancient Greeks are considered.

Kron has written an extensive article on husbandry in the Greco-Roman world in which he claims that the archaeological remains of the bones of their domestic animals reveal exceptional knowledge of breeding and animal upkeep, so that "a case can be made that the classical and Hellenistic Greeks should be credited for many of the critical innovations in animal husbandry."[227] These innovations should be dated to the fifth and fourth centuries BCE or earlier.[228] In areas in which Hellenization was slower to take root, some of these methods were likely taken on over time.[229] It is probably acceptable to delimit Hellenistic Egypt as one such region. Even still, there can be little doubt that Greek methods were used in Ptolemaic Egypt. These Greek methods were industrious and precise, the likes of which are praised to this day.[230] Kron provides another essential commentary specifically on breeding:

---

224 See p. 225.

225 See pp. 221–223.

226 Mélèze-Modrzejewski, "Papyrologie et histoire," 233–234.

227 Geoffrey Kron, "Animal Husbandry, Hunting, Fishing, and Fish Production," in *The Oxford Handbook of Engineering and Technology in the Classical World*, ed. John Peter Oleson (Oxford: Oxford University Press, 2009), 175.

228 Kron, "Animal Husbandry," 176.

229 Kron, "Animal Husbandry," 176.

230 See the references in Kron, "Animal Husbandry," 179. For the various ways in which the ancients increased their livestock size and improved their land fecundity, see pp. 180–183.

> The ancient agronomists had ably resolved all the technical problems involved in breeding and raising the young of that most delicate of domestic animals, the horse, and the same care was given to breeding the other major domestic animals. For example, *Columella advised farmers not only to use the best breeding stock, but also to use only sexually mature animals in their prime* (Rust. 7.3.6, 6.3, 6.8, 9.2); *to control the breeding process* (Rust. 6.37.1–2, 8–10; 7.3.11–16, 6.6–8); to provide prompt veterinary help in cases of difficult births (Rust. 7.3.16); and to show great care for the newborn young (Rust. 7.3.16–19). Unfortunately, the agronomists only occasionally allude to the more sophisticated methods used by breeders to consciously manipulate and improve their livestock. *They allude to crossbreeding with new breeds and even wild species* (Rust. 6.37.3ff; 7.2.4–5) *and show an awareness of recessive traits that had to be guarded against* (Rust. 7.3.1–2; Vergil, G. 3.355), but the skill of Greek and Roman breeders must be inferred primarily from their results. They were very successful, for example, in breeding sheep with a wide range of fleece types. These included several distinct breeds with fine wool, comparable to some of the finest modern merino wool.[231]

While Kron cites sources mainly from the late Hellenistic and Roman periods, he does claim these practices go back to the fifth century BCE or earlier. Given the strict control and care about breeding practices, whether with respect to sexual maturity, recessive trait control, or the like, it would not be acceptable to let wild animals interfere with this process. Such would be obvious to any ancient farmer. Animals were expensive commodities and raising those that were not desired could cause financial loss, especially since "an important stimulus to classical animal breeding came from its vigorous commercial development."[232]

This broad picture of ancient breeding could, at least to a degree, be judiciously superimposed on Ptolemaic Egypt. Fortunately, more information exists from that period, which substantiates such similarities to the picture Kron has sketched.

Rostovtzeff comments directly on the breeding practices in Ptolemaic Egypt:

> The Greeks in Egypt kept all their native habits and customs … [they] acclimatized the animals to which they were accustomed … We do not know how important sheep and goat breeding was in the Egypt of the

231 Kron, "Animal Husbandry," 179, emphasis added.

232 Kron, "Animal Husbandry," 179.

> Pharaohs, but under the Ptolemies certainly, and in the Fayum especially, sheep and goat breeding assumed very large proportions. The breeding of animals, like the planting of the vine, was one of the most common occupations of the Greeks in their mother country and represented on the other hand a good investment for Greek capital, the animals being the private property of their owners, as far as the Greek population of Egypt was concerned. On the estate of Apollonius sheep and goat breeding was a matter of great importance. Four paragraphs in the agenda of Zenon are devoted to this topic. Here again we have no statistics.[233]

These insights confirm that, at least as concerns Hellenes, animal breeding in Ptolemaic Egypt was under rigid control, as was the Greek practice. On top of using these methods, there is ample evidence of new, foreign breeds of animals being brought into Ptolemaic Egypt in order to acclimatize them and improve the stock of that region.[234] In fact, "the attempt to improve the native breeds of animals by importing better breeds from outside was common in the Hellenistic period."[235] With these incoming new breeds and the already meticulous breeding practices of the Greeks, it would be unacceptable to have some animals undesirably impregnated.

In addition, it must be emphasized that every animal owned by a farmer would be under the watch and taxation of the Ptolemies, a fact which itself would not promote the superfluous propagation of one's livestock. Commenting on C.Ord.Ptol. 21–22, Bagnall and Derow state, "Livestock are to be registered by a set date and taxes up to that date are remitted, provided that registration is made. If it is not, severe penalties await the violators. The pasture tax on livestock was a major source of tax revenue, and was based on the number of animals."[236] The Ptolemaic government required all citizens to count and report all animals owned for taxing.[237] New animals that were not planned would not be welcome within this system. And this is all the more the case when it is considered that a significant portion of the agricultural animals

233 Michael Rostovtzeff, *A Large Estate in Egypt in the Third Century* B.C.: *A Study in Economic History* (Madison: University of Wisconsin, 1922), 112–113. He cites PSI 368, 377 b and a, 346, 381; P.Lond.Inv. 2084.

234 Rostovtzeff, *A Large Estate*, 114, cites PSI 388. 56 for Arabian sheep and goats, "Edgar, P. Z. 24, Intr" for Milesian sheep, and P.Cair.Zen. 13 for "horses, donkeys and animals cross-bred by a donkey and a wild ass." Cf. ibid., 180, for another breed of sheep.

235 Rostovtzeff, *A Large Estate*, 114, fn. 85; cf. 115.

236 From Bagnall and Derow, *The Hellenistic Period*, 111. While these commands are for Syria/Phoenicia, the authors claim the same regulations for Egypt (111).

237 Clarysse and Thompson, *Counting the People*, 206–207. Cf. P.E.R. Inv. 24, 522; P.Hib. 2 238.

used and raised by the Ptolemaic citizenry were owned by the Ptolemaic government and were to be treated as such.

It is in Preaux's seminal work on the Ptolemaic economy that she emphasizes the role of these royal herds in the everyday life of Hellenised Egypt. She maintains,

> Le roi est propriétaire de gros bétail, mais ses sujets en possèdent également. Royal ou privé, ce cheptel est recensé, au III siècle, par les soins de l'économe, qui surveille en outre l'élevage des bêtes qui appartient au roi … Il faut donc que les animaux soient confiés à ceux qui, utilisant leur énergie, sont capables de tirer profit de ce capital vivant. C'est chez les agriculteurs, clérouques et paysans royaux, que doit se trouver réparti le bétail du roi … Bien des agriculteurs, en effet, n'ont ni boeufs, ni ânes, qu'ils puissent atteler à leur charrue. Leur dénûment s'étale dans plusieurs pièces des archives de Zénon. En effet, comme le roi prête à ses fermiers le bétail agricole, ainsi, le bénéficiaire de la dôréa pourvoit de bétail ceux qui cultivent la terre que lui a concédée le roi.[238]

The burden of caring for these animals falls on the Ptolemaic populace, while particular treatment is given to cattle that are solely dedicated to the purposes and enhancement of the Ptolemaic economy and bureaucracy.[239] If many cattle at various farms in Ptolemaic Egypt were owned by the royals and required extra special care, then it is no leap to assume that additional attention was given to keep these animals from being contaminated in their breeding practices.[240] Likewise, cattle rented or distributed to farmers by large land owners would also need to be taken care of in such a manner.[241]

If, then, the royal cattle were to some degree under the responsibility of the Ptolemaic populace, then there is warrant to pursue one further avenue of information on breeding practices: to make a connection between the obsession of Ptolemy II with the import and breeding of various animals and the trickle-down effect this *desideratum* had on the wider populace.[242] It has long been understood that "[royal] exploitations servirent de modèles pour les

238 Claire Préaux, *L'économie royale des Lagides*, (Bruxelles: Edition de la fondation égyptologique Reine Elisabeth, 1939), 208–210.

239 As seen e.g., in P.Tebt. 703, 3.64–70 and P.Petrie, 3 46 (4).

240 This is not to say all cattle were owned by royalty. See Préaux, *L'économie royale*, 210–213.

241 Cf. Préaux, *L'économie royale*, 213; PSI 577, 509 and P.Cair.Zen. 59165/59158.

242 It is unknown if the translation of Exodus came before the reign of Ptolemy II. It is probably fair to assume it did not based on his reign beginning at the outset of the third century.

expériences agronomiques conduites sur le « front pionnier » du Fayoum."[243] The royal farms and their breeding practices were copied by the rest of the populace. Indeed, "loin d'être en effet l'apanage des seuls souverains lagides ... ce souci d'acclimater des espèces nouvelles étaient au contraire largement partagés dans l'Égypte lagide."[244] So it is justified to ask how Ptolemy II viewed breeding, and then, at least in part, to assume such practice could make its way to the masses.

Ptolemy Philadelphus is known for his love of wild and exotic animals, which he paraded through the streets in honor of his parents.[245] He had a penchant to tame wild animals, a practice that was widespread and popular.[246] He also oversaw breeding experiments that occurred between wild and domestic animals.[247] For example, "that he was as deeply interested in introducing new breeds of domesticated animals into Egypt is attested by a papyrus (P. Cairo Zenon I. 59,075), written in 257 B.C., in which an Ammonite chief from east of the Jordan river says that he is sending the king a gift of horses, dogs, asses and several specimens of cross-breeding with the wild ass."[248] Other documents reveal his interest in Arabian and Milesian sheep, as well as other horses, donkeys or crossbred animals.[249] In his processions through Alexandria, he showed "a vast array of animals and birds, from elephants, zebras, ostriches, buffalos, caged lions, tigers, and panthers, to even a rhinoceros."[250] All these initiatives "témoignaient surtout des efforts très concrets déployés sur l'initiative du pouvoir royal pour acclimater en Égypte des races nouvelles, destinées soit à améliorer les races indigènes par de judicieux croisements, soit à être élevées pour elles-mêmes en raison de leurs qualités propres."[251] The goal of possessing these animals may also have been to improve Egyptian

---

243 Jean Trinquier, "Localisation et fonction des animaux sauvages dans l'Alexandrie lagide: la question du 'zoo d'Alexandrie,'" MEFRA 114 (2002): 892, fn. 139; cf. Claude Orrieux, *Les Papyrus de Zénon: L'horizon d'un Grec en Égypte au IIIe siècle avant J.-C.* (Paris: Macula, 1983), 88.

244 Trinquier, "Localisation et fonction," 894. cf. Orrieux, *Les Papyrus*, 92.

245 Joseph G. Manning, "Networks, Hierarchies and Markets in the Ptolemaic Economy," in *The Economies of Hellenistic Societies, Third to First Centuries BC*, ed. Zosia Archibald, John K. Davies, and Vincent Gabrielsen (Oxford: Oxford University Press, 2011), 311; Trinquier, "Localisation et fonction," 867–870, 873; cf. Diodorus Siculus, *Bib. hist.* 3.36.3; Theocritus, *Id.* 2.67–68.

246 Trinquier, "Localisation et fonction," 875; cf. 881–882; Cumont, *L'Égypte des astrologues*, 64.

247 Trinquier, "Localisation et fonction," 892.

248 Diodorus (Oldfather, LCL), vol. 2, 187, fn. 1.

249 See Rostovtzeff, *A Large Estate*, 114–15, and also fn. 85 for more examples.

250 Ian Worthington, *Ptolemy I: King and Pharaoh of Egypt* (New York: Oxford University Press, 2016), 205.

251 Trinquier, "Localisation et fonction," 891.

species.[252] It is interesting that Toubias, when charged with supplying an animal to Ptolemy II, "n'envoie pas à son royal protecteur un seul animal sauvage, mais, tout au plus, le fruit déjà moins rétif du croisement entre un animal sauvage et un animal domestique."[253] Ancients understood the difficulty that caring for wild animals brought, such that one would not send a mere wild animal to Ptolemy. It even seems to be the case that the Ptolemies kept their wild animals separate from their domestic counterparts.[254]

4.4.4.4 Conclusions on Animal Husbandry and Greek Law

It is evident that proper breeding with its appropriate timing, species, and concerns were promoted by the rulership, was within Greek husbandry practices, and from the evidence surviving, seems to have been carried out in Ptolemaic Egypt. For these reasons, a law prohibiting a wild animal from copulating with these carefully watched (and royally owned!) specimens would be more than welcomed by the populace, and especially by the royal benefactors. It should be noted that interspecies breeding can also yield sterile animals (e.g., the mule) and that only closely related species can produce any kind of offspring together. It is conceivable that the translation has this in mind, as in, "any (other species of animal) that lays with a (given species of) domestic animal." This reading is difficult to sustain because there is nothing in the context that directs towards it, whereas the antonymic relationship between κτῆνος and θηρίον provides contextual and semantic traction. Either way, one could make a case that the law in Exod 22:18 (22:19 LXX) would be viewed with particular pleasure by royal officials who have provided their precious cattle to various farmers; it ensures their livestock's safety and productivity. In this view, the law would be a command that is redirected back at the herdsman. It is his or her duty to keep the flocks pure—or else! At the same time, this law could also be viewed as a celebration of Greek excellency in animal breeding, which is a noted focus of Ptolemy and the broader culture at the time. All of this is not to say that the translator of Exodus is being influenced by an actual set of laws on breeding that existed somewhere in Ptolemaic Egypt. If they did exist, they do not survive. Rather, the translation should be seen as more reactionary. The intent is to get away from the bestiality law while still superficially representing the Hebrew text (SSF).

---

252 Trinquier, "Localisation et fonction," 892.

253 Trinquier, "Localisation et fonction," 893, fn. 145.

254 Trinquier, "Localisation et fonction," 912. Cf. p. 914, where the author is not certain if these groupings were permanent or just pre-processional.

Finally, it should not be considered likely, at least in light of Ptolemaic law at the time, that the animal lying with the κτῆνος in Exod 22:18 (22:19 LXX) is another domestic animal from another farm or pasturage. This is because an unwelcome domestic animal was not allowed even to be restrained, let alone killed, before a judicial decision was made concerning damages.[255] The offending animal would instead be returned. The translator could have removed the killing clause (θανάτῳ ἀποκτενεῖτε) and instead included an imprecation (θανάτῳ τελευτάτω) to circumvent this understanding.[256]

4.4.5 *Conclusion on Exodus 22:18 (22:19 LXX)*

Taken together, the translation-technical data, along with what is known about Greco-Egyptian law and husbandry practices, marshal a formidable case against reading the OG version of this law as little more than a reflection of the Hebrew *Vorlage*. There are good indications that the translator created a new law that anyone versed in Greek would appreciate and understand. As it stands, Exod 22:18 (22:19 LXX) in the OG might in fact be a law about animal husbandry, promoting proper breeding practice and not a law concerning bestiality.

4.5 Exodus 22:19 (22:20 LXX): On Sacrificing to the Gods

זבח לאלהים יחרם בלתי ליהוה לבדו

Whoever sacrifices to god, other than YHWH alone, shall be destroyed.

255 Helmis, “Crime et châtiment,” 100, referring to P.Petr. 3 26 (240 BCE).

256 Another possible reason Exod 22:18 (22:19 LXX) could have been changed would be that the original Hebrew law is all-encompassing when it refers to animals. In the Egyptian context, given that some animals were sacred and some were not, perhaps a translation that included all animals would have been divisive. Lying with some animals would have been a religious outrage (like certain bulls of the Apis variety), but others accepted (like the he-goat mentioned above). We know that the later Ptolemies even commanded the death penalty for those who killed sacred Egyptian animals (P.Yale 1 56 [100 BCE]), demonstrating their knowledge of and provisions for the morality of the Egyptian populace. Even still, this line of reasoning seems more difficult to establish. For sacred animals and the death penalty see Bluche, “La peine,” 167; Helmis, “Crime et châtiment,” 36–37; Méléze-Modrzejewski, “La sanction,” 254–255.

Ὁ θυσιάζων θεοῖς ἐξολεθρευθήσεται, πλὴν κυρίῳ μόνῳ.

The one officiating a θυσία for gods, except to the Lord alone, shall be destroyed.

Exodus 22:19 (22:20 LXX)

4.5.1 *Introduction*

A degree of suspicion is usually warranted when someone claims a new, unattested meaning for a documented lexical entry—especially when that new locution will act as the lynchpin of a larger and more controversial argument. I appreciate this skepticism. Despite this suspicion, when evaluating the use of θυσιάζω as compared to θύω—terms which, for all intents and purposes seem to be designated as synonymous in the current lexicons[257]—the former term shows itself through the extant contemporaneous evidence to be describing an action more distinct than that of the latter. The distinction is this: θύω describes an undefined sacrifice (it could be of any type or means) as compared to θυσιάζω which describes someone acting as the officiator of the θυσία sacrifice. This officiation always seems to be at an altar. If this distinction holds true, the importance of the use of θυσιάζω in OG Exod 22:19 (22:20 LXX) could hardly be overstated. Instead of being a law forbidding any sacrifice to foreign deities outside of the Israelite God, the law in the OG version prohibits only acting as the officiator in the formal θυσία ceremonial sacrifice at an altar. Participating in sacrifices or the slaughtering of animals with respect to other gods would then be tacitly permitted. I do not consider it fortuitous that such a change from the Hebrew text in the OG occurs, once again, in a law that seems to involve the death penalty (חרם) and that such a departure from the source text is in line with SSF.[258] Whether or not the OG texts refer to the death penalty with ἐξολεθρεύω is admittedly uncertain.[259] It must be stressed that the

257 E.g., LSJ, LEH; CGL, 697, has no entry on the term; MGS glosses with "celebrate a sacrifice" and it is unclear if this definition diverges from "sacrifice"; Muraoka, *A Greek-English Lexicon*, θυσιάζω, 1., 335, renders "to perform the cultic task of offering sacrifice." It is not certain how this definition differs from "to sacrifice," since any sacrifice to a deity in some sense belongs to a religious/cultic practice. Is his definition meant to refer to a more formal setting? If so, then he has discerned part of the semantics of this term that others have not.

258 חרם is a controversial term and concept which will be briefly discussed in turn.

259 Likewise, the text-critical variants with the fronted θανάτῳ will be considered in the relevant section.

translator only uses θυσιάζω once in the entire translation for זבח, while every other instance is θύω (17×).[260] This selectivity requires further consideration.

Consequent to this change in the OG, the rationale for this rendering could, like the other changes documented in this study, be sourced in Ptolemaic legal norms at the time of the translation. Living in Ptolemaic Egypt would almost certainly mean that one would be in constant proximity to foreign sacrifices. The conscription of citizens into services for the government in all likelihood meant that Jewish residents would also need to participate in such sacrifices. Added to this are occupations that would involve the same. Moreover, the push in the third century for the worship of Sarapis as the patron deity of the Ptolemaic dynasty could be on the horizon of the translation.

4.5.2 *Translation-Technical Analysis*

4.5.2.1 Defining θυσιάζω

It is not overly helpful to try to define a term by etymological or morphological analyses. Words—a verb in this case—find their meaning in their usage. However, in this particular instance such lines of reasoning merit a brief discussion, because of the type of verb θυσιάζω is, namely, a denominative verb. In Greek, denominative verbs (ίζω) "generally have either 'factitive' meaning ('make X Y'), or meanings having to do with types of behaviour."[261] These verbs are associated with "doing (rarely being) something connected with the basic noun."[262] In this case, that noun is θυσία. A non-contextual parsing of the verb would then associate it with the performance of the θυσία. Casabona comments on this term in his research on Greek sacrificial language, stating that, "Θυσία au point de départ d'un petit groupe de mots. Outre θύσιμος, attesté dès l'époque classique, la *koinè* connaît le dénominatif θυσιάζω, qui remplacera θύω, et demeure le verbe du grec moderne pour 'sacrifier'. Sur ce verbe, enfin, ont été créés θυσίασμα, θυσιαστήριον (Septante, Josèphe)."[263] He makes no further comment on the meaning of the denominative θυσιάζω outside of its etymological relation to θυσία. Of course, this prompts the questions, what is a θυσία? Who performed it? What kind of participants were there? Such questions might be helpful in determining the meaning of the verb, though, once again, its definition cannot be assumed to be the sum of its parts.

260 3:18; 5:3, 8, 17; 8:4, 21, 22(2×), 23–25; 13:15; 20:24; 23:18; 24:5; 32:8; 34:15. Note the forty occurrences in the Greek Pentateuch compared to θυσιάζω appearing only three times.

261 Boas et al., *Cambridge Grammar*, 275.

262 Mandēlaras, *The Verb in the Greek*, §69, p. 69. Cf. Smyth and Messing, *Greek Grammar*, 245.

263 Jean Casabona, *Recherches sur le vocabulaire des sacrifices en grec, des origines à la fin de l'époque classique* (Paris: Ophrys, 1966), 139.

θυσία derives from θύω, "to offer by burning" and "indicates that the burning of parts was the primary element in this form of sacrifice."[264] Casabona remarks, "Comme θύω, θυσία s'applique à des offrandes de toute nature ... le mot en lui-même est très général."[265] So, whatever the confines of such a ritual, they were relatively broad and could be associated with a myriad of contexts. Jews could perform a θυσία under their own religious constraints.[266] With respect to the act itself, New Pauly defines the θυσία as killing an animal "followed by a sacrificial meal."[267] Due to the value of domestic animals, they state, "The thysía could be eaten only under the restraint of a ritual context."[268] The process "involved the selection, consecration, killing, division, and burning of certain parts of a domestic animal. The procedure was used as a symbolic, expressive action to define both the relationships between humanity and the cosmic order and those that existed between men. It was also the primary—for most people the sole—means by which meat became available for consumption."[269] Such a ritual most often had a "cult official who performed the *thysia* [and] also took care of the table of the god ... the organization of the procession, the buying of the animal and the distribution of the meat to the members of the cult association after the sacrifice."[270] It was, despite its frequency, still "a special occasion."[271] In the end, "the *thysia* ... was a sacrifice at which both men and gods, as it were, received something to eat ... In the most common form of *thysia* ... the μηρία ... was burned on the altar, while the worshippers consumed the rest of the sacrificial animal in a sacral meal."[272] The officiator (priest/cultic official), from the fourth century on, seems to have received his own portion of meat as well as potentially that of the god's at a θυσία.[273]

264 David Gill, "Trapezomata: A Neglected Aspect of Greek Sacrifice," *HTR* 67, no. 2 (1974): 135.

265 Casabona, *Recherches sur le vocabulaire*, 127.

266 For the term's use in the LXX see Dirk Büchner, "The Thysia Soteriou of the Septuagint and the Greek Cult: Representation and Accommodation," in *Florilegium Lovaniense. Studies in Septuagint and Textual Criticism in Honour of Florentino Garcia Martinez*, ed. Hans Ausloos, Bénédicte Lemmelijn and Marc Vervenne (Leuven: Peeters, 2008), 85–100.

267 Jan N. Bremmer, "Sacrifice, III. Greece," *BNP*, 20 vols., ed. Francis G. Gentry (Leiden: Brill, 2004), 12:845.

268 Bremmer, "Sacrifice, III. Greece," 12:845 emphasis added.

269 Michael H. Jameson, *Cults and Rites in Ancient Greece: Essays on Religion and Society* (Cambridge: Cambridge University Press, 2014), 145 (cf. 147). For Greeks deriving most meat from sacrifice see pp. 181 and 198, and Paul Stengel, *Die griechischen Kultusaltertümer* (München: Beck, 1920), 105–106. Though this was not always true (Bartłomiej Bednarek, "The Sacrificial Ritual in Homer," *Classica Cracoviensia* 16 [2013]: 15).

270 Gill, "Trapezomata," 126.

271 Gill, "Trapezomata," 127.

272 Gill, "Trapezomata," 123.

273 Gill, "Trapezomata," 130–132.

All of this portrays the θυσία as a formal, ritualistic meal, instigated and frequently enacted by some sort of officiator, whether that be a temple official or the head of a household.[274] It was more than simply the killing of an animal under religious pretenses. Greeks could, albeit not often, slaughter animals for food apart from such ceremony.[275]

So, once again, if the denominative verb θυσιάζω were all one had to determine the word's meaning, perhaps it could refer to either acting as the officiator in the θυσία, being a participant in the ritual, or both. The LXX, literary, and documentary evidence strongly indicate that the verb was used in this first sense, that is, specifically to refer to the officiators of such a ritual.

4.5.2.2 θυσιάζω in the Greek Pentateuch

It has already been stated that the translator of Exodus only utilizes θυσιάζω once in 22:19 (22:20 LXX). Every other rendering of זבח is θύω, "to sacrifice" or "to slaughter." It is a generic term suitable to various forms of sacrifice or slaughter.[276] There is nothing contextually different about 22:19 (22:20 LXX) that would warrant not translating with θύω besides the fact that it is in a formal law code.[277] In Lev, θυσιάζω is used when referring to priestly sacrifice (7:6; 24:9), but θύω when referring to the people of Israel's personal sacrifices (17:5, 7; 19:5–6; 22:29).[278] These are the only uses of this verb in the Pentateuch.

274 For the θυσία possibly originating in household worship see Gill, "Trapezomata," 137; for heads of households offering on home altars see Jameson, *Cults and Rites*, 247. For more on the θυσία see Louise Bruit, "4.a. Banquet, C Les Théoxénies, 3. *Thysia* et Théoxénies, deux modes d'offrande," in *Thesaurus Cultus et Rituum Antiquorum II: Purification, Initiation, Heroization, Apotheosis, Banquet, Dance, Music, Cult Images* (California: The J. Paul Getty Museum, 2004), 226–228; Antoine Hermary, Martine Leguilloux, Véronique Chankowski, and Angeliki Petropoulou, "Le vocabulaire du sacrifice: Introduction," in *Thesaurus Cultus et Rituum Antiquorum I: Processions, Sacrifices, Libations, Fumigations, Dedications* (California: The J. Paul Getty Museum, 2004), 60–64.

275 Cf. Michael Jameson, "Meat, consumption of, I. Greece," BNP, 20 vols., ed. Francis G. Gentry (Leiden: Brill, 2004), 8:536; Bednarek, "The Sacrificial Ritual," 15.

276 See fn. 265 above. A good example of it being used generically where it could refer to sacrifice or slaughter is PSI 4 409, FrA.22 (275–226 BCE).

277 32:8 and 34:15 use θύω when referring to sacrifices to other deities, so it cannot be claimed that θυσιάζω is employed here simply due to idolatrous actions.

278 The translator seemingly read זבח as a verb in 7:6 instead of the nominal form found in the pointing of MT. It is also unclear if ἀπὸ τῶν θυσιαζομένων (24:9) is neuter passive, i.e., "from the things being offered as a θυσία," or masculine middle, i.e., "from those offering the θυσία on their own behalf." Given that θυσιάζω does not occur as a neuter in the BCE period, and since it does not occur in the passive either, a middle reading is probably warranted here. This is corroborated by the context where it refers to the priests sacrificing and then taking the proceeds for themselves.

In contrast, θύω is translated thirty-eight times by זבח.[279] One might perhaps expect a greater ratio of usage between θυσιάζω and θύω in the early translators had these terms been considered synonymous. The distinction found in Lev, namely, that θυσιάζω is used when sacrifices are being made explicitly by the priests instead of by the laity, is instructive. It begins to point at how this term is used in the literary and documentary sources.

4.5.2.3 θυσιάζω in the Documentary Texts

The documentary resources are presented here first because they represent uses of θυσιάζω that could not have been influenced by a transmission history like the literary texts. Their attestations continue to define θυσιάζω in the sense of "act as an officiator of a θυσία." It is quite interesting that, along with these references, there are only a handful of uses of this verb in the literary sources. In contrast, a term like θύω is attested nearly fifteen hundred times before the Common Era. Both terms find uses spanning the centuries, with the first attestation of θυσιάζω in the sixth century BCE. It is only helpful to contrast θύω with θυσιάζω when they are used in the same context, since the former term can cover the same ground as θυσιάζω. The verbal agents of θύω can be those officiating a sacrifice or lay people. It is a malleable term for sacrifice or animal butchery. However, θυσιάζω occupies a more restrictive semantic space in the source materials. In particular, the verb is found mostly in formal temple or altar-oriented scenarios, and there is always a focus on the specific leader of the sacrificial ritual. It is not used of laity but for the performer of the formal rite.

> καὶ τα[μ]ίας αἱρεθεὶς ὑπὸ τῆς βουλῆς εἴς τε τὰς̣ θυσίας τοῖς [ἱ]ε̣[ροῖς τὸν πόρον ἅπα]σιν μεμέρικεν τοῖς ἱεροποιοῖς, καὶ αὐτὸς συνεπιμε[μέ]λη̣τα[ι] θ̣υ̣σι̣άζ̣ων πάσας τὰς̣ θυσίας, ἔθυσεν δ̣[ὲ] καὶ ἐκ̣ τῶν ἰδίων καὶ π̣εφιλοτίμητ̣αι εἰς τὴν βουλὴν
>
> and (Nikokrates) chosen as treasurer by the Council has both allocated the [funds] to the religious officials for all the sacrifices and has shared in managing the conduct of all the sacrifices himself, and he sacrificed from his own resources and has shown love of honour for the Council[280]
>
> IG II^{3},1 921, II.12–15 (265 BCE)

279 σφάζω renders זבח once in Lev 17:5.

280 Translation from Sean Byrne, "Honours for the prytany of Aigeis," https://www.atticinscriptions.com/inscription/IGII31/921.

This excerpt comes from an honorific inscription praising one, Nikokrates, for his service. Nikokrates was responsible for giving funds to the religious authorities (ἱεροποιοῖς), and "shared in managing the conduct of all the sacrifices himself" (αὐτὸς συνεπιμε[μέ]λη̣τα[ι] θ̣υ̣σι̣ά̣ζων πάσας τὰς̣ θυσίας). The sacrifices here are those done by the cultic leaders and are designated to be θυσίας. Nikokrates went above and beyond in that he conducted the sacrifices himself.[281] It would be no specific praise if he were simply present for them. It seems as though θυσιάζω specifies his role in officiating at these offerings along with the priests.[282] In contrast, Nikokrates also "sacrificed from his own resources" (ἔθυσεν δ̣[ὲ] καὶ ἐκ̣ τῶν ἰδίων), where θύω is used.[283] This is the only aorist finite verb in the description of services rendered while the rest are formulated with the perfect tense (cf. lines 11, 14[2×], 15, 16). It is not clear, but by offsetting ἔθυσεν from the formal listing, ἔθυσεν might function as tertiary information to the main ways that he has served the Council. Moreover, it might separate the sacrifices with the priests from his personal sacrifices in that his personal sacrifices were an additional, separate sign of his piety. This makes sense, since ἔθυσεν is paired with his showing of love of honor for the Council—a marker of piety. The use of δέ may further demarcate that different sacrifices are in view. θυσιάζω seems to be used in the more formal cultic context, with a focus on the over-and-above performance of the θυσία ritual with the priests in contrast to more generic, unspecific sacrifices.

> Νικομάχου τοῦ θυ[
> [τύχαι ἀγα]θᾶι. ὁ πριάμενος τὰν ἱερωτε[ίαν]
> [τῶν θεῶ]ν τῶν δυώδεκα ἱερωτευσεῖ ἐ[πὶ]
> [ζωᾶς λ]αζόμενος τῶν θυομένων πάν[των]
> [τὰ] δέρματα καὶ τὰς κωλεάς, ὅσα κα τ[οὶ]
> [θια]σῶται θύωντι τοῖς δυώδεκα θεοῖς ἐν τ[ῶι]
> [κοι]νῶι τῶι Νικομαχείωι. ποταγόντω δὲ τ[οὶ—]
> [—το]ὶ ἑκαστάκι γινόμενοι τὰ ἱερεῖα ἅ κα [δέηι]
> [θυσιά]ζειν ποτὶ τὸν βωμὸν τὸν τῶν θε[ῶν]
> [τῶν] δυώδεκα καὶ ποιούντω τὰν θυσίαν
> [καὶ τὰν σπονδά]ν.

Nicomachus. Good luck. He who buys the priesthood of the twelve gods will be priest for life, receiving the skin and thighs of all the sacrifices, as

281 Note the use of emphatic αὐτός.

282 It could also be specifying that he did the sacrifices by himself.

283 θύω is also found in 1.3.

> much as the members sacrifice to the Twelve Gods in the common building instituted/given by Nicomachus. The respective [Sacrificial Servants] should take the sacrificial animals to be sacrificed to the altar of the Twelve Gods and perform the sacrifice and the drink offering.[284]
>
> IK KALCHEDON 13.1–11 (third century BCE)

Only a few tentative comments will be made due to the reconstruction necessary for this attestation of θυσιάζω. Merkelbach suggests that σφά]ζειν is a possible reconstruction here, but claims the lacunae better fit θυσιά]ζειν.[285] Likewise, he suggests to complete lines 7–8 as either τ]οὶ ἱε|ροὶ τοί] or τ]οὶ θιασῶ|ται].[286] The text is a set of provisions for the "Nicomachean" sanctuary, Nicomachus being the namesake and founder of the precinct. θύω and θυσιάζω are both used, with the former referring to sacrifices "in the common building" (ἐν τ[ῶι] [κοι]νῶι). Stroud claims the phrase ἐν τῶι κοινῶι refers specifically to the public domain where meat would be provided for all.[287] Those performing these sacrifices are labelled [θια]σῶται, which simply refers to members of the cult. If Merkelbach's reconstruction for lines 7–8 with τ]οὶ ἱε|ροί is correct, then the verbal subject of [θυσιά]ζειν is a different group. This group does not sacrifice in the common area, but instead are mandated ([δέηι]) to go "to the altar" (ποτὶ τὸν βωμόν). The potentially different group may be those who are religious officials who would officiate the θυσία, which is here distinguished as at an official altar rather than in the common area. This inscription, if the lacunae are being read correctly, would situate θυσιάζω in a context involving particular cultic leaders in contrast to lay-sacrificers, as well as a more formal offering at an altar.

> [—19 char.—ἐπαιν]ἐ̣σαι
> [—19 char.—Πα]τ̣αρέα, τῶν
> [ἀρχισωματοφυλάκων, ἀρχ]ιτέκτονα τῆς
> [—12 char.—τάξ]ε̣ως καὶ πρὸς τοῖς
> [πετροβολικοῖ]ς̣(?), καὶ στεφανῶσαι αὐτὸν
> [χρ]υ̣σῶι στεφάνωι καὶ ἀναθεῖναι
> εἰκόνα γραπτὴν ἐν τῶι ἱερῶι τῆς Παφίας
> Ἀφροδίτης, ἄγειν δ' αὐτοῦ καὶ ἡμέραν

284 Translation with help from Reinhold Merkelbach, Friedrich Karl Dörner, and Sencer Şahin, *Die Inschriften von Kalchedon* (Bonn: Habelt, 1980), 26.

285 Merkelbach, Dörner, and Şahin, *Die Inschriften von Kalchedon*, 27.

286 Merkelbach, Dörner, and Şahin, *Die Inschriften von Kalchedon*, 27.

287 Stroud, *The Athenian*, 26.

δι᾽ αἰῶνος, τοὺς μὲν νέμοντας τὸ
τάγμα τῶν πρεσβυτέρων ἀφετῶν
θυσιάζοντας ἐν Παλαιᾶι τῆι Ἀφροδίτηι,
τοὺς δὲ τὸ τῶν νεωτέρων νέμοντας
ἄγειν ἐν Πάφωι θυσιάζοντας τῆι Λητοῖ·
τὸ δὲ ψήφισμα τόδε ἀναγράψαι εἰς
στήλην παρίνην καὶ ἀναθεῖναι
ἐν τῶι ἐπιφανεστάτωι τόπωι τοῦ
ἱεροῦ.

the Council and People have resolved to praise …, citizen of Patara, one of the Principal Friends, chief engineer of the island, overseer of the city in charge of the ballistic engines, and to crown him with a golden wreath and to put up a painted portrait of him in the sacred precinct of the Paphian Aphrodite; in his honour the Members of the Corps of the Senior Artillerists shall forever observe a day with sacrifices in the Old City to Aphrodite, and the Members of the Corps of the Juniors with sacrifices at Paphos to Leto; a copy of this decree shall be inscribed on a limestone stele and set up at the most conspicuous spot within the sacred precinct.[288]

ABSA 56 (1961) 4,4.1–18 (163–145 BCE)

θυσιάζω is a participle twice in this honorific decree for military service (lines 12, 14). Mitford points out that "the Aphrodite temple of Old Paphos was the senior ἱερόν of the new city, for it was there that the Senior Gunners were to offer sacrifice, while their juniors were relegated to a shrine of Leto in New Paphos."[289] Paphos might have been "the headquarters in Cyprus of the Ptolemaic army and navy" in the third or second century BCE.[290] Concerning this text, Bucker surmises that the sacrifices "were celebrated in some sacred precinct maintained at Paphos by the Lycian troops."[291] He does not clarify whether the sacrifices at these two sites were officiated by the troops, but, given their specific role identified in the text, the single day of the year this occurred, the fact that this is a legal decree to be openly read in the precincts, and the responsibility placed on them, it seems as though this text is specifying that the troops were permitted to be the temple officials *on this specific day*

288 Translation from William H. Buckler, "Documents from Phrygia and Cyprus," *JHS* 55 (1935): 76.

289 Terence B. Mitford, "Helenos, Governor of Cyprus," *JHS* 79/80 (1959–1960): 106, fn. 37.

290 Buckler, "Documents," 78.

291 Ibid., citing *OGIS* 146, 147, 162 (fn. 42); emphasis added.

in their respective areas in order to honor their fellow serviceman. This text is similar to a context repeated by Diodorus where women are permitted to officiate at sacrifices (see literary texts below). If these troops were not being given permission to officiate, then why would a decree need to be made? Why would bringing a sacrifice in honor of their compatriot have been anything needing royal permission? Taking over official functions in the temple at the potential headquarters of the navy would, presumably, need such permission. In any case, θυσιάζω occurs here again in a formal, temple-oriented context.

> βασιλεῖ Πτολεμαίωι καὶ βασιλίσσηι Κλεοπάτραι τῆι ἀδελφῆι
> θεοῖς Φιλομήτορσι χαίρειν Θαυῆς καὶ Ταοῦς δίδυμαι αἱ λειτουργοῦσαι
> ἐν τῶι πρὸ\ς/ Μέμφει μεγάλωι Σαραπιείωι. καὶ πρότερον μὲν ὑμῖν
> ἐπιδημήσα[σι]ν ἐν Μέμφει καὶ ἀναβᾶσιν εἰς τὸ ἱερὸν θυσιάσαι
> ἐνετύχομ[ε]ν καὶ ἐπεδώκαμεν ἔντευξιν προφερόμεναι μὴ κομίζεσθαι
> τὴν καθήκουσαν ἡμῖν δίδοσθαι σύνταξιν τῶν δεόντων ἔκ τε τοῦ
> Σαραπιείου καὶ Ἀσκληπιείου.
>
> To King Ptolemy and Queen Cleopatra, his sister, divine *Philometores*, greetings (from) Thaues and Taous, the twins who perform the rites at the great Sarapion, in nearby Memphis. When previously you returned to the city and we caught up with you on the way to make sacrifices, we also handed you a petition, claiming that we had not received the assigned salary that should have been given to us for duties at the Sarapion and Asklepeion.[292]
>
> UPZ 1 42.1–7 (162 BCE)[293]

This is a petition to the king from twins who are seeking to gain compensation for their conscripted service.[294] At first glance this papyrus could be regarded as evidence contrary to the claim espoused thus far. *The king* is the one sacrificing in the temple (εἰς τὸ ἱερὸν θυσιάσαι). However, that the king was leading the θυσία is no problem, since Greeks did not have unbending regulations regarding who could or could not perform such an act, with the degree of strictness

292 Translation with help from Julio López Saco, *Fuentes Grecolatinas del Próximo Oriente, Egipto, Gracia y Roma: Inscripciones y otros materiales procedentes de la colección privada de K. C. Hanson*, trans. Fulvio Scarcia and Leonardo La Rosa (Escuela de Historia, UCV, 2007), 14.

293 The first petition that is essentially a copy of this one is found in UPZ 1 41.

294 It may also be that these twins worked at the temple and were not conscripted. The term λειτουργέω could indicate either. See discussion below.

often depending on the importance of the sacrifice and locale.[295] The king as head of Egypt had the prerogative to perform such an act, and it makes sense to use θυσιάζω here in order to emphasize that the king was himself leading sacrifices on behalf of his people. Even though the officiating aspect of θυσιάζω is not clear here, it is plain that the sacrifices involved with the verb are at the temple and, due to the king himself bringing the offering, could be assumed to be more formal in nature. With θύω, the agency of the king and the formality of the sacrifices would not have been explicit, and the king might have been assumed simply to be participating in the event rather than leading it instead of (or with) the priests. This text also serves to show that θυσιάζω does not need to refer to priests by trade.

> ἔν τε τοῖς γενεθλίοις τοῦ βασιλέως καθ' ἕκαστον μῆνα θυσιάζων ὑπὲρ τοῦ δήμου, διαδρομὰς ἐτίθει τοῖς τε ἐφήβοις καὶ τοῖς νέοις
>
> and with the family members of the king each month officiating the θυσία on behalf of the *demos*, he was setting up parades for the boys and the youth
>
> IK SESTOS 1.35–37 (133–120 BCE)

Due to the length of this text, the salient contextual aspects will be described rather than cited.[296] This inscription represents a panegyric to a priest who is doing exceptionally well ([ἐπὶ ἱ]ερ[έ]ως Γλαυκίου [το]ῦ Κιλλαίου [line 1]) named Manas (line 2). In his travels this man was appointed priest to the king (ἱερεύς τε ἀποδειχθεὶς το[ῦ] βασιλέως Ἀττάλου [lines 26–27]) and also became a gymnasiarch (lines 30–33). The document does not contrast θυσιάζω with θύω, but does emphasize that Manas was the one sacrificing on behalf of everyone else (συνετέλεσεν μὲν θυσίας … ὑπὲρ τῆς τοῦ δήμου καὶ τῆς τῶν νέων σωτηρίας [lines 62–64]; ἐπιτελῶν τὰς πρεπούσας θυσίας ὑπὲρ τῶν νέων [line 67]). Manas is the one with authority in these sacrifices (cf. lines 65–67) and it is emphasized that he *alone* served in religious duty (ὑφ' ἑαυτοῦ ἱερῶν; line 70). Lines 84–86 make explicit that these offerings were being performed at a formal celebration, and that for royalty. Given that the thrust of this panegyric is to focus on *Manas*'s benevolent religious performance, it would make sense for θυσιάζω to be used to clarify further that it was Manas performing the rituals at these celebrations. θυσιάζω makes clear that Manas took a lead role in these celebratory sacrifices, which were done "with the family members of the king." θύω in

---

295 Jameson, *Cults and Rites*, 246–247; cf. 183.

296 The full text is available online at https://epigraphy.packhum.org/.

this context would not specify that Manas was more than a mere participant in the offering involving the king's family. θυσιάζω puts the focus on Manas and his lauded role. The term is used again in a formal cultic context with a focus on the officiator of the sacrifice.

> [.....]ησ̣ει ἀρχιφυ[λακίτηι Βερενικίδος]
> Θεσμοφόρου καὶ το[ῖς σὺν αὐτῶι φυλακί-]
> ταις παρὰ Πορεγέ̣[βθιος τοῦ..... παστο-]
> φόρου καὶ ἰσιονόμ[ου ἀπὸ τῆς αὐτῆς]
> κώμης. τῆι ιε τοῦ [ἐνεστῶτος μηνὸς]
> θυσιάζοντος ἐμο[ῦ ἐν τῶι ἐνθάδε Ἰσιεί(?)-]
> ωι ὑπέρ τε τοῦ β[ασιλέως καὶ τῆς βασι-]
> λίσσης καὶ τῶν [τούτων τέκνων καὶ]
> προγόνων, οὐδ[εμιᾶς οὔσης πρὸς ἐμὲ]
> μέμψεως, ε̣π̣ο̣[- ca.18 -]
> Περῦτις Περύτ[ιος - ca.14 - ἐ-]
> μαστίγου
>
> To [...]esis, *archiphylakitês* of Berenikis Thesmophorou, and his *phylakitai*, from Poregebthis, priest and warden of the temple of Isis from the same village. On the 15th of the present month, while I was sacrificing in the temple of Isis there on behalf of the king and queen and their children and ancestors, totally innocent, ... Perutis, son of Perutis, whipped[297]
>
> P.Tebt. 3 1 797.1–12 (second century BCE)

This papyrus uses θυσιάζω to refer to the sacrifices of the "priest and warden of the temple," one of the people who is obviously responsible for performing sacrificial rituals. The formal cultic context is again apparent, and all the more so when this priest states that he was sacrificing on behalf of the royals on this occasion. One might presume these sacrifices were therefore ornate. Perhaps the petitioner also uses θυσιάζω in order to aggravate the severity of the crime, since, if the term does refer to officiating a θυσία, the priest would be claiming that he himself was in the middle of performing formal ritual for the Ptolemies when he was attacked. This, in a way, ups the ante of the heinousness acted out by Perutis, which could curry more favor for this royal petition. Not much else

297 Translation from John Bauschatz, *Law and Enforcement in Ptolemaic Egypt* (Cambridge: Cambridge University Press, 2013), 72.

can be derived from this text concerning the meaning of θυσιάζω, though its characterization could coincide with every other attestation.

> περὶ τᾶς κράνας. τᾶς δὲ κράνας τᾶς [ὠνομασμένα] διὰ τῶν ἀρχαίων ἐγγράφων Ἅγνας καὶ τοῦ γε[γε]νημένου ποτὶ τᾶι κράναι ἀγάλματος τὰν ἐπιμέλειαν ἐχέτω Μνασίστρατος, ἕως ἂν ζεῖ, καὶ μετεχέτω μετὰ τῶν ἱερῶν τᾶν τε θυσιᾶν καὶ τῶν μυστηρίων, καὶ ὅσα κα οἱ θύοντες ποτὶ τᾶι κράναι τραπεζῶντι, καὶ τῶν θυμάτων τὰ δέρματα λαμβανέτω Μνασίστρατος, τῶν τε διαφόρων, ὅσα κα οἱ θύοντες ποτὶ τᾶι κράναι προτιθῆντι ἢ εἰς τὸν θησαυρόν, ὅταν κατασκευασθεῖ, ἐμβάλωντι, λαμβανέτω Μνασίστρατος τὸ τρίτον μέρος· τὰ δὲ δύο μέρη, καὶ ἄν τι ἀνάθεμα ὑπὸ τῶν θυσιαζόντων ἀνατιθῆται, ἱερὰ ἔστω τῶν θεῶν. ὁ δὲ ἱερεὺς καὶ οἱ ἱεροὶ ἐπιμέλειαν ἐχόντω, ὅπως ἀπὸ τῶν διαφόρων ἀναθέματα κατασκευάζηται τοῖς θεοῖς, ἃ ἂν τοῖς συνέδροις δόξει.
>
> About the Fountain: Mnasistratos must take care of the fountain named "Hagna" by the ancient writings and the statue created near the fountain as long as he lives, and he is to share in both the sacrifices and Mysteries with the sacred men. Mnasistratos is to receive whatever those sacrificing at the fountain offer on the table and the skins of the sacrificial animals. Mnasistratos is to receive a one-third share of the income from whatever those sacrificing at the fountain offer or put into the treasury, when it is constructed. The other two portions and any dedication set up by those sacrificing are to be property of the gods. The priest and the sacred men must take care that from the funds dedications are made for the gods, whatever ones are decided by the *sunedroi*.[298]
>
> IG V,1 1390.84–89 (92 BCE)

This text is about the mysteries of Andania and "provides many details concerning the ceremonial and administrative context in which the mysteries were performed. In twenty-six sections, this document raises several issues: the supply of sacrificial animals, the penalty in case of infringement and the organization of the sacrificial meal or of the market during the festival."[299] The section with θυσιάζω (lines 84–89) concerns the involvement in the

298 Laura Gawlinski, *The Sacred Law of Andania: A New Text with Commentary* (Berlin/Boston: de Gruyter, 2012), 83.

299 Vinciane Pirenne-Delforge, "Mnasistratos, the 'Hierophant' at Andania (*IG*. 5.1.1390 and *Syll.*[3] 735)," in *Myths, Martyrs, and Modernity: Studies in the History of Religions in Honour of Jan N. Bremmer*, ed. Jutse Dijkstra, Justin Kroesen, and Yme Kuiper (Leiden: Brill, 2010), 221.

Mysteries of a wealthy benefactor, one Mnasistratos,[300] who is permitted and privileged to share in the θυσία and Mysteries with the sacred men[301] (μετεχέτω μετὰ τῶν ἱερῶν τᾶν τε θυσιᾶν καὶ τῶν μυστηρίων; lines 85–86) and also to share in "as much as the sacrificers might offer on the table at the spring" (ὅσα κα οἱ θύοντες ποτὶ τᾶι κράναι τραπεζῶντι; line 86, referring to meats) and "as much as the sacrificers might offer at the spring" (ὅσα κα οἱ θύοντες ποτὶ τᾶι κράναι προτιθῆντι; line 87 referring to monetary income).[302] Those bringing sacrifices are labelled οἱ θύοντες, whereas in the next lines a distinction is made: "and the two parts (of the income),[303] and whatever devoted thing might be devoted by τῶν θυσιαζόντων, will be holy to the gods" (τὰ δὲ δύο μέρη, καὶ ἄν τι ἀνάθεμα ὑπὸ τῶν θυσιαζόντων ἀνατιθῆται, ἱερὰ ἔστω τῶν θεῶν). Here a distinction is made between the group of sacrificers (οἱ θύοντες) coming to the shrine and those who have authority to designate devoted dedications to the gods (τῶν θυσιαζόντων).[304] Those who make up the group of τῶν θυσιαζόντων is made clear in the next line, which states that the priest and the sacred men will prepare the devoted items for the gods: "Now the priests and the sacred men will take care, so that devoted items might be prepared for the gods from the funds" (ὁ δὲ ἱερεὺς καὶ οἱ ἱεροὶ ἐπιμέλειαν ἐχόντω, ὅπως ἀπὸ τῶν διαφόρων ἀναθέματα κατασκευάζηται τοῖς θεοῖς; lines 88–89). Substantives of θύω and θυσιάζω are used in order to distinguish between groups of sacrificers, with the latter being those with formal tasks and authority at the cultic site. The lay-sacrificers, οἱ θύοντες, are separated from those in cultic authority who perform the rituals, τῶν θυσιαζόντων. This latter group also has authority over the monetary funds. This text clearly uses οἱ θύοντες and τῶν θυσιαζόντων as distinct groups and expected the reader to understand this.

> αὐτὸς ὁ θεὸς ἐπὶ βήματος μαρμαρίνου
> καὶ ἡ παρακειμένη τῶι θεῶι τράπεζα λίθου Λεσβί-
> ου ἔχουσα πόδας ἀναγλύπτους γρῦπας καὶ πρὸ αὐ-
> τῆς ἀβάκηον μαρμάρινον πρὸς τὴν χρῆσιν τῶν θυσιαζόντων

300 See Gawlinski, *The Sacred Law*, 195–196 and Pirenne-Delforge, "Mnasistratos," 221–222 for his role and privilege.

301 This term is transliterated by Pirenne-Delforge.

302 Gawlinski, *The Sacred Law*, 83.

303 The other third Mnasistratos receives (cf. lines 87–88).

304 Gawlinski does not comment on how θυσιάζω is used here (*The Sacred Law*, 83, 197–199).

> God himself on a marble pedestal. Adjacent to God a table of Lesbian stone with sculptured feet of a griffon and before it a marble dish to use for sacrificing.[305]
>
> SMYRNA 91.8–12 (Late BCE/Early CE?)[306]

This excerpt is a record regarding a religious site built by a priest named Apollonius Sparos (lines 3–6). The inscription describes the necessary components for this new site and acts as an inventory of sorts. It is a locked temple facility (lines 18–19) and thus can only be accessed by specific people. Speaking of this inventory, Thompson notes, "More was required, however, for the sanctuary to be a sacred site. Sacralization requires ongoing performance—devotees who regularly offer sacrifices and eat meals before God."[307] These devotees in this inventory seem to be referred to by τῶν θυσιαζόντων, since it makes little sense for generic lay-sacrificers to be mentioned here in a list prescribing the necessities for the temple itself to begin to function. These people would also run the facility and have the key to it. With respect to the "marble dish" (ἀβάκηον μαρμάρινον), Thompson speaks of the god associated with this bowl, saying, "In the inventory proper (lines 8–32), the cult deity is given greater status than the other five. Rather than being mentioned by name, he is referred to as 'God' (lines 29 and 33) or 'God himself' (line 8). Further, 'God himself' was present on a pedestal without any sculpted representation."[308] The sacrifices associated with this bowl, then, would be to the most revered God. This particular sacrificial spot was also elaborate and an important focal point in this temple.[309] This might again highlight the procedural and formal nature of offerings in this place and thus naturally associate the cultic officiators (τῶν θυσιαζόντων) with the most holy site. All these data suggest that the substantive τῶν θυσιαζόντων refers to cultic sacrificial officials who were in charge of particularly formal offerings and not to lay-sacrificers in general. This conclusion comports with every other use of θυσιάζω documented.

305 Translation from Leonard L. Thompson, "ISMYRNA 753: Gods and the One God," in *Reading Religions in the Ancient World: Essays Presented to Robert McQueen Grant on His 90th Birthday*, ed. Robert M. Grant (Boston: Brill, 2007), 102.

306 Gill, "Trapezomata," 120, says this is a first century CE inscription but most do not date it.

307 Thompson, "ISMYRNA 753," 104.

308 Thompson, "ISMYRNA 753," 106.

309 Gill, "Trapezomata," 119–120.

4.5.2.4 θυσιάζω in the Literary Texts

Examples from the literary resources will proceed chronologically with some texts providing more insight than others.[310] The accumulation of consistent usage among similar contexts, especially when paired with θύω for contrast, strongly favors that θυσιάζω continued to be defined in the way established thus far.

> "οὐδ᾽ ἄρα θύεις ἐρυσίχθον᾽;" "οὐκ," ἔφην, "ἐγώ.""βοῦν δ᾽ εὐρυμέτωπον;" "οὐ θύω βοῦν, ἄθλιε." "μῆλα θυσιάζεις ἆρα;" "μὰ Δί᾽, ἐγὼ μὲν οὔ, οὐδέτερον αὐτῶν, προβάτιον δ᾽." "οὔκουν," ἔφη, "τὰ μῆλα πρόβατα;" "⟨μῆλα πρόβατ᾽;⟩ οὐμανθάνω, ⟨μάγειρε,⟩ τούτων οὐδέν, οὐδὲ βούλομαι.
>
> "Aren't you sacrificing an earthbreaker?" "No, I'm not," I said. "A cow with a wide forehead?" "I'm not sacrificing a cow, you bastard." "So you're making a sacrifice of mēla?" "No, by Zeus, I'm not. Neither of these—just a little sheep." "Aren't mēla sheep?", he said. "Apples are sheep? I don't understand any of this, cook," I said, "and I don't want to."[311]
>
> STRATON, *Fr.* 1.21–22 (fourth to third centuries BCE)

In the flow of this comedic encounter, a chef questions his employer about how big his sacrifice will be. The size is whittled down from an "earthbreaker" (ἐρυσίχθον) to a "cow" (βοῦν) and then to μῆλα, which can be understood as either "sheep" or "apples." The joke here is that the chef is using obscure Homeric language that the employer does not understand. The progressively frustrated employer believes that the chef is mocking his sacrifice by claiming it was made of apples. The use of θυσιάζω here seems to be part of the comedic tension and mockery. The chef twice speaks of normal sacrificial items with θύω, but then when it comes to the pejorative claim about apples, he uses θυσιάζω. Now, it could be claimed that all that is occurring here is the employment of synonymous terms in order to forego bland repetition.[312] Yet such a line of

---

310 Aesop, *Fables*, 168, 1.3 has not been included in the formal analysis due to its late collection. So also Testament of the Twelve Patriarchs, 3.14.5.5. Both uses still corresponds to the rest of the entries.

311 Athenaeus (Olson, LCL), 271.

312 Werner suggests that it is only θυσιάζω and not θύω in this context that refers to sacrifice (Jaeger R. Werner, *Religion in Attic Middle Comedy* [PhD diss., University of Pennsylvania, 1962], 91, 116). This interpretation is correct in that it picks up on the subtleties of the comedic encounter with the sacrifice itself being meagre, but the context of a feast makes it hardly possible that the readers would not understand θύω as referring to an animal to be slayed in sacrifice. Moreover, if just the slaying of the animal were in view, it makes less

reasoning does not account for the flow of the comedic encounter. The humor lies in the ante-up effect of each subsequent term. The chef begins with a large animal (ἐρυσίχθον), then moves to a smaller yet still impressive one (βοῦν … εὐρυμέτωπον), and finally the Homeric homonym comes into play with μῆλα. It might be that the use of verbs here coincides with this progression. The playwright twice uses θύω when matching with the suitable sacrifices, but then uses θυσιάζω in order for the joke to have a greater effect. The term's specificity is where the humor is found. While the chef is not meaning to refer to anything but sheep here—an admittedly somewhat less impressive sacrifice than the others—still the audience would have heard, in essence, "So you're going to go through the formalities of a θυσία sacrifice *with apples*?" For one, this is absurd since the θυσία is a ritualistic feast of cooked *meat* that did not typically involve fruit.[313] But more importantly, if θυσιάζω does indeed refer to those acting as officiators of the ritual, here the employer is then the object of mockery through this double entendre. He would be officiating an apple sacrifice at his elaborate banquet.[314] This is meant to be absurd and impossible. Given that the employer and his increasing frustration is the brunt of the joke in this interplay, the employment of a more formal term (θυσιάζω) coincides with the humorous intent. The formality of the sacrifice is emphasized while the material of the sacrifice ("apples") is reduced to absurdity. θυσιάζω places the focus on the employer's own actions in "leading" the ridiculous sacrifice—actions which are completely indiscernible, since there is no meat in the sacrifice even to begin the normal preparations! Later on, when the chef slays the animal, the author returns to θύω and not θυσιάζω, since the chef is not the head of the household who would perform the θυσία rites (cf. 383a and ἔθυεν, ἔλεγεν ἄλλα ῥήματα). Had Straton merely been employing synonyms for the sake of rhetorical embellishment, why does he only use θυσιάζω this once, and that in the height of the comedic tension?

Unfortunately, due to the fragmentary nature of this section of Straton, we do not know anything more about the identity of the employer or the type of feast being set up. This sacrifice did occur at an altar during a feast.[315] It is the only employment of θυσιάζω in a household context from the attestations of the term. This is no problem since a θυσία could be performed in houses by the

sense that the chef would speak of the employer slaughtering the animal (θύεις) when it is the chef who does so (see 383a).

313 Cf. Gill, "Trapezomata," 132.

314 That this sacrifice is indeed more than a simple slaughter of an animal is implied further by the use of τὰς οὐλοχύτας (line 384), which Athenaeus (Olson, LCL), 271, fn. 88, notes to be a term used in sacrifices involving altars.

315 See previous footnote.

family head. Even still, the rhetoric in the comedy seems to continue to demonstrate the meaning proposed in this study.[316]

> οὗτος πρῶτος βοῦν ἐθυσίασε καὶ Ζῆνα προσηγόρευσεν,
> ὥς τινες.
>
> He [Kekrops Diphyes, the first king of the Athenians] was the first to sacrifice an ox and addressed Zeus by name, as some say.[317]
>
> PHILOCHORUS, *Fr.* F93.6–7 (fourth to third centuries BCE)

While there is little context available for this fragment, enough remains to highlight the use of θυσιάζω.[318] Here Philochorus is describing the origin of Athens and its first monarch. In the narrative, the belief espoused is that Kekrops Diphyes not only named Athens but also planted the first olive tree on the acropolis (lines 4–5). Subsequently, the region was called Κεκροπία because of him (lines 5–6). He is then touted to have been the first one to sacrifice (ἐθυσίασε) an ox and also to invoke the name of Zeus. There are a few things to note about the employment of θυσιάζω here. First of all, this is the first sacrifice at Athens with an ox. Whether the claim is that this is the first oxen sacrifice altogether is not clear, but the distinction remains that Kekrops is founding the great city and in this momentous occasion is performing the first bovine θυσία. If he is the first to do so, then he must be the one leading, officiating, and showing how the rite is done. Secondly, this event is associated with the origins of the unparalleled cult of Zeus, which further solidifies the solemnity and importance of the sacrifice. It is hard to imagine this occasion as impromptu or extemporaneous. It is portrayed as the crowning religious event of the city and of Greek religion. If Kekrops is being described as initiating the religious life of Athens, then the use of θυσιάζω is all the more fitting, since he is the first actor in the official rites of the cult of Zeus. Had Philochorus used θύω or the like here, it would not be explicit that Kekrops was *himself* formally initiating the cult of Zeus in official Greek sacrificial ritual (i.e., θυσία). With θυσιάζω, king Kekrops becomes the first Athenian θυσία-officiator and thus sets the precedent for such ritual and cultic involvement in Athens for the future. This fragment of Philochorus again fits the delimitations encountered so far,

316 There are no other uses of θύω available in Straton for contrast.
317 Translation from Phillip Harding, *The Story of Athens* (London: Routledge, 2008), 21.
318 There are a few other examples of θύω in the Philochorus fragments—enough to consider that θυσιάζω was not simply his preferred term for sacrifice if it were considered synonymous with θύω.

namely, that θυσιάζω is used in contexts of formal sacrifice with the focus being on the one performing the θυσία. There is no altar explicitly mentioned in this text, though it could be readily inferred.

> προσκυνήσαντα τὴν γῆν καὶ βωμὸν ἱδρυσάμενον καὶ θυσιάσαντα τοῖς θεοῖς γενέσθαι μετὰ τῶν ἐκβάντων τοῦ πλοίου ἀφανῆ
>
> After performing obeisance to the earth and setting up an altar and sacrificing to the gods, he and those who had disembarked from the ship with him disappeared[319]
>
> BEROSSUS, *Fr.* 7.34–36 (fourth to third centuries BCE)

Berossus is recounting a primordial myth about an all-encompassing flood that destroyed humanity and the environs. Xisuthrus (the Noah-like figure) makes a sacrifice directly after being delivered from the flood and disembarking the ship. Note that the author is intent to comment that an altar is built for this occasion (βωμὸν ἱδρυσάμενον). Xisuthrus is also, in the world of the narrative, the *de facto* leader of humanity and the one to rebuild it after the deluge. He is the religious leader who, in this act of sacrifice, reinitiates the act of formal offerings (θυσία) for the new world. Here there is an altar and ceremony with Xisuthrus at its head. In contrast, just a few lines later there is a distinction:

> Τοὺς δὲ ἀκούσαντας ταῦτα θῦσαί τε τοῖς θεοῖς καὶ πέριξ πορευθῆναι εἰς Βαβυλῶνα
>
> After hearing these things, they sacrificed to the gods and proceeded to Babylon on foot
>
> Berossus, *Fr.* 7.48–50

In this passage the survivors are peripatetically making their way to Babylon. It is in this transient state that they sacrifice to the gods and θύω is employed. There is no altar or formality, and Xisuthrus is not signaled out as performing the rite, but instead the whole group is described as sacrificing. This is not the reignition of the formal θυσία for the new humankind performed by its new patriarch, but simply offerings made in good will. This distinction suggests that, once again, θυσιάζω is used to point out a formal ritual being performed by a cultic leader at an altar. This text shares similarities with the Philochorus

319 Translations from Stanley Mayer Burstein, *The Babyloniaca of Berossus* (Malibu: Undena Publications, 1978), 20.

fragment in that it speaks of the primordial origins of a people group with a focus on their forefather setting up official sacrificial rites.

> Πόσσις δ' ἐν τρίτῳ Μαγνητικῶν τὸν Θεμιστοκλέα φησὶν, ἐν Μαγνησίᾳ τὴν στεφανηφόρον ἀρχὴν ἀναλαβόντα, θῦσαι Ἀθηνᾷ, καὶ τὴν ἑορτὴν Παναθήναια ὀνομάσαι, καὶ Διονύσῳ Χοοπότῃ θυσιάσαντα καὶ τὴν Χοῶν ἑορτὴν αὐτόθι καταδεῖξαι.
>
> Possis in the third book of Magnesian Affairs says that Themistokles, having accepted the office of crown-bearer (*stephanephoros*) in Magnesia, sacrificed to Athena and named the festival Panathenaia and, having sacrificed to Dionysos the Pitcher-Drinker (Choöpotes), also introduced the Festival of Pitchers (Choës) there.[320]
>
> POSSIS, *Fr.* 1.1–6 (fourth to third centuries BCE)

This fragment describes Magnesian history where one Themistokles becomes στεφανηφόρος, an important priestly role in the ancient Greek world.[321] Upon reception of the title, Themistokles sacrificed to Athena (θῦσαι Ἀθηνᾷ), and after θυσιάζω-ing to Dionysos, inaugurated the Festival of Pitchers. While it is difficult to be certain about the separate functions of θύω and θυσιάζω here, there are a few suspect differences in the events described. The sacrifices to Athena are linked directly to the reception of the priestly role. The aorist participle ἀναλαβόντα situates a prior event to the sacrifice, i.e., "after having accepted the office of crown-bearer, (he) sacrificed to Athena." Likewise, in parallel syntax, θυσιάσαντα is the prerequisite to the next event, i.e., "after having θυσιάζω-ed, (he) set up the Festival of Pitchers." These are, then, separate sacrifices. Banchich thinks that the second sacrifice here refers to an inaugural ceremony, whereas the previous sacrifice is undefined in its nature.[322] If it is a ceremony of inauguration, then it is certainly a formal event with all the associated rites. Perhaps θυσιάζω is part of the way the author is pointing out this illustrious occasion.

In contrast, Themistokles' reception of his new title and the subsequent sacrifices are, possibly, an act of obeisance and gratitude for this new office.

320 Translation by Thomas Banchich, "Possis of Magnesia (480)," in *Jacoby Online. Brill's New Jacoby, Part III*, ed. Ian Worthington (Brill: Leiden, 2007), http://dx.doi.org/10.1163/1873-5363_bnj_a480.

321 See Pauline Schmitt Pantel, "4.a. Banquet" in *Thesaurus Cultus et Rituum Antiquorum II: Purification, Initiation, Heroization, Apotheosis, Banquet, Dance, Music, Cult Images* (California: The J. Paul Getty Museum, 2004), §225, p. 246.

322 "Possis of Magnesia."

These may be more personal sacrifices showing his character and not an act leading others in a cultic ceremony like that of a brand new festival. It is possible then that this text uses the one (θυσιάζω) to describe his formal role in sacrifice and one (θύω) to describe his more personal devotion. In fact, this same distinction seems to be more clearly articulated in a similar context in one of the inscriptions previously discussed (IG II³,1 921, II.14 [265 BCE]). In any case, the inauguration of a festival is certainly a formal event in which the new religious leader would likely be involved as the one leading the ceremonies. He set the festival up, so it makes sense that he would lead the sacrifices in his new position.

> διὸ καὶ παρὰ πολλαῖς τῶν Ἑλληνίδων πόλεων διὰ τριῶν ἐτῶν βακχεῖά τε γυναικῶν ἀθροίζεσθαι, καὶ ταῖς παρθένοις νόμιμον εἶναι θυρσοφορεῖν καὶ συνενθουσιάζειν εὐαζούσαις καὶ τιμώσαις τὸν θεόν· τὰς δὲ γυναῖκας κατὰ συστήματα θυσιάζειν τῷ θεῷ
>
> Consequently in many Greek cities every other year Bacchic bands of women gather, and it is lawful for the maidens to carry the thyrsus and to join in the frenzied revelry, crying out "Euai!" and honouring the god; while the matrons, forming in groups, offer sacrifices to the god[323]
>
> DIODORUS SICULUS, *Bib. hist.* 4.3.3.1–5

Other references to sacrifices in the surrounding context of Book 4 in Diodorus often use θύω (18.3.5; 23.4.5; 23.4.7). This particular context refers to matrons performing sacrifices. They make offerings in a biannual formal gathering, which is apparently an unusual activity since Diodorus points out that such is only lawful (νόμιμον εἶναι) in this particular instance. In other words, matrons offering these sacrifices is not the norm and is permitted for this festival only. This context helps us understand the function of θυσιάζω, since there would be nothing strange about women being lay participants in a θυσία, that is, their sharing of the meal. Instead, this text is pointing out their role in actually officiating the ceremony, which would be abnormal and is legal only at this specific time. This citation from Diodorus makes relatively clear that θυσιάζω refers to someone acting in the leading role of a formal θυσία ceremony.

> Ὅτι ἡ σύγκλητος δεισιδαιμονοῦσα ἐξαπέστειλεν εἰς Σικελίαν κατὰ Σιβυλλιακὸν λόγιον. οἱ δὲ ἐπελθόντες καθ' ὅλην τὴν Σικελίαν τοὺς τῷ Αἰτναίῳ Διὶ καθιδρυμένους βωμούς, θυσιάσαντες καὶ περιφράγματα ποιήσαντες ἀβάτους

323 Diodorus Siculus (Oldfather, LCL).

ἀπεδείκνυον τοὺς τόπους πλὴν τοῖς ἔχουσι καθ᾽ ἕκαστον πολίτευμα πατρίους θύειν θυσίας.

The senate, prompted by religious scruples, sent a delegation to Sicily in accordance with an oracle of the Sibylline Books. They visited throughout Sicily the altars set up to Aetnaean Zeus; here they offered sacrifice and fenced in the areas, and forbade access to them except in the case of those in each state who had traditional sacrifices to perform.[324]

DIODORUS SICULUS, *Bib. hist.* 34/35.10

Once again θύω and θυσιάζω are used in the same context, with similar distinctions notable as before. This text mentions a group ("delegation") sent by the Roman senate. This event is mentioned by Cicero: "Then, *priests of the Roman people*, selected from the most honourable college of decemvirs" went on this journey.[325] So, the "delegation," not defined in Diodorus, is clarified to be priests in Cicero. Note that Diodorus never states that these were priests. Yet this would be clear if θυσιάζω were used to indicate that those travelling were cultic officials. Moreover, this delegation was clearly in charge of religious rituals since they were blocking access to altars. The use of θύω in this text is reserved for those laypeople who come to the altars with their traditional sacrifices. The text does not make clear if the laity were the ones officiating the θυσία ceremony or not. Yet, given that the delegation was acting with such authority together with the use of θυσιάζω, the text could indicate that it was this group of priests officiating the ceremonies while the townsfolk brought their sacrifices to the altar to participate in the meal. This is not completely clear. What is apparent is that this group is specifically priests of high authority who took control of local altars. It is hard to imagine that they did not directly perform the rites associated with these cults—they came in fact to fix religious practice. Whatever the case, this text again uses θυσιάζω to refer to the more authoritative group in contrast to θύω.

Ἐμοὶ μὲν οὖν καλῶς ἐνόμιζε περὶ ἑκάστων ἀπολογεῖσθαι· καὶ γὰρ ἐπὶ τῶν προσφερομένων ἔλεγε μόσχων τε καὶ κριῶν καὶ χιμάρων, ὅτι δεῖ ταῦτα ἐκ βουκολίων καὶ ποιμνίων λαμβάνοντας ἥμερα θυσιάζειν, καὶ μηθὲν ἄγριον, ὅπως οἱ προσφέροντες τὰς θυσίας μηθὲν ὑπερήφανον ἑαυτοῖς συνιστορῶσι, σημειώσει κεχρημένοι τοῦ διατάξαντος.

324 Diodorus Siculus (Walton, LCL).

325 Cicero, *Verr.* 2.4.108 (emphasis added): tum ex amplissimo collegio decemvirali sacerdotes populi Romani.

> He seemed to me to have made a good defense on all the points; for in reference also to the calves and rams and goats which are offered, he said that it was necessary to take them from the herds and flocks, and sacrifice tame animals and offer nothing wild, that the offerers of the sacrifices might understand the symbolic meaning of the lawgiver and not be under the influence of an arrogant self-consciousness.[326]
>
> Let. Aris. 170.1–6

The writer of Aristeas is here looking back on the priestly advice of Eleazar who explained the Mosaic sacrifices to him. The assumption, given the totality of the Mosaic legislation, is that priests would be offering these sacrifices and that they would be in line with the formal ceremonies prescribed in the Torah. The use of θυσιάζω is again situated in a formal context with respect to particular officiators of the rituals. Moreover, when referring pejoratively to the unmannerly sacrifices among the native Egyptian peoples, Aristeas had just previously used θύω (138.4). It may also be that Aristeas has chosen to use θυσιάζω based on his knowledge of the LXX.

4.5.2.5 Conclusion on θυσιάζω

It is relatively clear that θυσιάζω is used in the same way across the literary and documentary sources from before the Common Era. It is always found in a formal cultic context with a focus on the person performing the θυσία ritual. Often θυσιάζω is used in contrast to θύω in order to make these distinctions clear in contexts where they are being emphasized. There are no cases where the roles of θυσιάζω and θύω are switched when used together. It would be worthwhile to examine the later LXX texts to see if these distinctions hold out. They have been omitted from this study due to their uncertain dating and potential lexical influence from the Pentateuch. It can be noted that θυσιάζω is always used in contexts involving unlawful sacrifices in Kingdoms (2 Kgdms 15:12; 3 Kgdms 1:9, 19, 25; 22:44; 4 Kgdms 12:4; 14:4; 15:4, 35; 16:4; 17:35; 23:20),[327] and

---

326 Herbert T. Andrews, trans., "The Letter of Aristeas," in *The Apocrypha and Pseudepigrapha of the Old Testament in English. Volume II: Pseudepigrapha*, vol. 2 of *The Apocrypha and Pseudepigrapha of the Old Testament in English*, ed. Robert H. Charles (Oxford: Oxford University Press, 1913), 110.

327 It is uncertain whether the sacrifices of the priests are being perceived positively or negatively by the translator in 23:20. It may be that θυσιάζω is used ironically here, since the priests who were θυσιάζω-ing to the gods have now become the offering (θυσία) themselves. The fact that these texts are all associated with the Kaige recension also makes their contribution to the present data difficult to determine. This connection may be a fruitful avenue of research.

in 4 Kgdms 17:35, when looking back on the Mosaic prescriptions against sacrificing to other gods, the verbiage seems to be taken from Greek Exod 22:19 (22:20 LXX) with θυσιάζω.[328] A formal study of the influence of Exod 22:19 (22:20 LXX) on later texts could, then, be fruitful. As it stands, the sources outside of the LXX indicate that θυσιάζω would refer to one acting as officiator in a θυσία ritual. If the translator had chosen to render with θύω, this participation could have been conceived as mere butchery of the animal all the way up to the performing of specific rites, since θύω is generic and could refer to either. By using θυσιάζω in Exod 22:19 (22:20 LXX), the translator created a law that was only condemning those who officiate sacrifices to other gods and not merely those who participate in them, whether in slaughter or a meal.[329] Both θύω and θυσιάζω refer to the baseline concept of sacrificing, which comports with the translator's use of SSF with respect to זבח. But θυσιάζω is a strange choice. Anyone versed in the prescriptions of the Pentateuch, let alone condemnations of foreign sacrifices in Exodus (e.g., 34:15), would know that they are not permitted. Why then did the translator create such an exception in these laws?

One cannot help but think that perhaps the Exodus translation was expected to be read either apart from or as a guide to later laws. Was this translation, or even this set of laws, going to circulate on its own? If not, was the first prescription against foreign sacrifice in the Torah supposed to inform the rest, so that the reader would know that it is only officiating such sacrifices that was to be condemned?[330] Or, if this particular translation was expected to be viewed by Greeks or authorities, is the change merely a means of placating their whims? There are some aspects of Ptolemaic legal influence from the third century that could inform the choice to change this law. Before these can be evaluated, however, it is necessary to ask what the meaning of ἐξολεθρεύω in Exod 22:19 (22:20 LXX) might be. This term will determine whether or not this law should be categorized as one involving the death penalty—laws which, as we have seen, are often changed by the translator.

---

328 Chronicles uses it in both positive (1 Chron 21:28; 2 Chron 7:5; 33:16) and negative (2 Chron 34:4) contexts.

329 One wonders if a Jew at the time would assume that θυσιάζω in a Jewish context only referred to Israelite priests. This is possible.

330 Remember that θύω does not speak to the exact role of a sacrificer in a ritual, so later texts using θύω in their condemnations could be inferring officiation and not mere participation. This seems doubtful in my opinion.

4.5.2.6 Defining ἐξολεθρεύω[331]

There is a significant variant in the manuscript tradition that should preface a discussion on ἐξολεθρεύω. Rahlfs included θανάτῳ before ἐξολεθρευθήσεται, as based on the original reading of Vaticanus (B*) and a selection of other manuscripts.[332] The Göttingen edition relies on A and F for the non-prefixed version. Should θανάτῳ be original, it could change the tenor of how ἐξολεθρευθήσεται would be understood.

ἐξολεθρεύω is a compound verb formed from ὀλεθρεύω, both of which have no literary occurrences before the LXX. Neither are there documentary references before the Common Era.[333] These terms come from the cognate noun ὄλεθρος ("destruction," "ruin," "plague,")[334] which is attested as far back as Homer. ὀλεθρεύω is a denominative verbal form which usually indicates a condition or an action.[335] The prefix ἐκ- can mean that an "action is conceived as having reached its consummation."[336] Based solely on these data, the term would seem to indicate something like "to destroy completely" or "to completely bring to loss," or something of the like.[337] This definition does not fit the data particularly well. Some texts do not seem to indicate that destruction is intended. A look at the early sources can show this.

Instead of wading through the numerous uses of the term found in the Jewish materials, there is enough information within the Greek Pentateuch to determine what ἐξολεθρεύω might have indicated at this early period. First of all, I have already pointed out that when the translator of Exodus wrote laws with the death penalty full stop, the third person imperative seems to be employed. Exodus 22:19 (22:20 LXX) does not fit this pattern with the future tense, which should serve as a warning against reading ἐξολεθρεύω as the death penalty. Second and more importantly, ἐξολεθρεύω is used to translate כרת in contexts referring to removing a person from the community (Gen 17:14; Exod 12:15, 19; 30:33; Lev 17:4, 9, 14; 18:29; 19:8; 20:17, 18; 22:3; 23:29). Only in Exod 31:14 is it made explicit that *the means by which* the person is removed from the community is death. Such a means should not be assumed

331 I am indebted to Dr. Larry Perkins for conversation and research notes on this verb. Some of this work will be included in the upcoming *SBLCS* volume on Exodus.

332 58–82 56ᶜ–129–246.

333 Ziebarth, Neue Verfluchungstafeln 25, is a first century CE text that uses ἐξολεθρεύω. All others are later in date.

334 LSJ, ὄλεθρος, I.–II.

335 Smyth and Messing, *Greek Grammar*, 245, §866.4.

336 Friedrich Blass, Albert Debrunner, and Robert Walter Funk, *A Greek Grammar of the New Testament and Other Early Christian Literature* (Cambridge: Cambridge University Press, 1961), §318(5), p. 166.

337 Wevers, *Notes*, 351, glosses with "root out."

for the other uses of the term. Numbers 19:20 appears to indicate that the subject of ἐξολεθρευθήσεται is cut off from the people until he could be labelled "clean" once again, which might indicate that this individual is not to die (cf. vv. 20–22). The verb in and of itself, when used in this sense of "removal," seems only to indicate the removal of a person from the community; how and for how long is not specified.[338] This usage is almost always accompanied by a preposition or modifying phrase signifying the group from which one is being removed.[339] Yet, notably, when comparing Lev 17:9 and 17:14—a section on the same law—there is no prepositional phrase and the same meaning seems to be discernable: ἐξολεθρευθήσεται alone means to be cut off from the people. Admittedly, Dt translates various difficult terms with ἐξολεθρεύω[340] and mostly without any prepositional modifiers. The translation of Deuteronomy and its use of this term would need a study of its own.

What is problematic about understanding ἐξολεθρεύω as "to remove" is that the cognate noun and cognate verb both seem to mean "destruction." Of course, if "destruction" just means to make something no longer extant within a particular context, then "to remove" fits well. Perkins hypothesizes on this matter:

> Whether the action described by this Hebrew requires the death of the offender or their ostracism from the covenant community is not specified ... The Greek verb ἐξολεθρεύω, based on the meaning of the simple verb, seems to describe an act of destruction, not exclusion, and so brings into the Greek translation a different sense than that found in the Hebrew *Vorlage* ... Perhaps the translator considers the consequence of such exclusion from the covenant community, namely ruin and destruction, for the individual concerned, and this leads him to use ἐξολεθρεύω as the rendering.[341]

His reasoning would then be that "destruction" is the ultimate consequence of "removal," and the translator has rendered based on the final result of the action, not the action itself, per se. Whether or not this is the case, it is

338 ἐξολεθρεύω translates שחת in Exod 8:24: ἐξωλεθρεύθη ἡ γῆ ἀπὸ τῆς κυνομυίας. It seems as though the translator is indicating the fertile ground was removed because of the dog-fly. "Tilled land" is a common use for γῆ.

339 E.g., Gen 17:14; Exod 12:15, 19; 30:33; 31:14; Lev 17:4, 9; 18:29; 19:8; 20:17, 18; 22:3; 23:29; Num 9:13; 15:30; 19:20.

340 Including even ירש in 4:38, which indicates dispossession and not destruction.

341 Larry Perkins, from the first draft notes for the *SBLCS* volume on Exodus. Shared with permission.

exceedingly difficult to understand the nuances of ἐξολεθρεύω. Given the available data in the Pentateuch, it seems fair based on Num 19:20 and Lev 17:9/14 to claim that this term might not indicate death in and of itself, and that no prepositional phrase was necessary to convey this. Given that every use of ἐξολεθρεύω in Exodus outside of 22:19 (22:20 LXX) refers to the removal from a people group, it seems plausible that the term would be understood in the same way here.

Now, in Exod 22:19 (22:20 LXX) the translator is rendering the Hebrew חרם. There is considerable debate as to the meaning of חרם, which is not necessary to enter fully into here. Lev and Num render חרם with ἀνατίθημι and ἀναθεματίζω respectively (Lev 27:28–29; Num 21:2–3), while Dt uses multiple terms. If חרם did indicate the death penalty via a religious-sacrificial killing, which many modern interpreters believe it did, it is possible that by translating with ἐξολεθρεύω the translator has either muddled that indication or removed it.[342] It is uncertain whether Num 21:2–3 in the Greek refers to killing the Canaanites with ἀναθεματίζω.[343] Leviticus 27:28–29 does relate חרם/ἀνατίθημι to the act of putting to death. Perhaps the translator of Exodus wanted to avoid certain connotations that a translation like ἀνατίθημι might have brought, though that term itself is not decisively condemnatory.[344] The translator is, as we have seen, averse to the death penalty. There are simply not enough data or translation equivalents in Ex to make any firm conclusions here.

It seems fair to submit, though, that the term was probably not perceived as the immediate death sentence. It might be used with various senses, but it is often found referring to the removal of a person from a specific group or context with no specification as to how long or by what means that would be. Given that the translator of Exodus also translates without the third person imperative in the apodosis, the concept of "removal" seems to be the sense he was expecting his audience to understand. There is still regrettably little evidence to sustain this conclusion.

Now, if θανάτῳ were considered original to the translation, it is probably the case that the law would refer to the death penalty. The denominative verb ἐξολεθρεύω would probably point to an action of removal, and the means of removal would be identified through θανάτῳ.[345] The phrase would probably then be translated "by means of an early death he shall be destroyed/or

342 See a helpful overview of opinions on חרם in Charles Trimm, "Recent Research on Warfare in the Old Testament," *Currents in Biblical Research* (2011): 9–10.

343 LSJ, ἀναθεματίζω, I.–II., defines the terms as either "devote to evil" or "curse," neither of which necessarily indicate death.

344 See LSJ, ἀνατίθημι, II.1, or, e.g., Jdth 16:19.

345 See section 2.5.

removed." Perhaps θανάτῳ made it into the manuscript traditions so as to make the death penalty clear in this way, as might be aligned with חרם.

4.5.3 *Conclusion of Translation-Technical Analysis*

Despite the difficulties with ἐξολεθρεύω, the law in Exod 22:19 (22:20 LXX) does in fact change from a prescription against *any* sacrifice/slaughter to other gods except Israel's deity[346] to only proscribing the officiation of a formal θυσία to these gods. On the face of it, this permits the participation of Jewish peoples in sacrifice or even Greek animal butchery outside of this one constraint.

If this is true, is there a discernable legal framework from which such a translational change might have sprung? Part of the difficulty in discerning this is not knowing which line of reasoning to pursue. Exodus 22:19 (22:20 LXX) changes the type of participation prohibited in foreign sacrifices and also might remove the death penalty. Is the new translation motivated by the restrictive stance on sacrifice in the Hebrew *Vorlage* or the capital punishment that such sacrifices warranted? Could it be both? Given what we know about the death penalty in Ptolemaic Egypt, religious tenants like those exhibited in 22:19 (22:20 LXX) stemming from minority groups would likely be dismissed. This is even more the case when the attitude of the Ptolemies towards syncretism in the third century is considered. A law directly asking to kill anyone who participates in their extensively promoted cultic propaganda would never be accepted by the Ptolemies, since it would be antithetical to the entire religious establishment being so arduously set up. In this light, both the change regarding sacrifice/slaughter as well as the death penalty can be attributable to the influence of Ptolemaic syncretism in the surrounding culture. As an additional avenue for inquiry, it can also be considered that the Ptolemies conscripted all citizens to work for them at certain periods. This work more than likely involved participating in religiously-tied animal slaughter. Not to serve would be illegal. This same problem would also likely be encountered in the military and by many Jewish slaves. It is to these aspects of the Ptolemaic system that we now turn.

346 Muraoka, *A Syntax*, §38 iv), p. 467, states that πλὴν κυρίῳ μόνῳ "must read '... except to the Lord alone,' not 'to the only Lord,' let alone 'to an only lord' ... The lexeme in question, when anarthrous like in these cases, cannot mean 'sole'" (see the whole argument at pp. 466–468).

4.5.4 *Legal and Cultural Analysis*

As far as I am aware there are no laws existing from the Ptolemaic era that state that one must sacrifice to the Greek or Egyptian deities.[347] On the other side of things, there is evidence that Jews had already accommodated their sacrifices to Egyptian standards in the time before the Ptolemaic era.[348] Alternative sacrificial practices might have already been engrained in the communities before the translation was ever conceived of. However, this accommodation might not have been so prevalent at the dawning of the third century.[349] Whatever the case, there is still strong evidence pointing to the reality that anyone living in Ptolemaic Egypt would not only be inundated with pressures to participate in syncretistic religious practice, including sacrifice, but likely would be forced to do so in certain circumstances. So, while there is no direct law on foreign sacrifice, there are other cultural-legal forces that almost guarantee that some Jews living in this era would be under stress to participate in sacrifices/slaughter involving foreign gods. The first pressure comes more indirectly from the religious *Zeitgeist*, while the second involves mandatory services performed in Ptolemaic Egypt.

4.5.4.1 The Cult of the Monarchy and Sarapis

It is no secret that from the outset of the Ptolemaic era this new leadership made efforts to form novel religious practices. Pirenne writes, "La période ptolémaïque, en rendant à l'Egypte l'indépendance et, avec elle, une dynastie nationale, quoique grecque d'origine, exerça sur l'évolution du culte une

347 Tcherikover, *Hellenistic Civilization*, 306, comments that no surviving documents show exemption from respecting the gods. He believes this exemption was given without a formal statement. The present author finds this conclusion untenable given the kinds of situations that involved forced participation in foreign sacrifice (see below).

348 Here we could compare the Elephantine Papyri which may indicate that, upon the building of the new temple in place of one at the fortress of Yeb (around 400 BCE), animal sacrifices were no longer to be practiced (see Cowley 32.2–11 and Cowley 30.25–26 as well as James C. Vanderkam, *An Introduction to Early Judaism* [Grand Rapids: William B. Eerdmans, 2001], 149; cf. Cowley 33). Vanderkam notes that, "It is possible that animal sacrifices were considered offensive to Egyptians or it may be that there was some question about the propriety of offering such sacrifices in Egypt" (ibid., 149).

349 Hec. Ab. 3.4 (305–302 BCE in Egypt), where he says the Jews offered different θυσία than the rest of Egypt (Bezalel Bar-Kochva, *The Image of the Jews in Greek Literature: The Hellenistic Period* [Berkeley: University of California Press, 2010], 101, fn. 29 claims that the whole Jewish way of life is included in these lines [cf. 129–130]). The information in Hecataeus come from Egyptians themselves (ibid., 132). Ibid., 24–34, also comments that Theophrastus (319–314 BCE) may have had negative thoughts about Jewish sacrifice, which could echo Greek sentiments at the time. His thoughts would lend credence to the sacrificial system of the Jews being known to be antithetically different to the Greeks.

influence considérable. Le pharaon reprit la place qu'il occupait jadis dans le système religieux."[350] This new dynastic cult seems to have been established under Ptolemy II in 272 BCE, when he and his wife were labelled θεῖοι ἀδελφοί.[351] In conjunction with their cult was patronage of the deity Sarapis. This god acted "as a kind of divine counterpart of their own benevolent rule" from the outset of the Ptolemaic era.[352] Only Sarapis and Isis are found in the royal oaths of the papyri.[353] The Ptolemies did not invent Sarapis but rather introduced the cult or Hellenized image of this older god.[354] Sarapis was a mix of Osiris and the Apis bull of Memphis[355] though Sarapis was associated with many divinities and roles in the time he was worshipped.[356] The Egyptian form of Osiris-Apis maintained the appearance of the immensely popular Apis (Memphis) bull[357] whereas the Hellenized version of Sarapis did not.[358] The Apis bull and Sarapis were often worshipped together, with the Apis bull even having a shrine at the Serapeum in Alexandria, though in a separate location.[359] Here prayers were made for Ptolemaic dominance.[360] Such integration of Greek and Egyptian worship is well-documented and existed from the earliest points of the Hellenistic period.[361] It might have been through these religious means that the Ptolemies aimed to control the Egyptian political-social leadership,[362]

350 Jacques Pirenne, *La religion et la morale dans l'Égypte antique* (Neuchâtel: La Baconnière, 1965), 147. Préaux, "Les continuités," 237, questions whether this should be seen as Egyptian influence or as a development of previous Greek religion, the latter having some precedent.

351 Worthington, *Ptolemy I*, 205, who also claims Ptolemy I did not create such a cult for himself.

352 John E. Stambaugh, *Sarapis Under the Early Ptolemies* (Leiden: Brill, 1972), 94.

353 Stambaugh, *Sarapis Under the Early Ptolemies*, 33.

354 Stambaugh, *Sarapis Under the Early Ptolemies*, 13; cf. Worthington, *Ptolemy I*, 198–199.

355 Wilcken, *UPZ*, 18–29; Peter M. Fraser, "Two Studies on the Cult of Sarapis in the Hellenistic World," *OAth* 3 (1960): 1, fn. 2; Stambaugh, *Sarapis*, p. 5 and chapter 6.

356 Stambaugh, *Sarapis*, 4–6.

357 For the popularity of the Apis bull at the time see Pirenne, *La Religion*, 145.

358 Lewis, *Greeks in Ptolemaic*, 70; Stambaugh, *Sarapis*, 62–63.

359 Stambaugh, *Sarapis*, 65–66.

360 Lewis, *Greeks in Ptolemaic*, 70.

361 Siegfried Kreuzer, "Entstehung und Entwicklung der Septuaginta im Kontext alexandrinischer und frühjüdischer Kultur und Bildung," in *Septuaginta Deutsch. Erläuterungen und Kommentare zum griechischen Alten Testament. Band I: Genesis bis Makkabäer*, vol. 1 of *Septuaginta Deutsch. Erläuterungen und Kommentare zum griechischen Alten Testament*, ed. Martin Karrer and Wolfgang Kraus (Stuttgart: Deutsche Bibelgesellschaft, 2011), 5; cf. Préaux, "les continuités," 246, who notes that Egyptians may have been a bit more hesitant to adopt Greek religion.

362 Lewis, *Greeks*, 79–80.

although this might not have been the original intention of this cult.[363] Sarapis was likely intended to unite Egyptian and Greek religiosity, to some degree.[364] This deity and the dynastic cult paint a stark picture of a monarchy intent on directing some of the worship of its people.

This propagandistic push would have been well known to the Jews of third-century Egypt. How much it affected them probably varied. For example, CIJ II 1440/JIGRE 22 (246–221 BCE), an inscription for a Jewish prayer house in Schedia near Alexandria, is dedicated to Ptolemy III and Queen Berenike, yet without the divine epitaphs. On the other hand, P.Hib. 1 96 (260 BCE) has a Jew, Alexander, involved in a dispute that is ratified in some relation to θεῶν Ἀδελφ[ῶ]ν (r.2).[365] The extent to which Jews could excuse themselves from Ptolemaic religion on a daily basis is not exactly clear. It likely depended greatly on one's employment (e.g., if one is in the military; discussed below).

Enter into this milieu a Jew who produced a law that stated that any Israelite who involved themselves in sacrifice or animal slaughter for these causes was to be killed. How much easier would it be for the law only to proscribe officiating the formal θυσία sacrifice, with disobedience to that command only costing some sort of (temporary?) communal expulsion? One can imagine how this first law would run contrary to the aims of the powers that be, while the second is much more agreeable and practical. This becomes all the more pertinent when one considers that, on certain occasions, Jews would have been called upon by the Ptolemies for conscripted service in which there were almost certainly duties that involved sacrifices.

4.5.4.2 Mandatory Sacrifice in Ptolemaic Egypt

There is no dispute that the Ptolemaic administration often conscripted its citizenry into various tasks.[366] One assigned to this office (λειτουργία) was a λειτουργός, who was paid for their service. It is from the monarchy and not the classical *poleis* that this forced labor arises and the same types of work

363 Fraser, "Two Studies," 47, finds no correlation between political expansion and the introduction of the god; cf. Stambaugh, *Sarapis*, 95.

364 See, e.g., Stambaugh, *Sarapis*, 96. This is not agreed upon by all. See, e.g., Françoise Dunand, "The Factory of Gods," in *Alexandria, Third Century BC: The Knowledge of the World in a Single City*, ed. Christian Jacob and François de Polignac (Alexandria: Hapocrates Pub, 2000), 160, who argues that this cult was Greek-focused and simply the patron deity of the new dynasty in Alexandria; Coussement, *Because I Am Greek*, 192, who thinks that only the dynastic cult was to be worshipped while Sarapis functioned to create ties with Egyptian priesthoods.

365 This may have been unavoidable since this was a military quarrel.

366 Rostovtzeff, *A Large Estate*, 153.

are found throughout the Hellenistic world.[367] Lewis documents the different compulsory services in the Ptolemaic period: he includes labour and surveillance in irrigation and cultivation, transport, providing for travelling officials, billeting, and brickmaking, among other (less clear) compulsory positions of many assortments.[368] Rostovtzeff notes an inscription (SEG³ 1000) from Cos that represents taxation and some practice from the Ptolemaic period.[369] He claims that this text shows that "certain sacrifices were compulsory for particular groups of inhabitants taking active part in the economic life of the city."[370] The conscripted workers in this inscription were related to the navy and docks, and they were also contractors of taxes who would have been required to makes sacrifices in this line of service. There is some indication that full-fledged Greeks could be exempt from λειτουργία, provided they were not in the military.[371] Minorities like the Jews were, on the whole, not exempt. Often difficult work such as at quarries would be carried out for free by prisoners, with perhaps a smaller group of paid λειτουργοί.[372] UPZ 1 42 (162 BCE) could indicate that the twin sisters working at the Serapeum were conscripted into λειτουργία (they label themselves αἱ λειτουργοῦσαι; line 2), since they were complaining that they had not received the wages for this task (lines 5–7). This papyrus may be evidence that temple work was also assigned by the Ptolemies, which would be in close proximity if not actually participating in sacrifice.

These data make it hard to suggest that Jews in Ptolemaic Egypt would not be put into situations involving Greek sacrifice or animal slaughter on a somewhat regular basis. Their aid in carving meat to provide for a travelling Ptolemaic official or sacrificing as part of certain city events seems unavoidable. Moreover, we find λειτουργοί at military encampments (e.g., P. Hib. 1 96, r. 14–15)—a context that also is highly associated with sacrificial acts.

Perkins has gathered some of the data related to Jewish military service in the Ptolemaic period. He cites the Aramaic Cowley Papyrus 81 (310 BCE) that mentions ten Jewish settlements of which some were likely military groupings.[373] He also refers to Hengel's claim that Jewish slaves and soldiers were major

367 Naphtali Lewis, *Inventory of Compulsory Services in Ptolemaic and Roman Egypt* (New Haven: American Society of Papyrologists, 1968), 1.

368 Lewis, *Inventory of Compulsory Services*, 1–11. For the occupancies of Jews more broadly at this time period see Fraser, *Ptolemaic*, 84; Tcherikover, *The Jews in Egypt*, 6–16, for documentation regarding the Jews participation in all facets of life.

369 Rostovtzeff, *The Social & Economic*, 1:241.

370 Rostovtzeff, *The Social & Economic*, 1:241.

371 Préaux, *L'économie royale*, 247 (commenting on the claims of Oertel) indicates that the exempt names from the work are all Greek (barring soldiers).

372 See the discussion in Préaux, *L'économie royale*, 246–249.

373 Perkins, "Israel's Military," 562, fn. 54.

contributors to the Diasporic population.[374] Good examples would be P.Hib. 1 96, r.4 (260 BCE) that mentions a Jew in the army, or P.Enteux. 82 (221 BCE), which likely shows a Jewish man as the leader of a police force.[375] Jews seem to have been more prominently featured in the military in the Ptolemaic period.[376] Perkins claims that "documentary evidence indicates that their religious practices were intertwined with their military organization and life ... we have no evidence that the early Ptolemaic leaders specifically formed Jewish military units, even though they included Jewish people within their military organization."[377] One thinks back to ABSA 56 (1961) 4,4 (163–145 BCE)[378] where the military are given permission to officiate the θυσία in honor of a comrade. If it is true, then, that many Jews were soldiers in the third century and that military service involved sacrifices, then it is hard not to conclude that a large portion of Jews were confronted with foreign sacrifices regularly in this service. Not to be involved with the sacrifice would be to contravene their legal duties as soldiers. Finally, there is another large demographic of Jews that also points towards their necessary participation in foreign sacrifice.

Earlier I discussed the influx of Jewish prisoners of war at the turn of the third century and proposed the possible reason for the changes made to the law in 21:16 (21:17 LXX).[379] What is of concern here is that these prisoners of war were often enslaved. For example, in 302–301 BCE Ptolemy I took Jewish prisoners to Egypt and made them slaves, the same pattern that can be seen in 312 BCE when Ptolemy I took Marion on Cyprus and moved the inhabitants to Paphos (cf. Diodorus Siculus, *Bib. hist.* 19.79.4), when he sold the citizens of Mallos as slaves in Cilicia (Diodorus Siculus, *Bib. hist.* 19.79.6), and when after the battle at Gaza he moved eight thousand of Demetrius's soldiers to Egypt (Diodorus Siculus, *Bib. hist.* 19.85.3–4; Plutarch, *Dem.* 5.3).[380] Hengel's claim that many Jews were slaves in the Diaspora comports with what we know about prisoners of war and the Ptolemies. Now, if these Jews were enslaved to Greeks, is it feasible to think that they would never be tasked with the butchering of

374 Perkins, "Israel's Military," 562, fn. 54, and Martin Hengel, *Judaism and Hellenism. Volume One: Text*, vol. 1 of *Judaism and Hellenism* (Philadelphia: Fortress Press, 1974), 16. See also Marcel Launey, *Recherches ethniques*, vol. 1 of *Recherches sur les armées hellénistiques* (Paris: de Boccard, 1950), 541ff. for Jewish participation in Hellenistic armies.

375 For the latter claim see Aryeh Kasher, *The Jews*, 47.

376 LaCoste, *Waters of the Exodus*, 63.

377 Perkins, "Israel's Military," 562, fn. 55, working with Fraser, *Ptolemaic*, 280ff.

378 Discussed above on pp. 232–234.

379 See 3.4.

380 F. H. Thompson, *The Archaeology of Greek and Roman Slavery* (London: Duckworth, 2003), 16. See also Let. Aris. 12–15. There are other traditions that claim the Jewish move was voluntary (Josephus, *C. Ap.* 186–189, 209–212; *A. J.* 12.1–9; Appian, *Syr.* (11), 50; see Thompson. *The Archaeology*, 16.

animals that were devoted to the Greek deities? Remember that, had the translator used θύω in Exod 22:19 (22:20 LXX), that act would be undefined. It could be a ritual slaughter or a formal sacrifice. Anyone who has worked on a farm producing meat or has hunted game is well-aware of the strain involved in dissembling an animal. It is a dirty, difficult, and arduous task—work fit for a slave (at least on some occasions). It seems hardly possible that the Jewish slave force in Ptolemaic Egypt could avoid such behavior. So, once again, the change in the law to only prohibit officiating a formal θυσία, a task which would be saved minimally for the head of the household, would allow for Jewish freedom in the matter of pagan animal slaughter. This activity of a Jewish slave would be completely kosher, according to OG Exod 22:19 (22:20 LXX).

4.5.5 *Conclusion of Legal and Cultural Analysis*

The broader syncretistic push from the Ptolemies, as well as the on-the-ground reality that Jewish residents of Ptolemaic Egypt would necessarily and legally be involved with foreign sacrifices, both provide a rational basis as to why the translator of 22:19 (22:20 LXX) made the changes he did. These realities next to guarantee that the monarchy would not permit the death penalty as it stands in the Hebrew text and also direct us towards comprehending why the precise type of sacrificial activity represented by θυσιάζω was chosen.[381] As long as a Jew was not officiating a θυσία, there was no conflict between the text and the world outside of the translation. It is helpful to imagine that a Jew might even feel comfortable eating with Greeks at a θυσία, since at this time in history the meal itself seems to have been perceived more as a "divinely blest ... table-fellowship of the men" participating rather than a meal with a deity.[382]

4.5.6 *Conclusion on Exodus 22:19 (22:20 LXX)*

What is originally is a generic law against sacrificing to other gods except יהוה at the cost of death has become a prohibition against acting as the officiator of a formal Greek sacrifice (θυσία) at the cost of what is either death or expulsion from the community. That θυσιάζω means "act as an officiator at a θυσία" corresponds to every use found in Pentateuch as well as in the literary and documentary sources. Whether ἐξολεθρεύω conveys the removal from a community or death is admittedly uncertain. The Pentateuchal data leave the former option at least plausible.

381 If the text does refer to the death penalty, it could be imagined that Jews would infrequently be the officiator at a θυσία, as this was a role reserved for an honored person or head of a household and could probably be avoided quite easily.

382 Gill, "Trapezomata," 137.

CHAPTER 5

Implications and Conclusion

5.1 Implications for Septuagint Exodus

5.1.1 *Translation Technique*

If anything can be said about the translator's approach to the text it is that it is creative. This translator superficially represented the Hebrew text while at the same time transformed its meaning. Such a feat required a solid grasp of the source and target text's languages, idioms, and cultures that they were produced in. Finding a Greek term that shared some sort of conceptual commonality with the Hebrew text that at the same time suited his translational aims displays commendable innovation. I labelled this technique superficial semantic fidelity (SSF), and I documented it across the laws discussed.[1] There was no one way the translator superficially maintained the source text. For example, the translator exploited the Greek gender system when translating with πᾶν instead of πᾶς/πάντα in 22:18 (22:19 LXX), while he subtly made use of Greek legal norms when rendering מות יומת in similar yet distinct ways. Superficial semantic fidelity is not an absolute rule. There are also additions to the source text like τὸ κριτήριον in 21:6. This addition coincides with slave registration practices in Ptolemaic Egypt.[2] Superficial semantic fidelity also explains why the translator does not employ Greek legal terminology across the board. It appears formal legal terms are only used when the context and source text accommodated these renderings.

Above all, that SSF is present here in GCC ought to press those studying the Septuagint in the future to approach this translation cautiously and not to assume true semantic correspondence to the Hebrew text before appropriate lexicographic and translation-technical analyses have been undertaken. Moreover, the other Pentateuchal materials should be looked over again in light of both SSF and Lev–Num's use of legal syntax for the imperative (section 2.7). Given their shared use of the imperative for the death penalty, it should probably be concluded that there was some communication or mutual influence between these translators. Their translation practices and the intended audience of their translations should be re-evaluated in light of these findings.

1 This same technique is found elsewhere in the Code and will be the subject of later publications. For another example from Exod 21:7 see Korytko, "Slaves to the Septuagint."

2 See Korytko, "The 'Law of the Land,'" 48–57.

 | DOI:10.1163/9789004682047_006

The most pressing question that arises from the kind of translation method found in this portion of Greek Exodus is to ask what purpose it served. If the translator wanted to change the meaning of a particular law, why not just break from the source text and write whatever alternative he desired? Part of the answer could lie simply in translational scribal habits, as were already highlighted in section 1.7. Translators in that culture were expected to follow along with and maintain an outline of the source text.[3] If we layer upon this some sort of religious respect or belief in the divine origins of the source text, it is possible (though not a given) that a closer representation of that document could be expected.[4] However, we do not know whether the translator held the text in this regard. If the law code portion of Exodus were being written as some sort of pseudo-προστάγματα that were analogous to Ptolemaic royal decrees, then this might further entail a stricter accompaniment of the source text.[5] Another rationale for this superficial representation of the source text could correspond to the anticipated audience of the translation.

5.1.2 *The Translator and His Audience*

Much has been written on the identity of the Greek translators and who their hypothetical audiences might have been.[6] I do not intend to arbitrate between these views. Instead, I offer a few points of consideration to add into the mix. This kind of discussion is, of course, speculative.

To begin, what if Greco-Egyptian legal influences have indeed affected the translation in some of the ways described above? If this Greco-Egyptian influence was an innovation of the translator and not an inherited tradition, then the translator would be seen to be quite familiar with Hellenistic law and legal

---

3 See also Benjamin Wright, "The *Letter of Aristeas* and the Place of the Septuagint in Alexandrian Judaism," in *Alexandria: Hub of the Hellenistic World*, ed. Benjamin Schliesser et al., WUNT 460 (Tübingen: Mohr Siebeck, 2021), 243–244.

4 The perceived authority of the text is discussed below.

5 See section 2.7.

6 For a brief overview of positions see Leonard Greenspoon, "At the Beginning: The Septuagint as a Jewish Bible Translation," in *Translation is Required: The Septuagint in Retrospect and Prospect*, ed. Robert J. V. Hiebert, SCS 56 (Atlanta: SBL Press, 2010), 163–168. See also Siegfried Kreuzer, "Origin and Development of the Septuagint in the Context of Alexandrian and Early Jewish Culture and Learning," in *The Bible in Greek: Translation, Transmission, and Theology of the Septuagint* (Atlanta: Society of Biblical Literature, 2015), 3–46; Orth, "Ptolemaios," 97–114; Tessa Rajak, "Translating the Septuagint for Ptolemy's Library: Myth and History," in *Die Septuaginta—Texte, Kontexte, Lebenswelten*, ed. Wolfgang Kraus, Martin Karrer, and Martin Meiser, WUNT 219 (Tübingen: Mohr Siebeck, 2008), 176–193; Arie van der Kooij, "Perspectives on the Study of the Septuagint: Who Are the Translators?" in *Perspectives in the Study of the Old Testament and Early Judaism*, ed. Ed Noort and Florentino García Martínez (Leiden: Brill, 1998), 214–229.

values, which would as a consequence make him somewhat familiar with Classical law. Did he gain this knowledge through consultation with Greek legal scribes, or did he have this knowledge by virtue of living in Hellenistic Egypt? It is entirely plausible that the translator was trained as a legal scribe, but just as much that he simply grew up in a household that could afford Greek education, which would include studying classical texts and imbibing Greek values.[7] Still, if it is true that the deregulating imperative is an obscure trait of Ptolemaic legal syntax—which is by no means clear as it may have been comprehensible to average citizens—then this would also be an indication of his close familiarity with the legal scribal culture at the time. That Lev–Num also use this trait in their laws with the death penalty either informs us that their translators may have also been involved in that scribal world or that one of the translations was used as a template for the others when rendering the death penalty. Greco-Egyptian legal influence on the text might also be yet another indicator of the fluid ethnic boundaries and cultural influences apparent in early Hellenistic Egypt.[8] Jews in early Hellenistic Egypt enjoyed the legal tax status of one labelled "Hellene," were Hellenized in legal practice (see 1.6), and, even in the Fayum, participated such in the broader community that "they lived cheek by jowl with others."[9] That they (including the translator) had assimilated some Greek legal values would not be surprising, as the same kind of hybrid existence can be seen among Greeks who took on aspects of Egyptian identity yet remained, in their own eyes, Greek.[10] Why could a Jew not take on elements of Greek identity in their Scriptures and still remain, in their own eyes, Jewish? At the same time, it is hard to imagine that the translator made these changes unconsciously. The varying ways the Greek language

7 Clarysse and Thompson, *Counting the People*, 132, 147.

8 Honigman's tempered comments on ethnic labelling at the time are helpful: "Altogether, the evidence regarding Ptolemaic state regulation of status and inter-ethnic relationships remains too sketchy to allow any conclusions. That said, as the corpus of evidence grows—and in particular is supplemented by the Demotic papyri—the overall picture begins to controvert the claims of systematic ethnic discrimination that prevailed a few decades ago. Ethnic labeling was fluid, and as long as such changes were not merely a ruse for evading taxes, the Ptolemaic administration was relatively unconcerned. A consequence and perhaps a function of this fluidity was to constantly maintain a fair overlap between the segment of the population that Ptolemaic state policy identified as "Greeks" and the social elites of the country" ("The Shifting Definition of Greek Identity in Alexandria through the Transition from Ptolemaic to Roman Rule," in *Alexandria: Hub of the Hellenistic World*, ed. Benjamin Schliesser et al., WUNT 460 [Tübingen: Mohr Siebeck, 2021], 129; see also 131).

9 Clarysse and Thompson, *Counting the People*, 148; see also Honigman, "The Shifting Definition," 134.

10 Honigman, "The Shifting Definition," 125–126, 131, 135.

is exploited to accommodate the Hebrew text required forethought and ingenuity. Rendering the consistent penal מות in such varied ways likewise argues against unconscious adaptation. It comes across as though the translator (or perhaps predecessors on whom he relied) rendered this way with a purpose. The question is, which purpose and for whom?

One approach to this problem is to consider if the use of SSF was the translator's attempt to maintain some degree of bipartisanship among various groups in Ptolemaic Egypt, albeit in a relatively one-sided manner. The translator may have been maintaining a semblance of the Hebrew source text in order to placate a particular, perhaps more 'biblicist,' segment of the translation's expected audience, while the changes in accordance with Greco-Egyptian law would placate another anticipated readership. Some claim that there was little command of Hebrew and Aramaic in the third century among Jews in Egypt[11] and that knowledge of Hebrew was "exceptional."[12] That Hebrew was dying out among Jew in Egypt and that the LXX is a product of that problem "has become somewhat of a *communis opinio*."[13] If this line of reasoning is correct, then perhaps the translator used SSF so as to create the illusion that the source text was represented when in fact the meaning had changed. On the one hand, those who had no knowledge of Hebrew would have no idea this were going on. This would, in this view, comprise a large proportion of Jews at the time, especially since many would be illiterate. On the other hand, those who did know Hebrew

11 James Barr, "Hebrew, Aramaic and Greek in the Hellenistic Age," in *The Hellenistic Age*, vol. 2 of *The Cambridge History of Judaism*, ed. William D. Davies and Louis Finkelstein (Cambridge: Cambridge University Press, 1990), 79–114; LaCoste, *Waters of the Exodus*, 33, fn. 34; 72, fn. 31. Fraser states, "There are virtually no Hebrew or Aramaic inscriptions or papyri from Ptolemaic Egypt, whereas Jewish Greek documents abound" (*Ptolemaic*, 2:958). This suggests that the community was primarily hellenophone. However, Fraser is commenting about the start of the second century BCE. There are some papyri and ostraca in Aramaic found dated to the third century and at the start of the second (Tscherikover, *Corpus Papyrorum*, 30). Greek may have taken over more quickly in Alexandria, though (ibid.). The predominance of Greek names among Jewish societies in Egypt also suggests their thorough Hellenization (ibid., 28–29). For the Aramaic influence on the LXX see e.g., Anne-Françoise Loiseau, *L'influence de l'araméen sur les traducteurs de la LXX principalement, sure les traducteurs grecs postérieurs, ainsi que sur les scribes de la Vorlage de la LXX* (Atlanta: SBL Press, 2016); Jan Joosten, *Collected Essays on the Septuagint* (Tübingen: Mohr Siebeck, 2012), 53–66, and 65, where he claims that Aramaic may have persisted whereas Hebrew was an acquired language.

12 Arnaldo Momigliano, "The Hellenistic Discovery of Judaism," in *Emerging Judaism: Studies on the Fourth & Third Centuries B.C.E.*, ed. Michael E. Stone and David Satran (Minneapolis: Fortress Press, 1989), 142.

13 René Bloch, "How Much Hebrew in Jewish Alexandria?" in *Alexandria: Hub of the Hellenistic World*, ed. Benjamin Schliesser et al., WUNT 460 (Tübingen: Mohr Siebeck, 2021), 265.

would also need to have a significant competency in Greek to understand the intricacies of their idioms and the semantics/syntax of the Greek language and their laws. Besides, this presupposes that there was a Hebrew textual tradition present, known, and readily accessible in Egypt, which is not particularly clear at this time.[14] If, then, it is assumed that there was little knowledge of Hebrew in Egypt at the time, perhaps the translator knew they could get away with these changes because very few people could 'check their work.' However, the view that there was little proficiency in Hebrew in Ptolemaic Egypt has been increasingly challenged of late.[15]

There are indications that suggest Hebrew was still in use as a written language in Egypt at the time.[16] If Hebrew was still in use as a written language (and there were available Hebrew texts) then it is likely the case that many Jews in Ptolemaic Egypt could 'check the translator's work.' Even so, we must still assume that such a reader could pick up on the changed meanings found in the subtle shifts in Greek wording (e.g., θανάτῳ τελευτάτω vs. θανάτῳ θανατούσθω; πᾶς vs. πᾶν). But are we to imagine that this newly translated legal section was only 'really' comprehensible to the elite and legally-attuned? The ubiquity of spoken and written Greek among Jews in Egypt casts serious doubts on any such claim. It seems likely that someone immersed in the Hellenized culture with Greek as its prioritized language would be able to understand the differences in the Greek text. This still assumes that the translation was expected to be read broadly by Jewish constituents of Ptolemaic Egypt. There is the possibility that the translation was not intended to reach the masses at all and that the project was in fact chiefly for Ptolemy, his library, or his legal teams. In which case, would differences from the Hebrew even be a concern? Could they

14 B13 Passover Letter is from 419 BCE and is the first allusion to the Book of Exodus in Egypt (see Bezalel Porten, *Archives from Elephantine: The Life of an Ancient Jewish Military Colony* [Berkeley: University of California Press, 1968], 311). It is unclear if this letter indicates they had a text of Exodus in Egypt or if that text were being made known to them from Palestine so they could follow it. See Schwartz, "Law in Jewish Society," 55–59, for the scant evidence before the Ptolemaic period. Of course, the fact that the translation itself occurred in Egypt means that the Hebrew text was present to some extent.

15 Bloch, "How Much Hebrew"; Tessa Rajak, *Translation and Survival: The Greek Bible and the Ancient Jewish Diaspora* (Oxford: Oxford University Press, 2009), 38–63; Seth Schwartz, "Language, Power and Identity in Ancient Palestine," *Past & Present* 148 (1995): 41; Wright, "The *Letter*," 242. Surveys on the subject can be found in Siegfried Kreuzer, "Enstehung und Überlieferung der Septuaginta," *Einleitung in die* Septuaginta, Vol. 1 of *Handbuch zur Septuaginta*, ed. Sigfried Kreuzer (Gütersloh: Gütersloher Verlagshaus, 2016), 39–49, and Marguerite Harl, Gilles Dorival, and Oliver Munnich, *La bible grecque des Septante du judaïsme hellénistique au christianisme ancien* (Paris: Cerf, 1988), 66–78.

16 For the evidence and argumentation see Bloch, "How Much Hebrew."

originally have been no more than a means of placating this small group of elite Greek persons? We are here dealing with the problem concerning which niche the translation was intended to fill, the answer of which will inevitably inform how we might view these legal adaptations in GCC.[17] Of course, the translations of the Torah may also have served more than one purpose or audience (e.g., Ptolemy's officials and Jews in Egypt).[18]

If the translation of Exodus was for the masses, then many may have known that the Greek text differed from the Hebrew. The differences between the meaning of the Hebrew and the Greek version may not have been a secret the translator was trying to keep hidden. Such Hellenized renderings may not have been a matter to be concealed if Jews were already significantly Hellenized in their legal practice (see 1.6). Regardless of the Greek law that they used in court for what might have been practical reasons, it could be that their legal and moral values had become more Greek as well. Perhaps there were already reading traditions of the Torah that supported what we see in GCC.[19]

Only to add to the uncertainty and complexity of these inquiries is that the changes to the Hebrew meanings found in the translation of Exodus are not duplicated in parallel passages in places like Leviticus (e.g., there parental cursing/ill-speech is punished with death [20:9]; bestiality is condemned with death [20:15–16]). This could suggest that the niche that Greek Exodus (or even more particularly GCC) was intended to fill was not the same as the other books of the Torah.

It may be helpful at this point to examine how a few potential audiences that are not mutually exclusive could explain the adaptation towards Greco-Egyptian law hypothesized in this work. These audiences are Jews in Egypt, non-Jews in Egypt, and the Ptolemaic authorities.

Should the first be in view, then perhaps we can see the translator adapting the text so as to either conform it to what Jews were already practicing at the time—they were deeply Hellenized in law—[20] or perhaps to bring Jewish residents of Egypt legally in line with their full-fledged Greek compatriots as part of their integration into a Hellenic identity.[21] A significant part of Hellenic

17 This niche remains elusive despite this project's analysis of the translation and the translator's strategies (cf. Wright, "The *Letter*" 240).

18 Bloch, "How Much Hebrew," 266.

19 How the laws of the Torah may or may not have been perceived as binding is discussed below.

20 See section 1.6.

21 Whether this was out of compulsion, that is to say they were forced to follow other laws anyways, would probably depend on whether the translation was produced with the legal background of one of the major cities. See section 1.5.3.

identity at the time was the contrast of their culture and customs with the barbarians/foreigners.[22] Honigman comments on this Greek identity forming at the time among immigrants, including Jews, which

> crystallized around a set of elements, of which the most prominent were their service to the king, as soldiers and administrators; their linguistic assimilation into a common Greek dialect, the *koine*, and a common stock of personal names; their Greek way of life; their identification with tokens of loyalty to the king, in particular through the ruler cult (which was often linked to *gymnasia*), but also the use of personal names such as Ptolemaios and Berenike; and the worship of deities that were also endorsed by the king, in particular Sarapis … Of course, this list of defining items was open to internal contests … the Judeans would presumably have been happy to elide the cult of Sarapis from the abovementioned list.[23]

Putting aside whether or not the translational changes in Exod 22:19 (22:20 LXX) intimate that Judeans may not have completely elided participation in the cult of Sarapis (and other foreign sacrificial practices), the legal Hellenization of the Jews in Egypt may be further highlighted by the translation, and it could be another indicator that embracing Greek law and legal values were also one such "crystalizing element" of Greek identity. We also see Greek identity related to law in P.Hal. 1.260–265 where there was an exemption from the salt tax for those particularly participating in activities and employment that promoted Greek culture.[24] This is a strong indication that those who promoted the Greek way of life received particular favor from the Ptolemaic authorities.[25] Commenting on similar taxation records, Clarysse and Thompson state that, "the overall impression of privilege for the Greeks and those involved in the success of their system comes clearly through in our lists."[26] Should it come as a surprise that the translation may integrate certain legal values and expectations of the Greeks given this Hellenic impetus and the Greek identity already forming among Jews in other areas alongside legal practice?

This perspective gains further traction when we consider that "rather than being inextricably bound up with the individual, someone's ethnic identity is

22 Coussement, *Because I am Greek*, 12–15.

23 Honigman, "The Shifting Definition," 129–130.

24 Honigman, "The Shifting Definition," 128, points out that this tax exemption extended out to Egyptians as well and was less concerned with ethnicity.

25 Cf. Coussement, *Because I am Greek*, 146; Vierros, *Bilingual Notaries*, 34.

26 Clarysse and Thompson, *Counting the People*, 146.

a construct based on the ethnic groups one belongs to. In personal contacts, one could be judged to be an insider or outsider of an ethnic group not only on the basis of descent, but also language use, dress or other symbols that were considered relevant by members of the group."[27] What if a group's laws were added to such 'relevant symbols'? What if the translator has 'updated' the text towards Greek legal values as part of the burgeoning Greek identity of Jews at the time and, as it were, in what might represent one of the "tokens of loyalty to the king"? In this way the translation would also be pedagogical for Jews in Egypt.[28] Whether in practice or ideal, their legal values would align more closely with those of the Greeks. Perhaps a parallel could be drawn to Lycophron's *Alexandra* (second century BCE). In that poem "dialectical and foreign words were legitimate only insofar as they were mediated by the Greek classical tradition," which was itself "a statement about the Alexandrian Greek identity."[29] Ex could be a case where Hebrew law is mediated through classical Greek law inasmuch as it was received by Greco-Egyptian law in Hellenistic Egypt. Problematic to this view is that one might have expected a more systematic set of changes if this were the case. But we need not think in such absolute terms. A hybridization between Greek and Hebrew law might be expected in a hybrid culture that already held to a legal pluralism in many respects.[30]

A case can also be made that the translator might have expected full-fledged ethnic Greeks or other Hellenised peoples in Egypt to read this translation. We know that the story of Exodus and the figure of Moses were popular in the third-century BCE among Greeks.[31] In this literature we even see Hecataeus

27 Coussement, *Because I am Greek*, 158.

28 Greek education did in fact have the explicit goal of maintaining their cultural norms: "Education became a powerful agent for preserving 'Greekness' by maintaining fixed linguistic and social boundaries, excluding almost any form of Egyptian culture, and concentrating on transmitting Greek values, language, and literacy" (Rafaella Cribiore, *Gymnastics of the Mind. Greek Education in Hellenistic and Roman Egypt* [Princeton and Oxford: Princeton University Press, 2001], 9). Clarysse and Thompson point out the value of entering this educational system, stating that "a Greek education for the children might bring them later rewards; to 'go Greek' might bring different forms of advantage" (*Counting the People*, 147).

29 Honigman, "The Shifting Definition," 135.

30 Cf. Honigman, "The Shifting Definition," 135. For legal pluralism in Ptolemaic Egypt see section 1.5.3.

31 See the discussions of the various texts in Bar-Kochva, *The Image of the Jews*, 15–252. See also LaCoste, *Waters of the Exodus*, 69; Reinhard G. Kratz, "Greek Historians on Jews and Judaism in the 3rd Century BCE," in *Times of Transition: Judea in the Early Hellenistic Period*, ed. Sylvie Honigman, Christophe Nihan, and Oded Lipschits (University Park/Tel Aviv: Eisenbrauns/Emery and Claire Yass Publications in Archaeology, The Institute of Archaeology, Tel Aviv University, 2021), 263–278; Alison Salvesen, "'They Did Not Settle

(305–302 BCE) adapt his description of Jewish practice in such a way "so as to convey a message to the Ptolemaic authorities and the Greek-Macedonian population in Egypt."[32] A parallel could be drawn to Ex. Despite their Jewish authors, one thinks as well of Ezekiel the Tragedian's *Exagoge* and Artapanus's *On the Jews*, the latter of which also notably syncretises Jewish ideas, especially the figure of Moses, with that of Hellenistic Egypt.[33] A noted emphasis falls on the Exodus narrative in our early surviving sources. Perhaps the translator knew of this popularity and anticipated that Hellenised peoples would be reading his work. When they inevitably came upon GCC, the changes to the text ensured that it would not drastically butt up against their legal and moral values. In this way the translator may have felt a degree of embarrassment concerning the original content of some of these laws and made the changes in an apologetic manner. The popularity of Exodus might also explain why there is a proliferation of departures from the meaning of the Hebrew text in Greek Exodus's legal materials as compared to the other Pentateuchal legal corpora. Further investigations into these other legal texts are necessary before this claim can be verified.

Finally, if the Greco-Egyptian influence hypothesis is accurate, then it might be time to consider again the oft-dismissed testimony of *Aristeas*. What if the translation was expected to be read by the royal authorities? We need not necessarily envision Ptolemy himself, but what about his emissaries? We already know that other laws were being translated for these dignitaries to view.[34] What if GCC, and maybe then the rest of Exodus, were also a part of that translational movement? This could explain why the translator made these changes. In a similar way to what was stated above about Hellenised peoples reading the text, the adaptations towards Greco-Egyptian legal values in particularly acute places like the death penalty might have been a means of currying favor with the Ptolemaic government. The use of legal syntax with the imperative might make sense in this context and might have been appreciated by the legal authorities. They would be the ones to whom the deference is being made. Likewise, changes akin to the addition of τὸ κριτήριον in Exod 21:6 would fit well into this paradigm.[35] This plus, if made in light of Greco-Egyptian law, only

in the Land of the Lord: Ephraim Settled in Egypt' (Hos 9:3): Returning to Egypt in the Septuagint and Other Hellenistic Jewish Works," in *Israel in Egypt: The Land of Egypt as Concept and Reality for Jews in Antiquity and the Early Medieval Period*, ed. Alison Salvesen, Sarah Pearce, and Miriam Frenkel (Leiden: Brill, 2020), 150–177.

32 Bar-Kochva, *The Image of the Jews*, 127 (cf. 129).

33 LaCoste, *Waters of the Exodus*, 116–117.

34 See section 1.7.

35 See Korytko, "The 'Law of the Land,'" 48–57.

concerns proper slave registration protocol. This procedure is a chief concern of the bureaucratic administrators. Both examples are changes to the text that might make the translated laws amenable to the Greco-Egyptian context in the eyes of the royal authority. If the translational changes are not systematic and do focus on adapting legal content that prevents stepping into the sphere of Ptolemaic authority, then perhaps the changes are indeed something of a "token of loyalty" to the king.[36] A somewhat analogous case of Ptolemaic deference within Greek poetry at the time might be seen in the epigrams attributed to Posidippus.[37] Here we find both overt and subtle gestures of ingratiation to the authorities, and it is also possible "that the rest of the Alexandrian poets may have woven similar political concerns into their poetry."[38] To see the translator participate in this kind of nod to their rulers would be par for the course and representative of the translator's embeddedness in the literary culture at the time. This is not to mention some of the less amiable examples concerning the importance of displaying fealty to the king.[39] Does loyalty and deference to the Ptolemaic authority explain why Ex-Num all share the legal imperative in cases of the death penalty? Does this suggest that all three translators expected a Ptolemaic-bureaucratic readership? It is possible. Due to the uncertainty involved in interpreting the rationale for the imperative, it is probably not possible to know. Whatever the specific purpose and audience intended for the legal-syntactic imperative, it seems to be the case that the translators of Exodus, Leviticus, and Numbers had a unified agenda when rendering the death penalty.

It seems reasonable that any combination of the three aforementioned audiences could have been intended for Greek Exodus.[40] Further work needs to be done in order to gain a better grasp on the translator's identity and

36 This perspective could also lend credence to the view that these laws were circulated independently from the rest of the translation.

37 See Honigman, "The Shifting Definition," 134; Susan Stephens, "Posidippus' Poetry Book: Where Macedon Meets Egypt," in *Ancient Alexandria between Egypt and Greece*, ed. William V. Harris and Giovanni Ruffini, CSCT 26 (Leiden, The Netherlands: Brill, 2004), 63–86.

38 Honigman, "The Shifting Definition," 134, echoing Stephens.

39 For example, Honigman points out that Ptolemy II rooted out those who had authority in the Egyptian temples for generations and replaced them "with temple families of lower social status who readily offered their loyalty to the king" ("The Shifting Definition," 128).

40 For a discussion on the "apologetic" nature of Jewish diasporic documents, a trait that is particularly in line with the present volume's claims, see John Barclay, "Apologetics in the Jewish Diaspora," in *Jews in the Hellenistic and Roman Cities*, ed. John R Bartlett (London: Routledge, 2002), 129–148, specifically, 136–143, where he argues that multiple audiences could have been intended for works like the LXX.

audience. This research and the Greco-Egyptian legal influence hypothesis hopefully provide one such steppingstone on the path towards that goal. On the other hand, the translation-technical data in the present study should now enter into the conversations on Second Temple *halakhah* as a new dataset for discussion.

5.1.3 *Hermeneutics, Authority, and the Importance of the Reconfigured Death Penalty Laws*

Recent work in Ancient Near Eastern and Mesopotamian jurisprudence has indicated that law codes of the second and early first millenniums before the Common Era were likely not intended to be used in litigation as binding authorities.[41] This would have originally been the case for the Covenant Code.[42] Even so, Vroom highlights that, "if it is true that the Laws of Hammurabi or the Covenant Code did not function as binding law, it does not mean that these texts did not have authority for their communities. They may have held some sort of epistemic authority."[43] At some point in its history the biblical text does seem to take on a binding obligation/practical authority instead of this epistemic authority.[44] Vroom outlines how the Second Temple period displays differing indications as to how a given community perceived the authority and binding obligation of legal prescripts in the Hebrew Bible. The authority of the text often seems to be mediated through an authorized interpreter in this early period.[45] What is of particular relevance to the present study is that these authority figures "were able to make the Torah say things it does not say" because "the majority of the ... community did not have access the Torah. Rather, the practical authority of the Torah was mediated through qualified Torah interpreters."[46] It is not difficult to draw a line between this kind of interpretive authority and what we have seen in Ex. Some of these laws in

41 Jonathan Vroom, *The Authority of Law in the Hebrew Bible and Early Judaism: Tracing the Origins of Legal Obligation from Ezra to Qumran* (Leiden: Brill, 2018), 2, and fn. 3 for a bibliography.

42 See Bernard M. Levinson, *Legal Revision and Religious Renewal in Ancient Israel* (Cambridge: Cambridge University Press, 2008), 23–27; Bruce Wells, "What Is Biblical Law? A Look at Pentateuchal Rules and Near Eastern Practice," *CBQ* 70 (2008): 223–243; Raymond Westbrook, "The Laws of Biblical Israel," in *Cuneiform and Biblical Sources*, vol. 2 of *Law from the Tigris to the Tiber: The Writings of Raymond Westbrook*, ed. Bruce Wells and Rachel Magdalene (Winona Lake: Eisenbrauns, 2009), 317–340.

43 Vroom, *The Authority of Law*, 20.

44 See Vroom, *The Authority of Law*, 56 for bibliography and 70–71 for epistemic/practical authority.

45 See Vroom, *The Authority of Law*, 91–93, and 199 for the period of Ezra-Nehemiah.

46 Vroom, *The Authority of Law*, 200 (here speaking about Ezra-Nehemiah).

their Greek version now "say things they do not say"—regardless of whether these changes were based on influences from Greco-Egyptian law. It remains uncertain whether there was a greater access to the Torah in Hellenistic times than the period to which Vroom refers (i.e., Persian). The principle still holds: the translator may have been providing new, authoritative interpretations of the text as the community's "qualified Torah interpreter."

This discussion raises the question concerning what type of authority the translator vested in the text. Did the translator view the text more as an epistemic authority? This could explain the rather free departures from the source text's meaning documented throughout this volume. If the Hebrew laws were legal wisdom, the vicissitudes of culture, history, and time allowed for new, sensible rulings. At the same time, such rulings could plausibly be located in the translator's self-understanding as an authoritative interpreter with binding authority.[47] Either view could explain how the text could change its meaning without any significant repercussions from the community. It is, of course, entirely possible that the translation's theorized accommodations to Greek law were readily perceived and received by Jews in Egypt at the time. More work is required on this topic. Whatever type of authority was vested in the text, the changes hypothesized in this work fit within the evolutionary tradition of biblical law, beginning principally with Deuteronomy.[48]

Though Ex could be situated within discussions regarding the authority of the text in a few different ways, its treatment of laws with the death penalty is quite distinct when one surveys the ancient sources. As far as I am aware, all the ancient sources of the Second Temple period and beyond—from Jubilees to Qumran to the rabbis—maintain the scriptural injunctions concerning the death penalty. That is to say, while they might put up various hedges that prevent the practice of capital punishment, they do not actually remove capital

47 If Ex is influenced by Greco-Egyptian law, it would be rather ironic if Greek law was functioning as a practical authority that contravened an epistemic authority (i.e., the original Covenant Code).

48 This tradition continues throughout the Second Temple period: "Much as Deuteronomy appropriates the very language and literary characteristics of the Covenant Code as it transforms older Israelite legal material, the book of Jubilees, the Temple Scroll, the Damascus Document, and many of the sectarian legal texts among the Dead Sea Scrolls blur the boundaries between scripture and its interpretation. In so doing, all these texts harness the authority of their base texts in order to present a new and improved—sometimes dramatically different—vision of the legal institutions contained therein. Moreover, many of these texts simultaneously tap into the authority vested in the divine origins of the earlier texts" (Jassen, *Scripture and Law*, 27–28).

punishment from the biblical text, as is seen in Ex.[49] Some traditions add some capitally charged crimes to this scriptural list, but the list is never shorter than the biblical text.[50] If Ex was intended to be a stand-alone representation of the biblical text and not some sort of pseudo-commentary, then this text differs from the rest of these traditions. Moreover, what seems to be a dramatic transformation of Exod 22:18 (22:19 LXX) from a law about bestiality into a law concerning animal husbandry might be without precedent in the Second Temple period. The translator of Exodus is therefore unique with regards to the traditions on the death penalty and in some of his idiosyncratic translational practices. He is the odd man out who now needs to find his place and voice in this illustrious interpretive history. If some of this volume's preliminary observations concerning laws with the death penalty in Lev-Num prove true, then the translators of those texts might also need a seat alongside him.

5.2 Further Research and Dialogue

A sense of optimistic expectation comes with the publication of this work. Many other fields and disciplines can undoubtably shed further light on its data. Likewise, the implications for studies in Second Temple Judaism, Hellenism, Ptolemaic Egypt, and to some degree juristic papyri, will hopefully be a point of conversation. Within the field of Septuagint Studies more work will need to be done to determine if similar practices to those found here in

49 E.g., Rabbinic law narrowed the death penalty in Deut 22:13–21 so that it was only applied to cases where the woman was promiscuous after the betrothal (b. Ketub. 46a, Sipra Deut 235) (cf. Joseph Baumgarten, "The Avoidance of the Death Penalty in Qumran Law," in *Reworking the Bible: Apocryphal and Related Texts at Qumran*, ed. Esther G. Chazon, Devorah Dimant, and Ruth Clements [Leiden: Brill, 2005], 32). Qumran, on the other hand, prescribed that the woman with a bad reputation be examined before the man betrothed her, so that the situation in which the death penalty could be prescribed never occurred (4Q271 III, 12–15; ibid). Qumran also seems to have expelled members rather than capitally punish them (ibid. 34–35). The Targums also come to mind here with their "'converse translations,' where the Targum in effect provides an interpretation that is opposite to the meaning of the Hebrew text, either by removing or inserting a negation" (Staffan Olofsson, *Translation Technique and Theological Exegesis: Collected Essays on the Septuagint Version* [Winona Lake: Eisenbrauns, 2009], 95). Likewise, note the close parallel to Ex's apodotic curse with יומת מיתה בידי שמים found in the rabbis (previously noted and dismissed by Frankel, *Ueber den Einfluss*, 93–94).

50 Beth A. Berkowitz, *Execution and Invention: Death Penalty Discourse in Early Rabbinic and Christian Cultures* (Oxford: Oxford University Press, 2006), 58: "the Rabbis stay relatively close to the Torah's list of capital crimes, while the Qumran readers add freely to that list." For Qumran's additions see Baumgarten, "The Avoidance," 31.

Ex occur elsewhere. I have noted some in my analysis. More thought needs to be given to the genres of texts found within the LXX corpus and within books themselves. This is not to say that translators always considered such literary demarcations in a given book. Rather, some might have, as appears to be the case in for the translator of Exodus. Uncovering these kinds of translational choices does not come easily. Interdisciplinary measures must be taken and proficiency in the documentary and/or literary sources has to be achieved. I hope that the present study will capture the imagination of Septuagintalists and would-be Septuagintalists. New ground is broken, and there is more to be found.

5.3 Concluding Remarks

Since its production, the Covenant Code has influenced the legal, moral, and cultural imaginations of untold masses who heard its prescripts. It was often heard in echoes as time went on, and traditions emerged from it, even though it remained present. This is to be expected: as new contexts brought fresh and unforeseen demands, its original frame could not always support each of these burdens. At some time in the third century a translator took to the task of bringing this legal wisdom to another generation of a different culture and language. This translator's choice—should it be considered their own and not a received tradition—was to reimagine and reconstruct the Code in what seems to be an attempt to provide more suitable answers within the world he embodied. In this way, the translation of Greek Exodus bears witness to both a death and rebirth of Israel's most ancient proclamation of judicial wisdom. The alterations to laws concerning capital punishment attest to this. It is in the death of their penalties that this ancient code took on a new life. This recreation and its predecessor continued to face the same fate as the presence and influence of each waxed and waned in any given context. New meanings were ascribed to them, or their contents became outdated and contested. Such a fate is an unavoidable part of being bound to culture, history, and time. It is here now at this privileged point in the academic study of ancient texts that we can bridge these gaps and rediscover what was once together a death and a new-found life for the Covenant Code.

Appendix 1: Patterns in Command Verbs from Ptolemaic/Hellenistic Law

1.1 Documentation of Command Verbs

The following chart lists the decrees and some city/miscellaneous laws and the type of command verb they employ.[1] The first two categories can include commands with the infinitive, since it is a 'floating' form that sometimes appears with both imperatives and futures. Some texts are fragmentary and only include a single attestation. The various categories of mixed forms are explained in section 2.7.3. These mixed attestations follow what seem to be consistent rules and usage.

TABLE A1.1 Command verbs in hellenistic law codes

	πρόσταγμα	διάγραμμα	City law/other
Uses future for command	C.Ord.Ptol. 21 (260 BCE) C.Ord.Ptol. 11 (third century BCE) C.Ord.Ptol. 50 (124 BCE)	P.Rev. Col. 57–72[a] P. Rev. Col. 73–74[b]	(0×)

a Grenfell and Mahaffy, *Revenue Laws*, 122, states that section 57 is not part of the original section of 39–56, and as such the change in tense should not be related to the previous content. This text is assumed to be a royal decree/instruction based on tense and first person (royal) voice used in col. 57–58 (though col. 59–72 is a separate document; see ibid., xliii, 122–123). This is a διόρθωμα, which is a correction to a previous law. Col. 59–60.17 are a copy of the διόρθωμα from 58–59, which is likely caused by a scribe's blunder or carelessness, though it is uncertain (ibid., 122). It is worth noticing that the future tense is maintained

1 Texts without any syntax involving a command verb will not be cited (e.g., Inv. no. 25450 [Dossier arabe, no. 67–13–1] is a πρόσταγμα with no verbs cited in Peter M. Fraser, "A Prostagma of Ptolemy Auletes from Lake Edku," *JEA* 56 [1970]: 179). Likewise, some texts have an uncertain genre: with the imperative see, e.g., BGU 14 2367 (225–201 BCE); P.Hamb. 2 168 (275–226 BCE); SB 10 10494 (third century BCE); SB 6 9225 (third century BCE); with the future see, e.g., BGU 10 1901 (275–226 BCE). Other texts escape specific categorization: e.g., C.Ord.Ptol. 53bis and 53ter (105–99 BCE) are actions of the royals written with present tense and might be an announcement rather than something setting continuous precedent; C.Ord.Ptol. 30–31 doesn't seem to be actual prescriptions but rather an admonition to look at the prescriptions already sent (note the future tenses in lines 6, 23); C.Ord.Ptol. 37–38 contain fragments of the orders but it is not clear what aspects are the decree, if any. Again, perfectly categorizing and including every text is not essential to establishing the argument herein.

 | DOI:10.1163/9789004682047_007

TABLE A1.1 Command verbs in hellenistic law codes (*cont.*)

	πρόσταγμα	διάγραμμα	**City law/other**
	P.Yale 1 56 (100 BCE) C.Ord.Ptol. 73 (first century BCE) C.Ord.Ptol. 50 (124 BCE)[c] C.Ord.Ptol. 52 (124–116 BCE)[d] C.Ord.Ptol. 60 (115 BCE)[e] C.Ord.Ptol. 73 (50 BCE) C.Ord.Ptol. 81 (46 BCE)	P.Petr. 3 36 V (a).11–19 (218 BCE)[f] P.Col.Inv. 480 (198 BCE) St.Pont. III 278 (late second or early first century BCE)	
Uses imperative for command	SB 6 9454 (1) (270 BCE) P.Hib. 2 198 (242 BCE)	Syll.^{3} 306 (324 BCE)[g] Diodorus Siculus,	P.Hal. 1 (259 BCE)[h] P.Lille. 1 29 (third century BCE)[i]

throughout the document. While διόρθωμα does not mean διάγραμμα, the royal voice and first person is enough to establish this as a sort of royal correction/command, and as such it has been included here.

b Col. 73–78 is all διάγραμμα material according to Bikerman, "Διάγραμμα," 305. It could be argued that there should be no divide made between col. 74 and 75, and thus 75 changes to the imperative. Unfortunately, Grenfell and Mahaffy's edition notes that whatever came between col. 74 and 75 is lost (*Revenue Laws*, 50). Like col. 57 and 59 (see 40–42 in ibid.), another title of a διάγραμμα may have come before col. 75 and thus separated it from the previous one. The lacunae make it impossible to know what to do with the change from future to imperative. Grenfell and Mahaffy say that col. 73–78 "form a section by themselves" (173), but that need only refer to subject matter and not to the entirety of a single law. Indeed, Westermann calls col. 73–79 "shattered" (*Upon Slavery*, 29). Col. 73–74 could, then, have been included under "Imperative Dominant with Added Future (Not Payment Verb)."

c This text begins with a fragmented section of infinitives but then moves to futures. It is uncertain whether the large gaps earlier in the text contained futures or if the style switches in-between.

d Only one line with command, and it is possible that this should be read more as counsel rather than as formal law.

e Only one line with command, and it is possible that this should be read more as counsel rather than as formal law.

f διάγραμμα according to Westermann, *Upon Slavery*, 30.

g From Phokis. διάγραμμα according to Bikerman, "Διάγραμμα," 295, fn. 2. There are some future tense verbs that are first person after the formal laws in this decree. They are oaths and not part of the formal legislation.

h Note that this text contains some 250 lines of *compiled* city law, all of which use the imperative/infinitive like Classical city law.

i City law according to Youval Rotman, Reinhold Scholl, and Jean A. Straus, "Slavery in Greco-Roman Egypt," in *Law and Legal Practice in Egypt from Alexander to the Arab Conquest: A Selection of Papyrological Sources in Translation, with Introductions and Commentary*, ed. James G. Keenan, Joseph G. Manning, and Uri Yiftach-Firanko (Cambridge: Cambridge University Press, 2014), 447.

TABLE A1.1 Command verbs in hellenistic law codes (*cont.*)

πρόσταγμα	διάγραμμα	City law/other
C.Ptol.Sklav. I 90	*Bib. hist.* 18.56	
– C.Ord.Ptol. 77	(318 BCE?)	
– C.Ord.Ptol. 12–16	Hatzopoulos,	
C.Ord.Ptol. 20 (262 BCE)	Mac. Inst. II 12	
C.Ord.Ptol. 27 (237 BCE)	(200 BCE)[k]	
C.Ord.Ptol. 10 (245 BCE)	Hatzopoulos,	
C.Ord.Ptol. 5 (245 BCE)	Mac. Inst. II 13	
C.Ord.Ptol. 9 (245 BCE)	(221–197 BCE)[l]	
C.Ord.Ptol. 6 (245 BCE)	P.Hamb. 2 168, FrA	
C.Ord.Ptol. 17–18	(275–226 BCE)[m]	
(259 BCE = P.Rev. col. 36–37)	P.Hib. 1 29 FrA. r.	
C.Ord.Ptol. 24	1–11 (265 BCE)[n]	
(259 BCE = P.Hal. 1. 166–185)	P.Rev. col. 39.1–12	
C.Ord.Ptol. 27 (237 BCE)	(259 BCE)[o]	
C.Ord.Ptol. 25 (269–230 BCE)	P.Rev. col. 75–78[p]	
SB 6 8993 (175 BCE)[j]	P.Hib. 2 198, r,	
C.Ord.Ptol. 23 (157 BCE)	5.85–122 (242 BCE)[q]	
C.Ord.Ptol. 46 (144 BCE)	P.Petr. 3 26	
	(240 BCE)[r]	

j Very fragmentary with only one imperative remaining with the rest being infinitives. Called a decree by Rotman et al., "Slavery," 450. Assumed to be πρόσταγμα based on reconstructed line 1.1.

k From Macedonia. διάγραμμα according to Bikerman, "Διάγραμμα," 295, fn. 2.

l From Macedonia. διάγραμμα according to "Διάγραμμα," 295, fn. 2.

m διάγραμμα according to Mélèze-Modrzejewski, "Note sur la législation," 371, fn. 27.

n διάγραμμα according to Mélèze-Modrzejewski, "Note sur la législation," 369, fn. 16, and Wilhelm, *Beiträge zur griechichen*, 247. Westermann, *Upon Slavery*, 38, and fn. 108 comments that some think that this text is a νόμος.

o διάγραμμα according to Mélèze-Modrzejewski, "Note sur la législation," 369, fn. 17.

p διάγραμμα according to Bikerman, "Διάγραμμα," 305, along with Ulrich Wilcken and Ludwig Mitteis, *Grundzüge und Chrestomathie der Papyruskunde. Erster Band: Historischer Teil Zweite Hälfte: Chrestomathie*, vol. 1, part 2 of *Grundzüge und Chrestomathie der Papyruskunde* (Hildesheim: Olms, 1962), §181, 212–213.

q Mélèze-Modrzejewski, "Note sur la législation," 369, labels col. 5.85–122 and possibly r,6.123–140 as διάγραμμα. If the latter is, it seems to continue to display the imperative (line 125).

r διάγραμμα according to Mélèze-Modrzejewski, "Note sur la législation," 327; Helmis, "Crime et châtiment," 100.

TABLE A1.1 Command verbs in hellenistic law codes (*cont.*)

	πρόσταγμα	διάγραμμα	**City law/other**
	P.Gen. 3 136 R, FrA,v,i. 7	P.Hib. 2 197	
	(second century BCE)[s]	(275–226 BCE)[y]	
	C.Ord.Ptol. 58 (115 BCE)[t]	IG X,2 1 3	
	C.Ord.Ptol. 62 (99 BCE)[u]	(187 BCE)[z]	
	C.Ord.Ptol. 67 (75 BCE)[v]	O.Bodl. 1 277	
	C.Ord.Ptol. 70 (69 BCE)[w]	(125–101 BCE)	
	C.Ord.Ptol. 72 (57 BCE)[x]	IG V,1 1390	
	C.Ord.Ptol. 75 (41 BCE)	(92 BCE)[aa]	
Only uses	C.Ord.Ptol. 28 (229 BCE)	Priene 132	P.Hib. 2 196 Frag. II
infinitive for	C.Ord.Ptol. 78 (242 BCE)	(334/320 BCE)[ac]	(280–250 BCE)[ae]
command	C.Ord.Ptol. 79	P.Gurob 2.41–48	
	(third century BCE)[ab]	(226 BCE)[ad]	
	C.Ord.Ptol. 84		
	(third century BCE)		
	C.Ord.Ptol. 26 (242 BCE)		
	C.Ord.Ptol. 28 (229 BCE)		

s Possibly a πρόσταγμα as based on FrA,v,ii.12.
t Only one line with command.
u Only one line with command.
v Only one command verb.
w Only one command verb.
x Only one command verb.
y διάγραμμα according to Hans Julius Wolff, "Neue Juristische Urkunden VII—Neues Material zum Zwangsvollstreckungrecht der Papyri," *ZSS* 100 (1983): 452–453; the original editors believe it to be a civic law.
z From Macedonia.
aa From Messenia. It is called a διάγραμμα in faceA 1.114 and 193.
ab Very fragmentary with only one command verb surviving.
ac διάγραμμα according to Giuseppe Squillace, "Editto di Alessandro Magno per Priene," *Axon* 2 (2018): 153. This text also contains present tense announcements concerning the actions of the king (ll. 11, 14–16) akin to C.Ord.Ptol. 53bis and 53ter.
ad διάγραμμα according to Mélèze-Modrzejewski, *Loi et Coutume*, 203, fn. 25. The fragmentary nature of the citation only preserves two infinitives (line 48).
ae The genre of this text is uncertain and it is very fragmentary.

TABLE A1.1 Command verbs in hellenistic law codes (*cont.*)

	πρόσταγμα	διάγραμμα	City law/other
	C.Ord.Ptol. 29 (215–205 BCE)		
	C.Ord.Ptol. 33 (163 BCE)		
	C.Ord.Ptol. 34 (183 BCE)		
	C.Ord.Ptol. 35 (163 BCE)		
	C.Ord.Ptol. 39–40 (156 BCE)[af]		
	C.Ord.Ptol. 41–42 (145 BCE)		
	C.Ord.Ptol. 44 (144 BCE)[ag]		
	C.Ord.Ptol. 47 (139 BCE)		
	C.Ord.Ptol. 43 (135 BCE)[ah]		
	C.Ord.Ptol. 53 (After 118 BCE)		
	C.Ord.Ptol. 55 (118 BCE)		
	C.Ord.Ptol. 53 (118 BCE)		
	C.Ord.Ptol. 54 (118 BCE)		
	C.Ord.Ptol. 55 (118 BCE)		
	C.Ord.Ptol. 59 (115 BCE)[ai]		
	C.Ord.Ptol. 61 (114 BCE)		
	C.Ord.Ptol. 64 (96 BCE)[aj]		
	C.Ord.Ptol. 65 (95 BCE)[ak]		
	C.Ord.Ptol. 66 (93 BCE)[al]		

af Lenger (the editor) only includes lines 33 and 79 as orders.

ag Royal command is only found in one line in response to the petition (line 29).

ah Some texts like this include what seems to be a recounting of a decree and not a direct representation of the original text. This restating is expressed with 'προστάσσω + complementary infinitive.' Bikerman, "Διάγραμμα," 302–303 validates this form of expressing the διάγραμμα, indicating that it still represents the ordonnance. Whether the syntax has been altered from an original document is still a question left unanswered. It does not affect this study's argument.

ai Text is fragmentary and only one infinitive survives in the relevant section.

aj An imperative is at the end of this text and exhorts that the previous commands be followed (γίνεσθω; line 10).

ak Only one command verb.

al Only one command verb.

TABLE A1.1 Command verbs in hellenistic law codes (*cont.*)

	πρόσταγμα	διάγραμμα	**City law/other**
	C.Ord.Ptol. 69 (69 BCE)[am] C.Ord.Ptol. 71 (61 BCE) C.Ord.Ptol. 74 (49 BCE) C.Ord.Ptol. 83 (46 BCE)[an] C.Ord.Ptol. 76 (41 BCE) SB 26 16531 (third to first centuries BCE)		
Imperative dominant with future in relative clause	P.Hib. 2 198 r,5.119 C.Ord.Ptol. 82.8 (and 81.8[?])	P.Rev. 33.6[ao]	MDAI(A) 27 (1902) 47,71, col. III.141–142 (second century BCE)[ap] P.Freib. 3 34, Fr2.29 (173 BCE)[aq]
Infinitive dominant with future tense payment verb exception	C.Ord.Ptol. 8.6 (270–245 BCE) P.Hib. 2 198, r,2.17		
Imperative dominant with future tense payment verb exception	C.Ord.Ptol. 7.5 (245 BCE) P.Rev. 13.12; 14.13; 15.1, 9 (259 BCE) P.Hib. 2 198, r,2.36;[ar]	P.Hib. 1 29, FrA,1.23 (265 BCE)[at] Hatzopoulos, Mac. Inst. II 13.45 (221–197 BCE)	IG VII 3172, face B I.28 (222–200 BCE)[av]

am Only one command verb.

an There is a future verb in line 6, but it may have been part of a relative clause, as is the case in the related document C.Ord.Ptol. 82.8 (of which 81.8 likely read the same future verb in a relative clause). Cases with relative clauses are documented below.

ao The genre of this text is not clear and is unimportant due to the verb being in a relative clause.

ap Labelled βασιλικὸν νόμον in line 1.

aq Part of a royal land contract but demonstrates the same usage of the future in a relative clause.

ar The command verbs are lost in this decree and this example is included in this section due to the surrounding occurrences.

at The genre of this document is uncertain. Perhaps the financial focus could direct towards the classification of διάγραμμα.

av This is a decree from the city (ψήφισμα) and not a civic law, per se, but it still demonstrates the rule with future payment verbs. The text relates the payment to civic law as well: πραχθήσονται κατὰ τὸν νόμον.

TABLE A1.1 Command verbs in hellenistic law codes (*cont.*)

	πρόσταγμα	διάγραμμα	City law/other
	r,4 ctr.52; v,Fr4.2 (242 BCE)[as]	SEG 49:722.4 (Late third or early second century)[au]	
Imperative dominant with added future (not payment verb)[aw]	C.Ord.Ptol. 19.2–3, 18–19 (250 BCE) P.Rev. 3.2; 46.9–10; 53.4, 18–19, 23; 54.15; IG Iran Asie centr. nr. 66, fig. 66 (194 BCE)[ax]	SEG 9 1 (321 BCE) P.Rev. 40.9–20[ay] P.Rev. 56.14–18 P.Rev. 34.1–8	
Future-dominant with added imperative (**equivalent to Ex**)	SB 5 8008 (2).52–53 (260 BCE = C.Ord.Ptol. 22)	P.Paris 62 (203 BCE)[az]	SEG 9 72.31 (325–300 BCE)[ba]

as Included in this category based on surrounding materials; text is almost inexistant. Also labelled within C.Ord.Ptol.1–4 (barring r,4,ctr.52; v,Fr4).

au Either a διάγραμμα or more general regulation according to Angelos Chaniotis et al., eds., "SEG 49–722. Kassandreia (Poteidaia). Regulation concerning military service, late 3rd cent B.C. (or March 197 B.C.?)," *SEG* (2002), http://dx.doi.org/10.1163/1874-6772_seg_a49_722.

aw SEG 9 73 (second to first century BCE) not included due to its uncertain genre.

ax This text is included here because it shows the same traits as the others in this category. It does not use future tense verbs but present tense verbs. See the discussion in section 2.7.3.5 and below. This text also includes two future tense verbs within relative clauses (ll. 23–24) which fit within the same typology as "Imperative Dominant with Future in Relative Clause."

ay Part of a section of a διάγραμμα according to Grenfell and Mahaffy, *Revenue Laws*, 124; Mélèze-Modrzejewski, "Note sur la législation," 369, fn. 17.

az Given the parallels to P.Rev., this law code is possibly διάγραμμα materials (see G. M. Harper, "The Relation of Ἀρχώνης, Μέτοχοι, and Ἔγγυοι to Each Other, to the Government and to the Tax Contract in Ptolemaic Egypt," *Aegyptus* 14, no. 2/3 [1934]: 269; Grenfell and Mahaffy, *Revenue Laws*, 183, indicates that some of the text is a διάγραμμα but it is not certain if it all is).

ba That this document is from the Ptolemaic era is disputable. That it is Ptolemaic see Ulrich von Wilamowitz-Moellendorff, "Heilige Gesetze, eine Urkunde aus Kyrene," *SPAW* 19 (1927): 155 (cf. 176); Gaetano De Sanctis, "Le decretali di Cirene," *RFIC* 55 (1927): 187, calls the commands "decretali di diritto sacro;" Achille Vogliano, "Nuovi studi sulle decretali di Cirene," *RFIC* 56 (1928): 255–320, labels it a decree; Silvio Ferri, "La 'Lex cathartica' di Cirene," *Notiziario Archeologico del Ministero delle Colonie* 4 (1927): 100, says that this inscription comes from an older tradition or inscription. Whatever the nature of the document, which is highly disputed, the argument here still holds together. For the dispute on its genre and purpose see the introductory commentary in Carbon, Peels, and Pirenne-Delforge, "CGRN 99."

1.2 Other Examples of Imperative-Dominant Command Verbs with Added Future (Not Payment Verb)

[**παρα]λήψονται** δὲ οἱ [ἔχοντες τὴν ὠνὴν τ]ὸ προκη-
[ρυχθὲ]ν ἐφ' ἑκάστωι νομ[ῶι ἀποτίθεσθαι σήσ]αμον
[καὶ κρό]τωνα ἀφ' ἧς ἂν ἡμ[έρας τὴν ὠνὴν παραλάβ]ωσιν
[ἐν ἡμ]έραις γ, τοῦ ση[σάμου τὴν ἀρ(τάβην) (δραχμῶν).][, τοῦ σ]ησα-
[μίνο]υ τὸν με(τρητὴν) (δραχμῶν) [...][καὶ κρότωνος][καὶ κ]ίκιος \(δραχμῶν) ιζ/
[...]μωι [...] τιμῆς \ἧς [...]ται αὐτοῖς [...]ρ[...]/
\[...] εἰς τὸ κζ (ἔτος) καὶ τοῦ σησάμου καὶ κρότωνος καὶ κνήκ[ου] τι[μ]ὴν τὴγ γεγραμμέ-/
\νη[ν ἐν τῶι] διαγράμματι τῶι ἐκτε[θέ]ντι εἰς τὸ κζ (ἔτος)./

———

ἐὰν δὲ πλεῖον ἐγκαταλ[ε]ίπωσιν ἐξιόντες ἐκ τῆς
ὠνῆς, κομιζέσθωσαν παρὰ τοῦ οἰκονόμου τιμὴν
τοῦ μὲν σησαμίνου τοῦ με(τρητοῦ) ⟦(δραχμὰς) λα (τετρώβολον) (χαλκοῦς 2)⟧ \(δραχμὰς)
κθ (τριώβολον)/, τοῦ δὲ κί-
κιος τοῦ με(τρητοῦ) (δραχμὰς) κ ⟦α (διώβολον)⟧, τοῦ δὲ κνηκίνου τοῦ με(τρητοῦ)
{(δραχμὰς)} ⟦ιη (τετρώβολον)⟧ \(δραχμὰς) ιζ (ὀβολὸν)/,
τοῦ δὲ σησάμου τῆς ἀρ(τάβης) (δραχμὰς) η, τοῦ δὲ κρότωνος
τῆς ἀρ(τάβης) (δραχμὰς) δ, τῆς δὲ κνήκου (δραχμὴν) ⟦α (τριώβολον)⟧ \α (διώβολον)/

———

ὅσον δ' ἂν ἔλαιον
ὑποκηρύξωμεν λήψεσθαι \ἐξ/ ἑκάστου ν[ο]μοῦ εἰς
τὰ[ς] ἐν Ἀλεξανδρείαι διαθέσεις, **λημψόμε[θ]α** παρ' αὐ-
τῶν ἐν τῶι νομῶι τοῦ \[κίκ]ιος τὸμ με(τρητὴν) (δραχμῶν) ιθ (διωβόλου)/ ⟦μὲν ἐλαίου
τὸν με(τρητὴν) τὸν (δωδεκά)χο(υν)⟧
⟦χω[ρὶ]ς κεράμου (δραχμῶν) λα (τετρωβόλου) [(χαλκῶν 2)], τοῦ δὲ κίκι[ος] (δραχμῶν) κα (διωβόλου)⟧
⟦τ[οῦ] δὲ κνηκίνου (δραχμῶν) ιη (τετρωβόλου), [τοῦ] δὲ κολοκυ[ν]τί\ν/ου (δραχμῶν) ιβ⟧
κα[ὶ ὑ]πολογισθήσεται ἡ τ[ιμὴ] τοῖς ἔχουσ[ι] τὰς ὠνὰς
εἰς [τ]ὰς ἀναφορὰς τὰς γινομ[ένα]ς. τὴν δὲ τ[ιμ]ὴν τῶν φορ-
τ[ίω]ν καὶ τὸ κάτεργον καὶ τ[ὸ] ἀνήλωμα π[ροα]νηλισκέ-
τ[ω ὁ] οἰκονόμος.

The contractors shall receive the sesame and croton, of which a store (?) has been ordered for each nome, within three days from the day on which they take over the contract, paying for it at the rate of ... for sesame ... for a metretes of sesame oil, for croton ... for cici ... (altered to '17 dr.') ... But if, when they give up the contract, they leave behind them more oil (than they were ordered to store?) they shall receive from the oeconomus as the value of the sesame oil 31 dr. $4_{1/4}$ obols (altered to '28 dr. 3 obols') for a metretes, of cici 21 dr. 2 obols (altered to '20 dr.') for a metretes, of cnecus oil 18 dr. 4 obols (altered to '17 dr. 1 obol') for a metretes, and as the value of the sesame 8 drachmae for an artaba, of the croton 4 dr., and of the cnecus 1 dr. 3 obols (altered to '1 dr. 2 obols').

The oil which we hereinafter proclaim our intention of taking from each nome for disposal at Alexandria, we will take from the contractors in the nome, paying for it at the rate of 31 dr. $4_{1/4}$ obols for a metretes of sesame oil containing 12 choes without jars, and 21 dr. 2 obols for cici, 18 dr. 4 obols for cnecus oil, and 12 dr. for colocynth oil. (Altered to '18 dr. 2 obols for a metretes of cici.') This price shall be credited to the contractors in the instalments due from them, but the price of the produce, the wages of manufacture, and the miscellaneous expenses shall first be paid by the oeconomus.[2]

P.Rev. 53.4–26

The main verbs in question here are 53.4, 18–19, 23 (in bold). P.Rev. 53.4 begins with a future tense (here [παρα]λήψονται).[3] Beginning a section with a future has already been seen to be a trait of imperative-dominant laws with futures. The text is quite fragmentary, but Grenfell and Mahaffy suggest that this section refers to the incoming contractors who are about to take that office.[4] The translation would then be, "The [incoming] contractors shall receive the sesame and croton," of which the prices are then laid out (lines 7–8). It might be that the future here is like that in 40.9–20 in that it acts as preamble to the actual legislation to come. In this context the future tense may refer to the setting up of the new contractors in their role in that they are to be given charge over the goods they are receiving. This action would be much like the aforementioned

2 Translation from Grenfell and Mahaffy, *Revenue Laws*, 151–152.

3 That 53.4 onward forms its own section and is separate from the previous imperative laws, note that there is both a division line from the scribe, as well as a significant amount of space in which a corrector later came and inserted in small print another legal matter (cf. a replica of text 36 in Grenfell and Mahaffy, *Revenue Laws*, and the commentary at p. 151). The explanation here would be akin to what would be given for 52.4, if more of the text survived.

4 Grenfell and Mahaffy, *Revenue Laws*, 151.

appointments to various stations of authority. This conclusion must remain tentative based on the fragmentary nature of the text.

The imperative is used immediately following this section for the required payment to the outgoing contractor from the *oikonomos*. Here the responsibility and onus are on the contractor and *oikonomos*, and the imperative indicates that the preliminary information is over and the actions of the intendants are in view. Column 53.18 continues the future tense but now in the first person, which indicates the voice of the king.[5] Grenfell describes this section as referring to the king's future intentions, which are now being told to his servants. All these future intentions are written with the future tense, but right at the end, when it comes to the here-and-now activity of his subjects and their production of his goods, he declares that they will "first be paid" (imperative π[ροα]νηλισκέτ[ω) for the beginning of the work. The full payments, in contrast, will be credited to them in the future (ὑ]πολογισθήσεται). The future tense here sets up the prices to be paid later based on this new initiative as compared to the payments for production that are to be given immediately by the *oikonomos* (τ[ὸ] ἀνήλωμα π[ροα]νηλισκέτ[ω ὁ] οἰκονόμος; lines 25–26).[6] This section, then, uses the future to emphasize the royal voice and intentions (through the grammatical first person), sets prerequisite prices, and defers certain actions with their consequences to a later time (such as the full payments credited and owed). All these future tense actions lay outside of the abilities, purview, and here-and-now actions of the officials, and so are rendered with the future. Where the onus is on the officials, the imperative is used (e.g., lines 13, 26). The deferral of an act to a later time with the future tense is also parallel to the function of ὁ βασιλεὺς διαγνώσεται that was previously discussed.

> [τῆι Φιλαδέλφωι …]
> [οἱ δὲ πριάμενοι τὴν ὠνὴν ἐγγύους καταστή-]
> [σουσι τῶν ἐφεικ]όστων ἀφ' [ἧς ἂν ἡμέρας ἀγ]οράσωσιν̣
> ἐν ἡμέρα[ις] λ. τὰς δὲ κατ[αβολὰς(?) ποιή]σονται
> τῶν χρημάτων ἀπὸ Δίου ἕως [… κατ]ὰ̣ μῆνα τὸ
> ἐπιβάλλον.
> …
> ὅσος δ' ἂν ληφθῆι παρ' αὐτῶν οἶν̣[ος εἰς τὸ βασι]λικόν, ὑπο-
> λογεισθήσεται ἡ τιμὴ εἰς τὰς [γινομένας ἀνα]φοράς.

5 Grenfell and Mahaffy, *Revenue Laws*, 152–153.

6 Note the prefix προ- indicating that this passage is focused on when these events are occurring.

> The tax-farmers shall within thirty days from the day on which they purchase the tax, appoint sureties for a sum greater by one-twentieth than the price agreed upon for the tax, and the sureties shall register the property which they mortgage, in monthly instalments from Dius to …
>
> The value of the wine which is received from the tax-farmers for the Treasury shall be credited to the tax-farmers in the instalments due from them.[7]
>
> P.Rev. 34.1–8

The section after 34.1–8 is clearly demarcated with the large heading διαλογισμός (34.9). Five lines or so are lost before the start of the text in 34.1. This missing text makes it hard to distinguish why the future tense is employed here since 34.1 could be a new section/source with a heading that was lost. This section shares closes affinities with 56.14–18, a text that also exhibits the future tense.[8] It seems best to understand this future-oriented section as representing a one-time event in which the tax-farmer is to set up sureties for an allotted time. This would only happen once and as such it is viewed as a prerequisite matter and not a behavior that will be consistently performed. The prices are not laid out here because they are dependent on what is brought in daily and monthly.[9] Note that ὑπολογισθήσεται and similar wording are used as in the future tense section of 53.23. The tense indicates that in the future the price owed to the contractors will be given to them. It is a royal promise of which the details are not part of this legislation. The similarity in language between col. 34 and 56 and the references to prices, setting up institutions, and future crediting, all demonstrate close affinities between the texts with the future in P.Rev. despite their fragmentary nature.

> οἱ δὲ πριάμενοι τὴν ὠνὴν ἐγγύους καταστή-
> σουσι τῶ[ν] ἐφεικόστων καὶ διορθώσονται τὰ [μ]ὲ̣ν λο-
> γεύμα[τ]α̣ καθ' ἡμέραν [ἐ]πὶ τὴν τραπεζ[αν, τὴ]ν̣
> δ' ἀναφορ[ὰν τ]ὴν ἐπιβάλ[λ]ουσαν τῶι μηνὶ ἐν τ[ῶι ἐχ]ο-
> μένωι [πρὸ] τῆς διχο[μ]ηνίας.

---

7 Translation from Grenfell and Mahaffy, *Revenue Laws*, 111.

8 Both texts: begin with οἱ δὲ πριάμενοι τὴν ὠνὴν ἐγγύους καταστήσουσι τῶν ἐφεικόστων ("The contractors shall appoint sureties greater than by one twentieth …"; concern the ἀναφορά; end their respective section.

9 Cf. Grenfell and Mahaffy, *Revenue Laws*, 160.

> The contractors shall appoint sureties for a sum greater by one-twentieth than that which they have contracted to pay, and shall pay up the taxes collected every day to the bank, while the monthly instalment shall be paid up before the middle of the month following.[10]
>
> P.Rev. 56.14–18

As noted, this text seems to be connected to 34.1–8.[11] It is separated from the previous content by a line, and has different content from the previous section regarding a "Search," despite not having a title of its own.[12] Given the replicated language of 34.1–8 and that text's connection to col. 53, this section should probably be seen as using the future to indicate a one-time set up of sureties by the contractor (like col. 34) as well as the set prices they owed, which are not stated directly because they are dependent on what is brought in daily and monthly.[13] The use of the future here then fits into the general framework of prerequisite data and prices that prefigure the rest of the legislation.

IG Iran Asie centr. nr. 66, fig. 66 (194 BCE) also demonstrates this same structure including the royal first person voice (ll. 19–20 but in the present tense) and new roles being set up along with the preliminary information the royals want action towards. The first half of the letter contains the decision made to honor the queen and the appointment of a new high priestesses for her (κρίνομεν ... καὶ ταύτης κ[αθ]ίστασθαι ἐν τοῖς αὐτοῖς τό[ποι]ς, "we decide to appoint high priestesses of this one in the same places"). The second half of the letter contains the commands in the imperative mood (ll. 27, 30) to follow through with the vision they just cast and to erect steles with their vision inscribed. This is a similar pattern to other texts with the future tense amidst imperatives and should probably be categorized in the same way.

10 Translation from Grenfell and Mahaffy, *Revenue Laws*, 159–160.

11 Cf. Grenfell and Mahaffy, *Revenue Laws*, 159–160, who connect them.

12 "Search" is found in 55.17–56. 13; cf. Grenfell and Mahaffy, *Revenue Laws*, 158.

13 Grenfell and Mahaffy, *Revenue Laws*, 160.

Appendix 2: More Information on πᾶν/πάντα

2.1 πᾶν in the Documentary Sources

The following table does not include references to πᾶν when modifying a neuter noun since its gender is determined by the noun in that construction. It also does not include τὸ πᾶν due to this being a stock phrase that is unaffected by the gender or type of item it modifies.[1] Full citations included are from the third century with the rest (up until CE) being included in short form.

TABLE A2.1 πᾶν in the documentary sources

	Documentary source using πᾶν
Refers to persons	(0×)
Refers to animals/ inanimate objects	(16×) SEG 41:537.2 (450–400 BCE) πᾶν διαδασάμενος All bequeathed – refers to the testator's possessions Polis ed Olympieion 15.15 (350–250 BCE) πᾶν {20 tal., {3 sta.}} – refers to items and their price Polis ed Olympieion 28.10 (350–250 BCE) πᾶν • {193 tal., 10 lit.} – refers to items and their price IG XIV 645, I.111–112 (fourth to third centuries BCE) πᾶν τῶι πράτωι μισθώματι everything (decreed) in the first contract-price – refers to goods or perhaps to everything in the contract generally

1 See, e.g., τὸ πᾶν δραχμαὶ (P.Hamb. 2 184.4 [275–226 BCE]); τὸ πᾶν … ἀρ(τάβαι) (P.Cair.Zen. 3 59333, r. 30 [248 BCE]).

 | DOI:10.1163/9789004682047_008

TABLE A2.1 πᾶν in the documentary sources (*cont.*)

	Documentary source using πᾶν
	P.Cair.Zen. 2 59194, r.8 (255 BCE) εἰ δὲ μὴ δύνατον π̣ᾶ̣ν, τό γε ἥμυσυ and if not everything possible, indeed the half – refers to value/payment of the vases (cf. verso, line 2)
	P.Tebt. 3 1 815, Fr5,r.41 (223 BCE) π̣ᾶ̣ν ἀποδώσ⟨ου⟩σιν They will give all – refers to produce of crops (cf. line 38 τοὺς καρποὺς)
	PSI 4 422, r.24–25 (275–226 BCE) βέβρεκται γὰρ πᾶν For all has been inundated – refers to the land (cf. lines 22–24)
	Darmezin, Affranchissements 88,123.13–15 (late third century BCE) ἔττε πᾶν κα γένειτη ϝετίων ϝίκατι κὴ ἑνός until the entirety of twenty-one years have passed[a]
	UPZ 1 41.25–26 (161 BCE)
	P.Hamb. 1 57.19–23 (160 BCE)[b]
	IG XII,4 1:343.17 (150–100 BCE)
	P.Strasb. 6 564.5 (150–101 BCE)
	P.Herc. 1014 col. 4.6 (150–51 BCE)
	P.Merton 2 59.27 (143 BCE)[c]
	FD III 6:110.12–13 (138 BCE)
Generic/ abstract use	(38×) ZPE 14 (1974) 21,I.1 (300–250 BCE) ἀ̣[ντί]α πᾶν ἐπόνη̣[σεν] he laboured against all (the general problems)

a Translation from Toru Minamimoto, "Subordinators and the Supradialectal Formulas in the Dialectal Inscriptions from Mainland Greece (Excluding Attica)" (PhD diss., UCLA, 2017), 80.

b Example included due to neuter noun (ἄγριον) being provided in lacuna.

c This dispute involves a lost slave (lines 12–13, 21–28) and it is worth noting that the slave is not included in the "everything necessary" (πᾶν δέ[ον) to be paid, as "everything" only includes monetary costs and not the slave themselves (cf. line 27). This is potentially more evidence that πᾶν does not include persons, though of course slaves could be perceived as mere goods.

TABLE A2.1 πᾶν in the documentary sources (*cont.*)

	Documentary source using πᾶν
	IG II^{2} 3783.2 (303 BCE) σε [πᾶ]ν κατιδεῖν εὐξυνέτοις πραπίσι you have explored everything with your refined insights[d]
	PSI 6 622, r.7 (275–226 BCE) τὸ ὅλον δὲ πᾶν ποίει he does the whole and anything
	P.Petr. 2 13, Fr19.13–14 (255 BCE) ἀλλὰ πᾶν ἐ[μοὶ ἔστ]αι πεφροντισμένον τοῦ σε γενέσθαι ἄλυπον. but everything will have been considered by me in order that you will be without grief.
	PSI 4 361, r.4 (251 BCE) πᾶν ποιήσω τὸ δε⟨⟩ον I will do everything necessary
	IG XII,4 1:138.23–25 (241 BCE) ἀε]ὶ ὑπακούων εἰς πᾶν περὶ ὧν ἄν τι̣ς [αὐτὸ]ν̣ παρακαλῆι [the honored physician] always submits in everything concerning whichever someone might urge him.
	P.Tebt. 3.1 703, v.2.227–228 (210 BCE) πᾶν τ̣ὸ̣ [το]ιοῦτον ε[ἰ]ς ἐπίστασ̣ι̣ν ἧ̣κ̣ται All this has come for a cessation – refers back to the general situation or perhaps to ἀδίκημα in line 224
	IG V,1 1336.6 (third to second centuries BCE)
	Klazomenai 3.27 (200–150 BCE)
	P.Herc. 1420 fr. 2.4–6 (200–101 BCE)
	P.Herc. 1148 col. 8. 20–22 (200–101 BCE)
	BGU 6 1301.14 (200–1 BCE)
	Gonnoi II 41.13–14 (180–160 BCE)
	UPZ 1 59, r.15 (168 BCE)
	P.Phrur. Diosk. 15, r.17 (158 BCE)
	P.Herc. 1014 col. 56.8 (150 BCE)
	P.Herc. 1027 col. 15.4–6 (150–101 BCE)[e]

d Translation from Julia Lougovaya, "Medici Docti in Verse Inscriptions," *Greek Medical Papyri* (2019): 151.

e This example, πᾶν τὸ ματαίως ἡμᾶς παρενοχλοῦν, could refer to people, as in, "everyone vainly annoying us." This does not seem to fit the philosophical dialogue.

TABLE A2.1 πᾶν in the documentary sources (*cont.*)

	Documentary source using πᾶν
	P.Tebt. 1 60.2 (117 BCE)
	SB 20 14728 DAHT 164, r.18–19 (103 BCE)
	IG XII,1 980.8 (second century BCE)
	P.Herc. 1021 col. 19.9–11 (100–51 BCE)
	BGU 8 1785.9–10 (64–44 BCE)
	IG V,1 1432.26–27 (39 BCE)
	IG XII,4 1:294, frg. ab. 43 (first century BCE) (cf. SEG 51:1066)
	IC I xvii 21.7 (first century BCE)
	P.Herc. 339 col. 4.10–12 (first century BCE)
	P.Herc. 346 col. 5.3–5 (first century BCE)
	P.Herc. 1672 col. 15.38–39; col. 16.1 (first century BCE)
	P.Herc. 862 col. 11.15–18 (first century BCE)
	P.Herc. 1005 fr. 74.8–9 (first century BCE)
	P.Herc. 1050 col. 16.11–12; col. 20.15 (first century BCE)
	P.Herc. 1424, col. 12.32–33, 42–43 (first century BCE)
	P.Herc. 1471 col. 3b.7–8 (first century BCE)
	BGU 4 1130.5 (4 BCE)
	P.Herc. 1150 col. 3 inf. 28–29 (100 BCE–79 CE)
Disputable	(1×)
	IG XI,4 1299.48–49 (third century BCE)
	ἀλλ’ ὅτε καὶ τὸν γηραλέον λίπε μοῖρα, πάϊς γε μὲν ἐσθλὰ διδαχθεὶς ἐκ πατρὸς μεγάλως σέβεν ἱερά, πᾶν δὲ κατ’ ἦμαρ σὰς ἀρετὰς ἤειδεν But when also fate leaves old age, and indeed a child being taught uprightness from a father greatly reveres holy things, and everything/each (of them) sings everyday (of) your virtues …[f]

f It is uncertain if the πᾶν refers to the father and son, the father, son and fate, or to a generic "everything" pointing in a poetic way to the inanimate or abstract world. This last option is favourable given the tenor of the passage, which is itself a sort of panegyric about the lauded subject of the inscription.

2.2 πᾶν as a True Neuter Instead of πᾶν = πάντα

Thackeray cites a few passages where πᾶν, to him, represents a true neuter as opposed to this variant of πᾶν = πάντα.[2] He lists the following passages: Judg 3:29B, 4 Kgdms 15:20, 2 Chron 32:21, 2 Esd 7:17BA, Isa 23:9BSAΓ, Jer 9:26SAQ (cf. 32:9BA). Of these only Judg 3:29B, Isa 23:9BSAΓ and Jer 9:26SAQ (cf. 32:9BA) should be considered possible true neuters. 2 Esd 7:17BA refers to objects/animals and, as Muraoka has pointed out, is a mistake on Thackeray's part.[3] Fourth Kingdoms 15:20 and 2 Chron 32:21 were explained in section 4.4.2.4. Isaiah 23:9B ℵAΓ has been discussed in section 4.4.2.1, and it likely does reflect a true neuter, though not referring to humans.

The two texts that are not πᾶν = πάντα from Thackeray's list referring to humans that potentially use the neuter qualitatively are then Judg 3:29B and Jer 9:26SAQ (cf. 32:9BA). Note that both attestations are late. The former reads ὡσεὶ δέκα χιλιάδας ἀνδρῶν, πᾶν λιπαρὸν καὶ πάντα ἄνδρα δυνάμεως. πᾶν λιπαρὸν does seem to fit into a qualitative category of neuter that describes a human, and the immediately following πάντα seems to indicate that πᾶν is not πᾶν = πάντα, but this is not entirely clear. It is possible that πᾶν λιπαρὸν is a case of πᾶν = πάντα with its masculine counterpart (criterion 1 [section 4.4.2.4.1]) being represented through apposition with ἀνδρῶν. Whatever the case, besides the fact that πᾶν λιπαρὸν belongs to a later place in the text and language's history, the context here makes it unambiguous that πᾶν λιπαρὸν refers to the men as it is in apposition to the phrase δέκα χιλιάδας ἀνδρῶν and is further defined as πάντα ἄνδρα δυνάμεως. A qualitative use of πᾶν in a context like this is unlikely to be misunderstood. That is not the same as Exod 22:18 (22:19 LXX), which gives no further context or data to determine that πᾶν should be understood as referring to humans. Additionally, πᾶν λιπαρὸν seems to refer to distinct individuals and does not fit into the collectivizing sense of the neuter found *with the article* in the Classical and Post-Classical sources. This collectivizing sense is the type of neuter Muraoka claimed for Exod 22:18 (22:19 LXX) and is thus not analogous to Judg 3:29B. This is all the more the case if it is true that the collective neuter is used in a "generic, gender-neutral sense," since in Judg 3:29B it is specifically men who are signalled out.[4]

The cases in Jer 9:26SAQ/32:9BA with πᾶν περικειρόμενον/περικεκαρμένον are significant because they are syntactically parallel to Exod 22:18 (22:19 LXX).[5]

2 Thackeray, *Grammar*, 174.
3 Muraoka, *Syntax*, 661cg), fn. 1.
4 This gender-neutral function is the claim of Muraoka, *Syntax*, §20, ee, p. 102.
5 9:26 reads πᾶν in S*-130 A-410 Q^{txt}; 32:9 reads πᾶν in B A-106′ 130 239.

Despite their later dating, the change from πάντα περικειρόμενον/περικεκαρμένον to πᾶν περικειρόμενον/περικεκαρμένον in the Jeremian traditions could still ostensibly support Exod 22:18 (22:19 LXX) to be read as πᾶν = πάντα. If πάντα became πᾶν in that tradition, is this evidence that πάντα could be misread in this syntactic situation which would then warrant a change to πᾶν? This is possible.

πᾶν περικειρόμενον/περικεκαρμένον seems to describe an entire people group in a list of ethnicities, and it is this use of the neuter to collectively describe subjects, citizens, or close-knit people groups that is common in the Classical texts.[6] However, if 4 Kgdms 15:20 (and perhaps even Judg 3:29B) could serve as evidence that criterion 1 for πᾶν = πάντα is met when πᾶν is appositionally related to a masculine noun, then here in Jer 9:26SAQ we find πᾶν περικειρόμενον in apposition to τοὺς κατοικοῦντας ἐν τῇ ἐρήμῳ. The latter phrase is masculine and might therefore have served to indicate that πᾶν = πάντα. This reading could have emerged in the textual tradition due to the phenomenon found in Table A2.2 (below), which seems to indicate that without the article after πάντα, "πάντα περικεκαρμένον" might be read with πάντα as the object of the participle according to Classical Greek standards. πᾶν, on the other hand, is always the subject of the participle it modifies. Added to this is the neuter article found in the text: ἐπὶ πάντα περικειρόμενον τὰ κατὰ πρόσωπον αὐτοῦ. It is possible that πάντα may have come across as the nt.pl. object of περικειρόμενον (i.e., "one shearing all the things according to his face"). This syntactic problem could explain the impetus for the variation in the later MSS.[7] Later scribes could add the ms.sg. article or use πᾶν = πάντα in a context with a masculine noun in apposition to πᾶν in order to clear up the discrepancy. On the other hand, if this is a case of the collective neuter, it does not seem to fit the norms of the Greek language at the time of the original translation with respect to 'πᾶν + participles' (see Tables A2.3–A2.5 below), where the collective sense is rare and where the article would be required. Perhaps in this line of reasoning, Jer 9:26SAQ/32:9BA would have come across as stilted, particularly because there is no article, which seems to be the consistent way of indicating the collective neuter. Finally, that OG Jeremiah does not have any uses of πᾶν = πάντα should further serve to solidify its original absence in 9:26/32:9, though it is possible that Jer 9:26SAQ/32:9BA is a later example of this construction. This could make sense, since πᾶν = πάντα seems to be employed in places where πάντα could be misread, and that is the case here in Greek Jeremiah.

6 Kühner, *Ausführliche Grammatik*, 14.

7 τά is not found in the critical edition of Jer. 32:9, nor is direct apposition indicated. Perhaps the textual tradition represents conflation with 9:26, or πᾶν in the later history does represent a true neuter. Note that Q^{txt} has πᾶν in 9:26 but not 32:9, which could serve as evidence that 32:9 was not an instance requiring πᾶν = πάντα and that the manuscripts with this reading are a result of conflation with 9:26.

In the end, Jer 9:26SAQ/32:9BA are late and cannot be relied upon to determine norms at the time of the OG.

Appendix 2.3 πάντα/πᾶν and Participles

The following table lists the cases when πάντα functions as the subject or object of the verbal action of the singular medio-passive participle ending in -μενον.

TABLE A2.2 πάντα as the verbal subject or object of the singular medio-passive participle ending in -μενον

	πάντα as subject of participle ending in -μενον	**πάντα as object of participle ending in -μενον**
πάντα followed by articular participle	(17×)[a] Herodotus, *Hist.* 1.38.2 πάντα τὸν λαμβανόμενον; 3.84.9 πάντα τὸν βουλόμενον; 5.126.5 πάντα τὸν βουλόμενον; 6.36.3 πάντα τὸν βουλόμενον Aristotle, *Hist. an.* 555a.27 πάντα τὸν εἰρημένον[b] Diodorus Siculus, *Bib. hist.* 1.2.4 πάντα τὸν γενόμενον; 2.19.5 πάντα τὸν ὑφιστάμενον; 19.49.1 πάντα ⟨τὸν⟩[c] βουλόμενον SB 12 10867.5 (second century BCE) πάντα τὸν προσοφειλόμενον	(0×)

a Examples from periods up until the third century CE are included here due to the paucity of attestations earlier on and the necessity of proving this construction to be a rule of the Greek language.

b The whole line reads τὰ δ' ἀράχνια ὀχεύεται μὲν πάντα τὸν εἰρημένον τρόπον. It is uncertain whether πάντα goes with τὰ ἀράχνια or the following participle and noun. Both make sense in context. Given the long list of creatures that are similar to spiders which precede this section, it would make sense for the text to read "Spiders copulate in each previously spoken manner (that is, they match the previous creatures)" but Aristotle (Peck, LCL), 201, think πάντα goes with the subject τὰ ἀράχνια.

c The article should be included here according to Diodorus Siculus (Oldfather, LCL), 362, fn. 2.

TABLE A2.2 πάντα as the verbal subject or object of the singular medio-passive (*cont.*)

	πάντα as subject of participle ending in -μενον	**πάντα as object of participle ending in -μενον**
	2 Kgdms 20:12 πάντα τὸν ἐρχόμενον 3 Kgdms 22:17 πάντα τὸν Ισραηλ διεσπαρμένον Philo, *Migr.* 65 πάντα τὸν πορευόμενον Onasander, *Strat.* 11.6 πάντα τὸν βουλόμενόν Heraclitus, *Alleg.* 73.13 πάντα τὸν χρώμενον Dio Chrysostum, *Orat.* 31.19 πάντα τὸν βουλόμενον Galen, *Anat. admin. libri ix*, vol. 2, p. 230, line 18 πάντα τὸν γυμναζόμενον Aelian, Ἰσθμικὸς εἰς Ποσειδῶνα, Jebb p. 20, line 32 πάντα τὸν βουλόμενον	
πάντα in-between article and participle	(0×)	(5×) Anaxagoras, *Test.* fr. 46.14–15 τὸν πάντα διαταξάμενον Diodorus Siculus, *Bib. hist.* 1.2.5 τὸν πάντα τἄλλα λυμαινόμενον Arius Didymus, *Liber de phil.* p.+col. 95,1, line 27 τὸν δ᾽ ἔμπαλιν πάντα φοβούμενον Philodemus, Περὶ εὐσεβείας, fr. 53.1528–1531 τὸ μισόχρησ̣τον στόμα καὶ πάν̣τ̣α̣ [σι]νόμενον[d] MDAI(A) 32 (1907) 257,8, Col. II, bc.15 (70–50 BCE) τὸν πάντ[α] ποιούμενο̣[ν

d Dirk D. Obbink, "Philodemus, 'de pietate' I" (PhD diss., Stanford, 1987), 73, claims πάντα to be an object, and translates "the all-harassing (mouth of comedy)."

TABLE A2.2 πάντα as the verbal subject or object of the singular medio-passive (*cont.*)

	πάντα as subject of participle ending in -μενον	**πάντα as object of participle ending in -μενον**
πάντα followed by anarthrous participle and complementary infinitive	(0×)	(9×) Herodotus, *Hist.* 2.121A.2 πάντα ἐξηγησάμενον Xenophon *Cyr.* 7.2.15 πάντα ἐκείνῳ πειθόμενον Plato, *Ep.* 8, 353 α πάντα ἀρχόμενον Plato, *Resp.* 619c πάντα ἱκανῶς ἀνασκεψάμενον Heraclitus, *Incr.* 37,t Τοῦτον πάντα βουλόμενον Berossus, *Fr.* 7.16 πάντα εὐτρεπισάμενον Polybius, *Hist.* 30.18.4 πάντα βουλόμενον Diodorus Siculus, *Bib. hist.* 4.43.5 πάντα χαριζόμενον Nicolaus, *Fr.* fr. 88.4 πάντα ἀνακοινούμενον
πάντα with immediate gendered modifier and anarthrous participle[e]	(0×)	(2×) Demosthenes, *Epitaph.* 11 τἄλλα πάντα κατεστραμμένον Posidippus, *Fr.* Play Cho, fr. 1.6 πάντα τοῦθ' ἡγούμενον

e This category could be fused with the second category but these examples do not have infinitives following them.

The following tables document uses of πᾶν with participles. Examples within a prepositional phrase (e.g., κατά πᾶν), where τὸ πᾶν is used, or where significant reconstruction is needed, are not included. In addition, the referent of πᾶν is documented for each entry in order to show that πᾶν is not used to refer to humans.[8] This is not to say that πᾶν could not have that function in other literary texts with different constructions, but rather that the literary texts at the time of the translation do not find any parallels that would support reading πᾶν κοιμώμενον as referring to humans. Instances where there is no material referent (e.g., animals, monies) are labelled as "generic/abstract" (e.g., πᾶν τὸ κινούμενον, "any motion," πᾶν τὸ γινόμενον, "anything occurring," or πᾶν τὸ ἐρωτώμενον "every question"). Challenging translations are referenced in the footnotes.

TABLE A2.3 πᾶν and medio-passive participles ending in -μενον

	πᾶν as subject of medio-passive participle ending in -μενον	**πᾶν as object or adverbial modifier of participle ending in -μενον**
πᾶν followed by anarthrous participle (equivalent to Exodus)	*Animals*: Hermarchus, *Fr.* fr. 34.102 *Inanimate Objects*: Anaxagoras, *Test.* fr. 45.12 Aristotle, [*Probl.*] 967b.13 Theophrastus, *De igne*, fr. 3.9[a]	(0×)

a πᾶν καιόμενόν. See translation in Marlein Van Raalte, "The Nature of Fire and its Complications: Theophrastus' De Igne 1–10," *BICS* 53 (2010): 56–57, who argues that "fire" ought to be supplied.

8 The inscription database at inscriptions.packhum.org includes over 200 examples of πᾶν with some form of articular τάσσω, with πᾶν coming before or after the articular participle. The participle is never anarthrous and πᾶν is always the subject of the participle. These cases have not been included here due to the stock nature of the phrase, and the bulkiness that would ensue. They do continue to prove what is already obvious from the data presented here.

TABLE A2.3 πᾶν and medio-passive participles ending in -μενον (*cont.*)

	πᾶν as subject of medio-passive participle ending in -μενον	**πᾶν as object or adverbial modifier of participle ending in -μενον**
	Theophrastus, *Fr.* fr. 5.58.11[b]	
	Theophrastus, *Hist. plant.* 2.5.5.6	
	Generic/Abstract:	
	Herodotus, *Hist.* 1.97.1	
	Aristotle, *Phys.* 260a.32	
	Xenocrates, *Test. doc. fr.* fr. 87.6	
	Timon, *Fr. tit.* fr. 833.5[c]	
	Chrysippus, *Fr. log. phys.* fr. 221.6	
	P.Petr. 2 13, Fr19.13–14 (255 BCE)	
	SB 20 14728 DAHT 164, r.18–19 (103 BCE)	
	P.Phrur. Diosk. 15, r.17 (158 BCE)	
	With Neuter Noun:	
	Euripides, *Iph. taur.* 48–49	
	Xenophon, *Anab.* 4.7.11[d]	
	Plato, *Tim.* 45c	
	Aristoxenus, *El. harm.* p. 56, line 11	
	Theocritus, *Idyl.* 7.43[e]	

b πᾶν δὲ ἀργότερον διακεχυμένον. Translated as "everything is easier to work when made spreadable than when hardened" in Robert Mayhew, *Theophrastus of Eresus, On Winds* (Leiden: Brill, 2017), 65.

c πᾶν δ' ἐὸν αἰεὶ πάντῃ ἀνελκόμενον. Translated "all that exists, Drawn in every direction," in Timon (Laks and Most, LCL), 99.

d The article from the earlier τὸ στράτευμα may govern the participle here.

e οὕνεκεν ἐσσί πᾶν ἐπ' ἀλαθείᾳ πεπλασμένον ἐκ Διὸς ἔρνος. It may be that πᾶν here is functioning adverbially. The translation Hopkinson (LCL), 121, is "because you are a sapling molded for truth by Zeus." This does not take πᾶν adverbially. Perhaps the meaning is this: "you are every sapling molded for truth by Zeus" implies a comparison, as in "you are (like) every sapling molded for truth by Zeus." This fits the poetic context and fits with all other uses of πᾶν in this syntactic situation.

TABLE A2.3 πᾶν and medio-passive participles ending in -μενον (*cont.*)

	πᾶν as subject of medio-passive participle ending in -μενον	**πᾶν as object or adverbial modifier of participle ending in -μενον**
	Demetrius, *Fr.* fr. 192.3 Archimedes, *Con. sphaer.* vol. 1, p. 169, line 3; p. 202, line 22; p. 215, line 29 (3×) Archimedes, *Quadr.* vol. 2, p. 165, line 2; p. 185, line 18 (2×) Archimedes, *Erat. meth.*, vol. 3, p. 96, line 25; p. 108, line 8 (2×) Chrysippus, *Fr. log. phys.* fr. 603.4[f] Polybius, *Hist.* 6.11.9 (2×)	
πᾶν followed by articular participle	(119×) *Animals*: Aesop, *Fab.* 37, version 1, line 1 Aristotle, [*Plant.*] 816b.14[g] *Inanimate Object*: Aristotle, [*Probl.*], 870a Hecataeus, *Fr.*, Volume-Jacoby#-F 3a,264,F, fr. 25.1259 Chrysippus, *Fr. log. phys.* fr. 1048.6 *Generic/Abstract*: Aesop, *Fab.* 54, version 1.4–5 Aesop, *Fab.* (dodecasyllabic) F 249aliter.8 Thucydides, *P. W.* 6.89.4[h]	

f This is a predicate nominative.

g Also refers to plants.

h The text reads: πᾶν δὲ τὸ ἐναντιούμενον τῷ δυναστεύοντι δῆμος ὠνόμασται. Thucydides (Smith, LCL), 343, translates as "and as all that is opposed to despotic power has the name of democracy." Perhaps one could argue that δῆμος should be understood as "the People" and the phrase be translated "everything in opposition to tyranny is called the People," which could then make this an example of πᾶν referring solely to humans. However, πᾶν τὸ ἐναντιούμενον could be hyperbolic in that it semantically refers to everything in

TABLE A2.3 πᾶν and medio-passive participles ending in -μενον (*cont.*)

πᾶν as subject of medio-passive participle ending in -μενον	**πᾶν as object or adverbial modifier of participle ending in -μενον**
Xenophanes, *Test.* fr. 1.17	
Euripides, *Phoen.* 1334	
Sophocles, *El.* 40	
Herodotus, *Hist.* 6.4.5; 7.50.2	
Xeniades, *Test.* fr. 1.4–5 (2×)	
Plato, *Phaedr.* 245d	
Plato, *Tim.* 28a	
Aristotle, *Phys.* 232b.21; 235a.13–14; 236b.33; 237b.22; 239a.22; 242a.37, 39, 46, 49; 256a.13; 257b.1; 261b.28; 266b.28 (13×)	
Aristotle, [*Probl.*] 878a.28	
Aristotle, *Soph. elench.* 169a, 33	
Aristotle, *Top.* 103b.7;[i] 122b.28; 139b.16; 159b.37 (4×)	
Aristotle, *Phys. libr. sept. text. alt.* (post 267b26) 242a.3, 5, 13–14 (4×)	
Aristoxenus, *El. harm.* p. 71, line 18	
Xenocrates, *Test. doctr. fr.* fr. 120.2	
Eudemus, *Fr.* fr. 114.5; fr. 120.5; fr. 133.8 (3×)	
Speusippus, *Fr.* fr. 81b.6	
Epicurus, *Ep. Men.* 123.5	
Menander, *Fr. long. ap. al. auct. serv.* fr. 538.2; fr. 540.2 (2×)	
Clearchus, *Fr.* fr. 24.15	
Bion, *Fr.* fr. 17.4	
Chrysippus, *Fr. log. phys.* fr. 69.2; fr. 257.36; fr. 387.5; fr. 483.5; fr. 536.6; fr. 735.18; fr. 937.23; fr. 945.10; fr. 948.2, 3; fr. 1001.3	
Chrysippus, *Fr. mor.* fr. 145.3; fr. 221.1	

creation that opposes tyranny, which turns out then to be the People. Regardless, it is most probable that this is a collective sense indicated by the article in τὸ ἐναντιούμενον.

i The version referred to here is Aristotle (Tredennick and Forster, LCL), 292.

TABLE A2.3 πᾶν and medio-passive participles ending in -μενον (*cont.*)

	πᾶν as subject of medio-passive participle ending in -μενον	**πᾶν as object or adverbial modifier of participle ending in -μενον**
	Polybius, *Hist.* 1.44.5; 1.83.2; 4.51.2; 4.76.2; 5.68.3; 6.11.8; 8.3.5; 8.27.8; 10.24.5; 15.4.8; 21.19.10; 21.34.3; 24.12.3; 24.13.4; 24.13.6; 24.14.6; 24.15.1; 25.2.1; 27.7.7; 27.15.9; 29.7.4; 29.27.6; 36.5.4; 36.5.5; 36.6.3; 36.9.8; 38.5.6; 38.7.6; 38.11.8; 38.11.11; 39.3.1 Biton, Κατ. πολ. ὀργ. κατ. 7.19 P.Rev. 43,r.13 (259 BCE) BGU 6 1258 A.18 (154–142 BCE) IG IX,1^2 3:621, II.8 (second century BCE) IG IX,2 10a.4–5 (second century BCE) P.Grenf. 1.42 (169 BCE) ID 1517.24–25 (154 BCE) IG IX,2 5b.6–7 (130 BCE) *With Neuter Noun*: Anaxagoras, *Test.* fr. 92.15 Aristotle, *Top.* 100b, 25 (2×) Aristoxenus, *El. harm.* p. 23, line 5; p. 24, line 18 Anaximenes, *Fr.* Volume-Jacoby#-F 2a,72,F, fr. 11b.119 Theophrastus, *Sens.* 29.2 Archimedes, *Sph. cyl.* vol. 1, p. 8, line 3 Archimedes, *Con. sph.* vol. 1, p. 166, line 18 Archimedes, *Qaudr.* vol. 2, p. 193, line 4 Polybius, *Hist.* 5.4.8 Smyrna 14.43 (245 BCE)	(0×)
πᾶν after articular participle	*Animals*: Aristophanes, *Hist. an.* 2.359.16 P.Hamb. 1 57.19–23 (160 BCE)	(0×)

TABLE A2.3 πᾶν and medio-passive participles ending in -μενον (*cont.*)

	πᾶν as subject of medio-passive participle ending in -μενον	**πᾶν as object or adverbial modifier of participle ending in -μενον**
	Generic/Abstract: Herodotus, *Hist.* 3.14.29–30 Critias, *Fr.* fr. 19.21[j] Parmenides, *Fr.* fr. 1.19[k] Aristotle, *Phys.* 256b.5; 257a.11 (2×) Aristotle, *Phys. libr. sept. text. alt.* (post 267b26) 242a.16, 31 (2×) Eudemus, *Fr.* fr. 38.1; fr. 101.3 Epicurus, *Ep. Her.* 62.8 Eurytus, *Fr.* p. 88, line 6 Polybius, *Hist.* 5.84.10 SGDI II 1884.9 (170–156 BCE) P.Tebt. 1 60.2 (117 BCE)[l] *With Neuter Noun:* Heraclides, *Descr. Gr.* fr. 1.13.4 Demetrius, *Fr.* fr. 2.22	
πᾶν after anarthrous participle	*Inanimate Object*: Polybius, *Hist.* 1.48.8 *Generic/Abstract*: Plato, *Parm.* 165b Theophrastus, *De igne*, fr. 12.4[m] Chrysippus, *Fr. log. phys.* fr. 390.8	(0×)

j τὸ δρώμενον δὲ πᾶν ἰδεῖν δυνήσεται. This reads "And has the power to see men's every act" according to Sextus (Bury, LCL), 31.

k τὸ ἐν δόξῃ κείμενον πᾶν. "Everything that resides in opinion" according to Parmenides (Laks and Most, LCL), 99.

l It is possible that πᾶν modifies the neuter ἔδαφος here.

m συνηθροισμένον δὲ πᾶν ἰσχυρόν. It seems as though δὲ functions to separate συνηθροισμένον from πᾶν ἰσχυρόν, as aside from a parenthetical note, these are the only words in the sentence and thus must be in a predicative relationship, i.e., "Every strong (thing) is gathered together" (speaking here generically and abstractly in a conversation mainly about elements and temperatures).

The following tables include data up until the end of the second century BCE, and items not included in these charts follow the same rules as the previous table. Examples only include the nominative/accusative cases since the genitive and dative are morphologically indistinguishable in the masculine and neuter genders with both πᾶς and participles in the Greek language.

TABLE A2.4 πᾶν & the remaining medio/medio-passive participles

	πᾶν + remaining medio/medio-passive participles
Refers to animals/ inanimate objects	Ctesias, *Fr.* Volume-Jacoby#-F 3c,688,F, fr. 45n, Alpha.4 Aristotle, *Mete.* 355a.28 Polybius, *Hist.* 10.17.1; 16.21.9 Let. Aris. 76.4
Refers to Generic/ Abstract	Critias, *Fr.* fr. 19.19; fr. 25.34 Plato, *Tim.* Stephanus p. 41, a, line 8 Plato, *Leg.* 864a.4 Hippocrates, *Decent.* 3.14; 4.12 Aristotle, *Probl.* 922a.2[a] Callisthenes, *Test.* Volume-Jacoby#-T 2b,124,T, fr. 4.4 Anaxarchus, *Test.* fr. 3.10 Menander, *Fr. long.* fr. 215.7[b] Polybius, *Hist.* 6.12.8; 22.14.10; 24.15.2; 28.13.4; 29.4.2; 36.1.6; 36.8.6 Dionysius Scytobrachion, *Fr.* Volume-Jacoby#-F 1a,32,F, fr. 7.83
Refers to humans	(0×)

a See the translation of Mayhew and Mirhady (LCL), 570, where the τὸ ἥδιον (TLG) is replaced with τῷ ἡδίονι, which then categorizes this example within the parameters of this study.

b τὸ … ὑποληφθὲν … πᾶν "all man's supposings." This difficult translation is from Hicks (LCL), 87. The same text is also found under three other headings in TLG.

TABLE A2.5 πᾶν & singular active neuter participles

	πᾶν + singular active neuter participle
Refers to animals/ inanimate objects	Aeschylus, *Prom.* 126[a]
	Thucydides, *P. W.* 6.75.1
	Xenophon, *Mem.* 2.4.6[b]
	Xenophon, *Ages.* 9.3.6 (2×)
	Plato, *Tim.* 84a.5
	Plato, *Crit.* 111a.6
	Plato, *Resp.* 381a.10
	Hippocrates, *Epid.* 6, 294.4
	Hippocrates, *Coac.* 621.7–8
	Hippocrates, *Mul.* 1.37.15
	Aristotle, *Part. an.* 2.649b.11
	Aristotle, [*Probl.*] 889b.22
	Aristotle, [*Plant.*] 828b.24
	Theopompus, *Fr.* Volume-Jacoby#-F 2b,115,F, fr. 80.13
	Theophrastus, *Fr.* fr. 4, 65.4
	Theophrastus, *Caus. plant.* 6.6.5.1
	Hermarchus, *Fr.* 34.113
	Polybius, *Hist.* 3.46.12; 3.51.5;[c] 3.54.5[d]
	Aristophanes, *Hist. an.* 2.53.12;[e] 2.186.1; 2.549.24
	Dionysius Thrax, *Fr.* fr. 29a.10
	Agatharchides, *Mar. Erythr.* 102.2
	Comanus, *Fr.* fr. 7.7
	Posidonius, *Fr.* fr. 89.22

a In this text it is the Daughters of Oceanus who approach, but the author is speaking as one who does not know what is approaching and assumes it to be the sound of birds.

b πᾶν τὸ ἐλλεῖπον τῷ φίλῳ ("anything lacking to a friend"). This example could also fit under generic/abstract if more than goods are in mind.

c πᾶν τὸ παραπῖπτον ("any [animals] in the way"). This could also refer generically to anything that was on the path, but the context refers to pack animals and others.

d πᾶν τὸ παραπεσόν ("any [animal] stepping wide"). Paton, Walbank, and Habicht (LCL), 145, translate this as referring to humans and animals: "as both men and beasts could not tell on what they were treading owing to the snow, all that stepped wide of the path or stumbled were dashed down the precipice." This might be considered a mistranslation, as animals are the ones struggling with the paths. See οὔτε τοῖς θηρίοις οὔτε τοῖς ὑποζυγίοις δυνατὸν ἦν παρελθεῖν διὰ τὴν στενότητα in line 7. The consistent use of 'πᾶν + participle' in this study might cast doubt on their translation. Even if humans and animals are in view here, note the article, which is the way to signal a collective neuter according to classical standards.

e This text is cited as τὸ πᾶν in Agatharchides, *Mar. Erythr.* 55.16.

TABLE A2.5 πᾶν & singular active neuter participles (*cont.*)

	πᾶν + singular active neuter participle
Refers to generic/ abstract	Xenophanes, *Test.* fr. 35.10
	Thucydides, *P. W.* 4.59.2; 4.98.6; 4.126.6
	Euripides, *Fr. Hyps.* fr. 60.48 (cf. *Fr.* fr. 12.233)
	Herodotus, *Hist.* 1.24.4; 1.32.4–5; 9.11.15
	Zeno, *Test.* fr. 24.4, 6 (2×)
	Melissus, *Test.* fr. 5,974a.11
	Melissus, *Fr.* fr. 7.16[f]
	Parmenides, *Test.* fr. 46.14
	Plato, *Theaet.* 204d.10
	Plato, *Soph.* 245a.2
	Plato, *Parm.* 148e.4; 165b.5
	Plato, *Phaedr.* 238e.4; 261e.2
	Plato, *Resp.* 608e.4
	Aristotle, *Div. somn.* 463b.29–30
	Aristotle, *Eth. nic.* 4.19[g]
	Aristotle, *Ep.* Ep. 4.15
	Aristotle, *Vit. mort.* 1.323a.18; 1.327a.25
	Aristotle, *Metaph.* 1054b.27; 1071b.23; 1074a.25; 1075a.6
	Aristotle, *Mete.* 379a.20
	Aristotle, *Phys.* 202a.30; 209a.24; 212b.28; 224a.21; 234b.20; 235b.5; 237a.15; 237a.34 (pf.part.); 240b.25; 256a.22
	Aristotle, *Top.* 104b.25; 122b.21–22; 125a.21; 128b.7; 140a.5
	Ephippus, *Fr.* fr. 6.6
	Xenocrates, *Test. doc. fr.* fr. 231.7
	Eudemus, *Fr.* fr. 78.4, 6
	Theophrastus, *Sens.* 4.6
	Theophrastus, *De igne*, fr. 49.4
	Epicurus, *Dep. libr. rel.* fr. 29, 29.20[h]

f οὐ γὰρ ἂν πᾶν εἴη ἀλγέον ("for it [motion] can never be anything feeling pain"). Laks and Most (LCL), 247, translate this as "for it could not feel pain as a whole," which seems to take πᾶν adverbially. Given the patterns in this present study, this should probably be considered a mistranslation.

g τὸ δ' ἀγαθῷ ὑπερέχον πᾶν ἐντιμότερον ("everything superior in good is more honorable"). It is possible that Plato is referring to the honoured man abstractly here, but the thrust of the statement seems to be talking about moral abstractions. The rest of the language referring to the honored man does not use the neuter.

h Context is lacunae and the exact sense is unclear.

TABLE A2.5 πᾶν & singular active neuter participles (*cont.*)

	πᾶν + singular active neuter participle
	Carneiscus, *Phil.* (lib. ii) (P. Herc. 1027) 4, fr. 20.3[i] Cleanthes, *Test.fr.* fr. 489.3, 10, 13 Hecataeus, *Fr.* Volume-Jacoby#-F 3a,264,F, fr. 25.1489 Chrysippus, *Fr. log. phys.* fr. 1.17; fr. 140.3; fr. 283.3, 9, 13; fr. 339.2; fr. 387.1; fr. 387.4; fr. 799.12 Chrysippus, *Fr. mor.* fr. 86.4; fr. 499.1 Polystratus, *Fr.* (*P. Herc. 346*) fr. f3, col.8b.7 Polybius, *Hist.* 1.48.4; 3.12.6; 4.85.6; 8.24.1; 9.2.5; 10.45.6; 10.46.10; 11.4.5; 25.3.10; 38.5.6 Antipater, *Test.fr.* fr. 16.3; fr. 30.3; fr. 63.18; fr. 63.58 Archedemus, *Fr.* fr. 6.3 Diogenes, *Test.fr.* fr. 18.3
Refers only to humans	(o×)
Refers to all living beings	Plato, *Phaed.* 77c.8, πᾶν τὸ ζῶν ("every living being") Plato, *Phileb.* 20d.8, πᾶν τὸ γιγνῶσκον ("any intelligent being")[j] Plato, *Menex.* 237e.2, πᾶν γὰρ τὸ τεκὸν ("any creature that bears children") Aristotle, *An. post.* 1.78b.27, πᾶν γὰρ τὸ ἀναπνέον ζῷον ("for everything that breathes is an animal")[k] Aristotle, *Juv. sen.* 470a.20 Aristotle, *Somn. vig.* 454b.8; 454b.11 Ontas, *Fr.* p. 140, lines 13–14

i πᾶν τὸ ματαίως ἡμᾶς παρενοχλοῦν ("anything vainly troubling us"). Mario Capasso, *Il secondo libro del filista:* (*PHerc. 1027*) (Napoli: Bibliopolis, 1988), 200, renders this section "un ragionamento genuino sul piano di essa (la filosofia), avendo dissipato tutto quello che senza fondamento ci arreca tormento e provando riconoscenza per il sollievo che ne è derivato per l'essere grande e" (from δι[αλ]όγισμα γνήσ[ι]ον παρ' αὐτῆι, λελυκότ[α] πᾶν τὸ ματαίως ἡμᾶς παρενοχλοῦν καὶ εὐχαριστοῦντα τῶι περιγεγονότι κουφισμῶι διὰ τὸ μέγαν εἶναι καὶ). Capasso situates πᾶν τὸ ματαίως ἡμᾶς παρενοχλοῦν within philosophical discourse ("[la filosofia]") and thus this phrase should probably be understood as referring to ideas and not to specific opponents.

j πᾶν functions here to refer to any possible intelligent creature, imagined or real, and is not only referring to humans.

k Aristotle does not agree with this, but is using it as a syllogistic example; see line 26 and Tredennick and Forster (LCL), 89, fn. b, which indicates that ζῷον was too confined a term for such a broad statement, as only mammals breathed according to Aristotle.

While I focused on texts up until the end of the second century, a few possible examples of 'πᾶν + participle' referring to humans can be mentioned from later texts. All examples include the article, which again shows the necessity of that item (or definiteness) for the collective sense to be activated. The best example is Josephus, *Jewish War*, 3.463 with πᾶν τὸ νεωτερίζον ("all the revolutionary party"). It is a set term that is previously defined in *Jewish War* in 1.4 and in 4.133, both without πᾶν (cf. also Cassius Dio, *Roman History*, 62.11). Another example is Josephus, *Antiquities*, 5.226 with πᾶν τὸ προστυχὸν ("everything that was met"). Here one wonders if the neuter refers to all creatures in a hyperbolic way in order to express that the shocked soldiers were so surprised at the attack that they were killing everything they saw coming at them. This same hyper expressive use of πᾶν τὸ προστυχὸν to refer to anything and everything that was near is found in *Jewish War*, 3.304. This reading would be along the lines of the function of 'πᾶν + participle' from Deut 20:16 discussed in section 4.4.2.1. Semantically it refers to all creatures but pragmatically only to humans. At the same time, it is possible that Josephus wanted to indicate (somewhat comically, as is in line with the humor of the story) that even animals approaching the soldiers were being slaughtered. Regardless, these examples still have the article and would therefore fit as collective neuters. Similarly, *Antiquities* 7.61 reads τοὺς πεπηρωμένους τὰς ὄψεις καὶ τὰς βάσεις καὶ πᾶν τὸ λελωβημένον στησάντων ("they placed everyone who had been maimed in eye and in foot and in anything maimed"). This example is still with the article and is also within the normal confines of how a collective neuter is expressed in contrast to what is found in Ex.

Bibliography

Aejemeleaus, Anneli. "What Can We Know About the Hebrew *Vorlage* of the Septuagint." Pages 71–106 in *On the Trail of the Septuagint Translators: Collected Essays*. Leuven: Peeters, 2007.

Aeschines. *Aeschines with an English Translation*. Translated by Charles Darwin Adams. LCL. London: Harvard University Press; Heinemann, 1919.

Aitken, James K. "The Septuagint and Egyptian Translation Methods." Pages 269–293 in *XV Congress of the International Organization for Septuagint and Cognate Studies: Munich, 2013*. Edited by Wolfgang Kraus, Michaël N. Van Der Meer, and Martin Meiser. SCS 64. Atlanta: Society of Biblical Literature, 2016.

Aitken, James K. "The Septuagint—A Translation Among Translations," "The Septuagint, Editing, and Textual Production in Ancient Judaism," and "The Septuagint and Scribal Creativity in Egypt." The Grinfield Lectures. Oxford, Feb. 15–16, 24, 2021.

Aitken, James K. *The T & T Clark Companion to the Septuagint*. London: Bloomsbury, 2015.

Alessandrì, Salvatore. "IG II 2, 140 (Una Proposta Di Lettura)." *Annali Della Scuola Normale Superiore Di Pisa. Classe Di Lettere E Filosofia*, Serie III, 10, no. 4 (1980): 1131–1160.

Altshuler, David. "On the Classification of Judaic Laws in the Antiquities of Josephus and the Temple Scroll of Qumran." *AJS Review* 7 (1982): 1–14.

Amundsen, Darrel W., and Gary B. Ferngren. "The Forensic Role of Physicians in Ptolemaic and Roman Egypt." *Bulletin of the History of Medicine* 52, no. 3 (Fall, 1978): 336–353.

Amundsen, Leiv. "The Classical Greek background of Ptolemaic law and Administration of Justice." Pages 251–265 in vol. 1 of *Acta Congressus Madvigiani* (*Proceedings of the Second International Congress of Classical Studies*). Edited by Carsten Hoeg, Per Krarup, and P. J. Riis. Copenhagen: Ejnar Munksgaard, 1958.

Androutsos, Georges, and Aristide Diamantis. "La vie sexuelle des grecs anciens." *Andrologie* 17, no. 4 (2007): 343–352.

Antiphon. *Antiphon, Andocides, Minor Attic Orators, Volume I: Antiphon*. Translated by Kenneth J. Maidment. LCL. Cambridge: Harvard University Press, 1941.

Aristotle. *Aristotle in 23 Volumes*. Translated by Harris Rackham. LCL. 23 vols. Cambridge: Harvard University Press, 1952.

Aristotle. *Parts of Animals. Movement of Animals. Progression of Animals*. Translated by A. L. Peck, E. S. Forster. LCL. Cambridge: Harvard University Press, 1937.

Aristotle. *Posterior Analytics*. Translated by Hugh Tredennick and E. S. Forster. LCL. Cambridge: Harvard University Press, 1960.

Aristotle. *Problems*. Translated by Robert Mayhew and David C. Mirhady. LCL. Cambridge: Harvard University Press, 2011.

Arnaoutoglou, Ilias. *Ancient Greek Laws*. London: Routledge, 2010.

Arnaoutoglou, Ilias. "The Fear of Slaves in Ancient Greek Legal Traditions." Pages 133–144 in *Fear of Slaves—Fear of Enslavement in the Ancient Mediterranean (Actes du XXIXe colloque du GIREA—Rethymnon 4–7 novembre 2004)*. Edited by Anastasia Serghidou. Besançon: Presses universitaires de Franche-Comté, 2007.

Athenaeus. *The Learned Banqueters, Volume IV: Books 8–10.420e*. Translated by S. Douglas Olson. LCL. Cambridge: Harvard University Press, 2008.

Atkinson, Kenneth. "To the Reader of Psalms of Solomon." Pages 763–765 in *A New English Translation of the Septuagint and the Other Greek Translations Traditionally Included under That Title*. Edited by Albert Pietersma and Benjamin G. Wright. Oxford: Oxford University Press, 2007.

Baetens, Gert. "Demotic Petitioning." *JJP* 44 (2014): 29–69.

Bagnall, Roger S. "Some Notes on P. Hib. 198." *BASP* 6, no. 3/4 (1969): 73–118.

Bagnall, Roger S., and Peter Derow. *The Hellenistic Period: Historical Sources in Translation*. New York: Wiley & Sons, 2008.

Bagnall, Roger S., and Uri Yiftach-Firanko. "Law in Graeco-Roman Egypt: Hellenization, Fusion, Romanization." Pages 541–558 in *The Oxford Handbook of Papyrology*. Edited by Roger S. Bagnall. Oxford: Oxford University Press, 2011.

Banchich, Thomas. "Possis of Magnesia (480)." BNP. Second edition. Edited by Ian Worthington. Accessed online at http://dx.doi.org/10.1163/1873-5363_bnj_a480.

Barclay, John. "Apologetics in the Jewish Diaspora." Pages 129–148 in *Jews in the Hellenistic and Roman Cities*. Edited by John R Bartlett. London: Routledge, 2002.

Barkan, Irving. *Capital Punishment in Ancient Athens*. Chicago: University of Chicago, 1936.

Bar-Kochva, Bezalel. *The Image of the Jews in Greek Literature: The Hellenistic Period*. Berkeley: University of California Press, 2010.

Barr, James. *The Typology of Literalism in Ancient Biblical Translations*. Göttingen: Vandenhoeck & Ruprecht, 1979.

Barr, James. "Hebrew, Aramaic and Greek in the Hellenistic Age." Pages 79–114 in Vol. 2 of *The Cambridge History of Judaism*. Edited by William D. Davies and Louis Finkelstein. Cambridge: Cambridge University Press, 1990.

Baumgarten, Joseph. "The Avoidance of the Death Penalty in Qumran Law." Pages 31–38 in *Reworking the Bible: Apocryphal and Related Texts at Qumran*. Edited by Esther G. Chazon, Devorah Dimant, and Ruth Clements. Leiden: Brill, 2005.

Bauschatz, John. *Law and Enforcement in Ptolemaic Egypt*. Cambridge: Cambridge University Press, 2013.

Bechtel, Friedrich, Otto Kern, Karl Praechter, Carl Robert, Ernst von Stern, Ulrich Wilcken, and Georg Wissowa. *Dikaiomata. Auszüge aus alexandrinischen Gesetzen und Verordnungen in einem Papyrus des philologischen Seminars der Universität Halle* (*Pap. Hall., 1*). Berlin: Weidmann, 1913. Reprint: Milan, 1972.

Bedell, Ellen Dailey. "Criminal Law in the Egyptian Ramesside Period." PhD diss., Brandeis University, 1973.

Bednarek, Bartłomiej. "The Sacrificial Ritual in Homer." *Classica Cracoviensia* 16 (2013): 5–17.

Berkowitz, Beth A. *Execution and Invention: Death Penalty Discourse in Early Rabbinic and Christian Cultures*. Oxford: Oxford University Press, 2006.

Berneker, Erich. *Zur Geschichte der Prozesseinleitung im ptolemäischen Recht*. Ansbach: C. Brügel & Sohn, 1930.

Bickerman, Elias. *Institutions des Séleucides*. Paris: Geuthner, 1938.

Bickerman, Elias. "Διάγραμμα," *RPh* 12, (1938b): 295–312.

Bickerman, Elias. "Two Legal Interpretations of the Septuagint." Pages 201–224 in Vol. 1 of *Studies in Jewish and Christian History*. Edited by Amram Tropper. Leiden: Brill, 1976.

Biblia Hebraica Stuttgartensia: SESB Version. Electronic edition. Stuttgart: German Bible Society, 2003.

Blank, Sheldon H. "The LXX Renderings of Old Testament Terms for Law." *Hebrew Union College Annual* 7 (1930): 259–283.

Blass, Friedrich, Albert Debrunner, and Robert Walter Funk. *A Greek Grammar of the New Testament and Other Early Christian Literature*. Cambridge: Cambridge University Press, 1961.

Bloch, René. "How Much Hebrew in Jewish Alexandria?" Pages 261–278 in *Alexandria: Hub of the Hellenistic World*. Edited by Benjamin Schliesser, Jan Rüggemeier, Thomas J. Kraus, and Jörg Frey, with the assistance of Daniel Herrmann. WUNT 460. Tübingen: Mohr Siebeck, 2021.

Bluche, Frédéric. "La peine de mort dans l'Égypte ptolémaïque." *RIDA*, 3e série, 22 (1975): 144–175.

Boas, Emde, Evert Van, Albert Rijksbaron, Luuk Huitink, and Mathieu De Bakker. *Cambridge Grammar of Classical Greek*. Cambridge: Cambridge University Press, 2019.

Bons, Eberhard. "The Lord is the One who Crushes Wars: A Fresh Look at the Septuagint Translation of Exodus 15:3." Pages 158–167 in *Die Septuaginta—Geschichte, Wirkung, Relevanz*. Edited by Martin Meiser, Michaela Geiger, Siegfried Kreuzer, and Marcus Sigismund. WUNT 405. Tübignen: Mohr Siebeck, 2018.

Bontty, Mónica Marie. "Conflict Management in Ancient Egypt: Law as a Social Phenomenon." PhD diss., University of California, 1997.

Boochs, Wolfgang. *Strafrechtliche Aspekte im altägyptischen Recht*. Sankt Augustin: Academia Verlag, 1993.

Booth, Charlotte. *In Bed with the Ancient Egyptians*. Chalford: Amberly Publishing, 2015.

Botta, Alejandro F. *The Aramaic and Egyptian Legal Traditions at Elephantine: An Egyptological Approach.* New York: T&T Clark, 2009.

Boyd-Taylor, Cameron. "The Classification of Literalism in Ancient Hebrew-Greek Translation." Pages 121–142 in *Die Sprache der Septuaginta.* Vol. 3 of *Handbuch* zur *Septuaginta.* Edited by Eberhard Bons and Jan Joosten. Gütersloh: Gütersloher Verlagshaus, 2016.

Bremmer, Jan N. "Sacrifice, III. Greece." BNP 12: 845–850.

Brenton, Lancelot Charles Lee. *The Septuagint Version of the Old Testament: English Translation.* London: Samuel Bagster and Sons, 1870.

Brock, Sebastian P. "The Phenomenon of the Septuagint." *OtSt* 17 (1972): 11–36.

Brooke, Alan England, and Norman Maclean. *The Old Testament in Greek. Volume 2: The Latter Historical Books.* Part 2, Vol. 2 of *The Old Testament in Greek.* Cambridge: Cambridge University Press, 1930.

Brown, Francis, Samuel Rolles Driver, and Charles Augustus Briggs. BDB. Oxford: Clarendon Press, 1977.

Bruit, Louise. "4.a. Banquet, C. Les Théoxénies, 3. *Thysia* et Théoxénies, deux modes d'offrande." Pages 226–228 in *Thesaurus Cultus et Rituum Antiquorum II: Purification, Initiation, Heroization, Apotheosis, Banquet, Dance, Music, Cult Images.* California: The J. Paul Getty Museum, 2004.

Büchner, Dirk L. "On the Relationship Between *Mekilta De Rabbi Ishmael* and Septuagint Exodus 12–23." Pages 403–420 in *IX Congress of the International Organization for Septuagint and Cognate Studies, Cambridge 1995.* Edited by Bernard A. Taylor. SCS 45. Atlanta: Scholars Press, 1997.

Büchner, Dirk L. "The Thysia Soteriou of the Septuagint and the Greek Cult: Representation and Accommodation." Pages 85–100 in *Florilegium Lovaniense. Studies in Septuagint and Textual Criticism in Honour of Florentino Garcia Martinez.* Edited by Hans Ausloos, Bénédicte Lemmelijn and Marc Vervenne. Leuven: Peeters, 2008.

Buckler, William H. "Documents from Phrygia and Cyprus." *JHS* 55 (1935): 71–78.

Burns, Joshua Ezra. "Practical Wisdom in 4QInstruction." *DSD* 11, no. 1 (2004): 12–42.

Burstein, Stanley Mayer. *The Babyloniaca of Berossus.* Malibu: Undena Publications, 1978.

Cadell, Hélène. "Vocabulaire de la législation ptolémaïque: problème du sens de dikaioma dans le Pentateuque." Pages 207–221 in *Kata tous O' "Selon les Septante": Trente études sur la Bible grecque des Septante.* Edited by Gilles Dorival and Olivier Munnich. Paris: Cerf, 1995.

Calvert, Brian. "The Death Penalty in Plato's Laws." Pages 243–262 in *Justice v. Law in Greek Thought.* Edited by Leslie G. Rubin. Lanham: Rowman & Littlefield, 1997.

Canevaro, Mirko. "Making and Changing Laws in Ancient Athens." Pages 1–43 in *The Oxford Handbook of Ancient Greek Law.* Edited by Edward M. Harris and Mirko Canevaro. Oxford: Oxford University Press, 2015.

Canevaro, Mirko. "Thieves, Parent Abusers, Draft Dodgers … and Homicides? The Authenticity of Dem. 24.105." *Historia* 62/1 (2013): 25–47.

Cantarella, Eva. I *Supplizi Capitali in Grecia E a Roma*. Milano: Rizzoli, 1991.

Cantarella, Eva. *Les peines de mort en Grèce et à Rome: Origines et fonctions des supplices capitaux dans l'Antiquité classique*. Paris: Albin Michel, 2000.

Capasso, Mario. *Il secondo libro del filista: (PHerc. 1027)*. Napoli: Bibliopolis, 1988.

Carbon, Jan-Mathieu, Saskia Peels, and Vinciane Pirenne-Delforge. "CGRN 99." Collection of Greek Ritual Norms (CGRN). Liège, 2015. http://cgrn.ulg.ac.be.

Carmichael, Calum Morgan. *The Origins of Biblical Law: The Decalogues and the Book of the Covenant*. Ithaca: Cornell University Press, 1992.

Cary, M. "A Constitutional Inscription from Cyrene." *JHS* 48, pt. 2 (1928): 222–238.

Casabona, Jean. *Recherches sur le vocabulaire des sacrifices en grec, des origines à la fin de l'époque classique*. Paris: Ophrys, 1966.

Chaniotis, Angelos, H. W. Pleket, R. S. Stroud, and J. H. M. Strubbe, eds. "SEG 49–722. Kassandreia (Poteidaia). Regulation concerning military service, late 3rd cent B.C. (or March 197 B.C.?)." SEG. http://dx.doi.org/10.1163/1874-6772_seg_a49_722.

Chaniotis, Angelos, T. Corsten, N. Papazarkadas, and R. A. Tybout. "SEG 60–2024. Religion. Magic: Witchcraft and Divine Vengeance in Cases of (Untimely) Death." SEG. http://dx.doi.org/10.1163/1874-6772_seg_a60_2024.

Charles, Robert H., ed. *The Apocrypha and Pseudepigrapha of the Old Testament in English. Volume II: Pseudepigrapha*. Vol. 0 of *The Apocrypha and Pseudepigrapha of the Old Testament in English*. Oxford: Oxford University Press, 1913.

Childs, Brevard S. *The Book of Exodus: A Critical Theological Commentary*. Philadelphia: Westminster Press, 1974.

Clarysse, Willy, and Eddy Lanciers. "Currency and the Dating of Ptolemaic Papyri." *Ancient Society* 20 (1989): 117–132.

Clarysse, Willy, and Dorothy J. Thompson. *Counting the People in Hellenistic Egypt. Volume 2: Historical Studies*. Vol. 2 of *Counting the People in Hellenistic Egypt*. Cambridge: Cambridge University Press, 2006.

Clines, David J. A., ed. *Dictionary of Classical Hebrew*. 9 vols. Sheffield: Sheffield Phoenix Press, 1993–2014.

Colin, Jean. *Les villes libres de l'Orient gréco-romain et l'envoi au supplice par acclamations populaires*. Bruxelles: Latomus, 1965.

Cook, Johann. "Hellenistic and/or (Pre-)Rabbinic Traditions in the Septuagint." Pages 119–132 in *Florilegium Lovaniense: Studies in Septuagint and Textual Criticism in Honour of Florentino García Martínez*. Edited by Hans Ausloos, Bénédicte Lemmelijn, and Marc Vervenne. BETL 224. Leuven, Paris, and Dudley: Peeters, 2008.

Coussement, Sandra. *Because I Am Greek: Polyonymy as an Expression of Ethnicity in Ptolemaic Egypt*. Leuven: Peeters, 2016.

Cowey, James M. S. "Das ägyptische Judentum in hellenistischer Zeit—Neue Erkentnisse aus jüngst veröfftenlichten Papyri." Pages 2.24–43 in *Im Brennpunkt: Die Septuaginta. Studien zur Enstehung und Bedeutung der griechischen Bible*. Vol. 2 (3 vols.). Edited by Siegfried Kreuzer and Jürgen P. Lesch. BWANT 8. Stuttgart: Kohlhammer, 2004.

Cribiore, Rafaella. *Gymnastics of the Mind. Greek Education in Hellenistic and Roman Egypt*. Princeton and Oxford: Princeton University Press, 2001.

Darbo-Peschanski, Catherine. "La prononcé de la peine de mort en Grèce ancienne." Pages 129–137 in *La peine de mort: droit, histoire, anthropologie, philosophie*. Edited by Ioannis S. Papadopoulos and Jacques-Henri Robert. Paris: Université Panthéon-Assas, 2000.

Deissmann, Adolf. *Licht vom Osten. Das Neue Testament und die neuentdeckten Texteder hellenistisch-römischen Welt*. Fourth edition. Tübingen: Mohr Siebeck, 1923.

Deissmann, Adolf. *Bible Studies: Contributions, Chiefly from Papyri and Inscriptions, to the History of the Language, the Literature, and the Religion of Hellenistic Judaism and Primitive Christianity*. Edinburgh: T&T Clark, 1901.

Demosthenes. *Demosthenes with an English Translation*. Translated by Augustus T. Murray. LCL. London: Harvard University Press, 1939.

Demosthenes. *Demosthenes with an English Translation*. Translated by James H. Vince. LCL. London: Harvard University Press, 1930.

De Sanctis, Gaetano. "Le decretali di Cirene." *RFIC* 55 (1927): 185–212.

De Sola Pool, David. *Capital Punishment Among the Jews*. New York: Bloch, 1916.

Diggle, James, ed. *The Cambridge Greek Lexicon*. Cambridge: Cambridge University Press, 2022.

Dinarchus. *Minor Attic Orators in Two Volumes*. Translated by John O. Burtt. 2 vols. LCL. London: Harvard University Press, 1962.

Dines, Jennifer M., and Michael A. Knibb. *The Septuagint*. London: T&T Clark, 2005.

Diodorus Siculus. *Library of History, Volume 1: Diodorus Siculus*. Translated by Charles H. Oldfather. LCL Cambridge: Harvard University Press, 1933.

Diodorus Siculus. *Library of History, Volume XII: Fragments of Books 33–40*. Translated by Francis R. Walton. LCL. Cambridge: Harvard University Press, 1967.

Diogenes Laertius. *Lives of Eminent Philosophers, Volume II*. Translated by Robert Drew Hicks. LCL. Cambridge: Harvard University Press, 1925.

Dobias-Lalou, Catherine, in collaboration with Alice Bencivenni, Hugues Berthelot, with help from Simona Antolini, Silvia Maria Marengo, and Emilio Rosamilia. "Inscriptions of Greek Cyrenaica." IGCyr. Bologna: CRR-MM, Alma Mater Studiorum Università di Bologna, 2017. http://doi.org/10.6092/UNIBO/IGCYRGVCYR.

Dogniez, Cécile. "Le vocabulaire de la loi dans la Septante." Pages 350–354 in: *Die Sprache der Septuaginta*. Vol. 3 of *Handbuch zur Septuaginta*. Edited by Eberhard Bons and Jan Joosten. Gütersloh: Gütersloher Verlagshaus, 2016.

Dorival, Gilles. "The Septuagint Between Judaism and Hellenism." Pages 26–40 in *Die Septuaginta—Text, Wirkung, Rezeption*. Edited by Wolfgang Kraus and Siegfried Kreuzer, with Martin Meiser and Marcus Sigismund. WUNT 325. Tübingen: Mohr Siebeck, 2014.

Dover, Kenneth James. *Greek Homosexuality*. Cambridge: Harvard University Press, 1989.

Dover, Kenneth James. *Greek Popular Morality in the Time of Plato and Aristotle*. Indianapolis: Hackett, 2008.

Dozeman, Thomas B. *Eerdmans Critical Commentary: Exodus*. Grand Rapids: Eerdmans, 2009.

Dunand, Francoise. "Droit d'asile et refuge dans les temples en Égypte lagide." Pages 77–97 in *Hommages à la Mémoire de Serge Sauneron. Tome II: Egypte post-pharaonique*. Vol. 2 of *Hommages à la Mémoire de Serge Sauneron*. Edited by Jean Vercoutter. Paris: Institut Français D'archéologie Orientale du Caire, 1979.

Dunand, Francoise. "The Factory of Gods." Pages 152–162 in *Alexandria, Third Century BC: The Knowledge of the World in a Single City*. Edited by Christian Jacob and François de Polignac. Alexandria: Hapocrates Pub, 2000.

Evans, Trevor. *Verbal Syntax in the Greek Pentateuch: Natural Greek Usage and Hebrew Interference*. Oxford: Oxford University Press, 2001.

Evans, Trevor. "The Nature of Septuagint Greek: Language and Lexicography." Pages 91–104 in *The Oxford Handbook of the Septuagint*. Edited by Alison G. Salvesen and Timothy Michael Law. Oxford: Oxford University Press, 2021.

Farsedakis, J. J. "θανάτῳ ζημιοῦν: Contribution à l'étude du droit criminel athénien à l'époque classique." DPhil diss., Strasbourg, 1978.

Fernández-Marcos, Natalio. *The Septuagint in Context: Introduction to the Greek Versions of the Bible*. Boston: Brill Academic, 2001.

Ferri, Silvio. "La 'Lex cathartica' di Cirene." *Notiziario Archeologico del Ministero delle Colonie* 4 (1927): 91–145.

Ferri, Silvio. "Note d'epigrafia cirenaica." *Historia* 3 (1929): 381–400.

Feucht, Erika. "Family: II., Egypt." BNP 5:333.

Frankel, Zacharias. *Ueber den Einfluss der palästinischen Exegese auf die alexandrinische Hermeneutik*. Leipzig: J. A. Barth, 1851.

Frankel, Zacharias. *Vorstudien zu der Septuaginta*. Leipzig: F. C. W. Vogel, 1841.

Fraser, Peter Marshall. "A Prostagma of Ptolemy Auletes from Lake Edku." *JEA* 56 (1970): 179–182.

Fraser, Peter Marshall. "Inscriptions from Cyrene." *Berytus* 12 (1958): 101–128.

Fraser, Peter Marshall. "Inscriptions from Ptolemaic Egypt." *Berytus* 7 (1960): no. 1, 123–161.

Fraser, Peter Marshall. *Ptolemaic Alexandria: Text*. Vol. 1 of *Ptolemaic Alexandria*. Oxford: Clarendon Press, 2001.

Fraser, Peter Marshall. “Two Studies on the Cult of Sarapis in the Hellenistic World.” *OAth* 3 (1960): 1–54.

Fresch, Christopher. “The Peculiar Occurrences of οὖν in the Septuagint of Genesis and Exodus.” Pages 455–472 in *XV Congress of the International Organization for Septuagint and Cognate Studies: Munich, 2013*. Edited by Wolfgang Kraus, Michaël N. Van Der Meer, and Martin Meiser. SCS 64. Atlanta: Society of Biblical Literature, 2016.

Gagarin, Michael. *Drakon and Early Athenian Homicide Law*. New Haven: Yale University Press, 1981.

Gagarin, Michael. *Early Greek Law*. Berkeley: University of California Press, 1986.

Gagarin, Michael. “Early Greek Law.” Pages 82–94 in *The Cambridge Companion to Ancient Greek Law*. Edited by Michael Gagarin and David Cohen. Cambridge: Cambridge University Press, 2005.

Gager, John G. *Curse Tablets and Binding Spells from the Ancient World*. New York: Oxford University Press, 1992.

Gawlinski, Laura. *The Sacred Law of Andania: A New Text with Commentary*. Berlin/Boston: De Gruyter, 2012.

Gilbert, Gustav. *The Constitutional Antiquities of Sparta and Athens*. Translated by E. J. Brooks and T. Nicklin. New York: Macmillan, 1895.

Gill, David. “Trapezomata: A Neglected Aspect of Greek Sacrifice.” *HTR* 67, no. 2 (1974): 117–137.

Goldenberg, Robert. “The Septuagint Ban on Cursing the Gods.” *JSJ* 28, no. 4 (1997): 381–89.

Greenspoon, Leonard. “At the Beginning: The Septuagint as a Jewish Bible Translation.” Pages 159–170 in *Translation is Required: The Septuagint in Retrospect and Prospect*. Edited by Robert J. V. Hiebert. SCS 56. Atlanta: SBL Press, 2010.

Greenspoon, Leonard. “Textual and Translation Issues in Greek Exodus.” Pages 322–348 in *The Book of Exodus*. Edited by Thomas B. Dozeman, Craig A. Evans, and Joel N. Lohr. Leiden: Brill, 2014.

Grenfell, Bernard P., and John P. Mahaffy. *Revenue Laws of Ptolemy Philadelphus*. Oxford: Clarendon Press, 1896.

Gundel, Wilhelm. *Hermes: Neue Astrologische Texte Des Hermes Trismegistos; Funde Und Forschungen Auf Dem Gebiet Der Antiken Astronomie Und Astrologie*. München: Verlag Der Bayerischen Akademie Der Wissenschaften, 1936.

Gurtner, Daniel. *Exodus: Commentary on the Greek Text of Codex Vaticanus*. Leiden: Brill, 2013.

Hansen, Mogens Herman. *Eisangelia: The Sovereingty of the People's Court in Athens in the Fourth Century B.C. and the Impeachment of Generals and Politicians*. Odense: Odense University Press, 1975.

Harding, Phillip. *The Story of Athens*. London: Routledge, 2008.

Harl, Marguerite, Gilles Dorival, and Oliver Munnich. *La bible grecque des Septante du judaïsme hellénistique au christianisme ancien*. Paris: Cerf, 1988.

Harper, G. M. "The Relation of Ἀρχώνης, Μέτοχοι, and Ἔγγυοι to Each Other, to the Government and to the Tax Contract in Ptolemaic Egypt." *Aegyptus* 14, no. 2/3 (1934): 269–85.

Harris, Edward M. "How to Kill in Attic Greek. The Semantics of the Verb [ἀπο]κτείνειν and their Implications for Athenian Homicide Law." Pages 75–87 in *Symposion 1997, Vorträge zur griechischen und hellenistischen rechtsgeschichte (Altafiumara, 8–14 September 1997)*. Edited by Eva Cantarella and Gerhard Thür. Cologne/Vienna: Böhlau, 2001.

Harris, Edward M. "Did Solon Abolish Debt-bondage?" *CQ* 52, no. 2 (2002): 415–430.

Hauspie, Katrin. "Ἐν with Dative Indicating Instrument in the Septuagint of Ezekiel." Pages 201–224 in *XII Congress of the International Organization for Septuagint and Cognate Studies Leiden*. Edited by Melvin K. H. Peters. Leiden: Brill, 2006.

Hecht, Neil. S., B. S. Jackson, S. M. Passamaneck, Daniela Piattelli, and Alfredo Rabello. *An Introduction to the History and Sources of Jewish Law*. Oxford: Oxford University Press, 1996.

Helmis, Andréas. "Crime et châtiment dans l'Égypte ptolémaïque. Recherches sur l'autonomie d'un modèle penal." DPhil diss., Université de Paris X—Nanterre, 1986.

Hengel, Martin. *Jews, Greeks, and Barbarians: Aspects of the Hellenization of Judaism in the Pre-Christian Period*. Philadelphia: Fortress Press, 1980.

Hengel, Martin. *Judaism and Hellenism. Volume 1: Text*. Vol. 1 of *Judaism and Hellenism*. Philadelphia: Fortress Press, 1974.

Hermary, Antoine, Martine Leguilloux, Véronique Chankowski, and Angeliki Petropoulou. "Le vocabulaire du sacrifice: Introduction." Pages 60–64 in *Thesaurus Cultus et Rituum Antiquorum I: Processions, Sacrifices, Libations, Fumigations, Dedications*. California: The J. Paul Getty Museum, 2004.

Herodotus. *Histories*. Translated by Alfred D. Godley. LCL. Cambridge: Harvard University Press, 1920.

Hiebert, Robert. *The SBL Commentary on the Septuagint: An Introduction*. Edited by Dirk Büchner. Atlanta: SBL Press, 2017.

Honigman, Sylvie. "Jewish Communities in Hellenistic Egypt: Different Responses to Different Environments." Pages 117–135 in *Jewish Identities in Antiquity: Studies in Memory of Menachem Stern*. Edited by Lee I. Levine and Daniel R. Schwartz. Tübingen: Mohr Siebeck, 2009.

Honigman, Sylvie. "*Politeumata* and Ethnicity in Ptolemaic Egypt." *Ancient Society* 33 (2003): 61–102.

Honigman, Sylvie. "The Jewish *Politeuma* at Heracloepolis (review of J. M. S. Cowey and K. Maresch, *Urkunden des Politeuma der Juden von Herakleopolis [144/3–133/2 v. Chr.] [P.Polit.Iud.]*)." *SCI* 21 (2002): 251–266.

Honigman, Sylvie. *The Septuagint and Homeric Scholarship in Alexandria A Study in the Narrative of the Letter of Aristeas*. London: Routledge, 2012.

Honigman, Sylvie. "The Shifting Definition of Greek Identity in Alexandria through the Transition from Ptolemaic to Roman Rule." Pages 125–144 in *Alexandria: Hub of the Hellenistic World*. Edited by Benjamin Schliesser, Jan Rüggemeier, Thomas J. Kraus, and Jörg Frey, with the assistance of Daniel Herrmann. WUNT 460. Tübingen: Mohr Siebeck, 2021.

Horsley, Greg H. R., and Stephen R. Llewelyn. *New Documents Illustrating Early Christianity*. 10 vols. Sydney: Macquarie University, 1976–2008.

Horst, P. van der. "Thou Shalt Not Revile the Gods:" The LXX Translation of Ex. 22:28(27), Its Background and Influence." Pages 1–8 in vol. 5 of *The Studia Philonica Annual: Studies in Hellenistic Judaism*. Edited by David T. Runia, Alan Mendelson, and David Winston. Atlanta: Scholars Press, 1993.

Houtman, Cornelius. *Historical Commentary on the Old Testament: Exodus*. 4 vols. Leuven: Peeters, 1993–2002.

How, Walter W., and Joseph Wells. *A Commentary on Herodotus*. Oxford: Clarendon Press, 1964.

Hunt, Arthur S., and Josiah Gilbart Smyly. *The Tebtunis Papyri*. Vol. 3, pt. 1 of *The Tebtunis Papyri*. London: Milford, 1933.

Iwry, Samuel. "הנמצא—a Striking Variant Reading in 1QIs[a]." *Textus* 5 (1966): 34–43.

Jameson, Michael H. *Cults and Rites in Ancient Greece: Essays on Religion and Society*. Cambridge: Cambridge University Press, 2014.

Jameson, Michael H. "Meat, consumption of, I. Greece." BNP 8: 535–536.

Joosten, Jan. *Collected Essays on the Septuagint*. Tübingen: Mohr Siebeck, 2012.

Jannaris, Antonius. *An Historical Greek Grammar: Chiefly of the Attic Dialect*. London: Macmillan, 1897.

Janssen, Jac J. "Marriage Problems and Public Reactions." Pages 134–137 in *Pyramid Studies. Other Essays Presented to I. E. S. Edwards*. Edited by John Baines, T. G. H. James, Anthony Leahy, and A. F. Shore. London: Egypt Exploration Society, 1988.

Jassen, Alex P. *Scripture and Law in the Dead Sea Scrolls*. Cambridge: Cambridge University Press, 2014.

Jacobsthal, Hans. *Der Gebrauch der Tempora und Modi in den kretischen Dialektinschriften*. Strassburg: Trübner, 1907.

Kaplony-Heckel, Ursula. *Die Demotischen Tempeleide: Teil 1: Text*. Vol. 1 of *Die Demotischen Tempeleide*. Wiesbaden: Harrassowitz, 1963.

Kasher, Aryeh. *The Jews in Hellenistic and Roman Egypt: The Struggle for Equal Rights*. Tübingen: Mohr Siebeck, 1985.

Keenan, James G., Chrysi Kotsifou, Joseph Mélèze-Modrzejewski, Bernhard Palme, and Georg Schmelz. "The Judicial System in Theory and Practice." Pages 470–540 in *Law and Legal Practice in Egypt from Alexander to the Arab Conquest: A Selection of Papyrological Sources in Translation, with Introductions and Commentary*. Edited by James G. Keenan, Joseph G. Manning, and Uri Yiftach-Firanko. Cambridge: Cambridge University Press, 2014.

Kooij, Arie van der. "Perspectives on the Study of the Septuagint: Who Are the Translators?" Pages 214–229 in *Perspectives in the Study of the Old Testament and Early Judaism*. Edited by Ed Noort and Florentino García Martínez. Leiden: Brill, 1998.

Koehler, Ludwig, Walter Baumgartner, and Johann J. Stamm. *HALOT*. Translated and edited under the supervision of Mervyn E. J. Richardson. 4 vols. Leiden: Brill, 1994–1999.

Korytko, Joel F. "Slaves to the Septuagint: Applying Greek Legal Terminology for Slaves to Ex. 21.7." Forthcoming in *Themes and Texts, Exodus and Beyond*. Bloomsbury: T&T Clark.

Korytko, Joel F. "The Death Penalty in OG Exodus in Light of Graeco-Egyptian Legal Formulations." *JSCS* 54 (2021): 77–94.

Korytko, Joel F. "The 'Law of the Land' in the Land of the Lagids: A Comparative Analysis of Exodus 21.1–32." M.A. Thesis, Trinity Western University, 2018.

Kratz, Reinhard G. "Greek Historians on Jews and Judaism in the 3rd Century BCE." Pages 263–278 in *Times of Transition: Judea in the Early Hellenistic Period*. Edited by Sylvie Honigman, Christophe Nihan, and Oded Lipschits. University Park/Tel Aviv: Eisenbrauns/Emery and Claire Yass Publications in Archaeology, The Institute of Archaeology, Tel Aviv University, 2021.

Kreuzer, Siegfried. "Entstehung und Entwicklung der Septuaginta im Kontext alexandrinischer und frühjüdischer Kultur und Bildung." Pages 3–39 in *Septuaginta Deutsch. Erläuterungen und Kommentare zum griechischen Alten Testament. Band I: Genesis bis Makkabäer*. Vol. 1 of *Septuaginta Deutsch. Erläuterungen und Kommentare zum griechischen Alten Testament*. Edited by Martin Karrer and Wolfgang Kraus. Stuttgart: Deutsche Bibelgesellschaft, 2011.

Kreuzer, Siegfried. "Enstehung und Überlieferung der Septuaginta." Pages 29–88 in *Einleitung in die Septuaginta*. Vol. 1 of *Handbuch zur Septuaginta*. Edited by Sigfried Kreuzer. Gütersloh: Gütersloher Verlagshaus, 2016.

Kreuzer, Siegfried. "Origin and Development of the Septuagint in the Context of Alexandrian and Early Jewish Culture and Learning." Pages 3–46 in *The Bible in Greek: Translation, Transmission, and Theology of the Septuagint*. Atlanta: Society of Biblical Literature, 2015.

Kron, Geoffrey. "Animal Husbandry, Hunting, Fishing, and Fish Production." Pages 175–213 in *The Oxford Handbook of Engineering and Technology in the Classical World*. Oxford: Oxford University Press, 2009.

Kucharski, Jan. "Capital Punishment in Classical Athens." *Scripta Classica* 12 (2015): 13–28.

Kugler, Robert. "Dispelling an Illusion of Otherness? Juridical Practice in the Herakleopolis Papyri." Pages 457–470 in *The "Other" in Second Temple Judaism: Essays in Bibliography Honor of John J. Collins*. Edited by Daniel C. Harlow, Karina Martin Hogan, Matthew Goff, and Joel S. Kaminsky. Grand Rapids: Eerdmans, 2011.

Kugler, Robert. *Resolving Disputes in Second Century BCE Herakleopolis: A Study in Jewish Legal Reasoning in Hellenistic Egypt*. Leiden: Brill, 2022.

Kugler, Robert. "Uncovering a New Dimension of Early Judean Interpretation of the Greek Torah: Ptolemaic Law Interpreted by Its Own Rhetoric." Pages 165–175 in *Changes in Scripture: Rewriting and Interpreting Authoritative Traditions in the Second Temple Period*. Edited by Hanne von Weissenberg, Juha Pakkala, and Marko Marttila. BZW 419. Berlin: de Gruyter, 2011.

Kugler, Robert. "Uncovering Echoes of LXX Legal Norms in Hellenistic Egyptian Documentary Papyri: The Case of the Second-Century Herakleopolite Nome." Pages 142–153 in *XIV Congress of the International Organization for Septuagint and Cognate Studies, Helsinki 2010*. Edited by Melvin K. H. Peters. SCS 59. Atlanta: Society of Biblical Literature, 2013.

Kühner, Raphael. *Ausführliche Grammatik der griechischen Sprache: Satzlehre*. Vol. 1, pt. 2 of *Ausführliche Grammatik der griechischen Sprache*. Hannover/Leipzig: Hahnsche Buchhandlung, 1898.

LaCoste, Nathalie. *Waters of the Exodus: Jewish Experiences with Water in Ptolemaic and Roman Egypt*. Leiden: Brill, 2019.

Laronde, André. *Cyrène et la Libye hellénistique. Libykai historiai de l'époque républicaine au principat d'Auguste*. Paris: Centre National de la Recherche Scientifique, 1987.

Launey, Marcel. *Recherches sur les armées hellénistiques. Volume One: Recherches ethniques*. Vol. 1 of *Recherches sur les armées hellénistiques*. Paris: de Boccard, 1950.

Law, Timothy, and Alison Salvesen. *Greek Scripture and the Rabbis*. Leuven: Peeters, 2012.

Le Boulluec, Alain, and Pierre Sandevoir. *L'Exode*. Vol. 2 of *La Bible D'Alexandrie*. Paris: Cerf, 1989.

Lee, John A. L. *A Lexical Study of the Septuagint Version of the Pentateuch*. Chico: Scholars Press, 1983.

Lee, John A. L. "A Lexical Study Thirty Years on, with Observations on 'Order' Words in the LXX Pentateuch." Pages 513–524 in *Emanuel. Studies in Hebrew Bible, Septuagint and Dead Sea Scrolls in Honor of Emanuel Tov*. Edited by Shalom M. Paul, Robert A. Kraft, Lawrence H. Schiffman, and Weston W. Fields. VTS 94. Leiden: Brill, 2003.

Lee, John A. L. *The Greek of the Pentateuch: Grinfield Lectures on the Septuagint 2011–2012*. Oxford: Oxford University Press, 2018.

Lee, John A. L. "The Vocabulary of the Septuagint and Documentary Evidence." Pages 98–108 in *Sprache der Septuaginta*. Vol. 3 of *Handbuch zur Septuaginta*. Edited by Eberhard Bons and Jan Joosten. Gütersloh: Gütersloher Verlagshaus, 2016.

Lee, John A. L. "Translations of the Old Testament." Pages 775–784 in *Handbook of Classical Rhetoric in the Hellenistic Period: 330 B.C.–A.D. 400*. Edited by Stanley E. Porter. Leiden: Brill, 1997.

LeFebvre, Michael. *Collections, Codes, and Torah: The Re-Characterization of Israel's Written Law*. LHB/OTS 451. New York: T&T Clark, 2006.

Legras, Bernard. *Hommes Et Femmes D'Égypte: IVe S. Av. N. è.–IVe S. De N. è: Droit, Histoire Et Anthropologie*. Paris: A. Colin, 2010.

Lenger, Marie-Thérèse. *Corpus des ordonnances des Ptolémées* (*C. Ord. Ptol*). Bruxelles: Palais des Académies, 1980.

Levinson, Bernard M. "Is the Covenant Code an Exilic Composition? A Response to John Van Seters: Proceedings of the Oxford Old Testament Seminar." Pages 272–325 in *In Search of Pre-Exilic Israel: Proceedings of the Oxford Old Testament Seminar*. Edited by John Day. London: T&T Clark, 2004.

Levinson, Bernard M. *Legal Revision and Religious Renewal in Ancient Israel*. Cambridge: Cambridge University Press, 2008.

Lewis, Naphtali. *Greeks in Ptolemaic Egypt: Case Studies in the Social History of the Hellenistic World*. Oxford: Clarendon Press, 1986.

Levinson, Bernard M. *Inventory of Compulsory Services in Ptolemaic and Roman Egypt*. New Haven: American Society of Papyrologists, 1968.

Lippert, Sandra. "Law Courts." *UCLA Encyclopedia of Egyptology*. 2012. https://escholarship.org/uc/item/4136j3s7.

Lippert, Sandra. "What's New in Demotic Studies?: An Overview of the Publications 2010–2013." *JJP* 43 (2013): 33–48.

Lissarrague, François. "The Sexual Life of Satyrs." Pages 53–82 in *Before Sexuality: The Construction of Erotic Experience in the Ancient Greek World*. Edited by David M. Halperin, John J. Winkler, and Froma I. Zeitlin. Princeton: Princeton University Press, 1991.

Llewelyn, Stephen R. "'Slaves, Obey your Masters': The Legal Liability of Slaves." Pages 163–196 in vol. 7 of *New Documents Illustrating Early Christianity*. Sydney: Macquarie University, 1982–1983.

Loiseau, Anne-Françoise. *L'influence de l'araméen sur les traducteurs de la LXX principalement, sure les traducteurs grecs postérieurs, ainsi que sur les scribes de la Vorlage de la LXX*. Atlanta: SBL Press, 2016.

Lorton, David. "The Treatment of Criminals in Ancient Egypt Through the New Kingdom." *JESHO* 20, no. 1 (1977): 2–64.

Lougovaya, Julia. "Medici Docti in Verse Inscriptions." *Greek Medical Papyri* (2019): 139–160.

Lust, Johan, Erik Eynikel, and Katrin Hauspie. *A Greek-English Lexicon of the Septuagint: Revised Edition.* Stuttgart: Deutsche Bibelgesellschaft, 2003.

Lustig, Christian. "Moses eigenes Zelt. Zur Unterscheidung zweier Zelkonzeptionen im griechischen Exodusbuch." Pages 168–180 in *Die Septuaginta—Geschichte, Wirkung, Relevanz.* Edited by Martin Meiser, Michaela Geiger, Siegfried Kreuzer, and Marcus Sigismund. WUNT 405. Tübignen: Mohr Siebeck, 2018.

Lysias. *Lysias with an English Translation.* Translated by Walter R. M. Lamb. LCL. London: Harvard University Press, 1930.

MacDowell, Douglas M. *Athenian Homicide Law in the Age of the Orators.* Manchester: University Press, 1963.

Maehler, Herwig. "Greek, Egyptian and Roman Law." *JJP* 35 (2005): 121–140.

Mairs, Rachel. "Hermēneis in the Documentary Record from Hellenistic and Roman Egypt: Interpreters, Translators and Mediators in a Bilingual Society." *Journal of Ancient History* 8 (2020): 1–53.

Mandēlaras, Vasileios G. *The Verb in the Greek Non-Literary Papyri.* Athens: Hellenic Ministry of Culture and Sciences, 1973.

Manniche, Lise. *Sexual Life in Ancient Egypt.* London: Kegan Paul, 1997.

Manning, Joseph. "Hellenistic Egypt." Pages 434–459 in *The Cambridge Economic History of the Greco-Roman World.* Edited by Walter Scheidel, Ian Morris, and Richard P. Saller. Cambridge: Cambridge University Press, 2007.

Manning, Joseph. "Networks, Hierarchies and Markets in the Ptolemaic Economy." Pages 296–324 in *The Economies of Hellenistic Societies, Third to First Centuries BC.* Edited by Zosia Archibald, John K. Davies, and Vincent Gabrielsen. Oxford: Oxford University Press, 2011.

Markiewicz, Tomasz. "Security for Debt in the Demotic Papyri." *JJP* 35 (2005): 141–167.

Maurais, Jean. *Characterizing Old Greek Deuteronomy as an Ancient Translation.* JSJS 203. Leiden: Brill, 2022.

Maurais, Jean. "Translated Torah: Characterizing Old Greek Deuteronomy as an Ancient Translation." PhD diss., McGill University, 2020.

Mayser, Edwin. *Grammatik der griechischen Papyri aus der Ptolemäerzeit. Band II 1: Satzlehre, Analytischer Teil, Erste Halfte.* Vol. 2, pt. 1 of *Grammatik der griechischen Papyri aus der Ptolemäerzeit.* Berlin/Leipzig: De Gruyter, 1906–1934.

Meer, M. van der. "Papyrological Perspectives on the Septuagint of Isaiah." Pages 107–133 in *The Old Greek of Isaiah: Issues and Perspectives.* Edited by Arie van der Kooij and Michaël N. van der Meer. CBET 55. Leuven: Peeters, 2010.

Meisterhans, Konrad, and Eduard Schwyzer. *Grammatik Der Attischen Inschriften.* Berlin: Weidmann, 1900.

Mélèze-Modrzejewski, Joseph. "Jewish Law and Hellenistic Legal Practice in the Light of Greek Papyri from Egypt." Pages 75–91 in *An Introduction to the History and Sources of Jewish Law*. Edited by Neil S. Hecht, B. S. Jackson, S. M. Passamaneck, Daniela Piattelli, and Alfredo Rabello. Oxford: Oxford University Press, 1996.

Mélèze-Modrzejewski, Joseph. "La règle de droit dans l'Egypte ptolemaique: état des questions et perspectives de recherches." Pages 125–173 in *Essays in Honor of C. Bradford Wells*. Edited by Alan C. Samuel. ASP 1. New Haven: The American Society of Papyrologists, 1966.

Mélèze-Modrzejewski, Joseph. "La sanction de l'homicide en droit grec et hellénistique." Pages 245–259 in vol. 7 of *Mélanges P. Lévêque*. Edited by Marie-Madeleine Mactoux and Évelyne Geny. Paris: les Belles lettres, 1993.

Mélèze-Modrzejewski, Joseph. "La Septante comme nomos. Comment la Torah est devenue une loi civique pour les Juifs d'Égypte." *Annali di scienze religiose* 2 (1997): 143–158.

Mélèze-Modrzejewski, Joseph. *Loi et coutume dans l'Egypte grecque et romaine*. Varsovie: Faculty of Law and Administration of the University of Warsaw, 2014.

Mélèze-Modrzejewski, Joseph. "Note sur la législation royale des Lagides." Pages 365–380 in *Mélanges d'histoire ancienne offerts à William Seston*. Edited by Pierre Courcelle. Publications de la Sorbonne: Série Études 9. Paris: de Boccard, 1974.

Mélèze-Modrzejewski, Joseph. "Papyrologie et histoire des droits de l'antiquité." Pages 229–240 in *École pratique des hautes études. 4e section, Sciences historiques et philologiques. Annuaire 1973–1974*. Paris: École pratique des hautes études, 1974.

Mélèze-Modrzejewski, Joseph. "« Paroles néfastes » et « vers obscènes ». À propos de l'injure verbale en droit grec et hellénistique: Anthropologies juridiques." *Dike* 1 (1998): 151–169.

Mélèze-Modrzejewski, Joseph. "The πρόσταγμα in the Papyri." *JJP* 5 (1951): 187–206.

Mélèze-Modrzejewski, Joseph. "The Septuagint as Nomos: How the Torah Became a 'Civic Law' for the Jews of Egypt." Pages 183–200 in *Critical Studies in Ancient Law, Comparative Law and Legal History: Studies in Honour of Alan Watson*. Edited by John W. Cairns and Olivia F. Robinson. London: Hart Publishing, 2001.

Mélèze-Modrzejewski, Joseph, and Robert Cornman. *The Jews of Egypt: From Rameses II to Emperor Hadrian*. Princeton: Princeton University Press, 1997.

Merkelbach, Reinhold, Friedrich Karl Dörner, and Sencer Şahin. *Die Inschriften von Kalchedon*. Bonn: Habelt, 1980.

Minamimoto, Toru. "Subordinators and the Supradialectal Formulas in the Dialectal Inscriptions from Mainland Greece (Excluding Attica)." PhD diss., UCLA, 2017.

Mitford, Terence B. "Helenos, Governor of Cyprus." *JHS* 79/80 (1959–1960): 94–131.

Momigliano, Arnaldo. "The Hellenistic Discovery of Judaism." Pages 129–146 in *Emerging Judaism: Studies on the Fourth & Third Centuries B.C.E.* Edited by Michael E. Stone and David Satran. Minneapolis: Fortress Press, 1989.

Montanari, Franco. *The Brill Dictionary of Ancient Greek*. Edited by Madeleine Goh and Chad Schroeder. Leiden: Brill, 2015.

Montserrat, Dominic. *Sex and Society in Graeco-Roman Egypt*. London: Kegan Paul International, 1996.

Moore, Stewart Alden. *Jewish Ethnic Identity and Relations in Hellenistic Egypt: With Walls of Iron?* Leiden: Brill, 2015.

Mossé, Claude. *La fin de la démocratie athénienne. Aspects sociaux et politiques du déclin de la Cité grecque au IV siècle avant J.-C.* Paris: Presses Universitaires de France, 1962.

Moulton, James Hope. Wilbert Francis Howard, and Nigel Turner. *A Grammar of New Testament Greek. Volume 3: Syntax*. Vol. 3 of *A Grammar of New Testament Greek*. Edinburgh: T&T Clark, 1963.

Moulton, James H., and George Milligan. *The Vocabulary of the Greek Testament Illustrated from the Papyri and Other Non-literary Sources*. London: Hodder and Stoughton, 1930.

Muhlestein, Kerry. *Violence in the Service of Order: The Religious Framework for Sanctioned Killing in Ancient Egypt*. Oxford: Archaeopress, 2011.

Müller-Wollermann, Renate. "Todesstrafe und Folter im pharaonischen Ägypten." 147–161 in *Strafe und Strafrecht in den antiken Welten: unter Berücksichtigung von Todesstrafe, Hinrichtung und peinlicher Befragung*. Edited by Robert Rollinger, Martin Lang, and Heinz Barta. Wiesbaden: Harrassowitz Verlag, 2012.

Muraoka, Takamitsu. *A Greek-English Lexicon of the Septuagint*. Louvain: Peeters, 2009.

Muraoka, Takamitsu. *A Syntax of Septuagint Greek*. Leuven: Peeters, 2016.

Murphy, James J. "Demosthenes." *Encyclopaedia Britannica*. 2018. https://www.britannica.com/biography/Demosthenes-Greek-statesman-and-orator.

Neumann, Hans. "Death Penalty I: Ancient Orient." BNP 4:136–137.

Obbink Dirk D. "Philodemus, 'de pietate' I." PhD diss., Stanford, 1987.

Oliverio, Γ. "Iscrizioni di Cirene." *RFIC* 56 (1928): 183–239.

Olofsson, Staffan. *Translation Technique and Theological Exegesis: Collected Essays on the Septuagint Version*. Winona Lake: Eisenbrauns, 2009.

O'Neil, James L. "Royal Authority and City Law under Alexander and His Hellenistic Successors." *CQ* 50, no. 2 (2000): 424–31.

Orrieux, Claude. *Les Papyrus de Zénon: L'horizon d'un Grec en Égypte au IIIe siècle avant J.-C.*. Paris: Macula, 1983.

Orth, Wolfgang. "Ptolemaios II. und die Septuaginta-Übersetzung." Pages 97–114 in *Im Brennpunkt: Die Septuaginta. Studien zur Enstehung und Bedeutung der Griechischen Bibel*. Vol. 1 of *Im Brennpunkt: Die Septuaginta*. Edited by Heinz-Josef Fabry and Ulrich Offerhaus. Stuttgart: Kohlhammer, 2001.

Pantel, Pauline Schmitt. "4.a. Banquet." Page 246 in *Thesaurus Cultus et Rituum Antiquorum II: Purification, Initiation, Heroization, Apotheosis, Banquet, Dance, Music, Cult Images*. California: The J. Paul Getty Museum, 2004.

Parmenides. *Early Greek Philosophy. Volume v: Western Greek Thinkers, Part 2*. Translated by André Laks and Glenn W. Most. LCL. Cambridge: Havard University Press, 2016.

Pasinya, Laurent Monsengwo. *La notion de NOMOS dans le Pentateuque grec*. Rome: Biblical Institute Press, 1973.

Passoni Dell'Acqua, Anna. "Il Pentateuco Dei LXX Testimone Di Istituzioni Di Età Tolemaica." *Annali Di Scienze Religiose* 4 (1999): 171–200.

Passoni Dell'Acqua, Anna. "La terminologia dei reati nei προστάγματα dei Tolemei e nella versione dei LXX." Pages 335–350 in vol. 2 of *Proceedings of the XVIIIth International Congress of Papyrology*. Edited by Vasileios G. Mandēlaras. Athens: Greek Papyrological Society, 1988.

Passoni Dell'Acqua, Anna. "Ricerche Sulla Versione Dei LXX e i Papiri II. Nomós." *Aegyptus* 62, no. 1/2 (1982): 173–94.

Paul, Shalom M. *Studies in the Book of the Covenant in the Light of Cuneiform and Biblical Law*. Eugene, OR: Wipf & Stock, 2006.

Perkins, Larry J. "Exodus: To the Reader." Pages 43–51 in *A New English Translation of the Septuagint and the Other Greek Translations Traditionally Included under That Title*. Edited by Albert Pietersma and Benjamin G. Wright. Oxford: Oxford University Press, 2007.

Perkins, Larry J. "'Glory' in Greek Exodus: Lexical Choice in Translation and its Reflection in Secondary Translations." Pages 87–106 in *Translation is Required: The Septuagint in Retrospect and Prospect*. Edited by Robert J. V. Hiebert. SCS 56. Leiden: Brill, 2011.

Perkins, Larry J. "Israel's Military Characterization in Greek Exodus." Pages 550–563 in *Die Septuaginta—Orte und Intentionen*. Edited by Sigfried Kreuzer, Martin Meiser, and Marcus Sigismund. WUNT 361. Tübingen: Mohr Siebeck, 2016.

Perkins, Larry J. "Observations on the Plague Narrative in Greek Exodus: Strategies Used by the Translator to Shape the Narrative." *JSCS* 52 (2019): 73–90.

Perkins, Larry J. "The Greek Translator of Exodus—Interpres (translator) and Expositor (interpreter)—His Treatment of Theophanies." *JSJ* 43/3 (2012): 1–41.

Perkins, Larry J. "The Translation of משכן/מועד אהל and שכן in Greek Exodus." *JSCS* 48 (2015): 8–26.

Pestman, Pieter W. "Le manuel de droit égyptien de Hermoupolis." Pages 115–144 in *Textes et études de papyrologie grecque, démotique et copte*. Edited by Pieter W. Pestman. Leiden: Brill, 1985.

Philippi, Adolf. *Der Areopag und die Epheten: Eine Untersuchung zur athenischen Verfassungsgeschichte*. Berlin: Weidmann, 1874.

Philo. *Philo: In Ten Volumes [and Two Supplementary Volumes]*. Translated by Francis Henry Colson and George H. Whitaker. 10 vols. LCL. London: Heinemann, 1934.

Phillips, David D. *The Law of Ancient Athens. Law and Society in the Ancient World.* Ann Arbor: University of Michigan Press, 2013.

Piattelli, Daniela, and Bernard S. Jackson. "Jewish Law during the Second Temple Period." Pages 19–51 in *An Introduction to the History and Sources of Jewish Law.* Edited by Neil. S. Hecht, B. S. Jackson, S. M. Passamaneck, Daniela Piattelli, and Alfredo Rabello. Oxford: Oxford University Press, 1996.

Pierce, Richard H. *Three Demotic Papyri in the Brooklyn Museum: A Contribution to the Study of Contracts and Their Instruments in Ptolemaic Egypt.* Oslo: Universitetsforlaget, 1972.

Pietersma, Albert. "The Society of Biblical Literature Commentary on the Septuagint: Basic Principles." Pages 1–16 in *The SBL Commentary on the Septuagint: An Introduction.* Edited by Dirk Büchner. SCS 67. Atlanta: SBL Press, 2017.

Pietersma, Albert. "A Commentary on Psalm 15 in Greek: Text-Production and Text Reception." Pages 523–542 in *Die Septuaginta—Texte Theologien, Einflüsse.* Edited by Wolfgang Kraus and Martin Karrer with Martin Meiser. WUNT 252. Tübingen: Mohr Siebeck, 2010.

Pirenne, Jacques. *La religion et la morale dans l'Égypte antique.* Neuchâtel: La Baconnière, 1965.

Pirenne-Delforge, Vinciane. "Mnasistratos, the 'Hierophant' at Andania (*IG.* 5.1.1390 and Syll.3 735)." Pages 219–235 in *Myths, Martyrs, and Modernity: Studies in the History of Religions in Honour of Jan N. Bremmer.* Edited by Jutse Dijkstra, Justin Kroesen, and Yme Kuiper. Leiden: Brill, 2010.

Plato. *Plato in Twelve Volumes.* Translated by Robert G. Bury. Vol. 10–11 (12 vols.). London: Harvard University Press, 1967–1968.

Plato. *Plato in Twelve Volumes.* Translated by Harold N. Fowler. 12 vols. LCL. London: Harvard University Press, 1966.

Pliny the Elder. *Natural History.* Translated by John Bostock and Henry T. Riley. London: Henry G. Bohn, 1855.

Polybius. *The Histories, Volume I: Books 1–2.* Translated by W. R. Paton. Revised by F. W. Walbank, and Christian Habicht. LCL. Cambridge: Harvard University Press, 2010.

Porphyry. *Ancient Commentators on Aristotle.* Translated by Gillian Clark. LCL. London: Bloomsbury Academic, 2000.

Porten, Bezalel. *Archives from Elephantine: The Life of an Ancient Jewish Military Colony.* Berkeley: University of California Press, 1968.

Porten, Bezalel, and Jay Joel Farber. *The Elephantine Papyri in English: Three Millennia of Cross-Cultural Continuity and Change.* Atlanta: Society of Biblical Literature, 2011.

Préaux, Claire. *L'économie royale des Lagides.* Bruxelles: Edition de la fondation égyptologique Reine Elisabeth, 1939.

Préaux, Claire. "Les continuités dans l'Egypte gréco-romaine." Pages 231–248 in *Conclusions du Xe Congrès de Papyrologues, Actes du Xe Congrès International de Papyrologues, Varsovie-Cracovie, 3–9 septembre 1961*. Edited by Jozef Wolski. Wrocław: Zakład Narodowy im. Ossolinskich, 1964.

Propp, William Henry Covici. *Exodus 19–40: A New Translation with Introduction and Commentary*. New York: Doubleday, 2006.

Rahlfs, Alfred. *Septuaginta: With Morphology*. Electronic edition. Stuttgart: Deutsche Bibelgesellschaft, 1979.

Rajak, Tessa. "Synagogue and Community in the Graeco-Roman Diaspora." Pages 22–38 in *Jews in the Hellenistic and Roman Cities*. Edited by John R. Bartlett. London: Routledge, 2002.

Rajak, Tessa. *Translation and Survival: The Greek Bible and the Ancient Jewish Diaspora*. Oxford: Oxford University Press, 2009.

Rajak, Tessa. "Translating the Septuagint for Ptolemy's Library: Myth and History." Pages 176–193 in *Die Septuaginta—Texte, Kontexte, Lebenswelten*. Edited by Wolfgang Kraus, Martin Karrer, and Martin Meiser. WUNT 219. Tübingen: Mohr Siebeck, 2008.

Reinach, Théodore. "La charte ptolémaïque de Cyrène." *Revue Archéologique* 26 (1927): 1–32.

Rösel, Martin. "From the Torah to Nomos: Perspectives of Research on the Greek Pentateuch." Pages 65–73 in *Introduction to the LXX*. Edited by Siegfried Kreuzer. Waco: Baylor University Press, 2019.

Rösel, Martin. "The Septuagint: Translating and Adapting the Torah to the 3rd Century BCE." Pages 253–262 in *Times of Transition: Judea in the Early Hellenistic Period*. Edited by Sylvie Honigman, Christophe Nihan, and Oded Lipschits. Mosaics 1. Grand Rapids: Eisenbrauns, 2021.

Rostovtzeff, Michael Ivanovitch. *A Large Estate in Egypt in the Third Century B.C.: A Study in Economic History*. Madison: University of Wisconsin, 1922.

Rostovtzeff, Michael Ivanovitch. "Chapter 4: Ptolemaic Egypt." Chapter 4 in vol. 7, pt. 1 of *The Cambridge Ancient History*. Edited by John B. Bury, Stanley Arthur Cook, Frank E. Adcock, and Martin P. Charlesworth. Cambridge: Cambridge University Press, 1923.

Rostovtzeff, Michael Ivanovitch. *The Social & Economic History of the Hellenistic World*. 3 vols. ACLS Humanities E-book. Oxford: Clarendon Press, 1998.

Roth, Martha Tobi, Harry A. Hoffner, and Piotr Michalowski. *Law Collections from Mesopotamia and Asia Minor*. Atlanta: Scholars Press, 1997.

Rotman, Youval, Reinhold Scholl, and Jean A. Straus. "Slavery in Greco-Roman Egypt." Pages 442–469 in *Law and Legal Practice in Egypt from Alexander to the Arab Conquest: A Selection of Papyrological Sources in Translation, with Introductions and Commentary*. Edited by James G. Keenan, Joseph G. Manning, and Uri Yiftach-Firanko. Cambridge: Cambridge University Press, 2014.

Saco, Julio López. *Fuentes Grecolatinas del Próximo Oriente, Egipto, Gracia y Roma: Inscripciones y otros materiales procedentes de la colección privada de K. C. Hanson*. Translated by Fulvio Scarcia and Leonardo La Rosa. Escuela de Historia, UCV, 2007.

Safty, Essam. "Les principales catégories de crimes passibles de la peine capitale dans le droit attique aux temps des orateurs." *Cahiers des études anciennes* 33 (1997): 161–172.

Salvesen, Alison. "'They Did Not Settle in the Land of the Lord: Ephraim Settled in Egypt' (Hos 9:3): Returning to Egypt in the Septuagint and Other Hellenistic Jewish Works." Pages 150–177 in *Israel in Egypt: The Land of Egypt as Concept and Reality for Jews in Antiquity and the Early Medieval Period*. Edited by Alison Salvesen, Sarah Pearce, and Miriam Frenkel. Leiden: Brill, 2020.

Schäfer, Diedrich. "Zwei Spätptolemäische Ladungsprogrammata." *Aegyptus* 13, no. 3/4 (1933): 610–620.

Schaper, Joachim. "Exodos: Das zweite Buch Mose." Pages 258–324 in pt. 1 of *Septuaginta Deutsch. Erläuterungen und Kommentare zum griechischen Alten Testament*. Edited by Martin Karrer and Wolfgang Kraus. Stuttgart: Deutsche Bibelgesellschaft, 2011.

Schiemann, Gottfried. "Death Penalty II: Graeco-Roman." BNP 4:137.

Schiffman, Lawrence H. "The Septuagint and the Temple Scroll: Shared 'Halakhic' Variants." Pages 85–98 in *The Courtyards of the House of the Lord: Studies on the Temple Scroll*. Edited by F. García Martínez. STDJ 75. Leiden: Brill, 2008.

Scholl, Reinhold. *Corpus der ptolemäischen Sklaventexte. Teil 1: Text Nr. 1–114*. Vol. 1 of *Corpus der ptolemäischen Sklaventexte* Stuttgart: Steiner, 1990.

Schultz, Ferdinand. *Aeschinis Orationes*. Leipzig: Teubner, 1865.

Schwartz, Seth. "Language, Power and Identity in Ancient Palestine." *Past & Present* 148 (1995): 3–47.

Schwartz, Seth. "Law in Jewish Society in the Second Temple Period." Pages 48–75 in *The Cambridge Companion to Judaism and Law*. Edited by Christine Hayes. Cambridge: Cambridge University Press, 2017.

Screnock, John. *Traductor Scriptor: The Old Greek Translation of Exodus 1–14 As Scribal Activity*. VTSupp 174. Leiden: Brill, 2017.

Seidl, Erwin. "La preuve d'après les documents demotiques." *RecSocJB* 16 (1964–1965): 43–59.

Seidl, Erwin. *Ptolemäische Rechtsgeschichte*. Glückstadt: Augustin, 1962.

Sextus. *Against Physicists. Against Ethicists*. Translated by Robert Gregg Bury. LCL. Cambridge: Harvard University Press, 1936.

Shemesh, Aharon. "4Q251: Midrash Mishpatim." *DSD* 12, no. 3 (2005): 280–302.

Sissa, Giulia. *Sex and Sensuality in the Ancient World*. New Haven: Yale University Press, 2008.

Smyth, Herbert Weir, and Gordon M. Messing. *Greek Grammar*. Revised edition. Cambridge: Harvard University Press, 1956.

Sollamo, Raija. "The LXX Renderings of the Infinitive Absolute Used with a Paronymous Finite Verb in the Pentateuch." Pages 101–113 in *La Septuaginta en la investigacion contemporanea* (*V Congreso de la IOSCS*). Edited by Natalio Fernández-Marcos. Madrid: Instituto Arias Montano CSIC, 1985.

Spicq, Ceslas. *Theological Lexicon of the New Testament*. Translated and edited by James D. Ernest. 3 vols. Peabody, MA: Hendrickson, 1994.

Squillace, Giuseppe. "Editto di Alessandro Magno per Priene." *Axon* 2 (2018): 153–160.

Staalduine-Sulman, Eveline. "Between Legislative and Linguistic Parallels: Exodus 21:22–25 in its Context." Pages 207–224 in *The Interpretation of Exodus: Studies in Honour of Cornelis Houtman*. Edited by Riemer Roukema. CBET 44. Leuven: Peters, 2006.

Stengel, Paul. *Die griechischen Kultusaltertümer*. Third edition. München: Beck, 1920.

Strabo. *Geography*. Translated by Horace Leonard Jones, and J. R. Sitlington Sterrett. 8 vols. LCL. London: Heinemann, 1917–1932.

Stambaugh, John E. *Sarapis Under the Early Ptolemies*. Leiden: Brill, 1972.

Stephens, Susan. "Posidippus' Poetry Book: Where Macedon Meets Egypt." Pages 63–86 in *Ancient Alexandria between Egypt and Greece*. Edited by William V. Harris and Giovanni Ruffini. CSCT 26. Leiden: Brill, 2004.

Stolk, Joanne Vera. "Scribal and Phraseological Variation in Legal Formulas: ὑπάρχω + Dative or Genitive Pronoun." *JJP* 45 (2015): 255–290.

Stroud, Ronald S. *The Athenian Grain-Tax Law of 374/3 B.C.* Hesperia Supplements 29. Princeton: American School of Classical Studies at Athens, 1998.

Sundahl, Mark, David C. Mirhady, and Ilias Arnaoutoglou. *A New Working Bibliography of Ancient Greek Law, 7th–4th centuries BC*. Athens: Academy of Athens, 2011.

Swete, Henry Barclay, Henry J. Thackeray, and Richard Rusden Ottley. *An Introduction to the Old Testament in Greek*. Cambridge: Cambridge University Press, 1914.

Taubenschlag, Raphael. "Die action de pastu, de pauperie und de arborius casesis im Rechte der Papyri." *JJP* 7–8 (1953–1954): 387–388.

"Die Geschichte der Rezeption des griechischen Privatrechts in Ägypten." Pages 259–281 in *Atti del IV Congresso Internationale di Papirologia*. Milano: Società editrice "Vita e Pensiero," 1936.

Taubenschlag, Raphael. "The Ancient Greek City Laws in Ptolemaic Egypt." Pages 471–489 in *Actes du Ve Congrès international de Papyrologie, Oxford, 30 août-3 septembre 1937*. Bruxelles: Fondation égyptologique reine Élisabeth, 1938.

Taubenschlag, Raphael. "The Inviolability of Domicile in Greco-Roman Egypt." *Archív Orientální* 18(4) (1950): 293–297.

Taubenschlag, Raphael. *The Law of Greco-Roman Egypt in Light of the Papyri 332 B.C.–640 A.D.* New York: Harold Square Press, 1944.

Taubenschlag, Raphael. *The Law of Greco-Roman Egypt in the Light of the Papyri 332 BC–640 AD*. Revised edition. Warsaw: Panstwowe Wydawnictwo Naukowe, 1955.

Tcherikover, Victor, Alexander Fuks, David M. Lewis, and Menahem Stern. *Corpus Papyrorum Judaicarum*. Vol. 1 of *Corpus Papyrorum Judaicarum*. Cambridge: Harvard University Press, 1957.

Tcherikover, Victor, Alexander Fuks, David M. Lewis, and Menahem Stern. "Palestine Under the Ptolemies: A Contribution to the Zenon Papyri." *Mizraim* 4–5 (1937): 9–90.

Tcherikover, Victor, Alexander Fuks, David M. Lewis, and Menahem Stern. *The Jews in Egypt in the Hellenistic-Roman Age in the Light of the Papyri*. Jerusalem: Hebrew University Press Association, 1945.

Thackeray, Henry J. *A Grammar of the Old Testament in Greek*. Cambridge: Cambridge University Press, 1909.

Theocritus. Moschus, Bion. Translated by Neil Hopkinson. LCL. Cambridge: Harvard University Press, 2015.

Theophrastus of Eresus. *On Winds*. Translated by Robert Mayhew. LCL. Leiden: Brill, 2017.

Thompson, Dorothy. "Hellenistic Hellenes: The Case of Ptolemaic Egypt." Pages 301–322 in *Ancient Perceptions of Greek Ethnicity*. Edited by Irad Malkin. Cambridge: Harvard University Press, 2001.

Thompson, Dorothy. "Literacy and Power in Ptolemaic Egypt." Pages 67–83 in *Literacy and Power in the Ancient Near East*. Edited by Alan K. Bowman and Greg Woolf. Cambridge: Cambridge University Press, 1994.

Thompson, F. H. *The Archaeology of Greek and Roman Slavery*. London: Duckworth, 2003.

Thompson, Leonard L. "ISMYRNA 753: Gods and the One God." Pages 101–122 in *Reading Religions in the Ancient World: Essays Presented to Robert McQueen Grant on His 90th Birthday*. Edited by Robert M. Grant. Boston: Brill, 2007.

Thonissen, Jean-Joseph. *Études sur l'histoire du droit criminel des peuples anciens. (Inde brahmanique, Égypte, Judée)*. Vol. 1 of *Études sur l'histoire du droit criminel des peuples anciens*. Bruxelles, 1869.

Thucydides. *History of the Peloponnesian War*. Translated by Charles Forster Smith. LCL. Cambridge: Harvard University Press, 2015.

Thür, Gerhard (Graz). "Legal Pluralism." BNP. 2006. http://dx.doi.org/10.1163/1574-9347_bnp_e1019600.

Thür, Gerhard, and Hans Taeuber. *Prozessrechtliche Inschriften der griechischen Poleis: Arkadien (IPArk)*. Vienna: Verlag der Österreichischen Akademie der Wissenschaften, 1994.

Timon. *Early Greek Philosophy. Volume III: Early Ionian Thinkers, Part 2*. Translated by André Laks, and Glenn W. Most. LCL. Cambridge: Harvard University Press, 2016.

Tjen, Anwar. *On Conditionals in the Greek Pentateuch: A Study of Translation Syntax*. London: T&T Clark, 2010.

Todd, Stephen C. "How to Execute People in Fourth-Century Athens." Pages 31–51 in *Law and Social Status in Classical Athens*. Edited by Virginia Hunter and Jonathan Edmondson. Oxford: Oxford University Press, 2000.

Too, Yun Lee. "Legal Instructions in Classical Athens." Pages 111–132 in *Education in Greek and Roman Antiquity*. Edited by Yun Lee Too. Leiden: Brill, 2001.

Tov, Emmanuel. "Compound Words in the Septuagint Representing Two or More Hebrew Words." Pages 131–152 in *The Greek and Hebrew Bible: Collected Essays on the Septuagint*. Edited by Emmanuel Tov. VTSupp 72. Leiden: Brill, 1999.

Tov, Emmanuel. "Textual Harmonization in Exodus 1–24." *JBTC* 22 (2017): 1–16.

Trimm, Charles. "Recent Research on Warfare in the Old Testament." *CurBr* (2011): 1–46.

Trinquier, Jean. "Localisation et fonction des animaux sauvages dans l'Alexandrie lagide: la question du 'zoo d'Alexandrie.'" MEFRA 114 (2002): 861–919.

Tyldesley, Joyce A. *Judgement of the Pharaoh: Crime and Punishment in Ancient Egypt*. London: Weidenfeld & Nicolson, 2000.

Vahrenhorst, Martin. "Zwischen Alexandria und Tiberias—Berührungen zwischen dem Text der LXX und rabbinischen Traditionen." Pages 483–500 in *Die Septuaginta—Text, Wirkung, Rezeption*. Edited by Wolfgang Kraus and Siegfried Kreuzer, with Martin Meiser and Marcus Sigismund. WUNT 325. Tübingen: Mohr Siebeck, 2014.

Vanderkam, James C. *An Introduction to Early Judaism*. Grand Rapids: William B. Eerdmans, 2001.

Vandorpe, Katelijn, and Marc Waelkens. "Protecting Sagalassos' Fortress of the Akra: Two Large Fragments of an Early Hellenistic Inscription." *Ancient Society* 37 (2007): 121–139.

Van Heel, Koenraad Donker. *The Legal Manual of Hermopolis (P. Mattha). Text and Translation*. Leiden: Brill, 1990.

Van Minnen, Peter J. "Prisoners of War and Hostages in Graeco-Roman Egypt." *JJP* (2000): 155–163.

Van Raalte, Marlein. "The Nature of Fire and its Complications: Theophrastus' De Igne 1–10." *Bulletin of the Institute of Classical Studies* 53 (2010): 47–97.

Vélissaropoulos-Karakostas, Julie. *Ἀλεξανδρινοί νόμοι. Πολιτική αυτονομία καί νομική αυτοτέλεια της πτολεμαϊκής Ἀλεξάνδρειας*. Αθήνα: Σάκκουλας, 1981.

Vélissaropoulos-Karakostas, Julie. *Droit grec d'Alexandre à Auguste (323 av. J.-C.–14 ap. J.-C.): personnes, biens, justice*. Athens: Centre de Recherches de l'Antiquité grecque et romaine, 2011.

Vélissaropoulos-Karakostas, Julie. "He poine tou thanatou." *Archaiologia* 11 (1984): 36–44.

Versnel, Henk S. "Les imprecations et le droit." *RHD* 65 (1987): 5–22.

VerSteeg, Russ. *Law in Ancient Egypt*. Durham: Carolina Academic Press, 2002.

Vierros, Marja. *Bilingual Notaries in Hellenistic Egypt. A Study of Greek as a Second Language*. Brussels: Koninklijke Vlaamse Academie van België, 2012.

Verburg, Jelle. "The LXX of the Law of Deposit in Exodus 22:6–14." *JSCS* 51 (2018): 66–83.

Verburg, Jelle. "The Septuagint and Legal Traditions." DPhil diss., The University of Oxford, 2021 (forthcoming).

Vogliano, Achille. "Nuovi studi sulle decretali di Cirene." *RFIC* 56 (1928): 255–320.

Von Wilamowitz-Moellendorff, Ulrich. "Heilige Gesetze, eine Urkunde aus Kyrene." *SPAW* 19 (1927): 155–176.

Vroom, Jonathan. *The Authority of Law in the Hebrew Bible and Early Judaism: Tracing the Origins of Legal Obligation from Ezra to Qumran.* Leiden: Brill, 2018.

Wade, Martha Lynn. *Consistency of Translation Techniques in the Tabernacle Accounts of Exodus in the Old Greek.* SCS 49. Atlanta: Society of Biblical Literature, 2003.

Wallace, Robert W. "On not Legislating Sexual Conduct in Fourth-Century Athens." Pages 151–166 in *Symposion 1995: Vorträge zur grieschischen und hellenistischen Rechsgeschichte.* Edited by Gerhard Thür and Julie Vélissaropoulous-Karakostas. AGGHR 11. Cologne; Vienna: Böhlau, 1997.

Welles, Charles B. "New Texts from the Chancery of Philip v of Macedonia and the Problem of the <<Diagramma>>." *AJA* 42 (1938): 245–260.

Wells, Bruce. "What Is Biblical Law? A Look at Pentateuchal Rules and Near Eastern Practice." *CBQ* 70 (2008): 223–243.

Werner, Jaeger R. *Religion in Attic Middle Comedy.* PhD diss., University of Pennsylvania, 1962.

Westbrook, Raymond. "The Laws of Biblical Israel." Pages 317–340 in vol. 2 of *Law from the Tigris to the Tiber: The Writings of Raymond Westbrook.* Edited by Bruce Wells and Rachel Magdalene. Winona Lake: Eisenbrauns, 2009.

Westbrook, Raymond. "What Is the Covenant Code?" Pages 97–118 in vol. 1 of *Law from the Tigris to the Tiber: The Writings of Raymond Westbrook.* Edited by Bruce Wells and Rachel Magdalene. Winona Lake: Eisenbrauns, 2009.

Westermann, William Linn. "Enslaved Persons Who Are Free." *AJP* 59, no. 1 (1938): 1–30.

Westermann, William Linn. *Upon Slavery in Ptolemaic Egypt.* New York: Columbia University Press, 1929.

Wevers, John William. *Exodus*, vol. 2 of *Vetus Testamentum Graecum, Auctoritate Academiae Scientiarum Gottingensis editum.* Göttingen: Vandenhoeck & Ruprecht, 1991.

Wevers, John William. *Notes on the Greek Text of Exodus.* Atlanta: Scholars Press, 1990.

Wevers, John William. "PreOrigen Recensional Activity in the Greek Exodus." Pages 121–139 in *Studien zur Septuaginta—Robert Hanhart zu Ehren: aus Anlass seines 65. Geburtstages.* Edited by Detlef Fraenkel, Udo Quast, and John W. Wevers. Göttingen: Vandenhoeck & Ruprecht, 1990.

Wevers, John William. *Text History of the Greek Exodus.* Göttingen: Vandenhoek & Ruprecht, 1992.

Wiedemann, Thomas. *Greek and Roman Slavery.* London: Croom Helm, 1983.

Wilcken, Ulrich, and Ludwig Mitteis. *Grundzüge und Chrestomathie der Papyruskunde. Erster Band: Historischer Teil Zweite Hälfte: Chrestomathie.* Vol. 1, pt. 2 of *Grundzüge und Chrestomathie der Papyruskunde.* Hildesheim: Olms, 1962.

Wilcken, Ulrich. *Urkunden der Ptolemäerzeit. Erster Band: Papyri aus Unterägypten*. Vol. 1 of *Urkunden der Ptolemäerzeit*. Berlin & Leipzig: de Gruyter, 1927.

Wilhelm, Adolf. *Beiträge zur griechichen Inschriftenkunde*. Vienna: A. Hölder, 1909.

Willetts, Ronald F. *The Law Code of Gortyn*. Berlin: de Gruyter, 1967.

Williams, Margaret H. *The Jews Among the Greeks and Romans: A Diasporan Sourcebook*. London: Duckworth, 2001.

Winkler, John J. "Laying Down the Law: the Oversight of Men's Sexual Behavior in Classical Athens." Pages 171–210 in *Before Sexuality: The Construction of Erotic Experience in the Ancient Greek World*. Edited by David M. Halperin, John J. Winkler, and Froma I. Zeitlin. Princeton: Princeton University Press, 1991.

Winter, Franz. "Die dokumentarischen Papyri Ägyptens und die Septuaginta: Studien zu Köln." *Tyche* 17 (2002): 193–204.

Wolff, Hans Julius. "Law in Ptolemaic Egypt." Pages 67–77 in *Essays in Honor of C. Bradford Wells*. Edited by Alan C. Samuel. ASP 1. New Haven: The American Society of Papyrologists, 1966.

Wolff, Hans Julius. "Neue Juristische Urkunden VII—Neues Material zum Zwangsvollstreckungrecht der Papyri." *ZSS* 100 (1983): 444–453.

Wolff, Hans Julius. "Plurality of Laws in Ptolemaic Egypt." RIDA 7 (1960): 191–223.

Wonjae, Chris. "'For in the Day that You Eat of it, You Shall Surely Die': The Early Reception History of the Death Warning in Genesis 2:17." PhD diss., The University of Edinburgh, 2019.

Worthington, Ian. *Ptolemy I: King and Pharaoh of Egypt*. New York: Oxford University Press, 2016.

Wray, Alison. *Formulaic Language and the Lexicon*. Cambridge: Cambridge University Press, 2002.

Wright, Benjamin. "The *Letter of Aristeas* and the Place of the Septuagint in Alexandrian Judaism." Pages 229–244 in *Alexandria: Hub of the Hellenistic World*. Edited by Benjamin Schliesser, Jan Rüggemeier, Thomas J. Kraus, and Jörg Frey, with the assistance of Daniel Herrmann. WUNT 460. Tübingen: Mohr Siebeck, 2021.

Wright, Robert B. *Psalms of Solomon: A Critical Edition of the Greek Text*. New York: Bloomsbury Academic & Professional, 2007.

Xenophon. *Xenophon in Seven Volumes*. Translated by Carleton L. Brownson. 7 vols. LCL. Cambridge: Harvard University Press, 1979.

Yiftach, Uri. "Law in Ptolemaic and Roman Egypt." Pages 1–54 in *The Oxford Handbook of Ancient Greek Law*. Edited by Edward M. Harris and Mirko Canevaro. Oxford: Oxford University Press, 2020.

Younger, John G. *Sex in the Ancient World*. London: Taylor and Francis, 2009.

Index of Ancient Sources

Index of Modern Authors

Printed in the United States
by Baker & Taylor Publisher Services